THE ART OF ADVOCACY IN INTERNATIONAL ARBITRATION

SECOND EDITION

DOAK BISHOP
and
EDWARD G. KEHOE
Editors

JURIS

Questions About This Publication

For assistance with shipments, billing or other customer service matters, please call our Customer Services Department at:

1-631-350-0200

To obtain a copy of this book, call our Sales Department:

1-631-351-2100
Fax: 1-631-351-5712

Toll Free Order Line:

1-800-887-4064 (United States & Canada)

See our web page about this book:
http://www.jurispub.com

Printed in the United States of America
ISBN 978-1-933833-61-3

JurisNet, LLC
71 New Street
Huntington, New York 11743
USA
www.arbitrationlaw.com

PREFACE

Parties to a legal dispute start with a level playing field in that the law and the underlying facts will apply equally to the parties, forming the foundation upon which the ultimate decision rests. From this, one might conclude that if the judge or arbitrator is impartial, and all legal counsel involved are competent (both of which we assume to be the case), the outcome of the dispute should not be dictated or impacted by the respective quality of legal representation. Yet, throughout history and to the present day, persons and companies of means have been represented by the preeminent lawyers of the time in significant legal disputes. Competent legal counsel is not good enough for these parties. They want best. Why is that? The answer is not difficult to derive. Good lawyering makes a difference. A skilled and superior advocate marshals, analyzes and presents the law and the facts to the decision maker in a manner that increases the likelihood of success over his merely competent legal adversary. Success, of course, is a relative term in the arena of legal disputes. But history teaches us that the playing field does not remain level when a superior advocate enters the scene.

Mr. Bishop and I are honored and humbled to be the editors of this publication, which brings together the writings of esteemed and learned colleagues on the art of advocacy in international arbitration. The collective pages of this book are a roadmap for learning the myriad of skills to becoming a superior advocate in international arbitration disputes. Naturally, some will be more adept than others at putting this advice to practical use. But even superior advocates are likely to learn something of note between the covers of this publication. As Jan Paulsson observed in the Foreword to the first edition of *The Art of Advocacy in International Arbitration*: "The best of the best are quick to admit that they are always learning." The chapters of this second edition are authored by leading arbitrators, psychologists and counsel of this era who are remarkably candid in revealing the art and secrets of their craft. The arbitrators provide a looking-glass into the approaches and conduct that these ultimate decision makers find most effective; the psychologists explain why certain styles and techniques are so effective; and the advocates have cast aside competition, in favor of this collaborative and cooperative publication that strives to level the playing field in international arbitration disputes.

Edward G. Kehoe

ABOUT THE AUTHORS

DOAK BISHOP is a litigation Partner and a member of King & Spalding's Latin American Practice Group. Mr. Bishop has over 27 years experience focusing on international arbitration and litigation of oil and gas, energy, construction, and environmental disputes. He has developed a national reputation for his experience in international arbitration, serving both as an arbitrator and counsel in large business disputes. Mr. Bishop is Board Certified in Civil Trial Law by the Texas Board of Legal Specialization. Mr. Bishop presently serves as Vice Chairman of the Institute of Transnational Arbitration (1990-present) and as a member of the U.S. delegation to the NAFTA Advisory Committee on Private Commercial Disputes. He has previously served as Chairman of the Litigation Section of the State Bar of Texas (1998) and Co-Chair of the American Bar Association International Litigation Committee (1998-1999). His experience in litigation and arbitration includes: international litigation and arbitration; oil & gas and energy disputes; construction disputes; environmental disputes; high technology disputes. Mr. Bishop received his B.A. degree *with high honors* and *departmental distinction* from Southern Methodist University in 1973, and his J.D. degree *with honors* from The University of Texas in 1976 where he served as Research Editor of the *Texas Law Review.*

EDWARD G. KEHOE is the head of King & Spalding's New York Business Litigation Department, and he co-heads the Firm's International Arbitration Practice with Doak Bishop. Mr. Kehoe received his bachelor's degree in accounting at Lehigh University, and he graduated *cum laude* from St. John's Law School where he was a member of the *St. John's Law Review.* He has more than 19 years experience in international business arbitration and litigation, with a focus on energy, professional services liability, construction, pharma, and insurance. He is recognized in *Chambers USA* for international arbitration, where it states that he "*drew spontaneous applause from esteemed sources for his sophistication and success in handling a number of sizable* *matters.*" According to *The Legal 500* publication, clients and peers comment that he is "*held in very high regard*" for his international arbitration skills. He was selected by his peers as a New York Super Lawyer, and honored in the *Corporate Counsel Magazine* as one of the "Nation's Top Litigators" in business litigation. He is a member of the Panel of Neutrals for the AAA International Centre for Dispute Resolution. Mr. Kehoe also is a frequent writer and lecturer on international arbitration issues; he is a member of the Board of Editors of Global Arbitration Review, and the International Bar Association; and he sits on the Advisory Board of the Institute for Transnational Arbitration.

GUILLERMO AGUILAR-ALVAREZ is head of the International Arbitration Group at Weil, Gotshal & Manges. He concentrates his practice in international commercial and investment arbitration. He handles arbitration procedures under the rules of the International Court of Arbitration of the ICC, the AAA, the London Court of International Arbitration, ICSID, the Arbitration Institute of the Stockholm Chamber of Commerce, the Netherlands Arbitration Institute, the Inter American Commercial Arbitration Commission and UNCITRAL. Mr. Aguilar-Alvarez has also represented investors in investment disputes arising under Chapter 11 of the North American Free Trade Agreement, and other bilateral investment treaties. Mr. Aguilar-Alvarez has handled a wide variety of disputes (e.g., energy, engineering and construction, joint ventures, product distribution and franchising, purchase, and manufacturing) in many venues (the US, Europe and Latin America), under diverse legal systems (e.g., under the laws of Canada, several US states, Argentina, Brazil, Colombia, Chile, Costa Rica, Ecuador, Guatemala, Panama, Peru, Venezuela, Spain, France and Sweden) and involving parties of more than 30 nationalities. Mr. Aguilar-Alvarez served as Principal Legal Counsel for the government of Mexico for the negotiation and implementation of the North American Free Trade (NAFTA) and free trade agreements with Costa Rica, Bolivia, Colombia and Venezuela. Previously, Mr. Aguilar-Alvarez was Counsel and General Counsel of the ICC International Court of Arbitration. During the

2005-2006 and 2007-2008 (Fall Semester) academic years, Mr. Aguilar-Alvarez is a Visiting Lecturer in Law at the Yale Law School (2005-2009). He has been recognized by Chambers and by the International Who's Who of Arbitration Lawyers. Mr. Aguilar-Alvarez is fluent in English, Spanish and French, and has a working knowledge of Italian and Portuguese.

PIERRE BIENVENU, a Senior Partner of Ogilvy Renault LLP, practices international arbitration, corporate and commercial litigation and constitutional law. He has acted as counsel in many international arbitrations, both *ad hoc* and institutional, in relation to disputes in the fields of telecommunications, aeronautics, international distribution and joint ventures, mergers and acquisitions, and foreign investments. He is also frequently called upon to represent parties in court proceedings to enforce or set aside foreign awards, including before the Supreme Court of Canada. Mr. Bienvenu also regularly serves as an arbitrator in international arbitrations. He was co-chair of the IBA's Arbitration Committee in 2008-2009 and currently serves as co-chair of the IBA's North American Forum (2010-2011). A fellow of the American College of Trial Lawyers, Mr. Bienvenu is among the Canadian practitioners featured in the *Guide to the Leading 500 Lawyers in Canada, The Canadian Legal Lexpert Directory, The International Who's Who of Commercial Arbitration,* the *Chambers Global Guide, The Lexpert Guide to the Leading 100 Creative Lawyers in Canada, Global Arbitration Review 100* (2009) and *The Best Lawyers in Canada* (2010). He was awarded the distinction Advocatus Emeritus by the Bar of Quebec in 2008. In addition to appearing before administrative and arbitral tribunals, Mr. Bienvenu has pleaded before the courts of Quebec, the Federal Court of Canada and the Supreme Court of Canada. He has been involved in numerous challenges to the constitutional validity of provincial and federal legislation. Mr. Bienvenu represented the Attorney General of Canada in litigation concerning the legality, under both Canadian constitutional law and public international law, of the secession of the Province of Quebec from Canada, including in the highly publicized reference by the Government of Canada to the Supreme Court of Canada concerning the secession of Quebec. He also represented the federally-appointed judiciary before the Judicial Compensation and Benefits Commission as well as before the Supreme Court of Canada in the *Bodner* case, which concerned the standard of review of a government's rejection of a judicial compensation commission recommendation. Mr. Bienvenu is chair of the Executive Committee, of which he has been a member since 2001, and he was National Managing Partner from 2005 to 2009. He is co-chair of the firm's international arbitration practice. He is a Canadian national and is fluent in English and French.

NIGEL BLACKABY is a Partner in Freshfields Bruckhaus Deringer's international arbitration group and is head of both the US and Latin America international arbitration groups. He has acted as counsel and arbitrator in over 80 ad hoc and institutional arbitrations, both commercial and investor-state under bilateral investment treaties, with a focus on Latin America. He was recently named as one of the world's 20 most prominent arbitration specialists by "Who's Who of Commercial Arbitration". Nigel has represented states and foreign investors in arbitrations under the auspices of ICSID, the ICC, LCIA, AAA and UNCITRAL, both in English and Spanish. Recent ICSID matters include representing CMS Energy, BG Group plc and National Grid in three separate victories against Argentina as well as successfully defending Pakistan in the case of SGS v. Pakistan. He is currently acting in ten treaty arbitrations involving Argentina, Bolivia, Ecuador, Paraguay and Venezuela. He also represented Telecom Italia in five parallel arbitrations before the ICC concerning the control of Brasil Telecom. Nigel is an editor of *Arbitration International* and a member of the executive of the LCIA Latin America Users' Committee. He is co-author of *Law and Practice of International Commercial Arbitration* (Thomson Sweet and Maxwell, 2004), *Guide to ICSID Arbitration* (Kluwer, 2004), and *International Arbitration in Latin America* (Kluwer, 2003). He is a visiting lecturer in arbitration at the Université de Paris I Panthéon-Sorbonne. Nigel speaks English, French, Spanish and Portuguese and has law degrees from the University of Exeter (UK) and the Université d'Aix-Marseille III (France).

JAMES H. CARTER is a Partner in the New York office of Sullivan & Cromwell LLP and co-coordinator of its international arbitration practice, in which he is active as counsel and as an arbitrator. He is a graduate of Yale College and Yale Law School, attended Cambridge University as a Fulbright Scholar and served as law clerk to Hon. Robert P. Anderson of the U.S. Court of Appeals for the Second Circuit. Mr. Carter is a former Chairman of the Board of Directors of the American Arbitration Association and now chairs its Nominating and Governance Committee, and during 2004-06 he was President of the American Society of International Law. He is also a former Chair of the American Bar Association Section of International Law and Practice and served as Chair of its Committee on International Commercial Arbitration. Mr. Carter has chaired both the International Affairs Council and the Committee on International Law of the Association of the Bar of the City of New York, as well as the International Law Committee and the International Dispute Resolution Committee of the New York State Bar Association. He has served as a member of the London Court of International Arbitration and Vice President of its North American Council and is a member of the Court of Arbitration for Sport. He is co-editor of INTERNATIONAL COMMERCIAL ARBITRATION IN NEW YORK (Oxford University Press 2010).

JAMES CRAWFORD is a Whewell Professor of International Law, University of Cambridge. He was a member of the International Law Commission (1992-2001) and Special Rapporteur on State Responsibility. Professor Crawford is a member of the Australian and English bars and has an extensive practice before international courts and tribunals and as an arbitrator.

BERNARDO M. CREMADES is Senior Partner of the Spanish law firm B. Cremades y Asociados and Catedrático at the university in Madrid. His practice focuses on international commercial arbitration and transnational investment disputes. He has acted as counsel, party-appointed arbitrator and president of arbitral tribunals in more than 300 arbitrations. His professional experience in the field of arbitration includes acting in proceedings under the auspices of all major international arbitration institutions, including the ICC, ICSID, AAA, CRCICA or LCIA as well as "ad hoc" arbitrations. He is fluent in English, Spanish, French and German. Bernardo M. Cremades is the leading Spanish international arbitration practitioner ("number one practitioner in Spain for commercial arbitration legal expertise" and "one of the top names in the industry", *Who's Who legal*, July 2005). He is a member of many professional and international arbitration associations and institutions, and is a frequent speaker at conferences around the world. His international recognition includes Germany's distinguished Verdienstkreuz award, and the French distinction of Chevalier de l'Ordre National du Mérite. He is the author of *Arbitration in Spain* (1991), *Litigation in Spain* (1989) and numerous articles in arbitration-related law reviews.

STEPHEN L. DRYMER is a graduate of Yale University and the Faculty of Law of McGill University where he earned degrees in Common and Civil Law and is co-Chair of Ogilvy Renault's International Arbitration team. His practice focuses on domestic and international arbitration and alternative dispute resolution. He acts as arbitrator, mediator and as counsel to parties in international commercial and investment treaty disputes, and advises clients on issues associated with the design, negotiation and implementation of dispute resolution procedures. He has served in disputes in the manufacturing, petrochemical, oil & gas, financial services, IT, outsourcing, construction, transportation and telecommunication industries, among others. Stephen also advises and represents clients in disputes involving maritime delimitation and the negotiation of transboundary resource agreements. He is also particularly active in the resolution of sport-related disputes in Canada and internationally in which, in addition to extensive work as counsel, he has served as arbitrator and mediator in numerous cases involving a wide range of issues and sports. Stephen has been named by *Global Arbitration Review* as one of the world's leading international lawyers, and he is listed annually in such publications as *The International Who's Who of Commercial Arbitration*, *The International Who's Who of Business Lawyers*,

LEXPERT/American Lawyer Guide to the Leading Lawyers in Canada and *The Best Lawyers in Canada.*

DIETER FLADER is an expert on intercultural communication, Professor at the Free University of Berlin and at the University of Warsaw, and lectures in communication analysis, linguistics, sociology and psychoanalysis. He is director of the seminar "How to Solve Intercultural Conflicts and Improve Intercultural Management Skills" in Warsaw (in cooperation with the Polish company K2liders and the German Chamber of Commerce). He is communication consultant for international companies. Scientific background: Habilitation in Linguistics, Psychoanalysis and Communication Research; Professor at the Free University of Berlin, Faculty of Philosophy and Human Studies (since 1996), lecturing on Communication Analysis and Linguistics; Docent at the Graduate School for Social Research at the Polish Academy of Science in Warsaw(1996-2002), lecturing on Communication Theory and Psychopathology of Social Institutions; Lecturer on Inter-cultural Communication problems as visiting professor and docent at Vanderbuilt University (USA), Charles-University in Prague (Czech Republic), University of Tilburg (Netherlands), University of Salzburg (Austria), Adana University (Turkey), Warsaw University (Poland); Research work on strategies of advertisement, on psychoanalytic discourse, on the scientific foundation of psychoanalysis, and on inter-cultural communication problems in business in Poland. Professional Consulting background: Psychoanalytic expertise – clinical analysis, group dynamics training seminars for canidates of psychoanalysis in Berlin – (since 1979); Communication consultant for managers – training seminars, coaching, models of effective professional communications – (since 1989); Consultant on inter-cultural communication problems – training seminars, coaching, cultural audit – (since 1990)

L. YVES FORTIER is Chairman Emeritus of Ogilvy Renault LLP and is recognized as one of the top arbitrators in the world. Mr. Fortier has served as Chairman or party-appointed arbitrator on more than 100 arbitral tribunals, either ad hoc or constituted by different arbitral institutions, including the International Court of Arbitration of the International Chamber of Commerce (Paris), the London Court of International Arbitration (LCIA), the Hong Kong International Arbitration Court (HKIAC), the Singapore International Arbitration Centre (SIAC), the China International Economic and Trade Arbitration Commission (CITAC), the American Arbitration Association, the Court of Arbitration for Sport, the Zurich Chamber of Commerce, the International Centre for Settlement of Investment Disputes (ICSID), the Canadian Commercial Arbitration Centre, the British Columbia International Commercial Arbitration Centre and the ADR Chambers International Panel. From 1984 to 1989 he was a member of the Permanent Court of Arbitration at The Hague. From July 1988 until January 1992, Mr. Fortier took leave from his law practice to take up an appointment as Canada's Ambassador and Permanent Representative to the United Nations in New York. During his term at the United Nations, Mr. Fortier was Canada's Chief Delegate to the 43rd, 44th, 45th and 46th Sessions of the UN General Assembly. In September 1990, he was elected Vice-President of the 45th General Assembly. From January 1989 to December 1990, Mr. Fortier served as Canada's Representative on the Security Council of the United Nations and in 1989 he was President of the Council. As a trial lawyer Mr. Fortier has pleaded important cases before all court jurisdictions in Canada and before domestic and international arbitral tribunals. He has also served as counsel to many Royal Commissions and Commissions of Inquiry in Quebec and Canada.

MARK FRIEDMAN is a US trained litigation partner of Debevoise & Plimpton based in New York and London. His practice focuses on international arbitration and litigation. He represents clients in commercial and investment treaty cases. He also regularly advises clients in connection with internal investigations and US law matters, including matters involving the Foreign Corrupt Practices Act and similar legislation and regulations. Mr. Friedman's appearances in arbitration and court proceedings have earned him high regard as an advocate. His peers have said that "you know that you have a real fight on your hands when he's on the other side" (*Chambers UK*). He is ranked as a leading individual in *Chambers (Global, UK and US)*, *The International Who's Who of Commercial Arbitration*, *The International Who's Who of Commercial Litigation*, *PLC Which Lawyer? Yearbook*, *Legal Experts*, and as one of 45 stars under 45 by the Global Arbitration Review. He is Senior Vice-Chair of the International Bar Association's Arbitration Committee, a Vice-Chair of the International Dispute Resolution Committee of the International Section of the American Bar Association, and co-rapporteur of the International Law Association's Commercial Arbitration Committee. Mr. Friedman speaks and publishes on international arbitration and compliance topics, and sits as an arbitrador

EMMANUEL GAILLARD heads Shearman & Sterling LLP's International Arbitration practice and has represented corporations, States and State-owned entities in international arbitration matters for over 25 years. He has also acted as sole arbitrator, party-appointed arbitrator or chairman under most international arbitration rules, and is frequently called upon to appear as expert witness on arbitration law issues in international arbitration proceedings or enforcement actions before domestic courts. Through his practice, extensive writing and teaching, Emmanuel Gaillard has significantly contributed to the shaping of contemporary international arbitration law. His publications include *Fouchard Gaillard Goldman On International Commercial Arbitration* (1999), a leading treatise on international arbitration, *La Jurisprudence du CIRDI* (2 volumes, 2004 and 2010), a commentary on ICSID case law; and the first essay on the legal theory of international arbitration, based on his Course at The Hague Academy of International Law (*Aspects philosophiques du droit de l'arbitrage international*, 2008; *Legal Theory of International Arbitration*, 2010; *Teoría Legal del Arbitraje Internacional*, 2010). Emmanuel Gaillard is a Professor of Law at Paris XII University.

TERESA GIOVANNINI is a founding member at Lalive in Geneva. She specializes in International Litigation and Arbitration, and Art Law. She has acted as counsel, Sole Arbitrator, Co-Arbitrator and Chair in more than 130 international commercial disputes, under the rules of AAA/ICDR, CARICI, ICC, ICSID, LCIA, SCC, the Milan and Venice Chambers of Commerce, Swiss Chambers of Commerce and ad hoc (including UNCITRAL) under civil and common law. She is a lecturer and instructor at various research and training institutions, and at a number of international conferences on international arbitration, including AAA/ICDR (Neutrals training and conferences), IBA, ICC and ICC Institute of World Business Law, ICCA, ITA, Milan Chamber of Commerce, PLI (Practising Law Institute); SCC, UIA. Teresa is Vice President of the London Court of International Arbitration. She is a Fellow of the Chartered Institute of Arbitrators and a Council Member of the ICC Institute of World Business Law. Teresa is a Swiss Alternate Member of the International Law Association's Committee on International Commercial Arbitration, and a member of the Centre for American and International Law. She has been a Member of the Examination Board of the Chartered Institute of Arbitrators until 2010.

MICHAEL HWANG won a scholarship to Oxford University and read law at undergraduate and post graduate levels. He taught law at the University of Sydney before commencing private practice in 1968 at Allen & Gledhill (now Singapore's largest law firm) where he practiced for over 30 years, except for 1991 to 1992 when he served as a Judicial Commissioner (Fixed Term Judge) of the Supreme Court. He now practices as a Barrister and International Arbitrator in his own boutique practice. He is also an Adjunct Professor of Law at the National University of Singapore. In 1997 Mr. Hwang was appointed as one of the first twelve Senior Counsel of the Supreme Court of Singapore. From 2000 – 2003 he served as a United Nations Compensation Commissioner, assessing claims against Iraq arising from the First Gulf War. In 2003 he was appointed Singapore's Non-Resident Ambassador to Switzerland. In 2005 he was appointed Deputy Chief Justice of the Dubai International

Financial Centre. In 2008 he was elected the President of The Law Society of Singapore.

STEPHEN JAGUSCH specialises in international commercial and investment treaty arbitration at Allen & Overy, having acted as adviser and advocate in dozens of ad hoc and institutional international arbitrations, conducted in many countries over the world, and subject to a wide variety of governing substantive and procedural laws. A great many of Stephen's cases have been in favour of, or against, sovereign states or substantial multinational organisations, and in recent years Stephen has become recognised as an expert in the field of ICSID arbitration and disputes arising under bilateral or multilateral investment treaties.

TOBY LANDAU is a Barrister practising at Essex Court Chambers in London, and also a member of the New York Bar. He specialises in international arbitration both as counsel and arbitrator, and has extensive experience in this field. He has served as Arbitrator in over 50 major international cases in many countries, including ICSID (e.g. *Biwater v Tanzania*; *Impregilo v Pakistan*; *Hamester v Ghana*; *GEA v Ukraine*; *Cambodia Power Cambodia Power Company v Kingdom of Cambodia*), ICC, SCC, LCIA, and numerous other institutional and *ad hoc* arbitrations. As counsel, he has appeared in over 260 major international arbitrations, as well as many of the leading arbitration cases before the English courts. He is a Director of the LCIA; a Fellow (and previously Trustee) of the Chartered Institute of Arbitrators; the UK delegate to the UNCITRAL Working Group on Arbitration (since 2000); a member of the IBA sub-committee responsible for amending the IBA Rules on Evidence; and one of the draftsmen of the English Arbitration Act 1996, the Pakistan Arbitration Ordinance of 2005, and the Mauritius Arbitration Act of 2008. He is a Visiting Professor at Kings College London (arbitration law), and a visiting lecturer at the Pakistan College of Law in Lahore. He holds a first-class law degree and a first class BCL from Oxford University (Eldon Scholar), and an LL.M. from Harvard Law School (Kennedy Scholar). Before being appointed a QC in 2008, he received the Chambers & Partners Award for "Junior Barrister of the Year" in the field of international arbitration in both 2005 and 2007 (and was short-listed for the same award in 2006).

CHRISTOPHER LAU is an arbitrator in international and domestic arbitrations involving ICC, UNCITRAL, LCIA, SIAC, HKIAC & KCAB Rules and in ad hoc arbitrations in commercial disputes including disputes in relation to power plant projects, joint ventures, sale & acquisition of companies, international investments, maritime, insurance and building & construction. He has also been appointed as mediator by ICDR. Recent arbitral appointments include chairman of the tribunal in a marine insurance dispute in Indonesia; in a ship construction dispute in Australia and in Scandinavia; in a power plant dispute in South Asia; in a bridge construction dispute in East Asia; in joint venture/contractual disputes in China; in an oil rig construction dispute in the Middle East; as co-arbitrator in a synthesis gas plant dispute in North Asia; in a joint venture property development dispute in China; in an acquisition dispute in Asia; in a container terminal investment dispute in Asia; in an energy investment related dispute in the Americas; and as sole arbitrator in a dispute relating to a Bond Subscription & Joint Venture agreement and in a maritime dispute. Recent mediation appointment include mediator in an international contractual dispute governed by the laws of the State of New York. Christopher is a contributor to the Singapore Chapter in *Arbitration World, 2nd Edition*, Publishers, European Lawyer; a chapter on the process of obtaining evidence and discovery in Asia in Juris' *Asian Leading Arbitrators' Guide to Arbitration*; IGLG's *International Arbitration 2007, 4th Edition*; IGLG's *International Arbitration in Asia Pacific: Regional Overview and Recent Developments*; and a Consultant in Singapore Court Practice 2006.

JIM LAWRENCE, J.D., M.A. combines law, psychology and theatre, which he uses to provide legal professionals with the communications skills they need to succeed. He has studied acting/performance for more than 20 years. At the University of

Houston Law Center, Mr. Lawrence currently directs a highly successful Moot Court Program. Over the past four years, the program has won 16 national and regional titles and awards. Before working with the moot court program, he served as Program Director for the Trial Skills Program. Mr. Lawrence serves as a consultant to The Advocates, a national jury science firm.

PETER LEAVER was called to the Bar by Lincoln's Inn in July 1967, and was appointed Queen's Counsel in April 1987. He has practised at the Commercial Bar in England, and has also acted in commercial cases in other jurisdictions. In the last few years he has spent most of his time sitting as an arbitrator in international commercial cases under the rules of many institutions, including the ICC, the LCIA and SIAC. In addition, he is a member of ACICA and the Chartered Institute of Arbitrators, and was for many years an arbitrator at the Court of Arbitration for Sport. He is currently the Chairman of the Board of Directors of the London Court of International Arbitration.

IGNACIO MADALENA is an associate with B. Cremades y Asociados in Madrid. His practice is entirely focused on arbitration. He acts as adviser and advocate in institutional and ad hoc arbitrations under all the major arbitration rules, including proceedings between States and investors under the Washington Convention on the Settlement of Investment Disputes. Ignacio has particular experience in relation to disputes arising out of major infrastructure projects, as well as in the oil and gas industry, particularly in Latin America. Ignacio holds an LL.M. Degree in Public International Law from Georgetown University Law Center and an LL.M. Degree in International Business Law from the University of Leuven. He is fluent in English, Spanish and French.

CRAIG MILES is a partner in King & Spalding's International Arbitration Group, residing in the Houston office. His practice focuses on representing foreign investors in disputes with host governments, primarily before the World Bank's International Centre for Settlement of Investment Disputes (ICSID), and private parties in commercial disputes before the International Chamber of Commerce (ICC), the American Arbitration Association (AAA), and other domestic and international arbitral institutions. Mr. Miles has first- or second-chaired dozens of arbitral hearings involving disputes throughout North and South America, Europe, Asia, Africa and the Middle East, with particularly strong experience in bilateral investment treaty (BIT) disputes in the oil and gas sector and in Latin America. Among his recent cases are four of the largest ICSID BIT awards ever obtained by foreign investors, three against the government of Argentina and one against the government of Egypt. He presently represents investors in disputes with the governments of Argentina, Bolivia, Ecuador, Egypt, Romania and Venezuela. Mr. Miles also acts as lead outside counsel to the Arbitration Committee of the USA Rice Millers Association, a trade group that regularly administers arbitrations involving the rice industry worldwide. Mr. Miles routinely appears in peer-reviewed rankings such as *Chambers*, *Who's Who*, *Best Lawyers in America* and *Latin Lawyer. Chambers Global* has described Mr. Miles as an "up and comer" in international arbitration who is "tipped for greatness by peers," while *Latin Lawyer 250* describes him as a "key name in this field," and *Global Arbitration Review 100* calls him "a name to know." Mr. Miles frequently speaks and writes on international arbitration issues, occasionally in Spanish, in which he is proficient along with French. Among other memberships, he currently serves on the ICC's Task Force on Investor-State Arbitration and on the Advisory Board of the Institute for Transnational Arbitration.

SOPHIE NAPPERT is a dual-qualified lawyer in Canada and in the UK. She is an arbitrator in independent practice, based in London. Before becoming a full-time arbitrator, she was Head of International Arbitration at a global law firm. Sophie is trained and has practiced in both civil law and common law jurisdictions. Sophie is ranked in Global Arbitration Review's Top 30 List of Female Arbitrators Worldwide and is listed in the International Who's Who of Commercial Arbitration. She is commended in the legal directories as *'one of the top new-generation arbitrators'* and was peer-nominated as a co-Moderator on OGEMID, the online discussion forum on current issues of international law and arbitration. Areas of expertise include: energy and natural resources, construction, infrastructure, hotel and leisure, telecoms, joint ventures, concession agreements, Russia, Kazakhstan and the Caspian region, the Energy Charter Treaty, investment treaty disputes and disputes against State parties. Sophie is a regular speaker at conferences and seminars on issues of arbitration and international law. She is also a guest lecturer at Columbia Law School, Harvard Law School and McGill University Faculty of Law. Education: University of London: LL.M. (Masters Degree in Law) with Merit, King's College London; McGill University (Canada): Bachelor of Laws (Common Law), (LL.B.), Bachelor of Civil Law (B.C.L.); Institute of International and Comparative Law (Magdalen College, Oxford): Diploma in Public International Law.

JAN PAULSSON is co-head of Freshfields Bruckhaus Deringer's international arbitration and public international law groups. He holds degrees from Harvard, Yale and the University of Paris. He has acted as counsel or arbitrator in hundreds of international arbitrations. He has conducted cases under the ICC, UNCITRAL, ICSID, LCIA, and AAA Rules, as well as before the International Court of Justice. He is President of the London Court of International Arbitration, the World Bank Administrative Tribunal, and the EBRD Administrative Tribunal; and is a member of the Permanent Court of Arbitration in The Hague. Mr. Paulsson holds the Michael Klein Distinguished Scholar Chair at the University of Miami and is a Visiting Professor at the London School of Economics. He is a *Profesor Honorario* of the *Universidad Peruana de Ciencias Aplicadas.* He is the author of several textbooks and numerous articles, in particular the standard reference work *ICC Arbitration* (3rd edition 2000) which he co-authors with Messrs WL Craig and WW Park. His monograph *Denial of Justice in International Law* was published by Cambridge University Press in 2005. He speaks English, French, Spanish and Swedish.

PHILIPPE PINSOLLE is a Partner at Shearman & Sterling LLP in Paris, and specializes in international arbitration. He has been involved, as counsel or arbitrator, in more than a hundred and twenty international arbitrations, both institutional (ICC, ICSID, LCIA, SCC, AFA, Swiss Rules, etc.) and *ad hoc*, concerning such activities as investment, oil and gas, energy, telecom or defense industry. He is a member of the Paris Bar and of the Bar of England & Wales (Gray's Inn). He is a lecturer on international arbitration at the Universities of Aix-Marseille III, Versailles-St Quentin and Paris 12. Philippe Pinsolle is the former President of the International Arbitration commission of the Union Internationale des Avocats (UIA) and a co-founder of the Young Arbitration Practitioners (YAP). He is the author of numerous articles and case-notes on international arbitration. He holds a J.D. degree from the University of Paris II, a M.Jur. from Oxford University, Hertford College, and an MBA degree from Essec.

LUCY REED is co-head of the global international arbitration group of Freshfields Bruckhaus Deringer LLP. Lucy acts as advocate for private and public clients and sits as arbitrator in international arbitrations under the major institutional and ad hoc rules. She is past President of the American Society of International Law and Chair of the ITA. Lucy has served as an arbitrator on the Eritrea-Ethiopia Claims Commission, co-director of the Claims Resolution Tribunal for Dormant Accounts in Switzerland, U.S. Agent to the Iran-United States Claims Tribunal, and the State Department's Deputy Assistant Legal Adviser for International Claims and Investment Disputes.

DAVID W. RIVKIN, a litigation Partner in Debevoise & Plimpton's New York and London offices, has broad experience in the areas of international litigation and arbitration. He has handled international arbitrations throughout the world and before virtually every major arbitration institution, including the ICC, AAA, LCIA, ICSID, IACAC and the Stockholm Chamber of Commerce. Subjects of these arbitrations have included long-term energy concessions, investment treaties, joint venture agreements, insurance coverage, construction contracts, distribution agreements and intellectual property, among others. Mr. Rivkin also represents European, Latin American and Asian companies in transnational litigation in the United States, including the enforcement of arbitral awards and arbitration agreements. Mr. Rivkin is consistently ranked as one of the top international dispute resolution practitioners in the world. Most recently, he was ranked among the top six international arbitration practitioners worldwide in *Chambers Global* (2009).

CATHERINE ROGERS is a law professor who teaches a range of comparative and international law subjects at two schools, the Paul M. Hebert Law Center, Louisiana State University, in Baton Rouge, Louisiana, and Istituto Diritto Comparato (IDC), Università Commerciale Luigi Bocconi, in Milan, Italy. The primary focus of her scholarship is international arbitration, with a special emphasis on the development of international standards of professional conduct for attorneys and arbitrators, as well as more generally the nature of the public/private divide in international dispute resolution systems. She has lectured and published extensively on lawyers' and arbitrators' ethics in international arbitration, and her scholarship has been recognized through several awards, including the Stanford-Yale Junior Faculty Forum (2001 and 2004) and the CPR Professional Article Award (2002). She is an appointed member of the Academic Council of the Institute of Transnational Arbitration, and she sits on the Advisory Board of the Penn State Dickinson School of Law's Institute of Arbitration Law and Practice. Before going into teaching, Professor Rogers received her B.A. from University of California at Berkeley, her J.D. from University of California at Hastings College of Law and her LL.M. from Yale Law School. Following law school, she clerked for Judge Melvin Brunetti on the U.S. Ninth Circuit Court of Appeals, and practiced international litigation and arbitration in New York, Hong Kong and San Francisco.

AUDLEY SHEPPARD is a Partner at Clifford Chance where he is an expert in International Commercial Arbitration and International Law, and has many years experience in the resolution of disputes arising out of major infrastructure projects and international contracts, as counsel and arbitrator. He is also Co-chair of the International Bar Association arbitration committee; Visiting professor at the Queen Mary School of Arbitration, London; Member of the ICC Commission on arbitration; and Fellow of the Chartered Institute of Arbitration.

ANTHONY SINCLAIR is a member of the International Arbitration Group of Allen & Overy LLP. He has been counsel in both commercial (administered and ad hoc) and investor-State arbitrations including numerous bilateral investment treaty (BIT) and Energy Charter Treaty (ECT) arbitrations under ICSID and UNCITRAL arbitration rules, as well as twice in ICSID annulment proceedings. Anthony is co-author of the second edition of *The ICSID Convention: A Commentary* (Cambridge University Press, 2009) with Christoph Schreuer, Loretta Malintoppi and August Reinisch.

HENRY FORBES SMITH is a Barrister practising international commercial litigation and arbitration at One Essex Court in London. He is a member of the bars of England, New York and New Zealand. He has a LLB (Hons) from the University of Otago, a BCL from the University of Oxford, where he was a Vinerian Scholar and a Domus & Harmsworth Senior Scholar, and a PhD in the conflict of laws from the University of Cambridge, where he was a WM Tapp Student. Before joining the English bar, he practised U.S. law with Davis Polk & Wardwell. He originally trained as a New Zealand lawyer with Chapman Tripp.

GUIDO SANTIAGO TAWIL is a Chair Professor of Administrative Law at the University of Buenos Aires and a Senior Partner at M. & M. Bomchil, in Buenos Aires where he heads the international arbitration and regulatory practices of the firm. Dr. Tawil is the Co Chair of the IBA's Arbitration Committee, a Council member of the International Council for Commercial Arbitration (ICCA), a Court member of the London Court of International Arbitration (LCIA), the ICC's Latin American Arbitration Group, ITA´s Academic

Council, the Administrative Law Institute of the National Law Academy, among other institutions. He has published seven books and over 120 articles and papers in matters related with his fields of practice. He has been awarded with the Law School Award for the best doctoral dissertation and by the Buenos Aires Bar with the Shaw Award for the best legal contribution. Dr. Tawil received his law degree, a master degree and a Ph.D. with the highest academic qualifications, all of them from the University of Buenos Aires.

MARTIN VALASEK, a Partner of Ogilvy Renault LLP, is a leading practitioner in the area of international arbitration. He regularly acts as lead counsel in arbitrations to resolve investor-State and commercial contract disputes. He also practices corporate and commercial litigation, with a particular focus on cross-border disputes. He has acted in many international arbitrations, covering a wide range of legal systems and industries, including aerospace, airport development, banking, construction, mining, energy, environmental remediation, pharmaceuticals, IT outsourcing, lotteries and steel manufacturing. He has extensive experience with arbitrations conducted under the ICC, LCIA, ICSID and UNCITRAL Rules, and has also handled other *ad hoc* arbitrations and matters under the auspices of many other institutions, including the AAA, the CPR Institute and Hong Kong International Arbitration Centre. Mr. Valasek has been recognized in the *2009 Guide to the World's Leading Experts in Commercial Arbitration* and the *International Who's Who of Commercial Arbitration 2010*. He was Editor-in-Chief of the *McGill Law Journal* and clerked for Mr. Justice Gonthier of the Supreme Court of Canada. In 2007, he was named one of Lexpert's "Top 40 Lawyers Under 40" for Canada. Mr. Valasek is a member of the bars of Québec, Ontario and New York. He is a member of the Canadian Bar Association and the International Bar Association. In October 2009, he was elected to the Panel of International Commercial Arbitrators and accepted as a member of the ICC National Committee of the Canadian Chamber of Commerce. In September 2007, he commenced a three-year term as President of the Young Canadian Arbitration Practitioners (YCAP). In 2008, he was selected to be the Canadian representative of the Young Arbitrators' Forum (YAF) of the International Chamber of Commerce (ICC). He served as Regional Representative for North America (Canada) of the Young International Arbitration Group (YIAG) of the LCIA from 2006 to 2009. He is a director of the Andover Canadian Fund Inc. and Bach-Académie de Montréal, and a member of the Advisory Board of the *McGill International Journal of Sustainable Development Law and Policy*. Mr. Valasek is fluent in English, French and Czech, and has a working knowledge of Spanish.

RICHARD C. WAITES, J.D., Ph.D. is a board certified trial attorney and social psychologist, is an internationally recognized expert in jury and courtroom decision maker research, a field he helped to develop and that he continues to advance. Waites practiced law as a trial attorney for 13 years. During this time, Waites represented hundreds of individuals and corporations in litigation matters, including more than 70 jury trials.. Waites is one of the founders of Advocacy Sciences, Inc., the largest jury and trial consulting firm in the United States. The Advocates has 23 professional trial consultants and offices in 17 major cities throughout the nation. Waites serves as the CEO and as Chief Trial Psychologist for The Advocates. The firm's clients include trial attorneys and law firms as well as domestic and international corporations who use the firm's expertise in accurately assessing the persuasive strengths and weaknesses of their litigation cases and in developing creative and successful trial and arbitration strategies. Since 2004, Waites has continued in private practice as a trial consultant and is engaged to assist trial attorneys and corporations in litigation.

ALEXANDER A. YANOS is a partner in Freshfields Bruckhaus Deringer LLP's dispute resolution practice in New York. He has spent over twelve years litigating and arbitrating commercial and financial disputes. Alex has acted as arbitration counsel in matters before the ICJ, ICSID, the ICC, the Stockholm Chamber of

Commerce, the AAA, the Hong Kong International Arbitration Center, the Inter-American Commercial Arbitration Commission and the LCIA. He has specialised in disputes involving sovereigns, handling arbitrations on behalf of claimants in disputes against Argentina, Venezuela, Russia and the US before the ICC, ICSID and the ICJ, while representing Lithuania and Pakistan in ICSID arbitrations and Paraguay in the US courts. As a litigator Alex has focused on multijurisdictional disputes involving US securities, banking, antitrust and insurance laws on behalf of US and international clients. He has handled matters before federal and state courts in New York, Georgia, Texas and Virginia. He is a member of our insurance, construction and Latin America practice groups. Before beginning his private practice, Alex clerked for the Honorable Jerome Farris, in the Court of Appeals for the Ninth Circuit. He is admitted in New York State and in the Eastern and Southern Districts of New York.

TABLE OF CONTENTS

Introduction

Doak Bishop

The theme of this book is that good lawyering matters. A good case rarely happens by itself. A case that is thoroughly prepared, sharply focused, supported by concrete evidence, and properly presented is far more likely to be persuasive than one that is not. While the facts and the law form the fundamental matrix, a good case is the product of substantial efforts by good lawyers painstakingly reviewing documents, interviewing witnesses, researching the law, strategizing and focusing the case, and developing compelling written and oral presentations. How to perform these tasks properly is the subject of this book.

The starting point of this inquiry should be the scientific research that has been conducted into how people make decisions and what persuades them. Decision-making and persuasion are well studied subjects in the fields of consumer marketing, politics and psychology, and certain types of decision-making have recently become the subjects of scientific study by neuroscientists who observe and record the neuronal activity of the brain during decision-making.

There is a rich social science literature on the psychology of persuasion. In the United States, because the jury system has produced some very large verdicts, trial lawyers often employ jury psychologists in significant cases to conduct focus groups and mock trials to help fashion the most persuasive message in a case. In fact, thousands of mock trials have been conducted for jury cases in the United States over the past 30 years, and numerous articles and several practical books have been published discussing the research and findings of jury psychologists. Of course, arguing a case to a US jury, which generally does not read the documents, take notes or ask questions, is not the same as presenting a case to an experienced international arbitral tribunal. The decision-makers are differently trained and skilled, and subject to a very different adjudicatory system. Chapter 4, by Dr. Richard Waites and James Lawrence, addresses some of the key findings of US jury psychologists on persuasion in a judicial context. Unfortunately, however, there has been very little research focusing on decision-making and persuasion in international arbitration. Chapter 5, by Prof. Dieter Flader and Sophie Nappert, discusses some of the research currently ongoing to fill this gap. But international advocates can turn at least to the literature of psychology and the studies of US jury psychologists, however imperfect a fit for international arbitration, to provide some assistance in understanding the fundamental psychological principles of decision-making and persuasion.

An arbitral case, like a case in a national court system, is not just a simple mathematical equation, summing the facts and the law and arriving at a precise answer. Arbitral decision-making is neither mathematics nor science. Neuroscience has demonstrated that decision-making is often not limited to a single part of the brain, nor is it typically a simple step-by-step process of conscious reasoning. Human decision-making involves a complex and constantly shifting tension between the reasoning (neo-cortex) and emotional/instinctive (amygdala) parts of the brain, much of it at a subconscious level. Neuroscience is currently documenting both the pervasiveness of subconscious decision-making and the complex patterns of neurons firing in different sequences in various parts of the brain when people are faced with ethical decisions, which might be considered analogous to the types of decisions made by arbitrators.

Some commentators have suggested that all decisions are ultimately made at a subconscious level for emotional or instinctive reasons, although they are consciously justified in a rational manner. In this view, the driving force of all decisions is emotion or instinct, while reasoning merely provides the justification. This may come as a surprise to many lawyers as it appears on the surface to be inconsistent with the typical human experience of apparent conscious, step-by-step reasoning leading to conclusions. Whatever the ultimate truth of this debate, whether our decisions are really made subconsciously or consciously, solely by emotion or by reasoning, or by some combination of both, in international arbitration they are at least rationally justified in a reasoned decision.

The lesson of this research, however, is that a cautious and thoughtful advocate should identify both the emotional and rational appeal of his[1] case, and ignore neither.

It is this complex decision-making process that advocacy seeks to influence. While there are many tactical tools that the advocate may employ, there are at least two fundamental strategic mechanisms for persuasion that should be considered. The first is the obvious process of logical, step-by-step reasoning as the means of interpreting a contract or a law, or applying the facts to the law. The process of logical reasoning occurs in the rational part of the brain, the neo-cortex, which is generally well developed in lawyers by training and experience. It is generally accepted in international arbitration that it is this process that appeals to lawyers. Logical reasoning should always be an important part of the advocate's toolkit and should not be neglected, even if one subscribes to the view that all decisions are driven by emotion. If logic does not itself drive the decision, it is at least necessary for justifying that decision, and it seems likely that it at least influences and at times may even reverse an impression or decision. Judges sometimes talk of a tentative decision that "won't write," meaning that the attempt to draft an opinion justifying a decision failed, forcing a reassessment of the tentative decision. This seems to be a vindication of the view that logical reasoning at least partially influences judicial and arbitral decision-making.

The second basic mechanism, and one that may not be as well known to all lawyers, is the use of the narrative story as the mode of communicating the essential facts of the case. Humans have difficulty remembering or making sense of a number of random or disconnected facts, or even a long list of discrete but connected facts. So people tend naturally in their minds to organize a set of facts into a narrative story as a mechanism to store and remember them efficiently. The story provides a mental structure with a chronological flow and causal connections, sometimes providing an affective (emotional) meaning that transcends the facts themselves.

---

1 The words "he," "his" and "him" are used in this chapter in a neutral gender sense as shorthand references to persons of either gender.

But a story can also distort the evidence, especially causal inferences, by subtly altering or ignoring certain facts or selectively emphasizing certain causal factors. Historians have commented on this problem in the writing of history. Thus, care is necessary in constructing the story. In an arbitral setting, a story should reconcile and make sense of the evidence. Consistency of the story with both the evidence and common sense is critical for a story that is both credible and plausible, and thus, for its acceptance. In advocacy, a narrative story that credibly reconciles the evidence is greater than the sum of its parts, and can be highly persuasive.

The story should be articulated at an early point in the case because the arbitrators will likely start to construct a storyline for themselves, either consciously or subconsciously, as soon as they begin to learn the facts. Discrete facts that cannot be fit into the storyline often get overlooked or ignored as outliers. Once the arbitrators have structured the evidence into a story in their own minds, it can be more difficult to persuade them because it requires them to disregard an entire structure of the evidence and construct a new one. This is indicative of the importance of first impressions in advocacy.

One point to note is that the stories constructed by the arbitrators in their own minds will probably differ one from another, sometimes significantly. The advocate should not assume that all of the arbitrators understand the facts in the same way. This again points to the need for counsel to argue a credible story that can be accepted by all of the arbitrators as common ground for how to understand the evidence. A final point about the story is that while a claimant should certainly present a storyline of the evidence, the respondent should also consider presenting a just-as-plausible counter-story with the same evidence, or by supplementing the evidence. Since a counter-story presents an overall structure of how the facts fit together, it is more likely to be persuasive than simply poking discrete holes in the claimant's story.

One way to approach the emotional-rational duality of the human thought process is to create a subtle emotive appeal for the case by identifying the facts that are particularly persuasive, sometimes referred to as the "equities" of the case. The equities are the particular facts that evoke our human sense of right and wrong, of fairness and unfairness, of damage and suffering, in short, of justice. These facts have an affective (emotive) quality to them that appeal to the emotional / instinctive part of the brain, but they should also have strong appeal to our rational side as well. Facts that are especially persuasive can also include any admissions of the opposing party — statements admitting the existence of a fact that hurts that party's case. US trial lawyers often try to build their cases as much as possible on admissions of the opposing party. An advocate should pay particular attention to both the equities of the case and the opposing side's admissions during argument.

One of the most important tasks of the advocate is to strategize the case. The strategic plan should plot out how the case will proceed from Point A to Point Z. It should show *precisely* how and why the client's case should prevail, taking into account the facts and the law, and anticipating the opposing side's likely arguments. One aspect of strategizing is to focus the case. "Focus" is a key word for advocacy. Think of going to see an eye doctor. He asks you to look through a lens. What do you see? Is the image sharp or fuzzy? Then he rotates the lens. Is the image sharper or fuzzier? A legal case is not synonymous with the complete and raw facts of a situation. Due to time constraints and cost, the full facts of a situation, all documents related to it, and all possible witnesses can rarely be presented to the tribunal. Providing a tribunal with all of the documents and general propositions of law presents a fuzzy image. The arbitrators are left to figure out from a mass of material what is really important. There may be many ways they could perceive the case, and without the advocate's focus, they could arrive at any one of ten different conclusions, nine of which could be bad for the advocate's case. As part of his preparation, a good advocate turns the lens until the image is sharp, and the case compelling. In the context of arbitral advocacy, this involves a substantial amount of work, much of which involves strategic decisions: deciding which documents are really important, which witnesses to present, which claims or defenses to assert, and how to present this information in a simple, clear and concise manner. This effort, undertaken in the right way, rotates that lens until the patient's eye is focused sharply on the subject matter. This is the task of the advocate: to present the right arguments in a sharply focused manner, which structures how the arbitrators perceive the case. The strategic plan should consider these issues. The chapters by David Rivkin, Emmanuel Gaillard, and Philippe Pinsole address the critical issue of strategizing an arbitral case, and deserve careful attention.

One of the authors of the chapter on the psychology of persuasion, US lawyer and psychologist Dr. Richard Waites, identifies in his book, *Courtroom Psychology and Trial Advocacy,* four elements of persuasion: (1) the communicator, (2) the content of the message, (3) the way the message is presented, and (4) the audience. This classification can be helpful in understanding the complex subject of persuasion. For international arbitration, Dr. Waites' categories might be understood in the following way.

What is important about the communicator is credibility; "credibility is critical to persuasion."[2] Credibility involves two elements: (1) honesty (trustworthiness), and (2) expertise (demonstrating a mastery of the facts and law). Credibility means that the audience will be less skeptical of the messenger, and more accepting of the message. Lack of credibility, on the other hand, raises the audience's level of skepticism and makes it more difficult to persuade. Gaining and maintaining credibility are thus key factors for an advocate's ability to be persuasive.

For an audience consisting of arbitrators, the content of the message generally should be rational, analytical and thoughtful, not *overtly* emotional. An overtly emotional appeal may provoke resentment from the tribunal. This is not inconsistent with the foregoing discussion on how decisions are made. The emotive content of the case should not be overlooked, but should be presented in a low key manner. The key facts presented (*i.e.*, the equities), the order in which they are presented, and the advocate's

---

2 Richard C. Waites, Courtroom Psychology and Trial Advocacy, p. 26 (ALM Publishing 2003).

voice inflection and body language will necessarily all convey some emotion, but generally it should not rise to the conscious level. The message should focus the case by emphasizing the concrete evidence (*i.e.*, tangible, objective or clearly proven), showing precisely how it satisfies the elements of the legal claims or defenses. For arbitrators, the governing law will provide the societal values applicable to the dispute. Generally, the arbitrators will be able easily to accept arguments that clearly fit within the parameters of the applicable law. But if an argument requires an extension of the law or a new interpretation or application, or if the true facts fall outside the normal range of a plausible story (such as presenting unusual motivations), then the advocate needs to anticipate this problem, often addressing it directly and demonstrating that the facts or the novel legal interpretation are plausible, perhaps supported by analogues in other areas.

The message should be communicated both orally and in writing. Oral messages generally have more affective appeal than writings and can be more powerful in persuasion, but the spoken word is "fleeting and memories fade."[3] The dominant sense of learning for some people is listening to the spoken word, but for most international arbitrators with legal training, their dominant sense of learning is likely to be the written word. This means that they will prefer and digest information more easily from the written submissions. One can sometimes observe this objectively in arbitrators who spend the oral hearing largely reading the real-time written transcript being contemporaneously made of the proceeding. When the oral hearing is concluded, the arbitrators are left with the written submissions and witness statements to which they will generally turn in writing the award, which may take weeks or months. Thus, the message should be clearly, thoroughly and persuasively inscribed in the written memorials, but sharply focused in the oral presentation. Very importantly, however, the message should not be overstated. Arbitrators are generally critical thinkers who will subject the message to critical scrutiny. Overstatement of the case may lose credibility.

---

3 *Id.* at p. 32.

Thus, if an advocate is to err, it should be on the side of understatement, not the contrary.

Finally, the audience, of course, consists of the arbitrators. It is often said that the most important thing that counsel will do in a case is to select the arbitrators. The values, beliefs and attitudes that the arbitrators bring to the case can be critical to the outcome. What is important is that their pre-existing attitudes allow them to be open to the message to be delivered so that persuasion is possible. Thus, an advocate should research the awards, writings, speeches, and opinions of the arbitrators to the extent possible, in advance of appointment. But the depth of information that one would need of the arbitrators' values, beliefs and attitudes to be truly predictive given the overriding importance of the facts, and the unique facts of each case, is almost never available. Thus, the advocate typically must make decisions based on incomplete and generally inadequate information. The best the advocate can do in most situations is to determine the general attitude of the arbitrator toward certain situations and whether any published decisions or writings indicate a prejudgment on key legal issues in the case. Fortunately, most arbitrators take the standards required by the arbitral rules — impartiality and independence — very seriously, and the community values that govern a decision are objectively set forth in the relevant law. Experienced arbitrators adhere to the standards of the rules and generally try to apply the governing law, even if it differs significantly from that to which they are accustomed.

An often neglected aspect of advocacy in international arbitration is that of ethics. It is generally considered that lawyers carry their own country's ethical rules with them when they practice abroad. But the absence of a truly international code of ethics for international advocates means that the subject is often overlooked, partly because of a lack of knowledge or confusion as to which rules apply. While the International Bar Association has prepared an International Code of Ethics for lawyers, that Code is insufficient: it is not well known, it is not specific to advocacy, it does not contain all rules necessary for international advocacy in light of the conflicting national ethical rules to which different advocates are subjected, and it is not mandatory for international advocates. The result of the present practice is that opposing advocates from different countries may have very different ethical obligations in the same case (*e.g.*, produce or withhold key documents), which can potentially affect the outcome of the case. The work over the past decade of certain scholars such as Prof. Catherine Rogers has pointed to the need for a mandatory code of ethics for international advocates. Prof. Rogers' chapter persuasively makes the case for such a code.

Advocacy in international arbitration is unique, different from that used in both national legal systems and standing international tribunals and its unique quality is due largely to its diversity and that of its subject matter. It is not a single monolithic style, but instead consists of different procedures and styles drawn from various national judicial systems or standing international tribunals. Its practitioners — both advocates and arbitrators — come from all of the world's major legal systems and cultures, including international tribunals. It is practiced generally before *ad hoc* arbitral tribunals, whose members are selected for a single, specific case. The arbitrators are diverse, often from different countries, continents, cultures, and legal systems, often speaking different languages, and representing various legal specialties or even professions. The advocates may be just as diverse. A single case may involve issues of the laws of different countries, even different legal systems, or of public international law or the *lex mercatoria.* The procedural law that must be applied may differ from the substantive law. The standards of a relevant trade or profession may differ from region to region, and conflict in a given case. All of this diversity makes international arbitration a game of three dimensional chess.

International arbitration involves an amalgamation of different procedures and styles of advocacy. The mixing of the oral advocacy and adversarial traditions of Great Britain, the Commonwealth countries, and the United States with the largely written advocacy and inquisitorial legacy of Continental Europe has resulted in a flexible procedure that can lean toward one or the other of the great traditions, given the necessities of the case and the proclivities of the arbitrators and counsel. But in recent years, a trend can be observed toward harmonizing the procedures of the different judicial systems, at least when the arbitrators and advocates are from different legal systems and are experienced in international arbitration. In this homogenized style, much of the burden of advocacy is carried by the written memorials, with the supporting evidence attached, yet the oral hearing (including US or British-style cross examination) can be essential, changing the outcome of some cases because of the cross examination of a witness or the clarity and focus of the oral arguments. A unified style of international arbitral advocacy should aim toward a common denominator: a presentation that is simple, clear, concise, and sharply focused.

A final point with respect to advocacy concerns the perspective of the arbitrator. Before concluding his preparations for an oral hearing, the advocate should stop and consider the oral presentation from the perspective of the arbitrators. What will be of interest to them? How should the presentation be ordered? To what style of advocacy are they accustomed? The author has learned more about advocacy by serving as an arbitrator than from his many years of experience as counsel. The reason is that serving as an arbitrator allows the advocate to perceive the case from the very different perspective of the decision-maker. There is often a "disconnect" between the arbitrator and the advocate. The arbitrator's job is to decide the issues in dispute and to draft an award that rationally justifies that decision. He is interested in learning about the facts and the law that are relevant to deciding those issues and justifying the decision. Any arguments or evidence that are not helpful in performing those specific tasks are unwelcome. Ad hominem arguments, "cheap shots" at the opposing party or counsel, and overly-strident advocacy are generally not well received. The advocate should assume the role of assisting the tribunal in performing its job properly. Consider starting the oral presentation with a list of the issues to be decided by the tribunal. For the arbitrators, it is often helpful to have such a list at the outset in order to know what is important to look for in the evidence to follow. Put yourself in the arbitrators' shoes and ask questions of the witnesses that will assist the arbitrators in deciding the case. Fit the evidence together into a plausible and credible story that the tribunal can use to justify the decision. Structure the presentation in a way that will assist the tribunal in drafting a reasoned award. By considering what the arbitrators need to decide the case favorably and to justify that decision rationally, the advocate both assists the arbitrators and simultaneously provides the client with the best chance of prevailing in the case. Chapters 10, 24 and 25 by Pierre Bienvenu, Bernardo Cremades and Yves Fortier address the subject of advocacy from the arbitrator's standpoint. These chapters provide important advice for the advocate.

The previous edition of this book was the first ever to address the subject of advocacy in international arbitration. Surprisingly, the editor had difficulty in attracting chapter authors for that edition. The reason may have been that many prospective authors had never really thought about the techniques of successful advocacy. But the first edition attracted substantial attention to its subject matter, focusing advocates and would-be advocates on some of the techniques of advocacy.

While the first edition focused mainly on the cultural differences in advocacy in various regions of the world and before specialized tribunals, this second edition differs significantly. It focuses more on functionality and technique while preserving a section on the cultural differences in arbitral advocacy. It is designed to address each functional aspect of an international arbitration and the techniques that have been developed for good written and oral advocacy. In this respect, it has been devised to assist both the novice in learning the techniques of advocacy and the experienced advocate in improving his skills.

The organization of this book proceeds according to the following plan. Part I of this book provides introductory material, discussing cultural differences in advocacy, differences in witness evidence in different legal systems, and the ethics of advocacy in international arbitration. Part II addresses the often overlooked but vital topic of the psychology of persuasion. The two chapters in this Part include contributions both by lawyers and psychologists who specialize in the field of persuasion. A working knowledge of the psychology of decision-making and the psychological principles of persuasion is essential for the consistent success of an advocate. These chapters introduce this subject matter and are a must-read for both new and experienced advocates.

Part III focuses on the important subject of strategy. Strategizing a case is certainly a critical component of advocacy. Part IV begins the practical application of the principles of persuasion, addressing the various aspects of written advocacy. Because many if not most international arbitral proceedings include an extensive phase of written submissions, it is these written submissions that "make" the case and carry the primary burden of persuasion. Therefore, preparing those submissions in a compelling manner is crucial to winning the case. This Part will discuss the principles of effective written advocacy; advocacy in pleadings, memorials and post-hearing submissions; witness statements and expert reports; and the organization and presentation of documents.

Part V discusses the various aspects of oral advocacy. It is at this phase of the case that the advocate has the opportunity to speak directly to the tribunal, to focus the arguments sharply, and to answer the questions of the tribunal. This Part will discuss oral advocacy in pre-hearing arguments, opening statements, and closing arguments, and will also address direct and cross examination of witnesses. Part VI addresses the subject of the regional differences in advocacy, and Part VII concludes the book with a discussion of advocacy from the perspective of the arbitrator.

It is hoped that this book will attract even more attention to the subject of advocacy in international arbitration. In the bigger picture, the point of good advocacy is not for one advocate or party to win a given case, but to level the playing field for all advocates and to assist tribunals in arriving at the right results in their cases.

Part I.

ADVOCACY IN INTERNATIONAL ABITRATION

Chapter 1

CULTURAL DIFFERENCES IN ADVOCACY IN INTERNATIONAL ARBITRATION

Jan Paulsson

If you want to observe a real clash of cultures, one might be tempted to say, it is hard to find more sound and fury than what emerges when rival French lawyers appear *on both sides*, or rival Londoners on both sides, or Cairenes or New Yorkers! For then, it often seems, the combatants leave no prisoners, and urge vehemently that starkly different procedural arrangements be adopted, each camp insisting all the while that what they seek is but the normal course of well-ordered events. Their opponents, of course, are the ones attempting to mislead the tribunal with self-serving requests that make a mockery of due process!

How can this be, when both lawyers are members of the same bar association or law society? The answer is that on any given day one set of lawyers embodies the culture of claimants, while the opponent represents the culture of respondents. Here is the real clash, it may seem: the "*justice delayed, justice denied*" school vs. the "*nothing's settled until it's settled right*" school.

Confirmation of this observation seems to be provided, by the way of contrast, in the polite diffidence often exhibited when opposing counsel truly come from different cultures, as each side outdoes the other in proffering well-mannered, tentative suggestions, full of solicitous understanding for the other side, as though all feel it incumbent to act as goodwill ambassador attesting to the decency and urbanity of their own legal community.

Is there then no true clash of cultures in international arbitration? Are there only the different procedural preferences that commend themselves to lawyers in light of tactical objectives – which preferences are, moreover, likely to be attenuated when adjustments are made for the different origins of the participants? There is certainly something to be said for this startling proposition. Nearly three decades of successive editions of the IBA Rules on the Taking of Evidence in International Commercial Arbitration have led to the emergence of a remarkable series of effective *compromises* with respect to important issues of due process which had once seemed intractable. Similarly, successive editions of rules of leading arbitral institutions have incorporated refinements that reflect steady *convergence.* And of course, the UNCITRAL Model Law on International Commercial Arbitration has been embraced by legislatures in countries of all stages of development in all regions of the world—impressive testimony to the emergence of *harmonious conceptions* of the international arbitral process.

Yet to conclude that we can cease to worry about clashes of culture would be premature and exaggerated. In relation to the theme of this book, it would be perilous for the advocate to ignore the potential for misunderstanding, and indeed occasionally mistrust, that still lies under the surface of cosmopolitan good manners. To get a proper sense of the prevalence of such disaffection, one would have to know what parties say internally, behind closed doors, reacting to a disappointing ruling; and what arbitrators whisper to each other in deliberations as they reflect on the behavior of the parties and their counsel.

The effect of cultural differences on perceptions of the legitimacy of the international arbitral process as a whole is, of course, a matter of fundamental importance. In these pages, however, the focus is narrower. In seeking to master the art of advocacy, we need to consider *the value to advocates of sensitivity to the attitudes of both their opponents and the arbitrators.*

That skilled advocates need to be attuned to the culture of the arbitrators they face is self-evident; it is an obvious and essential element of the internationally active advocate's credibility and persuasiveness.

But it is also of capital importance to understand the opponent, lest one make false assessments of the latter's degree of attachment to given features of the process. Why expend precious political capital, fighting tooth and nail in written submissions for an important point which in all likelihood the opponent would readily concede anyway? Why waste ammunition to secure fleeting satisfaction with respect to a secondary issue to which the opponent turns out to be attached with passionate intensity? Above all, why run the risk of creating needless resentment by operating in ignorance of opposing counsel's conceptions of fairness and ethics? After all, loyalty between opponents is the first step toward mutual respect—the precondition for the kind of constructive dialogue that may lead to amicable settlement. It needs hardly be said that since good advocacy aims to contribute to the attainment of this client's concrete objectives, so much the better if it is achieved without fighting to the end.

Let us begin with the consequences of misreading the cultural predispositions of *arbitrators*. We are here naturally dealing with the types of tension which are likely to be latent; written and oral exchanges with the tribunal are unlikely to be confrontational. Yet situations may emerge that raise the tribunal's ire, as indeed happened in one case when a traditionalist European arbitrator entered the room on the first day of witness hearings to see that one party's American counsel had already invaded the scene to display an elaborate panoply of screens and demonstrative exhibits, or when a sole arbitrator from the Middle East was handed a "draft judgment" by another American lawyer. In the first example, the lawyer had innocently but ignorantly assumed that it was understood and expected that his expert witnesses would be able to put on a forensic show of the kind routinely seen in U.S. courtrooms. The European arbitrator, on the other hand, considered that it was for the tribunal to direct the course of the testimony, and therefore presumptuous—if not suggestive of an untoward degree of collusion between advocate and expert— for counsel to set the stage without as much as a by-your-leave. In the second example, the lawyer had innocently but ignorantly assumed that the sole arbitrator would be assisted by a formal statement of the relief requested as matters stood at the end of the case, quite normal in his home courts, whereas the arbitrator, perhaps a fortiori because he was sitting alone and because the respondent had refused to participate in the proceedings and to contribute to his fees, rejected the text with distaste, as an unacceptable attempt to excise undue *ex parte* influence.

Not all advocates will go so far as to procure and study the available prior ruling of every arbitrator. But surely it is irresponsible for an advocate who comes from a different legal environment not to seek to determine the procedural do's and don'ts that are likely to be part of the tribunal's expectations, if not requirements. (It is not impermissible simply to ask the tribunal!) This consideration permeates the pages of this volume, in the many different ways reflected in the titles of the contributions of various authors.

Before shifting our focus away from the arbitrators, we may well ask whether in some environments arbitrators do not in fact perceive and adhere to a higher standard in international cases than in domestic ones. This may seem an odd and somewhat disturbing supposition, because arbitral propriety should not be variable. Yet one may well perceive in some countries that the community of prominent lawyers is quite small, and characterized by a density of interrelations which in turn gives rise to a rather singular culture of influence and tacit expectation. It seems humanly impossible in such an environment to constitute a collegium whose members are unaffected by the identity of their fellows and of those who appear before them, and all that goes with it: personality and status, past encounters and future prospects, reputation and influence in the community. In such a context an unadulterated objective assessment of the merits of the case may seem unattainable. Understanding this to be so, arbitrators in the local setting may make adjust their behavior, consciously and subconsciously, to account or compensate for myriad contextual factors. The result may be deemed fair, or at least tolerable but the path less than straight-forward in the view of outsiders, and therefore unacceptable to them. Yet when individuals ventures forth to act in a transnational setting, unencumbered by the density of local factors and thus free to concentrate on doing the ablest and fairest job possible in the particular case, they may well give a far better account of themselves. To bring the point home concretely, consider the more extreme but still analogous situation of very capable arbitrators who live under oppressive political regimes; it may be wholly unrealistic to expect them to deal impartially with a dispute between a national and a foreigner although they would perform very well in a dispute between foreigners only.

We turn now to issues that may trouble relations between *advocates*. They are not limited to matters of arbitral procedure strictly speaking, but also extend to more general behavioral patterns. Indeed, true cultural clashes are more likely to occur outside the arbitral hearings, and relate to such important matters of culture as relations among members of the bar; or between lawyers, on the one hand, and clients, witnesses, and judges or arbitrators on the other. Members of different bars may, for example, have a clear understanding of the rules pertaining to professional privilege; yet fail to understand that the accuracy of that understanding is geographically limited.

Similarly, in some places the confidentiality of lawyer-to-lawyer communications is presumed; in others, it depends on an explicit notice of confidentiality. In some places, the confidentiality of attorney-client communications may be waived; in others not—for fear that the powerful would otherwise routinely obtain waivers by coercion. In some places, advocates can act on the assumption that clients will understand that their lawyer may have a duty to the court to bring relevant information to its attention even if it is unfavorable; in others, an advocate who expresses such ideas is likely to be summarily fired. In some places, a lawyer who calls witnesses to the stand without attempting to determine the tenor of their testimony would be guilty of professional negligence; in others it is said that no advocate may even *meet with* a witness beforehand.

Incidentally, in France the members of the bar seem to be in unison in believing that it is improper for an *advocat* to discuss the case with a *témoin* in advance of the hearing. Yet it seems impossible to find such a rule in any code of deontology. It is likely that French advocates, unused to the appearance of witnesses in *any* court case, and alarmed at the comprehensive and well-written witness statements put forth by Anglo-American lawyers, have transformed the proscription of *suborning* witnesses into an illusory blanket rule against even making the effort to determine what a witness may know. This example illustrates one of the paradoxes of international arbitration; in a domain characterized by much sophistication about many things—e.g. the law of treaties; rules pertaining to conflicts of laws and conflicts of jurisdiction; and the mechanics of trans-border finance and industry it is often possible to get away with all manner of shaky approximations when making allegations about the way things are done under one's own national regime, because others in the room are not able or inclined to verify them.

Those who would deny the persistence of cultural differences in international arbitration must bear the burden of explaining why the hearing of the same case, if it took place in Paris, would notwithstanding the applicability of the same international rules likely require but a fraction of the time one would expect to be devoted to it if it conducted just across the Channel in London (on the assumption that that the affair in each place is conducted under the direction of French and English presidents, respectively.) This does not, of course, denote different objectives: fairness, efficiency, and reliable awards are equally prized by all good arbitrators. And we can certainly observe that the international arbitral process has gone a long way toward evolving something of a culture of its own when we consider that although these hearings will be conducted in quite different ways, each of them will also look very different, and *more like each other*, than cases before the High Court or the *Tribunal de grande instance*. Still, it is obvious that there is a French conception of priorities in the proper presentation of a case that is different from the English one. The essence of this difference simply cannot be distilled into a single sentence. Even at the level of detail, it remains elusive to anyone who would want to impart the lessons of experience to a neophyte anxious to get his or her hands on a reliable instruction manual. We are of course talking about culture.

Knowing that what is sought under all decent methodologies is *insight*; does it help to refer to the French admiration for synthesis and the English desire to get to the bottom of things? That one approach is that of the surgeon, interested only in what is decisive for the particular problem that has arisen, seeing no need to learn *everything* about the anatomy and history of the patient indeed would view it as noise and distraction? That the other believes that the ability to determine what is truly relevant, if not decisive, requires a complete understanding of the facts? That the French broadly view witnesses as unreliable and are rather certain that it is pointless to hear their self-serving statements? That the English advocate, without having any particular illusions about human nature, believes that a skilled professional can derive much evidence of value from witnesses by confronting them with facts and propositions that reveal self-serving declarations to be significant indicators of untruth? Of course, the premise of this belief is that the skilled professional is given all the time he needs to build the foundation for his cross-examination. To this the French reply might be that their courts have never been given the luxury of such limitless investigations, that the litigants want a quicker answer, that at any rate there are other litigants awaiting their turn, and finally that the Ministry of Justice does not have a budget adequate to fill the courtrooms that would be needed if one were to give advocates *carte blanche*—and why should we assume anyway, that justice is served by a contest between the forensic "development" of facts after the dispute has arisen rather than the intelligent application of legal analysis to a written record as it stood, frozen (as it were) in the hands of the parties at the moment they began to fight?

Of course, there is no way to answer these questions with any degree of certainty or finality. We cannot even be sure that we learn all that much from experience. No culture is a mechanical "system"; the variables are infinite; experiments are not reproducible. Even if they were monolithic, cultures evolve. International arbitration involves innumerable constellations of different cultures, as reflected in the assumptions of behavior of all participants. We go to work not knowing exactly what to expect. This is part of the exhilaration of the *métier*. Who is complaining?

Chapter 2

DIFFERENCES IN THE APPROACH TO WITNESS EVIDENCE BETWEEN THE CIVIL AND COMMON LAW TRADITIONS

Anthony C. Sinclair*

I. Domestic Influences on the International Arbitration Bar

The differences in approach that can bear upon international arbitration proceedings have, in the past, been expertly illuminated in a great many settings.[1] For all but the most senior arbitrators, with decades of practice behind them involving a great diversity of parties and jurisdictions, to update and offer a modern overview of differences in the approach to witness evidence in civil and common law countries is a daunting task. These observations fortunately benefit not only from the author's own experience but that of an integrated global arbitration practice within a multinational firm, in which colleagues routinely work together, share and learn from each other's practices. What follows are, nevertheless, observations of a generalised nature to which it is freely admitted there will be a great many more exceptions and qualifications than can be mentioned here.

Many of the differences that one can observe in the practice of international arbitration stem from the different levels and range of experiences of the counsel involved. Some differences in approach

---

* International Arbitration Group, Allen & Overy LLP.

1 See e.g. H. M. Holtzmann and G. Bernini, "Hypothetical Case for Use in a Comparative Study of Arbitration Practice in Various Legal Systems" in P. Sanders (ed.), *Comparative Arbitration Practice and Public Policy in Arbitration* (1986) *ICCA Congress Series – No. 3*, 19. See also the contributions to the first edition of this book, R. D. Bishop (ed.) *The Art of Advocacy in International Arbitration* (Huntington: Juris, 2004).

may be more directly cultural, linked to the practice of litigation in the courts of different jurisdictions. One should not over simplify the differences between civil and common law approaches, since there are differences both subtle and substantial within these systems.[2] Nevertheless there are striking differences in the approach of civil and common law courts and tribunals when it comes to witness evidence. Some of the differences found in a selection of jurisdictions are as follows.

In the case of England and Wales, the United States, Singapore, Australia, New Zealand, Hong Kong, and many other common law jurisdictions, there is a highly developed regard for evidence committed to paper in the form of witness statements, with extensive cross examination of the witnesses to test their evidence at trial. In New York, in particular, there is still the prospect of jury trials in civil cases, which may have an impact on the style and substance of advocacy. In these jurisdictions, the result is an extensive practice of witness "proofing", assistance with the production of witness statements, preparation of witnesses for trial and cross examination by highly skilled advocates.

Practice is markedly different in the case of litigation conducted in the civil law jurisdictions. The practice of the Belgian courts, for example, is rarely to admit witness statements in commercial disputes.[3] Witness statements are occasionally produced, but they are afforded little probative weight. Where there is live testimony at trial, the court will take the lead with questioning, not counsel or parties. Likewise in French litigation, witnesses are extremely uncommon,

---

[2] See e.g. J. Paulsson, "Overview of Methods of Presenting Evidence in Different Legal Systems", in A. J. van den Berg (ed.), *Planning Efficient Arbitration Proceedings – The Law Applicable in International Arbitration* (The Hague: Kluwer, 1999) 112 and cf. Lord Justice Staughton, "Common Law and Civil Law Procedures: Which is the More Inquisitorial? A Common Lawyer's Response" (1989) 5(4) *Arbitration International* 351; C. Reymond, "Civil Law and Common Law Procedures: Which is the More Inquisitorial? A Civil Lawyer's Response (1989) 5(4) *Arbitration International* 357.

[3] H. Van Houtte, "Counsel-Witness Relations and Professional Misconduct in Civil Law Systems" (2003) 19(4) *Arbitration International* 457.

with the courts favouring practices such as neutral court-appointed experts to resolve disputed questions of fact. Where witness statements are produced, examination by the judge is the norm. In Italy, the court drives the process of obtaining information from witnesses. Cross examination is not typically available.

In Germany, potential witness evidence is identified in written submissions, but this does not entail the preparation of witness statements. Instead, if the judge considers witness evidence necessary to resolve an issue in dispute, witnesses previously identified or nominated by the parties in their written submissions may be called to testify, but examination at the hearing is by the judge, with the parties' counsel having the right to put follow-up questions. In Poland, there is no cross examination of witnesses, but as in Germany judges may put questions to experts (typically court-appointed) and the parties themselves. The parties may present follow-up questions to experts. In Luxembourg and the Netherlands, witnesses may be produced for examination at trial. In the Netherlands, examination is conducted by the court, but the parties can put forward questions. In Luxembourg, cross examination by counsel is permitted.

In China, there has traditionally been little credence given to signed witness statements in the course of litigation, but witnesses can and do give evidence in person in court, where they are typically examined by the judge alone. Cross examination is only available with the court's permission. In Japan, it is possible to adduce witness evidence at trial, but the requesting party must convince the court that this is necessary in order to determine the issues. Attendance in person is preferred, in which case written statements will normally not be produced. For litigation in the UAE, arguments and evidence are normally introduced by way of written submissions. However, witness evidence may be presented if the claim exceeds a certain value (AED 5,000 at the time of writing) and a party requests it. Witnesses may be called and questioned at trial by both the parties and the judge.

It is readily apparent that many differences in the practice of international arbitration are likely to be the product of the differing experience levels of counsel more familiar with the procedures and techniques of the national courts of their home jurisdiction where they acquired their training as litigators. Given the approach followed in domestic litigation in many of the civil law jurisdictions just cited (and others not mentioned), it is not surprising that, in domestic arbitration proceedings and arbitration proceedings dominated by litigators steeped in those local traditions, witness statements are rare and cross examination almost never practised.

For example, in Brussels-based Belgian Centre for Mediation and Arbitration ("CEPINA") arbitration, it is quite unusual to use witnesses, no doubt reflecting the practices of the Brussels bar. It is also no surprise that there is not a well-developed system for handling of witnesses, including cross examination, in international arbitrations held in China given prevailing practices in Chinese litigation. This is changing slowly, with the 2005 revisions to the China International Economic and Trade Arbitration Commission ("CIETAC") Arbitration Rules, and Rule 29(3) in particular, specifically allowing parties to agree on a more adversarial (common law) rather than inquisitorial (civil law) approach to arbitration proceedings. As a result it is possible to observe more frequent use of witnesses and witness examination in recent CIETAC arbitrations. However, it remains the case that local lawyers are relatively unfamiliar with witness statements, their form and content, or the skill of cross examination.

Whilst witness statements in general may be more readily accepted in complex international arbitration proceedings, lawyers from many civil jurisdictions still tend to consider that witness statements from persons who are employees or officers of a company that is a party to proceedings are self-serving (if not inadmissible) and can be surprised when confronted with them in international arbitration. Arbitrators trained in France, Germany and Russia, for example, may be reluctant to hear witness evidence from certain persons, especially senior officers of a company which is a party to the dispute since they are considered not to be sufficiently independent. They may be heard, but their evidence is taken to be the explanation of the parties, evaluated as such and therefore may be afforded different weight.

But not all arbitration proceedings are alike. Proceedings dominated by domestic procedural considerations are not in both spirit and substance "truly international" arbitrations, inspired by the New York Convention and the UNCITRAL Model Law, conducted under one of the leading institutional or ad hoc sets of rules for international arbitration proceedings, within the transnational framework of the IBA Rules on Taking of Evidence in International Commercial Arbitration (the "IBA Rules"). Rules 4(4) to 4(8) of the IBA Rules, Article 25(5) of the UNCITRAL Arbitration Rules (the "UNCITRAL Rules"), Article 20(5) of the AAA International Centre for Dispute Resolution ("ICDR") International Arbitration Rules, and Articles 20(3) to 20(6) of the London Court of International Arbitration Rules (the "LCIA Rules") all expressly contemplate the use of witness statements in arbitration proceedings. The use of witness statements is also widespread in arbitration under the ICC Arbitration Rules (the "ICC Rules"),[4] albeit not expressly mentioned in those rules. Likewise, it is also now generally accepted in international commercial arbitration, if it was not before,[5] that any person, including the parties and their legal representatives, should be permitted to testify as a witness in international commercial arbitration.[6] This is confirmed in Rule 4(2) of the IBA Rules, which a prudent advocate or tribunal may reference at the outset of proceedings if there is the risk of misunderstanding later. The tribunal is of course free to attribute such weight as it deems appropriate to any witness evidence, as expressly confirmed by most arbitration rules.[7]

---

[4] Y. Derains and E. A. Schwartz, *A Guide to the ICC Rules of Arbitration* (2nd edn., The Hague: Kluwer, 2005) 276-277.

[5] Cf. ICC Case No. 7319, Decision, 30 October 1992, in which the Tribunal ruled that the directors of a company that was a party could not give evidence as witnesses.

[6] Cf. ICC Arbitration Rules, Rule 20(3) of which appears to retain a distinction between a witness and "any other person" who may testify.

[7] Article 22(1)(g) of the LCIA Rules; Article 20(6) of the ICDR International Arbitration Rules; Article 25(6) of the UNCITRAL Rules; Rule 34(1) of the ICSID Arbitration Rules.

Truly international proceedings are conducted by an increasingly specialised and multicultural "international arbitration bar",[8] in the leading seats for international arbitration, especially London, Paris, Geneva, Stockholm, Singapore, Hong Kong, New York and Dubai (amongst others). Proceedings of this kind are the primary focus of this chapter. Here the differences in the approach of counsel to witnesses and witness evidence are less stark. For modern civil law trained arbitration practitioners, techniques surrounding the introduction and testing of witness evidence are now a familiar part of their cases,[9] and thus, the differences between the civil and common law practice of arbitration are almost certainly diminishing.[10] According to Hans Van Houtte, "in Europe witnesses are now becoming a substantial element in arbitration proceedings, not only for transatlantic or cross-Channel cases, but also for continental disputes and even for purely domestic disputes".[11] Civil lawyers readily grapple with witness statements and oral testimony in this form of arbitration, but clearly on the basis that these features are an Anglo-American import and do not come as second nature. Nevertheless, the differences that remain are potentially important, since truly international arbitration proceedings often pit against each other counsel harking from very different cultural and legal traditions.

The purpose of this chapter is not to promote any single approach to witness evidence, which is not likely to be apt given the diversity of arbitral proceedings and the fundamental principle of party autonomy. Rather, it is to recall some effective techniques of advocates observed in practice, and a few less effective ones too. Section II addresses the witness statement and its preparation. Section III is concerned with the role of the advocate in preparing witnesses to give evidence in hearings. Section IV concerns the questioning of witnesses at hearings themselves.

---

[8] See C. Reymond, "Le Président du Tribunal Arbitral", *Etudes offertes à Pierre Bellet* (Paris: Litec, 1991) 467, 474.

[9] Van Houtte, above note 3, 459.

[10] Also e.g. J. Paulsson, above note 2, 112; G. Von Segesser, "Witness Preparation in International Commercial Arbitration" (2002) 20(2) *ASA Bulletin* 222.

[11] Van Houtte, above note 3, 458.

II. The Witness Statement

A. The advocate's role in the preparation of witness statements

In some civil law jurisdictions, local bar rules forbid counsel from interviewing prospective witnesses. The same is true of the English bar, but not English solicitors. In some jurisdictions such actions may attract legal sanctions in addition to the discipline of the bar regulatory body. But frequently it is expressly acknowledged, as with the code of ethics for the Brussels Bar, that such rules do not apply to foreign or transnational arbitration whenever the rules governing that arbitration permit contact with witnesses.[12]

In the practice of international commercial arbitration, it is acknowledged that "the drafting of a Witness Statement requires contacts between the witness and the party that is presenting him",[13] and presumably that party's lawyers too. This is confirmed in Rule 4(3) of the IBA Rules, which provides that "It shall not be improper for a Party, its officers, employees, legal advisors or other representatives to interview its witnesses or potential witnesses". Similarly, Article 20(6) of the LCIA Arbitration Rules provides that a party or its legal representative may interview a witness or potential witness for the purpose of presenting his testimony in written form or producing him as an oral witness, subject to the mandatory provisions of applicable law. These rules have been said to "reflect the current consensus in the international arbitration community".[14]

If the applicable rules do not provide as much, or there is potential for disagreement or doubt, it would be appropriate to adopt a provision such as that set out in Rule 4(3) of the IBA Rules in the first procedural order. There should be no doubt as to whether counsel or the parties may meet with actual or potential witnesses, in order to obtain witness statements. Counsel from different cultural

---

12 *Ibid*, 459.

13 IBA Working Party, "Commentary on the New IBA Rules of Evidence" (2000) *Business Law International* 14.

14 Von Segesser, above note 10, 223.

backgrounds and legal traditions may still hold difference conceptions as to the content of those meetings, in the light of their own professional conduct rules, but ought to share a common goal, which is to help the witnesses to produce truthful but also effective witness statements. The question that must be asked is whether their efforts constitute effective advocacy.

In arbitration proceedings influenced by civil law practices, witness statements are frequently written in their entirety by the witnesses themselves. Counsel may do little more than help the witness to structure arguments or provide copies of the relevant documents for review. This accords with the expectations of many civil law arbitrators, who prefer a first hand impression and may admit distrust of a witness statement that is "too polished", or a witness that is "too smart" when answering questions. As a result, witness statements are often not to the point and include emotional language. They may lack precision as to people, dates and figures. They are often cast in the passive voice. Where lawyers have been involved, the language may be formalistic or repetitive of a party's submissions. These deficiencies are tolerated by civil lawyers: witness testimony is not considered very reliable in the first place, writing it down does not make it more reliable.

As between the common law traditions, frequent experience (both in observing opposing counsel but also working together as co-counsel) supports the generalisation that US lawyers tend to be more directly involved in the drafting of witness statements than most other arbitration practitioners. Witness statements adduced in support of parties represented by US counsel are from time to time noted for not being in the witnesses' own words (or not appearing to be so). English common lawyers will declare their departure from US practices, stating that they prefer their witnesses to "hold the pen" and draft their statements in their own words, or at least that they adhere very closely to the witness's own phrases and terminology. The reality may not always be quite so different from US colleagues, however, as English lawyers will rigorously test a witness's evidence against the documents, resulting in numerous iterations of a witness statement before it is finalised. It is easy to imagine that something of the lawyer might find its way into the statement during this process.

There is no doubt that there are occasions where the lawyers cannot resist taking the pen, or the witness's own resources (available time, language and drafting skills) mean that the lawyers must be involved in producing drafts of what the witness tells them in witness interviews. Here there is a risk that the lawyer may undermine the witness (and their party's case) if insufficient care is taken to ensure without exception that the evidence is the witness's own, and in the witness's own words. The influence of the lawyers in drafting a witness's evidence can be particularly evident when, during a hearing, it becomes clear that the witness does not have a command of English to match the eloquence of his or her written statement. For example, in one case, a witness used rather elegant metaphors in his written statement, which was in English, yet insisted on testifying in his native language at the hearing. During the hearing, it became abundantly clear that the witness had no comprehension of the meaning of the metaphor in English, which also appeared in that party's written submissions. This adds nothing to the witness's credibility and may detract from it.

Other forensic anomalies sometimes arise, such as when a witness testifies in a language different from the language of the signed written statement (even more so when there is no native language version), or when certain distinctive phrases recur in the statements of other witnesses. This can happen even when there is no native language issue: lawyers may include overly legalistic or formal phrasing that is not part of the witness's natural idiom. In cross examination, it may be possible to undermine the credibility of the witnesses by identifying the hand of the lawyers at work here. Arbitrators tend to be interested in such anomalies, but only to a degree. Counsel themselves are likely to be much more excited than arbitrators in establishing, through the minutiae of phrasing, formatting and vocabulary, that the witness statement was not drafted solely by the witness.

A common lawyer, particularly a US-trained advocate, will routinely cross examine on the manner in which a witness statement was prepared with questions such as: "who drafted your statement?"; "how many times did you meet Lawyer X?"; "for how many hours?"; "did Lawyer X tell you what to say in your statement?"; and quite possibly, "are you being paid for giving this evidence and appearing here today?" A well-prepared witness will also have standard and well-accepted answers: "Lawyer X prepared a first draft of my statement, based on my answers to questions he posed to me when we met. I carefully reviewed and made several revisions to the draft to make sure every word reflected what I said. My statement accurately reflects the facts as I recall them". For the arbitrators, this can be a fairly uninspiring routine.

Of course, arbitrators have seen it all before,[15] and are not surprised when witness statements are drafted by the lawyers. Or they come from a legal tradition in which there is relatively little weight given to witness statements anyway. A consistent message one hears from arbitrators, of all cultural or jurisdictional backgrounds, is that witness statements are far more compelling if they are in the witness's own words, including their own colloquialisms. Many civil and common law trained arbitrators alike are evidently uncomfortable with witness statements prepared under the influence of counsel. One view is that:

> "Drawn up with the party or its legal advisors the witness may be influenced in formulating his or her Statement which has to be signed and affirmed by him or her as being the truth. In my opinion these Witness Statements, preceding the hearings of the witnesses in person, are not in accordance with the expectations of many parties in an international arbitration".[16]

Other arbitrators simply find the advocate's efforts unconvincing. One English-trained arbitrator has observed that the "massive

---

[15] A. V. Schlaepfer, "Witness Statements" in L. Lévy and V. V. Veeder (eds.), *Arbitration and Oral Evidence* (Paris: ICC Publishing, 2005) 68.

[16] P. Sanders, *Quo Vadis Arbitration? Sixty Years of Arbitration Practice* (The Hague: Kluwer, 1999) 262.

efforts" of advocates "at reshaping the testimony of their client's factual witnesses" are ineffective, if not counter-productive.[17]

Telltale signs of the lawyer's influence upon the language used tend to diminish a witness statement's probative value in the eyes of arbitrators empowered to determine for themselves the weight of the evidence.[18] And if arbitrators are not persuaded, it must be poor advocacy. This guidance might lead lawyers to be careful not to over-finesse, if involved in producing the drafts. One approach to dispense with any charade may be to include, in the witness statement itself, a declaration that the witness has been assisted in drafting the witness statement by the lawyers, but that nevertheless the evidence remains the witness's own. Leading arbitrators frequently acknowledge that such preparation is permissible and to be expected. Hwang says, for example, that "Witness statements are particularly helpful in putting across the testimony of witnesses who are not fluent in the language of the arbitration more effectively to the arbitral tribunal. This ensures that the key points of what the witness is trying to put across in his evidence are not confused or lost simply because the witness is unable to communicate effectively through an interpreter".[19] Such an admission may diminish the weight of the written statement, but may also defuse any challenge to the witness's credibility at the hearing and ensure that focus remains on the witness's recollection and the substance of the evidence. Such transparency may also assist the arbitral tribunal to appreciate more immediately "how spontaneous the statement actually is".[20]

B. Scope and Content of the Witness Statement

Article 4(1) IBA Rules provides that each party "shall identify the witnesses on whose testimony it relies and the subject matter of that

---

[17] V. Veeder, "The Lawyer's Duty to Arbitrate in Good Faith" (2002) 18 *Arbitration International* 431.

[18] IBA Rules of Evidence, Rule 9(1).

[19] M. Hwang and A. Chin, "The Role of Witness Statements in International Commercial Arbitration" (2006) 13 *ICCA Congress Series – No. 13* 650, 651.

[20] *Ibid*, 652.

testimony". The parties must give this information within any time period ordered by the tribunal. Beyond this, there is great flexibility as to the form and content of witness statements.

The role of the advocate extends to the scope and content of the witness statements put forward in support of the claim or defence. Witness statements are an opportunity to introduce to the tribunal the human side of one's case, to win both the arbitrator's heart as well as the mind. A witness statement can be used to present and explain arguments that will appeal to the commercially-minded arbitrator who may prefer to give effect to the parties' agreement even at the expense of minor technical or procedural concerns. A witness statement can be used to "tell the story", but above all, it can focus on the justice of the case.

Beyond these aspirations, there are certain practical concerns for the advocate. The witness statement must generally be confined to matters within the witness's personal knowledge or belief. Hearsay may be included, given that there are no particular rules of evidence in international arbitration,[21] but it should normally be identified as such. Fact and opinion should be demarcated too, again not because any particular rules of evidence apply but because witnesses are likely to lose credibility if their written statements contain speculation about matters beyond their knowledge, provide argument on the law, make conclusionary or inflammatory statements, or generally seek to argue the case.

With counsel from the civil law tradition, one observation is that they frequently see the "witness statement" as a short summary of the evidence, or topics on which the witness may address the tribunal at the hearing, but not the evidence itself. Witness statements may be just a page or two in length, but counsel and the witness expect the evidence during the hearing to go well beyond the statement. This form of witness statement is observed, from time to time, in arbitrations involving parties from the Middle East and Asia, in

---

[21] See e.g. UNCITRAL Model Law on International Commercial Arbitration, Article 19.

particular. The reaction of the tribunal to such practices is also likely to be driven by their background and experience levels.

On the other hand, an English lawyer may tend towards the other extreme, making sure to cover every point in issue (however small), in order to be sure to have proved every element of the case. This may be a product of English court experience, where lawyers are anxious to provide substantiation for every allegation or point of defence. This approach, if not carefully controlled, can lead to overly cumbersome witness statements, risk confusing the arbitrators with non-essential details and, potentially, increase the cost of proceedings.

One sometimes encounters more unusual forms of witness statement. In one case, where the parties had agreed to apply the IBA Rules, one of the parties produced unusual statements, in tabular format, which apparently sought to comply with the letter of Rule 4(5) (b) of the IBA Rules by setting out in a separate column a source for almost every sentence of the statement. It is advisable to address possible differences of understanding about the scope and content of witness statements in the initial procedural directions. A possible formulation, adopted by a tribunal in one case, spells out the expectations of the parties and the tribunal. In the initial procedural order in that case it was agreed that:

> "without prejudice to the power of the Tribunal to request or allow the parties to produce further evidence at any stage of the proceedings, signed witness statements and expert reports shall be... sufficiently detailed so as to constitute the evidence-in-chief of each factual or expert witness. This means that the witness statements and expert reports shall contain everything that the witness or expert has to say about the facts and issues in dispute, and counsel introducing the witness or expert shall not ask any questions of that witness or expert at the hearing other than in relation to facts or issues which arose after the statement or report in question was prepared".

Such an order is generally consistent with the expectation that the other side should know in advance of the hearing the evidence a witness offers so that they, and the tribunal, can better engage with the issues raised.

III. Preparation for the Hearing

Common lawyers, as a class, will acknowledge that "effective witness preparation is one of the most important components of successful advocacy in international commercial arbitration,"[22] and will each have their own approach and internal check list.[23] Generally civil lawyers engaged in international arbitration also appreciate the need to prepare their witnesses for trial even though it may not sit comfortably with them, given their particular training and legal traditions.

As to the extent of preparation, counsel may review the documents with the witnesses and challenge the witnesses' recollection or answers in the light of those documents, but would violate most bar rules (as well as other legal duties) if he or she were to propose that a witness should give evidence that is untrue. On the other hand, a witness should be able to recall in detail the content of his or her written statement, have an appreciation of how that evidence relates to the overall dispute and be familiar with the key documents. An unprepared witness, unfamiliar with the key documents concerning their testimony, is unlikely to be a persuasive witness.

When it comes to preparation for hearings, US counsel tend to stand apart from all others, perhaps due to their tradition of jury trials even in commercial matters. Many US counsel, if speaking candidly, will reveal with some pride the extent of witness preparation they undertake prior to an important hearing. They will acknowledge the risk that preparation may undermine the persuasiveness of the witness's evidence at the hearing, to which the solution in their eyes is yet more preparation. Preparation can continue right up to the

[22] D. Roney, "Effective Witness Preparation for International Commercial Arbitration: A Practical Guide for Counsel" (2003) 20(5) *Journal of International Arbitration* 429.

[23] Roney provides a useful guide for practitioners, *ibid.*

moment before the witness gives evidence. For some US counsel, the most traumatic experience in international arbitration proceedings can be witness sequestration, even more so if they suspect opposing counsel is not abiding by the tribunal's direction.

Heavy-handed preparation can become evident to sophisticated arbitrators and opposing counsel during the course of the hearing. A witness coached to produce the "right" answers can lack spontaneity and authenticity in cross examination, or become terrified of making a mistake and forget or confuse key points. The personality of the particular witness needs to be kept in mind. There can also be amusing unintended consequences, such as one witness, told to maintain eye contact and address his answers to the tribunal, who refused to look at counsel putting the questions and appeared to unsettle the arbitrators by his unswerving gaze. In addition to preparation on the evidence, many US counsel seem adept at providing witnesses with techniques or rote answers that allow them to duck difficult questions and retreat into a safe harbour. This can act as an effective form of damage limitation, but again can appear entirely transparent in the hearing room and raise doubts as to the witness's overall reliability. This is counter productive, given that the primary function of the evidentiary hearing is to test the credibility of witnesses and their written statements. If counsel's efforts are producing these effects, there must be doubt whether they contribute to effective advocacy.

IV. The Hearing

Hearings occupy a central place in complex international commercial arbitrations and the witnesses are key players on this stage. Whilst documents-only arbitrations can and do occur (most commonly in London Maritime Arbitrators Association arbitrations, but sometimes in cases concerning letters of credit, for example), they are rare in complex commercial cases. In these cases, there is typically a hearing primarily devoted to the receipt of evidence. The hearing assumes a paramount importance for common law counsel. The primary function of the hearing is to hear and test the evidence of the witnesses in person.

Witnesses will not normally be allowed to appear in international arbitration proceedings if they have not produced, in advance, a written statement of their evidence, save with the tribunal's permission perhaps where a witness is being compelled to appear.[24] Conversely, the written statement of a witness who is requested to appear for testimony at an evidentiary hearing but does not appear may be disregarded, absent good reason for their absence. In the English common law tradition, arbitrators would tend to give little weight to written witness statements in the absence of an opportunity for counsel and tribunal alike to probe the witness's recollection of events. This approach is confirmed in Rules 4(7) and 4(8) of the IBA Rules:

> "7. Each witness who has submitted a Witness Statement shall appear for testimony at an Evidentiary Hearing, unless the Parties agree otherwise.
>
> 8. If a witness who has submitted a Witness Statement does not appear without a valid reason for testimony at an Evidentiary Hearing, except by agreement of the Parties, the Arbitral Tribunal shall disregard that Witness Statement unless, in exceptional circumstances, the Arbitral Tribunal determines otherwise".

The opposing party is not compelled to request an opportunity to cross examine a witness, and may decide not to call a witness without being taken to have accepted that witness's evidence. Rule 4(9) of the IBA Rules usefully allows the parties to agree to dispense with cross examination of certain witnesses, without being taken to agree with their evidence:

> "9. If the Parties agree that a witness who has submitted a Witness Statement does not need to appear for testimony at an Evidentiary Hearing, such an agreement shall not be considered to reflect an agreement as to the correctness of the content of the Witness Statement".

---

[24] Also M. Bühler and C. Dorgan, "Witness Testimony Pursuant to the 1999 IBA Rules of Evidence in International Commercial Arbitration – Novel or Tested Standards" (2000) 17(1) *Journal of International Arbitration* 3, 11.

The decision not to call a witness is a judgement often weighed by experienced advocates. A party is most likely to take this approach if the events the witness speaks to are peripheral, or the evidence does little damage to the other party's case. Another possibility is not to call a witness, or expert in particular, who has produced a "dense and impenetrable" statement or report on technical issues in the case. As one expert has observed, if the witness or expert is not called for cross examination, an "obtuse report is then left to stand on its own and to confuse tribunal and counsel alike".[25] The witness or expert is thereby deprived of the opportunity to clarify their evidence, leaving a tribunal that is confused by the statement and most likely not to adopt its conclusions or recommendations.

Where witnesses are called to testify in person, it is normally for the party offering them to determine the order in which they will be heard. Of course, the tribunal may have its own views on the order in which it would wish to hear the witnesses, but otherwise this can involve some strategic consideration. Witnesses may simply be offered in chronological order, by issue, due to the need to set the foundation for and explain important exhibits to be discussed by others, or simply as a matter of convenience and availability. They may also be offered, for example, by strength of witness with counsel preferring to lead with a strong witness first, or keep one to the end to "mop up" issues and repair damage done in cross examination of other witnesses.

A. Direct Examination

In the common law tradition, the witnesses, both of fact and expert opinion, will have submitted detailed statements of evidence in advance of the hearing, which stands as their evidence-in-chief.[26] For common lawyers, written witness statements are generally

---

[25] R. E. Walck, "Observations on Expert Engagements" (2007) 4(3) *Transnational Dispute Management* 3.

[26] J. Beechey, "Advocacy in International Commercial Arbitration: England", in R. D. Bishop (ed.) *The Art of Advocacy in International Arbitration* (Huntington, N.Y., Juris, 2004) 233, 247.

understood to contain not just a summary of what they might say at the hearing, but all that they have to say. If this principle is followed, there should only be relatively confined, or no, direct examination at the hearing, with the result that the evidentiary hearing may be substantially reduced, and examination of the witnesses much better focused. This treatment of witness statements is indeed contemplated in Rule 8(3) of the IBA Rules, which provides: "The Parties may agree or the Arbitral Tribunal may order that the Witness Statement or Expert Report shall serve as that witness's direct testimony".

In contrast to this, the brief or summary style of witness statement one sometimes sees with Asian or Middle Eastern parties, for example, is frequently coupled with an expectation on the part of counsel that there is scope to introduce further evidence at the hearing in the form of direct examination, and that the written statements themselves do not stand as evidence-in-chief. Supplemental evidence-in-chief presents certain procedural risks, insofar as opposing counsel (and the tribunal) may be surprised by new material. Tribunals are likely to be irritated by this practice, if it comes as a surprise. For its part, opposing counsel may require an adjournment to take instructions or, if required to press on, may complain that they are deprived due process as they are not able to conduct as effective a cross examination as they might.

It should be possible to avoid such divergences in approach by agreeing in advance—along the lines of Rule 8(3) of the IBA Rules—that at the hearing, witnesses may generally only give supplemental evidence-in-chief to correct an error or clarify an ambiguity in their statement, to address facts which emerged or events which occurred since they filed their statements, or to respond to allegations made subsequently by the opposing party's witnesses or in its submissions. On top of this, it is frequently agreed that counsel for the party offering the witness may ask a few introductory questions in order to "relax the witness".

B. Cross Examination

The success of a case often turns on the performance of the witnesses at the hearing, and their performance often turns on the skill and personality of the cross examiner. It has been said that cross examination—"the greatest engine ever invented for the discovery of truth"—distinguishes common law proceedings from those under any other legal system.[27] It is a core feature of adversarial proceedings, in which the attitude is that the judge or arbitrator will be reluctant to accept the truth of the unsworn written statements of a witness, without the opportunity to test those statements in person, under cross examination. Witness statements normally offer a framework for the cross examination (as will depositions, which are rare in international commercial arbitration, but occasionally do take place in US-influenced and domestic arbitrations), hence the need to ensure they accurately reflect what the witness will say under cross examination.

The function of cross examination generally includes one or more of the following purposes:[28] (1) to elicit the confirmation of known facts or admissions not mentioned in witness statements or direct examination that help develop the case; (2) to correct misstatements of fact; (3) to ensure that facts are set in their proper context; (4) to identify or reconcile apparent contradictions; and (5) to cast doubt upon the reliability and credibility of a witness—thereby undermining pillars upon which the other side's case is built, or repairing damage done to one's own case.

Different considerations may arise that affect the approach taken to the cross examination of expert witnesses, but the purpose is broadly the same. In the contest of the experts, the advocate will wish to ensure that one's own expert's credentials—both in terms of expertise and objectivity—remain intact. To do so, the advocate may have briefly directed evidence as to the expert's background and professional experience, or invited the expert to clarify any aspect of

---

[27] I. Younger, *An Irreverent Introduction to Hearsay* (American Bar Association, 1977) 2.

[28] See also e.g. J. W. Cooley and S. Lubet, *Arbitration Advocacy* (2nd edn., NITA, 2003) 142.

their experience on redirect, if damage has been inflicted on cross examination. The advocate may also wish to cast doubt on the expertise or objectivity of the opposing expert. This may require questions focused on methodology, the facts and assumptions underpinning the conclusions, or the views of other experts. Another tactic may be not to doubt the opposing expert's qualifications but simply to point out that they are ill-suited to the issue in hand, as properly defined. At the heart of the cross examination will be an attempt to doubt that there is a sound and widely accepted basis for the opinion expressed. For civil lawyers more familiar with the practice of court-appointed experts, they are likely to find the concept of cross-examining an expert disconcerting, but for common lawyers this is routine.[29]

C. Leading Questions

Cross examination is typically conducted by means of tightly controlled and "leading" questions, which suggest the answer within their own terms. This is the norm in most arbitrations. (In contrast, leading questions are discouraged in direct examination, especially if they are many, if not actually excluded.)[30] Leading questions in cross examination are not considered a problem for two main reasons, first because the tribunal determines the weight to be accorded to any witness evidence, and secondly, because the opposing party's witnesses are relatively unlikely simply to agree with propositions put to them by the other side's lawyer on cross examination.

But not all arbitrators are familiar with cross examination. In one recent arbitration, a German sole arbitrator admonished the English cross examiner for asking leading questions, and instructed him only to ask questions commencing Who, What, Where, When, How and Why. This is of course diametrically at odds with normal practice and the advice repeated throughout the leading advocacy manuals for

---

[29] R. Kreindler, "Benefiting from Oral Testimony of Expert Witnesses: Traditional and Emerging Techniques" (2007) 4(3) *Transnational Dispute Management* 4.

[30] See e.g. M. F. Hill, A. V. Sinicropi and A. L. Evenson, *Winning Arbitration Advocacy*, (Washington, DC: Bureau of National Affairs, 1997) 147.

common law practitioners, which insist that "every question on cross-examination should be leading".[31]

D. The Art of Cross Examination, and its Risks

Most modern arbitration practitioners appreciate that their role as counsel may include cross examination of witnesses. Their differing cultural and legal traditions are, however, likely to mean that counsel outside the common law are relatively inexperienced in this practice. In common law jurisdictions, cross examination is a highly specialised art. For counsel relatively inexperienced in this skill (which will include not only most civil law-trained litigators new to arbitration but also those English solicitors more accustomed to instructing counsel from the English bar) at best they may struggle to draw out helpful responses. At worst, they run the risk of severely damaging their case; indeed, a poor "cross examination may provide you with a chance to lose it".[32] One reason is that ill-judged questions may present the witness with the perfect opportunity, which he or she is sure to be looking out for, to bolster the other side's case and undermine your own.

As for counsel steeped in cross examination, most differences in approach or technique are likely to be the product of different training and individual personalities and not any cultural divide. Occasionally different expectations as to the process can be identified. Lévy and Reed suggest, for example, that "a US litigator representing the respondent may not appreciate that the time spent cross examining claimant's witnesses counts against his or her own time, and… may not appreciate that the time his or her own witnesses spend answering tribunal questions may count against respondent's time".[33] Similarly, the English barrister or common law litigator unfamiliar with arbitration may, for example, "lay foundations", object to hearsay, and generally adhere to particular

---

[31] See e.g. Cooley and Lubet, above note 27, 148.

[32] *Ibid*, 139.

[33] L. Lévy and L. Reed, "Managing Fact Evidence in International Arbitration" (2006) *ICCA Congress Series – No. 13* 663, 640.

national courtroom practices and expectations associated with those proceedings that are frequently not appropriate in arbitration. As for cultural differences, it is occasionally heard that an English arbitration practitioner may be more upfront with witnesses, whilst US lawyers may skirt around issues in order to elicit useful responses more inferentially, but this is a broad generalisation to which there are no doubt a great many exceptions.

E. Scope of Cross Examination

It is often debated whether questions may be asked outside of the subjects addressed in the witness statement.[34] This is a relevant consideration, since it is sometimes apparent that counsel have tightly controlled the scope of a witness's written statement in the hope that this should limit the topics that may be raised under cross examination. That is unlikely to be a successful strategy. Whilst there are frequently different expectations, even between common law trained counsel, as to whether one can cross examine on matters outside the witness statement or the broad credibility of the witness, most arbitrators will accept that a witness may be cross examined on events of which the witness has personal knowledge, or about documents on the record authored or received by that witness, regardless of the scope of the witness statement. Proof of this in the form of an extreme example is a case in which the typed transcript of the cross examination of a key witness, who had proffered only a cursory witness statement, stretched to 200 pages. In another case, a civil law arbitrator became irritated by a four- or five hour-long cross examination of a witness who had submitted a half-page witness statement; counsel of course sought to explain that the witness was integral to and had personal knowledge of many of the events in dispute not covered in the written statement. Despite the irritation, the telling point is that the arbitrator allowed the cross examination to develop in that way and for that length of time.

---

[34] *Ibid*, 637.

F. Cross Examination through Interpreters

Where witnesses testify in a language other than that of the arbitration, it is a great asset if the advocate is proficient in that other language. This is the case even if the proceedings are not bilingual. For an important witness, there may be a role for a local counsel to conduct the cross examination, if the lead counsel is not versed in that language,[35] since it is almost impossible to cross examine a witness with any force when you are doing so through an interpreter. On the other hand, when dealing with a witness being examined through an interpreter, language skills can give the advocate a distinct advantage in terms of handling the witness, because it is possible to understand everything that is being said and therefore have more ability and time to adjust the questions or approach.

G. Use of Media to Enhance Cross Examination

A further observation is that US counsel frequently seem more comfortable with the integration of electronic media into their presentations, including cross examination of witnesses. One effective approach is to confront witnesses with documentary evidence in the form of extracts contained in a "PowerPoint" or projector screen presentation, allowing counsel to control precisely what paragraphs or sentences the witness and the tribunal focus upon, to the exclusion of others. Both the witness and the tribunal remain free, of course, to request or refer to the full document in hard copy in front of them, but the effortless and rapid pace of an electronic presentation can put subtle pressure on witnesses. Even though counsel for the party presenting a witness may encourage that witness to request or use a paper copy, the lure of the screen may be too great, especially where it takes time to locate documents in paper files and the witness is anxious not to be seen to be holding up proceedings.

---

[35] Occasionally more than one counsel will cross examine a single witness, but this practice is uncommon and likely to attract objections.

V. Witness Conferencing

The contribution of the advocate may be diminished where the witnesses are examined through "witness conferencing",[36] this being a technique consisting of the simultaneous joint hearing of all fact witnesses, or experts, on a particular topic. It is a practice adopted most by civil law arbitrators. Depending on how it is engineered, the scope for traditional cross examination may be negligible or even non-existent. Indeed, Wolfgang Peter acknowledged in his seminal article on the subject that with witness conferencing, "The debate takes place among the informed and specialized witnesses; it is expert knowledge v. expert knowledge and no longer the lawyer's questioning technique v. the witnesses' expert knowledge".[37] Witness statements prepared in advance may also seem to be set aside in favour of the arbitrator's inquisitorial approach. These two consequences of witness conferencing can cause some anxiety for common lawyers who place great store in both written witness statements and the opportunity to test them through cross examination.

On the other hand, witness conferencing can be efficient. Moreover, counsel will not normally be excluded entirely,[38] but will have an opportunity to direct questions to the witnesses. However, more than one of the witnesses may wish to respond to any particular question, which may generate further interventions from yet other witnesses, leading to a full blown debate. It can be a frustrating process for the common law advocate who would wish to have greater control and opportunity to pin a particular witness down on a specific point of detail. The fact that witnesses are not sequestered can also make it more difficult to isolate a particular witness's recollection of particular events and thus, their credibility and reliability. Nevertheless, witness conferencing does offer its advantages and is certainly effective in appropriate cases. Therefore

---

36 See W. Peter, "Witness Conferencing" (2002) 18 *Arbitration International* 47.

37 *Ibid.*

38 *Ibid*, explaining that "...witness conferencing does not eliminate cross examination, but places it in an enlarged context, where counsel involve further members of both teams".

counsel need to find the flexibility to accommodate it, since it is surely here to stay.

VI. Redirect

When it comes to redirect, there are striking differences in approach between US counsel and the more traditional English approach. US counsel frequently go to some lengths to prepare for redirect, even to the point of special bundles and slide presentations. For the English lawyer, redirect examination should only deal with matters raised in cross examination, excluding the giving of fresh evidence at this stage, so it is difficult to contemplate how this sort of material for redirect may be prepared in advance. Faced with a highly orchestrated redirect by US counsel, English lawyers will be alert to whether questions are confined to the scope of cross examination or in fact new evidence is being introduced, in which case the English counsel is likely to object to the line of questions or request permission to conduct further cross examination. The solution, to avoid technical squabbles whilst the witness is giving evidence, is for such expectations to be raised and addressed in advance in a procedural order at the outset of the proceeding, or in a preparatory conference call shortly before the hearing.

VII. Conclusion

There are a great many differences in the practice of international arbitration that are the product of the differing experience levels of counsel, and the influence of the procedures and techniques of the national courts of their home jurisdiction where they acquired their training as litigators. There is, however, a growing international arbitration bar, which specialises in the conduct of truly international proceedings. Civil and common lawyers alike engage in the preparation and drafting of witness statements, the preparation of witnesses to give evidence, and the questioning of witnesses at hearings. Amongst the most regular arbitration practitioners differences in approach are more likely to be traced to personality-type and particular professional experience, not merely differences in culture or legal tradition. The same is even more likely to be true for the younger generation of arbitration practitioners, born of the modern boom in arbitration, who have had considerably less exposure to domestic litigation than their predecessors. Out of these groups, the latter following in the footsteps of the former, it may be that a "harmonized approach to advocacy in international arbitration"[39] will finally emerge.

[39] R. D. Bishop, "Toward a Harmonized Approach to Advocacy in International Arbitration" in R. D. Bishop (ed.), above note 1, 451.

Chapter 3

THE ETHICS OF ADVOCACY IN INTERNATIONAL ARBITRATION

Catherine A. Rogers*

I. Introduction

Traditionally, attorneys are subject to ethical rules that are created and enforced by national and sub-national regulatory authorities. As dispute resolution has gone global,[1] however, attorney ethics increasingly defy this traditional regulatory model.[2] In many systems, there are doubts about whether the ethical regulations of an attorney's "home state" extend extraterritorially, for example, into international arbitrations occurring elsewhere.[3] Even when home

---

* Professor of Law, Pennsylvania State University, Dickinson School of Law, University Park, Pennsylvania & Università Commerciale Luigi Bocconi, Milan, Italy.

[1] *See* Thomas E. Carbonneau, *The Remaking of Arbitration: Design and Destiny* 27, in LEX MERCATORIA AND ARBITRATION (Thomas E. Carbonneau, ed., 1998).

[2] *See* Ronald A. Brand, *Professional Responsibility in a Transnational Transactions Practice*, 17 J.L. & COMM. 301, 335 (1998) (noting that a bar opinion permits parties to international arbitration to be represented by non-state-licensed attorneys); Toby S. Myerson, *The Japanese System*, in RIGHTS LIABILITY AND ETHICS IN INTERNATIONAL LEGAL PRACTICE 69 (Mary C. Daly & Roger J. Goebel, eds., 1994) (noting that even traditionally restrictive Japanese law changed recently to permit non-Japanese-licensed attorneys to engage in international arbitrations in Japan).

[3] *See* Detlev Vagts, *International Legal Ethics and Professional Responsibility*, 92 AM. SOC. INT'L L. PROC. 378, 378 (1998) (noting that it is unclear whether the Model Rules apply in arbitration proceedings); Peter C. Thomas, *Disqualifying Lawyers in Arbitrations: Do the Arbitrators Play Any Proper Role?*, 1 AM. REV. INT'L ARB. 562 (1990) ("When an English barrister suggested a couple of years ago that an advocate in a private commercial arbitration was not bound by the same duties owed by counsel to a court, the immediate (near unanimous) response was shock and indignation.").

state ethical rules are applied extraterritorially, however, they most often conflict with the rules that govern opposing counsel from a different jurisdiction. At best, therefore, attorneys in an international arbitration are each abiding by different and often-conflicting national ethical rules. At worst, they are operating in an ethical no-man's land.

When the topic of ethics in international arbitration is discussed, the assumption is that the only real concern is the content of the substantive rules that guide and regulate attorney conduct. However, just as the substantive ethical rules in any national legal system exist within the framework of a larger regulatory regime, so too must any ethical rules developed for the international arbitration system. This Chapter reviews some of the well-known conflicts and ethical ambiguities that arise in international arbitration, and examines some of the problems in developing a uniform set of rules that are increasingly regarded as a necessary development. Beyond the substantive rules, however, this Chapter also takes up the related problems inherent in implementing and enforcing those rules.

II. The Nature and Substance of Ethical Conflicts

Michael Reisman and Detlev Vagts long ago recognized that the conflicts among national ethical rules require development of international ethical rules to govern attorney conduct in the context of international tribunals, specifically international arbitration.[4] Since then, a number of other important scholars have added their voices to a growing chorus calling for new ethical rules for international arbitration.[5] The topic is increasingly popular at international

---

[4] *See* W. MICHAEL REISMAN, NULLITY AND REVISION: THE REVIEW AND ENFORCEMENT OF INTERNATIONAL JUDGMENTS AND AWARDS 116-17 (1971); Detlev F. Vagts, *The International Legal Profession: A Need for More Governance?*, 90 AM. J. INT'L L. 250, 250 (1996) (describing problems in Iran Claims Tribunal caused by lack of ethical consensus among attorneys).

[5] *See* Charles N. Brower & Stephan W. Schill, *Regulating Counsel Conduct Before International Arbitral Tribunals* in MAKING TRANSNATIONAL LAW WORK IN THE GLOBAL ECONOMY: ESSAYS IN HONOUR OF DETLEV VAGTS (forthcoming 2010);

arbitration conferences, and as a corollary to various efforts to address the ethics of lawyers engaged in transnational legal practice. Literally dozens of new international codes of ethics have been drafted.

For a long time, the only international ethical rules were found in the 1956 International Bar Association (IBA) International Code of Legal Ethics. Although called a "code" and referred to as "rules," that effort is most accurately characterized as a set of professional notions rather than rules that provide any meaningful guidance.[6] More recent efforts include the IBA "Core Values" Resolution, which began in 1998, and the IBA General Principles of the Legal Profession of 2006, for which new commentary is currently being drafted. In addition, the Bar Association Presidents' Meeting developed in 2005 a Statement of Core Principles, which was adopted by 100 bar associations from around the world, and the *Union Internationale des Avocats* (UIA) developed the Turin Principles in 2002.[7]

In addition to these efforts, some international tribunals, such as the International Criminal Tribunal for the Former Yugoslavia and the International Criminal Court in The Hague, have developed codes of ethics for defense counsel. There has also been a virtual

---

Pierre Heitzmann, *Confidentiality and Privileges in Cross-Border Legal Practice: The Need for a Global Standard?*, 26 ASA BULLETIN 205 (2008); Carrie Menkel-Meadow, *Are Cross-Cultural Ethics Standards Possible or Desirable in International Arbitration?*, Georgetown Public Law Research Paper No. 1130922; University of California Irvine School of Law Research Paper No. 2008-2, at 19, http://ssrn.com/abstract=1130922; Jan Paulsson, *Standards of Conduct for Counsel in International Arbitration*, 3 AM. REV. INT'L ARB. 214 (1992); John M. Townsend, *Clash and Convergence on Ethical Issues in International Arbitration*, 36 U. MIAMI INTER-AM. L. REV. 1 (2004); *see also* Brian Cooper, *Ethics for Party Representatives in International Commercial Arbitration: Developing a Standard for Witness Preparation*, 22 GEO. J. LEGAL ETHICS 779 (2009).

6 Mary C. Daly, *The Dichotomy Between Standards and Rules: A New Way of Understanding the Differences in Perceptions of Lawyer Codes of Conduct by U.S. and Foreign Lawyers*, 32 VAND. J. TRANSNAT'L L. 1117, 1158 (1999).

7 For a detailed survey of these and other reform efforts to date, *see* Laurel S. Terry, *A "How To" Guide for Incorporating Global and Comparative Perspectives into the Required Professional Responsibility Course*, 51 ST. LOUIS U. L.J. 1135, 1140-46 (2007).

explosion of auxiliary regulation of attorneys through national legislation and international agreements aimed at controlling money laundering, corruption, terrorism, tax evasion and trade in legal services.[8] These various sources demonstrate increased recognition of the need to regulate attorneys, but they only address a limited range of ethical issues, and even then only partially and with limited success.

The seminal and most familiar example used to illustrate the need for international ethical rules is the clash between national ethical rules relating to pre-testimonial contact with witnesses. As one scholar recounts, lawyers from different jurisdictions have starkly different opinions about pre-testimonial communication with witnesses:

> An Australian lawyer felt that from his perspective it would be unethical to prepare a witness; a Canadian lawyer said it would be illegal; and an American lawyer's view was that not to prepare a witness would be malpractice.[9]

There are also significant national divergences about the nature and scope of disclosures that can or should be made. In many jurisdictions, communications with in-house counsel are confidential, while in others they are not.[10] In jurisdictions like the United States, where there is a tradition of opposing parties exchanging of

---

[8] For an overview of these developments, see Laurel S. Terry, *et al.*, *Transnational Legal Practice*, 42 INT'L LAWYER 833 (2008).

[9] Karen L.K. Miller, *Zip to Nil?: A Comparison of American and English Lawyers' Standards of Professional Conduct*, CA32 ALI-ABA 199, 204 (1995). For additional discussion of these issues, see Mary C. Daly, *The Cultural, Ethical and Legal Challenges in Lawyering for a Global Organization*, 46 EMORY L.J. 1057 (1997).

[10] Pierre Heitzmann, *Confidentiality and Privileges in Cross-Border Legal Practice: The Need for a Global Standard?*, 26 ASA BULLETIN 205 (2008); Bernhard F. Meyer-Hauser & Philipp Siber, *Attorney Secrecy v. Attorney-Client Privilege in International Commercial Arbitration*, 73 ARB. 148 (2007); Richard M. Mosk & Tom Ginsburg, *Evidentiary Privileges in International Arbitration*, 50 INT'L COMP. L. Q. 345 (2001); Taru Spronken & Jan Fermon, *Protection of Attorney-Client Privilege in Europe*, 27 PENN ST. INT'L L. REV. 439 (2008).

documents before trial, attorneys have an ethical obligation to search for and disclose non-privileged documents in response to authorized requests. In other jurisdictions, where there is no tradition of document exchange, and hence no related ethical obligations, many counsel regard it as a betrayal of their obligation of loyalty to disclose documents that are damaging to their client.

Meanwhile, the French doctrine of "*sous la foi du Palais*" may require that an attorney maintain as confidential as against his own client a communication conveyed by opposing counsel, even if such communication contains a proposed settlement that U.S. ethical rules mandate that the attorney disclose to the client.[11] In a newer development, the UK Proceeds of Crime Act of 2002 mandates that attorneys disclose certain information to law enforcement agencies (while withholding the disclosure from the client), even if such disclosure is forbidden under the ethical rules of many other jurisdictions.[12]

There is also wide divergence regarding the nature and degree of permissible *ex parte* communication between judges or arbitrators, on the one hand, and parties or their counsel on the other hand. In China, for example, it is not only permissible but also probable that an arbitrator (or judge) will act as a mediator in the same case in which she presides as ultimate decision maker.[13] The substance of

---

[11] Laurel S. Terry, *An Introduction to the European Community's Legal Ethics Part 1: An Analysis of the CCBE Code of Conduct*, 7 GEO. J.L. ETHICS 1, 36-7 (1993).

[12] *See* Galvin F. Leckie & Anthony E. Woods, *Developments in Ethics*, SJ027 ALI-ABA5 221, 223 (2003) (describing the Proceeds of Crime Act as a "troubling development" that erodes the relationship between lawyer and client and the duty of confidentiality); Hans-Jürgen Hellwig, *At the Intersection of Legal Ethics and Globalization: International Conflicts of Law in Lawyer Regulation*, 27 PENN STATE INT'L L. REV. 395, 399 (2008) (describing a German attorney imprisoned in London for refusing to disclose information deemed confidential under German law).

[13] Jun Ge, *Mediation, Arbitration and Litigation: Dispute Resolution in the People's Republic of China*, 15 UCLA PAC. BASIN L.J. 122, 127 (1996) (noting that the Chinese Civil Procedure Law requires judges to conduct mediation if the parties do not object). This approach translates into arbitration rules in China and other Asian countries. *See, e.g.*, China International Economic and Trade Arbitration Committee Arbitration Rules, arts. 46, 47 (1994); Japan Commercial Arbitration Association

these *ex parte* conversations may be (but is not necessarily) communicated to other parties. Similarly, many Continental systems permit some *ex parte* communications and do not presuppose that all parties will always be in the courtroom during fact-finding proceedings. Relatedly, many national ethical rules expressly permit some contacts.[14] In the United States, by contrast, there are absolute restrictions against *ex parte* communications, except in certain rare procedural contexts. In an interesting twist, which has historically caused some complications in international arbitrations,[15] the stringent U.S. rules prohibiting *ex parte* communications are not followed in U.S. domestic arbitration, where party-appointed arbitrators have routinely communicated with their appointing party, even about crucial issues involving strategy.

Although not an exhaustive survey of all the ethical conflicts that arise in international arbitration, it is a daunting list nonetheless. Lawyers engaged in transnational legal practice have little or no guidance about how these rules fit together, and even less guidance about how to manage such conflicts when appearing before international arbitration tribunals.

Commercial Arbitration Rules, Rule 39 (1992); Hong Kong Arbitration Ordinance §§ 2(A), 2(B), ch. 341, Laws of Hong Kong (H.K.), cited in Philip J. McConnaughay, *Rethinking the Role of Law and Contracts in East-West Commercial Relationships*, 41 VA. J. INT'L L. 427 n.102 (2001).

[14] *See, e.g.,* Code of Conduct—Germany § 8.3 ("A lawyer may contact or submit documents or exhibits to a judge without the knowledge of the lawyer(s) or the opposing client(s) in the case."), *cited in* Terry, *supra* note 11, at 36 n.159.

[15] Ambassador Malcolm Wilkey, *The Practicalities of Cross-Cultural Arbitration*, in CONFLICTING LEGAL CULTURES IN COMMERCIAL ARBITRATION: OLD ISSUES AND NEW TRENDS 86 (Stefan N. Frommel & Barry A.K. Rider, eds., 1999); Nicholas C. Ulmer, *Ethics and Effectiveness: Doing Well by Doing Good*, in THE COMMERCIAL WAY TO JUSTICE: THE 1996 INTERNATIONAL CONFERENCE OF THE CHARTERED INSTITUTE OF ARBITRATORS 167, 171 & n.8 (1996) (noting that it is "not [an] uncommon practice" for one arbitrator to be communicating with the appointing party).

III. The Consequences of Ethical Conflict

Back when international arbitration was predominantly a compromise-oriented system governed by informal procedures, the absence of clear ethical guidance was not a serious concern.[16] Today, these conflicts are quite pronounced and they create two distinct but related problems. The first problem is sometimes referred to by ethicists as the "double deontology" problem. An attorney may be licensed in more than one jurisdiction or otherwise be subject to the regulatory power of more than one jurisdiction, for example the rules of both the jurisdiction where an attorney is licensed and the jurisdiction where that attorney has an office or is appearing before a tribunal. In these instances, the different rules may impose obligations that are impossible to comply with simultaneously and the attorney is faced with the prospect of professional discipline regardless of what action he takes.

The second problem is that, when attorneys who are bound by different ethical rules participate in a single international proceeding, the proceedings may be structurally unfair. As Detlev Vagts cogently explains:

> [I]t would not be workable to allow the counsel for opposing sides in a civil case to enter the courtroom subject to different rules. . . . It would not do to prohibit one lawyer from a civil law jurisdiction from interviewing a witness before the trial while the American lawyer would not only be allowed to do so but would be guilty of professional negligence if he or she presented an un-interviewed witness. [17]

There are numerous other potential conflicts, described above, that may produce inequalities and affect the fairness of the proceedings.

---

[16] For an extended discussion of the structural reasons why ethical conflicts in international arbitration are receiving greater attention, see Catherine A. Rogers, *Fit and Function in Legal Ethics: Developing a Code of Attorney Conduct for International Arbitration*, 23 MICH. INT'L L.J. 341 (2002).

[17] Detlev Vagts, *Professional Responsibility in Transborder Practice: Conflict and Resolution*, 13 GEO. J. LEGAL ETHICS 677, 690 (2000).

Both the double deontology problem and what might be referred to the inequality-of-arms problem have asserted themselves with increasing frequency in international arbitration. As a result, despite the fact that they have no formally delegated powers to enforce ethical rules,[18] arbitral tribunals are increasingly being pressed into service. They resolve such conflicts on an *ad hoc* basis, for example when ordering production of documents, when making evidentiary rulings, when ruling on claims of alleged conflicts of interest, asserted privileges[19] and requests for disqualification,[20] when drawing (or refusing to draw) adverse inferences based on alleged misconduct, [21] and when awarding costs and fees.

---

[18] *But see* Paulsson, *supra* note 5, at 215 (stating that "[a]rbitrators are named to resolve disputes between parties, not to police the conduct of their representatives, and therefore do not rule on complaints of violations of codes of conduct").

[19] Klaus-Peter Berger, *Evidentiary Privileges: Best Practice Standards Versus/and Arbitral Discretion*, 22 ARB. INT. 501 (2006).

[20] Historically, arbitrators were regarded as not having the jurisdiction or authority to disqualify counsel. *See, e.g.*, Munich Re America Inc. v. Ace Property & Casualty Co., 500 F.Supp.2d 272, 275 (S.D.N.Y. 2007) (holding that "disqualification of an attorney for an alleged conflict of interest, is a substantive matter for the courts and not arbitrators," and reasoning that "[a]ttorney discipline has historically been a matter for judges and not arbitrators because it requires an application of substantive state law regarding the legal profession"); *see also* Simply Fit of N.Am. v. Poyner et al., 579 F.Supp.2d 371 (E.D.N.Y. 2008). These are domestic cases, but reportedly have been relied on by some international commercial arbitration tribunals. More recently, a distinguished tribunal in an investment arbitration concluded that it did possess such power. *See* Hrvatska Elektroprivreda, d.d. v. The Republic of Slovenia, ICSID Case No. ARB/05/24, Tribunal's Ruling regarding the participation of David Mildon QC in further stages of the proceedings of 6 May 2008, available at http://icsid.worldbank.org/ICSID/FrontServlet?requestType=CasesRH&actionVal=showDoc&docId=DC950_En&caseId=C69. Arguably, while there may be compelling reasons to require that ethical issues in domestic cases be brought to domestic regulatory authorities, the arguments against arbitrator authority are much less compelling in the international arbitration context, particularly if the rules being applied are international and not domestic ethical rules. For an excellent discussion of disqualification in the investment arbitration context, *see* Brower & Schill, *supra* note 5.

[21] Vera van Houtte, Stephan Wilske & Michael Young, *What's New in European Arbitration?*, 62-JAN DISP. RESOL. J. 12 (2008) (describing findings by

At a substantive level, *ad hoc* innovations have also prompted development of some specialized ethical rules for international arbitration. For example, as noted above, there are significant conflicts between national traditions and ethical rules regarding the permissibility of pre-testimonial communication with witnesses.[22] These conflicts have over time been largely displaced in international arbitration by a generally accepted customary rule of practice permitting such communication. This customary practice has, in turn, been translated into an explicit rule in the IBA Rules on the Taking of Evidence in International Commercial Arbitration (IBA Rules),[23] and Swiss and French authorities have expressly ratified it as an exception to otherwise applicable national ethical rules.[24] Although

Swiss federal tribunal that drawing negative inferences for a party's refusal to produce documents was an element of the arbitrator's assessment of the evidence).

[22] Mirjan R. Damaska, *Presentation of Evidence and Factfinding Precision*, 123 U. PENN. L. REV. 1083, 1088-9 (1975) (explaining the classical view that "'[c]oaching' witnesses [in inquisitorial systems] comes dangerously close to various criminal offenses of interfering with the administration of justice" as well as being contrary to professional canons of ethics); John H. Langbein, *The German Advantage in Civil Procedure*, 52 U. CHI. L. REV. 823, 834 (1985) (The German lawyer "virtually never [has] out-of-court contact with a witness," because, under the German rules of ethics, a lawyer "may interview witnesses out of court only when it is justified by special circumstances. He has to avoid even the appearance of influencing the witness and is, in principle, not allowed to take written statements.").

[23] Article 4(3) of the IBA Rules provide that "[i]t shall not be improper for a Party, its officers, employees, legal advisors or other representatives to interview its witnesses or potential witnesses." Although framed as a rule of evidence, use of the word "improper" reveals its real purpose in resolving the ethical conflict.

[24] In Switzerland, while pre-testimonial contact with witnesses is generally prohibited, Article 7 of the *Code Suisse de Deontologie* provides with respect to *Contact avec les témoins* (contact with witnesses): "*L'avocat s'abstient d'influencer les témoins et experts. Demeurent reservée les règles particulières des procédures d'arbitrage et procédures devant les Tribunaux supranationaux*" (prohibiting attorneys from contacting witnesses, but suspending such prohibition in proceedings before arbitral or supranational tribunals). *See also Bulletin du Bâttonnier n. 9 du 4 Mars 2008* (resolution of the *Conseil de l'Ordre de Paris* permitting members of the Paris Bar to prepare witnesses in international arbitration proceedings located in France or abroad in accordance with "applicable rules").

these innovations provide important gap-fillers, there is a distinct need for a more systematic resolution to the conflicts between national ethical rules.

While providing a useful stop-gap, in some instances these *ad hoc* innovations create new, more subtle problems. For example, in systems like the United States, where pre-testimonial communication with witnesses is broadly permitted, there are more specific rules setting boundaries for such communications. Other systems that traditionally prohibit such communication have resolved some issues by creating specific exceptions to those prohibitions for international arbitration, but those exceptions do not include any guidance about the extent and limits of their application.[25] As a result, conflict remains regarding the manner and extent to which pre-testimonial communication with witnesses is permissible, even after new rules were developed in a direct attempt to resolve the primary underlying conflict.[26] Moreover, as described below in the context of another international tribunal, if new rules are promulgated, their application is limited unless they officially displace contrary national rules, for example through a choice-of-law provision.

IV. Ethical Rules as More than Text

The need for a systematic response to conflicting national ethical rules has been drawing more attention, particularly in the form of

---

[25] Notably, while U.S. attorneys have wide latitude to interview witnesses, there are some important limitations, particularly with respect to former employees who may have confidential information. *See* Habib Hasrullah, *Interviews with Former Employees: Strategies and Pitfalls*, 16 No. Prac. Litigator 47 (2005); *DC Bar Opinion 287: Ex Parte Contact with Former Employees of Party-Opponents*,http://www.google.it/search?sourceid=navclient&aq=0h&oq=dc&ie=UTF-8&rlz=1T4SKPB_enIT326IT327&q=dc+bar+opinion+287; *see also* James Castello, *Q&A: Is Arbitration an Ethical Wasteland?*, GLOBAL ARB. REV. (17 June 2009).

[26] Lucy Reed & Jonathan Sutcliffe, *The "Americanization" of International Arbitration?*, 4 MEALEY'S INT'L ARB. RPT. 37, 42 (2001) (suggesting that while some consensus has emerged about the possibility of preliminary communication with witnesses, there remains conflict as to the extent permitted).

proposals to develop an international code of ethics.[27] As described above, there are a number of generally applicable international codes of ethics, and new efforts to draft a code specifically for international arbitration.[28] Developing a workable code of ethics is not as simple as drafting good substantive rules. Instead, the rules must be distilled from, and integrated into, the legal culture of international arbitration.

In national legal systems, ethical rules do not reflect simply an abstract decision made by a bar association about where to draw an ethical line. They instead shape and are shaped by shared understandings of what is proper based on history, culture, education and training of a national legal profession.[29] Ethical rules for international arbitration must also be a meaningful expression of the shared ethical values and assumptions that inform attorneys' role in an international arbitration or it will be difficult for attorneys to comfortably step away from their national traditions and ethical precepts.

---

[27] *See, e.g.*, Malini Majumdar, *Ethics in the International Arena: The Need for Clarification*, 8 GEO. J. LEGAL ETHICS 439, 451-52 (1995); John Toulmin, *A Worldwide Common Code of Professional Ethics?*, 15 FORDHAM INT'L L.J. 673 (1991-1992).

[28] For example, the IBA has announced creation of a Task Force specifically to address the issue and work on a possible code of ethics. *See* http://www.ibanet.org/LPD/Dispute_Resolution_Section/Arbitration/Overview.aspx. Some doubt the viability of actually developing such a multi-national code since ethical rules are so closely linked to national procedures and national legal cultures. *See* Menkel Meadow, *supra* note 5; University of California Irvine School of Law Research Paper No. 2008-2, at 19, http://ssrn.com/abstract=1130922 (concluding that cultural differences make it impossible to develop universal ethical standards for international arbitration); Kristen Weisenberger, *Peace Is Not The Absence Of Conflict: A Response To Professor Rogers's Article "Fit and Function in Legal Ethics,"* 25 WISC. INT'L L.J. 89 (2007) (arguing that extant rules of conduct are adequate for the purpose of regulating international arbitrations, and a conflict-of-laws approach is the best option).

[29] Judith A. McMorrow, *Creating Norms of Attorney Conduct in International Tribunals: A Case Study of the ICTY*, 30 B.C. INT'L & COMP. L. REV. 139, 146 (2007) (describing how legal education, malpractice standards, market and informal social controls, and applicable mechanisms of self-regulation shape the ethical obligations of attorneys in domestic contexts).

In this respect, efforts to draft ethical rules for international arbitration should look to the experience of the International Criminal Tribunal for the former Yugoslavia (ICTY). Although a criminal tribunal, it has many features that are similar to international arbitration, particularly with respect to accommodating a multitude of national legal cultures. There are twenty-five judges at the ICTY, coming from twenty-three different countries and "[t]he defense bar of the ICTY has 257 members, drawn from multiple legal traditions, with roughly half of the defense bar from the former Yugoslavia. . . ."[30] As part of their participation in ICTY proceedings, "[c]ivil and common law lawyers" are reoriented to the "new hybrid trial model [of the ICTY] and their role within that model."[31] All attorneys at the ICTY undergo this re-orientation, which has been particularly important with respect to Soviet-era trained lawyers, who viewed the role of the criminal defense lawyer as an enemy of the state. Once the role of attorneys before the ICTY was established, new ethical norms appropriate to that new role had to be and were developed and eventually codified.[32] All this occurred despite the fact that "[t]here was no shared history, background, or culture to help determine the best course of action."[33] This example is, of course, a compelling response to those critics who regard with skepticism the entire project of drafting a code of ethics for international arbitration.

While harmonized rules are much needed, a single code that applies generally to international arbitration may not be right. While arbitration is often discussed as a monolithic system, in fact there is a remarkable degree of variation among different institutions and arbitral rules, and even among arbitrations administered under a single set of rules. For ethical rules to be workable across the range of international arbitral regimes, they must have a degree of flexibility to facilitate the diversity and flexibility that exists in arbitration

---

[30] *Id.* at 148.

[31] *Id.*

[32] *See id.* at 966-68 (outlining the development of the ICTY Code of Professional Conduct).

[33] *Id.* at 148.

proceedings. An example will illustrate the inherent limitations of a single, inflexible code. A rule that generally permits pre-trial witness communication, even though clearly the working consensus, might not be suitable in an arbitration in which the parties have adopted procedures based on a so-called "inquisitorial model," under which the arbitral tribunal controls the presentation of evidence and conducts all of the questioning of witnesses.[34] Party communication with witnesses in this context would interfere with the arbitrator's role, and a general, inflexible ethical rule allowing it would be awkward, if not counterproductive.

V. Cooperative Integration of the New Rules

The challenges involved in developing substantive ethical rules reveal other related questions. Who should promulgate such codes or rules? How will new codes or rules inter-relate with otherwise applicable national ethical rules? How would such ethical rules be enforced? What role would national bar associations or regulatory authorities have? While a detailed examination of each of these issues is beyond the scope of this Chapter, it is useful to sketch out the broad outlines of a proposal.[35]

First, the need to avoid a one-size-fits-all approach relates to differences among arbitral institutions and even among individual proceedings administered by the same institution. Distinctions among arbitral institutions suggest that they should be primarily responsible for developing codes or "menus" of ethical rules that are specially tailored to the general contours of proceedings they

---

[34] *See* Catherine A. Rogers, *Context and Institutional Structure in Attorney Discipline: Developing an Enforcement Regime for Ethics in International Arbitration*, 39 STAN. INT'L L. REV. 1, 28 (2002).

[35] For an extended discussion of how to implement new codes of ethics that are specially tailored to specific institutional and procedural regimes, *see id.* Many of these proposals will be reconsidered, expanded and further developed in CATHERINE A. ROGERS, GLOBAL LEGAL ETHICS IN INTERNATIONAL ARBITRATION (forthcoming Oxford University Press, 2010).

generally administer.[36] Since parties can still modify the procedures under a given set of arbitral rules, any codes that are developed should be subject to some modification by parties and arbitrators to accommodate or address specific procedures or cultural preferences implicated in an individual arbitration.

Beyond efforts from within the arbitration community, there is a need to coordinate with national regulatory authorities. Any rules developed for international arbitration must necessarily displace otherwise applicable national ethical rules, or there is a risk the new rules will only complicate the conflicts instead of resolving them. This unfortunate result can currently be observed in the ICTY, where defense counsel are permitted by the ICTY's code of ethics to engage in pre-trial communication with witnesses. Because those counsel's home bar associations do not provide for specific exemptions or choice-of-law rules, however, many defense counsel remain obliged to refrain from such communication. In other words, an international rule addressing the substantive conflict is not enough to remove the underlying conflict between the rules without cooperation from national bar associations.

Several bar associations have demonstrated a willingness to permit their attorneys to be subject to special rules applicable in international tribunals. In addition to the Swiss and French exceptions regarding witnesses, described above, bar associations are starting to develop choice-of-law rules that would provide more systemic exemption from national rules in favor of rules that specifically govern international arbitration. For example, U.S. Model Rule 8.5 was expressly extended to encompass transnational activities,[37] and provides that "for conduct in connection with a matter pending before a tribunal, the rules of the jurisdiction in which the tribunal sits [shall apply], unless the rules of the tribunal provide otherwise . . . ." For a number of reasons, the details of

---

[36] *See* Brower & Schill, *supra* note 5; Rogers, *supra* note 34, at 26-29.

[37] Specifically, Comment 7 provides "[t]he choice of law provision [contained in Rule 8.5] applies to lawyers engaged in international practice[.]" MODEL RULES OF PROF'L CONDUCT R. 8.5 cmt. 7 (2002).

which are beyond the scope of this Chapter, Model Rule 8.5 produces some highly problematic and ultimately unsatisfactory results when applied to international arbitration.[38] The UK Solicitors Regulation Authority's ("SRA's") Rule 15 regarding "Overseas Practice" extends well beyond the rather clunky approach provided in Model Rule 8.5. It includes an extensive preface that explains how its various provisions apply and careful, and individualized guidance about how rule applies to activity abroad.[39] For example, U.K. confidentiality and conflict-of-interest obligations continue to apply to activities abroad, but the U.K. prohibition against contingency fees does not apply to representation in foreign jurisdictions.

Perhaps even more telling than the partial successes of general choice-of-law rules in the U.S. and UK ethical codes are the failed attempts at providing choice-of-law. The CCBE Code was specifically drafted to provide guidance to attorneys engaged in cross-border activities in Europe and is arguably the most advanced and successful international code of ethics to date.[40] Given this purpose, the double deontology problem is of paramount importance, but the CCBE Code does not offer any real guidance other than to suggest that attorneys from different nations inform themselves about the rules of other jurisdictions.[41]

Similarly, in developing a substantive code of conduct for the International Criminal Court, the International Bar Association

---

[38] For an extended discussion of the textual ambiguities in, and problems applying to Rule 8.5, see Catherine A. Rogers, *Lawyers Without Borders*, 30 U. PENN. INT'L L. REV. 1035 (2009).

[39] *See* SOLICITORS REGULATION AUTHORITY ("SRA") CODE OF CONDUCT, Rule R. 15 (providing the rules regarding overseas practice, ranging from conflicts of laws to fee practices).

[40] Terry, *supra* note 11, at 36-37.

[41] Article 2.4 of the CCBE Code provides:

> "When practising cross-border, a lawyer from another Member State may be bound to comply with the professional rules of the Host Member State. Lawyers have a duty to inform themselves as to the rules which will affect them in the performance of any particular activity." CCBE Code of Conduct, Art. 2.4.

considered specific precedents that clearly illustrated the need for tribunal ethical rules to supersede home state rules.[42] In light of these precedents, it debated the issue extensively.[43] Despite these efforts, however, the delegates were unable to reach agreement on "strategies" for preventing conflicts between national ethical rules and the newly proposed supranational ethical rules.[44]

The limited national efforts in Switzerland and France, and even the more general choice-of-law rules in the U.S. and UK Rules, seem like important developments. But a multitude of inconsistent and conflicting national choice-of-law rules only adds a layer of complexity and confusion to the existing conflicts. The real need is for an international choice-of-law rule that designates, and coordinates priority for, international ethical rules that are specifically developed for international arbitration.[45]

Alas, even if such an international choice-of-law rule seems essential, Jonathan Goldsmith, the Secretary-General of the CCBE, has expressed extreme hesitancy about the prospects for such a rule.[46] It is tempting, however, to ponder whether his skepticism is based on the challenges to consensus that have encumbered efforts by the CCBE. By contrast to a top-down regulatory entity like the CCBE, the international arbitration community may be both more motivated since the potential benefits for the system are more palpable.

---

[42] *See* Daniel D. Ntanda Nsereko, *Ethical Obligations of Counsel in Criminal Proceedings: Representing an Unwilling Client*, 12 CRIM. L. FORUM 487 (2001).

[43] Michael Walsh, *The International Bar Association Proposal for a Code of Professional Conduct for Counsel Before the ICC*, 1 J. INT'L CRIM. JUSTICE 490, 499 (2003).

[44] *See id.*

[45] *See* Catherine A. Rogers, *Cross-Border Bankruptcy as a Model for Regulation of International Attorneys*, in MAKING TRANSNATIONAL LAW WORK IN A GLOBAL ECONOMY: ESSAYS IN HONOUR OF DETLEV VAGTS (forthcoming 2010); Laurel S. Terry, *The Future Regulation of the Legal Profession: The Impact of Treating the Legal Profession as "Service Providers,"* 2008 J. Professional Lawyer 189, 192 (2008) (proposing an international choice-of-law provision to be implemented through the "additional commitments" provisions under GATS, drafted in cooperation with the IBA); Vagts, *supra* note 4, at 378 (arguing that "rules of private international law or conflicts of law to determine which countries' standards should apply").

[46] *See id.*

Moreover, the international arbitration community has arguably already been more successful at influencing national bar authorities, if the Swiss and French carve-out rules are any indication.

VI. Conclusion

There are many pragmatic reasons why a new ethics regime is needed in international arbitration. Attorneys need more guidance about what constitutes proper conduct. Parties need to understand better how to plan their legal representation and related case strategy. Arbitrators need more clear guidance and support in making rulings on ethical issues. And bar associations need assurance if they are to relinquish at least partial control over aspects of transnational practice that there is a reliable regime in place to protect client and societal interests implicated in attorney conduct.

Perhaps even more importantly, however, developing an effective ethical regime for international arbitration implicates fundamental issues about the health and vitality of the international arbitration system itself. The professional status of international lawyers is in part what confers legitimacy, both real and perceived, on the international arbitration system. Party consent, the jurisdictional predicate of the entire international arbitration system, is orchestrated by international lawyers. International lawyers are the ones who select the rules, laws, location, and often the presiding arbitrators on behalf of the client-party. As Charles Brower and Stephan Schill explain:

> The need for uniform rules concerning counsel conduct before international tribunals stems not only from a need to ensure that counsel and parties operate on a level playing field. At issue may ultimately be the legitimacy of the international arbitral system as a whole, in particular inasmuch as, in the case of investment treaty arbitrations, it operates not only retrospectively as a review mechanism for the legality of State conduct under international law, but also prospectively as a mechanism of global governance.[47]

---

[47] Brower & Schill, *supra* note 5.

If at least one *end* of a new ethical regime for international arbitration is to reify the international arbitration system, that goal has implications about the *means* for developing the needed ethical regime. Systemic cooperation that involves all relevant actors—parties, counsel, arbitrators, arbitral institutions, and national and international regulatory authorities—is necessary to not only developing the content of the new ethical rules, but to implement them and ensure their meaningful enforcement.

Part II.

PSYCHOLOGICAL PERSUASION

Chapter 4

PSYCHOLOGICAL DYNAMICS IN INTERNATIONAL ARBITRATION ADVOCACY

Richard C. Waites and James E. Lawrence

I. Introduction

One of the inherent strengths of the current system of international arbitration is the unique opportunity for advocates and students of advocacy from so many different cultures to learn from each other about ways to enhance the effectiveness of their arguments and presentations. Some approaches to effective advocacy that might at one time been seen as radical have become routine as they were tested and found to be effective, while other approaches once thought to be expected and normal have been abandoned.

In addition to cross-cultural learning, we are all benefitted by the influences of disciplines other than law as we work to improve the effectiveness of our advocacy. For example, scientific research in the field of psychology has provided valuable information about how to improve communications and persuasion in arbitration and other types of legal decision making, and thus, assist arbitration panels and individual arbitrators in better understanding the evidence and positions of the parties in an arbitration.

There is a substantial body of research and writing relating to the use of scientific methodology as applied in the context of both court trials and domestic arbitrations within the United States. For example, scientific methodologies have been used to study various aspects of lay jury and domestic arbitrator selection, lay juror and domestic arbitrator perceptions, the impact of using visual aids during the trial and arbitration process, and decision making processes throughout court trial and domestic arbitration proceedings. The use of scientific methodology in preparing for court trials and domestic arbitrations in the United States is so widely accepted that the subject of such research has become popularized as exemplified by the success of the John Grisham novel and movie, *The Runaway Jury*. Conversely, until now there has been a dearth of research and writing related to the use of scientific methodology as applied to the study of advocacy and arbitrator decision making in international arbitrations.

One of the premises of this chapter is that scientific methodology can and should be used in the international arbitration process for the purpose of improving the quality and effectiveness of advocacy. As shown in the context of the United States, all of the participants in the decision making process – decision maker, party, and advocate – are likely to benefit greatly from resulting improvement in communication. The same human qualities that are exemplified in the court and domestic arbitration process are also at play within the international arbitration context.

In this chapter, we will explore some principles and findings that we have discovered through the use of scientific research dedicated to better understanding of the decision making processes of arbitrators as well as other type of legal decision making. In the process, we will also explore ways to make this information useful to every advocate for a party in international arbitration.

Science is a foundation for art. The more we understand the science of psychological dynamics, both of the self and of the group decision making process, the more skilled we become in the art of advocacy.

II. The Arbitrator-Oriented Approach to Advocacy

A. What is Arbitrator-Oriented Advocacy?

When we ask an arbitration panel to accept our arguments and to decide a case in our favor, we are asking them to allow us into their world. It is like asking them to let us come into their homes. They must be the one to unlock and open the door from the inside.

Arbitrators, like all people, are complex. They use their logic and emotions in varying degrees to make decisions that will help them to experience pleasure and avoid pain. One way in which all legal decision makers experience pleasure is to make decisions that make them feel good about themselves. This principle is absolutely true in persuading international arbitrators.

To motivate arbitrators to listen to us and to take action in our favor, we must understand their needs and what inspires them. Using the most correct and appropriate advocacy technique is not enough.

Persuading arbitrators involves meaningful two-way communication between the lawyer and the arbitrator(s) he or she wishes to convince. When it comes to interaction between lawyers and arbitrators, lawyers cannot dominate the fact finders and decision makers. Lawyers can only inspire them and motivate them. The arbitrators choose for themselves how they will respond.

No matter who the arbitrators are in your cases, their individual perceptions and interpretations of the circumstances of the case are uniquely their own. For decades interviews of arbitrators have revealed that each of them develops their own version of a case story by the end of the arbitration. Most of them have begun to form the story before the end of the opening statement.

It is not <u>our</u> power as advocates that results in a favorable decision. It is the power within the decision maker that creates the magical experience and results in a decision.

As lawyers, we give homage to the power of the decision maker. We honor and respect their power and should not try to upstage it. To the contrary, one of our goals is to empower fact finders by acknowledging their supreme authority.

B. The New Age of Advocacy and Arbitration

The world around us is changing. The practice of advocacy is changing. Historically, we have depended solely upon self-reliance and intuition in developing and presenting cases in arbitration as we were taught to do. We have relied solely upon advocacy skills that we learned from law professors, seminar speakers, mentors, and sometimes opposing advocates. We have developed our themes and case theories from ideas that sounded persuasive to us that we generated ourselves or that we borrowed from other sources.

However, despite our emphasis upon self-reliance, a revolution has occurred in how we develop and present cases to judges, juries, and arbitrators. This revolution began more than thirty years ago with the founding of the National Institute for Trial Advocacy (NITA) in the United States (www.nita.org), more recently with the founding of the Foundation for International Arbitration Advocacy (FIAA) in Switzerland (www.fiaa.com), as well as other teaching organizations that are dedicated to assisting lawyers in enhancing their trial and arbitration advocacy skills. NITA, FIAA, and these other groups believe that the ideals of our system of justice are furthered when attorneys work to develop their skills as advocates. The effect that these research and teaching organizations are having is profound.

One of the effects of the drive to become more successful as an advocate has been the need for more reliable and useful information about how our case presentations will be perceived by arbitrators. Scientific decision maker research is just one source of this information. There are many others.

As we learn more about how arbitrators make decisions, we discover new ways to apply this information to make every advocate's work more effective and more useful for the arbitration panel. By focusing case presentations on the needs of the arbitrators to better understand cases and their meaning, they can do a better job of making appropriate decisions. In the final analysis, then, the arbitration advocacy system itself is improved.

In this chapter, we spend a great deal of time looking at the results of scientific research and how to apply what we have learned. In the process, however, we may sometimes fail to acknowledge that advocacy is an art. It is one of the highest forms of art. It involves the use of oratory and expression that focuses on the meaning of life's circumstances.

Until now, we have spent years making sacrifices to learn this art. But now the basic learning is over. It is now time to use our skills and all of the resources we now have to create a masterpiece that is meaningful in the lives of our clients and the arbitrators as well.

C. How Do We Inspire Arbitrators to Decide in Our Favor?

Being the most competent lawyer in arbitration is not enough. It takes more than oratorical skills and arbitration savvy to convince arbitrators to enter a decision for our client. To win a case, the substance of our presentation must be compelling, meaningful, and inspiring.

Some of the most brilliant lawyers across the world tell us that they view themselves as messengers. They tell us that fact finders are more persuaded by the message and content of their arguments. They tell us many war stories about trials and arbitrations in which a less skilled advocate defeated them because the substance of the winning argument was more compelling.

Developing an effective arbitration strategy that will make an arbitration panel enthusiastic about deciding in our favor is dependent largely upon framing an argument in a way that is meaningful and motivational to them. The themes and case theory we rely upon must be in accordance with their attitudes about specific issues in the case, relevant life experiences, and other characteristics of the decision maker which will influence their decision.

People do not make decisions in a vacuum. No arbitrator has ever made a decision without first taking into consideration their perceptions of the world around them and their previous life experiences.

D. The Secret to Motivating Arbitrators

The world of international arbitration advocacy is unique in many respects, but the fundamental dynamics of persuasion are the same everywhere. Because arbitration advocacy takes place within a legalistic environment laden with complicated rules and procedures, we sometimes forget the people we try to persuade in arbitration are the same people who spend most of their time outside the arbitration.

Whether we want to admit it or not, arbitration advocacy is selling. It is the highest form of selling in the sense that we are selling ideas that will affect people's lives.

Why do people buy products or ideas? The answer is simple. They buy out of self-interest. Benjamin Franklin, a famous author, diplomat and scientist from the United States, once said, "If you would persuade, you must appeal to interest rather than intellect."

The practice of persuading people in arbitration seems complex because of the hundreds of details that are present in every case and the fact that different arbitrators will view the case differently. Nevertheless, the objective is to frame the issues and presentation of a case to address the needs of the arbitrators. They want to learn as much information as they can and they need to make a decision that makes them feel good about themselves.

In essence, therefore, they make important decisions the same way you do. Think about how you go about making decisions about family matters, law practice matters, and other personal matters. Do you make important decisions completely rationally and considering only the information that someone tells you is admissible? Probably not.

The more we are sensitive to the needs of arbitrators to form a story about what happened and why things happened the way they did, the better equipped we will be to develop themes and messages in the case which are meaningful and powerful to them. They need to know the important aspects of the case as clearly and simply as possible. Drenching them with unnecessary details makes their work more difficult and can dilute the possibility of presenting a cogent and persuasive argument.

Therefore, the secret to motivating arbitrators is to understand the subject of the arbitration from their perspective and to appeal to their self-interest in a world as they see it. Arbitrators, like all legal decision makers, have strong senses of the importance or lack of importance of evidence and issues. Likewise, they have a strong sense of how to fashion a solution that makes them feel comfortable and fits contentedly into their view of the world.

There is also another important aspect of presenting a case that all successful lawyers must understand. Arbitrators will make their decision in your case based on their own attitudes about specific issues in the case, their own life experiences, and their own set of life's influences.

III. The Dynamic of an Effective Advocate in International Arbitration

Advocacy is persuasion and psychology is the foundation for persuasion. Unfortunately, preparation for practicing law rarely includes instruction on the science and art of persuasion. Consider the amount of time devoted to communication theory and cognitive processing theory in legal education. Analytical reasoning is presumably developed through the legal education pedagogy but the study of the psychology of the advocacy process is rare. The goal of this chapter is to provide information and insights relating to the science of persuasion that is rarely found in legal education, legal literature, and legal training.

The foundation for understanding the science of persuasion begins with the concept of internal roadmaps. A basic knowledge of internal roadmaps then provides a framework for discussing how the science of persuasion is applied in international arbitration.

A. The Internal Roadmap

Psychological roadmaps are the neural pathways along which the brain sends and receives information. The send/receive process operates primarily on two levels that we will refer to as *surface structure* and *deep structure*. *Surface structure* is what a person observes through the five senses: words, tonality, body language, visual images, and gestures. However, the information processed through the surface structure pathway is only factual data. The surface structure pathway does not give meaning or emotional value to the observation data. The meaning and emotional value to the observed data comes from the *deep structure* pathway. A person's *deep structure*, on the other hand, contains that person's experiences, values, biases, prejudices, dreams, fears, and beliefs.

A simple illustration of the surface structure/deep structure dynamic is the "Ocean Test" as we refer to in teaching trial advocacy. The "Ocean Test" may be demonstrated by a comparison between a word's definition (i.e. surface structure] with the images that use of the word conjures up (i.e. deep structure).

The necessity of understanding the differential between a fact (as presented by the advocate) and the image(s) that the fact generates in one's mind of the arbitrator is what makes the surface structure/deep structure dynamic so critical in international arbitration advocacy. In the final analysis, then, the foundation for successful persuasion is understanding the significance of the arbitrator's internal roadmap.

The interplay between the individual advocate, the arbitration panel, and scientific methodology can be exemplified by the geometric shape of a triangle. In 1816, Dr. A. L. Crelle, a German mathematician, described a triangle, stating that "[i]t is indeed wonderful that so simple a figure as the triangle is so inexhaustible in properties".[1] Specifically, the simple figure of the triangle here is: Side 1) the dynamic of an effective advocate, Side 2) the decision making processes of international arbitration panels, and Side 3) using scientific decision maker research in arbitration advocacy. (*The triangle analysis has been used in the study of domestic lay jury and arbitration in the United States.*) Side 1 (the advocate) and Side 2 (the arbitration panel) are both well-chronicled concepts in international arbitration. However, the international arbitration literature does not include discussions of the psychological dynamic of the effective advocate or of the arbitration panel. Also absent in the majority of literature regarding international arbitration is analysis of how to connect the two concepts (the advocate and the arbitration panel) through scientific research and, thus, to complete the triangle. The triangle

---

[1] Crelle, A. L. "Einige Bemerkungen über die dreiseitige Pyramide." *Sammlung mathematischer Aufsätze u. Bemerkungen* **1**, 105-132, 1821 as reported in Wells, David. *The Penguin Dictionary of Curious and Interesting Geometry*. London: Penguin, p. 21, 1991.

analogy, with the sides identified above, may be illustrated in the following sections – demonstration what Crelle reasoned to be "so inexhaustible in properties."[2]

Consider the following diagram:

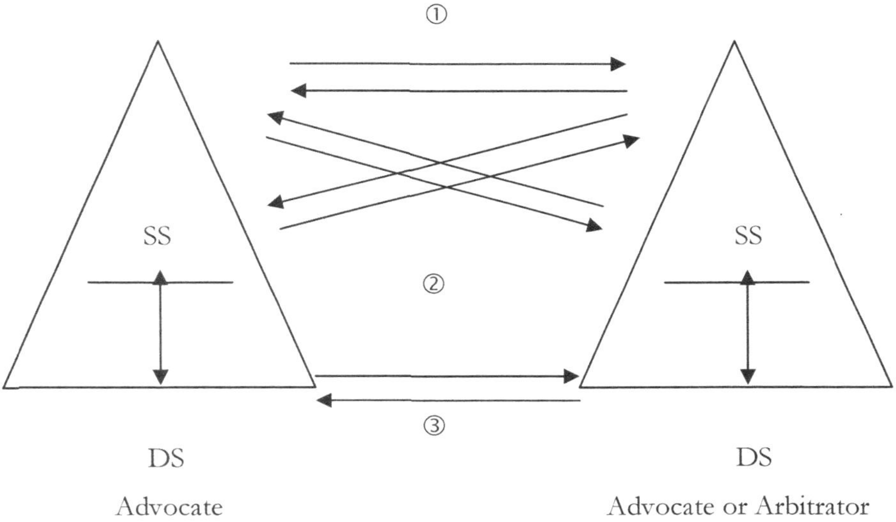

SS = Surface Structure
DS = Deep Structure

The diagram illustrates the complexity of an interaction between an advocate or opposing counsel – with an arbitrator – in an arbitration hearing. Each set of arrows represents an element of the interaction.

a. Surface Structure to Surface Structure.

The "factual" exchange between the advocate or opposing counsel and the arbitrator includes information gained by the advocate through words, gestures, tone, body language, and other observations sent/received through the five senses.

---

[2] *Id.*

b. Surface Structure to Deep Structure.

The exchange between a person's surface structure and another's deep structure is perhaps the most underutilized and unrecognized of the three exchanges shown in the diagram.

It is underutilized because the information sent/received in this exchange often reveals information about fears, biases, dreams, and prejudices that people often have difficulty acknowledging about themselves. For example, perhaps the opposing counsel is wearing an ill-fitting suit that is unduly wrinkled. Remember, however, that an ill-fitting, wrinkled suit observation (surface structure) only identifies that the opposing counsel is wearing an ill-fitting, wrinkled suit. It is the observer's deep structure that creates a meaning for that observation.

What does an ill-fitting, wrinkled suit mean? It *could* carry an infinite number of meanings because experience tells us that no two people have exactly the same life experiences and perceptions, and therefore, there is little chance that the deep structures of two different arbitrators, even though they may have similar backgrounds, will be alike. To one arbitrator, the meaning suggested by the images might reveal a negative bias or prejudice the observer has about individuals who wear ill-fitting, wrinkled suits. To another arbitrator, the meaning might be that the advocate is "down-to-earth", self-confident, and more credible than an advocate dressed quite fashionably.

The simple example of the "ill-fitting, wrinkled suit is useful in understanding a much more important concept – that every detail of the evidence or of an argument has the potential to be interpreted differently by different arbitrators and to be applied differently by each arbitrator in interpreting the circumstances of a case and making an important decision. Therefore, the need for thorough and objective study of likely arbitrator perceptions is of enormous importance.

One of the most curious aspects of this constant dynamic taking place during an arbitration proceeding is that most of the time neither arbitrators nor advocates recognize that this important underlying interpretive process is taking place. In those instances where an arbitrator or advocate recognizes that some underlying interpretation is taking place, the ability to accurately identify it and articulate it is missing. In science, for example, we recognize a phenomenon we call "fundamental attribution error" where we attribute an event or outcome wrongfully to one factor when, in truth the event or outcome was caused by something else entirely.

As a result of a lack of understanding of the existence or pervasiveness of underlying interpretations and misinterpretations, neither arbitrators nor advocates question the meaning their deep structure gives to a factual observation. Simply stated, observers make assumptions about their observations.

c. Deep Structure to Deep Structure.

If the exchange from surface structure to deep structure is mostly underutilized and unrecognized, then the exchanges between the deep structures of arbitrators and advocates are perhaps the most difficult to understand and deal with effectively.

The opportunity to persuade is dramatically increased when there is an exchange between the advocate's deep structure and the deep structure of the opposing counsel or arbitrator. Because the deep structure holds the meaning for factual data, the advocate who understands how to create a deep structure exchange has an advantage. The difficulties in creating a deep structure exchange are: 1) individuals do not generally like to talk about their fears, biases, prejudices, goals, and dreams, 2) attorneys believe they only need the facts, and 3) it takes time and patience to develop the techniques necessary to create this exchange.

B. Effective Applications

A discussion of the science of persuasion is incomplete without exploring how the theory applies to the international arbitration hearing context. The applications are endless but, due to space limitations, the focus here will be limited to three of the most common applications: 1) the importance of narrative, 2) using scientific evidence, and 3) questioning witnesses.

(1) The Importance of Narrative

A narrative, for the purposes here, is the story of the case. The story of the case is often overlooked in the international arbitration context because advocates focus primarily on the factual data (surface structure) of the case. The use of an effective narrative, however, provides a context (deep structure) for the factual data. The context then creates an anchor point, or theme, for the advocate to use during the process of a hearing. It is important to note that a theme is *not* an emotional appeal but rather it is one way to create a deep structure to deep structure exchange.

For example, consider a shipping contract dispute between an Indian company and a Chinese company. The arbitration panel consists of arbitrators from Sweden, United States, and France. The way for an advocate to reach the deep structure of every person involved in this process is either to select a universal theme, an anchor point that transcends culture, or to develop separate themes directed to each arbitrator, but that are complimentary to each other. A possible single theme in this case might be "doing what is right". While cultures differ in how "doing what is right" is applied, no culture is without a concept that mirrors this theme. An effective advocate would return to the "doing what is right" anchor point throughout the course of the hearing in order to continually remind the arbitral panel of the essence of the dispute.

Perhaps the most eloquent explanation of the role of narrative meaning (meaning in the context of a story) is reflected in the writings of Jerome Bruner, a famous educational and developmental psychologist, in his work *Acts of Meaning*.[3] In this work, Bruner explains that the central concept of human psychology is *meaning* and the processes and transactions involved in the construction of meaning. Bruner states that culture shapes human life and the human mind and gives meaning to the events and behaviors by creating an interpretive system. He states that our interpretations and

---

[3] Bruner, *Acts of Meaning*, (Cambridge, Massachusetts: Harvard University Press, 1990).

perceptions are highly individualized in many ways, but that they are highly influenced by forces around us. He refers to this interpretive system as *folk psychology* or *common sense.* Bruner writes that this *folk psychology* is a system by which people organize their experience in, knowledge about, and transactions with the social world.

The vehicle with which people learn, organize and relay meaning and understanding is the *narrative* or *story* as Bruner recognizes. In his work, Bruner states that the function of *story* is to create an explanation, to give understanding, and to rationalize events, behaviors, and mental states of other people with whom an individual interacts. In this way, an individual and group can compare acceptable and normal cultural patterns with actions which deviate in matters of legitimacy, moral commitment, and values.

Another interesting and provocative writer on this subject was Joseph Campbell, the great social philosopher and cultural anthropologist. In his work, *The Power of Myth*,[4] Campbell explains his belief that the basic driving force for mankind is the search for *meaningful experience.* Throughout his lifetime he immersed himself into the cultural philosophies of human societies around the world and reached back into prehistoric times. Before his death in 1987, he stated in his last interviews and writings that he had reached the conclusion that it was not enough for man to discover the meaning of something intellectually in an objective way. He determined that it was more important for us to actually *experience* the meaning – to internalize it and feel its effects – a more subjective reaction.

The use of stories, myths, parables, and fables to proscribe acceptable behaviors and motivations is well documented in most every primitive and modern culture. Anthropologists who have studied dispute resolution in Western and non-Western societies have found clear and convincing evidence that laws or codes for conduct are represented and passed from generation to generation in the form of stories.

The conclusions of these authors are important to us in international arbitration in one significant respect – we must make

---

[4] Campbell & Moyers, *The Power of Myth* (New York: Anchor Books, 1991).

the effort to develop and present a case presentation that offers real substantive meaning and experience for every arbitrator. Otherwise, we are simply going through the motions of advocacy and will wind up with a case presentation that offers neither meaning nor experience to which an arbitrator can identify and commit.

(2) Using Scientific Evidence

Scientific evidence may, at first glance, seem to be merely a factual (surface structure) element of a dispute. Indeed, from an intellectual point of view, scientific evidence includes data, findings, and perhaps discoveries that should be useful in helping the arbitration panel understand an important point(s). We also know from historical practice that in order to be considered useful, scientific findings must offer reliability which may be defined as the consistency of a measurement, or the degree to which an instrument measures the same way each time it is used under the same condition with the same subjects.

However, providing scientific evidence to support advocacy is much more than an intellectual exercise. To the arbitrator, scientific evidence must not only have scientific reliability and validity, but it must also have meaning in a much deeper sense that supports the overarching themes and narrative of the case. In this sense, the use of scientific evidence, including the way it is presented, creates a higher level of meaning and application for the data to support the advocacy points.

When an advocate uses scientific evidence, the reliability aspect of the evidence accesses the element of assurance in a person's deep structure. Assurance is important in the science of persuasion because it creates confidence that the conclusive outcome will be the same each time the data is processed. Confidence in the conclusive outcome of scientific evidence establishes elements of trust and rapport – both of which are components of a deep structure to deep structure exchange.

In practice, therefore, a successful advocate will want to develop ways to persuade arbitrators that the scientific evidence supports the advocate's positions on central themes and narrative of the case. Presentation and discussion of the detailed aspects of the actual scientific research questions, methodologies, research designs, and findings should be as brief, concise, and comprehensive as necessary, but without unnecessary discussion and detail. Only in this way can the advocate help the arbitrator to understand the important meaning that the scientific evidence has for the entire case.

We might look at the example of a communications technology issue in a patent dispute. The plaintiff might argue that the defendant was aware of the plaintiff's patented technology and specifically tried to design the defendant's technology in a way that would skirt the claims in the plaintiff's patent. Focusing on a possible defense strategy, the defendant could bring forth a stream of reputable scientists all of whom might claim that the defendant's technology was unique and did not mirror the plaintiff's technology. The defendant could bombard the arbitrators with a steady stream of evidence focusing only on the scientific evidence for weeks, which in the end might overwhelm the plaintiff's expert witnesses and cause a pro-plaintiff decision, if the arbitrators were still interested in the case.

However, in the minds of the arbitrator in our example, the plaintiffs have actually brought a patent infringement dispute that is grounded in allegations of deception by the defendant, thus focusing on the defendant's character, which was not addressed in the steady stream of scientific evidence. Query whether it might be helpful for the defendant to address the deception allegation first and then go on to show with more concise proof that the defendant's technology is different from that of the plaintiff. The defendant might offer the actual inventor of its own technology to show the world-class trend-setting expertise of the defendant's inventor and the independent process by which the defendant's technology was developed. Furthermore, instead of offering a mind-numbing string of experts, to offer only 2-3 selected world-class experts to support the defendant's contentions with casual mention of others who would concur.

Therefore, in the final analysis, it is best to squarely meet the core issue(s) from the arbitrators' perspective which usually involves issues that give meaning to the behavior of the parties in the evidence and give meaning to the dispute as a whole and how best to create a decision that gives meaning and significance to their decision.

(3) Questioning Witnesses

Asking questions is an essential skill for an attorney, regardless of whether the context is in an office setting, a trial setting, or an arbitration setting. However, many attorneys focus on the factual information (surface structure) because they do not know how to access information from a witness' deep structure that can effectively provide information to enlighten and persuade an arbitrator's deep structure. Accessing information from one's deep structure requires discipline and willingness for the attorney to seek information rather than simply establishing power or control.

The most effective technique for accessing information from the deep structure of a witness, arbitrator or even another advocate is with *clean* questions. A *clean* question is one where the questioner refrains from including any personal bias, prejudice, or preconception in the question. Examples of clean questions are "what is important about...", "tell me more about...", and "what else is important about..." When a clean question is presented, it requires the answerer to reconsider an initial answer and give more information than in the initial answer. Each reconsideration pushes the answerer further into the deep structure and so as the exchange continues, the questioner begins to learn more and more about the meaning (deep structure) of the factual information (surface structure).

No discussion about clean questions is complete without a brief explanation of the technique of "looping". Looping is taking a part of the answer and using it in the next question. The technique communicates that the questioner is listening and that what the answerer said is important. When the answerer feels that what has been said is heard and is important, the willingness to give more information increases significantly.

The following is an example of a Q & A where the technique of asking clean questions is combined with the technique of looping.

Q: Why did your company include this clause in the contract?
A: We wanted to know that we could count on receiving the widgets in a timely fashion.

Q: What was important about your company receiving the widgets in a timely fashion? (an example of a clean question with looping)
A: We had a deadline to meet and we couldn't meet the deadline if we didn't have the widgets.

Q: What was important about meeting your deadline? (an example of a clean question with looping)
A: If we didn't meet the deadline, we'd have to pay a penalty.

Q: What else is important about meeting the deadline? (an example of a clean question with looping)
A: This is our first contract with this company and we've worked hard to get their business. We'd like to do more business with them and if it looks like we aren't dependable, then they may not want to sign additional contracts with us.

As this exchange demonstrates, using clean questions in combination with looping creates the rapport necessary for the questioner to get in-depth information from the answerer that is useful to address the needs of an arbitrator's deep structure.

IV. The Decision Making Processes of Arbitrators

A. Overview of the Communication/Persuasion Process

The persuasive process begins with basic communication as we have noted. Let's begin our discussion of the communication and persuasion process with an analysis of the communication process as it relates to persuasion and then examine the core principles involved in effective persuasion.

B. The Process of Communicating

(1) Basic Characteristics of Effective Communication

Because communication is inherently interactive, the communicator and the observer are both interdependent. In each of our communications with arbitration panels, we are dependent upon the arbitrators for response, whether spoken or unspoken. Otherwise, the interaction rapidly disappears.

Certainly some conversation is *interactive* but not necessarily communicative. Quite often in arbitration, for example, people say things that are meaningless and intended only to fill silence. Sometimes these meaningless interactions detract from the message to be communicated and sometimes they do not.

The best communicators, however, remain true to their message. They remain focused on the idea to be communicated. They work hard to make sure that all of their words, actions, and tools communicate *pure* messages without any distractions.

Regardless of the culture or setting, we think and communicate in symbols. A symbol is a sound, behavior, letter, or visual image that stands for something else. The most highly organized symbols we usually call *language*. A typical arbitration is filled with symbols, each of which will mean something special to one or more arbitrators. Therefore, we have to pay attention to the symbols we use and project so that the correct message is presented, and hopefully received.

(2) Inner Selves and Communication

Our internal states are both the beginning and the end of communication. The perceptions and mental state of the communicator are the source of the information to be communicated. Conversely, the perceptions and mental state of the listener form the end product of the communication.

One might argue that the things in our environment about which we are communicating are definite and that perceptions of the same object must be identical. After all, the sky is usually blue and trees are usually green. However, our memories and perceptual systems are highly selective about what they let in, and even more selective about the information that is stored in temporary or long term memory. Each person perceives the sky or a tree in a very unique way. In this sense, our perceptions are not directly tied to specific events or objects, but are created by our individual perceptual systems.

(3) Tools for Creating and Changing Perceptions

There are actually many interesting tools that humans have created or used over the millennia to create, maintain, and change perceptions. These tools are derived from our understanding about our cognitive (thinking) processes and our affective (feeling) processes. We will look at three of these tools that are most useful in arbitration. They are language, schema and affect.

Language is a powerful communication tool in many respects. In a very basic way, it helps us to organize our thoughts and information in systematic ways. Language can be used in the form of words, concepts, or style of expression. Words convey meaning and concepts and the same words can be spoken or displayed in many ways. Language is flexible and, in this sense, is a tool, not a constraint.

As children, we acquire language early on as symbols and concepts. It is not until later that we learn the spelling of the words and the rules of grammar. For this reason, in presenting a case in arbitration, it is more important to be concerned about the concepts and the connotations of our presentation, than the actual words used. Once the concepts are right, then the words will follow.

However, many times as lawyers we perceive language as a technical construct rather than a free flowing modem of communicating. We tend to be hyper-technical about our use of particular words that fit legal patterns rather than focused on central concepts and messages that arbitrators will need to hear and see that positively affects their deep structure if we are to be persuasive.

As human beings, we tend to form preconceptions and expectations around our previous life experiences. Technically, psychologists refer to these preconceptions and expectations as schemas.

A schema is a group of concepts and perceptions and the systems we use to organize them. They are a type of mental shorthand. Schemas help us to quickly make sense of the things that are happening around us. For example, when we are following a car down the freeway and the car begins to swerve from a blown tire, we consult our schemas to try to understand what is happening and what, if anything, we need to do about it. Our brains tend to store information in an order that seeks to make sense or order out of life's events and to avoid disorder or inconsistencies.

When arbitrators are listening and observing your presentation, they are constantly testing and comparing the thoughts and messages in your presentation with their own life experiences in order to make sense out of the presentation. If there is an identical match between arbitrators' schemas and the messages in the presentation, they will readily accept the new information (matching schemas is an example of a deep structure to deep structure exchange). If the arbitrators' schemas are different from the messages or ideas in the presentation, they will generally feel uncomfortable with them and may even reject them. If the arbitrators have no schema with which to compare the ideas in the presentation, they will consider the attendant circumstances and how much they trust the presenter in order to form a new schema. Or they might reject the ideas in the presentation altogether.

Consider this example. If a lawyer tries to paint his corporate client as a company that makes decisions based upon their business interest in keeping customers happy, arbitrators will likely accept the message, assuming there is supportive evidence. This message will make sense to them, based upon their own life experiences. On the other hand, if the lawyer tries to paint his corporate client as a company that makes decisions solely on the basis of humanitarian considerations, arbitrators will likely reject the message. Their experience tells them that this message is not true.

When there is a match between the arbitrators' schemas and the messages, the relationship between the arbitrators and the lawyer is enhanced. When arbitrators reject a message, however, the relationship between the arbitrators and the lawyer suffers.

One of the primary reasons for conducting pre-arbitration decision maker research is to identify the schemas that arbitrators will use to process the case and reach a decision. We have learned through experience that when we try to guess the schemas that arbitrators will use, we are often wrong. Scientific mock arbitration panel research also helps us to identify which of the schemas arbitrators will use that will be dominant in reaching a decision.

Arbitrators, like the rest of us, often form schemas around subjects. Consider the example of banks. With reference to banks, arbitrators expect to see a bank president, loan officers, tellers, vaults, cash drawers, expensive rugs, and elegant wood paneling. We expect banks to make loans to people, companies, and governments with good credit and to deny loans to those who have bad credit. We often expect bankers to be more interested in making money than benefiting society. Besides these perceptions, each of us has many other perceptions of banks and the people who work there. If an arbitration involves a bank or banking issues, these schemas will possibly come into play. The question, then, in pre-arbitration development of the case is to discover ahead of time how these schemas and representations will figure into arbitrators' thinking.

Schemas are formed primarily by perceptions and ideas that have been related to us by others. Socialization is perhaps the most powerful influence on how schemas (and stereotypes) are formed, maintained and changed. The significant people in our lives have a profound influence on how we view the world.

Arbitrators' perceptions are highly individualized. Even when the facts of a case are not disputed, each arbitrator will likely have a different version of the same schema to figure out what happened, why things happened as they did, and what the decision should be. Since arbitrators' schemas are pre-existing, therefore, the objective for a lawyer is to set the stage with powerful messages that will cause an arbitrator to put these schemas into motion.

Interestingly, within the framework of our schematic structure often lies the key to changing attitudes or perceptions. Our value structure forms the backbone of our belief system and can often be of great use to a lawyer who wishes to change the perceptions that arbitrators might have at the outset of arbitration.

The last tool that we will discuss is affect. In contrast to our thinking processes, we share other experiences with arbitrators through our feelings. To demonstrate the differences, let's assume that you missed an important filing deadline. On one hand, you know what happened factually from your cognitive processes. On the other hand, you are probably quite upset and perhaps even frightened about the possible consequences. These emotional reactions or emotional states we call affect.

In our example, the cognitive processes brought about the emotional state because we have learned because of our experience to associate the two together. In other words, we have learned to link certain cognitive thoughts and perceptions to certain sets of emotions (which form our deep structure). The emotions only come as a result of our perception that a certain state of events or facts exist.

Now let's work on changing the perception and observe what happens. What would happen if the arbitration panel extended the deadline? The facts have now changed. Our perception of the state of the world has changed. And of course, our mental state changes from anxiety to calm.

Let's see what happens when we apply these principles to a particular case. This time let's consider a contract and fraud dispute between two businesses. One company is a Fortune 500 company that manufactures computer hardware and software. The company uses small companies to manufacture certain parts of their computer equipment. One such small company complains that the big company promised to order one million parts a year for 10 years. It claims that in reliance on this promise, it borrowed and spent money to expand its plant size and machinery capacity. It also complains that the big company now orders only 200,000 parts per year. The big company replies by saying that the one million parts number was only a projection, not a promise. Furthermore the big company says that it would order more parts when the economy in the industry improved and its customer demand increased.

What will arbitrators think? How will they feel about the big company? Will they mistrust the officers of the big company under the assumption that officers of big companies will tell a lie just to protect their jobs? Will they feel sorry for the small company because it had less power and control? Will they believe that the drop in the number of parts ordered was due solely to the unexpected changes in the industry, and therefore, not a breach of contract or result of fraud?

To be sure, each new set of facts and circumstances in the case will prompt different cognitive and emotional responses from arbitrators based upon their attitudes, life experiences, personality traits, values, and demographic influences. The keys to success, therefore, lie in understanding the arbitration panel's attitudes, life experiences, and beliefs with respect to specific issues in the case. By understanding which attitudes, life experiences, and beliefs will dominate the arbitration panel's thinking, we have a better chance of developing a targeted presentation that will be persuasive. In addition, by understanding the breadth and depth of thinking or feeling about the issues that an arbitration panel will experience, we can shape the arguments and communication opportunities so that they coincide with arbitrators' schemas as well as their cognitive and affective processes. This important information about arbitrators is also one of the objectives of pre-arbitration decision maker research.

The construction of a powerful argument is the product of systematic analysis and methodical development of messages and information that can be communicated effectively.

(4) Measuring Effectiveness of Communication

There are generally two ways to measure the effectiveness of communication. The first is to judge the quality of the communication by comparing the actual communication to its purpose. The second, is to observe whether the recipient of the communication is motivated to behave in accordance with the purpose of the communication. The first measure is a more subjective measurement, while the second is more objective.

Regardless of how you judge effectiveness, the central question is *Does the communication have its desired effect?*

The reason this topic is so important for lawyers is that the effectiveness of advocacy is so often measured subjectively (i.e. whether the lawyer believes he or she did a good job in presenting the case), rather than the more objective standard. As a result, the communication efforts of the lawyer are often ineffective even though the lawyer has communicated with great social skill.

C. The Importance of Listening and Making Arbitrators Want to Listen

Some people say that listening is an art. Perhaps that is true. Certainly one of the best ways to understand another person is to listen to them. But the ability to listen is also a skill that can be enhanced with understanding and practice. Listening is an active behavior, not a passive one. Our success in listening to judges and arbitrators and getting them to listen to us can be markedly improved once we consider how the listening process works.

(1) How Listening Works

Listening in arbitration is critical to the process of communication and persuasion. Arbitrators must listen to understand the case. Lawyers must listen to arbitrators in order to understand arbitrators' perceptions and to measure how well the case is being presented and accepted. Lawyers must listen to them in order to pick up procedural cues.

However, as human beings, we do not listen to everything we hear and not everything we hear is important enough to seriously consider. Many things affect our listening ability. For example, we are sometimes accused by others of selective listening. Sometimes the selection process is deliberate and other times it is unconscious.

As attorneys, we have an obligation to train ourselves to listen carefully to arbitrators, witnesses, and other lawyers and to minimize the selectivity that we might be tempted to use outside the arbitration. Arbitrators, on the other hand, do not have the same motivations. They feel quite free to listen when they want, or alternatively, not to listen, either consciously or unconsciously. Selective listening by judges, juries, and arbitrators is not the result of any disrespect to the presenter, but is a coping mechanism that legal decision makers use to survive the decision making process and make a decision based upon the most important evidence and ideas presented to them.

The average person's attention span is approximately 10-12 minutes. Therefore, during a 5 day arbitration, for example, any particular arbitrator would have "tuned in and out, then tuned in again" roughly 200 times. Given the monumental amount of detail in most international arbitrations, the struggle of an arbitrator to remain focused on the important aspects of the case (in the perceptions of an arbitrator) is a mighty struggle indeed.

For the most part, arbitrators will listen to the things which coincide with their self-interest in knowing about the case and making a decision which makes them feel good about themselves. They will generally listen to a lawyer unless the lawyer has made them angry or created some other obstacle to acceptability.

Arbitrators, like most people, also listen selectively due to unconscious attitudes about the subject, the speaker, or some other element of the case. In addition, there are always competing stimuli in an arbitration.

By and large, however, the biggest obstacle to communication in the middle of arbitration is the striking difference between the presentation rate of information and the assimilation rate with which arbitrators absorb information. Most speakers talk at a rate of between 80 and 120 words per minute. However, arbitrators, like most people, can absorb words, images, and pieces of information at a much faster rate.

The difference in the presentation rate with which most arbitration teams present their cases and the assimilation rate at which arbitrators absorb it generally leads to some difficulties. Daydreaming, sleeping, and sometimes even frustration and anger are often the result of arbitration presentations, which are unnecessarily detailed and could be presented in more interesting and efficient ways.

(2) Memory and Retention of Information

Retaining information long enough to make a decision is an essential part of arbitration panel decision making. Retention involves memory. To better understand how memory works try this exercise. Answer the following questions using your memory:

1. What is the name of the street you live on?

2. What was your mother's maiden name?

3. What major cities in the world are located on a coastline?

To be able to answer these questions, the answer must have been encoded, stored, and retrieved. Memory refers to our ability to acquire, retain, and use information or knowledge.

Arbitrators retain information in several ways. Memories are stored in either short-term memory or long-term memory. Short-term memory is that part of our memory which is currently active and can change quickly when our focus of attention is shifted. We usually keep short-term information active in our minds for less than ninety seconds. For example, you might be trying to remember a telephone number when suddenly a friend asks you a question such as, "What time does the train arrive?" You may instantly forget the telephone number you were trying so hard to remember.

Long-term memory, on the other hand, is the repository of everything that we know. Generally, any piece of information that we hold onto in our brains for more than an hour is considered to be long term. Long-term memory is virtually limitless. However, memory can fool us. Sometimes we remember things differently than the way they actually were. On the other hand, sometimes we fail to remember things that we thought we knew very well.

In these ways, human memory is different from computer memory. Computers store information digitally in exactly the same form that was input. Computers do not create nuance or context without being instructed. Computers do not make judgments. Computers do not color memory with emotional responses. On the other hand, human memory does all these things.

Computers can generally recall every bit of data that was input even once. Human beings only store information in long-term memory that appears to be important or useful for future reference.

What is the benefit of short-term memory in arbitration? The most effective communicators are usually good at short-term listening. For example, during interactions with the arbitrators and during examination of witnesses, listening to the other person's responses is important in creating a productive flow of conversation.

In persuasion, we attempt to activate an arbitrator's long-term memory in a number of ways. The most typical ways involve association and repetition. The general idea is that if we can associate new information with information already stored in an arbitrator's long-term memory, storage of the new data will be facilitated. In addition, if new data is repeated long enough, it will usually be transferred to long-term storage.

The psychological messages that are the most persuasive and powerfully compelling in arbitration are those which are reflected already in an arbitrator's long-term reference memory. For this reason, some attorneys and trial scientists have mused that a case is decided before arbitrators ever come to the arbitration hearing.

D. How Persuasion Works - The Elements of a Persuasive Argument

Persuasion is communication that is intended to reinforce, shape, or change responses of the audience. In terms of arbitration persuasion, a lawyer or advocate is trying to reinforce, shape, or change attitudes and behavioral intentions (decision making) of the arbitration panel and individual arbitrators. This idea implies that persuasion is more than just communicating objective facts and information as we noted in our discussion of surface structure and deep structure. If persuasion in arbitration simply consists of relating the facts of the case, we wouldn't need lawyers and arbitrators. We would simply type in the facts to a computer and the computer would decide who wins the case.

Human beings are more complex, however. For the most part, persuasion takes place when a credible source of information presents an idea or attitude that differs from the ideas or attitudes already held by the audience in some way. The audience may have no preconceived ideas about the topic or may have different ideas or attitudes about the same topic. As a result of the presentation of a new or different idea, the audience will feel momentary tension that produces a kind of dissonance or incongruity. Because of the discomfort that the audience feels, they are motivated to try to remove the dissonance by either accepting the new idea readily, or rejecting it, or reconciling it with previously held ideas and attitudes.

Realistically, most arbitrators will have pre-existing attitudes and opinions about some or all of the topics that will arise in the arbitration. Nonetheless, there seems to be a great deal of extra space available for new ideas and attitudes for most arbitrators. As long as these new ideas or attitudes conveniently fit in with previously held ideas and attitudes, the job of persuasion is relatively simple. On the other hand, sometimes these new ideas or attitudes run head-on against an arbitrator's pre-existing beliefs. In that case, the job of persuasion is more challenging. In other cases, the difficulty of the task falls somewhere in between, such as when new ideas or attitudes do not actually conflict with pre-existing beliefs, but some adjustment is required. Indeed, where one set of beliefs is bad for your case, you should identify a different set of beliefs that provide a more helpful framework for your case. In other words, you will want to reframe the case and change the perspective.

Attitudes are visceral and implicit for most people. Clearly the best option in the face of a pre-existing attitude is to try to find a way to reconcile it with the new idea that we want the audience (the arbitration panel) to accept. For example, if we want arbitrators to believe that our corporate client has a justifiable defense to the claimant's demands to punish the corporation, we would find it quite difficult to make an arbitrator believe that punishment is not justified in a case where a corporation has acted badly. On the other hand, if we state that we agree that punishment can be justified in the unusual instance where a corporation has acted badly, but that this particular corporation has demonstrated its contrition and punishment is not necessary, the persuasion process becomes easier.

E. The Elements of Persuasion

In order for us to be persuasive in arbitration, we must understand the elements that make up a persuasive communication. There are essentially four elements to a persuasive presentation: the communicator, the message, how the message is communicated, and the audience.

(1) The Communicator and Credibility

Credibility of the advocate and the advocate's message is important in persuasion. Credibility or the lack of it is the result of the arbitrator's observations of the quality and integrity of an advocate's character and behavior.Arbitrator perceptions of credibility are a threshold through which they all will pass before an arbitrator can ever seriously consider an advocate's arguments.

Source credibility (i.e. the credibility of the source of a piece of information) often diminishes over time and the message may fade as the source of the message is forgotten or even dissociated from the message. Conversely, the effect of a message sometimes increases over time even though the messenger may not have had perceived credibility (no perceived expertise or trustworthiness). It may be, for example, that one of the advocates is obviously young or inexperienced, but has a powerful message, while the opposing advocate is obviously more experienced and steady in arbitration. In these instances, arbitrators will often tend to remember the message longer than the messenger. We sometimes refer to this as the *sleeper effect.*

In discussing expertise and persuasiveness, it is important to note the difference between similarity and credibility. Have you ever noticed that when people are buying things in the hardware store, they will rely upon other people who have experienced the same problem before they will trust the word of an expert? On the other hand, when discussing a more technical topic such as the composition of ozone, people tend to rely solely upon experts and will scoff at the opinion of a neighbor down the street.

After much research we now understand that in some cases similarity is more important than credibility. If the topic relates to a subjective preference (i.e. personal choice), people tend to prefer the opinion of someone who shares their personal values, tastes, or way of life. But when making judgments about facts or objective reality, such as whether Madrid receives more rainfall than Rome, people prefer the opinion of someone with objective credibility.

Research in social psychology has supported the principal that only a credible speaker (someone hard to discount) can cause marked change in an arbitrator's thinking when advocating an idea that is greatly discrepant (different) from the preexisting attitude held by an arbitrator. It is also helpful to couple a difficult argument with other persuasive tools to help an arbitrator feel more comfortable considering an argument that seeks to cause an arbitrator to adjust his or her views.

One of the most important goals for an attorney at the outset of arbitration is to gain credibility as soon as possible. It is like building up the balance in a bank account before spending the money. Experience tells us that no matter how strong an argument appears to be, there will come a time during the arbitration when an advocate will need the extra credibility to get over a difficult spot in the arbitration.

(2) The Content of the Message

When we talk about the content of a message, we are referring to the substantive information that is being transmitted as well as the style with which it is being conveyed. There are many lively debates in arbitration advocacy about a number of issues that relate to the content of our messages. Consider the following questions.

1. Which is more persuasive - a carefully reasoned message or one that arouses emotion?

2. Is it better to advocate an idea that is slightly different from an arbitrator's or to advocate an extreme point of view?

3. Should a message express only one side of the argument, or should it try to refute the opposing view?

The answers to these questions are found in the great body of published and private scientific research available to us as arbitration advocates.

In the reason versus emotion debate, the correct answer comes from an understanding of the particular audience. If an arbitration panel is comprised of well educated or analytical people, the rational appeal will usually obtain better response than with less educated or less analytical people. Thoughtful and involved arbitrators are generally more responsive to reasoned arguments. Arbitrators who are not interested in the subject tend to make their decisions based upon their perceptions of the communicator and the message, as opposed to the logic of the argument.

The content of messages also becomes more persuasive if it is associated with good feelings. Likewise, happy (contented) people tend to make fast decisions and unhappy people tend to make decisions more slowly. Therefore, if you cannot make a strong case, it would be smart to put the arbitration panel in a good mood. It does not always work, but if both cases have equally powerful messages, the odds are better that you will win.

Conversely, some messages are very effective by invoking negative emotions. For example, fear and anger are strong motivators.

How do you handle a situation when you know in advance that some arbitrators will find one of your arguments hard to accept? Do you try to soft peddle the new idea or do you present it head on in its most blunt form? We know that some new ideas or attitudes will produce discomfort and sometimes discomfort causes people to change their opinions in response to the new idea. So, we might argue that a more direct and bold approach is preferable. On the other hand, sometimes a message that is uncomfortable causes the lawyer to lose credibility or interest of the arbitrator.

For example, there have been many instances where politicians and news reporters have taken positions different from a listener and the listener then interpreted the speaker as biased, inaccurate, and untrustworthy. For the most part, therefore, people are most open to conclusions within their own the range of acceptability. Greater disagreement between the new idea and the listener's pre-existing attitude will produce less change in the arbitrator's attitude.

Research has indicated that arbitrators who are deeply involved in the subject of the arbitration will be able to accept only a narrow range of perceptions and attitudes. To these people, a moderately different message may seem radical, particularly if the message argues an opposing view to that of the arbitrator as opposed to an extreme version of the view the arbitrator already holds. Therefore, if you have gained credible authority and the arbitrator is only moderately involved in the issue, you should feel freer to advocate a more radical position.

One final thought about advocating a different view from an arbitrator. Most arbitration panels consist of people with widely ranging views on most topics. The smart advocate will construct an argument that will appeal to people from all these different perceptions. To be in a position to do that, it is most important to identify these widely ranging viewpoints using scientific arbitration panel research or other research techniques and to experiment with the combinations of messages that will form a stronger composite argument.

As for addressing the opponent's arguments, there is no one common sense answer. There are times when we run the risk of weakening our own argument and confusing the audience. On the other hand, our message might seem more fair and perhaps even disarming if it recognizes and then refutes the opposition's arguments.

(3) How the Message is Conveyed

Technically speaking, there are many methods with which to convey a point of evidence or argument. The primary considerations for determining which method(s) to use include: 1) whether the arbitrators will pay attention to the message embedded in the information communicated, 2) whether they will understand the information and the point to be made, 3) whether they will believe what they see and hear, and whether they will behave accordingly.

Perhaps one of the most frustrating aspects of communication and persuasion is that rarely does one medium of communication seem to be the most powerful. Let's consider for example, the spoken word. Over the years we have heard, and perhaps delivered, stirring and powerful speeches and lectures. But try as we might, words are fleeting and memories fade. In addition, only approximately 30% of people rely primarily on the sense of hearing to learn new information. For most people, including arbitrators, however, the message in the speech is more powerful and lasting than the speech itself.

With respect to written words, we know from experience and research that arbitrators rely heavily on the words contained in written agreements and communications. However, in the scheme of things, arbitrators make their decisions based upon the overall messages that stimulate their belief systems. On the other hand, written words in evidence and demonstrative aids that convey messages are more powerful than written words that have no message, despite their being technically accurate. Therefore, a lawyer or advocate would be well advised to use words judiciously and to use words in visual aids that convey messages and mental pictures.

With respect to graphics and video presentations, research has indicated that the messages that are simple to understand are most persuasive when supported by some type of video presentation. Complex or difficult messages are more persuasive when written (they force the listener to think through the idea). Therefore, the level of difficulty of the message interacts with the medium to determine how persuasive the message is.

Regardless, it would be wise to use more than one medium to convey the most powerful messages in a case. There is a powerful anchoring effect that builds confidence in a message when they see and hear it repeated in different forms in different media.

(4) The Audience - The Arbitration Panel

Regardless of the audience, it is important to have an understanding of the decision making and perceptive characteristics of members of the audience before developing or presenting a persuasive argument. The characteristics to consider generally fall into five categories: attitudes about specific issues in the case, life experience relevant to specific issues in the case, personality traits, general values/beliefs, and influential demographics.

Attitudes and life experiences relevant to specific issues in a case are often significantly or moderately related to decisions. Research by social psychologists has found that the relationships between the attitudes or life experiences and the attitudes about specific issues in a case that exist for an individual arbitrator are perhaps the most important characteristic to know about the arbitration panel before attempting to persuade them. One of the many advantages to performing scientific mock arbitration panel research in advance of arbitration is to identify the case specific attitudes and life experiences that will shape the listening and mental processing of the likely arbitration panel in the case.

For the most part, general personality traits of arbitrators will not predict their responses to an argument. A particular trait may enhance the effectiveness of one argument or another or, alternatively, may work against it.

The characteristics most often used (although least reliable in predicting behavior) are demographics. As a general subject, the demographics of arbitrators are not helpful in predicting how they will process the case or how they will vote. But a demographic characteristic can often raise a question or create a hypothesis in a particular case that can be helpful in forming a composite understanding of an arbitrator. Consider this example of an arbitrator's demographics. In a case that involves technical issues, such as patent, trade secrets, or toxic waste, an arbitrator who has a background in science may find it easier to comprehend the details and arguments, but may also have preexisting ideas that favor one side or the other of the argument.

There are certain hypotheses that can be formed by knowing a limited amount of information about the audience. However, until enough information is obtained which confirms or refutes the hypotheses, it is best to keep all options open.

F. Cultural Differences and Arbitrator Decision Making

Although a great deal of attention is focused on the legal and procedural differences between the cultural customs, approaches, and styles of arbitrators and advocates from different countries and continents, perhaps the most frustrating issues for many participants are the differences in the methods of communication, meaning of communications, mental interpretations, and behavioral expectations that arise for arbitrators and advocates who come from different cultures.

It is beyond the scope or capacity of this chapter to fully explore the precise differences that exist between international arbitration participants from different parts of the world. However, we will discuss some of the thornier issues and recommend ways of preparing to effectively deal with them in a particular case.

To illustrate how the issue of cultural differences appears in the course of an arbitration, we note the observations of Pierre Lalive, a senior partner and founder of Lalive, a Swiss law firm in Geneva, and one of the world's leading specialists in international disputes. Professor Lalive has over fifty years of experience in international law and arbitration and has acted as arbitrator or counsel in several hundred international arbitration proceedings.

> "Cultural differences or even conflicts between such a counsel and the international arbitrator(s) are, as a result, numerous and sometimes costly, all the more so when the

arbitrator also is lacking in international or comparative outlook. The task of counsel being to persuade the arbitration panel (i.e. the majority of its members, in particular its chairman), a rather elementary condition of success would seem to be for an attorney to understand the arbitrator's background and culture, both legal and non-legal.

. . .

"I have stressed on other occasions the "need to pay more attention to questions of communication between the arbitration panel and the representatives of the parties" and mentioned a few practical examples which, hopefully, could serve as a warning against the prevailing habit of so many lawyers of "transposing", sometimes most undiplomatically, national practices and forensic attitudes to the field of international arbitration.

"I shall always remember my embarrassment when, many years ago, as I was acting as junior counsel to a distinguished New York attorney in an international arbitration in Europe, I was summoned by the chairman (a former law professor of mine), who bluntly asked me whether my New York colleague considered him and his fellow arbitrators as either stupid or untrustworthy, since he had pressed the tribunal to adopt his draft of a very detailed set of procedural rules, presumably hoping thereby both to protect himself and help the tribunal!

"In another case, a famous French arbitrator became increasingly irritated, over months of proceedings, by the practice of an English counsel of answering in detail every single letter or point of the other side, presumably on the assumption that, unless every point made was expressly refuted, even when marginal or irrelevant, it would be considered as conceded. Similarly, it appears that many experienced arbitrators, particularly Europeans, complain about the lack of "synthetic spirit" or mere courage to select arguments or documents, of certain litigators, in particular American, an attitude which results in the arbitration panel being submerged by tons of (partly irrelevant) documents.

. . .

"A last example, known amongst specialists of arbitration, may be taken from the manner in which arbitral proceedings are conducted: plaintiff's counsel was an English barrister, while defendant's counsel was a French avocat. Both of them, returning to their respective offices, were questioned about the proceedings and gave the same answer: "Well, I was asked two questions by the chairman!" This identical answer conveyed in that case two completely different meanings. The Frenchman was surprised, if not shocked, that his well-structured "plaidoirie" should have been interrupted at all, while the Englishman was dismayed to have received so little reaction or guidance in his presentation from the arbitrator!"[5]

The identification and objective analysis of the ways in which cultural differences manifest themselves in a particular arbitration are difficult and sometimes frustrating for most arbitrators and advocates at one time or another. However, there is a great deal that can be learned from science about how to deal successfully with the differences that arise from divergent languages, practices, interpretations of meaning, or some other culturally based aspect of mental processing and behavior.

From a psychological perspective, the study of the differences between cultures extends into two separate approaches. The first is a field we refer to as *cultural psychology* which is the study of the way cultural traditions and social practices regulate, express, and transform human behavior and mental processes within separate and

---

[5] Lalive, Pierre. "Cultural Differences and international arbitration", 9 *Euromoney* 13-15 (1995).

distinct cultures, resulting in a focus on ethnic divergences in mind, self, and emotion.[6] *Cultural psychology* includes the study and impact of culture, tradition and social practices on members of any particular culture. The second is a more recently developed field we refer to as *cross-cultural psychology* in which psychologists generally use culture as a means of testing the universality of psychological processes across cultures while at the same time determining how local cultural practices shape psychological processes. For instance, a *cross-cultural psychologist* would focus on the aspects of social interaction that are universal across a variety of cultures, whereas a *cultural psychologist* would be interested in how the social practices of a particular set of cultures shape the development of cognitive processes of members of a culture in different ways.

To further our work in understanding and utilizing information helpful in successful international arbitration, we borrow information and study methods from both of these branches of psychology. The most important principle here that international arbitration advocates can learn is that deeply held mental and behavioral differences between arbitration participants from different cultures does exist in a way that can be studied and understood scientifically. The awareness that is created from this principle should serve to remove the issue of cultural differences from a subjective analysis that fosters continued misunderstandings and to place it squarely on the examining table to allow for more objective analysis for use in any particular setting.

Once we accept that decision making and successful persuasion can be studied using scientific methodologies, we can then utilize the tools that science offers us to study ways to enhance the effectiveness of advocacy in international arbitrations. By objectively studying the cultural differences that are likely to play a dynamic role in an arbitration, the knowledge gained through the use of a scientific approach is also likely to enhance the experience of arbitrators, advocates, and parties.

---

[6] Shweder, Richard (1991). *Thinking Through Cultures.* Harvard University Press (at p. 72).

V. Psychology and the Decision Making Process of the Arbitration Panel

Every day professional men and women sit as arbitrators in international arbitrations. Each of them has a private story to tell about their successes and failures in life. Each of them has a family history that has helped make them who they are. Each of them has a unique life outside the arbitration that influences the way they will view the issues during arbitration.

This section will explore some of the things we know about the mental processing of arbitrators in arbitration and how it affects their behavior when deciding how a case should be resolved. We will discuss what *common sense* for arbitrators really is and how we can understand how it will be applied by a likely arbitration panel in a given case. We might even discover something about ourselves in the process.

A. An Overview of a Panel's Decision Making Process

For many centuries, collective (small group) decision making in both private and public affairs has been a hallmark of most societies. The conventional wisdom is that small groups of individuals who share a common purpose make better quality decisions than individuals acting alone. To better understand group decision making in an arbitration setting, one must analyze the social structure and process within an arbitration panel as they affect each individual arbitrator and the arbitration panel as a whole.

The influences that will shape the way an arbitrator feels and thinks about a case begin long before arbitration. As a result, the decision making process for an arbitrator in any particular case begins as soon as he or she enters the arbitration and begins making assessments of the people and the information that are presented.

Researchers who have studied the decision making behavior of arbitrators have identified three levels of analysis. The first level refers to the decision making behavior of individual arbitrators. The second refers to the social events that occur before and during the deliberation of the case. The third level of analysis is a review of the cognitive and affective experiences of individual arbitrators in the context of social interaction before and during deliberation (i.e. how the arbitration panel as a whole reaches a decision).

Understanding how an arbitration panel reaches its decision requires a review of each of these levels, so we should explore each one separately. The practical reason for doing so is that the most effective arbitration presentations should incorporate powerful themes that appeal to both individual arbitrators and the arbitration panel as a whole.

(1) Arbitration Panel Decision Making Model for Arbitrators

Scientific research into arbitration panel decision making and that of other legal decision makers has concluded that there is a three stage model which best describes the process a typical arbitrator goes through on his or her journey to making a decision. First, the individual arbitrator evaluates the facts, arguments, and technical evidence and constructs a mental summary in the form of a narrative story. Second, the arbitrator comprehends the questions to be answered at the end of the arbitration concerning the legal decision alternatives that are available as decision categories. Third, the arbitrator attempts to find a match between his or her story of the case and a decision category in order to classify the story in the category it best fits. Upon completing this mental procedure, the arbitrators then interacts with the rest of the arbitration panel to negotiate a solution that helps each arbitrator to reach the maximum goal of making a decision that gives meaning to their experience and helps them to feel good about themselves.

This general three-stage model for decision making is referred to by social scientists as an *explanation-based model.* Within this mental structure, the arbitrator attempts to summarize the case by forming an explanation and creating a story of the case which is used in reasoning toward a decision. This process begins as soon as the arbitrator begins learning about the case from direct and indirect cues in arbitration.

There are both cognitive (thoughtful and intellectual) and affective (emotional) processes which occur during this first stage of individual arbitrator decision making. This formation of a summary of the evidence is the same process that occurs when each of us tries to make sense of the other events we encounter in everyday living. Beginning during the initial stages of the arbitration presentation, arbitrators assign meaning to the case by incorporating or over-laying on the actual case one or more reasonable explanations or narrative stories that explain the events that the lawyers and the witnesses have talked about. This search for meaning is perhaps the most profound explanation for why arbitrators decide cases as they do as we have already discussed.

A typical arbitrator concludes the initial stage of the decision making process with a single dominant story in mind. In fact, researchers have determined that a sizable percentage of arbitrators and other legal decision makers have established a clear leaning in the case by the end of the opening statement (prior to any exposure to witnesses or evidence). This would mean that for most arbitrators, the actual arbitration presentation is a process of filtering through the evidence to test their individual hypothesis about the case – to either confirm or to alter their original notion of what the case story really is.

How Arbitrators Make Decisions

1. **Form a story of what happened**
2. **Filter through the evidence to find support**
3. **Compare their story to the allegations**
4. **Try to make them fit together**
5. **Negotiate with other arbitrators**

As we have discussed, in the course of determining the narrative story of the case, each arbitrator will refer back to their life experiences, stereotypes, schemas, attitudes, and any other references in their minds that will help them to understand and find meaning within the particular facts and issues in the case. Arbitrators' cognitive structures (everything they know and how they reason) are fairly inflexible and they will make every effort to fit their perceptions of the facts and circumstances of the case into the story they have formed.

(2) Direct Influence of Attitudes in Decision Making By Arbitration Panels

Every arbitrator evaluates what transpires in arbitration on the basis of his or her life experiences, attitudes, and pre-dispositions. Arbitrators obviously do not come to the arbitration with blank minds. Their beliefs, values, attitudes, and morals are well entrenched, and everything that is heard and experienced will be filtered and colored by them.

Research in the field of cognitive psychology has indicated that attitudes take on a role of directing or guiding human behavior in one direction or another, as opposed to motivating particular behavior. Therefore, attitudes may be considered to enter the picture predominantly at crucial decision junctures. There are literally thousands of published scientific studies designed to understand the formation, maintenance, and change of attitudes that are available to us as reference tools.

In the context of decision making in arbitration, salient beliefs and attitudes will guide individual arbitrators and the entire arbitration panel to reach a decision which conforms to their beliefs and attitudes about the specific issues present in the case.

(3) How Arbitrator Attitudes and Beliefs Are Formed and Changed

Understanding the role of attitudes in arbitration panel decision making requires an acknowledgement that individual arbitrators bring their life experiences (including ideas they have learned as well as their learned thinking processes) with them in their roles in arbitration. It is beyond the scope of our discussion to explore the myriad of earlier life experiences which arbitrators bring with them into the decision making process. However, it is important to explore the role these experiences play in the decision making process as well as the role that socially shared experience plays in arbitration decision making process.

As we have seen, the results achieved by recent social science studies have clearly demonstrated that an arbitrator's cognitive life experiences have shaped the arbitrator's emotional processing, personality, persuadability, perceptions of causal attribution, perceptions of damages and reactions to attorneys and witnesses. It is equally clear that individual arbitrators and the arbitration panel as a whole are influenced by emotional or affective processing despite their inability to recognize and articulate it.

An arbitrator's appraisals of attitude objects (e.g. people, events, institutions, etc.) are likely to influence their subsequent emotional reactions to them. Conversely, an arbitrator's emotional reactions to an attitude object can yield information for us by inducing thoughts about it. In practical terms, it does not matter if the sequence is either a) emotion influences thoughts or, alternatively, b) thoughts influence emotion, the result is the same: an attitude which influences the outcome of a decision is, as a rule, based on an arbitrator's emotional and intellectual experience.

Arbitrators' attitudes and beliefs are formed in response to information learned through personal experience, through information relayed by other people, and through personal observation. The formation of attitudes and beliefs is an arbitrator's way of understanding and experiencing the rest of the world around them. As a result, in order for us to understand how arbitrators perceive the issues, parties and facts of our case, we must make the effort to identify the likely attitudes and beliefs of arbitrators and understand how they were formed, why they have been maintained, and how they might be changed if necessary.

Attitudes are comprised of affect (emotions and instincts), cognition (perceptions, thoughts, and interpretations), and behavior (intention to act in accordance with the attitude). For example, consider an arbitrator's reaction in a trade secret case. An arbitrator may feel strongly that anyone who steals a secret and sells it to someone else is a bad person (feeling), that anything that a company keeps private is a secret (perception), and if given a chance to punish someone for stealing a secret, he would do so (behavioral intention). This same pattern can be adapted to any attitude about any subject.

In scientific mock arbitration panel research, we closely study these types of patterns in order to identify areas of weakness and strength of a particular issue in a case. We want to understand arbitrators' attitudes, the life experiences that are associated with them and the role they will play in arbitrator decision making about the case. By studying attitudes, we learn a great deal about how to successfully deal with the attitudes that likely arbitrators will have. We will learn about the attitudes that may come into play that are beneficial to us as well as those that are not and how to disarm or change them.

This brings us to an interesting observation about attitudes: arbitrators will only apply those attitudes that are *salient.* Salient attitudes are those that are actually prompted to appear in arbitrators' minds by the case presentation as opposed to attitudes that we forecast should apply to the case, but which arbitrators do not find to be applicable. Every arbitrator, like every other person, has thousands of attitudes about something. The question is always, "Which ones will you encounter in this case?"

The only way to know which attitudes, beliefs, values, life experiences, and mental processes likely arbitrators will utilize to decide a particular case, is to conduct some kind of pre-arbitration research (whether scientifically conducted or not) to identify them, to understand them, and how to work with them to develop a powerful and persuasive case. There are many different methods to conduct such research that will be discussed in a separate chapter on scientific arbitration panel research.

For the most part, arbitrators form attitudes that are consistent with their view of the world around them and consistent with their other attitudes and beliefs. Arbitrators have many belief systems about almost every object, person, institution, life challenge, etc. that they have encountered in their lifetimes.

Lest one be frustrated by attitudes that at first appear to be insurmountable, there are a number of important characteristics of attitudes that are important for a lawyer or advocate to understand. While it is true that arbitrators are committed to their own perceptions, it is also true that there are a number of weaknesses in the attitude formation process that make many of them more susceptible to adaptability and change.

The first is that there is a value hierarchy that most people have in their overall belief system that often allows one attitude to be trumped by another, more important, attitude. Let's imagine a case against a major financial news publisher which involves allegations that the newspaper wrongfully published a critical expose' of an investment brokerage company. The company alleges that the article was based upon false or misleading information, and, as a result, that the company had to close its doors due to the adverse effects of the article on its reputation. At arbitration, the claimant argues that the author of the article and the publisher had bad motives that interfered with objectivity. The claimant argues that the publisher knew the kind of effect that critical articles could have on such a company. It argues that because of the loss of the company, 100 innocent employees lost their jobs at a company they loved working for.

In defense, the publisher states that it had no ill intent and that if the information was false, the fault lay with the sources of information, not the publishing company. The publisher also infers that the reason for the failure of the company was poor management.

Even the most experienced lawyers and advocacy consultants cannot always accurately predict which of the attitudes and belief systems of a likely arbitration panel will be activated in a particular case without conducting empirical arbitration panel research before arbitration. However, once the attitudes and perceptions of an arbitration panel are activated, they will most surely influence the arbitration panel's decision in the case.

B. Individual and Group Decision Making in Arbitration

At the heart of the decisions reached by an arbitration panel are decisions which are made by individuals which make up the group. In this context, it is important to understand the cognitive and affective factors which affect the decisions of each individual as well as the entire arbitration panel group.

(1) Role of Individual Arbitrators in Panel Decision Making

It is difficult if not impossible for a single arbitrator to comprehend all of the facts, events, and nuances contained in an arbitration case presentation. No matter how intelligent or experienced an arbitrator is in making important decisions, every arbitrator, like every person, has limitations. For example, individual arbitrators engage in a variety of coping mechanisms which "filter" information and shape perceptions so as to create understanding and comfortable feelings and to minimize dissonance. Individual arbitrators are also limited in their decision making abilities by varying emotional reactions, differing assessments of attribution, varying intellectual capacities, varying abilities to recall, differences in cultural views and sensitivities, widely varying life experiences, and many other factors.

As a result, arbitrators construct different stories or assessments of cases even though every arbitrator was exposed to the same facts, evidence and arguments in the case. They construct their own version of the facts and motivations with respect to each of the arbitration participants. This process of applying an arbitrator's understanding of life and the creation of a narrative or story for the case being presented to them in arbitration is the driving force behind an individual arbitrator's decision about the case as we have stated. Once a narrative has become firmly visualized, arbitrators will rarely change their opinions about what happened, although they will occasionally change their minds about how the events in the case should be legally classified.

Ironically, the same limitations and characteristics of arbitrators which give meaning to individuality are also strengths with which the arbitration panel group as a whole can arrive at a fair and equitable decision. Differing insights and differing views of events and motivations provide the group with a more complete perspective out of which better quality decisions can be made.

(2) Group Influences on Individual Arbitrator Decision Making

There are a number of ways in which various processes within an arbitration panel influence another arbitrators' individual decision making. For example, in the context of group decision making, information is exchanged as a by-product of the social interaction which occurs within the group. Knowledge may be acquired that might not have otherwise occurred to individuals without the interaction because of inexperience or lack of knowledge. It is in this critical point in the arbitration panel deliberation process, for example, that arbitrators with relevant life experience will generally speak up, and sometimes apply their own expertise in the subject matter of the arbitration.

It is human nature for arbitrators to talk to each other about the case during the arbitration and certainly during deliberations. But regardless of when the substantive interaction begins, each member of the group typically begins with a set of ideas about his or her own goals and the alternative choices.

The information exchanged by members of the group includes both cognitive and affective information (i.e. how each of the arbitrators thinks and feels about the issues in the case). The differences in the effects of each are interesting and profound. As a practical matter, it is difficult if not impossible to separate one's thinking about a set of circumstances from one's emotional reaction to them. However, in the process of sharing cognitive and affective information, the recipient of a shared idea will likely react differently than the originator, although the recipient may be motivated to act in complete concert with the originator. As a result, arbitrators will often (if not usually) arrive at the same conclusion, although their thoughts and feelings (rationale) about the case may be different.

Similarly, in the quest to comprehend and solve any dilemmas presented in a case, arbitrators almost always learn and understand the case more completely only after discussion within the panel. There are many reasons which form the basis for this principle. For example, the panel as a whole usually has a more complete data base than any of its members for problem-solving. It is not likely than any individual member of the arbitration panel has acquired or has access to all of the pieces of information needed to solve the group's problem.

Because of the limitations that an individual arbitrator experiences in the formation of a story which explains the case, a narrative which at first appears to be complete to those of us on the arbitration team, is often determined to be inadequate or inappropriate once expressed before the rest of the arbitration panel. The checks and balances offered by a multiple person arbitration panel are intended to insure what is often referred to as *justice*.

Finally, the interaction between members of a panel can provide motivation to arrive at a more complete and morally supportable decision than one individual arbitrator acting alone. Interpersonal energy among arbitrators, either positive or negative, tends to enliven and stimulate more complete and acceptable discussion and results.

C. Comparing the Decisions of Arbitration Panels with Those of Lay Juries

As we have noted, there are virtually no known scientific studies of the decision making behavior of arbitrators in international arbitration. However, there are some significant studies of domestic arbitrations in the United States which have been organized in the same fashion as most international arbitrations. One such study was conducted by Professor Donald Wittman of the Economics Department at the University of California at Santa Cruz, California in the United States.[7] By way of background, the State of California has provided for court-annexed arbitration in certain kinds of cases. This essentially means that before a case could be tried to a jury, it must be tried to an arbitration panel. The arbitration decision would not be binding.

Wittman's study looked into a number of questions, including, "How do the decisions made by arbitrators compare to the decisions made by juries?" To answer this question, the researchers reviewed the decisions made by professional arbitrators and juries in 383 automobile accident cases that were tried in the State of California over a nine year period. The results of the trials were published in a publication entitled *Jury Verdicts Weekly*. The researchers studied the average awards, the percentage of pro-plaintiff (pro-claimant) verdicts and possible explanations for any variances.

The results of this study are consistent with the studies of other researchers who have compared the decisions of arbitration panels and lay juries. They found that arbitrators ruled in favor of the plaintiff ninety-eight percent (98%) of the time while juries ruled in favor of the plaintiff seventy-three (73%) of the time.[8] In addition, they found that the average arbitration verdict was $22,521, whereas the average jury verdict was only $19,227. In other words, arbitration verdicts were on the average seventeen percent (17%) higher than jury verdicts.[9]

In statistical terms, the correlation between jury awards and arbitration awards in Professor Whitman's study was seventy-four percent (74%). (This means that a jury award and an arbitration award would be the same seventy-four percent (74%) of the time.) The data from the study also indicates that twenty-six percent (26%) of the time, the arbitration award would be higher or much higher than a jury verdict.

---

[7] Wittman , Donald. "Arbitration in the Shadow of a Jury Trial Comparing Arbitrator and Jury Verdicts." 58 *Dispute Resolution Journal* 59 (November 2003/ January 2004).

[8] Id.

[9] Id.

The differences in the decisions between arbitrators and juries may be understood in a number of ways. Before relying on any hypothesis, however, a more in-depth review of the actual arbitrators' characteristics and their likely perceptions in the case would be advisable.

VI. Scientific Research and Mock Arbitrations

Decades of scientific research in the fields of psychology, marketing, social science, and others have allowed us to develop scientific research designs and methods that are directly applicable to studying likely perceptions of arbitrators in an upcoming arbitration. The most useful scientific tool we have in preparing for an arbitration hearing is a mock arbitration panel study. A mock arbitration panel study is conducted in an arbitration hearing style setting using mock arbitrators who have characteristics which match those of the actual arbitrators in a case. Such research studies are created and conducted in a laboratory setting as if the case were going to hearing the day of the study.

Recruiting mock arbitrators requires attention to detail. The recruiter will need to match the type of practice, academic background, demographics, general attitudes about the issues in the case, and as many other characteristics as possible after researching the backgrounds of the actual arbitrators.

Procedures for setting the agenda (which will mirror the actual anticipated proceedings) and for collecting and analyzing useful, accurate, and reliable data from the mock arbitrators should be instituted. The information gathering stage of the research study will include each mock arbitrator's views in the case prior to the proceedings (based upon the written documents) and after the mock presentations for each of the opposing parties. The mock arbitrators will discuss the case using the anticipated actual format selected. The trial team and client can observe the discussions either by audio link or audio-visual link as preferred by the trial team and the mock arbitrators. Afterwards, the research scientist will engage the mock arbitrators in a qualitative interview similar to that of a mock trial study, often followed by a live and frank discussion directly with the advocacy team.

In general, scientific mock arbitration research offers a unique opportunity to bring the arbitration process into the laboratory for study and analysis that can be used to improve the advocacy process. Successful mock arbitration research takes into account the peculiarities of the arbitration process in a particular case, while at the same time providing a rigorously scientific process for objective study. Thirty years of mock arbitration research has taught us that there are a number of special steps that must be taken to insure a smooth and productive process.

Because normally only three research arbitrators are used in such research, it will be hard to generalize their decision to the actual case unless you have conducted extremely conscientious sampling in choosing who the research arbitrators will be and strictly followed scientific protocols. If the mock arbitrators are an almost identical match to the real arbitrators and strict scientific study methods are used, the perceptions and decisions which the mock arbitrators reach in the mock arbitration study will be more likely to forecast the perceptions and decision of the actual arbitration panel.

The degree to which there are differences in characteristics may or may not indicate that there will be differences in the perceptions of the actual panel. Nonetheless, experience tells us that there is much inherent value in conducting the mock arbitration panel study. Many, if not most, of the perceptions of the mock arbitrators will be close enough to those of the actual arbitration panel that the data will be valuable in developing recommendations for themes, case story, and other aspects of the actual presentation.

VII. Conclusion

In this chapter we have devoted most of our discussion to creating an awareness of the psychological aspects of the complex decision making processes that exist in all international arbitration. We have described the importance of arbitrator-oriented advocacy in the successful quest for a favorable decision. We have suggested principles and methods for every advocate to use in understanding the likely perceptions of arbitrators in a particular arbitration. It is our hope that the information here is useful in helping an advocate to create a powerful and positive persuasive experience for arbitrators and clients, and indeed, for the advocate.

Chapter 5

PSYCHOLOGICAL FACTORS IN THE ARBITRAL PROCESS

Sophie Nappert* and Dieter Flader**

I. Introduction

This project has its genesis in the creation of a Special Issue on Arbitrator Bias for the online journal Transnational Dispute Management.[1] Our reflection on various forms of bias in arbitral decision-making, conscious or unconscious, positive or negative, led to the realisation that insufficient attention was being given to the psychological factors at play in the arbitral process. In the wider context, the implications of the cognitive element of professional activity are a growing field of practical interest and academic study.[2]

---

* Arbitrator, 3 Verulam Buildings, Gray's Inn, London. E: snappert@3vb.com.
**Professor, Free University of Berlin, Habilitation in Linguistics, Psychoanalysis and Communication Research. E: multitex@zedat-fu-berlin.de.

The authors are most grateful to the following colleagues, who provided early support, assistance and feedback on this project: Prof. Frédéric Bachand, Prof. Andrea K Bjorklund, Mark Kantor, Joanna Kolber, Dr Julian Lew, Michael McIlwrath, Mark G Peacock J.C.S., Prof. Regine Reichwein, Dr Catherine Rogers, Dr Diego V Rosales, Arthur W Rovine, Prof. Donna Shestowsky, Laurence Shore. Our sincere thanks also go to the arbitrators who returned completed questionnaires.

1 See the editorial: Sophie Nappert, 'Bias: The Other Four-Letter Word?' (2008) *Transnational Dispute Management* Vol. 5 Issue 4, available at http://www.transnational-dispute management.com/samples/welcome.html.

2 See notably Frederick Schauer, 'Is There a Psychology of Judging?', in D E Klein and G Mitchell, eds., *The Psychology of Judicial Decision-Making*, OUP, 2010, Dan Simon, 'In Praise of Pedantic Eclecticism: Pitfalls and Opportunities in the Psychology of Judging', in *The Psychology of Judicial Decision-Making*, ibid.; Jean R Sternlight and Jennifer K Robbenholt, 'Good Lawyers Should Be Good

More specifically, what triggers which decision-making processes in the mind of international arbitrators? What persuades an international tribunal and why? Thus we stepped into the 'twilight zone' of the human dimension of arbitration.

We initiated a pilot study based firstly on *qualitative evaluation research*, a method designed to improve professional qualifications in various areas.[3] We explain our approach below. We are now seeking to refine this method by applying research findings in modern neuroscience and cognitive psychology concerning the decision-making process generally. Our aim is to find out whether these findings can be applied to arbitration in practice and if so, how they assist arbitrators and counsel engaged in the process. At the time of writing, this is a work in progress,[4] with a view to eliciting further scholarship, as well as a series of practical workshops on how psychological insight assists the international arbitration process on both sides of the 'bench'. Although this project presents undeniable academic interest, we feel that it is important to emphasise its practical perspective, and to stress that its primary purpose is to provide a set of tools for the use of arbitration practitioners.

This chapter therefore looks at the art of persuasion in international arbitration from the psychological angle, on the basis of

---

Psychologists: Insights for Interviewing and Counseling Clients' (2008) *Ohio State Journal on Dispute Resolution*, Vol.23:3, 437, available at http://ssrn.com/abstract=1127724; David J Arkush, 'Situating Emotion: A Critical Realist View of Emotion and Nonconscious Cognitive Processes for the Law', available at http://ssrn.com/ abstract=1003562; C R Drahozal, 'A Behavioral Analysis of Private Judging' (2004) 67 *Law and Contemporary Problems* 105, available at http://transnational-dispute-management.com.

[3] House, E.R./Howe, K.R. (1999): *Values in evaluation and social research*, Sage Communications Inc.: "*We want to cast the core fact-value distinction* [fact as objective, value as subjective] *another way. We want to contend that fact and value statements are not dichotomous; rather, the two blend together. Evaluative statements consist of fact and value claims intertwined, melded together, and so do most claims in evaluation. Furthermore, we want to contend that evaluators can draw objective value conclusions by collecting and analyzing evidence and following the procedure of their professional discipline.* (...) *The concept of IQ is a good example: it has both fact and value elements to it.*"

[4] On which the authors welcome feedback and comments.

what our project has yielded so far, and examines issues for the continuation of our work.

II. What are We Hoping to Achieve? Why does this Matter?

What is the value of a better awareness of the psychological factors at play in the arbitral process? What can be achieved with psychological self-awareness that cannot be achieved without? On a basic level, one might posit that self-awareness through psychological insight is in itself valuable to make international arbitration a more enlightened process overall. These authors, however, would go further. We argue that some of the very core features of international arbitration are such as to make psychological insight essential to the maintenance of the quality and integrity of the arbitral process. Psychological insight also has the potential to provide arbitration professionals with a powerful tool to assess *from within* concerns about and criticisms of the process, and of arbitral decision-making, and address them.[5] Psychological research findings on human decision-making as an everyday occurrence, based on neuroscience,[6] provide the following helpful elements.

---

[5] An area where calls are increasingly being made for some measure of qualitative evaluation: see, by way of example, Susan D Franck, 'The Role of International Arbitrators' (2006) *ILSA Journal of international & Comparative Law*, available at http://ssrn.com/abstract=885381; Franck, 'The Liability of International Arbitrators: A Comparative Analysis and Proposal for Qualified Immunity'(2000) *New York Law School Journal of International and Comparative Law*, Vol.20 No.1, available at http://ssrn.com/abstract=821104; Catherine A Rogers, 'The Ethics of International Arbitrators' in L W Newman and R D Hill, eds., *The Leading Arbitrators' Guide to International Arbitration*, 2nd ed., Juris Publishing, 2008; Rogers, 'The Vocation of International Arbitrators' (2005) *American University International Law Review*, Vol.20, available at http://ssrn.com/abstract=691470; Rogers, 'Regulating International Arbitrators: A Functional Approach to Developing Standards of Conduct' (2004) *Stanford Journal of International Law*, Vol.40, available at http://ssrn.com/abstract=622482.

[6] Klein (1999). *Sources of Power. How People Make Decisions*, Cambridge, MA, MIT Press.

A. The Autopilot

The limbic system (the centre of emotion) in the human brain continuously classifies incoming information as 'important' or 'unimportant'. The same information is then evaluated again as being 'positive' or 'negative', on the basis of past experience and connection with pleasant or unpleasant emotions. The limbic system thus stores and evaluates a large amount of information, strongly associated with memories of emotion. It sifts through and computes this information unconsciously, using heuristics (initial impressions, educated guesses or intuitive judgments based on past experience), to find its way through the complexity of impressions and information. We will call this process the 'autopilot'.

The autopilot works like an automatic system of information management and control of attendant activities. Its primary use is to 'unburden' the brain. A good everyday example is the routine of driving a car. Once the routine is mastered, the driver need not concentrate constantly on driving technique, perception of information and traffic rules. These are managed automatically so that the driver's mind is, so to speak, 'free' to do something else: speaking to a passenger, say, or thinking about the day ahead.

The autopilot is particularly well-developed in trained professionals, whereas beginners use the different strategy of 'switching on' conscious analytical thinking more frequently when presented with information they need to process. The coexistence of these two separate systems of reasoning in the human brain is well-recognised, and in the context of other research on decision-making the 'autopilot' is referred to as 'intuitive' judgment and conscious analytical thinking as 'cognitive reflection' or 'the ability or disposition to resist reporting the response that first comes to mind'.[7]

Let us take an example connected with the environment of a law firm: that of junior lawyers following a training seminar aimed at

---

[7] Chris Guthrie, Jeffrey J Rachlinski and Andrew J Wistrich, 'Blinking on the Bench: How Judges Decide Cases' (2007) 93 *Cornell Law Review* 101, 109, at footnote 49.

teaching them client interviewing techniques. The purpose is to develop communication skills that will elicit from the client the elements of information necessary to identify the applicable legal issues. The junior lawyers learn that they cannot simply rely on the clients' characterisation of the problem. As a further step, the junior lawyers should also be taught that it is not sufficient to identify the legal issues. In addition, various possible solutions should be outlined. Experienced lawyers know that this further step is a crucial one, which must be practised early and honed on, so that clients are not only given a statement of their problem, but ways in which it may be solved.

Let us now assume that a junior lawyer who, improperly or insufficiently supervised, fails properly to assimilate the last step of offering solutions. After some time in practice, the junior lawyer will come to master the client interviewing technique, but keeps coming short of outlining proper solutions. The incomplete technique becomes the autopilot, without the junior lawyer realising its shortcomings.

Here lies the problem: the autopilot lets us down. It provides a false sense of familiarity and security, even where some of the information presented to us (the clients' information for the junior lawyer in the above example; evidence, in the case of arbitrators) would not be classified in the same way as the autopilot process suggests were it analysed by conscious thought. Thus in excluding important information *ab initio*, or classifying it as unimportant, or underrating its complexity, the decision-making process is hampered from the start.

Linking this to the task of persuasion, the advocate facing an international arbitration tribunal will want to 'play to' the autopilot to advance the best arguments of his or her case. For complex or novel issues, the advocate will ensure that the tribunal collectively does not underrate or dismiss certain important elements that may stand in the way of a neat, simple outcome. The arbitrator who is aware of these psychological processes will 'switch on' the analytical thinking process more systematically, and compare the outcome of his/her analytical thinking with his/her initial impressions (the autopilot).

III. Relevant Elements of International Arbitration

The arbitral process, with its specific components and features, presents several elements which lend themselves to psychological probing. The following areas are just a sample.

A. Choice of Decision-makers

One distinguishing feature of arbitration as a means of dispute resolution is that the parties can choose to have a say in the composition of the tribunal. This feature comprises several built-in psychological elements.

First, in a privately paid-for process where party appointments are valued or seen as a 'fundamental right',[8] parties may feel empowered with an element of control over, if not the entire tribunal, at least their nominee. The fine line walked by the party-appointed arbitrator in terms of impartiality, integrity and loyalty has long been the subject of criticism and comment.[9] In ensuring that their appointing party's case is properly understood by the tribunal (to use the oft-heard description of the role of the party-appointed arbitrator),[10] the party-appointed arbitrators may tend to discount the more complex, or weaker, aspects of the nominating party's case.

Second, arbitrators are free agents. Unlike judges, they have no tenure, and operate in a competitive market for services. The quest for future appointments may colour the arbitrators' behaviour, and impact on their decision-making. They may be reticent to render difficult, or unpopular, decisions and prefer to split cases down the middle. In a three-member tribunal, they may tend to rely on dissents rather than look for consensus in deliberations, which could imply a degree of compromise that they consider would affect their eligibility for reappointment. They may have a perception of their own

---

[8] Jan Paulsson, 'Are Unilateral Appointments Defensible?' 2 April 2009, at http://kluwerarbitrationblog.com.

[9] Nigel Blackaby, Constantine Partasides, Alan Redfern, Martin Hunter, *Redfern & Hunter on International Arbitration,* OUP, 5th ed. 2009.

[10] *Ibid.*

impartiality and independence in a given case, or their ability to keep hermetically separate their role as counsel in one case, arbitrator in another, that is at odds with that which an outsider would consider acceptable.

Third, arbitrators operate within a (restricted) peer group of fellow arbitrators and counsel, whose overall view of each other's performance essentially dictates the potential success and longevity of an arbitrator's career. At the same time, there are few, if any, instances in which arbitrators individually obtain specific, reliable feedback on their skills and performance. Likewise there are few, if any, fora where arbitrators can freely exchange views on difficult ethical questions or disclose their uncertainty of approach in certain situations without being concerned about affecting their reputation and future appointments. Arbitrators therefore need to develop, and maintain, a strong internal compass of values, which they are prepared to defend and stand by, whilst at the same time constantly auto-evaluate the accuracy and soundness of their performance and measure it in terms of their 'marketability'.

B. Impartiality (and Contrast with Personal Preferences)

Impartiality is a *sine qua non* feature of the function of an arbitrator. Individual arbitrators may "translate" this requirement into different attitudes. Some will stick to a regimented, detached manner before the parties, giving no indication of their reaction to what is unfolding before them. It is very difficult for these arbitrators to engage with the case, and reliance on the autopilot becomes harder to gauge. Also, lack of communication with counsel prevents the clarification of the more difficult points, and thus the 'switching on' of the analytical thought process occurs less systematically than perhaps it should be.

Yet these same arbitrators inevitably have personal preferences as to a style of case or presentation. This jars with the detached attitude they adopt, creating a tension that remains unresolved. Hence in a sense they may be more prone to be persuaded by the advocate whose style or approach they happen to favour. In deliberations with their fellow arbitrators they may adopt the same detached, apparently inscrutable manner, giving off the impression that their mind has been made up from an early stage, without being willing consciously to verify the premises on which their decision rests, relying, they say, on their judgment and experience.

Other arbitrators, unfettered by the outward attitude of perfect control, are more readily prepared to engage with counsel on both sides in equal measure. Thereafter in deliberation they reflect upon the experience and consciously assess the elements of the case on each side before making their decision.

C. Privacy Versus Public Scrutiny and Precedent

The international commercial arbitration process has historically been private. Only the parties were privy to the arbitrators' behaviour, exercise of judgment, values and thought process. In issuing an award in a given case, arbitrators did not look to make pronouncements beyond the four corners of that particular case. In a system in which awards were not publicly disseminated, they did not look to make legal history. Similarly, the desirability or marketability of a given arbitrator was not primarily measured by the contents of his/her awards. Rather it may have been his/her contribution to a process perceived by the parties as inherently fair as a whole, and where they had an opportunity to air their grievances to a tribunal willing to listen.[11] Or his/her standing as a scholar in the community, or retired judge, or business person of high repute.

Lack of precedent, historically a staple of arbitration, is less prevalent in the current age of corporate governance and transparency of process. In certain areas of international arbitration dealing with issues of public interest (namely investor-to-State arbitration), many disputes are in the public domain from the start. The vulnerability of arbitrators is correspondingly exacerbated, for

---

[11] Donna Shestowsky, 'Misjudging: Implications for Dispute Resolution' (2007) *Nevada Law Journal* 487 (arguing that disputants are not primarily guided by outcome accuracy considerations when evaluating dispute resolution procedures, and that they focus more on how they were treated).

whilst the arbitration process has been forced to become more public, no corresponding protection has been afforded to the decision-makers, whose every utterance in an award is pored over and dissected by the investment arbitration community with exacting standards. The investment arbitration awards that have been branded poorly reasoned, unpredictable, and downright irreconcilable in this field may to an extent be a symptom of this phenomenon. Calls are being made for the implementation of a review or appeal system that, assuming it is feasible, may provide as much of a safety net for arbitrators as it would assist consistency in development of this nascent legal field.

Until this phenomenon is addressed, there is room for argument that it can present a real threat to the integrity of the international arbitration process, both investor-to-State and commercial, as the same arbitrators often straddle both disciplines.

D. Lack of Appeal or Review

In a process that allows limited or no review of decisions, it is hard to resist the thought that there is little room for error. This is a tall order for any human decision-maker, hence perhaps the criticism that certain arbitrators tend to 'split the baby' – a Solomonic outcome with which arbitration as a process is regrettably associated, to a greater or lesser degree.[12] A review or appeal system in investment arbitration could also, arguably, bring the case-by-case decision-making process of arbitrators closer to that of State judges. Psychological studies have aimed to show that one factor setting apart judicial decision-making from a layperson's, or even a lawyer's, is what is termed 'second-order reasoning'[13]: the 'higher-order decisions trumping reasons that would otherwise provide a valid basis for a decision',[14] such as, for example, precedent.

---

[12] Gary B Born, *International Arbitration and Forum Selection Agreements: Drafting and Enforcing*, Kluwer Law International, 2nd edition, 2006.

[13] Schauer, supra, note 1.

[14] Simon, supra, note 1.

E. Global Aspects of International Arbitration

To the practitioners of international arbitration, both counsel and arbitrators, the multi-cultural nature of the process is a reality they encounter under many guises in their daily practice. Many experienced international arbitration practitioners do not give it a second thought. In order to reflect this practical reality, international arbitration practice has developed guidelines on procedure and arbitrators' conflicts of interest,[15] to name but two, that seek to provide a common ground between common law and civil law traditions, with a view to accommodating practitioners hailing from different legal cultures. Such is the truly international character of the international arbitration process that there are proponents of the application of a self-standing transnational 'arbitral legal order' as overarching applicable law in international arbitration.[16]

A closer look at some of the ramifications of the global nature of international arbitration highlights the specific challenge that it presents to arbitrators and counsel, which offers fertile ground for psychological insight. This challenge can be summed up as one of communication which arises not only between counsel and arbitrators from different legal and cultural backgrounds, but also between arbitrators on the same panel, and the perception by arbitrators of the witness evidence presented to them. Because the processes involved in communication have deep roots in culture, emotion and education, the autopilot may prove especially influential.

The multi-layered process of putting across a message in the international arbitration procedure, and ensuring it is understood, calls for the development of particular skills. Reliance on 'instinct' and one's own perceived 'open-mindedness' is likely to prove

---

[15] The IBA Rules on the Taking of Evidence in International Commercial Arbitration; the IBA Guidelines on Conflicts of Interest in International Arbitration, both available at http://www.ibanet.org/Publications/publications_IBA_guides_and_free_materials.aspx.

[16] Most recently, and vigorously, defended by Prof Emmanuel Gaillard, *Aspects philosophiques du droit de l'arbitrage international*, (2008) Les Livres de Poche de l'Académie de droit international de la Haye, Martinus Nijhoff Publishers.

insufficient in the face of calls for measurable standards of arbitrator behaviour. For counsel, the awareness of the psychological factors at play is bound to enhance the persuasive quality of their case. For arbitrators, it will help chart a course in what can be a minefield of potential misunderstandings and misperceptions.

F. Overall Picture

In a confidential process, operating under the gaze of a restricted and demanding peer group, with few external means of testing the soundness of one's skills and judgment, how vulnerable are arbitrators to persuasion? Either overly vulnerable, or so unwilling to step out of their comfort zone as to resist persuasion completely. Hence the need for a measure of psychological insight to restore the balance.

The above features provide a good example of the workings of our research method. How helpful to arbitral decision-making is the maintenance of a regimented, detached manner before the parties? It may be deliberately adopted by an arbitrator as a strategy to fulfil the requirement of impartiality. The arbitrator may believe that the strategy can be dropped as soon as he or she becomes aware that it does not work. However, applied persistently, this manner can culminate into a permanent outward attitude of perfect control and become a 'value-based' attitude, learned in the course of practice as an arbitrator, or even as early as in law school.

How helpful to arbitral decision-making is the belief that the arbitrator must master all details and materials of the case 'first off' not to endanger the perception of his/her authority, and to ensure that no important part of the case is misunderstood? Where these attitudes are routinely adopted, we would expect to see them reflected in the replies to the questionnaire, which constitute the 'data' used in the first step of our evaluation.

In the next step of our evaluation, we confront these attitudes with other requirements of the arbitration process: for example, the requirement to ensure that the arbitrator obtains missing information, or a clearer understanding of certain issues, necessary to draft the award. The arbitrator could turn to the parties for assistance, 'There is an uncertainty on my side on issue XY. Please help me get a better understanding of this issue.' This scenario, however, may be perceived as incompatible with the permanent outward attitude of perfect control, or mastery of the evidence or issues. Therefore the 'perfect control' demeanour may be considered unhelpful to the performance of the arbitrator's role, as it prevents the arbitrator from communicating frankly the reality of uncertainty.

For arbitration counsel, knowledge of these likely reactions will provide insight into the most effective persuasion strategy for a given tribunal, and in developing criteria for choosing arbitrators in the first place. It places a few objective points of analysis on that trigger point that makes one think, "This is the right arbitrator for us", or "This tribunal will follow our argument on this".

The multi-cultural nature of international arbitration in turn provokes the following thoughts. Advocates (and parties) hailing from countries with a strongly-established litigious culture tend to perceive arbitration as a competition to be won. The evidence and legal arguments presented to the tribunal are determined by the question: will it help me to win the case?

With this basic criterion of evaluation, these advocates and parties have a deeply- embedded tradition of competition amongst individuals. This is true of many fields of human activity: sports, politics, and business. (We call this a 'value-based attitude', a concept further explained below). In the international arbitration context, the advocate holding this value-based attitude may well misread the impact of a certain style of presentation of evidence on arbitrators holding different value-based attitudes – a well-known occurrence is the reluctance of arbitrators hailing from a civil law background towards the aggressive, or prolonged, cross-examination of witnesses. Similar situations occur in cases where one party and its advocate come from a less litigious legal tradition, or a country with little or no tradition of arbitration. Arbitrators may misread the advocate's presentation as lacking a certain conviction or 'fighting spirit'. The advocate may view the attitude of strong individual competition as superficial. Our project aims at examining ways in which arbitrators and counsel in these situations can be aware of the influence of the autopilot and find workable, and effective, channels of communication.

IV. Challenges and Methodology

In order to probe areas such as persuasiveness, the brain's approach to and handling of complex facts and concepts, cultural bias, emotion, and collegial and isolated decision-making in international arbitration, we face three main challenges: first gathering data, second analysing it, and third identifying objective criteria to be used by practitioners in evaluating the psychological dimension of persuasion in the arbitral process.

Before we delve further into methodology, it is also important that we emphasise what our method of research is **not.** Studies on arbitration-related decision-making carried out on domestic arbitrators and juries in the US (for example, Professor Donald Wittman's study)[17] generally proceed along the following lines: they focus on a limited number of pre-determined parameters to the exclusion of others (in the Wittman research: are arbitrators and juries likely to make higher awards where the Respondent has deep pockets?) and aim to provide a statistical overview of the outcome of decision-making within these limited parameters (Wittman: yes, both arbitrators and juries in 383 cases will award higher compensation where the Respondent has deep pockets).

These studies, whilst they isolate one possible factor of decision-making, shed no light on other possible intervening factors (e.g. emotion) or triggers. In the words of John Dewey, this method "sets forth the *results* of thinking, it has nothing to do with the *operation* of thinking."[18] As such, therefore, these studies shed little light on the theory of persuasion in decision-making.

In contrast, our study – at this stage a pilot study – is focused on international arbitration. It seeks to identify precisely that which is

---

[17] Donald Wittman, 'Arbitration in the Shadow of a Jury Trial: Comparing Arbitrator and Jury Verdicts', Dispute Resolution Journal, Nov 2003-Jan 2004, available at <http://findarticles.com/p/articles/mi_qa3923/is_200311/ai_n9463732/?tag=content;col1.> See also Drahozal, supra note 2.

[18] John Dewey, 'Logical Method and the Law', (1924) 10 *Cornell LQ* 17, 22, cited in Dan Simon, 'A Third View of the Black Box: Cognitive Coherence in Legal Decision Making', (2004) 71 *Univ. of Chicago Law Rev.* 511, 514.

less developed in the statistical approach used in other studies: what persuades and triggers decision-making in international arbitrators, who operate in a process characterised by several unique features, each carrying psychological components (we do not single out only a few parameters). In Dewey's words, we seek to focus on the 'operation' of decision-making. In order meaningfully to focus on the 'operative' part of decision-making, we need a methodology that provides heightened 'explanatory strength', by which we mean that it explains possible motivations, rather than stop at observing these motivations. The 'explanatory strength' of the statistical methodology is comparatively low.

Consider, again, Professor Wittman's study on arbitrators and juries as an example. Arbitrators and juries are likely to make higher awards where the respondent has deep pockets. This leaves unanswered the question why this is the case. Why are these arbitrators and juries guided in the decisions by the Respondents' financial means? In the terms of our study: what underlying values are guiding – as an unstated, implicit knowledge of this professional group – their decision-making with regard to the financial means of the Respondents?

Our first step is to identify the psychological issues faced by arbitrators, and to find the appropriate categories for them. To this end, qualitative evaluation research is more effective than other research methods, statistical or experimental, because it proceeds, not from an outcome-orientated, statistical mode of research (where data is slotted into pre-determined parameters and categories), but 'from the inside', using anecdotal information from a cross-section of the arbitrators themselves.

A. Gathering Data: Getting Arbitrators to Open Up

The first challenge is that the application of a psychological angle to international arbitration is uncharted territory in many respects,[19] not least of which the fact that there is no representative empirical data regarding international arbitrators and practitioners of international arbitration. In addition, unlike court trials, the vast majority of arbitration hearings are not open to the public, ruling out field work. So we set about finding a way to obtain relevant data.

We started with the arbitrators, a fairly contained group which is well-suited to our methodology. *Qualitative evaluation methodology*, rather than placing statistical emphasis on a large number of case studies, proceeds from the basis of a limited sample of 'information-rich', and illuminative, participants. Qualitative data is especially useful where different participants are expected to manifest varying outcomes based on their own individual experience and circumstances. For our target group of arbitrators, this data is obtained by circulating questionnaires[20] and conducting interviews.[21]

The data documents the existing practical knowledge of arbitrators about the arbitral process. There are various components to this knowledge. Some of the components are explicit, and easily reflected on. Others are implicit, and never reflected on. Yet all these components of professional knowledge are used by arbitrators to guide the way in which they conduct themselves and communicate in professional situations.

---

[19] With the exception of studies carried out comparing arbitral decision-making to decision-making by jurors in the domestic American context. See, e.g., Drahozal, supra note 2; also Wittman, supra note 17. The methodology in these studies is, as we explain above, the polar opposite of that which we are adopting for this project.

[20] An initial round of questionnaires was circulated on the OGEMID and Arbitral Women online discussion groups, between July and September 2009. OGEMID: http:// www.transnational-dispute-management.com. Arbitral Women: http://www. arbitralwomen.com.

[21] Forthcoming.

B. *Analysing Data: The Documentary Method of Interpretation*

How is it possible to access the implicit, never-reflected-upon components of the arbitrators' professional knowledge? By means of a method of analysing answers called the *documentary method of interpretation*.[22] It is a partly inductive, and partly deductive, method. In contrast to the traditional quantitative method of research, which fits data into pre-ordained categories, the qualitative method is data-led: the categories emerge from a deepening study of the data itself. It is well-known and applied in various modern scientific disciplines such as linguistics, sociology and pedagogy.

The documentary method of interpretation takes into account all social phenomena that are considered meaningful. In everyday communication between individuals, these phenomena might comprise activities like telling a story, passing judgment on a professional performance, or answering questions. These phenomena are considered as data documenting underlying patterns – either the patterns of an individual's thinking and social acting, or those of a social group (say arbitrators). The process of interpretation consists in finding and identifying these patterns by placing the data within initial 'categories'. As investigation into the data progresses, the initial identification of categories is constantly being reassessed in light of the deepening information, so as to allow the natural emergence of certain patterns. The application of this method ensures that we remain 'within the data': we avoid subsuming it in pre-labelled categories which may turn out to be inadequate. As the process evolves, more connections amongst the data become evident, thus unveiling the underlying patterns.

The patterns lie in structural regularity, rather than statistical regularity: they may evidence a collective form of telling a story; a way of performing evaluations by using a set of specific criteria; a

---

[22] H Garfinkel, 'Common Sense Knowledge of Social Structures: The Documentary Method of Interpretation', in Manis, J/Meltzer, B (1972): *Symbolic Interaction: A Reader in Social Psychology*, 2nd ed., Allyn & Bacon Inc.

mode of thinking to identify an issue. These structural regularities of thinking and social acting belong to the existing practical knowledge of arbitrators, and are used to give meaning to the arbitrator function and mode of being. The scientific component lies in the process of making explicit, and reflecting upon, what is done without reflection in everyday life: identifying social phenomena by using structural regularities which make them meaningful.

C. Deeper Analysis: Identifying Values

As a next step following qualitative evaluation research, we distinguish (i) evaluation, (ii) social values, and (iii) value-based attitudes.

Evaluation incorporates value judgments referring to programs, social institutions, or politics; value judgments are made on the basis of certain procedures and in accordance with certain given criteria.[23]

Social values build up a value system in which they are inter-related, especially by a structure whereby values are distinguished according to a preference ranking.

The notion of **value-based attitudes** concerns the 'implicit', never-reflected-upon knowledge referred to above. This notion is needed to carry out the empirical reconstruction of social values in practical, everyday life. The reconstruction in turn is necessary, given the abstract and vague character of the information obtained when people are asked to identify their prime values. By way of example, Americans might answer: 'It is individuality, of course' or 'It is success'. But what is the practical manifestation of individuality or success? How does this social value determine their practical everyday activities? Value-based attitudes provide insight into the process of 'how-it-is-done' because these attitudes are determined by an existing implicit practical knowledge.[24]

---

[23] House/Howe, supra, note 3.

[24] E. Stake, (1995), *The Art of Case Study Research*, Thousand Oaks, CA, Sage Communications Inc.; I. Shaw, (1999) *Qualitative Evaluation*, London, Sage.

D. The Example of the 'Rationalist'

How does the documentary method of interpretation work in this context? Let us take as an example the approach to arbitral decision-making which can be termed 'rationalistic'. Let us assume that this approach includes a certain value-based attitude. Let us assume further that a person (who will be called the 'rationalist') has an implicit practical knowledge about his/her 'rationalistic' approach – practical in the sense that he/she will make use of this knowledge in the professional activity of arbitration. By looking for data documenting this approach, we get access to the value-based attitude of a rationalistic approach.

What are the relevant types of values? In our initial search for preliminary categories, we could go back to the period of the history of philosophy termed 'rationalism'. We do so, not because we believe that the history of philosophy will have a direct influence on the value-based attitudes on professionals of our time, but to see how rationalism emerged, and its influence on Western culture. History tells us that the era of rationalism (the 17th and 18th centuries) saw the development of a new concept of science (led by Descartes, Spinoza, Leibniz). 'Science' was equated to 'natural science' and 'mathematics'. 'Scientific' meant 'represented by the formal language of mathematics'. Rationality was seen to rule the world. The thinking process held unlimited power. Connected with these beliefs were a strong optimism and conviction that a solution could ultimately be found to any problem.

Historical information thus provides indications of certain implied preferred values that may be taken into account in analysing the rationalistic approach to arbitration. Firstly, there is a clear and highly-held appreciation of cognition (thinking), endowed with the power of absolute control. Emotions are sharply distinguished from thinking, and thinking can control emotions absolutely – a control that is considered necessary to all academic (scientific) professional pursuits. Only by excluding emotion from the outset can another high value be reached: the objectivity of research findings. Emotional reactions are considered to jeopardise this objectivity.

Secondly, mathematics and natural sciences were then the ideal model of science. Use of the formal language of mathematics and logic allowed the perfect realisation of the above concept of objectivity.

What of rationalism nowadays? A strong influence of rationalism can still be found in many fields of natural science, albeit in a modified way, including psychology oriented towards natural science as the ideal model of scientific research. Finally, on this topic, we must stress the fact that the following questions are empirical in nature: What is the rationalistic approach to arbitration? How does it manifest itself? The concept of value-based attitudes will help us build adequate categories for identifying the rationalistic approach in the form of an underlying pattern – a pattern of behaviour underlying the data received in the questionnaires, and revealed by this data.

E. Measuring Arbitral Decision-making

The third methodological challenge of our research is to identify an objective measure for the evaluation of arbitral decision-making. In other words, how do we identify what arbitrators need to know and apply in the psychological dimension of the arbitral process? How do we elaborate applicable criteria for this evaluation? Going back to the data, we evaluate it on two distinct levels: (i) the use of the implicit knowledge of arbitrators as the basis for a value-based attitude (a rationalistic approach); and (ii) gauging this implicit knowledge against certain features of the role of arbitrator.

The relevant features for level (ii) of the evaluation are found with the help of research findings of modern neuroscience and cognitive psychology, which refer to decision-making processes similar to those of arbitration; with the help of psychoanalysis, referring to psychological conflict structures potentially of relevance to the arbitral process; and with the insight provided by experienced arbitrators (in the questionnaires and in interviews). Taking again the example of a rationalistic approach to arbitration, its strong belief in the unlimited power of the thinking process is questioned, both by modern neuroscience and cognitive psychology, as well as by psychoanalysis. It is submitted that arbitrators ought to consider these research findings, not as arguments for "irrationalism", but towards the development of a higher level of rational professional behaviour.

At the time of this writing, with our project still in its early stages of analysis, it is premature to attempt definite answers to these questions. However a number of avenues have already begun to emerge from the data collected so far, and we outline below these initial elements for further reflection.

V. The Questionnaire and What it has Revealed So Far

This chapter is based on nineteen (19) completed questionnaires. The questionnaire is reproduced in Annex 1. The respondents were asked to react to seventeen (17) statements, some of which broken down into several sub-propositions. Each statement or sub-proposition was to be ranked with a number from 1 to 5 according to the respondent's level of agreement, with 1 meaning total agreement and 5 meaning complete disagreement. The statements were organised under the following headings: Approaching a case; The Arbitral Process; Sympathies and Antipathies; External appearances and internal feelings; Sole arbitrator/panels.

A. Individuality of the Arbitrator

The first finding to emerge from the replies was the wide variety of the ratings to any given statement. Data analysis in our research method looks for 'clusters of similarities' – trends and patterns in the answers that provide clues as to the applicable categories. There are very few such clusters in our data. The questionnaire includes certain statements that were expected to attract consensus, for or against. The heading 'Approaching a case' comprised a list of mental techniques, including '(a) Breaking the difficulty down into components that I consider manageable'. It was expected that there would be little, if any, disagreement with (a), yet three (3) respondents completely disagreed, and two (2) rated the statement 'in the middle'

– presumably neither agreeing nor disagreeing. Further down the same list, the technique mentioned as (c) 'Working out a desirable outcome and working backwards', was expected not to attract strong agreement – yet two (2) respondents strongly agreed, and three (3) gave it a middle ranking.

How can these findings be interpreted? Although it is premature to attempt a definite answer, the following questions arise, to be probed in the future steps of our research: Does the variety of replies indicate that arbitrators cultivate strongly individualistic approaches to decision-making? If so, where does the individualism take its source? Is it as a result of legal training? Is it one of the consequences the lack of appropriate fora for arbitrators to 'test' their approach, and have an opportunity to measure it against that adopted by others?

Reaching level (ii) of the evaluation, we can gauge the apparent professional individuality against the desirability of reappointment. Assuming that individuality is considered a 'winning formula' bringing repeat appointments, arbitrators would be asked to consider the following challenge: a deliberately individualistic approach to decision-making may be risky if the approach forms part of a routine that turns out to be incomplete, or wrong.

B. Strength of Resolve About Chosen Approach

As mentioned above, one source of identification of the features against which to gauge the findings is the insight of experienced arbitrators. Some respondents to the questionnaire provided several additional written comments, or expanded on the reasons behind the ratings given to the various statements. One comment was critical of the approach whereby arbitrators should achieve absolute mastery of the material put forward by the parties. The respondent felt that arbitrators should be able to admit that they do not understand everything about a case, and ask for help. Furthermore, the respondent stressed that fellow arbitrators on a tribunal are an important source of help, by filling in information such as cultural background or commercial aspects of a case.

Yet, unexpectedly, a majority of respondents (9) disagreed with the following statement in the questionnaire: 'I often get the sense that I am missing an important part of a party's case and rely on discussing with my fellow arbitrators to fill in the missing parts.' What inference may be drawn from these disagreements? A lack of intellectual humility, or lack of awareness of limitations? How can this attitude be explained? If the data reveals indications of a rationalistic approach to arbitration, this value attitude might be consistent with a rationalistic approach to arbitration. We might add that this is a prime instance where a 'rationalistic' approach does not necessarily mean a 'rational' approach.

C. Refusal to Allow Recognition of Emotions or Unconscious Preferences

The interplay of emotions in the course of arbitration has been mentioned above. One important area where this happens has not yet been alluded to. We mention it here because it was raised by some respondents in their replies. One important tenet of arbitration is the equal opportunity given to the parties to tell their story and express their grievances. The arbitrator, in trying to understand properly the whole story, necessarily makes use of what is called in micro-sociology 'taking on the role of the other', seeing things from the other's perspective. In so doing, the arbitrator will mentally refer to his/her stock of knowledge about everyday life and situations – and about emotions.

The arbitrator who tries to understand the case presented by the parties without factoring in the parties' emotions is discounting ab initio an important factor to his/her understanding of the case, and ultimately to his/her decision-making. Of course parties resort to arbitration precisely because they trust arbitrators not to allow their own emotions to clutter their judgment. This, however, does not mean that arbitrators cut off all contact with their own emotional responses in order to gain an objective understanding of a party's case.

An important distinction should be made between one's emotional reactions and the process of understanding the emotions of others. Whilst arbitrators must control their own emotional reactions to a case, failure to give proper recognition to the parties' emotional reactions arguably hampers the arbitrators' understanding of the case as it discounts the part played by the parties' emotions in the circumstances leading up to the dispute.

The following example illustrates our point. Let us assume a high-value case between an investor and a State entity, in which allegations are made that the agreement between the parties was procured by bribery or influence peddling in the former government of the State entity, and is therefore void. Direct evidence of such transactions is hard to come by; on occasions it is restricted to innuendoes, and counsel's emotionally-charged rhetorics. Allegations of this type are met by arbitral tribunals in different ways. Certain tribunals tend to refuse to acknowledge such allegations absent hard evidence (which admittedly is unobtainable); others will allow them as a factor in their decision, albeit according them relative importance in accordance with the perceived robustness of the allegations. In all cases, however, these are troubled waters in which arbitrators feel distinctly ill at ease.

Allowing for a full overview of the case, bribery allegations included, is likely to inform the arbitrators' understanding of other aspects of the dispute in a way that excluding them does not. One of the aims of the project is to seek to provide tools for arbitrators and counsel to navigate these troubled waters.

VI. In Lieu of a Conclusion: Avenues for Further Insight

The early findings of the pilot study show that the psychological paths to persuasion appear more multi-faceted than was anticipated. This project is, in many ways, an incremental learning process. We learned that certain expectations of what might be "typical" reactions have to be modified because the respondents' approaches to the arbitration process turn out to be more individualistic than initially expected. We also learned that the preliminary category of the rationalistic type of approach is more nuanced than had been anticipated. Objectivity in the project rests in its readiness to rethink presuppositions (including personal bias, habits of culture, and theoretical preferences). Also, knowledge is principally gained as the study unfolds, rather than just in its final outcome.

The next step of our study will include interviews based on these initial findings. We propose to focus on the respondents' awareness of some of the psychological challenges posed by the arbitral process: sympathies and antipathies (with parties and advocates), internal feelings (including the outward attitude of control, the personal ideal of an arbitrator's professional behaviour, the importance of the judgment of fellow arbitrators), and personal experiences as sole arbitrators and in a panel. We are aiming for a deeper understanding of the reactions and motivations of arbitrators, which will inform in due course the elaboration of tailored psychological tools to assist international arbitration practitioners. It is unlikely that we will get to the bottom of the fascinating and complex motivations behind the persuasion of international arbitrators, but every step is valuable knowledge, which hopefully can contribute to the progress of international arbitration.

ANNEX I: THE QUESTIONNAIRE

Thank you for filling out this questionnaire. Please return it before 30 September 2009 to Prof Flader at multitex@zedat.fu-berlin.de or via the OGEMID anonymous reply facility at http://www.transnational-dispute-management.com/ogemid/anon.asp.

Methodology:
Please rate each statement below with a number from 1 to 5, indicating your level of agreement, with 1 meaning that you totally agree with the proposition, and 5 that you completely disagree with it. Please also feel free to add any comments of your own.

These are not multiple choice questions. Where there are several statements in a paragraph, each statement must be rated.

Background

Age:

Male or female?

Nationality:

Number of cases as an arbitrator:

Today's date:

Approaching a case

1. I make regular use of mental techniques such as the following to see through a complicated case. My usual technique is:
   a. Breaking the difficulty down into components that I consider manageable;
   b. 'Boxing in' similar facts as they come along;

   c. Working out a desirable outcome and working backwards;
   d. Discussing with fellow arbitrators;
   e. Asking parties for clarification;
   f. I do not believe in techniques and rely on my training, experience and personal judgment.
2. I often get the sense that I am missing an important part of a party's case, and rely on discussions with my fellow arbitrators to fill in the missing parts.
3. As a sole arbitrator I am constantly concerned about misunderstanding a party's argument or evidence.
4. As an arbitrator my greatest worry is to find that I change my mind about the outcome of the case mid-way through writing my award.

The Arbitral Process – Sympathies and Antipathies

5. I am sensitive to the way in which an advocate appearing before me presents his/her case. I find that I am better disposed towards a party's case if the style of advocacy used by their counsel appeals to me.
6. I approach every case in the same manner and try to be as detached and regimented as I can, so as to give every party an equal chance, and not to prejudice a party who may be less at ease with the process.
7. I am of the view that parties will be satisfied with the arbitration process, regardless of the outcome, if they have had the opportunity to tell their story to the tribunal and air their grievances.

External appearances and internal feelings

8. In the course of a case in which I am sitting as an arbitrator, I feel that I must adopt an outward behaviour of control and assurance, when in fact inwardly there are feelings of uncertainty, inadequacy and uncertainty of thought.

9. The outward attitude of control which I feel I must adopt as an arbitrator is prompted by:
   a. My own perception of an arbitrator's behaviour;
   b. The expectations of fellow arbitrators sitting with me on the panel;
   c. The expectations of the parties and their counsel.
10. My personal ideal of an arbitrator's professional behaviour is:
    a. The legal scholar;
    b. The diplomat;
    c. The reasonable commercial business person;
    d. The judge;
e. The parental figure.
11. The judgment of my fellow arbitrators and other colleagues in the arbitration field is an important gauge of my perception of my capabilities as an arbitrator.
12. In a professional career there is a progression from a junior, inexperienced status to an experienced one. As an arbitrator, I feel that I am always learning and never quite graduate to the 'experienced' status.
13. I am very much aware of the fact that my decisions as an arbitrator must be "right". I feel my decisions are always "right" to the best of my abilities.
14. The reward of a job well done, to the best of my abilities and knowledge, is:
    a. A feeling of personal accomplishment;
    b. The anticipation of future appointments;
    c. Peer recognition in my field;
    d. Enhanced prestige in my professional circles.

<u>Sole arbitrator /panels</u>

15. When acting as a sole arbitrator I feel:
    a. Isolated as I do not have anyone to turn to;
    b. I cannot completely trust my own reactions and prefer the collegiality and comfort of two other arbitrators on the panel;

    c. Vulnerable;
    d. All-powerful.
16. When acting on a panel of three arbitrators, I feel:
    a. Proud to have been selected alongside distinguished colleagues;
    b. Conflicted; I will have to make compromises to my judgment and findings;
    c. Confident that I can bring them round to my point of view;
    d. Confident that as peers and professionals, we will find a common ground;
    e. Most of the time I feel sidelined as the two other arbitrators always seem to get along better with each other than they do with me.
17. To me the 'dark side' of arbitration could be described as:
    a. The ever-present possibility of reaching a totally wrong decision;
    b. Losing visibility in professional arbitration circles;
    c. Not knowing how I rate amongst my peers;
    d. My rate of appointments diminishing for no apparent reason;
    e. Being 'black-listed' by certain law firms because of an unpopular decision.

Part III.

STRATEGY

Chapter 6

STRATEGIC CONSIDERATIONS IN DEVELOPING AN INTERNATIONAL ARBITRATION CASE

David W. Rivkin*

I. Introduction

The original meaning of strategy hails from the military sphere. In Greek history, the *strategos* was the commander-in-chief or chief magistrate in Athens, and the *strategia* was his command or office. Strategy later took on its present meaning of "the art of projecting and directing the larger military movements and operations of a campaign."[1] In warfare, strategy is distinguished from tactics, which designates the handling of forces in deployment. Strategy determines the way in which the overall war should be fought, while tactics focus on the means of fighting the individual battles. As the famous strategian Sun Tzu famously said, "All men can see these tactics

---

* The author is a litigation partner of Debevoise & Plimpton LLP, where his practice focuses on international arbitration and international litigation. Subjects of his arbitrations have included long-term energy concessions, investment treaties, joint venture agreements, insurance coverage, construction contracts, distribution agreements and intellectual property, among others. He is immediate past chair of the 30,000 member Legal Practice Division of the International Bar Association, where he formerly headed the Arbitration Committee. He currently serves in leadership positions for the London Court of International Arbitration, the Arbitration Institute of the Stockholm Chamber of Commerce and the Singapore International Arbitration Centre, among others. The author gratefully acknowledges the assistance of Ina Popova of Debevoise & Plimpton LLP in the preparation of this chapter.

1 OXFORD ENGLISH DICTIONARY (2nd ed. 1989).

whereby I conquer, but what none can see is the strategy out of which victory is evolved."[2]

Similarly, in arbitration developing the strategy of a case for arbitration should go beyond notions of offense and defense in individual battles. The advocate and his or her client should at all times focus on the goals that they hope to achieve. At the beginning of the case, they must develop a clear, consistent strategy that will move them in a straight line to that goal. A reactive strategy, developed as the case proceeds, places the client at a tactical disadvantage and risks undermining the overall case.

In doing so, the advocate and client need to keep in mind the differences between international arbitration and state court litigation. Arbitration affords enormous flexibility to tailor the resolution process to the wider context of the dispute, and any arbitration strategy should take that context fully into account. It also provides opportunities to create an efficient procedure that focuses the evidence on the issues that need to be decided. Developing this strategy requires an appreciation of the priorities of the parties and the sensibilities of the tribunal, a candid evaluation of the factual and legal issues in dispute, and a long-term view of what the arbitration can achieve.

The first step in preparing a case for arbitration is to consider the underlying relationship between the parties, both before and after the arbitration. Are the parties fighting over control of a business or seeking monetary damages? Is the goal to reconcile them or to dissolve a situation that has reached an irreconcilable impasse? If the dispute is between an investor and a government, does the dispute involve the investor's only activity in that country, or must the government's reaction and potential retaliation against other activities also be considered? These considerations should not be abandoned after a decision has been made to proceed with arbitration. Keeping the client's business goals always in mind helps formulate targeted submissions and assess which procedures would be most appropriate. It should also underlie the development of the entire arbitral process.

---

2 SUN TZU, THE ART OF WAR (6th century B.C.), Ch. VI.

Arbitration is not, of course, typical combat. The goal is not subduing the opponent but winning the hearts and minds of three experienced professionals. The tribunal's background and professional experience can influence their views on both procedural and substantive issues, and so they should also inform many of the choices to be made by the advocate throughout the course of the arbitration. An English-trained arbitrator might, for example, expect common exhibit bundles and a skeleton brief of oral submissions in advance. A civil law tribunal, on the other hand, might be more receptive to arguments of good faith, deductive reasoning or reliance on *lex mercatoria.* In any event, the tribunal's role is to help the parties achieve their objectives, and the advocate's role is to help the tribunal in that task.

With these considerations in mind, I will discuss some of the choices facing the parties before and during the arbitration, and propose ways to think about these choices that I have found useful in my own experience.

II. Before Arbitration

A. To Arbitrate or Not to Arbitrate?

As international arbitration practitioners, our clients often come to us in a state of mild desperation. Frequently, arm's length negotiations have proved unfruitful; crucial commercial relationships or the solvency of business entities may be at stake.

Whether arbitration is the best avenue for resolving these difficulties will depend, in the first instance, on the robustness of the potential case. Are all the elements of a claim reasonably satisfied? What are the possible defenses? What witnesses are available? Would privilege or data protection restrictions hinder one's ability to access documentary evidence?

The relationship between the parties should guide the next stage of the analysis. Investment disputes, for example, involve particular issues owing to the vulnerable position of the investor and the nature of the arbitral process involving sovereigns. The immediate business goal of preserving good relations with the host state will often set a higher threshold for pursuing remedies on an international level. One must consider how the host state would react to the filing or to an adverse award: what is the risk of retaliation against existing investments? Would provisional measures be required, and is the state likely to comply? Wider political considerations will also play a role, as most recently illustrated by the corruption allegations leveled at the former Bolivian Minister of Legal Affairs, Cecilia Rocabado, in connection with agreeing to a revised procedure in the Entel nationalization dispute before ICSID.[3]

The participation of a sovereign state will likely impact the arbitral procedure and timetable. Investment cases are likely to take much longer. It can take several months to constitute a tribunal, for example, and once constituted, the tribunal may be more deferential to the sovereign's procedural requests. Jurisdictional objections are more likely than in commercial arbitrations, and tribunals often do not proceed with the rest of the case until those objections are decided.

One must also consider substantive issues, such as whether claims are ripe for arbitration. Arbitration may not be timely if the available claim matures with time, such as denial of justice or arbitrary impairment. On the other hand, a forced expropriation may leave the investor little choice than to proceed to arbitration quickly. When local law issues are involved, as often they are, the advocate and client must consider potential obstacles such as fork-in-the-road clauses and the risk of waiver. These will require a delicate analysis of the availability of effective local relief and chances of success in domestic courts.

Finally, from the investor's perspective, the prospects for enforcing an award against the host state are of particular importance, and, even though enforcement may be years away, they must be

---

[3] *See* Los Tiempos, January 19, 2010, *Acusan a ex ministra de corrupción en caso ETI*, *available at* <http://www.lostiempos.com/diario/actualidad/economia/20100119/acusan-a-ex-ministra-de-corrupcion-en-caso-eti_54279_96242.html>, *last accessed* January 26, 2010.

considered before any arbitration is commenced. Some light can be shed on this issue by investigating the host state's history of voluntary compliance with awards or sovereign debt judgments; by assessing the proportion of disputes against the state that were settled after filing or in which the respondent state sought review; and by identifying jurisdictions in which the state is likely to have assets, based on its main sources of revenue.[4]

Commercial disputes, on the other hand, often allow for greater flexibility. The stronger business-oriented impulse in these cases should encourage the parties to craft a procedure that is both efficient and conciliatory. However, just as in investment disputes, the advocate and his or her client must consider the eventual endgame. Will the tribunal be able to issue an award in time for any relief to be meaningful? Is an award ultimately enforceable? If the dispute is between joint venture partners who are finding it difficult to co-exist, will an award truly resolve the situation or will it simply allow one party to claim a victory but leave the parties in the same untenable situation?

Mediation can be an effective alternative to arbitration in certain circumstances. It should be considered if the primary goal is to preserve the parties' future business relationship or if the answers to the questions posed above are negative. Mediation can also help the client achieve a reasonable business solution if the arbitration case has substantial hurdles. One of the undisputed advantages of mediation is that the decision-makers on both sides can discuss their business objectives in a non-adversarial setting. If one believes that the other party has an unrealistic view of its likelihood of success, mediation can be especially effective, because the mediator can convey the strengths and weaknesses of each side's case in an even-handed manner.

---

[4] David W. Rivkin and Christopher K. Tahbaz, "Attachment and Execution on Commercial Assets," in *Enforcement of Arbitral Awards against Sovereigns (D. Bishop, Ed.) (JurisNet 2009)*

B. Setting the Stage

Assuming that a decision has been made to proceed to arbitration, the advocate should set the stage in the manner that is appealing to the tribunal and effectively conveys the client's story.

(1) Frame the action

a. Investigate as soon as possible.

Substantial factual investigation at an early stage is essential to the successful resolution of a case. Unless the advocate has a clear sense of the issues, the facts that will support the case and the ones that need to be explained or made irrelevant, it is difficult to develop a strategy that will be clear, consistent and persuasive. Similarly, one cannot make proper decisions as to the procedures that should be followed without that understanding. Such an early investigation may add some early expense, but more often than not, it leads to savings eventually, through a more efficient arbitration procedure, a better appreciation of alternative resolutions or through a victorious award. Once the advocate has a sufficient understanding of the case to develop the themes of the case and the strategy that will be consistently followed, then each step of the case – such as selecting the tribunal, framing the arguments, obtaining additional evidence, and determining appropriate procedures – should reflect that determination.

Although most arbitration rules do not require the claims to be exhaustively stated within the Request for Arbitration, presenting the case as fully as possible early begins the process of convincing the tribunal at their introduction to the case. By framing the case in the manner in which the advocate wants the tribunal to understand it, the advocate also increases the chance that the tribunal will accept the procedures that will be proposed to resolve it.

Early fact development also creates other advantages. It avoids surprises later in the case. Establishing a rapport with potential witnesses at an early stage also helps gain their trust, which enhances their candor and benefits them as they prepare for testifying later in the case.

b. Identify the necessary parties

With the theory of the case in mind, the advocate needs to consider which parties are necessary to the proceedings. Multi-party arbitration can sometimes present certain advantages: including the opponent's parent company may maximize the chances of recovery on the award; another party may contribute helpful documentary or testimonial evidence; and consolidated proceedings minimize the risk of inconsistent awards in complex group contract situations. On the other hand, any potential advantages should be weighed against the danger of a challenge to the tribunal's jurisdiction. Jurisdictional objections dilute valuable time and resources and divert the tribunal's attention from the merits of the dispute. Depending on the arbitration rules being used, multiple parties may also complicate the selection of the tribunal. Because many rules provide that the institution will select all arbitrators if the parties cannot agree on who shall be appointed and by whom, adding parties may lead to losing the ability to select an arbitrator of one's choice. For all these reasons, it is generally preferable to bring into an arbitration only those parties for whom consent to arbitration can be established and that are strictly necessary to the proper resolution of the dispute.

c. Consider providing early notice

Some arbitration clauses and many investment treaties require that notice be provided at some time period before an arbitration may be commenced. In those circumstances, the advocate and client should consider how soon it makes sense to provide that notice to start that cooling off period. One needs to consider the positions of the parties and whether a notice at that time is more likely to terminate any ongoing settlement negotiations or, by showing the willingness to move to an adjudicatory stage, to facilitate such negotiations. Providing a notice may sometimes also start the running of interest on sums that are due. Thus, it may be advantageous to provide a warning that arbitration is about to be filed even when a contract does not require it.

For the reasons described above, however, it is generally not advisable to provide this notice until the advocate and client have sufficient knowledge of the case to know that they will pursue the arbitration if the case is not settled – and to know the strategy and themes they will consistently pursue if so.

d. Anticipate the support required

In arbitration, we are lucky to work with professionals of different backgrounds and areas of expertise. The advocate should consider whether the case would benefit from the support of a local law firm or of experts.

- Local law firms. Collaborations with other firms can be highly productive, and there are a variety of ways to obtain useful support from a law firm in another jurisdiction. Where that jurisdiction's law is the applicable law for the arbitration, the advocate should consider whether that law is best presented in the written memorials or through an expert opinion. Increasingly, tribunals prefer the former, since cross-examination of legal experts is rarely more helpful than simply presenting argument on those issues. Where the collaboration is as co-counsel, the advocate needs to think critically about the most effective division of labor between the two firms. Local counsel may have a proximity to witnesses and documents and possess language capabilities that would allow them better to develop the evidentiary record. If the two law firms are working across time zones or producing collaborative work product, be prepared for the logistics of managing a larger team.

- Experts. Many international arbitrations involve technical factual issues, economic phenomena, or complex valuation questions for which an expert opinion can be indispensable. In those cases, it is best to engage an expert as early as possible, so that the advocate and client can obtain the expert's understanding of the issues and fold that understanding into the development of the strategy and themes to be followed in the case. Again, it is important to avoid having to retract or revise a position that was taken without a complete understanding. Similarly, the expert needs to understand how his or her issues fit into the overall case and the positions of the parties, so that the expert can effectively focus any report on the issues that are meaningful to the tribunal.

At all times, the expert should provide to the advocate candid opinions that allow the advocate properly to prepare the case. In the report, the expert should not stretch to support a party by asserting a position that is difficult to defend. As with all witnesses, an expert's credibility is paramount to his or her effectiveness.

(2) Cast the perfect tribunal

The parties' choice of the decision-makers is one of the advantages of arbitration and has major strategic implications. The first question in choosing the tribunal is whether a three-member panel would be appropriate. If the issues are relatively straightforward and the amount in dispute modest, a sole arbitrator presents significant advantages in terms of case management and cost control. Even if the arbitration agreement provides for three arbitrators, the advocate should consider whether to propose a sole arbitrator instead.

A complex factual or legal situation, on the other hand, may be best served by healthy debate among different points of view. One can be more comfortable that three intelligent arbitrators who can consult with one another will understand difficult factual or legal issues. The parties also appreciate having greater control over the choice of decision-maker in a three-member panel, because they are able directly to appoint one of the members. On the other hand, a three-member tribunal will inevitably raise complications in scheduling hearings, and will move more slowly in making decisions and drafting the final award. One technique that is often useful with three-arbitrator panels is to empower the presiding arbitrator to make procedural orders without consulting the other arbitrators.

In determining whom to nominate as arbitrator, the advocate has to take into account, as always, the theory of the case and the client's overall goals. One should consider how the arbitrator may approach certain issues, how the arbitrator's background fits the case, whether the arbitrator has any special technical, financial or legal expertise that will be useful, whether the arbitrator's cultural perspective is important to one's client. An arbitrator should be able to understand the business issues underlying the dispute and what the parties hope that the arbitration can achieve. A good party-appointed arbitrator will not risk losing credibility by becoming a party advocate, but is rather someone who will ensure that you have a fair opportunity to present your case.

The advocate should also think about how the arbitrator will approach the procedural choices to be made. It is important to consider the arbitrator's reputation for availability and for moving a case efficiently. An arbitrator in demand may be more desirable for many reasons, but one should make sure that he or she will be able to devote the time and effort required to understand the issues and to manage the arbitration efficiently in the hoped-for timeframe. Depending on the case, an advocate may prefer an arbitrator who is not shy about making preliminary determinations, will resist excessive discovery requests, or favors bifurcation. Case management skills are especially important when proposing or approving the presiding arbitrator.

III. During Arbitration

Once the arbitration has begun, the advocate's challenge becomes telling the story in a way that will persuade his or her audience. Unlike advocates in domestic court litigation, advocates in international arbitration often have an ability substantially to shape the process. Strategic considerations should be an integral part of constructing that process and then presenting a compelling story.

A. Determining the Appropriate Procedures

In setting the procedural framework for the arbitration, the advocate needs to think critically about how complex the supporting structure truly needs to be. I have proposed elsewhere the "Town Elder" paradigm: an approach for international arbitration that seeks to return the process to its basics. The approach posits the original arbitrators, the town elders, listening to both sides explain their version of the dispute. The town elder would not have put in place a complex procedure, but would have asked for additional information – perhaps a document that one side says supports its case or a witness or an expert to explain what happened – only as needed. The Town Elder approach borrows from the economics concept of zero-based budgeting.[5] Zero-based budgeting creates a budget from scratch by determining the expenses necessary for the upcoming year, as opposed to starting from the previous year's budget and modifying it. The latter approach inevitably continues projects that are no longer necessary or effective, but which have a momentum of their own.

While international arbitration today often involves complex disputes, substantial damages and public policy issues that require careful consideration and appropriate procedures, the approach should nevertheless be the same. In international arbitration, practitioners should consider the wide range of available procedural choices as features to be custom-picked on a case-by-case basis, according to the needs of the dispute at hand, and not automatically continued because that is how prior arbitrations were conducted.

Determining in advance how best to use various procedural options in a strategic manner will help the advocate achieve the client's goals and success in the arbitration. The advocate should discuss with opposing counsel procedures that will lead to an efficient resolution of the case and then urge those procedures to the tribunal at an early procedural conference. Under most rules, the tribunal retains control over the procedural aspects of the arbitration, so the advocate will need to convince the tribunal that these procedures are the best ones for the arbitration.[6]

The case management conference will also be an opportunity to set clear goals and expectations regarding time. Decisions about time can be broken down into two broad categories: when, and for how long.

- Fast track. Many institutional rules, including the ICC Rules, provide for fast track procedures that allow the parties to

---

[5] David W. Rivkin, *Towards a New Paradigm in International Arbitration: The Town Elder Model Revisited*, 24 Arb. Int'l 375 (2008).

[6] *See, e.g.*, International Chamber of Commerce, *Rules of Arbitration* ("ICC Rules"), *available at* <www.iccwbo.org/uploadedFiles/Court/Arbitration/other/rules_arb_english.pdf>, Preamble; Int'l Center for Dispute Resolution, *International Arbitration Rules*, art. 16, *available at* <www.adr.org/sp.asp?id=33994>.

shorten the time periods specified for certain phases of the arbitration, such as the time limit for rendering the award.[7] If used wisely, this can be an effective strategic tool. On the other hand, avoid the temptation to set unrealistic deadlines, as extensions will disrupt the entire process.

- Bifurcation and phasing. Bifurcation can contribute to the early resolution of the dispute, for example, if a significant part of the claims are dismissed for lack of jurisdiction, or if an award on liability sets the framework for settlement discussions before a damages phase. Whether bifurcation is appropriate, however, will depend on the extent to which the dispute can be neatly severed into stages such as jurisdiction/merits or liability/damages. Separate phases for liability and damages can make sense where, as for valuation disputes, the issues are relatively self-contained. Bifurcation allows the parties and the tribunal to concentrate on each issue at a time, making the case more manageable and submissions more effective.

  Conversely, bifurcation can be a disservice if the issues are intertwined, causing the parties to expend time and effort in presenting evidence multiple times. If both stages rely on the same key documents and witnesses, bifurcation will not be a good strategic choice.

  Similarly, as discussed below regarding preliminary determinations, an advocate should consider whether to propose separate hearings on issues that can be decided discretely. The client and the case may benefit substantially, for example, by having the tribunal rule, at an early stage, on an important issue of contract interpretation that does not require much evidence. That determination may permit the

---

[7] *See, e.g.*, ICC Rules, Article 32; Int'l Institute for Conflict Prevention & Resolution, *Global Rules for Accelerated Commercial Arbitrations* (effective August 20, 2009), *available at* <www.cpradr.org/ClausesRules/GlobalArbitrationRules/tabid/422/Default.asp>.

parties to focus their evidence regarding other issues, or it may even pave the way to meaningful settlement discussions.

- Submissions. The substantial knowledge of the case gained by the early investigation should facilitate the advocate's decision as to how written submissions should be structured. With an understanding of the evidence in hand and how much of the opposing party's case remains to be understood, the advocate can encourage either simultaneous or consecutive submissions. The advocate also needs to consider whether the client's case is best presented in writing or orally. While substantial written memorials are now common, there are many cases where credibility of key witnesses and their version of the events will be most important. In such cases, the parties may wish to limit or even eliminate pre-hearing submissions and proceed straight to testimony that can allow a tribunal to make those credibility determinations. The presentation of the case.
- Chess clock method. Many practitioners are averse to the "chess clock" method, in which each side has a fixed number of hours to present its case (direct and redirect examinations of its own witnesses, cross-examinations of opposing witnesses, and oral arguments, if any). However, use of these time limits can often present an advantage for the client and for the process. The chess clock method usually makes a case more compelling. A limited time frame forces both sides to focus on what really matters to the tribunal's decision-making. It also avoids repetitive testimony and undue emphasis on peripheral issues, both of which are key to persuasive advocacy and an efficient process. In my experience as arbitrator and counsel, I have never felt that the method has prevented a party from fully presenting its case.

B. Preliminary Determinations

Preliminary determinations can be a useful tool for achieving your strategic objectives and streamlining the arbitral process. The attitude of arbitrators towards such motions has changed perceptibly in recent years. Many arbitrators now view determining preliminary issues as a useful case management tool.

While arbitrators have always had a general power to issue partial awards, the AAA/ICDR was the first institution to include a provision specifically granting arbitrators the authority to hold hearings and rule on preliminary issues. Its Article 16.3 provides in relevant part: "[t]he tribunal may in its discretion . . . bifurcate proceedings, . . . and direct the parties to focus their presentations on issues the decision of which could dispose of all or part of the case." [8] Now, many institutional arbitration rules, including ICSID,[9] allow the tribunal to dispose of unmeritorious claims at an early stage or to render partial awards on severable issues. Arbitrators have the benefit of being able to focus the evidence and argument on only those matters necessary to determine that issue. Unlike similar summary judgment proceedings in litigation that are generally limited to issues on which there is no real factual dispute, advocates and tribunals in international arbitrations can focus on any issue warranting an early determination and hold fact-based hearings on those issues.

The proper use of partial awards for preliminary determinations can be a substantial advantage to international arbitration and to

---

[8] AAA International Dispute Resolution Procedures, International Arbitration Rules ("ICDR Rules"), Article 16.3, *available at* <http://www.adr.org/sp.asp?id=33994#INTERNATIONAL%20ARBITRATION%20RULES>.

[9] ICSID Rule 41(5) provides, in relevant part, "a party may . . . file an objection that a claim is manifestly without legal merit. The party shall specify as precisely as possible the basis for the objection. The Tribunal, after giving the parties the opportunity to present their observations on the objection, shall, at its first session or promptly thereafter, notify the parties of its decision on the objection." International Centre for Settlement of Investment Disputes, Rules of Procedure for Arbitration Proceedings, Article 41(5), *available at* <http://icsid.worldbank.org/ICSID/StaticFiles/basicdoc/basic-en.htm>.

advocates who properly use them. Preliminary determinations should be pursued if a threshold question could dispose of a major issue and either resolve the entire case or significantly limit the remaining evidence to be heard. Examples include legal or contract interpretation issues such as whether lost profits or consequential damages are recoverable, what the applicable law should be, or whether a *force majeure* defense applies. The availability of an estoppel limitations defense may also be worth deciding early. In one case, we convinced an arbitrator to hold a separate hearing, before any liability hearing, on whether the claimant's net asset value was negative at the time of the alleged breach. If it was, then even if there was liability, the claimant was not entitled to any damages under the contract. After hearing evidence, the arbitrator agreed with our position and issued a final award on that basis. This motion thus saved substantial costs and time that would otherwise have been unnecessarily spent on the liability issues.

C. Evidence

A successful arbitration depends on effective marshalling of the evidence. The advocate should consider how to deal with all evidentiary issues in light of the overall strategy of the case and the client's goals. For example, is witness or expert evidence required? Are there particular documents within one's opponent's possession that would advance the case?

(1) Document Production

Despite being a common feature of international arbitration, discovery need not be pursued in every case, and when it is sought, the advocate should carefully tailor the discovery requests. The advocate should seek only what is truly needed, and he or she should frame the requests to focus on as narrow a category of documents as possible. The standards of the IBA Rules of Evidence have become generally universal since their adoption in 1999. The Rules require that any request for documents include only a "narrow and specific category of documents" if the individual document cannot itself be identified, and they further require the proponent to demonstrate, among other things, that the requested documents are relevant and material to the arbitration.[10] Although advocates and clients are often drawn by the temptation of the unknown and the desire to know what their opponent was really thinking, the advocate should always consider if discovery will be helpful to the client's case and whether it will justify the added time and expense.

Discovery may not always obtain anything helpful. In investment disputes, for example, governments are unlikely to produce many documents unless they are very clearly identified and easy to locate. Otherwise, bureaucracy and objections about state secrets and government deliberations will likely lead to few produced documents. Even in commercial arbitrations, discovery often leads to prolonged objections and heated privilege debates. In one recent arbitration, for example, our opponent produced a letter in which, but for the date line, every word had been redacted. In addition, of course, the client may have to disclose something unhelpful. Through the early fact investigation described above, the advocate can identify the weaknesses of the case and assess whether it would be strategically better to rely on documents already in the client's possession.

If the advocate believes that discovery will be useful, he or she should assess the most "efficient, economical and fair" way to conduct it.[11] Numerous copies of voluminous paper bundles may not be the most manageable or cost-effective way to share documents between the parties or with the tribunal. Arbitration institutions are working hard to offer flexible alternatives to boxes of

---

[10] Int'l Bar Association, Rules on the Taking of Evidence in International Commercial Arbitration (1999) ("IBA Rules"), Article 3.3. The revised 2009 draft of the Rules, currently under discussion, proposes adding that the documents requested be "material to the outcome and relevant to the case." *See* Int'l Bar Association, Arbitration Committee, *Draft revised IBA Rules on the Taking of Evidence in International Arbitration* (2009) ("Draft revised IBA Rules"), Article 3.3 (b), *available at* <http://www.ibanet.org/Document/Default.aspx?DocumentUid=0F703EBD-9ECA-4926-9A1E-EF91C008156D>.

[11] Draft revised IBA Rules, Article 2.

exhibits. The AAA/ICDR has issued Guidelines for Arbitrators Concerning Exchanges of Information; and CPR has published a Protocol on the disclosure of documents and presentation of witnesses.[12] The AAA/ICDR Guidelines provide that arbitrators "should be receptive to creative solutions for achieving exchanges of information in ways that avoid costs and delay."[13] The ICC, for example, has electronic storage services to facilitate exchanging documents. An entirely paperless arbitration may be far into the future, but exploring creative avenues for exchanging documents in a manner most helpful to all involved is a wise strategic investment, allowing the advocate to devote greater energy and resources to the heart of the dispute.

Drafting document requests should again be consistent with the overall strategy of the case and be focused carefully to achieve those goals. If the request is overly broad, it is likely to be denied by the tribunal, and it is also easier for the opponent to interpret in a manner that will lead to producing limited documents. In particular, tribunals do not like broad requests such as those for documents "relating to" a particular subject. Specific requests are more likely to yield useful documents, and they are consistent with the generally accepted standards of the IBA Rules of Evidence. For electronic documents, the draft revised IBA Rules and the ICDR Guidelines envisage providing search terms.[14]

Finally, the advocate should consider whether document requests are better served before the parties make their memorials or after a first round of submissions if there are two rounds. Conducting discovery then, after the parties have a better understanding of the

---

[12] Int'l Centre for Dispute Resolution, *ICDR Guidelines for Arbitrators Concerning Exchanges of Information* (2008) ("AAA/ICDR Guidelines"), *available at* <www.adr.org/si.asp?id=5288>; Int'l Institute for Conflict Prevention & Resolution, *CPR Protocol on Disclosure of Documents and Presentation of Witnesses in Commercial Arbitration* ("CPR Protocol"), *available at* <http://www.cpradr.org/Portals/0/CPR%20Protocol%20for%20distribution.pdf>.

[13] AAA/ICDR Guidelines, Article 6(a).

[14] *See* Draft revised IBA Rules, Article 3.3(a); AAA/ICDR Guidelines, Article 4.

other side's case and its principal contentions, often permits much more targeted requests and therefore leads to more useful documents.

However discovery is conducted, it should not distract from the strategic goals and the focus on the core questions at issue. For that reason, an advocate should avoid vexing the tribunal with petty objections. Try to work out a reasonable scope to problematic document requests and only involve the arbitrators in deciding objections when absolutely necessary. Of course, tribunals will be much more sympathetic to reasonable objections if one's own document requests have been carefully and narrowly tailored. Objections that an opponent's request is burdensome are rarely successful when both sides have submitted overly broad, "related to" requests.

(2) Witness Testimony

Testimonial evidence should be evaluated in similar terms. The advocate should make sure that the testimony is carefully focused on the core issues and in a manner that will be persuasive to the tribunal. Tribunals are rarely swayed by multiple witnesses repeating the same story. A clear, consistent story, well told by the witness with the best personal knowledge and supported by contemporaneous documents, is much more convincing.

- <u>Who</u>? Consider which witnesses can shed the best light on particular elements of your case and help the tribunal to understand certain issues. The tribunal will often want to hear from at least one fact witness who can speak to the parties' intentions and contemporaneous understanding. They may not want to hear from a witness whose testimony does not add to that of witnesses who are closer to the events. Conversely, not making key individuals available as witnesses can betray a lack of confidence in your case.
- <u>What</u>? A cardinal rule when working with witnesses and experts is to consider which topics are properly the subject of that person's testimony. Neither fact nor expert witnesses are

credible when testifying on issues with which they are insufficiently familiar. When in doubt, many witnesses will try to say what they believe is most helpful to their side, without a full appreciation of the fact that such testimony is actually harmful to the party. The advocate should prepare witnesses to testify as to their own understanding and to be forthcoming about the limits to their own recollection. Expert witnesses present challenges of their own. Strong expert witnesses are able to bolster the advocate's case while persuading the tribunal, through the rigor of their analysis, that their interpretation is correct. However, an expert who comes across as an advocate loses credibility with the tribunal.

- How? Much has been said about the advantages and disadvantages of cross-examination in international arbitration, and I will not discuss them here. Witness testimony is usually now presented in international arbitration through written, sworn, direct testimony. The witness then appears at the hearing for cross examination. In general, this presents an advocate with an excellent way to present one's case in a clear and consistent manner. However, the advocate must ensure that the witness statements are the witness's and not the lawyer's. The witness must be entirely comfortable with every word of the witness statement, or that will soon become evident on cross examination. Moreover, the language and tone of the witness statement must be that of the witness and not the lawyer. When portions of the witness statement are cut and pasted from a brief or another witness statement, the credibility of that witness disappears.

Experts of course usually present their opinions in writing in advance of the hearing. International arbitration has developed two techniques to allow tribunals better to judge the weight to be given expert evidence, and advocates should consider how best to use these techniques to persuade the tribunal that his or her expert is the one upon whom the tribunal should rely. Prior to a hearing, experts may sometimes meet to discuss each other's reports and to draw up a common list of issues on which they agree and disagree. The meeting is held without lawyers, so the experts can exchange views candidly. Often, they know each other through professional associations and want to be credible to each other. As a result, the meeting often is successful in focusing the areas on which the experts agree and disagree, which saves us a substantial amount of time at the hearing. In addition, it is often very useful at the hearing to have the two experts testify simultaneously, with questioning by both sides and by the tribunal. This is known as witness conferencing. This technique allows the tribunal to hear the experts' views together and allows each expert to comment on why he or she agrees or disagrees on particular points. The tribunal is more easily able to understand the basis for any disagreements and to come to its own determinations on those issues.[15]

D. Argument

The ultimate aim of any dispute resolution strategy is to convince the decision-maker to agree with the advocate's position. The advocate must make his or her client's point of view clear, but do so in a way that is palatable to the tribunal. For example, arbitrators are frequently chosen for their expertise in the field. Factual and legal development should be tailored to that expertise, reflecting a level of detail that neither underestimates nor alienates the tribunal.

Just as much as the content, the structure of one's argument can make a strategic contribution to your case. The advocate should raise important claims from the beginning; any additional claims raised during the hearing or in final submissions may be seen as a desperate move to overcome difficulties shown in other arguments. Similarly, the advocate should make sure that the place of each argument in the theory of the case is sufficiently clear from its presentation. The advocate should resist the urge to give unwarranted attention to

---

[15] *See also* ICC Techniques, Point 70; IBA Rules, Article 8.2.

supplemental or alternative arguments that may weaken the overall position. As Sun Tzu advises, "On marginal ground, do not stop."[16]

With this in mind, avoid unnecessary procedural motions that do not advance the case (and may in fact be detrimental to it). Emotional or purely tactical – as opposed to strategic – objections fragment the dispute, test the tribunal's patience, and dilute the strength of one's case. They can also be costly to one's client. The ICC Techniques, for example, instruct arbitrators to use their authority to allocate costs to discourage unreasonable behavior such as: "excessive document requests, excessive legal argument, . . . dilatory tactics, [and] unjustified interim applications."[17]

One type of objection that has become regrettably more frequent is the partiality challenge to an arbitrator. The threshold for bringing such a challenge should be as high as the stakes, for losing such a challenge often upsets the entire tribunal, not just the challenged arbitrator.

Forsaking excessive positions also entails avoiding arguments that overreach or unnecessarily impugn the character of the parties involved. Allegations of corruption or fraud should be avoided unless the advocate has compelling proof. If one does make such a claim, treat it as sensitively as possible. The advocate should allow the persons in question a fair opportunity to respond to such serious allegations, and be prepared to establish his or her case over their denial. An allegation of fraud that is not sufficiently supported and appears to be made mainly for the emotional impact almost always insults a tribunal and undermines all of that party's arguments.

IV. Conclusion

"Know thyself, know thy enemy," Sun Tzu said.[18] In international arbitration, I would add, "know thy tribunal." This is perhaps the most important principle of advocacy in international

---

16 Tzu, *op. cit.*, Ch. XI.

17 ICC Techniques, Point 85.

18 Tzu, *op. cit.*, Ch. X.

arbitration. Putting oneself in the tribunal's position provides the proper perspective on the multiple choices and obstacles an advocate faces when developing a case strategy for arbitration. Although this will take time and perseverance, it should lead to victory in the end.

Chapter 7

ADVOCACY IN PRACTICE: THE USE OF PARALLEL PROCEEDINGS

Emmanuel Gaillard and Philippe Pinsolle

I. Introduction

In the first edition of this book, we had taken the view that, in international arbitration, advocacy was not limited to the oral performance of counsel. In our view, advocacy encompassed all the aspects of the dispute and all the strategic decisions to be made in the case. Strategy in arbitration is multidimensional. Unlike court proceedings, arbitration leaves open a wide range of possibilities for the litigants and it is for their advocate to make the best possible use of these possibilities. The role of the advocate should thus not be limited to delivering the best oral performance, but should also extend to any important strategic decision to be made. Some authors have expressed doubt as to the accuracy of this far-reaching definition of advocacy.[1] The reasons are understandable. However, it seems that limiting advocacy to the oral argument of the advocate or indeed to the examination of witnesses does not do justice to this concept. We believe that the role of the advocate in an international arbitration is much wider than that and that the input of a good advocate can make the difference by choosing the right option from the very beginning of a case.

Against this background, we have described in the first edition of this book various scenarios where a choice had to be made in an attempt to identify what was the best choice for the good advocate.

---

[1] See David J.A. Cairns, Advocacy and the Function of Lawyers in International Arbitration, to be published in Liber Amicorum for Bernardo Cremades.

In this new edition, we propose to focus on a very intricate issue for advocates: parallel proceedings. With the proliferation of complex deals and the corresponding proliferation of a related contracts and agreements drafted in a different manner, there is room for playing with parallel proceedings that can really make a difference on the outcome of the case. Moreover, depending on the national legislations which may come into play in the arbitration, it will be more or less easy to have recourse to parallel proceedings. The first part of this contribution will be devoted to the study of actual situations where the parties have had recourse to parallel proceedings for obviously tactical purposes. This analysis is based on reported case law which came into the public domain. The second part of this contribution will be devoted to the analysis of the conditions which permit recourse to parallel proceedings as well as the possible limits of other tactical use. This chapter is not intended to provide a road map for derailing an arbitration, but rather to identify the fundamental issues underlying the very notion of parallel proceedings.

II. Examples of Parallel Proceedings Initiated for Tactical Purposes

Practice shows many examples of parallel proceedings initiated in order to gain a tactical advantage. For example, a party can start an action before State courts in breach of an arbitration agreement (A), a party may also start an action before an arbitral tribunal in response to the other party's violation of the arbitration agreement (B). Another option is to seize two different arbitral tribunals on the basis of the same agreement (C).

A. Going to Courts in Breach of the Arbitration Clause

A party may seize State courts (in most cases its home courts), either before the initiation of arbitral proceedings or once arbitration has been initiated, in order to either have the arbitration agreement annulled or have a judgment rendered on the merits. This happened in the well-known *West Tankers* case where the ECJ ruled on the compatibility of anti-suit injunctions with EU law.[2] In this case, the Italian company Erg Petroli SpA had chartered a tanker owned by West Tankers Inc. The charter-party was governed by English law, and contained an arbitration agreement providing that disputes would be submitted to arbitration in London. Following a collision in Syracuse between a tanker and a pier owned by Erg Petroli, the latter sought compensation from its insurers up to the limit of its coverage and initiated arbitral proceedings in London against West Tankers for the surplus. The Italian company's insurers, for their part, filed a claim against West Tankers before the court of Syracuse in order to recover the sums they had paid to Erg petroli, under the insurance policy.

Considering that they were not bound by the charter-party, and the arbitration agreement it contained, the insurers submitted that the Italian courts had jurisdiction under Article 5.3 of the Brussels Regulation, which, in relation to tort claims, grants jurisdiction to the courts located where the damage took place.[3] The tactical interest, for the Italian insurers, was to bring proceedings before an Italian court rather than before an arbitral tribunal in London. They thus hoped to argue their case in Italian and under Italian law. In this case, their strategy turned out to be successful. West Tankers tried, in vain, to obtain an anti-suit injunction from English courts, restraining the insurers from pursuing proceedings before Italian courts.

In response to the House of Lords' reference for a preliminary ruling, the ECJ deemed that such anti-suit injunction was not compatible with the Brussels Regulation since each court within the territory of the Union has exclusive jurisdiction to decide whether or not it has jurisdiction to settle a dispute under Article 5.3 of the

---

[2] ECJ, February 10, 2009, case C-185/07, Allianz SpA, formerly Riunione Adriatica di Sicurtà SpA v. West Tankers Inc., in Les Cahiers de l'arbitrage, Gazette du Palais 2009, July 17-18, 2009, p. 51.

[3] (EC) Regulation N° 44/2001 of the Council dated December 22, 2000 regarding jurisdiction, the recognition and enforcement of judgments in civil and commercial matters, OJEC N° L 012, January 16, 2001, p. 1-23.

Regulation.[4] The proceedings initiated in Italy have therefore been pursued and, to the best of our knowledge, are still pending. Another strategy would have consisted in West Tankers initiating arbitration on the merits, and disregarding the Italian proceedings, as, in all likelihood, the arbitration award would have been rendered before a final decision of the Italian Courts and would have been enforced notwithstanding the Italian proceedings.

B. *Starting Proceedings before an Arbitral Tribunal in Response to the Violation of the Arbitration Agreement*

Another alternative is for a party to seize an arbitral tribunal on the merits against a party who had first seized a State court in breach of the arbitration agreement. A primary example is the *Fomento* case, which was filed with the Swiss Federal Tribunal in 2001.[5] Fomento de Construcciones y Contratas S.A., a Spanish company, undertook to provide civil engineering services for the construction of a port in Panama. Although the agreement between it and a Panamanian company contained an ICC arbitration clause, the Spanish company filed an action before the Panamanian courts against the Panamanian

---

[4] Regarding the preliminary question put forward by the House of Lords, see House of Lords, February 21, 2007, *West Tankers Inc. v. RAS Riunione Adriatica di Sicurtà SpA and others*, Revue Critique DIP, 2007, p. 434, note L. Usunier. See also S. Bollée, « *Quelques remarques sur les injonctions anti-suit visant à protéger la compétence arbitrale* (on *The Front Comor* decision of the House of Lords) », Revue de l'Arbitrage 2007, 223.

[5] Swiss federal tribunal (1st Civil law division), May, 14 2001, *Fomento de Construcciones y Contratas S.A v. Colón Container Terminal S.A.*, Decision of the federal Tribunal 127 III 279, ASA Bull, 2001, n° 3, p. 544. See on this decision J.-F. Poudret, Note, Revue de l'arbitrage 2001, p. 835 ; M. Scherer, « When Should an Arbitral Tribunal Sitting in Switzerland Confronted with Parallel Litigation Abroad Stay the Arbitration ? », ASA Bull, 2001, n° 3, p. 451 ; E. Geisinger and L. Lévy, « Lis Alibi Pendens in International Commercial Arbitration, Complex Arbitrations », ICC Bulletin 2003, special issue., p. 53 ; C. Oetiker, « The principles of Lis Pendens in International Arbitration: The Swiss Decision in *Fomento v. Colon* », *Arbitration International*, 2002, Vol. 18, No. 2, p. 137 ; F. de Ly and A. Sheppard, « ILA Final Report on *Lis Pendens* and Arbitration », *International Arbitration* , 2009, Vol. 25, n° 1, p. 3 *et seq.*, special p. 27-28.

company, most likely to delay or paralyze arbitral proceedings it believed to be imminent. The Panamanian company immediately responded by initiating an arbitration with it seat in Switzerland, and the Spanish company asked the arbitral tribunal to stay the proceedings until the Panamanian courts had rendered a decision. The arbitral tribunal refused to do so and rendered its award. Proceedings for setting aside the award were initiated before the Swiss Federal Tribunal, which decided that *Lis Pendens* rules under the Swiss Statutes on private international law (PIL) applied to the arbitral tribunal, and that the latter should have stayed its proceeding given that the Panamanian courts were first seized of the same dispute. The award was thus set aside

This decision was evidently unfavorable to arbitration. Any party anticipating that an arbitration would be initiated against them could commence proceedings before any State court in order to paralyze the arbitration. The Swiss legislators thankfully put an end to this situation by amending Article 186 PIL on October 10, 2006, which now provides that *[the arbitrator] shall rule on its own jurisdiction, notwithstanding an action on the same matter, between the same parties, pending before a State court or another arbitral tribunal, unless serious reasons require the suspension of proceedings.*[6]

In a more recent case, the Swiss Federal Tribunal ruled on a dispute between a French and an Italian company that had entered into a put and call agreement for the shares of a third party company in Italy (company X).[7] The agreement contained an arbitration agreement stating that all disputes relating to the interpretation and/or the execution thereof, whether deriving from the agreement or in connection with it, shall be submitted to arbitration in Switzerland.[8] Several months later, the parties initiated discussions on

---

[6] Swiss federal act on private international law (PILA), December 18, 1987, Art. 186 para. 1 bis, E. Gaillard, NYLJ.

[7] Swiss Federal Tribunal (1st Civil law division), March 6, 2008, 4A_500/2007, ASA Bull, 2009, Vol. 27, n° 1, p. 94.

[8] The arbitration agreement was drafted as follows: « [...] tutte le controversie relative all'interpretazione e/o all'esecuzione del Contratto, o comunque derivanti dal Contratto o in relazione allo stesso, saranno devolute alla competenza esclusiva

the possibility of extending the put and call agreement to warrants issued by company X. The parties had exchanged several letters on the matter and the Italian company claimed that two of these letters reflected the intention of the parties on the repurchase of the warrants and thus constituted an agreement. The Italian company seized the Tribunal of Milan, on the basis of Italian contract law, in order to assert such theory. The French company reacted by immediately submitting the dispute to an arbitral tribunal pursuant to the arbitration agreement contained in the put and call agreement. Before the arbitral tribunal, the French company submitted that the arbitration agreement included all disputes relating to the put and call agreement, including the dispute on the extension of the agreement to the repurchase of the warrants. This is what West Tankers should have done instead of requesting an anti-suit injunction before State courts.

By immediately initiating parallel proceedings before an arbitral tribunal without awaiting the decision of the Italian courts on their own jurisdiction the French company made a key strategic move which was manifestly advantageous for several reasons. First, it brought the case before its natural judge. Second, the provision of Swiss law and the case law of the Swiss Federal Tribunal regarding the scope of arbitration agreement are more liberal than those of Italian law and case law. It was therefore likely that the arbitral tribunal would decide that it had jurisdiction to settle the dispute, whereas arbitral jurisdiction would probably have been denied by Italian courts as the criteria applied by both judges is different.

This is what happened in this particular case. The Arbitral Tribunal decided that it had jurisdiction and rendered an award within a very short time-frame, rejecting the Italian company's claims. A few months later, the Tribunal of Milan held the exact opposite by stating that the arbitration agreement contained in the put and call agreement did not cover the dispute relating to the exchange of letters relating to the repurchase of the warrants, which was under the jurisdiction of the Italian courts. The French party was however in a

---

di un collegio arbitrale nominato, e che deciderà, in conformità al Regolamento d'arbitrato della Camera di Commercio e dell'Industria di Ginevra [...] ».

much more advantageous position before the Italian courts since it was able to rely on the international arbitral award rendered in its favor. The award most likely influenced the final decision at the Tribunal of Milan, which turned out to be entirely in favor of the French party.[9]

C. Seizing Two Arbitral Tribunals on the Basis of a Same Agreement

Litigants' imagination having no limits, a recently published decision of the Swiss Federal Tribunal mentions a case in which a party decided to commence parallel proceedings, not before a State court or on the basis of a different agreement, but on the basis of the same agreement before a different arbitral tribunal[10]. In this case, a professor of pharmaceutical sciences, who discovered a substance likely to have a therapeutic effect on certain forms of cancer, entered into a know-how license agreement with a Swiss pharmaceuticals company (company X). The agreement contained an ICC arbitration clause, with a seat in Geneva. Several years later, the same professor transferred all the rights and obligations resulting from the license agreement to a third company (company Y). A dispute arose between companies X and Y relating to the payment of royalties, and company Y submitted the dispute to an arbitral tribunal.

In a partial award, the arbitral tribunal acknowledged the right of company Y to receive payment of royalties, and the question of quantum was deferred to a subsequent phase of the arbitration. On the basis that the arbitral tribunal's interpretation of the agreement did not reflect its intention at the time it entered into the agreement, company X therefore informed Company Y that it considered that the agreement was void for mistake, and seized a second arbitral

---

[9] Tribunal of Milan, Judgment of February 13, 2008, 8th civil division, case. N° 32406/2006.

[10] Swiss Federal Tribunal, (1st civil law division), 4A_210/2008/ech, October 29, 2008, *X. SA v. Y Limited*, ASA Bull, 2009, Vol. 27, n° 2, p. 309.

tribunal to declare the agreement void. The claim of company X before the second arbitral tribunal was in fact an invitation to review the merits of the award rendered by the first tribunal. The direct consequence of the agreement being declared void, if granted, was that company Y would be deprived of its right to perceive royalties, which was precisely the object of the partial award rendered by the first tribunal.[11] The Federal Tribunal did stress the tactical aspect of the party's decision to commence the second proceeding: *"Speaking of claim is questionable when dealing with a mere declaratory relief, the only aim thereof being, other than deferring the outcome of the pending case regarding the payment, a case in which the Claimant has lost on the principle of liability, at least to give support to the request for partial release of this party's debt arising out of the case".*[12]

The Federal Tribunal consequently dismissed the claim to set aside the partial award, which lead the first arbitral tribunal to refuse to stay the proceedings whilst awaiting the second tribunals' award. It was nevertheless a clever attempt to derail the first arbitration proceedings on the part of company X.

These examples lead to the conclusion that there are various ways of initiating parallel proceedings and that they are sometimes successful. In light of the above, two questions arise: what elements permitted a party to commence a parallel proceeding, and the limits of these procedural tactics.

---

[11] This is what the Federal Tribunal clearly stated in its recitals: "It is surprising to observe that in its arbitration request, the complainant did not make any request for relief apart from the one aiming at obtaining a declaration on the validity of the nullification of the second amendment. Had it done so, it would only have been in a position to partly reject the financial claims put forward by the respondent, a claim that the arbitral tribunal granted, on the principle, in its partial award. This shows, once again, that the two aforementioned questions are inseparable owing to their obvious connexity" ibid, p. 316-317.

[12] *Ibid*, p. 319.

II. Elements Enabling a Party to Have Recourse to Parallel Proceedings and the Limits Thereof

The study of the above cases reveals three different scenarios. Cases of parallel proceedings between an arbitral tribunal and a State court (A), cases of parallel proceedings between two arbitral tribunals ruling on different agreements (B) and cases of parallel proceedings between two arbitral tribunals ruling on the same agreement (C). Each of these cases calls for different analysis.

A. Cases of Parallel Proceedings between Two Arbitral Tribunals Ruling on Different Agreements

This is the standard scenario in parallel proceedings. It leads to the *West Tankers*, *Fomento* and Italian cases. National legislations generally address this situation, albeit in different ways, encouraging or discouraging, as the case may be, the use of state proceedings.[13] Some legislations – the most arbitration friendly – reduce the judge's intervention to a minimum and, consequently, the possibilities of having recourse for tactical purposes to parallel judicial proceedings. Such is the case, for example, of French legislation and, since the *anti-Fomento* law entered into force, Swiss legislation.

In France, the issue is tackled by the so-called negative effect of the principle of competence-competence. Pursuant to Article 1458 of the French Code of Civil Procedure, which also applies to international arbitrations, State courts have to declare that they do not have jurisdiction whenever the dispute has already been submitted to an arbitral tribunal in application of an arbitration agreement. When no arbitral tribunal has been seized, the same Article provides that the State court must also refrain from hearing the dispute, unless the arbitration agreement is manifestly null and

---

[13] For a comparative study of national provisions on the matter, see the International Law Association's report on *Lis* Pendens and arbitration, F. de Ly and A. Sheppard, "ILA Final Report on *Lis Pendens* and Arbitration", *op. cit.*, spéc. pp. 25-30.

void. This calls for a *prima facie* control of the existence and validity of the arbitration agreement.[14] Case law nevertheless extended this *prima* facie control to manifestly non-applicable clauses.[15] It is in practice particularly difficult, if not impossible, for a litigant to seize French courts, for tactical purposes, in order to derail arbitration proceedings.

This is also the case in Switzerland. Aware of possible international repercussions following the *Fomento* decision, which is generally perceived as contrary to the interests of international arbitration, the Swiss legislator amended Article 186 of the PIL Act relating to the jurisdiction of the arbitral tribunal, by adding Article 1 bis thereto, which explicitly provides that: *"[the arbitrator] rules on its own jurisdiction notwithstanding an action on the same matter already pending between the same parties before a State court or another arbitral tribunal, unless serious reasons require the suspension of proceedings".*[16] In addition, Switzerland, like France, applies the negative effect of the principle of competence-competence when the seat of the arbitration is in Switzerland.[17] The procedural strategy which consists in submitting a

---

14 Article 1458 CPC : "When a dispute that has been submitted to an arbitral tribunal by virtue of an arbitration agreement is brought to a State court, the latter must declare that it lacks jurisdiction unless the arbitration agreement is manifestly null and void. In both cases, the court cannot automatically reveal that it lacks jurisdiction". On the negative effect of the principle of competence-competence in French law, see E. Gaillard and J. Savage (eds.), Fouchard Gaillard Goldman on International Commercial Arbitration, Kluwer, 1999, para. 661 et seq.; E. Gaillard, note ad 2nd civil chamber of the Court of cassation, May 10, 1995, Coprodag, Revue de l'arbitrage 1995, 618 ; E. Gaillard, « L'effet négatif de la compétence-compétence », in Etudes de procédure et d'arbitrage en l'honneur de Jean-François Poudret, Université de Lausanne, 1999, pp. 387 et seq.

15 1st chamber of the Court of cassation, February 20, 2007, Revue de l'arbitrage 2007, 775, note F.-X. Train.

16 Swiss federal act on private international law (PILA), December 18, 1987, art. 186 para. 1bis. For reactions of the doctrine against the *Fomento* decision, see above mentioned references, note 6.

17 On the negative effect of the principle of competence-competence when an arbitration seat is located in Switzerland, see E. Gaillard « L'effet négatif de la compétence-compétence », *op. cit.*, p. 393 ; J.-F. Poudret, « Le pouvoir d'examen du juge suisse saisi d'une exception d'arbitrage », ASA Bulletin 2005, 401 ;

dispute to State courts of a third-country, in order to paralyze arbitral proceedings, has no longer any practical effects if the seat of arbitration is in Switzerland.

Conversely, other legislations give broader powers to State courts to intervene during arbitration proceedings and consequently allow parties more opportunities of having recourse to parallel proceedings for tactical purposes. This is the case for example in England where, notwithstanding the existence of an arbitration agreement, parties are allowed to have recourse to State courts in four different situations. First, Section 32 of the Arbitration Act provides under certain conditions parties with the possibility to obtain a preliminary decision from a State court on the arbitrator's jurisdiction.[18] Second, Section 45 of the Arbitration Act authorizes the State court to determine of a preliminary point of law under certain conditions (notably the agreements of all parties concerned or the permission of the arbitral tribunal), provided that this point of law affects the rights of either of the parties to the arbitral proceedings.[19] Finally, Section 72 enables a

---

G. Kaufmann-Kohler and A. Rigozzi, *Arbitrage International. Droit et pratique à la lumière de la LDIP*, Schulthess, 2006, *paras.* 438 *et seq.*

[18] Arbitration Act, Section 32 (1) and (2) : "Determination of preliminary point of jurisdiction (1) The court may, on the application of a party to arbitral proceedings (upon notice to the other parties), determine any question as to the substantive jurisdiction of the tribunal A party may lose the right to object (see section 73). (2) An application under this section shall not be considered unless— (a) it is made with the agreement in writing of all the other parties to the proceedings, or (b) it is made with the permission of the tribunal and the court is satisfied— (i) that the determination of the question is likely to produce substantial savings in costs, (ii) that the application was made without delay, and (iii) that there is good reason why the matter should be decided by the court ".

[19] Arbitration Act, Section 45 (1) and (2) : "Determination of preliminary point of law (1) Unless otherwise agreed by the parties, the court may on the application of a party to arbitral proceedings (upon notice to the other parties) determine any question of law arising in the course of the proceedings which the court is satisfied substantially affects the rights of one or more of the parties. An agreement to dispense with reasons for the tribunal's award shall be considered an agreement to exclude the court's jurisdiction under this section. (2) An application under this section shall not be considered unless— (a) it is made with the agreement of all the other parties to the proceedings, or (b) it is made with the permission of the

person involved in an arbitration, but who takes no part in the proceeding, to seek from the courts a declaration, or an injunction, on the validity of the arbitration agreement, on the scope thereof or on the proper constitution of the arbitral tribunal.[20] Admittedly, English law subjects these recourses to a number of more or less constraining conditions, but it still offers the litigant a wider range of possibilities to initiate parallel proceedings than French or Swiss law.[21]

More fundamentally, Section 9 of the Arbitration Act provides that where a court is seized of a matter which is to referred to arbitration under an arbitration agreement, the court should settle the matter if it considers the arbitration agreement to be *"null and void, inoperative, or incapable of being performed"*. This wording, inspired by the New York Convention and the UNCITRAL model law,[22] echoes

---

tribunal and the court is satisfied—(i) that the determination of the question is likely to produce substantial savings in costs, and (ii) that the application was made without delay".

20 Arbitration Act, Section 72 (1) : "Saving for rights of a person who takes no part in proceedings (1) A person alleged to be a party to arbitral proceedings but who takes no part in the proceedings may question—(a) whether there is a valid arbitration agreement, (b) whether the tribunal is properly constituted, or (c) what matters have been submitted to arbitration in accordance with the arbitration agreement, by proceedings in the court for a declaration or injunction or other appropriate relief".

21 Recourses provided for by Sections 32 and 45 are only open in a limited number of cases, notably when the parties agree to apply them or when the arbitral tribunal is convinced that this solution aims at reducing important costs. Recourse in Section 72 however is not subject to any particular condition. See *Fiona Trust v. Yuri Privalov and Others* [2007] EWCA 20 at [34], taking into account that the judge must be very "cautious" before accepting a recourse based on Section 72.

22 UNCITRAL model law on international commercial arbitration, 1985 (amended in 2006), Art. 8(1): "The tribunal seized of a dispute on a question that is the object of an arbitration agreement will refer the parties to arbitration if one on them requests this, at the latest when it submits its first conclusions on the merits of the dispute, unless such judge establishes that said agreement is null and void, inoperative and not likely to be enforced".

Article 7 of the Swiss PIL[23]. It is however on the basis of that Article that the Swiss courts applied the negative effect of the principle of competence-competence in Switzerland and limited their review to a *prima facie* review of the arbitration agreement in question.[24] It should be noted that, on the basis of a quasi-similar wording, English courts decided, on the contrary, that, a detailed review of the validity and scope of the arbitration agreement was necessary at such a preliminary stage. English case law is unanimous in this regard.[25] In this specific case, judicial tradition, in addition to the law, encourages parties to have recourse to State courts, even at the beginning of the arbitration

The possibilities of having recourse to parallel proceedings between an arbitral tribunal and a State court thus largely depends on the applicable law in the State where the court is seized and on the judicial tradition of its courts. There is no doubt, in this context, that the reform relating to the Brussels Regulation proposed by the European Commission in its Green paper dated April 21, 2009, if adopted, would directly result in an increase of the opportunities to derail arbitration proceedings by initiating parallel proceedings within

---

23 Swiss PILA, December 18, 1987, Art. 7: "Arbitration Agreement If the parties have entered into an arbitration agreement on an arbitration dispute, the Swiss tribunal will decline jurisdiction unless: a. the defendant has taken steps in the proceedings relating to the merits, without reserve; b. the tribunal established that the agreement is null and void, inoperative and is not likely to be enforced; or c. the arbitral tribunal cannot be formed for reasons that are clearly owed to the defendant to the arbitration".

24 Regarding decisions having *prima facie* control of the compromissory clause, see for example Swiss federal tribunal, (1st civil law division), Decision of the federal Tribunal 122 III 139, April 29, 1996, *Fondation M. v. Banque X.*, ASA Bulletin, 1996, 527 ; Swiss Federal Tribunal, (1st civil law division), 4P.114/2004, March 29, 2004, ASA Bulletin, 2005, 145.

25 See, for example, Sunlife Assurance Co of Canada v. CX Reinsurance Co Ltd [2004] Lloyd's Rep. I.R. 58 ; Elektrim v. Vivendi Universal [2007] EWHC 11, [123]-[132] ; Downing v. Al Tameer [2002] EWCA Civ 721; Janos Paczy v. Haendler & Natermann GmbH [1981] 1 Lloyd's Rep. 302, CA.

the European Union.[26] By allowing judgments relating to arbitration to be automatically recognized within the European Union,[27] and by giving priority to the judge of the seat of the arbitration to rule on the validity of the arbitration agreement by a declaratory judgment,[28] the proposed reform will undoubtedly encourage a "race to the courts" between the parties.[29]

All that a party seeking to derail arbitral proceedings will have to do is to seek from a State court a decision that will render an arbitration agreement invalid, preferably in a State where legislation is not favorable to arbitration, in order for this decision to be automatically recognized in all EU member States, thus preventing the enforcement (exequatur) of a possible arbitral award within these States. To avoid this situation, the party wishing to have recourse to arbitration will be forced to obtain from the courts of the seat of the arbitration, as a preventive measure, a decision recognizing the validity of the arbitration agreement. In both cases, proceedings will

---

[26] Green paper on the amendment of (EC) Regulation n° 44/2001 of the Council relating to jurisdiction, the recognition and enforcement of judgments in civil and commercial matters, April 21, 2009, COM(2009) 175 final. On this paper and on the consequences it will have on the future of arbitration within the European Union, see notably P. Pinsolle, "The Proposed Reform of Regulation 44/2001: A Poison Pill for Arbitration in the European Union?", Int A.L.R, 2009, Issue 4, p. 62 ; A. Mourre, « A propos de la portée de l'exclusion de l'arbitrage dans le règlement n° 44/2001, notamment après l'arrêt West Tankers de la CJCE », *in Les Cahiers de l'arbitrage*, GP July 17-18, 2009, p. 20-28, as well as the numerous contributions published at: http://ec.europa.eu/justice_home/news/consulting_public/news_consulting_0002_en.htm.

[27] Green paper p. 9: "[...] a (partial) deletion of the exclusion of arbitration from the scope of the Regulation could improve the interface between arbitration and judicial proceedings. As a consequence of this deletion, judicial proceedings in support of arbitration could come within the scope of the Regulation".

[28] Green paper, p. 9 : "More generally speaking, we could watch over the coordination between proceedings concerning the validity of an arbitration agreement brought before a court or before an arbitral tribunal. We could, for example, give priority to the member State courts where the arbitration is taking place, in order to rule on the existence, validity and scope of an arbitration agreement".

[29] As per Lord Hoffmann in GAR.

hence take place before a State court, and not before arbitrators, contrary to the parties' agreement. Moreover, in the absence of choice of seat by the parties, the Green paper recommends that the seat be fixed in the country whose courts would have jurisdiction over the dispute in the absence of an arbitration agreement.[30] In practice, given the options of forum offered by the Regulation (respondent's place of residence and, if applicable, place of execution of the agreement, delivery of the object, damage, etc), one can imagine the number of possibilities that the Commission's reform will make available to the litigants desiring to escape or delay arbitration. Notwithstanding the intention behind the European proposal, which was most certainly laudable, this proposal is troublesome to say the least from the point of view of the efficiency of proceedings.

B. Cases of parallel proceedings between two arbitral tribunals ruling on different agreements

The existence of parallel proceedings before two arbitral tribunals ruling on different agreements that belong to the same underlying economic transaction is almost as frequent as parallel proceedings before a State court. This does not involve a conflict between the jurisdiction of a State court and that of an arbitral tribunal, but one between the *ratione materiae* jurisdiction of two arbitral tribunals.

The arbitrators are very cautious in this regard as the scope of their jurisdiction is fully reviewed by State courts with the risk to see their award set aside.[31]

---

[30] Green paper, p. 9, note 14: "If such approach were elected, uniform criteria should enable the seat of arbitration to be chosen. The general study suggests referring to the parties' agreement or to the arbitral tribunal's decision. If a seat cannot be chosen pursuant to this, it is recommended to turn to the courts of a member State that ruled on the dispute by virtue of the Regulation in the absence of an arbitration agreement".

[31] This is the case, for example, in France (Art. 1502 of the Code of civil procedure, that makes provision for the annulment of the award when the arbitrator has ruled *"without an arbitration agreement or based on an agreement that was null*

Several examples exist. In a case that was recently referred to the Paris Court of Appeal, two Cuban companies had initiated arbitral proceedings against a Mexican bank on the basis of a loan agreement and a farm-out agreement, both providing for an ICC arbitration, without mentioning the seat of the arbitration.[32] The parties had agreed on Paris as the seat of the arbitration. The Mexican bank soon hereafter expressed its intention to refer additional disputes to the arbitral tribunal, relating to a second loan agreement, which was linked to the first, and which also contained an ICC arbitration clause, but with a seat in Madrid this time. The Cuban companies objected to the arbitral tribunal's jurisdiction to decide on the second loan agreement and referred the matter to a second arbitral tribunal. However, given that the claims under the loan agreements were closely related and that, save for the seat, the arbitration clauses were similar, the first tribunal declared that it had jurisdiction to rule on all claims. This is the reason why the Paris Court of Appeal decided to partially set aside the award on the grounds that, on the one hand, no variation of the seat of the arbitration chosen by the parties in the second loan agreement could be implied from the parties' agreement to arbitrate in Paris the disputes relating to the first loan agreements, and, on the other hand, that the fact that the claims under the agreements were closely related had no influence over the parties' desire to organize separate proceedings in Paris and Madrid.

---

or had expired" or *"without complying to the mission it had been assigned"*), in the United Kingdom (Section 67 of the Arbitration Act, that provides for recourse due to the arbitral tribunal's lack of jurisdiction to rule on the merits, this recourse including the validity and the scope of the compromissory clause), in Germany and the UNCITRAL model law (§ 1509 para. 2 ch. 1 let. c ZPO and Art. 34 para. 2 let. A ch. 3 of the model law, providing for the annulment of the award if the tribunal ruled on a dispute that is not mentioned in the compromissory clause or that surpasses the compromissory clause) or in Switzerland (Art. 190(2) (d) of the PILA, that provides that the award can be annulled when an arbitral tribunal wrongfully declared that it had jurisdiction or when lacking jurisdiction).

32 Paris Court of Appeal, 1st Chamber, November 16, 2006, Société Empresa de Telecomunicaciones de Cuba SA v. SA Telefonica Antillana and SNC Banco Nacional de Commercia Exterior, Revue de l'arbitrage 2008, 109, note M. de Boisséson.

Consequently, if recourse to parallel proceedings based on different agreements that are part of a same transaction is relatively common, the success of such strategies will essentially depend on the drafting of the arbitration agreement contained in the agreements in question. In the presence of different arbitration clauses, even within a contractual group, it will be very difficult for a party to impose the jurisdiction of a single tribunal, at least as long as the other party objects to it. The existence of a single economic transaction can, however, lead one of the two tribunals to stay the proceedings (see paragraphed I.C above).

C. The case of two tribunals ruling on the basis of the same agreement

The case of two arbitral tribunals ruling on the basis of the same agreement is more delicate. It raises the problem of the allocation of jurisdiction between two tribunals that are equally competent to rule on questions referred to them. By definition, these questions are included within the scope of the clause. In practice, we believe that the question will not be resolved by delimitating the jurisdiction *ratione materiae* of each tribunal, but by deciding on the admissibility of the claims referred to a second tribunal.

It has been argued that the tribunal second seized would lack jurisdiction to settle the dispute since the arbitration agreement would no longer have any effects as a result of the first tribunal being seized.[33] This reasoning is appealing, but seems nevertheless slightly artificial. In reality, it is an application by analogy of a reasoning applicable to a specific submission to arbitration (*compromis)*, that is an arbitration agreement which is entered into after the dispute has arisen, for the purpose of resolving this specific dispute. However, contrary to a submission agreement, an arbitration clause remains effective when an arbitral tribunal is seized. It is still possible to refer

[33] P. Mayer, «Litispendance, connexité et chose jugée dans l'arbitrage international », *in Liber Amicorum Claude Raymond, Autour de l'arbitrage*, Bredin, Lalive, Poudret, Terré (editions), Litec, 2004, p. 185 *et seq.*

an additional question and, in theory, the same question to a second arbitral tribunal. The second tribunal seized has supposedly as much jurisdiction to deal with these issues, as the first tribunal as its powers emanate from the same clause. The arbitration clause, contrary to a *compromis*, remains valid and effective even if the dispute was referred to an arbitral tribunal.

Other authors suggested the application, by analogy, of international *lis pendens* rules, as fundamental procedural rules recognized by nearly all legal systems as a mean of protection against dilatory tactics and increase in the number of proceedings.[34] However, such factors do not seem to justify the obligation for a second seized arbitral tribunal to stay its proceedings whilst awaiting the award of the first. Ever since the anti-Fomento law entered into force, Swiss law expressly provides for the contrary, since Article 186 para. 1 bis PIL states that when a claim, with the same object and between the same parties is brought before two arbitral tribunals, the second does not have to stay the proceedings, unless "serious reasons" require it to. Case law of the Federal Tribunal will specify what these serious reasons are, but the principle is that the decision to stay proceedings remains a discretionary decision for the arbitrator. A stay would appear to be an appropriate measure whenever one of the parties attempts to bring the same claim before a second arbitral tribunal, for tactical reasons.[35]

---

[34] See G. Born, *International Commercial Arbitration*, Vol. 2, Kluwer Law International, 2009, p. 2048-2049.

[35] See on this subject the recommendations of the International Law Association (ILA) on Lis Pendens, Res Judicata and arbitration: "[…] (5) Where the Parallel Proceedings have been commenced before the Current Arbitration and are pending before another arbitral tribunal, the arbitral tribunal should decline jurisdiction or stay the Current Arbitration, in whole or in part, and on such conditions as it sees fit, for such duration as it sees fit (such as until a relevant determination in the Parallel Proceedings), provided that it is not precluded from doing so under the applicable law and provided that it appears that: (1) the arbitral tribunal in the Parallel Proceedings has jurisdiction to resolve the issues in the Current Arbitration and (2) there will be no material prejudice to the party opposing the request because of (i) an inadequacy of relief available in the Parallel Proceedings; (ii) a lack of due process in the Parallel Proceedings; (iii) a risk of

The Swiss Federal Tribunal's above mentioned decision is a perfect example of this situation, insofar as the question that was referred to the second tribunal was only the other side of the coin of the question that was referred to the first. Once the award is rendered by the first arbitral tribunal, the question shall therefore be resolved in terms of admissibility of claims brought to the second tribunal, in account of *res judicata*.[36] In our opinion, the second tribunal should, through a definitive award, decide that the claims that have already been referred to a first tribunal and those that are necessarily included in the scope of the issues already referred to the first tribunal are inadmissible.

annulment or non-recognition or non-enforcement of an award that has been or may be rendered in the Parallel Proceedings ; or (iv) some other compelling reason […]", F. de Ly and A. Sheppard, « ILA Recommendations on Lis Pendens and Res Judicata and arbitration », Arbitration International, 2009, Vol. 25, n° 1, p. 83 et seq., spec. p. 84.

[36] On *Res Judicata* in international arbitration, see notably D. Hascher, « L'autorité de la chose jugée des sentences arbitrales », *Trav. Com. fr. dr. int. privé*, 2000-2002, Paris, Pedone, 2004 ; B. Hanotiau, "The Res Judicata Effect of Arbitral Awards", CCI Bull. 2003, spec. suppl., p. 43. as well as P. Mayer, *op.cit.*

Part IV.

WRITTEN ADVOCACY

Chapter 8

EFFECTIVE WRITTEN ADVOCACY

Guillermo Aguilar Alvarez

I keep six honest serving men. (They taught me all I know); Their names are What and Why and When and How and Where and Who
Rudyard Kipling

There is only one opportunity to make a first impression. For advocates, this opportunity comes in the form of a written submission. While naturally there is a chance to address the court orally, it comes much later, and by that time the parties' written submissions will have already set the stage of the dispute. The court's approach to the hearing and to adjudication will be influenced by preliminary views formed in reviewing the memorials of the parties, the documentary and testimonial evidence, and the legal authorities tendered in support for their respective positions. Whether in the context of domestic litigation or international arbitration, the orientation, strength and permanence of these views will be determined by the focus, clarity and effectiveness of the advocate's written argument.

Persuasion in the context of international arbitration presents additional challenges.[1] Arbitrators and counsel from different nationalities, cultural backgrounds and legal instruction converge in a single proceeding. A diversity of languages is frequently involved.

---

1 "Many of today's largest and most important legal disputes have changed almost unrecognizably from traditional court litigation: they are resolved by private arbitral tribunals, apparently apply multiple legal systems to achieve their final award and, at times, involve a stunning number of languages and cultures." (Sourgens, "Comparative Law as Rhetoric: an Analysis of the Use of Comparative Law in International Arbitration", 8 Pepperdine Dispute Resolution Law Journal 2007).

Competing normative frameworks may govern the merits of the dispute and the conduct of the proceedings. It is not uncommon in international arbitration for counsel to face the challenge of arguing at venues, in languages and under legal norms that are not familiar to all of the arbitrators. Finally, upon completion of the arbitral proceedings, an international legal regime looms over the recognition and enforcement of the award.

This chapter briefly explores how advocates meet the challenge of written persuasion in international arbitration. Part I addresses the preparatory stages of a written submission. Part II discusses the drafting process.

I. Preparation

There is a perception that British and American influence has been the engine of an arbitration proceeding that places great emphasis on oral advocacy. This perception overstates reality because it underestimates the importance of the written record.[2] International arbitration comprises several stages of written submissions. Typically the sequence goes something like this: claimant will file statement of claim, respondent submits its statement of defense, claimant presents a reply and respondent concludes with a rejoinder. In addition, the parties may request the right to file simultaneous or successive post-hearing briefs. Having said this, factors that might affect the number and cadence of written submissions include the participation of a State or a State enterprise, the type and complexity of the case, the

---

2 Article 31 of the ICSID Rules of Procedure for Arbitration Proceedings provide for two rounds of written submissions. The UNCITRAL Arbitration Rules (article 22), the AAA International Arbitration Rules (article 17.1) and the LCIA Arbitration Rules (article 15) provide for one round, although it is possible for the arbitrators to determine if the parties shall file a second round of memorials (see Tawil, "Advocacy in International Commercial Arbitration: Argentina", in *The Art of Advocacy in International Arbitration*, Doak Bishop Ed., Juris, Huntington, 2004, p. 385). The ICC Rules of Arbitration provide for a Request for Arbitration and an Answer (articles 4 and 5) but then grant the arbitrators discretion to determine the procedural timetable in consultation with the parties (article 18.4).

nature of jurisdictional objections, applications for interim measures of protection or bifurcation of the proceedings,[3] and the existence of counterclaims or cross-claims.

In any event, long before counsel address the tribunal orally at the hearing, written submissions provide an opportunity to present, improve, and rebut factual and legal arguments. Fact and expert witnesses are also generally required to file written testimony that will replace their direct examination at the hearing. Finally, arbitrators have little tolerance for surprise documents or testimony at the hearing – all documentary and testimonial evidence that a party intends to rely on must at the latest be filed with the last pre-hearing written memorial,[4] and a rule requiring the parties to exchange demonstrative exhibits before the hearing may also be enforced. As a result, ". . . arbitral counsel will have little chance to dazzle [the] audience at the merits hearing . . . Perry Mason-styled advocacy simply fails to convince in international arbitration due to a process strongly favoring balanced written advocacy."[5] While the oral hearing is designed for the parties to test the accuracy and strength of each other's evidence and arguments, the risk of exposure of inconsistencies and weaknesses can largely be avoided by careful preparation and drafting of the written submissions.

Paradoxically, the bulk of time required to prepare a written submission is not spent writing. Rather, an advocate must set aside a considerable amount of time to investigate the facts of the case, research the relevant legal principles, and find a place to stand – a place where the facts and the law converge to maximize the likelihood of success.

A. The Facts

Good advocates know their case cold. But, perhaps more importantly, successful advocates know the other party's case better.

---

[3] For instance jurisdiction and the merits, or liability and *quantum*.

[4] Exceptions may be made for justifiable cause, with the leave of the tribunal.

[5] Sourgens, *cit*, p. 5.

Getting to this point requires mastering the underlying contract and its genesis, and working with the client in the meticulous investigation of the facts.

In commercial arbitration counsel's starting point is usually the disputed contract. The relevant agreement or agreements and their negotiating history will be carefully reviewed to provide an initial understanding of the parties' bargain and to put preliminary questions to the client as to the ensuing dispute. Comprehension of the deal will facilitate identification of the relevant facts and development of a strategy – facts fall into place more naturally and persuasively when they tell the story of the parties' shared expectations at the time of contracting.[6] Moreover, the approach towards contract interpretation ordinarily applied in international commercial arbitration often focuses on the intentions of the parties, since the transactions with which it is concerned are between individuals and commercial entities from different linguistic and cultural systems, between whom the possibilities of lack of congruence in the use of terms is comparatively high. Even between sophisticated parties served by

---

[6] In investment arbitration under bilateral investment treaties, the investor and the host State do not typically "contract" with each other – the treaty is entered into by the host State and the State of the investor, and the investigation tends to focus not on "shared" expectations but rather on the expectations of the investor at the time of making the investment [*See, Plama Consortium Limited v. Bulgaria*, ICSID Case No. ARB/03/24, Award of August 27, 2008; *Técnicas Medioambientales Tecmed S.A. v. Mexico*, ICSID Case No. ARB(AF)/00/2, Award of May 29, 2003; *Enron Corp. v. Argentina*, ICSID Case No. ARB/01/03, Award of May 22, 2007; *LG&E Enercy Corp., LG&E Capital Corp., LG&E International, Inv. v. Argentine Republic*, ICSID Case No. ARB/02/1, Award of October 3, 2006; *CMS Gas Transmission Company v. Argentine Republic*, ICSID Case No. ARB/01/8, Award of May 12, 2005; *Occidental Exploration and Production Company (OEPC) v. Ecuador*, UNCITRAL case UN3467, Award of July 1, 2004); *Rumeli Telekom A.S. v. Kazakhstan*, ICSID Case No. ARB/05/16, Award of July 29, 2008; *Biwater Gauff Ltd. v. Tanzania*, ICSID Case No. ARB/05/22, Award of July 24, 2008; *PSEG Global Inc. v. Turkey*, ICSID Case No. ARB/02/5, Award of January 19, 2007); *Saluka Investments BV v. Czech Republic*, UNCITRAL, Award of March 17, 2006; *MTD v. Chile*, ICSID Case No. ARB/01/7, Award of May 25, 2004].

competent counsel it would not be at all surprising that key terms might be misunderstood, or have different acceptances on each side.[7]

For many reasons, it is important to develop a good working relationship with the client's general counsel. Close cooperation is key to a common understanding of the estimated duration, cost and possible outcome of the arbitration. Additionally, the general counsel will gauge adaptation of the advocate's strategy to the client's goals and, where appropriate, seek business guidance from senior management. The client's legal department also provides an organized central point of access to the relevant cast of characters and to documentary evidence.[8] The general counsel will identify the location of documents, employees who may have left the company, employees or documents not under the control of the client, or individuals who may be cooperative or harmful. In sum, the client's legal officer is the advocate's point of entry to witnesses and documents, the necessary inputs of the factual investigation.

Counsel will gather available documents in the client's from the designated locations. Counsel will also interview personnel with first hand knowledge of the underlying project and the dispute. These interviews will yield not only a better understanding of events, they also lead to the location of additional relevant documents, to the identification of possible fact witnesses and to early determination as to the need for expert evidence.

---

[7] Under some legal systems the court may review the negotiating history to determine which party is responsible for inserting the disputed contractual provision. Under the *contra proferentem* rule of interpretation, an ambiguous term will then be construed against the interests of the party that imposed its inclusion in the contract. This rule applies only where the ambiguous clause was included at the unilateral insistence of one party. However, even counsel who has determined that it is in the client's best interest to argue strict application of the contract should review the negotiating history and be mindful of a possible *contra proferentem* defense.

[8] Some multinational companies keep project-specific databases with remote access capabilities, or that are easily transferable. This considerably facilitates the investigation of the facts, and it saves time and money in the preparation of electronic files for the Tribunal.

Counsel will organize the facts, frequently in the form of a timeline supported by documents and notes from interviews. Analysis of the facts and supporting evidence in chronological order provides insight into motivations and permits spotting of evidentiary gaps. This is typically the first of many readings, one that will provide the big picture. Subsequent visits to the counsel's record will be more focused, and they will produce a preliminary sense of strengths and weaknesses. This preliminary assessment may subsequently vary, as the gaps in available evidence are filled.

B. The Law

It is beyond the scope of this chapter to explore the much debated issue of the proper substantive or procedural rules in international arbitration. Nonetheless, a brief assessment of the normative framework in international arbitration is a useful reminder of the diversity in which the international arbitration bar operates.

National laws,[9] international conventions,[10] authoritative international instruments[11] and commentators[12] recognize the right of

---

[9] Argentina (article 14 of the Civil Code); Austria (*see* Melis, "National Report Austria", Sanders and van den Berg, eds., *ICCA International Handbook on Commercial Arbitration* (Kluwer, The Hague), vol. I; Denmark (section 12 of the Arbitration Act of 1972); England (*see* Steyn and Veeder, "National Report England", *ICCA International Handbook on Commercial Arbitration*, vol. II); Finland (article 31(2) of the Arbitration Act of 1992); France (article 1496 of the New Code of the Civil Procedure); Mexico (article 1445 of the Code of Commerce); the Netherlands (article 1054 of the Code of Civil Procedure) and Switzerland (article 187 of the Swiss Private International Law Act).

[10] Article VII of the 1961 Geneva Convention and Art. 42 of the 1965 Washington Convention (ICSID).

[11] Article 28(1) of the UNICTRAL Model Law.

[12] *See,* for instance, , Battifol, "L'affirmation de la loi d'autonomie dans la jurisprudence francaise", *Festschrift fur Hans Lewald* (Basel 1953); Goldman, "La volonté des parties et le role de l'arbitre dans l'arbitrage international", Revue de l'arbitrage (1981) p. 469; Ionasco and Nestor, " The Limits of Party Autonomy – I", Schmitthoff, ed., *The Sources of the Law of International Trade* (London) 1964; Klein, "Autonomie de la Volonté et arbitrage", Revue Critique de Droit International

the parties to designate the substantive rules that will govern in case of dispute. In fact, parties make that choice in an overwhelming majority of cases. According to ICC statistical information for 2008, the parties selected the proper law in 86.8% of the relevant contracts. In 84% of cases, the choice was a national law.[13] However, parties also specified international rules in 3% of their contracts: *e.g.*, the U.N. Convention on Contracts for the International Sale of Goods, the UNIDROIT Principles of International Commercial Contracts, the Law of the Organization for the Harmonization of Business Law in Africa, EC law, international law or universally recognized principles of law. Consider, however, the geographic origin of the parties (120 countries), the arbitrators (74 countries) and the arbitral venues (93 cities in 50 countries),[14] and realize how rare it is to find a case in which counsel on both sides and the three arbitrators are all trained in the law selected by the parties, or in the law of the place of arbitration. By design, advocates in international arbitration face the challenge of persuasion using tools that are frequently foreign to them, and to a majority of the arbitrators.

Advocates are drawn to legal principles quite early, as they gather the facts. However, this process is quite dynamic. Legal research intensifies and expands as relevant facts are organized and analyzed, and as the opposite side presents rebuttal factual and legal arguments. While the starting point is typically the contract, if a clear solution does not readily emerge from the ordinary meaning of the agreement, apposite rules will be researched in the applicable statutes, in the decisions of the courts, in the works of legal scholars, or in other relevant sources mandated by the stipulated arbitration rules. For instance, article 17(2) of the ICC Rules of Arbitration directs the arbitrators to ". . . take account of the provisions of the contract and the relevant trade usages." Interestingly, while article 17(1) of the

---

Privé (1958) p. 255; Yntema, "Autonomy in Choice of Law", American Journal of Comparative Law (1953), p. 341.

[13] ICC International Court of Arbitration Bulletin, "Statistical Report", volume 20 No. 1, 2009, p. 12.

[14] All for 2008 (*cit.*, pp. 6, 10 and 11).

ICC Rules is a testament to the importance of the parties' choice of law, article 17(2) provides arbitrators with some common ground: the contract and relevant trade usages. Journals and commentators report on arbitral awards where, the choice of the parties notwithstanding, arbitrators applied other rules on grounds that the law selected by the parties was insufficient to solve the dispute. There has been controversy over the appropriateness of this *demarche*.[15] This chapter does not dwell on this debate. Rather, it highlights the importance of matching the selection of an arbitrator to the nucleus of the advocate's legal arguments. If counsel's legal case hinges on the interpretation of a contractual provision, the nationality of the arbitrator is not a compelling factor that restricts the advocate's choice. Conversely, if the matter turns on the interpretation and application of domestic law, counsel may be well-advised to consider an arbitrator that is familiar with that law.

Finally, advocates must decide how best to convey the law to the tribunal. In general, counsel deal with the applicable law as a matter of evidence. Written expert witness statements are submitted and the legal experts are cross-examined at the hearing, such that the members of the tribunal that are not conversant with the applicable law may contrast this evidence with the views of their colleague

---

[15] In *SPP v. Arab Republic of Egypt* (ICSID award of 20 May 1992), the arbitrators resolved the question of calculation of interest by reference to international law, on grounds that the law selected by the parties (Egyptian law) was silent on this point. *See* also ICC award 7792 (1995 *Journal de Droit International* 993), were the arbitrators circumnavigate the contractual choice of Argentinean law to interpret a provision of the contract in the light of Texas precedents. For a critical view, *see* Mustill, "The New *Lex Mercatoria: The First Twenty Five Years*", Liber Amicorum for Lord Wilberforce (Oxford 1987), p. 104 ([t]he arbitrator is mandated to decide the dispute in accordance with the contract; and the contract includes an agreement to abide by the denominated law. An arbitrator who decides according to some other law, whether anational or otherwise, presumes to rewrite the bargain. He has no right to do this. However good his motives, he does a disservice to the parties and to the institution of international arbitration".) For a different view, *see* Gaillard, "Thirty Years of *Lex Mercatoria*: Towards the Selective Application of Transnational Rules, ICSID Review – Foreign Investment Law Journal (1995).

arbitrator who is trained in the relevant law. Alternatively, other tribunals may take a more direct approach and require counsel to present the law directly, without the support of legal experts. Either way, counsel not trained in the proper law of the contract will be assisted by local counsel.

C. Cracking the Code

The advocate's central contribution lies in finding the place where the facts and the law intersect to yield the outcome sought by the client in the arbitration. Law and facts are critical inputs, but they are not the only source for the theory of the case. It is equally important that the advocate understand the client's business, and that the theory of the case leads to an award that achieves the desired business objectives. For instance, law and fact may support a finding of termination of contract. However, if the client's business objective is to preserve the contract as a means to gain leverage, counsel must find a different place to stand.

Like judges, arbitrators are also sensible to the equities of the case. A good advocate will develop a case plan that seeks to compel victory not just as a matter of law, but also as a matter of fairness. Bishop writes:

> Inherent in the facts are the "equities" of the case – the human sense of "fairness" or "unfairness" arising from the acts of the parties in their dealings, the "wrongs" that were committed by one party against another, and the injury that was suffered by one party as a result. These are the engines that drive the case. The saying goes that the law follows the equities. This means that the law may often be molded or interpreted to do justice as the equities dictate. The advocate should focus on the equities to persuade the arbitrators.[16]

---

[16] Bishop, "Toward a Harmonized Approach to Advocacy in International Arbitration", in *The Art of Advocacy in International Arbitration*, Doak Bishop Ed., Juris, Huntington, 2004, p. 454.

Naturally, the theory visualized by the advocate may falter with the development of the facts or the law as the case progresses. A skilled advocate will recognize this and will make adjustments to strategic decisions by asking new questions and developing new areas of investigation.[17] It is also inevitable that one of the two parties to the arbitration will have the stronger connection between facts, law and equities. If so, the case plan should also be viewed as a useful tool in the management and adjustment of client expectations. For instance, an advocate with a losing hand on liability may still have a winning hand on quantum. Greed often turns the moral compass of the arbitrators against the party with the stronger case on liability.

As a final point, the case plan is also a valuable scheduling and strategic tool. It will provide the advocate and the client with a roadmap setting out:

- staffing details;
- dates for completion of a first draft of the written submission;
- dates for the client to provide comments on the first draft;
- an indication of areas for fact or expert testimony, and a calendar for witness and expert witness interviews;
- dates for completion of written witness and expert witness statements;
- an inventory of available and required documentary evidence, productions lists and privilege logs;
- target dates for a possible mock arbitration to simulate the hearing and the outcome of the arbitration;[18] and
- a more accurate cost estimate to completion of the arbitration.

---

[17] Bishop, *cit*, p. 464.

[18] See Bishop, *cit*, p. 467 (". . . parties have conducted mock arbitrations in some major international arbitrations in recent years in order to refine both the issues to be argued and the presentation of the case. These parties have selected mock arbitrators, subject to strict obligations of confidentiality, whose backgrounds are similar to the real arbitrators in the case. For example, a party will select mock arbitrators of the same nationality as each real arbitrator and from the same profession – professor, barrister, practicing international lawyer, etc.).

II. Drafting

The theory of the case developed by the advocate must be effectively communicated to the arbitrators if it is going to translate into a favorable decision. A strident prose, hyperbole, poor organization, and bad translation may all be fatal to even the most brilliant theory. On the other hand, an effective written submission may greatly enhance the persuasiveness of an otherwise weaker case.

First, advocates must be mindful of their audience. Their dispute will be adjudicated by arbitrators, not judges or a jury. This carries immediate style implications. While an aggressive style of advocacy may be the norm in domestic litigation, it does not go over well in international arbitration. In fact, clients who expect hostile advocacy must be educated on the advantages of courteous restraint in international adjudication:

> Within the United States, many . . . clients have come to expect a rather aggressive style of advocacy. This is what they are accustomed to. This is what they've come to expect. And there are times they don't feel they're being well served unless they see you taking that sort of aggressive stance. And yet, within the context of an international arbitration under other choices of law and in other *fora*, it may be the worst possible thing you can do."[19]

Second, it is very helpful to sketch out the legal and factual theory of the case in the form of an outline that brings out the themes developed by the advocate, and leads the arbitrators through the issues of fact and law to the desired outcome. Use of full sentences to identify the headings and sub-headings in the outline will later assist counsel in the drafting process, and the arbitrators in navigating the

---

[19] Opinion expressed by Bill Cason in the context of the *King & Spalding-Sponsored Roundtable*, "Complex Issues in International Arbitration: Inside and Outside Counsel Debate Best Practices for Resolving Important Transnational Disputes" held on November 4, 2002. At the time, Bill Cason was listed as Vice-President and Assistant General Counsel of Oceana International Ltd.

memorial.[20] Arbitrators also appreciate an accurate table of contents, and a table of authorities that separately identifies domestic court decisions, arbitral awards, statutes, international legal materials (*e.g.*, international treaties or the resolutions of international organizations) and scholarly writing. Arbitral tribunals frequently also require that exhibits be bound separately and numbered sequentially throughout the proceedings, and that they be preceded by an index that identifies each document, its exhibit number and the volume where it is located. While this requirement may sound trivial, it is key to all future reference to the record, and to the drafting of the award by the arbitrators.

Third, style is, well, a question of style. Personal habits or preferences will yield different approaches and there is nothing wrong with this. However, personal styles should not interfere with the persuasive quality of a written submission. Here are some recommendations on effective written briefing by Justice Scalia of the U.S. Supreme Court and Bryan Garner:

(a) master language;[21]

(b) be clear;[22]

(c) be brief;[23]

---

20 "Without subheadings, the reader would face a vexatious reading experience." (Vaughan, "Persuasion Is An Art . . . But It Is Also An Invaluable Tool In Advocacy", 61 *Baylor Law Review* 635). See also Scalia and Garner, *Making Your Case: The Art of Persuading Judges*, Thomson/West, 2008, p. 59 ("The primary purpose of written submissions in legal proceedings is to assist the court in the adjudication of a dispute.")

21 Scalia and Garner, *cit*, p. 61 ("Lawyers possess only one tool to convey their thoughts: language. They must acquire and hone the finest, most effective version of that tool available. They must love words and use them exactly.")

22 *Id*, p. 107 ("In brief-writing, one feature of a good style trumps all others. Literary elegance, erudition, sophistication or expression – these and all other qualities must be sacrificed if they detract from clarity".)

23 *Id.*, p. 98 ("Judges often associate the brevity of the brief with the quality of the lawyer. Many judges . . . say that good lawyers often come in far below the page limits – and that bad lawyers almost never do.")

(c) make it interesting;[24]

(d) don't misstate the facts;[25]

(e) don't misstate the law;[26]

(f) don't stray from your legal argument;[27]

(g) keep it simple;[28]

(h) use examples;[29] and

(i) revise, revise, revise.[30]

---

[24] *Id.*, p. 112 ("Three simple ways to add interest to your writing are to enliven your word choices, to mix up your sentence structure, and to vary your sentence lengths. With words, ask yourself whether there is a more colorful way to put it. With sentences, guard against falling into a monotonous subject – verb – object rut – especially when it's the same subject sentence after sentence. And remember that an occasional arrestingly short sentence can deliver real punch.")

[25] *Id.*, pp. 93 ("Omitting a fact crucial to your case is a critical mistake. An even worse one is misstating a fact. Nothing is easier for the other side to point out, and nothing can so significantly damage your credibility.") and 95 ("A fair statement of the facts includes relevant facts that are adverse to your case. They will come out anyway and if you omit them you simply give opposing counsel an opportunity to show the court that you're untrustworthy.")

[26] *Id.*, p. 123. ("The impression you want to make on the court – that you're knowledgeable and even expert – will be compromised by any misdescription that opposing counsel brings to the court's attention. If a case is only close but not completely on point, say so. Then explain why the difference is insubstantial and should not affect the outcome.")

[27] *Id.*, p. 98 (". . . keep your eye on the ball. Write down at the outset, and keep before you throughout your drafting of the Argument, the syllogism that wins your case. Each aspect of the argument must be consistent with this and should be no more sweeping than necessary to support it. Nothing should be irrelevant to it.")

[28] *Id.*, p. 113 ("Banish jargon, hackneyed expressions, and needless Latin".)

[29] *Id.*, p. 111 ("Legal briefs are necessarily filled with abstract concepts that are difficult to explain. Nothing clarifies their meaning as well as examples.") In international arbitration, recourse to comparative law may also be a valuable device to explain the contours of legal concepts that may be foreign to one or more of the arbitrators (for use of comparative law as an instrument of persuasion *see* Sourgens, *cit.*)

[30] *Id.*, p. 80-81.

Keeping to these simple guidelines will produce a written submission more likely to assist the arbitrators in the efficient adjudication of the dispute, and it will also strengthen the credibility of counsel.

Chapter 9

PLEADINGS, MEMORIALS AND POST-HEARING BRIEFS

Mark Friedman*

I. Introduction

There is nothing like a gripping courtroom drama. As the advocate summarizes the facts in a way that makes the just result obvious regardless of what the law says, or the cross-examiner springs the trap on an unsuspecting witness, we are moved, stirred, transfixed. Dynamic, clever and filled with tension, we are captivated by courtroom confrontations in plays and films ranging from *To Kill a Mockingbird* to *Inherit the Wind*, from *The Verdict* to *The Caine Mutiny*, from *The Merchant of Venice* to *My Cousin Vinny*. For example, in the play *A Few Good Men*, a military prosecutor, Lieutenant Kaffee, on cross-examination provokes the arrogant, imperious Colonel Jessup into a self-righteous tirade in which he insists he is above the law, above the truth:

> KAFFEE: [The members of the jury are] entitled to the truth.
> JESSUP: Is that right?
> KAFFEE: Do you disagree?
> JESSUP: Certainly not in principle. I disagree only inasmuch as I disagree that a paraplegic is entitled to foxtrot. It'd be nice, it just isn't possible.
> KAFFEE: Are you saying it's not possible for this court to hear the truth?
> JESSEP: This court? I don't know what that means. I'm saying it's not possible for you to hear the truth.
> . . .

* I thank my Debevoise & Plimpton LLP colleagues Ina Popova and Pedro De Oliveira for their assistance in preparing this chapter.

KAFFEE: Why is it impossible—?
JESSEP: Because you can't handle it, son. You can't handle the truth.

And so begins Colonel Jessup's downfall, in which he ultimately admits the truth – that he ordered the murder of a soldier under his command.

How can written advocacy compare to that? It lacks the frission, the immediacy and responsiveness of oral advocacy. It has none of the glamour or excitement. It is not the stuff of movies and plays. It is the poor cousin to oral advocacy, sharing some fundamental family traits but perpetually confined to the background.

Written advocacy can nevertheless be vital, powerful and essential in its own right. Since as a practical matter it often provides an international arbitration tribunal with its introduction to the case, identifies the disputed issues, reflects the universe of evidence the parties expect to rely upon and summarizes legal positions and the authorities offered in support of them, it is arguably at least equally and perhaps have more importance than oral advocacy. After all, if you get to an oral hearing down 40-love, it is not certain you will lose, but the odds are against you.

Let me use an historical example, far removed from modern international arbitration, to illustrate some of written advocacy's particular benefits. In 1787, when the United States was in its infancy, delegates of the various American states convened over a hot summer in Philadelphia, Pennsylvania and produced the Constitution of the United States. Despite the painstaking labor of these delegates, ratification of the Constitution by the states was not assured. There was in fact strong opposition to it, as many feared the creation of a national government would reproduce in the new world the very kind of old world "tyrannical" government they had just fought a long war to escape. As part of the effort to convince skeptical New Yorkers to support the Constitution, three lawyer-statesmen – writing under the *nom de plume* Publius – produced an extraordinary series of written arguments confronting the naysayers' fears, and attempted to articulate the central tenets of a never before tried system of government. For example, in *Federalist* No. 69, Publius addressed one of the "hot button" issues of the day – that the new President was simply a king by another name. To rebut this contention, Publius contrasted the fundamental qualities of the constitutional president and a monarch, starting with:

> The President . . . would be an officer elected by the people for four years; the king of Great Britain is a perpetual and hereditary prince.

Publius then listed seven more similarly significant differences between the president and a king, building to the following:

> The one has no particle of spiritual jurisdiction; the other is the supreme head and governor of the national church! What answer shall we give to those who would persuade us that things so unlike resemble each other? The same that ought to be given to those who tell us that a government, the whole power of which would be in the hands of the elective and periodical servants of the people, is an aristocracy, a monarchy, and a despotism.

That is heady and rhetorically effective, even after more than two centuries. The Constitution's proponents of course ultimately carried the day: the Constitution was ratified in 1789 and today survives as the oldest written constitution in use by any nation.

For our present purposes, however, the *Federalist* illustrates some of the special benefits of written advocacy:

- Through writing, arguments can be developed, and facts marshaled and developed, with *care, precision and detail.*
- It offers *convenience*, permitting a reader to consider the argument at her own pace, and even for consideration by readers not present for an oral argument.
- Additionally, written advocacy *endures.* Arguments presented in writing are fixed and unchanging. They can accordingly be referenced, reconsidered at another time, quoted, and examined. Even now, more than two centuries after they were penned, *The Federalist Papers* remain persuasive and are

routinely cited by courts and scholars seeking to understand and apply the Constitution. *See Printz v. United States*, 521 U.S. 898 (1997) (*citing* The Federalist Nos. 15, 18-20, 27-28, 33, 36, 39, 44-45, 51 & 70).

In these perhaps unglamorous but essential qualities, written advocacy is irreplaceable. When the drama of the oral hearing subsides and the memory of it begins to fade, the written work persists with the same force and clarity as the day it was submitted.

In this chapter I will attempt to identify some of the features of effective written advocacy in contemporary international arbitration. I do so with great caution. The range of views about what constitutes good advocacy is probably about as wide as the range of advocates and arbitrators. Also, there are many forms of written advocacy – pleadings, letters, briefs, memorials. These might have different objectives and call for different approaches. There are also various potential audiences in addition to arbitrators, including clients, adversaries, the press, government agencies and many more. These many variables counsel against attempting to articulate prescriptive rules.

Instead, I will first describe what I understand to be the aim of written advocacy; I will then explore five qualities that tend to make written advocacy effective; finally, I will identify a few bad habits to avoid.

II. Written Advocacy Should Persuade

It is almost too obvious to state, but the purpose of any kind of advocacy, including written advocacy, is to persuade. The Oxford English Dictionary defines "persuasion" as, among other things, "the addressing of arguments or appeals to a person in order to induce cooperation, submission, or agreement." OXFORD ENGLISH DICTIONARY (2nd ed. 1989). For international arbitration practitioners seeking to persuade sophisticated and experienced tribunals, "cooperation" or "submission" may be setting the bar too high, but we can safely aim for tribunal agreement with and even endorsement of the points we urge.

While this observation is elementary, it is also fundamental. It implies that the overarching question for the advocate must be: what will the *tribunal* find persuasive? It requires viewing the case from the tribunal's perspective, and doing so from the beginning, when the tribunal knows nothing about the dispute, right up through post-hearing submissions, when they may be sick and tired of hearing about it.

So what is the tribunal's perspective? A tribunal has no client. It does not come to the case with an agenda. Instead, a tribunal has a job to do. Its members must decide a dispute that is often complex and subject to many potential outcomes, as cases whose results are obvious tend to be settled rather than litigated. Good written advocacy helps a tribunal do its job. How would you go about it if you were the arbitrator? Would the tribunal benefit from a timeline of relevant events? A graph translating a collection of facts into a graphically compelling trend? A table collecting all the instances in which the other party acted in a way that conformed to your client's interpretation of the contract? A decision tree setting out the relevant steps of the analysis with reference to both parties' positions on each point? What the arbitrator needs is what you need to present. If you write the award for your tribunal, they will not have to.

Attempting to be helpful to an international arbitration tribunal may require abandoning certain parochial, national practices. There are some practices that make perfect sense within a national court system and hence may be transposed to domestic arbitrations where all participants share the similar training. But they may not get you very far in international arbitration, where very often the tribunal includes members from different legal traditions. For example, litigation in the United States begins when a plaintiff files a "complaint," to which the defendant responds with an "answer." Complaints frequently contain a great deal more speculation and surmise than one would expect in international arbitration – the assumption is that gaps in evidence and knowledge can be filled in by liberal discovery that typifies U.S. litigation. Answers are often studies in avoidance; they tend to say very little, and often address a plaintiff's allegations in the most cursory way. For example, a complaint might allege:

> The acts and practices of Defendants as herein alleged have had the purpose or effect, or the tendency or capacity, to restrain competition unreasonably and to injure competition in the following ways, among others: restraining competition in the Relevant Markets for [certain drugs]; fixing, raising, stabilizing, or otherwise tampering with the prices for [certain drugs]; raising the cost nationwide that pharmacies, hospitals, insurers, managed care organizations, wholesalers, government agencies, consumers, and others must pay for [certain drugs]; depriving Plaintiff and other third party payors of prescription benefit cost controls by eliminating their ability to employ cost containment programs for [certain drugs]; and depriving Plaintiff of the benefits of competition among generic pharmaceutical manufacturers and entry from new competitors.

Second Amended Complaint at ¶ 71, Health Care Serv. Corp. v. Mylan Lab., Inc., No. 1:01CV02646 (D.D.C. Mar. 5, 2002), *available at* 2002 WL 34112035. A typical answer might respond:

> Defendants deny the allegations in Paragraph 71 of the Second Amended Complaint.

Joint Answer of Defendants to Second Amended Complaint at ¶ 71, *Health Care Serv. Corp. v. Mylan Lab., Inc.*, No. 1:01CV02646 (D.D.C. Oct. 31, 2003), *available at* 2003 WL 25438888.

This kind of pleading, entirely appropriate in U.S. litigation, would likely be considered unhelpful, and therefore unpersuasive, in an international arbitration.

In thinking about the tribunal's perspective, it is also important to consider the extent to which any given arbitrator may himself be the product of national habits and traditional practices. In some legal cultures arguments tend to be presented as a series of propositions, one following the other, with the reader invited to draw a certain conclusion that presumably follows as a matter of course. This deductive model aspires to present legal argument as logical syllogism. Often such an argument has an academic quality, with general principles laid out first, followed by discrete propositions drawn from the facts of the current case. The conclusion is often reserved to the end, so the reader follows the path of the argument without knowing the ultimate destination in advance.

A typical judgment of the French *Cour de cassation* illustrates such an approach. The famous *Hilmarton* decision is based on citation to one article of the Civil Code and just a single paragraph of reasoning:

> Given article 1351 of the Civil Code;
>
> Whereas the two decisions being challenged granted exequatur to the [Swiss court] judgment dated 17 April 1990 and the [second arbitral] award dated 10 April 1992, despite the decision of the Cour de cassation of 23 March 1994 rejecting the appeal;
>
> Whereas in so doing, despite the fact that the existence of an irrevocable French judgment on the same issue between the same parties precludes the recognition in France of judicial decisions or arbitral awards rendered abroad that are incompatible with it, the Court of Appeal acted in violation of the above-mentioned provision;
>
> THEREFORE, and without it being necessary to address the remaining grounds of appeal,
>
> ANNULS AND REVERSES . . . .[1]

---

[1] Free translation of the following excerpt from Cass. Civ. 1e, Jun. 29, 2007, *Hilmarton*:

> Vu l'article 1351 du Code civil ; . . . Attendu que les deux décisions attaquées ont, malgré l'arrêt de rejet de la Cour de Cassation du 23 mars 1994, accordé l'exequatur à l'arrêt du 17 avril 1990 et à la sentence du 10 avril 1992 ;Attendu qu'en statuant ainsi, alors que l'existence d'une décision française irrévocable portant sur le même objet entre les mêmes parties faisait obstacle à toute reconnaissance en France de décision judiciaire ou arbitrale rendue à l'étranger incompatible avec elle, la cour d'appel a violé le texte susvisé ; . . . PAR CES MOTIFS, et sans qu'il y ait lieu de statuer sur les autres griefs : . . . CASSE ET ANNULE . . .

In contrast, in other legal cultures, arguments have a more inductive quality. That is, from the outset they announce the conclusion, which is then justified by supporting law and facts. This model aspires to identify the central point and then analyze it, as though it were a scientific hypothesis subject to testing and experimentation. This does not mean the argument is any less closely reasoned or logical than one reflecting a different legal tradition, but only that it attempts to tether such reasoning to an already identified end-point. The decision in *Chromalloy Aeroservices v. Arab Republic of Egypt*, 939 F. Supp. 907 (D. D.C. 1996), which reached a similar result substantively to *Hilmarton*, illustrates this approach. Its opening paragraph announces:

> The Court grants Chromalloy Aeroservices' Petition to Recognize and Enforce the Arbitral Award, and denied Egypt's Motion to Dismiss, because the arbitral award in question is valid, and because Egypt's arguments against enforcement are insufficient to allow this Court to disturb the award.

The decision continues for 8 pages, and includes passages such as:

> This Court *must* grant CAS's Petition . . . "unless it finds one of the grounds for refusal . . . of recognition or enforcement of the award specified in the . . . Convention. . . ." Under the Convention, "Recognition and enforcement of the award *may* be refused" if Egypt furnishes to this Court "proof that . . . [t]he award has . . . been set aside . . . by a competent authority of the county in which, or under the law of which, that award was made." . . . In the present case, the award was made in Egypt, under the laws of Egypt, and has been nullified by the court designated by Egypt to review arbitral awards. Thus, the Court *may*, at its discretion, decline to enforce the award. . . .
>
> [U]nder the Convention, CAS maintains all rights to the enforcement of this Arbitral Award that it would have in the absence of the Convention. Accordingly, the Court finds that, if the Convention did not exist, the Federal Arbitration Act would

> provide CAS with a legitimate claim to enforcement of this arbitral award. . . .
>
> Egypt's complaint that, "[T]he Arbitral Award is null under Arbitration Law, . . . because it is not properly 'grounded' under Egyptian law," reflects this suspicious view of arbitration, and is precisely the type of technical argument that U.S. courts are not to entertain when reviewing an arbitral award. . . .
>
> The Court's analysis thus far has addressed the arbitral award, and, as a matter of U.S. law, the award is proper. . . . The Court now considers the question of whether the decision of the Egyptian court should be recognized as a valid foreign judgment. . . .

The foregoing examples are from judicial decisions, not arbitration pleadings. But I have used them because they illustrate deeply ingrained, even habitual approaches to legal reasoning that lawyers often mimic in their arbitration submissions. An advocate could make the same points under either model, but the intended audience may respond more receptively to one approach rather than the other. Those familiar with the deductive approach may consider the inductive approach to be mercenary, blunt and illogical; those familiar with the inductive approach may consider the deductive approach to be aimless, evasive and pretentious.

Other vestiges of national legal culture may also influence an arbitrator's receptivity to written submissions. For example, some arbitrators may expect submissions that are comprehensive, festooned with evidentiary detail; others may desire concise, even stripped-down papers or "skeleton" arguments centering on the key legal propositions. Some arbitrators may be comfortable with an aggressive, hard-hitting, "take no prisoners" tone; others prefer understatement or academic dispassion.

The point is not that any one approach is right and the others wrong, or even that one approach should be preferred to another in a prescribed set of circumstances. Instead, the point is that advocacy is more likely to be effective if it satisfies the expectations and predilections of the arbitrators, or at least in its manner of presentation does not create obstacles to the arbitrator's understanding. To the extent possible, the method of presentation should be adapted to the tribunal.

This is not to say that effective written advocacy begins and ends with knowing your tribunal. It is certainly useful before writing to know all that you can about your arbitrators. Do they come from a particular legal background that will act as a lens through which they are likely to view the case? Is there some aspect of their experience that has familiarized them with the topics addressed in the arbitration? Have they joined prior awards or authored articles that provide some insight into arguments that might resonate with them? All of that is important. But I hope in the balance of this Chapter to show that there is a great deal more that can be said about key elements of written advocacy that if not universal are at least likely to be effective most of the time with most tribunals.

III. The Elements of Effective Written Advocacy

While there are many cultural and situational variables to take into account, there may be some more universal elements to effective written advocacy in international arbitration. This would not be surprising:

- Each of us who practices regularly in this field is constantly subjected to legal traditions and approaches that differ from our own, and if we are wise we will shamelessly copy the best of what those other cultures offer.
- Law firms increasingly are populated by lawyers hailing from different traditions.
- Rules and guidelines attempt to harmonize disparate practices.
- Extensive publications and frequent professional conferences encourage cross-pollination of ideas and approaches.

Here I focus on five qualities that I believe make for effective written advocacy in international arbitration, at least in most circumstances. These are: (1) define the essence of your argument; (2) frame the argument; (3) present coherently; (4) maintain pace and balance; and (5) appeal to equities.

A. Define the Essence of Your Argument

Just about every argument has a core, a central proposition that expresses what the argument is *really* about. If you can discern that essence of the argument, it will provide the clarity and focus that causes the rest of the argument to fall into place. It may also help you "sell" the arbitrators on the most difficult aspects of the case. For example, when faced with differing interpretations of a disputed piece of evidence, a strong underlying theme will help the arbitrators to give your client the benefit of the doubt.

It is not always easy to define the essence of the argument. Many cases are factually and legally complex. They might involve several contracts, multiple parties, various potential claims and counterclaims and convoluted facts. I have seen many pleadings where the advocate simply launches into description of the facts, or tries hurriedly to reference all the key documents, or focuses on a particular legal proposition even if it is not one that will be dispositive.

Instead, consider whether there are some basic, common-sense ideas that undergird the entire messy situation. For example, the claimant might contend: "Despite all of the complexities the respondents may attempt to exploit, the dispute centers on respondents' failure to meet detailed specifications that were exactingly negotiated by the sophisticated parties, their legal counsel and their respective engineers and for which claimant paid a premium over what otherwise would have been the contract price." Such an approach packs a strong communicative punch into a single sentence. It informs the tribunal that the specification is important to the case; it suggests that the parties knew exactly what they were getting when they agreed to that specification; and it signals to the tribunal that the respondents may try to "junk it up," which may put the respondents in a bind: if they offer complex technical arguments – even ones that have some validity – the tribunal may suspect that they are trying to avoid the key issue.

When trying to define the essence of an argument, I often follow a practical rule of thumb: if I cannot express all salient elements of my point in a single paragraph (or, in shorter submissions, even a single sentence), I have not yet successfully defined the essence of my argument. I tend therefore to write topic paragraphs iteratively. I prepare initials drafts of them at an early stage to rough out themes and get myself headed in the right direction. Later, however, I return to this paragraph and keep revising it again and again until it I think it says exactly what I want, and no more. After all that polishing, it should be like a Tiffany diamond – compact yet elegant, multifaceted yet clear, appealing yet honed to a point that can cut steel.

B. Frame the Argument

How an argument is framed can literally define the terms of the debate. If I tell you that I live in a place that suffers from more than one murder every day of the year, including weekends and holidays, it may sound like a pretty dangerous place. If instead I tell you that I live in a city of over 8 million inhabitants with a murder rate of merely 0.005%, which is one of the lowest in the world and in which murder by strangers has nearly been eradicated, it sounds like I live in a pretty safe place. All of these facts are accurate. Changing how they are framed and selected, however, strongly changes the impression they convey.

Consider another example demonstrating the critical importance of framing, which I came across in a book called *How We Decide*, by Jonah Lehrer (2009). In a study, physicians were asked to consider the following scenario:

> The United States is preparing for the outbreak of an unusual Asian disease, which is expected to kill six hundred people. Two different programs to combat the disease have been proposed. Assume that the exact scientific estimates of the consequences of

> the programs are as follows: If program A is adopted, two hundred people will be saved. If program B is adopted, there is a one-third probability that six hundred people will be saved and a two-thirds probability that no people will be saved. Which of the two programs would you favor?

Physicians are generally risk averse. Not surprisingly, 72% of them chose the certain life saving results offered by Option A, and only 28% chose the higher risk/higher reward Option B.

However, the experimenters then changed the framework, and posed the same scenario but focusing on the lives that would be lost rather than those that would be saved:

> The United States is preparing for the outbreak of an unusual Asian disease, which is expected to kill six hundred people. Two different programs to combat the disease have been proposed. Assume that the exact scientific estimates of the consequences of the programs are as follows: If program C is adopted, four hundred people will die. If program D is adopted there is a one-third probability that nobody will die and a two-thirds probability that six hundred people will die. Which of the two programs would you favor?

With this scenario, the results were completely upended: 78% of physicians chose the risky Option D, and only 22% chose the more certain results of Option C. As Lehrer observes, "Of course, this is a ridiculous shift in preference." The actual outcomes in the scenarios did not change; only the framework did.

Advocacy in international arbitration works on the same basic cognitive and psychological processes. If you can help the tribunal ask the right questions, you are more likely to get the right answers. In one case, we represented a sales agent whose principal had refused to pay commissions. The principal had conducted an internal investigation and concluded that our client had paid bribes. Some of the evidence looked troubling, including notes of an interview with our client in which the investigators had understood our client to have confessed. However, as we dug into the facts, we realized that the investigation had been flawed; what it actually uncovered was a plot among the principal's own employees to pay bribes, in which they tried to enmesh our client on false pretenses. Accordingly, we put the investigation on trial. The focus shifted from our client's actions to an unseemly conspiracy among the principal's employees. By the end of the case the investigation's mistakes and misunderstandings had been exposed. Our client prevailed.

Written submissions are a good place to begin framing the case. In one very concrete sense, written submissions *literally* frame the case. The claims a party chooses to assert, the evidence and analysis supporting or rebutting those claims, formulation of the relief requested and similar components of written advocacy define the parameters of the dispute and the issues that the tribunal will have to decide. Furthermore, as a practical matter, written submission typically provide the tribunal with all it knows about the case for some time, and perhaps a considerable time. In many international arbitrations, the parties do not engage with the tribunal about the merits until a year or more after the proceeding has commenced. In the meantime, all the tribunal knows about the merits comes from the parties' written advocacy.

To determine whether I have the right framework, I ask myself: Am I arguing on the ground most favorable to my client? Is my argument one that plays to my client's strengths? This is akin to the oversimplified but venerable litigator's adage: "if you have bad law, argue the facts; if you have bad facts, argue the law." In a written submission that initiates a process – like a request for arbitration, a statement of case or a motion – it is relatively easy to ensure that you argue on grounds favorable to your client because you are writing on a blank slate. You will need to take into account whether positions you articulate can be sustained through subsequent briefing and argument, but all of this is reasonably within the advocate's control. Getting on the right ground can be more challenging in a responsive submission. The slate is no longer blank. That does not, however, mean you need simply to buy into your opponent's framing of the debate. Instead, you might consider addressing the arguments in a different order than they were presented, or starting with some crucial facts your adversary has omitted, or attacking an implicit assumption on which your adversary's argument is based. These and other devices may permit you to change the framework and get the tribunal viewing the case in a light more favorable to your client.

C. Present Coherently

The most effective written advocacy is not just analytically correct, it is also coherent. By this I mean that it hangs together, and makes it easy for the reader to comprehend both the overall "big picture" and where the various legal or factual details fit into it. A well written submission should resonate like a musical chord – its individual elements combining into something stronger and more appealing than any individual strand alone.

Coherence may sound like an elusive quality, and one that is difficult to describe or explain how to achieve. One legal writing instructor has explained the need for coherence as follows:

> [B]egin by seeing your document from your readers' perspective. To you, it is a finished product you can grasp as a whole. For them, as they are reading it, the document as a whole never exists. At any one point, they will remember only a few sentences, if that, in relatively precise form. What has gone before will have been winnowed and compressed to fit into their memory, and what lies ahead is largely a mystery.
>
> When you write a document, therefore, you are organizing a complex process: the flow of information through your readers' minds.
>
> ARMSTRONG & TERRELL, THINKING LIKE A WRITER: A LAWYER'S GUIDE TO EFFECTIVE WRITING AND EDITING 14 (2003)

I believe three qualities contribute significantly to organizing that flow of information and attaining coherence: structure, logic and consistency.

A sensible *structure* promotes clarity. It indicates to the reader the relative priority of arguments, where particular facts or propositions of law fit into those arguments, and how the various arguments relate to each other. In other words, it reveals to the reader the pattern of the argument, which is often easier to retain than so many unconnected details.

I have often found drafts that pay insufficient attention to structure. Sometimes, for example, a draft suggests that subsidiary points are on par with primary points. Consider an outline that says:

I. The claimant is entitled to exercise the right of first refusal

II. The respondent's attempted share transfer triggered claimant's right of first refusal

III. The respondent's attempted share transfer involved the shares that are subject to claimant's right of first refusal

IV. The claimant's prior share transfer does not relieve the respondent of its obligations under the right of first refusal clause

This structure suggests there are four discrete, equally important arguments. However, the first three of them are actually very closely related. It is not self-evident what the difference is between them, or how one relates to the other. These relationships would be more transparent if the structure were:

I. The claimant is entitled to exercise the right of first refusal

   A. The respondent's attempted share transfer triggered claimant's right of first refusal

   B. The respondent's attempted share transfer involved the shares that are subject to claimant's right of first refusal

II. The claimant's prior share transfer does not relieve the respondent of its obligations under the right of first refusal clause

Now the second and third propositions become supportive of the first, more general proposition, and the fourth proposition becomes more distinct. It is easier for the reader to see the overall pattern of the argument, to make sense of it, to hold it in mind.

Logic also contributes to coherence. One proposition should lead naturally to another. This makes it easy for the reader to follow the sequence of propositions without breaking the flow. To continue with our above example, its logic might be further strengthened by reversing the second and third propositions, so it would read:

I. The claimant is entitled to exercise the right of first refusal

   A. The respondent's attempted share transfer involved the shares that are subject to claimant's right of first refusal

   B. The respondent's attempted share transfer triggered claimant's right of first refusal

II. The claimant's prior share transfer does not relieve the respondent of its obligations under the right of first refusal clause

In this example, you are almost tempted to insert the word "therefore" into what is now I.B – so it would read: "The respondent's attempted share transfer therefore triggered claimant's right of first refusal" – as that proposition seems like a natural conclusion from I.A's point that the relevant shares were part of the attempted transfer.

Finally, *consistency* helps convey the sense that the entire document works together. A document at war with itself leaves the reader confused and questioning what in the document to trust. I have read briefs that in one section confidently assert some categorical legal proposition, and then in a subsequent section quote a legal authority that suggests that the very same legal proposition cannot be treated categorically and is actually highly fact sensitive. This kind of internal tension raises questions in the arbitrator's mind not only about what the law actually provides, but also about the credibility of the document's author.

Consistency may also require paring back or foregoing some alternative arguments. Particularly at more advanced stages of a case, alternative arguments imply a lack of confidence in your position and may even force you to assert propositions that are in such tension that they have the effect of reducing the prospects of winning on any of the alternative grounds. For example, in one recent case, the respondent defended against a claim for breach of a "no transfer" provision by arguing that there had been no agreement to sell. The same respondent then brought a counterclaim for frustration of the sale, arguing that it *had* concluded an agreement to sell, which had failed at the last minute due to the claimant's actions. The counterclaim thus seems to undermine the defense, creating confusion about what actually happened – had there been an agreement to sell or not – and what position respondent actually espouses.

Consistency also implies a consistent tone and approach. Many significant international arbitrations are conducted by teams comprised of several lawyers from a firm, or even from two or more firms. Arguments can get parceled out among the various team members. This kind of "piece work" approach can be highly efficient for clients, but requires extra work when stitching back together the various pieces to ensure that the document speaks in one voice.

One quick and dirty way to test coherence of a longer document is to review the table of contents for its substance. The table of contents is a graphical outline of the entire document. Particularly after having anguished over the particulars of each paragraph and sentence, studying the table of contents enables you to step back from the trees and take in the forest. Does it make sense? Do the sections trace a natural progression? Is there tension or inconsistency between components of the document? If from the table of contents you could not sensibly explain the progression of the argument to a lawyer who is unfamiliar with the case, you may want to consider further whether your document is sufficiently coherent.

D. Maintain Pace and Balance

Good written advocacy should be like any good writing – it should be a pleasure to read. In the international arbitration community we are fortunate often to have cases that are challenging and interesting, filled with complex issues and personalities. A brief or memorial should be correspondingly lively, vital and engaging. It should have an arc-like trajectory, maintain momentum as it progresses through arguments without getting bogged down, and keep the various components in balance and proportion to each other. It should hum along with the confidence, authority and purpose of a bullet train gliding on silken steel rails toward its announced destination.

There is a lot of advice available about how to write well. Provide strong topic sentences. Use active voice. Vary sentence length. Employ accessible diction. The list of such helpful and well intentioned nostrums goes on and on. Here, however, I want to focus more particularly on some aspects that can contribute to or confound good writing in international arbitration.

First, before drafting, establish a notional page target. Should this be a 10 page document? A 25 page document? A 40 page document? A 75 page document? Such an exercise may feel artificial. After all, substance, not an artificial page constraint, should dictate the document's length; it should be as long as it needs to be to cover the ground that needs to be covered. However, I find that envisioning what the end product ought to look like overall helps me map out the argumentative path, and begin to assess how different elements of the document can be brought into balance.

Notional page limits also impose discipline and rigor. In legal writing, shorter is often better. There is a familiar saying, often attributed to Blaise Pascal (and also to many others fabled for their witticisms): "I would have written a shorter letter if I had more time." *See* BLAISE PASCAL, LETTRES PROVINCIALES (1657), Lettre XVI.[2] Writing economically hones your message and excises distractions. Recently we and our co-counsel kicked back and forth a draft brief and when the dust settled we had 42 pretty good pages. The problem was, we had a strict 25 page limit. I worked through several nights trimming, rearranging, condensing, summarizing, focusing. What

---

[2] "*Je n'ai fait celle-ci plus longue que parce que je n'ai pa eu le loisir de la faire plus courte.*" ("I made this [letter] longer only because I did not have the opportunity to make it shorter.").

emerged was far more forceful. We lost nothing of substance. To the contrary, we said more, and more effectively, in 25 pages than we had in 42 pages.

Self-imposing limits may also force difficult but ultimately rewarding choices about what to include and what to omit. There is often a great temptation to include every fact you have learned, even trivial ones, and every argument you can imagine, even weak ones. Who knows what will appeal to the tribunal, especially early in the case, so isn't it safer to throw everything against the wall and see what sticks? You should struggle to resist this temptation, for you may drown out your main argument in a flood of unnecessary detail, abstract hypotheticals, and ill formed collateral points. "[T]he more you say, the less well the hearers retain . . . By dint of burdening their memory you will overwhelm it; just as . . . plants are choked by immoderate irrigation." FRANÇOIS DE SALIGNAC DE LAMOTHE FELELON, THREE DIALOGUES ON PULPIT ELOQUENCE 157 (Samuel J. Eales trans., 1897) (internal citations omitted).

Second, break up the document into manageable chunks. Even the most intellectually ravenous arbitrator can digest only so much new information at once. Finding ways to divide the document can help the arbitrator keep together constellations of facts and arguments. One method for accomplishing this is of course by adding more substructure to the document, but that runs the risk of fragmenting it and could be counterproductive. Instead, consider other ways of providing narrative breaks: use of bullet point summaries, block quotes, tables and graphs, maps, pdfs of exhibits, and other devices that relieve monotony and keep the arbitrator looking forward to the next page.

Third, eliminate redundancy. Reading should be a journey of discovery for the arbitrator. Redundancy interrupts narrative flow and gives the arbitrator the impression that he is going around in circles. (I find the same to be true of substantive footnotes, which often are a dumping ground for underdeveloped arguments, and I therefore try not to use them at all in my own written submissions.) Also, if the same idea is referenced later in the document but in a slightly different way, the arbitrator may wonder which of the two descriptions is accurate.

You should aim to address each issue once and only once. For example, in an investor-State case, a treaty, national law and a contract may all provide for similar standards of conduct. Instead of analyzing the conduct three times in the sections of the document that address respectively the treaty, national law and the contract, consider first explaining why under each of those three sources of obligation the test is effectively the same, and then analyzing the conduct in such a way that it can be applied to each head of claim. As a practical test, if you find a phrase like, "as explained above," repeatedly cropping up in your document, you may have a redundancy problem.

Avoiding redundancy can be especially challenging in reply and rejoinder submissions. There you have to walk a line of alluding to arguments asserted against you without becoming unmoored from your own earlier submission. One strategy that is often helpful in this situation is to frame the argument by identifying the points of explicit or implicit agreement between the parties, and using that as the platform from which to attack the remaining points of disagreement. For example, imagine a case under English law; the claimant in pre-hearing brief explains and cites cases stating that the law forbids interpreting a contract based on statements made in pre-contractual negotiations; the respondent's pre-hearing brief does not deny that legal principle, but introduces some pre-contractual negotiation documents anyway. The claimant in reply does not want to walk through the same pre-contractual negotiation authorities he already cited; that would be redundant. Instead, the claimant might say, "Although the respondent does not deny that settled English law forbids use of pre-contractual negotiation documents to interpret a contract, the respondent without justification offers such negotiation documents precisely for that purpose." This kind of introduction anchors you in your previous submission, but keeps the spotlight on the responsive aspect of the reply.

Finally, keep your sense of proportion. By allocating less space to alternative or merely supplemental arguments, you communicate to the tribunal that you appreciate the relative importance of various issues and, as a result, inspire a confidence that your understanding is correct. This is equally true of the treatment of your opponent's arguments. Ignoring or glossing over strong opposition arguments diminishes the arbitrator's confidence.

E. Appeal to Equities

An appeal to the equities is a powerful persuasive device. It can transform a collection of disparate legal technicalities into the "right" resolution, not only on the law but on the facts. Nearly all human beings – and even international arbitrators, I am reliably informed – possess a deep-seated sense of justice and fairness.

Equitable appeals are no substitute for careful analysis, compelling facts and controlling law. However, they provide another dimension to the case. In the damages phase of an investment treaty arbitration our adversary pointed out that the amount we sought on behalf of our client represented approximately $100 for every man, woman and child in a country where the average annual income was only around $2,500, and was more than the entire budget for certain ministries that provided important public services. None of this changed the legal standard for damages, or the facts and expert evidence that the parties had presented to the tribunal. I nevertheless believe it was at least a sobering thought that weighed on the arbitrators' minds and induced additional caution as they worked through the damages analysis and its many moving parts. In the end the tribunal rendered a substantial award for our client, but it was only about half of what we had requested.

Writers should take care to explain how legal authority relied upon is fair and just. Pedantic reliance on technical arguments is often not convincing and may leave the tribunal searching for a more satisfying result. Commercial disputes often involve make-or-break situations, such as granting control of a corporation or potentially putting one side out of business. To be persuasive, a submission must reduce resistance to such troubling outcomes by making your position appealing to the arbitrator's, and society's, sense of the equities. For example, you could explain that even though you seek substantial pecuniary relief, the opposing side had obtained other benefits as a result of the disputed transaction.

In one case the claimant contended that our client, through an M&A transaction up the corporate chain, had breached a contract provision barring sale of a certain asset. We counterclaimed that the claimant had engaged in a similar transaction just a few months before, so if they were right about the contract interpretation then they had breached first. We ultimately contended that the tribunal could decide under a literal construction that neither party had breached the contract, or under a purposive construction that they both had, but in either event the result ought to be the same – the tribunal should dismiss the claim and the counterclaim and leave the parties to their respective M&A transactions because that was the only fair result under the circumstances. That is exactly what the tribunal did. The equitable result did not supplant the legal analysis, but it sure helped inform it.

IV. Avoid Bad Habits

In this final section I offer some thoughts about qualities that almost always make written submissions less effective with tribunals.

First, avoid petulance, vituperation, sarcasm and *ad hominem* attacks. These are not effective. Ask anyone who has served as an arbitrator and this will appear as one of his top pet peeves with counsel. The reason is that such behavior simply does not help the arbitrator do his job of deciding the case and writing the award. Your ultimate objective as an advocate is effectively to write the award so that the tribunal in substance appropriates your written submission as its decision. Written submissions that contain insults and an unprofessional tone, however, will never be adopted by a tribunal no matter what other merit they may have.

Second, do not be a coward. Every case has its problematic aspects. Do not shirk from or ignore them. They will not go away. Instead, determine how you can best confront them. Any submission that responds to another should presumptively respond comprehensively and confront all of the arguments. One delicate judgment call is when to initiate discussion of a point adverse to your client, where the adversary has not yet done so. If it is a matter you are legally or ethically obligated to raise – such as a truly controlling authority – the answer is easy. Where there is no such obligation, it still might make sense to raise the adverse issue under some circumstances. You might consider doing so where you anticipate that the issue will arise anyway, or that if it does arise you might look like you were hiding the ball from the tribunal, or that you can take the sting out of the issue by acknowledging it and getting it out of the way.

Third, do not dissemble or cheat. Preserving your integrity and the trust of the tribunal is especially important in arbitration. Do not distort or take liberties with the record or the law. The chances are that you will be caught and everything else you say will be suspect. The tribunal will usually conduct its own thorough review of the facts and relevant evidence, and will not fail to notice instances of misquoting evidence or less than forthright argument.

Fourth, be wary of categorical statements and overclaiming. Advocates often make assertions like "the adversary has no evidence that . . . ," that a claim is "completely baseless," and many others that admit no exceptions. This can be dangerous. You run the risk of setting the bar too high. Must you really show that a claim is "completely baseless" to prevail? Moreover, life is full of exceptions. If you are wrong about a categorical claim, you create an easy opening for your opponent.

V. Conclusion

Carnegie Hall is one of America's most famous performance spaces. The top talent plays there. This has given rise to an old joke: A woman from out of town is lost in New York City and approaches a policeman on the corner. The woman, befuddled, map crumpled in her hands, asks, "How do I get to Carnegie Hall?" The policeman sizes her up and replies, "Practice, practice, practice."

Effective written advocacy likewise requires practice, practice, practice. It is the kind of thing you can get better at with work, the kind of thing that rewards the effort devoted to it. I recall when I was a young lawyer and a senior partner kept fiddling with my draft of a letter to the court, returning it to me with comments again and again. I exclaimed, "at this rate, the letter will cost the client $5,000." Without missing a beat he said, "sometimes a letter is worth $5,000." These days I spend a lot of time with younger lawyers planning, crafting and honing our written submissions. For important matters we may go through twenty drafts or more before we have it just right. Through all that effort, these talented lawyers from top schools grow to be better writers – and so do I.

Most of us in our written advocacy will never conjure the passion, capture the revolutionary zeal or enjoy the enduring legacy of Publius and the *Federalist*. But we can aspire to achieve similar success in the much smaller world of the arbitrations in which we appear. Reflecting on how we go about our written advocacy, and keeping at it, can help us get there.

Chapter 10

WITNESS STATEMENTS AND EXPERT REPORTS

Pierre Bienvenu and Martin J. Valasek

I. Introduction

In the context of international arbitration, it could well be argued that written advocacy is advanced primarily through the written submissions containing <u>argument</u>, namely the submissions that identify the relevant legal principles, explain why those particular principles are applicable in the circumstances, and apply those principles to the facts that have been established (or are to be established) through the evidentiary phase of the arbitration. Mark Friedman addressed this type – the archetype – of written advocavy in an earlier chapter of this book. Understandably, that is likely the most common perception in relation to written advocacy in an international arbitration. A written submission containing argument – a brief or memorial – is certainly the vehicle through which a lawyer can most visibly and directly practice his or her written advocacy. After all, in the written sphere, what could be more characteristic of the advocate than the vision of the skilled and experienced practitioner pulling together all of the strands of the case – law and fact – into a compelling brief that is well-organized, logical and going to the essence of the issues at the heart of the dispute? To that extent, pre- or post- hearing briefs are to written advocacy what the opening statement or closing argument are to oral advocacy.

As Guillermo Aguilar Alvarez aptly demonstrates in his introductory chapter on written advocacy, however, the brief is only one of several components that make a party's written case convincing. If the brief is the recipe that guides the Tribunal to the conclusions that are sought by the advocate, its success depends on the ingredients, namely law and fact. The advocate finds the law as it exists, be it in the legal codes or statutes promulgated by a jurisdiction's legislative body in the judgments written by its judges and magistrates, and sometimes even in general principles. In this respect, not all legal systems are equal. They differ in their sophistication, particularly in commercial law. They also differ in the clarity and quality of expression of their legislation or court judgments. While in most commercial or contractual contexts parties should exercise their prerogative to choose an applicable law well before a dispute arises, based, in part, on the quality of that legal system, the advocate dealing with a case can rarely influence the choice of law, still less the clarity of the applicable legal principles and rules as expressed in the primary source material.

From a certain perspective, the same is true of facts: the material events have already occurred by the time the lawyers get involved. If the events have occurred, one might ask, how could the facts of the case not be in the same category as the law – namely something that the lawyer simply must accept as a pre-packaged bundle? From this perspective, the lawyer cannot alter the course of events that occurred prior to his or her involvement in the case any more than the lawyer can alter or influence the applicable legal principles and rules.

There is, however, an important difference, from an advocacy perspective, between the legal principles and the facts with which the advocate must work in the written submissions. The difference stems from the fact that while legal principles and rules have already been reduced to written form by third parties prior to the commencement of the case,[1] the facts and any expert analysis of the facts have not. Prior to the commencement of the arbitration, the events that have given rise to the dispute exist merely as recollections in the memory of one or more individuals. While a significant documentary (and, increasingly, electronic) record also often exists in disputes that are commonly resolved by arbitration (such as disputes in the document-

---

[1] Not just any written form, either, but the formal and official form of statute, regulation or judgment.

intensive world of large-scale construction projects, commercial joint-ventures, etc.), more often than not that documentary record, just like individual recollections, is incomplete, inaccurate and perhaps even contradictory, and must be interpreted with the help of witness evidence. In other words, unlike law, the facts of a case do not exist in a convenient, formal, logical, and consistent written form.

This chapter deals with the advocacy that can be applied or exercised through the written submissions typically used in international arbitration to convey the facts of the case, and the expert investigation or analysis of those facts, namely witness statements and expert reports. As compared to the open and direct advocacy engaged in drafting briefs and memorials, or in presenting oral argument, this is the "invisible" written advocacy of international arbitration. Indeed, the less visible it is, the more effective it should be.

II. Witness Statements

A. Introduction

Witness statements have now become common place in international arbitration. Their prevalence in practice is illustrated by the provisions of the *IBA Rules on the Taking of Evidence in International Commercial Arbitration* (the "**IBA Rules**") dealing with witnesses of fact.[2] This was not always so. A decade ago there were still some who questioned the utility of witness statements. In the late 1990s, Professor Pieter Sanders wrote:

> Witness Statements may alleviate the hearing but, drawn up with the party or its legal advisors, the witness may be influenced in formulating his or her Statement which has to be signed and affirmed by him or her as being the truth. In my opinion, these Witness Statements, preceding the hearings of the witnesses in

---

[2] IBA Rules, Art. 4(4)-4(9). At the time of writing, revisions to the IBA Rules are being considered by the IBA's Arbitration Committee. References in this chapter to the proposed revisions to the IBA Rules are to the revised Rules that were submitted for adoption by the IBA Council in May 2010.

person, are not in accordance with the expectations of many parties in an international arbitration.[3]

More recently, most practitioners have come to recognize the significant advantages of witness statements. For example, Michael Hwang has identified the following advantages of a witness statement:

- It saves considerable hearing time (usually the most expensive part of an international arbitration).
- It prevents the other party from being taken by surprise at the trial.
- It enables the opposing Counsel to prepare his cross-examination more efficiently, thus again reducing cross-examination time.
- It obviates the necessity for sterile arguments about whether questions asked of the witness are leading.
- It helps to define the issues for argument at the hearing more clearly, allowing the parties and the Tribunal a more focused examination of the matters in dispute.[4]

---

[3] Pieter Sanders, *Quo Vadis Arbitration?: Sixty Years of Arbitration Practice* (Massachusetts: Kluwer Law International, 1999) at 262.

[4] Michael Hwang, "Advocacy in International Commercial Arbitration: Singapore" in Doak Bishop, ed., *The Art of Advocacy in International Arbitration* (New York: Juris Publishing, 2004) 413 at 422. See also Laurent Levy, "Testimonies in the Contemporary Practice: Witness Statements and Cross Examination" in *Arbitral Procedure at the Dawn of the New Millennium: Reports of the International Colloquium of CEPANI, October 15, 2004* (Brussels: Bruylant, 2005) 107 at 113 (noting also that a witness statement "assists the parties and the arbitral tribunal in determining whether the testimony of a specific witness is necessary"). Hwang also notes (*ibid.*) that these advantages come at a price:

- It deprives cross-examining Counsel of the opportunity of seeing and hearing the witness give his oral testimony-in-chief, and therefore a valuable guide to deciding whether the words of the witness in evidence-in-chief are really the witness' own, or someone else putting words in the witness' mouth.
- It also deprives cross-examining Counsel and the Tribunal of a tool in determining the initial credibility of the witness in assessing the truthfulness or accuracy of the witness evidence-in-chief.

Witness statements are particularly helpful in large arbitrations or arbitrations that deal with complex issues, be they of a financial, technical or other nature, as they give all participants in the process sufficient time to study and understand the allegations and cross-allegations in advance of the hearing. In practice, witness statements are submitted by individuals of all rank and stripe. This follows from the general rule that any person may present evidence as a witness in an international arbitration, including a party or a party's officer, employee or other representative.[5] Witness statements, while written, are not to be regarded as documentary evidence, but as a means of presenting testimony from witnesses of fact. The IBA Rules, at Art. 4(4)-(9), explain the mechanics of how the written statement typically fits into the process of taking evidence from a witness in an international arbitration. The IBA Rules provide, in relevant part:

> 4. The Arbitral Tribunal may order each Party to submit within a specified time to the Arbitral Tribunal and to the other Parties a written statement by each witness on whose testimony it relies, except for those witnesses whose testimony is sought pursuant to Article 4.10 (the "Witness Statement").[6] [...]
>
> [...]
>
> 7. Each witness who has submitted a Witness Statement shall appear for testimony at an Evidentiary Hearing, unless the Parties agree otherwise.
> 8. If a witness who has submitted a Witness Statement does not appear without a valid reason for testimony at an Evidentiary Hearing, except by agreement of the Parties, the Arbitral Tribunal shall disregard that Witness Statement unless, in exceptional circumstances, the Arbitral Tribunal determines otherwise.

---

[5] IBA Rules, Art. 4(2).

[6] Article 4.10 addresses the situation where a Party wishes to present evidence from a person who will not appear voluntarily. The preparation of a witness statement in such a situation is obviously not possible.

9. If the Parties agree that a witness who has submitted a Witness Statement does not need to appear for testimony at an Evidentiary Hearing, such an agreement shall not be considered to reflect an agreement as to the correctness of the content of the Witness Statement.

The idea is that a witness statement should be disregarded unless confirmed orally and, conversely, that a witness should not be heard unless he or she has previously submitted a witness statement. This is the spirit of the IBA Rules, and is a manifestation of the overriding principle expressed in the preamble of these rules that each party should be entitled to know reasonably in advance of any evidentiary hearing, the evidence on which the other parties rely. Witness statements have, accordingly, been referred to as a "prelude to oral testimony"[7] or as "draft" testimony.[8]

Although a witness statement can technically be considered "draft" testimony, and as non-binding until it is confirmed by the witness at the hearing, this should by no means suggest that counsel and witness should not take utmost care in preparing the statement. First, the content of a witness statement (if it is sufficiently detailed) can and often does serve as a witness's evidence-in-chief,[9] and will influence the scope of questions at the hearing. Indeed, Art. 4(5)(b) of the IBA Rules provides that a witness statement's description of the facts should be "full and detailed" and "sufficient to serve as that witness's evidence in the matter in dispute." Furthermore:

> There may be uncontroversial witnesses whose entire testimony may be received in written form. These may include formal witnesses who depose to matters which are admitted by the other

[7] Levy, *supra* note 4 at 117.

[8] Pierre-Yves Tschanz, "Advocacy in International Commercial Arbitration: Switzerland" in Doak Bishop, ed., *The Art of Advocacy in International Arbitration* (New York: Juris Publishing, 2004) 195 at 225.

[9] David W. Rivkin, "Procedural Issues to Consider" in Rufus V. Rhoades, Daniel M. Kolkey & Richard Chernick, eds., *Practitioner's Handbook on International Arbitration and Mediation*, 2d (New York: JurisNet, LLC, 2007) 133 at 152.

> party, or other witnesses of substance where the other party considers the evidence to be immaterial or irrelevant to the matters in issue. In all such cases, where the opposing party elects not to cross-examine the witness on his witness statement or affidavit, that evidence will be received without the need for a physical appearance by the maker of the statement or affidavit.[10]

Second, decision-makers can begin forming opinions about a case at an early stage, and first impressions (even on paper) are therefore important.

Third, in time-controlled arbitrations, the rules will allow the respondent to choose who from the claimant's list of witnesses is actually to be heard in the hearing, and vice versa. As John Tackaberry has cautioned, if the practitioner has "under proofed" his witness, the risk exists that the other side does not call that witness and whatever oral evidence he might have given beyond the content of his statement will not be heard by the Tribunal. Indeed, the other side may recognize that not all of the evidence which that witness could give is in the statement and, as a result, decide not to call the witness for cross-examination in order to seek to keep that evidence out of the hearing.[11]

Finally, a witness statement will provide predictability to the party tendering the evidence in that it will (and fairly so if the witness statement has been adequately prepared) "box" the witness into the stated version of his or her testimony.

There are therefore very good reasons to prepare the witness statement with care. In the next section, we address the issue of counsel's involvement in the preparation of witness statements, before turning to the heart of the topic, namely what constitutes effective advocacy with witness statements.

---

[10] Hwang, *supra* note 4 at 431.

[11] John Tackaberry, "Practical Considerations for Conducting the Hearing" in Rufus V. Rhoades, Daniel M. Kolkey & Richard Chernick, eds., *Practitioner's Handbook on International Arbitration and Mediation*, 2d (New York: JurisNet, LLC, 2007) 155 at 174-175.

B. Involvement of Counsel in the Preparation of Witness Statements

It is now generally accepted in the field of international arbitration that it is proper for counsel to interview witnesses or potential witnesses,[12] and to assist in the preparation of a witness statement. The IBA Rules provide:

> It shall not be improper for a Party, its officers, employees, legal advisors or other representatives to interview its witnesses or potential witnesses.[13]

Similarly, the LCIA Rules (at Article 20.6) expressly permit it, subject to "the mandatory provisions of any applicable law." In a recent article, Peter Schlosser noted that he found no indications or obstacles in the ethical rules of the Bar of any civil law country that would prevent a lawyer from preparing a witness in an arbitration.[14] This is a relatively recent shift, as explained by Bernard Hanotiau:

> Until a few years ago, however, members of the Bar in various civil law countries were prohibited from having direct contact with a potential witness. In other words, preparing a witness was strictly forbidden and any one who breached the rule would incur disciplinary sanctions. Recently, the rule has been relaxed in international cases to avoid putting civil law lawyers at a disadvantage with English barristers or American attorneys.[15]

---

[12] Michael Bühler & Carroll Dorgan, "Witness Testimony Pursuant to the 1999 IBA Rules of Evidence in International Commercial Arbitration – Novel or Tested Standards?" (2000) 17:1 J. Int'l Arb. 3 at 11, and sources cited at footnote 38. See also Levy, *supra* note 4 at 112 (noting that it is generally accepted "that counsel may liaise with witnesses and prepare the hearing with them").

[13] The revised IBA Rules propose to add to Art. 4(3) "and to discuss their prospective testimony with them."

[14] Peter F. Schlosser, "Generalizable Approaches to Agreements with Experts and Witnesses Acting in Arbitration and International Litigation" in Gerald Asken *et al.*, eds., *Global Reflections on International Law, Commerce and Dispute Resolution* (Paris: ICC Publishing, 2005) 775 at 780-781.

[15] Bernard Hanotiau, "The Conduct of the Hearings" in Lawrence W. Newman & Richard D. Hill, eds., *The Leading Arbitrators' Guide to International*

Notwithstanding these changes, Hanotiau notes that "a certain number of civil law advocates are still unwilling to interview their witnesses and refuse therefore to submit witness statements."

While the rules on counsel's involvement in the preparation of witness statements have undoubtedly been relaxed in recent years, there are obvious limits on the practice, as noted by various authors. Redfern and Hunter illustrate the point as follows:

> For example, it would be gross misconduct for a lawyer to try to persuade a fact witness to tell a story that both the lawyer and the witness in question knew to be untrue, and to prepare the witness to make the story sound as credible as possible.
>
> [...]
>
> The role of counsel should be to assist witnesses in developing the confidence and clarity of thought required to testify truthfully and effectively based upon their own knowledge or recollection of the facts.[16]

Bernard Hanotiau expresses the limits in the following terms:

> In any case, the lawyers have the ethical duty to avoid attempts to induce the witness to make false testimony. Witness preparation should not become witness manipulation. The starting point for any witness preparation is to remind the witness to tell the truth. Moreover, the witness who has been "over-prepared" may quickly lose credibility in the eyes of the Arbitral Tribunal.[17]

Some codes of professional conduct address counsel's contact with witnesses in international arbitration and include specific

---

Arbitration, 2d (Huntington: Juris Publishing, 2008) 359 at 365 [Hanotiau, "Hearings"].

16 Alan Redfern *et al.*, *Law and Practice of International Commercial Arbitration* (London: Sweet & Maxwell, 2004) at 207.

17 Bernard Hanotiau, "Civil Law and Common Law Procedural Traditions in International Arbitration: Who Has Crossed the Bridge?" in *Arbitral Procedure at the Dawn of the New Millennium: Reports of the International Colloquium of CEPANI, October 15, 2004* (Brussels: Bruylant, 2005) 83 at 92 [Hanotiau, "Procedural Traditions"].

directives. For example, Section 16 of the Professional Rules of the Dutch-speaking Brussels Bar provides:

> In his contacts with the witness, the lawyer will in all circumstances take into consideration the appropriate prudence, decency and integrity. He will strictly refrain from influencing the witness or from inciting him to deviate from the truth.[18]

The reality is that counsel are often very involved in the drafting of witness statements, and visibly so. For example, it is typical that the final version of the witness statement will be filed with the witness's signature on a final signature page transmitted by fax or in a format different from the body of the statement, highlighting that counsel and the witness are in different locations (which is quite common) and that the final version of the substantive part of the witness statement came from counsel, not from the witness. Another clue as to counsel's involvement in witness statement preparation is when a witness who is not fluent in the language of the arbitration submits a statement in that language that is perfectly correct and even sophisticated in style. In some cases, the witness even includes a declaration that counsel assisted in the preparation of the statement.

As explained in the next section, the good advocate need not hide the fact that he was involved in the preparation of a witness statement. Rather, the good advocate should make it easy for the Tribunal to forget about counsel's involvement, allowing the voice of the witness to come through the document.

C. Effective Advocacy with Witness Statements

(1) Basic Form and Content Guidelines

Article 4(5) of the IBA Rules provides useful guidance on the basic form and content of witness statements. Article 4(5) provides that witness statements should contain:

---

[18] As quoted in Bühler & Dorgan, *supra* note 12 at footnote 67.

(a) the full name and address of the witness, his or her present and past relationship (if any) with any of the parties, and a description of his or her background, qualifications, training and experience, if such a description may be relevant and material to the dispute or to the contents of the statement;

(b) a full and detailed description of the facts, and the source of the witness's information as to those facts, sufficient to serve as that witness's evidence in the matter in dispute;

(c) an affirmation of the truth of the statement; and

(d) the signature of the witness and its date and place.

According to Bühler and Dorgan, other points to consider when preparing written witness statements include the following:

- The text of the witness statement may be in narrative form. Depending upon the nature of the information contained in the statement, it may be more convenient to present it in some other form, such as a listing of relevant events by way of "bullet points" drafted in "telegraphic" style. It is helpful where each paragraph in a witness statement is limited, as far as possible, to a distinct portion of the subject, and then numbered separately. It facilitates references to specific passages in the witness statement, which assists the tribunal and the parties, in particular at the hearing.
- Excessive length of the witness statement should be avoided, as well as needless repetition. ...[19]

For rebuttal witness statements, the content should be restricted to material that is responsive to matters contained in another party's witness statement or expert report. Article 4(6) of the IBA Rules provides:

> If Witness Statements are submitted, any Party may, within the time ordered by the Arbitral Tribunal, submit to the Arbitral Tribunal and to the other Parties revised or additional Witness

---

[19] Bühler & Dorgan, *supra* note 12 at 13-14.

> Statements, including statements from persons not previously named as witnesses, so long as any such revisions or additions only respond to matters contained in another Party's Witness Statement or Expert Report and such matters have not been previously presented in the arbitration.

In the Introduction to this part, we listed the advantages of witness statements, as explained by Michael Hwang. Michael Hwang also notes that in order to obtain the various advantages offered by a witness statement, the statement must be in terms of exactly what the witness would say if he were giving oral evidence-in-chief in court proceedings.[20] This suggests that a "full and detailed" statement is best. Indeed, as Hwang points out, the witness may not be allowed to add further oral evidence at the hearing, unless:

- he wishes to correct an error or ambiguity in the statement or affidavit;
- he wishes to elaborate on some small matter of detail; or
- he wishes to respond to some statement made in the opposing witness statements or affidavits which he had not seen at the time his own statement or affidavit was filed.[21]

A "full and detailed" statement may not be required in all cases, however. According to Doak Bishop, there are three types of witness statements:

- a simple statement, listing general topics of the witness's testimony;
- a statement containing a full and detailed testimony of the witness; and
- a statement that adopts an intermediate approach, identifying key points of a witness's testimony without all of the relevant facts and details.[22]

---

[20] Hwang, *supra* note 4 at 423.

[21] *Ibid.*

The same author goes on to advise:

> Which of these types of witness statements to provide is a strategic decision for counsel, but it is a decision that must be made in a manner that meets the requirements and expectations of the tribunal. Since it is relatively easy to determine, counsel should ask the panel at the preliminary hearing which of these types of witness statements is preferred and then comply with the panel's directions in this regard.[23]

Given the range of possibilities as to what level of detail to provide in a witness statement, what is therefore important is for all counsel to know and understand the "rules of engagement" at the outset, so that each side benefits from a level playing field.[24]

Having reviewed the basic guidelines for the form and content of a witness statement, we turn now to address each element of the witness statement in greater detail.

(2) Identification of the Witness

As suggested by Article 4(5)(a) of the IBA Rules, the witness statement should provide:

- the full name and address of the witness,
- his or her present and past relationship (if any) with any of the parties, and
- a description of his or her background, qualifications, training and experience, if such a description may be relevant and material to the dispute or to the contents of the statement.

---

[22] Doak Bishop, "Advocacy from the Arbitrator's Perspective" in Doak Bishop, ed., *The Art of Advocacy in International Arbitration* (New York: Juris Publishing, 2004) 441 at 476.

[23] *Ibid.*

[24] Levy, *supra* note 4 at 112.

Some suggest that it is also useful to attach a picture of the witness to the witness statement, so that arbitrators can more easily recall the oral testimony of a witness in reviewing a statement after the hearing.

The identification of the witness presupposes the selection of that individual as an appropriate or necessary witness. As we saw earlier, it is now generally accepted in international arbitration that any individual may testify, including a party or party representative. In selecting a witness, the good advocate will already be thinking of the impact that witness might have on the Tribunal in comparison to other possible or necessary witnesses, and how the various subject matters to be covered in evidence should be "allocated" to the different witnesses that are available to the party. The advocate needs to consider that certain individuals are under his client's control (e.g., a party's existing employees), and thus will likely testify voluntarily, while other individuals (e.g., a party's former employees) may refuse to testify or dispose of less time to prepare a witness statement setting out their evidence.

(3) Description of the Facts: Telling the Story

The description of the facts to which the witness is prepared to attest is the core of the witness statement, and the part that presents a challenge for the advocate. The advocate can be of great assistance to the witness, but the advocacy that he or she exercises through the witness statement should be "invisible." Its aim should be to allow the witness to discover and amplify the witness's own voice, and not to bury the witness's story under layers of "facts" constructed by an overzealous lawyer.

a. Getting Started: Preparing the First Draft

To start, counsel should avoid presenting a suggested draft of the statement to the witness. Doing so heightens the risk that the witness will assume that it is acceptable or even expected that he or she adopt the lawyer's version of events. Recall that the witness is typically a stranger to legal proceedings of any kind, let alone proceedings at the international level. It may not dawn on the witness that he or she must be actively involved in preparing the witness statement, and thus should challenge inaccuracies or untruths in any version prepared by the lawyer.

Having the witness adopt someone else's version of the events, apart from raising ethical issues, poses obvious problems for counsel at the hearing. A written statement delivered by a witness is, in principle, always subject to testing at a hearing, where the statement must be presented (in direct testimony) and/or defended (in cross-examination) by the witness himself or herself. If the written statement, as the precursor to the oral testimony, is not delivered in the witness's own voice, then counsel has taken a big risk. At the hearing, the witness may attempt to follow the script of the written statement, adopting as his or her own the story presented therein. A seasoned arbitrator, however, will likely pick up on the discrepancy, particularly when an experienced counsel challenges the script through cross-examination. It is also possible that the witness testifying orally at the hearing will start to tell his or her own story, precisely because it is what comes naturally, leaving exposed the discrepancies between the oral testimony and the "ill-fitting" written statement. Bühler and Dorgan are correct in cautioning that:

> A witness statement should not simply repeat a party's pleadings, which sometimes occurs when counsel, rather than the witness, does the drafting. Counsel can legitimately assist the witness in the preparation of the statement to avoid lack of clarity, repetition and irrelevance; but the substance of the statement must come from the witness. A "lawyer's statement" will have little or no credibility.[25]

In an ideal world, and the option is available in certain instances, counsel would ask the witness to prepare the first draft of his statement. In doing so, the lawyer should ask the witness to deliver a full and frank account of everything related to the dispute that the witness knows or about which he has information. This, however, is often not feasible or practical. For example, the witness may be

[25] Bühler & Dorgan, *supra* note 12 at 13-14.

extremely busy and unlikely to be able to deliver a draft within the required time period. The witness may also be intimidated or embarrassed by the prospect of having to draft a written statement. In all such cases, the lawyer should schedule a meeting with the witness and, through open, non-leading questions, ask the witness to describe the relevant events of which he has knowledge in as much detail as possible. Ideally, the meeting should be in person, and the lawyer should have a junior colleague or assistant present to take notes (in some cases, it might be helpful to audio-record the session). The notes (checked against the audio recording, if available) may then be used to prepare the first draft of a statement for the witness's review. It may be efficient for counsel to provide the witness, in advance of the meeting, with a list of topics to be discussed for possible inclusion in the witness's statement.

If counsel and witness speak the same language, all of this is relatively straightforward. If not, then translation and/or interpretation are required. In such cases, it is most efficient to have the witness (or local counsel who speaks the witness's language) prepare the first draft of her statement in her mother tongue, and to have it translated into the language of the arbitration. We discuss the particular challenges raised by language issues in the separate section on language, below.

Doak Bishop's commentary on witness statements in our view provides helpful guidance on what elements the witness should be requested to include in the first draft:

> ... they should fully develop the relevant background, the events, acts and omissions in dispute, any relevant conversations (being as precise as possible in relaying statements made), and the motivations of the witness. Motivations should not be neglected, although this is an area that the advocate may desire to save for the oral hearing. Even when motives are not directly relevant to the elements of a claim or defense, an arbitrator may want to know why the witness took a particular position, made a particular

statement or engaged in a particular act or omission. Supplying that information can create credibility and assist in persuasion.[26]

b. Getting it Right: Completing a Comprehensive Draft

The first draft of the facts is the "raw material" of the statement. The quality of the first draft depends on many factors, and it can sometimes be very good. Even if it reads well, however, it is rarely a document that should be submitted to the Tribunal without considerably more work on the part of both the witness and the advocate. It is not the witness's "best possible testimony," and in certain cases is just plain awful! The first draft of a statement is often limited by a combination of one or more of the following common shortcomings of the witness: incomplete knowledge about, or initial misunderstanding of, certain events; poor memory or faulty recollection; and poor writing or communication skills, leading to difficulties in the witness's "telling of the story."

As Mark Baker has written: "a good advocate can work within ethical bounds to bring out the best possible testimony from any witness."[27] In practical terms, this means assisting the witness with a second draft, and subsequent drafts. The work will typically involve follow-up meetings or conference calls to discuss the outstanding matters, and the exchange of marked-up drafts. The lawyer may wish to send a mark-up of the first draft with questions and comments, and request that the witness send back a second draft with answers and/or responsive comments. This "dialogue" should be sustained for as many rounds as it takes to get the testimony right.

What does it mean to get the testimony "right"?

First and foremost, it means ***removing the errors and inconsistencies***. By the time witness statements are being prepared in a case, counsel should have a very strong command of the documentary record and of what each witness is testifying about. It

---

[26] Bishop, *supra* note 23 at 476-477.

[27] C. Mark Baker, "Advocacy in International Arbitration" in Lawrence W. Newman & Richard D. Hill, eds., *The Leading Arbitrators' Guide to International Arbitration*, 2d (Huntington: Juris Publishing, 2008) 381 at 395.

is counsel's responsibility to challenge each witness on internal inconsistencies in his or her testimony, as well as on inconsistencies between his or her testimony and both (i) the testimony of each other witness and (ii) the documents in the record.

Counsel should also ensure that, as part of the witness's testimony, the witness is ***referring to key documents***, whether the document is relevant to a factual issue in dispute, or to issues of credibility. Documents should be leveraged, bearing in mind that arbitrators tend to give greater weight to contemporaneous documents than to uncorroborated witness testimony.[28] This question is further addressed below.

Getting the testimony right also means ***addressing the difficult facts***[29] – the "inconvenient truths." These will invariably surface in the arbitration, and it is better for a witness to get ahead of them in the statement, rather than being forced to deal with them for the first time on cross-examination.

Another way of perfecting the testimony is ***reviewing the opponent's submissions***, including the allegations in its pleadings and especially the evidence adduced by the other side in support of its position. Where a witness is preparing a statement in support of the respondent's submission, and the claimant has already submitted witness statements in support of its position, this step will be crucial. In preparing a responsive statement, counsel should be asking his witness what he or she has to say about what the other side claims, and what the other side's witnesses have declared. After all, at the hearing and in deliberations, the Tribunal will be focusing on the confrontation of the opposing claims and the evidence and arguments presented in support of each. A witness's testimony is most material – and potentially most effective – when it directly supports a party's position and opposes the other side's position, so long as the opposition is limited to facts and falls short of engaging

---

[28] Redfern *et al.*, *supra* note 16 at 298, 308.

[29] James L. Loftis, "Advocacy of Private Disputes before International Claims Resolution Bodies" in Doak Bishop, ed., *The Art of Advocacy in International Arbitration* (New York: Juris Publishing, 2004) 39 at 73.

the witness in argument. Such crucial evidence must be carefully reviewed with the witness, to ensure that it is as solid as possible.

By effectively communicating the questions and comments arising out of the various areas addressed above, the good advocate will be leading the witness on a journey of rediscovery, providing documents and other materials to refresh the witness's recollection. This involves being efficient and diplomatic, and avoiding a process that becomes overly burdensome, time-consuming, or just plain unpleasant. Counsel must do his or her best to maintain a good relationship with witnesses throughout the process, using tried and true techniques to keep them on side, such as timely notification of relevant dates in the arbitration and preparation process, timeliness in the delivery of the lawyer's own work product, and respectful communication that favours humility (and, where appropriate, even humour) over hubris.

Finally, counsel should be aware of the risk that lawyer's communications to a witness who is not a client of the lawyer could be subject to discovery, although the risk in an international arbitration is much lower than it is in litigation, given the usually much narrower scope of discovery allowed under the applicable rules and/or by the Tribunal. In her book *The Attorney-Client Privilege and the Work-Product Doctrine*, Edna Selan Epstein addresses the issue in the context of witness preparation in U.S. litigation:

> Deposition questions regarding witness preparation often raise issues involving the work-product protection. Although the rule does not explicitly apply to questions that seek to discover a lawyer's statements made to the witness during preparation to testify, the principles enunciated in *Hickman*[30] are nonetheless invoked to protect a lawyer's intangible work product as it may be reflected in conversations the lawyer has with a witness who is not a client of the lawyer. If a witness is instructed not to testify about certain matters in the course of the deposition, courts will review

[30] *Hickman v. Taylor*, 329 U.S. 495 (1947).

the questions asked and sort out those areas of inquiry that are protected as opinion work product from those that are not.[31]

c. Making it Better: Polishing the Final Draft

Once a comprehensive draft has been completed, the work is not yet done. The testimony is now "right", but it may not yet be the "best possible" testimony.

A first consideration that goes beyond the strict facts being related by the witness is whether the witness' story is properly sequenced. The usual way to tell a story is chronologically, but blind adherence to chronological order should be avoided, and other ways considered. For example, depending on the matter in dispute, a travelling salesman's story may well be easier to follow organized by sales territory ("During the year, I returned to Calgary twice, resulting in sales of ... During the same period, I was in Vancouver five times, resulting in sales of ...") rather than in the strict order in which sales were made ("In January, I sold ... in Calgary. I then flew to Vancouver ...."). Hwang notes that "Where a number of separate issues are involved, chronological narrative can be divided into different sections according to issue."[32]

A related question is organization through headings and sub-headings. In a longer statement, sections should be clearly identified by short descriptive headings, and longer sections further sub-divided by descriptive sub-headings. The headings and sub-headings, collected in a table of contents at the beginning of the statement, give the Tribunal a helpful summary-at-a-glance of what is otherwise a long statement.

Beyond sequence is the question of "back story". Is there sufficient background information to make the key evidence stand out? Although such information is not essential, it can make all the difference for the Tribunal's understanding of the case.

---

[31] Edna Selan Epstein, *The Attorney-Client Privilege and the Work-Product Doctrine*, 3d ed. (Chicago: American Bar Association, 1997) at 382.

[32] Hwang, *supra* note 4 at 424.

Conversely, is there too much non-essential information in the witness statement clouding the important facts, or too much unnecessary detail confusing the message? It is important, once the comprehensive draft has been completed, to examine critically whether even whole parts of the testimony are really required. For example, perhaps another witness is already covering certain elements that could therefore be dropped from a witness's statement, and replaced with a sentence of the following kind: "I have read paragraphs 75-90 of Mr. Smith's statement, and I am in full agreement with his description of the trade show, which I attended with him."

A related consideration is the need to protect the witness on cross-examination. Perhaps not surprisingly, this concern is voiced most effectively by American practitioners, especially those who also do trial work in the courts. For example, Doak Bishop writes:

> A carefully crafted witness statement should also anticipate the attacks and cross-examination of the opposing party and the questions of the arbitrators. Thinking through the testimony to ensure that it has the proper level of detail and consistency is important for it to be ultimately persuasive.[33]

Similarly, Mark Baker advises:

> When drafting the statement, it is important for the witness to limit his or her testimony to important issues and not stray beyond the facts necessary to develop the party's case. This would help ensure that the witness does not unnecessarily open too many doors for opposing counsel on cross examination. The advantages of fully developing testimony must be balanced with the risks associated with providing more opportunities for the cross examination on various issues.[34]

Finally, in reviewing the comprehensive draft, the good advocate should ask herself whether the testimony is not only "right", but also

---

[33] Bishop, *supra* note 23 at 476-477.

[34] Baker, *supra* note 27 at 393.

accessible to the Tribunal? Is there jargon that can be converted into plain language? Are there long descriptions that can be replaced with a map or diagram? Would a glossary of key technical terms, abbreviations and/or acronyms be helpful? How about a list of all individuals mentioned in the statement, together with their respective titles, job descriptions and the dates during which they held any given position, where the statement relays facts relating to complex internal dynamics at a company?

d. Staying within Ethical Bounds

Assisting the witness with the development of the statement from first draft to polished draft is the very essence of the "invisible" advocacy practiced by counsel in international arbitration. It is ethical as long as the final product remains a statement of the testimony of the witness, and not of testimony that has been made up by the lawyer for purposes of the arbitration.

To conclude this section with a metaphor, it is the witness who carries the tune, while the good advocate acts merely as sound engineer. The witness must not be asked to "synch" his testimony to counsel's words, written to satisfy the demands of the case. Instead, counsel should use his toolkit of methods to bring clarity, definition, tone and volume to the witness' voice. Such involvement by counsel is widely accepted in international arbitration.

In his article "Effective Witness Preparation for International Commercial Arbitration," David Roney presents certain generally accepted ethical guidelines for counsel engaged in witness preparation, a process which, in many cases, involves the step of submitting written witness statements:

> Counsel is entitled to review the case in detail with each of their own witnesses and to challenge any inconsistencies and point out any weaknesses in the evidence of the witness.
>
> By contrast, counsel must not propose, either directly or indirectly, that a witness should tell a specific "story". This is not only unethical, it is also invariably counterproductive. A witness who is coached to recount a specific story will not be credible and, in all

> likelihood, this story will not hold up under questioning from opposing counsel or the arbitral tribunal.[35]

Laurent Levy goes so far as to say that:

> The arbitrators would not actually benefit from a statement, which a witness drafted on his own. The help of counsel in drafting the witness statement enables the witness to focus on the relevant issues, which in turn proves a useful tool for the arbitrators.[36]

Michael Schneider touched on this point when he eloquently contrasted authenticity with accessibility during an ITA workshop on arbitral advocacy. He said:

> This discussion raises a question about authenticity in witness statements. I don't think there is a need for authenticity, because what counsel is doing is translating into a form that is accessible to the Tribunal what the witness, in substance, has to say. I think it is perfectly all right to reformulate what the witness had said because it has a different function. So, I think sometimes we are overestimating this question of authenticity. But then you can put at the end of the witness statement: 'this witness statement has been discussed with my counsel who drafted it and I confirm that it is my testimony'.[37]

(4) Documents and Evidentiary Issues

Practitioners need not be too concerned with technical rules on the admissibility of evidence, including the documents attached to witness statements. Experienced international arbitrators, "whether they are from common law or civil law countries, tend to focus on

---

[35] David P. Roney, "Effective Witness Preparation for International Commercial Arbitration: A Practical Guide for Counsel" (2003) 20:1 J. Int'l Arb. 429 at 430.

[36] Levy, *supra* note 4 at 115.

[37] As quoted in "Advocacy with Witness Testimony" (2005) 21:4 Arb. Int'l 583 at 592.

establishing the facts necessary for the determination of the issues between the parties, and are reluctant to be limited by any rules of evidence that might prevent them from achieving this goal."[38] This is consistent with Article 9(1) of the IBA Rules, which provides:

> The Arbitral Tribunal shall determine the admissibility, relevance, materiality and weight of evidence.

But as Hwang correctly notes:

> Although the strict rules of evidence normally do not apply to arbitrations, some regard should be paid to those rules, as many of them are based on common sense. For example, while most Tribunals will consider hearsay evidence, they will also recognize that such evidence will be inconclusive and may even be unreliable.[39]

As already mentioned, witness statements should incorporate references to contemporaneous documents, as evidence of contemporaneous documents will invariably be given greater weight than uncorroborated witness testimony.[40] The contemporaneous documents should be explained by the witness, and attached to the witness statement (if not already submitted separately).

Bühler and Dorgan write:

> The witness should identify the documents he has been given when preparing the statement. The reference may be done in general fashion; it may also be appropriate to state when the witness saw a document for the first time. Where the witness refers to documents on record in the arbitration, it is convenient to include the appropriate exhibit references. Counsel for the parties generally supply the references.[41]

Hwang provides the following guidance:

---

[38] Redfern *et al.*, *supra* note 16 at 296.

[39] Hwang, *supra* note 4 at 424.

[40] See Redfern *et al.*, *supra* note 16 at 298, 308.

[41] Bühler & Dorgan, *supra* note 12 at 13-14.

> All relevant documents should be referred to in the body of the statement or affidavit so that those documents can be read and understood by the Tribunal in proper perspective and order.[42]

(5) Language

The question of what language the statement should be prepared in is an important one. It is typical for at least some witnesses in an international arbitration not to be fluent or even functional in the language of the arbitration. In his commentary at the ITA, Gerald Aksen highlighted this problem, and offered his advice as to the best way to deal with it:

> The biggest problem I have seen in witness statements is where the witnesses do not speak the language of the arbitration. If the lawyer prepares that written statement up front, he or she prepares it in the language of the arbitration, and then translates it back to the language of the witness who is testifying. That is not fair, because no one can do adequate translations, and the statement doesn't come out the way the witness would have made it. It is very difficult to deal with those kinds of settings. My advice always is to have the witness prepare his own statement in his own language. It is then translated into the language of the arbitration. There is a better chance that that will work out, certainly to the satisfaction of the witness, because you don't want your witness embarrassed at that moment.[43]

Similar guidance is provided by the Commercial Courts Guide in England & Wales, from which arbitration practitioners may draw inspiration:

> Fluency of witnesses

---

[42] Hwang, *supra* note 4 at 424.

[43] As quoted in "Advocacy with Witness Testimony", *supra* note 38 at 589.

H1.4 If a witness is not sufficiently fluent in English to give his evidence in English, the witness statement should be in the witness's own language and a translation provided.

H1.5 If a witness is not fluent in English but can make himself understood in broken English and can understand written English, the statement need not be in his own words provided that these matters are indicated in the statement itself. It must however be written so as to express as accurately as possible the substance of his evidence.

The proposed revisions of the IBA Rules would require that witness statements include a statement as to the language in which the witness statement was originally prepared and the language in which the witness anticipates giving evidence at the evidentiary hearing.[44]

(6) Affirmation of the Truth

The IBA Rules state that a witness statement should contain "an affirmation of the truth of the statement" by the witness.[45] In other words, the witness statement need not be sworn like an affidavit. Indeed, because the statement must normally be confirmed at the hearing, and does not stand alone as evidence unless accepted as such by the parties, one of the principal reasons for swearing an affidavit is not present.

It is good practice for the witness to distinguish between assertions made in the witness statement based on the witness's own knowledge, and those which are made on the basis of information or belief. In the latter case, the witness should give the source for any assertion made on information or belief.[46]

---

[44] Revised IBA Rules, Art. 4(5)(c).

[45] IBA Rules, Art. 4(5)(c).

[46] See Art. 4(5)(b) of the IBA Rules.

III. Expert Reports

A. Introduction

Depending on the nature and subject-matter of the dispute in an international arbitration, evidence based on the documents and the testimony of witnesses of fact will not be sufficient to provide the Tribunal with a basis to come to a decision. For example, a manufacturing process may have come to a halt because of an alleged breakdown of a piece of equipment in the factory, while nobody who witnessed the breakdown really understands how or why the machine failed. In such cases, an expert may be required to investigate the causes of the failure, or to explain the significance of the circumstances surrounding the failure, or both. Another typical scenario in which an expert is required is the valuation of an asset or enterprise, for example in the context of a dispute between co-owners or shareholders or a dispute involving compensation for the destruction or expropriation of property. In such a case, the expert, having been provided with the factual financial data about the asset or enterprise, applies one or more methodologies to develop an opinion on "fair value" or "fair market value", for example. Engineering and accounting, however, are only two of the more common fields among many more that are regularly encountered in international arbitration.

The role of an expert is conceived differently in civil law countries and common law countries, and each tradition has found a reflection in the practice of international arbitration. Bernard Hanotiau explains the difference as follows:

> 33. [...] In the countries of Roman law tradition, an expertise is a procedure in which the advice of one or several technical experts is requested by the Court. Moreover, experts are often appointed after the exchange of written submissions and the presentation of oral arguments. In fact, an expertise is often used to discover information that in common law systems would be obtained through discovery.
>
> 34. In common law systems, expert witnesses are not appointed by the Court. Like witnesses of fact, they are produced by the parties

> to supply specialized information to the tribunal. Like witnesses of fact, they are examined and cross-examined by Counsel.[47]

The IBA Rules accommodate both types of experts, namely "party-appointed experts" (Art. 5) and "Tribunal-appointed experts" (Art. 6). In each case, the expert's report is said to be a means of evidence on certain "specific issues".

Neither approach to expertise is wholly satisfactory, as has been noted by several practitioners. John Tackaberry makes the following observations:

> To begin, we reiterate that many civil law panels regard the evidence of experts retained and paid by the parties as irremediably tainted. And with some justice, perhaps. Equally, a panel appointed expert is also unsatisfactory in some respects. For example, unless the Panel itself includes someone who is expert in the same field, it may be that the expert's conclusions will be very difficult to challenge effectively. And the expert does not have the same incentive to question and reconsider his or her own views as would be the case if he or she had to deal with the views of someone else in the same field on the same topic.[48]

Martin Hunter is similarly ambivalent:

> The main disadvantage of the common law system is that the expert "evidence" presented to the arbitral tribunal is "bought" by the party presenting it. The party in question simply would not present the testimony to the tribunal if the expert's opinion was unfavourable to its case. The civil law system suffers from the disadvantage that the parties (or their advocates) tend to think that their disputes will be decided by the tribunal-appointed expert, rather than by the arbitral tribunal that was appointed by the parties to resolve it.[49]

---

[47] Hanotiau, "Procedural Traditions," *supra* note 17 at 92-93.

[48] Tackaberry, *supra* note 11 at 181.

[49] Martin Hunter, "Expert Conferencing and New Methods" in Albert Jan Van Den Berg, ed., *International Arbitration 2006: Back to Basics?* (The Netherlands: Kluwer Law International, 2007) 820 at 820-821.

This text is not the place to dwell on the differences in the two approaches to expert evidence in international arbitration, or even to argue in favour of one approach over another. In this chapter, we are dealing necessarily with expert reports prepared by party-appointed experts, since counsel has no direct written advocacy role with respect to the expert report prepared by a Tribunal-appointed expert.[50] As mentioned below, however, in some cases, there is both a Tribunal-appointed expert and party-appointed experts, in which event the existence of a Tribunal-appointed expert can be a relevant consideration in the advocacy exercised through the reports of the party-appointed experts.

B. Involvement of Counsel

(1) Involvement of Counsel in the Selection of an Expert

In international arbitration, just as in domestic legal proceedings, counsel is typically involved in the selection of the expert, and for good reason: a party's choice of expert is crucial in a case requiring technical or specialized knowledge, and a lawyer's experience from prior dealings and interactions with experts can be of great assistance to a party making such a choice.

What should a party and its counsel look for in an expert? Naturally, the kind of expert that should be retained depends on the facts and circumstances of the particular case, and the issues for which the expert is required. However, there are certain common characteristics shared by effective experts in any field and for any case. An effective expert:

- has a comfortable command of the specialized knowledge and/or techniques that are specific to the expert's field of expertise;

---

[50] The revised IBA Rules propose an expanded description of the required content of expert reports, including reports by Tribunal-appointed experts; see Art. 6(4) of the revised IBA Rules.

- is well-known and respected in his field, with significant publications to his credit in his area of expertise;
- is able to maintain his independence and objectivity – and thus his credibility – while effectively advancing the position being put forward by a party and its advocate;
- is professional and thus committed to devoting to the preparation of his report and cross-examination sufficient time to ensure that the opinion is credible, and presented in clear and accessible terms; and
- has strong communication skills, and particularly the ability to explain complex matters in simple language, and in discrete steps; and the ability to respond effectively to questions from a cross-examiner, or member of the Tribunal (the ideal expert is thus fluent or fully functional in the language of the arbitration).

Dushyant Dave suggests that counsel consider the following battery of questions and factors in selecting an expert:

– How many times has the expert acted as consultant?

– In how many cases has the expert actually testified?

– Were the issues in previous cases similar to the issues in the case before the tribunal?

– Has the expert expressed views to the contrary, at any time in publications or testimony, on the subject upon which he is now expected to opine?

– Has the expert ever been employed by the opposing party or counsel?

– Has the expert been repeatedly engaged by the law firm or the counsel representing the party?

– Is the expert going to be available for cross-examination on the future dates that may be fixed by the tribunal? Has the expert disclosed unused material or any contrary tests or opinions (even if carried out by someone else) of which he/she is aware?

- It would be greatly helpful to remember the principles set out by the US Supreme Court in *Daubert v. Merrell Dow Pharmaceuticals*[51] and *Kumho Tire*[52] while choosing an expert because it must be clear that his testimony will constitute "scientific knowledge" or "technical and other specialized knowledge" required to assist the tribunal in reaching the ultimate conclusion.
- To know the exact nature of the dispute to be decided in Arbitration and whether the expert is indeed proficient in the particular subject. For example, in a dispute involving chemical technology it would be unwise to choose an expert from the field of civil engineering.[53]

Doak Bishop advises, for his part, that

> [w]hen expert evidence is to be used, the expert should be carefully selected for his credentials and expertise on the specific issue requiring expert evidence. Nothing can substitute for the necessary expertise in an expert witness, although expertise alone may not be sufficient. The expert witness must also be able to articulate his opinions and reasons both in writing and orally, and to have sufficient mental agility and character to withstand cross-examination.

---

51 509 U.S. 579 (1993) (in this decision, the U.S. Supreme Court established that, in any case in the federal courts involving expert scientific testimony, the trial judge must determine whether the reasoning or methodology underlying the testimony is scientifically valid and whether that reasoning or methodology properly can be applied to the facts at issue).

52 *Kumho Tire Co.* v. *Carmichael*, 526 U.S. 137 (1999) (expanding the *Daubert* test of reliability and relevancy to all expert testimony based on "technical" or "other specialized" knowledge).

53 Dushyant Dave, "Contemporary Practice in the Conduct of Proceedings: Techniques for Eliciting Expert Testimony – How Party Appointed Experts Can Be Made Most Useful" in Albert Jan Van Den Berg, ed., *International Arbitration 2006: Back to Basics?* (The Netherlands: Kluwer Law International, 2007) 813 at 815.

For these reasons, it is wise for counsel to consult other lawyers that have worked with the expert candidate being considered in order to get a first-hand impression of how effective the expert was in an actual arbitration setting, and in dealing with the pressures of cross-examination, witness conferencing and questioning from members of the Tribunal.

(2) Involvement of Counsel in the Preparation of the Expert Report

Once the expert is selected, his or her tasks include: educating a party's counsel on the specific issues for which the expert has been retained; gathering and/or observing the raw data and information that requires processing, explanation or analysis; analyzing the data and information by application of various methodologies or models; and preparing a report setting out and explaining the expert's opinions and conclusions. In an ideal world, the expert would always craft the perfect expert report. In reality, many experts do prepare excellent reports. In that regard, many experts have an advantage over witnesses of fact in that they are professionally trained and experienced in drafting their written testimony.

At the same time, it is not uncommon for an expert to both need and welcome the assistance of counsel in the preparation of an expert report. It has been pointed out that, in international arbitration, "[b]ecause communication between a party and its expert remain undisclosed, expert testimony and reports may be the result of extensive collaboration."[54] By contrast, in some jurisdictions, counsel involved in litigation are justifiably cautious in engaging in extensive collaboration with an expert because the expert may be required to disclose the nature of the collaboration during discovery.[55] This could

---

[54] Dana H. Freyer, "Assessing Expert Evidence" in Lawrence W. Newman & Richard D. Hill, eds., *The Leading Arbitrators' Guide to International Arbitration*, 2d (Huntington: Juris Publishing, 2008) 429 at 431, citing Rachel Kent, *Expert Witnesses in Arbitration and Litigation Proceedings*, www.transnational-dispute-management.com (June 2007) 4:3 at 2.

[55] For example, in the U.S., the Federal Rules of Civil Procedure provide that a

result in the revelation of sensitive discussions between counsel and expert concerning counsel's strategy or counsel's assessment of the case. Even in an international arbitration, counsel should be cautious, and confirm what rules and obligations are likely to apply to the disclosure of communications between counsel and expert in their particular case.

C. Effective Advocacy with Expert Reports

(1) Basic Form and Content Guidelines

According to Article 5(2) of the IBA Rules, an expert report prepared by a party-appointed expert should contain:

> (a) the full name and address of the Party-Appointed Expert, his or her present and past relationship (if any) with any of the Parties, and a description of his or her background, qualifications, training and experience;
>
> (b) a statement of the facts on which he or she is basing his or her opinions and conclusions;

---

party "may depose any person who has been identified as an expert whose opinions may be presented at trial" (Rule 26(b)(4)(A)) and, in exceptional circumstances, may "by interrogatories or deposition, discover facts known or opinions held by an expert who has been retained or specially employed by another party in anticipation of litigation or to prepare for trial and who is not expected to be called as a witness at trial" (Rule 26(b)(4)(B)). Similarly, Part 35.10 of the Civil Procedure Rules of England sets out the rules governing disclosure of information by experts, including as follows:

> (3) The expert's report must state the substance of all material instructions, whether written or oral, on the basis of which the report was written. (4) The instructions referred to in paragraph (3) shall not be privileged against disclosure [...]

By contrast, in Quebec, for example, the general rule is that communication between counsel and expert, whether oral or written, is protected by the privilege of "professional secrecy" (see *Poulin v. Prat*, [1994] R.D.J. 301 (C.A.)).

(c) his or her expert opinions and conclusions, including a description of the method, evidence and information used in arriving at the conclusions;

(d) an affirmation of the truth of the Expert Report; and

(e) the signature of the Party-Appointed Expert and its date and place.[56]

Article 5(3) of the IBA Rules provide:

> The Arbitral Tribunal in its discretion may order that any Party-Appointed Experts who have submitted Expert Reports on the same or related issues meet and confer on such issues. At such meeting, the Party-Appointed Experts shall attempt to reach agreement on those issues as to which they had differences of opinion in their Expert Reports, and they shall record in writing any such issues on which they reach agreement.

In the revised IBA Rules, it is contemplated that such a meeting may be ordered by the Tribunal even before the party-appointed experts have submitted their reports in order to identify areas of disagreement and assist in focusing the expert reports.[57] This would obviously need to be reflected in the expert report.

(2) Expert's Qualifications, Training and Experience

Undoubtedly, the credibility of the expert's opinion begins with the Tribunal's perception that the expert witness has the qualifications, training and experience necessary to understand the

[56] The revised IBA Rules propose to replace the language of paragraph (d) with the following : "an affirmation of his or her genuine belief in the opinion expressed in the Expert Report", and to add a paragraph dealing with the language in which the report was prepared. Another proposed addition reads as follows: "if the Expert Report has been signed by more than one person, an attribution of the entirety or specific parts of the Expert Report to each author." Reports signed by more than one persons are discussed later in this chapter.

[57] See Art. 5(4) of the revised IBA Rules.

specific issues that he or she is considering, and to be in a position to advise the Tribunal on those issues. As mentioned earlier, it is crucial, at the stage of selecting an expert, that an individual with the proper qualifications, training and experience is identified and chosen.

Having made the right choice, however, it is just as important that the report communicate the specifics of the expert's background to the Tribunal. This is typically done by including, as the first exhibit to the expert report, a detailed *curriculum vitae*, listing the expert's educational background, publications, conferences, and prior engagements as a consulting or testifying expert. This information will likely have been carefully vetted during the selection process. Counsel should review it again carefully before it is included in the expert report, since any aspect of the expert's background will be fertile territory for cross-examination by opposing counsel. Indeed, one approach to discrediting an expert is to highlight weaknesses in his or her background, or occasions on which the expert took a somewhat different approach to the issue as compared to the approach taken in the expert report.

(3) Expert's Independence and Objectivity

The IBA Rules provide that the expert should disclose in the expert report "his or her present or past relationship (if any) with any of the Parties." An expert's independence is perhaps the most important determinant of his or her credibility in the eyes of the Tribunal. For this purpose, a mere formal statement of independence is insufficient. In every aspect of the expert's work, including in the expert report, party-appointed experts must maintain their independence and objectivity, and avoid crossing the line from effective expertise to acting as advocates for a party. As Mark Baker has written:

> [...] The expert, while presenting a position that benefits the advocate's client, must be – and come across as – unyieldingly scrupulous and trustworthy. The arbitrators will not be swayed, or

amused, by an expert who clearly has shed his or her professional integrity for a large sum of money.[58]

Some would question whether this is a realistic expectation. Vera Van Houtte has written:

> An expert witness' position is generally described as one holding the middle between that of a witness of fact and that of the parties' counsel.
>
> Although he is expected to be impartial and objective when submitting an expert report, experience has shown that the desired objectivity often fails (hence the expression "hired gun").[59]

Doak Bishop, for his part, recommends that

> [a]n expert, both in his written report and in any oral testimony, should emphasize his independence and credibility. Merely saying it obviously is not enough. The report must show it. The methodology used should show it. The instructions to the expert should also show it. The expert should be able to say and show that the methodology used and the opinions reached would be no different if he were hired by the opposing party.[60] (Emphasis added.)

Thus, for example, the credibility of a quantum expert may be enhanced if she explains in her report that she has carefully considered an element of the damages claimed by the party that has retained her but, contrary to her conclusions for the other elements of the claim, has determined that, although well-founded, this particular element of the claim does not give rise to any significant damages.

---

58 Baker, *supra* note 27 at 394.

59 Vera Van Houtte, "Party-Appointed Experts and Tribunal-Appointed Experts" in *Arbitral Procedure at the Dawn of the New Millennium: Reports of the International Colloquium of CEPANI, October 15, 2004* (Brussels: Bruylant, 2005) 135 at 136.

60 Bishop, *supra* note 23 at 466.

(4) The Substantive Content of the Expert's Opinion

Just as the description of the facts is the core of the fact witness's statement, the expert's opinion is the core of the expert report. After all, the expert's opinion on the specific issue relevant to the dispute is the very reason for which the expert was retained. The objective must be to present the opinion in the most credible and convincing way. It is obviously entirely insufficient for an expert simply to formulate the conclusion that he or she has drawn in the case. No Tribunal will find that an expert's educational and professional background, and formal independence from the retaining party, are sufficient bases for the credibility of that opinion.

No matter how impressive the expert, his or her conclusion must be built up step by step, working through (a) the underlying facts and assumptions, (b) the available methodologies, (c) an explanation for the expert's choice of one or more such methodologies, and (d) the application of the chosen methodology(ies) to the facts and assumptions of the case. In other words, as Doak Bishop has pointed out:

> What is most persuasive about expert reports and testimony is not the opinions themselves; arbitrators will assume the expert would not be sponsored by a party unless his ultimate opinion was helpful to the party's case. What is most persuasive about an expert is twofold: (1) the expert's credibility; and (2) the support for the opinion–the supporting evidence, reasoning[,] and methodology. In working with an expert, the advocate should emphasize these areas.
>
> . . .
>
> The evidence supporting the conclusions should be carefully marshaled to demonstrate that it logically leads to the deductions drawn from it. The reasoning of the expert should be stated step-by-step, again logically leading to the inferences drawn. The methodology should be standard and well accepted for the issues involved. Each of these matters should be detailed in the expert's

report, along with any assumptions employed. The assumptions should also be shown to be standard, whenever possible. [61]

Where more than one expert has authored a single report, it is advisable for the respective experts to identify for which particular parts of the report each is responsible.[62] This allows the Tribunal to match the particular expertise of each expert to the identified subject matter, and thus assists the Tribunal in evaluating the evidence. It also signals to everyone involved in the arbitration how the subject matter will most likely be divided among the multiple expert witnesses for purposes of direct oral testimony and cross-examination.

Proper support for the expert's opinion, convincingly explained, also maximizes the chances that the expert's report will stand up to the opposing expert. In a typical case, each side has reputable experts taking opposite positions on the relevant issues.[63] The Tribunal will therefore evaluate an expert report "not only on its face value, but also in view of the opposing expert testimony, if any."[64]

"Witness conferencing", which consists of the simultaneous joint hearing of expert witnesses (and sometimes fact witnesses), is becoming increasingly prevalent, for the simple reason that it is effective. Experience shows that an expert's testimony is often best tested not by opposing counsel, but by the opposing expert.[65] In witness conferencing, "[t]he debate takes place among informed and specialized witnesses; it is expert knowledge versus expert knowledge

---

[61] *Ibid.*

[62] Art. 5(2)(i) of the revised IBA Rules provides that if the expert report has been signed by more than one person, it should contain "an attribution of the entirety of specific parts of the Expert Report to each author."

[63] This explains why some have defined an expert, only half-jokingly, as "a person who differs in opinion with his colleague." See Sanders, *supra* note 3 at 264, recalling this definition from his days at Leiden Law Faculty.

[64] Van Houtte, *supra* note 56 at 153.

[65] Indeed, as Van Houtte explains: "the competence and impartiality of a party-appointed expert may often be tested only by the other party's expert." See Van Houtte, *supra* note 56 at 150.

and no longer the lawyer's questioning technique versus the witnesses' expert knowledge."[66]

While reviewing an expert's draft report, counsel should therefore keep the opposing expert in mind. This means carefully reviewing any expert report already submitted by the opposing party, and ensuring that the draft report under review addresses any weaknesses or shortcomings in the other side's report in a methodical and scientific way. If the party-appointed experts are submitting simultaneous reports, it means being aware of the positions that the opposing expert is likely to adopt, and ensuring that one's own expert is well positioned for the anticipated confrontation of experts. Similarly, in cases where the Tribunal has appointed its own expert, and the party-appointed experts must therefore convince the Tribunal-appointed expert, counsel must ensure that the party-appointed expert engages the issues in her report in a way that will connect with the approach likely to be taken by the Tribunal-appointed expert (as disclosed, for example, in his earlier writings or by the comments he may have made during an initial meeting with the parties).

In cross-examination, good counsel will rarely choose to go head-to-head with a competent expert in his or her area of expertise. Instead, counsel will exploit weaknesses in the facts and assumptions underpinning the expert's opinion. In reviewing an expert's draft report, counsel should therefore carefully check that the facts stated in the report are aligned with the record (i.e., the fact witness statements and documents being submitted along with the expert report), and that the expert's assumptions are reasonable and properly justified.

Beyond the reasonability of the underlying assumptions, and the consistency of the underlying factual record, it is the clarity of the reasoning of the expert that determines whether or not the Tribunal will accept his opinion. It is thus essential that the Tribunal be able to follow each step in the expert's logic and reasoning. This is particularly challenging when an expert is presenting complex technical evidence. In such cases, "the good advocate should not

---

[66] Hanotiau, "Hearings", *supra* note 15 at 377.

throw the arbitrator into the deep end of the pool without swimming lessons."[67] In the words of Doak Bishop:

> In complex cases, the advocate should define – and even provide a written legend to the arbitrators defining – the technical terms used by the experts. Photographs, diagrams and demonstrative evidence should be used to illustrate technical terms and processes so the Panel can visualize them. Once the arbitrators visualize the concepts, verbal descriptions can be understood and can refine them. But the advocate should provide sufficient background in the experts' reports, pre-hearing memorials, opening statements, and the early moments of the experts' oral testimony, slowly building the arbitrators' knowledge and understanding, before honing in on the disputed points. An alternative approach is to proceed immediately to the disputed points, pausing then to provide background on each technical point sufficient to fully understand it before moving to the next.[68]

The expert opinion is the core element of an expert report, and it is the expert's evidence on that point on which the Tribunal and the opposing expert will focus. It is ineffective and likely to undermine the expert's credibility for him or her to adopt an opinion that he/she cannot sincerely and convincingly defend. Counsel should therefore avoid seeking to twist an expert's opinion so that it responds in all respects to the client's wishes. Instead, as discussed, good counsel should work with the expert to ensure that his or her reasoning is solid, and that the report is written as clearly as possible.

(5) The Special Case of Legal Experts

Special considerations apply to legal experts, where again the different traditions of the civil law and common law are relevant to

---

[67] Doak Bishop, "Advocacy in International Commercial Arbitration: United States" in Doak Bishop, ed., *The Art of Advocacy in International Arbitration* (New York: Juris Publishing, 2004) 309 at 337.

[68] *Ibid.* at 337-338.

understanding how the practice in international arbitration has evolved in this respect. Hanotiau explains as follows:

> Anglo-Saxon practice treats issues of "foreign" law as matters of fact, to be proved by appropriate evidence. It therefore envisages expert testimony. In civil law, "*la Cour sait le droit*": the Court is supposed to know the law. In international arbitration, the Arbitral Tribunal will often include at least one member familiar with the "foreign" applicable law. Many tribunals will therefore instruct the parties to argue their points of law as part of the legal argument. In this context, they will sometimes submit expert legal testimony or affidavits.[69]

Redfern and Hunter echo this practice:

> It takes only a brief moment of reflection to appreciate that the convenient fiction that "foreign law is fact" does not work in the context of an international arbitration.
>
> (...)
>
> In practice, the international arbitration community has solved this dilemma in a pragmatic and efficient way. In the twenty-first century, in almost all international arbitrations, "law" is treated as "law". Each party usually has a duly qualified lawyer, often an academic, from the relevant jurisdiction in its team of counsel. Written expert opinions on disputed issues of the applicable law will be submitted with the memorials (with replies if necessary), and the relevant counsel from each team are ready to answer questions from the tribunal and to make oral submissions by reference to legal authorities from the relevant jurisdiction.[70]

El-Kosheri makes the distinction between three situations in relation to the use of a legal expert in international arbitration. In his view, the decision whether to use a legal expert on a disputed question of law hinges on whether the question is governed by:

---

[69] Hanotiau, "Procedural Traditions," *supra* note 17 at 96.

[70] Redfern *et al.*, *supra* note 16 at 410, paras. 6.170, 6.172.

(a) international law;

(b) the rules of a particular domestic legal system; or

(c) usages of trade, *lex mercatoria*, *lex petrolia*, or another similar code applicable to a specific industry or association.[71]

When dealing with matters of international law, El Kosheri opines that a Tribunal is expected to know the law and therefore parties should not be required to produce expert legal opinions.[72] El Kosheri suggests that a similar situation exists in the third category, as arbitrators hearing international commercial cases are usually familiar with frequently raised issues pertaining to trade usages or particular transactions.

According to El-Kosheri, the position may be different, however, when the rules applicable to an issue in dispute are legislative provisions or established jurisprudence of a given domestic legal system. On certain issues, the applicable rules may differ substantially from one jurisdiction to another, such as in relation to prescription, importing and exporting rules and regulations, the convertibility of local currency, etc. For cases in which such issues are material, El-Kosheri's view is that it may indeed be important to present expert evidence of the applicable rules.

In the authors' experience, there seems to be a trend away from recourse to expert opinion evidence on legal issues in international arbitration in favour of counsel simply arguing the point. This may reflect a realization that too often legal experts called upon to testify become advocates for the party's position and that, accordingly, it is

---

[71] Ahmed S. El-Kosheri, "The Different Types of Experts with Special Emphasis on Legal Experts (Jura Novit Curia)" in Albert Jan Van Den Berg, ed., *International Arbitration 2006: Back to Basics?* (The Netherlands: Kluwer Law International, 2007) 797 at 798.

[72] Prof. James Crawford explains that, in his view, "it is usually unhelpful for expert testimony to be produced on the very questions of international law which an international tribunal has to decide". See James Crawford, "Advocacy Before the International Court of Justice and Other International Tribunals in State-to-State Cases" in Doak Bishop, ed., *The Art of Advocacy in International Arbitration* (New York: Juris Publishing, 2004) 11 at 32.

best for them to address the Tribunal as part of the party's counsel team, rather than as expert witnesses. There are cases, however, where expert opinion evidence on legal issues may be helpful to the Tribunal. One example would be when the nature of a legal issue is such that the Tribunal needs to be informed through expert evidence about the very legal framework within which the issue arises. For example, in a dispute arising out of a joint-venture agreement governed by English law, it may be advisable to inform the Tribunal through expert evidence about the tax regime of the host state in which the joint venture has invested, if the issue is the tax treatment of certain expenditures to be borne by the joint venture. In such a case, the members of the Tribunal may draw assistance from evidence about the tax regime of the host state in order to understand the parties' respective positions and be in a position to resolve the issue. This situation assumes that no member of the Tribunal is trained or qualified as a tax lawyer of the host state.

The strategy is far more difficult to establish for an advocate if one of the arbitrators knows the law applicable to the relevant issue. Indeed, it is impossible to simplify the matter into a neat set of guidelines. This was well illustrated by Prof. Gabrielle Kaufmann-Kohler in the luncheon address she delivered at the workshop on arbitral advocacy organized by the ITA in June 2004, entitled "The Arbitrator and the Law: Does He/She Know It? How? And a Few More Questions".[73] On that occasion, Prof. Kaufman-Kohler opined that there existed no well-settled arbitration practice on the issue of whether applicable law is like a fact that needs to be proven, or rather a subject that the arbitrator can or must research him or herself.[74] As a result, arbitrators from different legal traditions or with contrasting experiences from prior cases may have dissimilar assumptions about what elements of the law need to be proven.[75] In light of this, how should counsel approach the issue? Prof. Kaufman-Kohler's reflections on this topic are helpful, and reproduced here in the same

[73] Reproduced in (2005) 21:4 Arb. Int'l 631.

[74] *Ibid.* at 636.

[75] *Ibid.* at 632.

spirit in which they were originally offered, namely in the hope "that they may contribute to better case management and advocacy":[76]

> What about the advocate's perspective? What should his or her strategy be? How does he/she best educate the arbitrator? he answer is typically a lawyer's answer: it all depends. On what does it depend?
>
> Before going into this issue, a threshold question needs to be addressed: should a party appoint an arbitrator who knows the applicable law? Not necessarily.
>
> Other factors may prevail: professionalism, case management skills, experience, availability, knowledge of the trade or the industry. Knowledge of the applicable law may, however, play a more prominent role when outcome turns on a very technical legal issue.
>
> After the appointment, on what considerations does the advocate's strategy depend? Three factors must be taken into account:
>
> - Does the arbitration involve a lot of complex legal issues?
> - Does a member of the tribunal have knowledge of the governing law? If so, who? The Chair? One of the co-arbitrators? The one you have appointed or the other one? If it is the other one, can he or she be expected to give competent and reliable input on the applicable law to the Chair?
> - Do the arbitrators come from legal cultures where the law must be proven, or will they consider that they have control over the law (*iura novit arbiter*), or will they be used to a mixed approach like the one adopted in the procedural rule set forth earlier?
>
> Counsel's choice will then depend on the combination of these factors. My purpose is not to give a cookbook recipe; it would be useless, because it would necessarily be oversimplistic. Let me just highlight a few thoughts:
>
> - First, if there are a number of complex legal issues and the Chair comes from a legal culture where the law must be

[76] *Ibid.* at 638.

proven, it is advisable to file an opinion by a legal expert and, depending on the case, offer his or her oral testimony as well.

- Further, if no one on the Tribunal, or possibly only the co-arbitrators, but not the Chair, have expertise in the applicable law, it will often be advisable to tender legal evidence.
- But one should not file a legal opinion in an arbitration where the Chair comes from a country in which he or she expects to have control over the law and is an authority in the field. For instance, do not submit an opinion to a Swiss contract law professor in which one of his colleagues purports to teach him about how to construe a contract. He may resent being given lessons and be negatively influenced, or simply ignore the opinion. If proof of the law is sometimes insufficient, it can also be overdone. As always, the best rule is to use reasonable judgment.
- By contrast, when the case raises a very technical issue of law which is not settled, it may make sense to produce legal evidence even if the arbitrators know the legal system at issue, provided it is given by someone whose authority they are likely to recognize.
- Moreover, whether you offer legal evidence or not, you should make sure that the arbitrators have easy access to the necessary legal materials, court decisions, excerpts from treatises, cases, together with translations – good translations; legal translation is an art in [and] of itself, which does require attention because it can make a significant difference.
- Finally, whenever you have doubts on the expectations of the arbitrator about proof of the substantive law, it is best to raise them at the initial procedural hearing.[77]

In all cases in which the advocate decides to present evidence of the applicable law through an expert, the legal expert should enlighten the Tribunal on the applicable rules, but avoid expressing

---

[77] *Ibid.* at 636-638.

an opinion on how those rules should apply to the specific facts and circumstances of the case:

> Legal experts are supposed to provide the tribunal with opinions on the legal issues arising in the arbitration. In principle, the legal experts provide general opinions on the issues rather than specific conclusions regarding the specific circumstances of the case.[78]

IV. Conclusion

In the Introduction, we noted that the facts of a case, together with the applicable law, are the ingredients with which counsel must work in pulling together the argument in support of his or her client's position. The facts and the law are the ingredients of any legal recipe, and the outcome of a lawyer's argument will, in the end, depend greatly on those ingredients. In this chapter, we have explored the advocacy that counsel can deploy in the "development" of some of those ingredients, namely the written statements prepared by witnesses of fact and the written reports prepared by expert witnesses. We have noted that such advocacy is most effective when it is "invisible", and merely serves to clarify and amplify the voice of the fact witness or expert witness. A final, overarching point to make is that the "flavours" being advanced in the legal recipe must have a basis in the ingredients. Accordingly, counsel should always keep in mind the broad themes of his or her client's case – the theory of the case being advanced on behalf of that party – and, to the extent possible, seek to ensure that those themes are also reflected in, and advanced by, all witness statements and expert reports.

---

[78] Kap-You (Kevin) Kim & John P. Bang, "Commentary on Using Legal Experts in International Arbitration" in Albert Jan Van Den Berg, ed., *International Arbitration 2006: Back to Basics?* (The Netherlands: Kluwer Law International, 2007) 779 at 784.

Chapter 11

ORGANISATION AND PRESENTATION OF DOCUMENTS TO THE TRIBUNAL[1]

Stephen Jagusch

I. Introduction

The practice of international arbitration would be dull indeed if there existed a single form of effective advocacy. Most cases can be presented effectively and persuasively by entirely difference approaches. Add to this that different arbitrators will be persuaded by different presentations and in relation to different aspects of a single case, and one quickly comprehends why advocates in international arbitration find their work so stimulating. The international element – in particular foreign arbitrators and advocates – creates an environment most unlike routine national court cases. Only rarely do two international arbitrations, even if involving similar facts and law, have the same look and feel. Although advocates share the common goal of doing the best for their client there is no one-size-fits-all to the approach of the advocate at any stage of the arbitration process. There is no uniform method of commencing proceedings, developing and proving arguments, identifying and discharging burdens of proof or organising and presenting documentary, witness and other evidence.[2] At every stage there is tremendous scope for an

---

[1] This chapter represents a substantial development of a presentation by the same title delivered at the October 2007 annual meeting of the IBA in Singapore as part of a session on the Art of Advocacy in International Arbitration. The author acknowledges the assistance in preparing this chapter of Ioanna Thoma, an associate formerly within Allen & Overy's International Arbitration Group.

[2] It is often suggested that common approaches are developing, or should be encouraged to develop. See for example William D. Park's "Arbitration's Protean

impact on the arbitrators and the opposition, and hence tremendous scope for advocacy. The role of the advocate in international arbitration is, therefore, about so much more than what is merely written and said. It is about all aspects of the proceedings. This includes the manner in which counsel organise and present to the arbitrators large quantities of documents – the subject of this chapter.

The broader opportunities and suggestions for effective advocacy are described more fully by the authors of other chapters of this book, as well as by the contributors to its first edition.[3] What any experienced advocate has learned, however, is that most arbitrators, at least in their deliberations, are heavily influenced by the documentary record. Given the near certainty therefore of the key role of the documents, counsel who fail to produce the most effective organisation and presentation of the documents do so at their and their clients' peril.[4] Indeed, so fundamental is the management of the evidence that any failure to make the most of the documents may fairly be described as a failure of advocacy.

The purpose of this chapter is to share reflections on this very important subject – dealing with large quantities of documents. It is useful however to reflect first on the broader role of advocacy and the principles to be borne in mind when approaching any task undertaken by the advocate. Advocacy – the art of persuasion – has at its core the presentation of logical arguments, the arousal of emotions and the character of the advocate.[5] These are the tools with which the advocate fashions his case from the facts and the law.[6]

Nature: The Nature of Rules and the Risks of Discretion", Arbitration International, Volume 19 Number 3.

3 Doak Bishop (ed), The Art of Advocacy in International Arbitration (1st ed Juris Publishing Inc. New York 2004) hereafter "**The Art of Advocacy**".

4 Experienced practitioners are never short of war stories about cases that ought to be won but which were lost through the mismanagement and poor presentation of documents.

5 Respectively the *logos*, *pathos* and *ethos*: see Aristotle, Rhetoric – Book I, Chapter I [1356a] available at: http://www.public.iastate.edu/%7Ehoneyl/Rhetoric/index.html.

6 Doak Bishop, Toward a Harmonised Approach to Advocacy in International Arbitration, The Art of Advocacy (hereafter "**Bishop**") at 452.

Too frequently, however, counsel consider that advocacy is concerned only with written or oral presentations. This ignores, at the expense of the advocate and his client, that (and especially in international arbitration) advocacy encompasses every decision counsel makes from the moment he takes on the case, including interactions with clients, witnesses and document reviews and organisation, categorisation, evaluation and presentation of the documentary record.[7]

Whilst strong legal and analytical skills are the cornerstones of good advocacy, personality – the 'character' of an advocate – also plays a vital role. It manifests itself in the tone and style of the written submissions as well as how the advocate seeks to breathe life into the file at the hearing through their oral submissions, questioning of witnesses and their interaction with the arbitrators. This includes how the advocate chooses to present documentary evidence. The better advocate is the one who understands and plays not only to the strengths of their case, but to the strengths of their personality and what they anticipate to be the preferences of the particular arbitrators. Very few arbitrators survive entire proceedings without being influenced, for better or for worse, by the relationship that develops between them and counsel, and, in document heavy cases, by the tools and tactics deployed by counsel to present and explain the facts and the documentary record.

So how, then, does the advocate deal with these challenges when faced with large quantities of documents? The somewhat clichéd expressed that effective advocacy is that which maximises the chances of winning a case,[8] whilst true, provides no practical guidance. As this chapter seeks to explore, there are numerous opportunities to make a good (or bad) impression on the arbitrators and what may improve your chances of winning before the

---

[7] Donald Francis Donovan, Introduction to the Fifteenth Annual International Commercial Arbitration Workshop: Arbitral Advocacy, 22 Arbitration International (2005) at 537.

[8] Judge Charles Brower, Act IV - Oral Advocacy, 21 Arbitration International (2005) at 629.

arbitrators in one case may not do so, or may not be available or affordable, in another.

II. Large Quantities of Documents – A Contemporary Problem

The first role of the advocate is to master the facts, which cannot be accomplished without mastering the evidence. Few would deny that good advocacy, after all, depends on good preparation.[9] A challenge for advocates in international arbitration is that an increasing number of cases are very complex: as well as substantive issues (of which there may be many claims, defences, counterclaims, set-offs) and related disputes in multiple jurisdictions, there may also be preliminary issues concerning for example jurisdiction of the arbitrators or the admissibility of claims or evidence. The documentary evidence alone may be tendered in a variety of languages and in paper and a variety of electronic forms. So how does one go about organising, analysing and presenting such material? It is rare that arbitrators get involved in this aspect of any proceeding, it being a matter considered the domain of the advocates.[10] Institutions and rules do not tend to deal with the management of evidence. Even in arbitrations administered by dispute resolution bodies of international organisations such as the ICJ, PCA, or ITLOS, or claims commissions such as the UNCC, CRT-DA and GFLCP where the role of counsel is more limited due to the increased role of the staff of the tribunal,[11] document management remains the core of counsel's organisation and presentation of the case.[12]

---

[9] Michael Hyam, Advocacy Skills (Blackstone Press Limited London 1990) at 10.

[10] That said, there is much to be said for the tribunal intervening early in document heavy cases to ensure that all appropriate steps are being taken to minimise the time, cost and environmental impact of counsels' presentations.

[11] James Loftis, Advocacy of Private Disputes Before International Claims Resolution Bodies, The Art of Advocacy at 47-48.

[12] The burden of substantial documents does not rest with how best to organise and present them. Other challenges arise from counsel's duty to act with

This challenge in relation to documents – which arises even in arbitrations involving straightforward issues or where the amounts at stake are modest – is exacerbated by the growing number of types or categories of documents which are produced in international arbitration proceedings. This has led to criticism both by parties, principally on account of the additional costs involved, and arbitrators, who complain of being swamped with documents[13]. Disputes even of the narrowest issues can produce large quantities of documents, for example copies of emails (and their attachments) sent and received not only on servers but also on handheld devices (such as Blackberries), and stored elsewhere such as on laptop hard drives, CDs, DVDs and 'memory sticks' (most commonly USB drives). Even devices more typically used for storing music, photographs and videos can be and frequently are used for storing documents and other communications.

The ease alone of making electronic communications has led to its proliferation and hence the population of potentially relevant or material documents. Messages are often sent on the spur of the moment simply because it is possible to do so. Communications are made that in the days of letters and faxes people would never have bothered with. Moreover, multiple addressees, 'blind copies' and forwarding can be achieved at the touch of a button or two – a temptation which many find too great to resist, even in respect of the most pointless of communications. As if that were not enough, today the use of 'distribution lists' and auto-forwarding or copying often to

---

scrupulous care and diligence (see the 1988 edition of the International Code of Ethics of the International Bar Association providing that: "*[l]awyers shall at all times give clients a candid opinion on any case. They shall render assistance with scrupulous care and diligence*") thus, arguably, requiring counsel also to consider the authenticity and provenance of documents produced. This could present a substantial burden in document heavy cases: see also Marvin Hill, Anthony Sinicropi and Amy Evenson, Winning Arbitration Advocacy (Bureau of National Affairs Washington DC 1997) at 221, 228.

[13] Yves Derains, Towards Greater Efficiency in Document Production Before Arbitral Tribunals – A Continental Viewpoint, in: ICC Bulletin – Document Production in International Arbitration (ICC 2006 Special Supplement) (hereinafter "**ICC 2006 Special Supplement**") at 85.

large numbers of recipients is commonplace. Moreover many organisations store – and some even automatically convert into emails – the voice messages left on telephones.

Add to this that each recipient of an electronic communication comes into possession of a separate 'document' for disclosure purposes, which then frequently develops a life of its own as it too gets processed through the multiple reproductions described above, often with comments or annotations which themselves take on the character of 'new documents'. The treatment or *mere existence* of an electronic communication without comment or annotation can itself be relevant or material evidence, for example concerning the fact or timing of receipt. In some cases a *failure* to comment, forward, file or annotate can also be relevant or material, for example where it might indicate acceptance or indifference to the subject matter of the communication.

Until relatively recently little thought was given to the consequences of the frequently vast trails of records of communications and documents, especially those that begin their lives as seemingly innocuous messages. However the growing acceptance in international arbitration that documents for the purposes of disclosure includes electronic data[14] establishes the need for counsel to identify these trails in order properly to analyse the facts, to provide advice, to ascertain what documents ought to be sought and from whom and what documents may need to be produced to the arbitrators and the opposition.

Another cause for the proliferation of cases involving large numbers of documents is what some describe, with varying degrees of accuracy, as the *Americanisation* of international arbitration. By this description it is suggested that US-style extensive discovery is creeping

---

[14] See for example the definition of 'document' for the purposes of the IBA Rules on the Taking of Evidence in International Commercial Arbitration:

> *"Document" means a writing of any kind, whether or not recorded on paper, electronic means, audio or visual recordings or any other mechanical or electronic means of storing or recording information.*

into international arbitration.[15] Whether or not that is occurring, it is nevertheless clear – and noted generally with disdain by civil lawyers – that disclosure has become customary in international arbitration and that it involves broadly the steps envisaged by the IBA Rules for the Taking of Evidence in International Commercial Arbitration (the "**IBA Rules**").[16] The IBA Rules provide that parties are entitled to seek documents (including electronic records) in their opponent's possession, custody or control which are specifically identified and which are relevant and material to the outcome of the case.[17] The trend in contemporary international arbitration is to permit disclosure within the confines of the IBA Rules.[18]

For these various reasons, having to manage vast quantities of documents has become a contemporary reality of international arbitration. The process is both time consuming and expensive. That alone is good reason to be wary of permitting disclosure to become disproportionate to the issues and amounts at stake, but that may not be consistent with the parties' respective strategies in any given case. A more powerful argument against wide ranging disclosure is that not all documents produced by the parties end up relevant and helping the arbitrators to decide the case. In the majority of cases only a small fraction of the documents produced become relevant in the deliberations. This problem is contributed to not only by overzealous

---

[15] Whilst some argue that the IBA Rules on the Taking of Evidence in International Commercial Arbitration are a move in that direction, in the better view is that such rules in fact seek to limit permissible the categories of permissible disclosure requests. (It is often overlooked that only one of the 16 members of the Working Party that produced the rules practised in the USA.)

[16] Presently subject to revision but not in any manner that is expected significantly to limit their scope or application.

[17] Relevance is a broader concept compared to materiality. Relevance pertains to the case generally while materiality pertains to specific propositions to be established. In that sense 'relevance' is somewhat redundant as anything 'material' will by definition be relevant.

[18] Sometimes, however, counsel and arbitrators may prefer the application of the rules of the jurisdiction where they usually practise, or at the seat of the arbitration, either because of lack of sufficient experience and exposure to international arbitration practice or for strategic reasons.

requests for production, but also by the thoughtless (though sometimes strategic) flooding of the proceedings with knowingly irrelevant documents[19] in order to conceal or obscure harmful issues or evidence.[20] But whatever the reason for a substantial documentary record, advocates must recognise this phenomenon and ensure that their approach to the documents sufficiently separates the wheat from the chaff.

Just as with other aspects of the advocate's role, including the organisation and presentation of written and oral presentations, there is no recognised best practice for the organisation and presentation of large quantities of documents. There are no rules or guidelines on how documents should be managed. It will depend on the nature of the case, the party in question (and its objectives) and the view taken on what is most likely to impress the arbitrators. The following observations reflect the author's view of best practice. The approach taken is to separate organisation from presentation. The very foundations for any slick presentation of documents is that they have first been understood, which requires in turn that they have been logically and sensible organised.

III. How to Organise Large Quantities of Documents

Document identification and review is not required only in order to develop targeted requests for documents from the opposition,[21] or to enable proper responses to requests or orders to produce. It should form part of counsel's own investigation into the facts. But *how* it is done is up to counsel. And how it is done in the days and

---

19 Horacio Grigera Naon, Document Production in International Commercial Arbitration: a Latin American Perspective, ICC 2006 Special Supplement at 15.

20 Whilst there is an argument that counsel who succeed in hiding or diverting attention from weakness through unnecessary disclosure have demonstrated effective advocacy, counsel must be careful to respect their ethical obligation to respect and contribute to the integrity of the process including by not taking positions known to be false by virtue of secreted documents: Bishop at 474.

21 Nicholas Fletcher, The Use of Technology in the Production of Documents, ICC 2006 Special Supplement (hereafter "**Fletcher**") at 101.

weeks after initial instruction may well be different from how it is done as the case develops and the facts and issues evolve or become clearer. In this respect, counsel should be open to occasional reorganisation of the documents during the lifetime of the proceedings with a view to having prepared, well in advance of the hearing, an organisation that will facilitate the most effective presentation to the arbitrators. The organisation of documents required to enable a full understanding of the complete matrix of facts and to enable the giving of advice thereon will usually be quite different to the organisation required to present specific facts and issues to the arbitrators.

Considerations such as the parties' respective burdens of proof and the production regime negotiated with the opposition or mandated by the arbitrators[22] will often influence how documents are organised. As will the manner in which the client has organised the papers (if at all) and the timing of the client's delivery of all or parts of record to counsel. The development of the issues during the lifetime of the proceedings will also have a role to play. But few would deny that an effective identification and organisation of voluminous documents – the arrangement counsel seek ultimately to achieve - is one that fits the facts together in a reasonable story, does not overlook or leave issues unconsidered and is supported by a user-friendly index.[23] The key documents should be able to be identified with ease, whether by subject or chronologically, and documents should be cross referenced to related documents and issues and if necessary the fact or expert witnesses. This is where there is tremendous room for creativity. Counsel must create clarity our of what will often, at the outset, be chaos. There should be something *obvious* about the organisation achieved. If a disinterested observer cannot see immediately the sense in the organisation proposed, start again.

In the early stages, prudent counsel should first put in place – and maintain – a chronological file of the relevant documents. This is the

---

[22] Horacio Grigera Naon, Document Production in International Commercial Arbitration at 18.

[23] Bishop, The Art of Advocacy at 442-446.

best way to ensure that the story of the case is understood in its proper context. It also enables counsel to understand and analyse how the facts and issues fit together as a whole. But when the chronological bundle becomes unwieldy, it is useful to consider ways of organising the evidence that can be accomplished in parallel with the chronological bundle. The most basic of approaches, by which is meant the *minimum* expected of competent counsel, is to organise the documents into bundles in a manner that best suits the approach being taken to the issues. In most cases, a chronological approach is the best starting point, though in certain situations documents are best organised thematically or by witness (and chronologically within each category).[24] However it is achieved, the documents need to be sorted out in a way that is easy for counsel to find quickly, retrieve and review the document he wishes to refer to.[25] Organising dozens of categories of documents in this particular fashion is no great challenge, though it is time-consuming. The inevitable consequence to most clients is cost.[26] Maintenance of the bundles is also vital – they must be organised in away that permits new or replacement documents to be added, as invariably happens frequently throughout the life of arbitral proceedings. If parallel bundles are in use (themes, witnesses etc) these too will require simultaneous updating. In most cases there will be more than one set of bundles in use which will also require updating; usually one for counsel and perhaps another one or two for members of his or her team, one or two for the in-house and commercial client teams, one or more for any key fact witnesses and one or more for the experts. The most efficient teams are those who all have access to the same material at the same time. This requires considerable efficiency, and effort.

A key decision which ought to be made early is whether to deploy information technology to assist in the organisation of the

---

[24] Bishop at 474.

[25] Michael Hyam, Advocacy Skills at 14.

[26] Understandably, few clients appreciate paying the high hourly rates of even the most junior office employees to conduct this basic document-sorting work. Many clients now seek to in-source such work.

documents. All cases involving large quantities of documents demand that serious consideration be given to computer-based assistance, and most will demand its implementation.

The non-IT, paper based approach to bundles is fraught with problems. The creation, indexing, management and updating alone of paper bundles is enormously time consuming, to say nothing of the analysis of the and interrogation of the bundles once prepared. Mastering the contents of paper bundles is subject to the many utility-limiting foibles of our species – concentration, sight, memory and intelligence among them. Post-it notes and highlighters are useful in their own right, but of extremely limited value when trying to come to terms with multiple issues within a substantial volume of paper. The reading alone of substantial volumes can take days or weeks. Moreover, the developing bundle will require multiple re-reads: when first read the issues of importance to counsel are likely to be quite different from the issues as they develop in the proceedings. The problems with paper bundles are in deed numerous. The routine reorganisation of or removal from or addition to paper bundles, even ignoring the issues with multiple copies of the bundle, can itself create significant indexing, tabbing or page numbering issues.[27]

As if any more need to be said against traditional paper bundles, it should not be forgotten that they are susceptible to wear, destruction and loss, they are heavy and can take up considerable space and they are very expensive to ship around the world – to the many global destinations (and back) where arbitrators and counsel and clients and witnesses and experts reside, and that serve as arbitration venues.

At the other end of the spectrum are highly sophisticated electronic storage, analytical and retrieval systems. Many large law

---

[27] One is also increasingly sensitive these days to the environmental impact caused by the creation of large numbers of folders of documents, from which other copies are routinely created for other counsel team members, client representatives, witnesses, opponents and the arbitrators. All of this takes time and is expensive and generates, often wholly needlessly, substantial volumes of paper.

firms now offer these systems as part of their IT infrastructure and companies which specialise in the organisation and presentation of large quantities of documents are cropping up in most jurisdictions. These systems, whilst also expensive (though becoming cheaper), offer numerous very useful benefits. For example, electronically stored documents can, at the push of a button, be ordered and indexed in an almost limitless variety of ways: chronologically, thematically, by sender or recipient or even by reference to their containing particular words or phrases. Special software enables the classification of documents by inputting relevant parameters or keywords in a database, producing summaries and creating sub-classifications where desirable.[28] When accompanied by appropriate software, individual documents amongst collections of many thousands can be accessed on one or more computer screens, or printed out, in seconds. Whilst on screen they can be annotated, highlighted, enlarged, and electronically 'linked' to other documents, or 'allocated' to particular issues or witnesses or paragraphs in pleadings or witness statements. Copies can be stored on highly portable devices such as CDs or DVDs or USB/memory sticks and can be sent electronically and simultaneously across the globe to multiple recipients in moments, thereby saving time and reducing the cost of printing and transporting substantial quantities of paper.

Another significant advantage of electronic document organisation – especially the highly sophisticated systems available today – is that 'de-duplication' can be performed at great speed and at little cost. This is a process whereby documents which are mere duplicates of other documents (created by the many duplicating effects of the electronic communications systems described above) can be identified and removed from the bundles, thus in many cases reducing substantially the number of documents requiring individual, human analysis.

The organisation of documents electronically also aids the sharing and combining of bundles and hence the preparation and

[28] Fletcher at 102-104.

organisation of core and hearing bundles.[29] This offers counsel the possibility to create joint exhibits accompanied by explanations on who prepared the exhibit and why it has become part of the evidence submitted.[30] Most contemporary systems also enable secure, controlled access over intranets or the internet, and for use on computers of all types, and hence fully accessible and portable to all who require it: multiple members of the external, in-house and commercial client teams, fact witnesses, experts and arbitrators.

Perhaps the greatest benefit for counsel of sophisticated electronic document systems is the speed with which ideas, memories and arguments can be tested against the factual record. This greatly aids the preparation of submissions, witness statements and cross-examination. During the hearing itself, such systems can be worth their weight in gold – especially when dealing with unexpected issues, questions from the arbitrators or answers from witnesses under cross-examination. The ability to check submissions and answers and evidence against an electronic record inevitably produces 'safer' advocacy, in that counsel has an added degree of confidence in their presentation. Confidence is, after all, necessary for effective advocacy and is best demonstrated to the arbitrators by a complete mastery of the facts, law and issues of the case. This confidence creates, in the eyes of the arbitrators, an impression that helps to build and maintain the credibility of the advocate – a vital ingredient in the process of persuasion.

For all that can be said for electronic systems, they are not flawless and are by no means the only prudent option. Documents do not transport *themselves* onto electronic management systems, and even electronic 'originals' do not always synchronise with their new electronic home. In many cases, electronic originals will need to be converted, or printed then freshly scanned, either way involving considerable time and expense. This data entry process is susceptible

---

[29] Although some electronic document storage systems have particular software that does not communicate well with others, there is a growing convergence of technology which enables the various forms of storage to be recognised and understood by other systems.

[30] Marvin Hill, Anthony Sinicropi and Amy Evenson, Winning Arbitration Advocacy at 126.

to that old adage "garbage in, garbage out", a problem that is magnified when the process of transferring documents and content that is transferred is left to humans.[31] In order for any electronic system to be effective, it must receive the documents in a manner that enables vital information to be read electronically, otherwise such information must be entered manually. Where documents require manual data entry, the data that is required to enable the system to deliver to its potential is considerable – dates, type (letter, fax, email, memo, contract, other), sender, recipient, subject, content etc. Any failure at the data input level can cause inaccuracy and instability across the entire database. If crucial documents (or the information contained within them) are incorrectly entered into the database then key information may be missed from the electronic searches of the database. When counsel is let down by the system, the whole technological endeavour will have failed and the advocate can end up *losing* credibility. Further, despite the technological development of most document management systems, it is still the case that not all documents are readable by all software programmes with the result that traditional search and production of paper documents may nevertheless become necessary.[32] In other words, whilst electronic systems for organising large quantities of documents have much to be said for them, they are not foolproof and great care must still be taken in the early stages of the transfer of information onto the relevant databases and in their maintenance.[33]

For the most part, the circumstances of the case will dictate how the documents are best organised. Where large quantities are concerned, in most cases it will be a false economy to seek to save the costs of electronic storage and management. It will also be a false economy to limit the bundle to one chronological set as it will be too

---

[31] Especially if those chosen to perform the task are not heavily involved in the case or are relatively unskilled (and hence cheaper that counsel) as often occurs when mundane work like data entry is delegated or outsourced to juniors.

[32] Fletcher at 103.

[33] And back-up. All electronic storage systems are vulnerable to loss due to the failings of harmful interference of software, hardware, power supply and the like. Routine and comprehensive back-up is essential.

cumbersome for the efficient management of discrete issues. As the case develops, and with the aid of electronic storage, counsel should develop mini-bundles of documents pertaining to specific issues in the case, highly relevant or controversial periods in time, the personal knowledge or involvement of key witnesses and so forth. This approach to the organisation of the documents enables counsel, when presented simultaneously with the entire chronology and the mini bundles to dip from one onto another with relevant ease. It also facilitates the delegation of specific tasks to counsel's support team, such as the preparation of particular witnesses or the analysis of specific periods of time. Finally, with hands-on clients, electronic and subject or date specific categorisation of documents enables their demands to be met more quickly and efficiently.

Having carefully arranged the documents enable the most efficient use and analysis of them, and having built the case around those documents, the next challenge to the advocate faced with large quantities of documents is how to present them to the arbitrators.

IV. How to Present Large Quantities of Documents

It is one thing to organise documents for one's own use. It is another to present them to the arbitrators. Once the advocate has established his or her theory of the case and pleaded the facts and law thought best to win the case, attention must turn to proof. In this respect the effective presentation of the documents is one that proves or disproves the relevant facts or arguments. Here, what works for one arbitrator may not work for another – the challenge for the advocate is to find the presentation (timing, substance, choice of media) that most likely appeal to the arbitrators. The experienced advocate will be all too aware that he or she gets no second chance to make a first impression.

Although there are few rules in this area, certain approaches will be expected by most arbitrators and if not respected may well incur their wrath. The documents presented to the arbitrators should be divided into those which substantiate the facts (i.e. the evidence), those establishing the law and those containing the pleadings and witness evidence. Beyond that, and as with the organisation of large quantities of documents, the panoply of options for presenting them extends from the rudimentary to the highly sophisticated. As one might expect, in most properly handled cases there is a positive correlation between sophistication, efficiency and ease of presentation. However, sophistication comes at a cost, and a very substantial cost for the high-end technology, and this cost often rules it out of contention for modest claims. However, as is the trend generally with new technology, the cost is steadily falling. Further, the pressure of competition from specialist providers of these services is also forcing the cost downwards. However, it still remains the case that, except for claims involving at least several hundred thousands of dollars, the current cost of high-end presentational hardware and software is considered by many clients to be disproportionately high.

Another great advantage of electronic systems is the greater flexibility that they afford to counsel in the presentation of their case. In traditional paper-based document systems, when a few documents are unexpectedly required to illustrate a certain point, there are few things more infuriating to counsel than being unable to find them, and few things are *less* persuasive to the arbitrators than the sight of (and the delays created by) counsel faffing about amidst numerous bundles desperately looking for that elusive document – and more so if it is thought to relate to a point of marginal relevance. Because of this, when as frequently happens a nice point occurs to counsel dealing with traditional paper-based bundles, the moment will pass, often because the articulation and presentation of the point would involve work and effort out of proportion to the weight of the point sought to be made. These frustrations can be substantially avoided, if not completely eliminated, when the documents are electronically indexed and organised in a sensible fashion with well-designed software and the use of suitable viewing screens. In other words, the assistance offered by electronic systems enhances presentations and, thus, improves advocacy.

It is also difficult to deny the presentational benefits of large screens and software which enable documents to be displayed quickly and enlarged, or key words or extracts to be highlighted, or two or more documents or extracts to be placed side-by-side on a screen for comparison purposes. Documents submitted by both sides can be searched and grouped very quickly, in order to create clusters of documents relevant for different aspects of the case during the course of the proceedings. Large visual presentations can also be enormously useful to advocates when trying to explain complicated processes, interactions, sites or equipment. It is undoubtedly true that a picture can speak a thousand words. In international arbitration where time tends to be precious and submissions necessarily brief, the power and persuasiveness of visual presentations is often overlooked by advocates. Technology boosts counsel's confidence and contributes to the completeness, simplicity and succinctness of his presentation. It can also help to win the panel's first impressions about which party's case is best supported by the documentary record.

Recalling that presentation is at the heart of all advocacy, it follows that key to any good presentation, let alone the presentation of considerable amounts of evidence, is clarity, efficiency, timeliness and confidence without overstatement.[34] When the advocate is able to bring documentary record to life through speedy and clear projection onto large screens, and navigate the arbitrators through documents but otherwise 'let the documents do the talking', many of these objectives will be satisfied.

Another benefit to electronically enhanced visual displays is that arbitrators, as with all human beings, have limits to their patience and concentration.[35] These limits are arrived at much sooner when surrounded by copious quantities of paper. Any technological tools that can facilitate the processing and combination of multiple pieces of information and enhance the general impression that documentary evidence constitutes a reliable and trustworthy source of evidence[36] that supports the advocate's case, should be grabbed by the advocate with both hands.

---

[34] Sir David Napley, The Technique of Persuasion at 93.

[35] Bishop at 471.

[36] Philipp Habegger, Document Production – An Overview of Swiss Court and Arbitration Practice, ICC 2006 Special Supplement at 22.

The use of electronic aids to locate and present evidence will not in and of itself turn a poor presentation into a good one. The *method* of presentation is key. The mere projection of a long series of documents will soon have the undesired effect of *losing* the arbitrators' attention. In selecting the best method of presentation, it is useful to remember that advocacy is not mere unilateral persuasion[37] It is also about presentation of the case in a useful and workable manner.[38] A successful advocate must keep a lively tone and provide a road map that he or she will follow during the presentation of the case.[39] This must be integrated within the presentation of the documents.

A related consideration is that the advocate most likely to engage the arbitrators fully is the one who respects the principles of primacy and recency.[40] Arbitrators tend to remember best the things they read and hear first and last. But other than to bear that concern in mind, there is no favoured order in which large volumes of documents are usually presented in international arbitrations. In some cases it may make sense to present the documents in chronological order[41] – but usually only when the advocates best points lie in the *sequence* of events. When the case involves discrete issues there is much to be said for the advocate taking each in turn, treating each as a chapter of the presentation. On occasion the advocate will be best served by presenting the documents in the order they are referred to in the pleadings. This assumes that the pleadings – the written advocacy – tell the story as the advocate would prefer to present the case orally. For the most part, however, arbitrators will have read the papers and will be less stimulated by oral presentations that merely track the recently read submissions.

---

[37] James Crawford, Advocacy Before the International Court of Justice and Other International Tribunals in State-to-State Cases (hereafter "**Crawford**", in The Art of Advocacy at 35.

[38] *Ibid.*

[39] Marvin Hill, Anthony Sinicropi and Amy Evenson, Winning Arbitration Advocacy at 112.

[40] John Cooley and Steven Lubet, Arbitration Advocacy at 132.

[41] Crawford at 35.

The Roman rhetors might have dealt with far simpler and less sophisticated cases than we do these days. However, Quintilian's maxim is still very relevant: an advocate's aim is not to put an arbitrator *in a position* to understand the advocate's argument but to counsel him to meet it.[42] Persuasion goes well beyond laying all the facts and law before the arbitrators and stepping back to let them decide.[43] Good advocates assist the arbitrators in navigating the case whilst trying at the same time to convince them that his client is right. This involves taking a view on what is most likely to persuade the arbitrators in question. It might seem that the move to providing arbitrators with the wherewithal to study the record electronically makes common sense, but be careful with these assumptions. Though not something one will likely heard or spoken of in years to come, there are still arbitrators who do not own laptops and who cannot tolerate non-paper bundles or presentations. Even within the realm of paper presentations, a small but move away from large A4 lever arch folders to the far more efficient double-sided, spiral–bound A5 folders is frequently rejected by some arbitrators.[44] This has been due not only to poor sight but also to the discomfort caused by change *per se*. By contrast, there are arbitrators who *ask* for documents, and in word-searchable form, to be presented on CDs, DVDs and USB/memory sticks, and who can be observed in the hearings checking through the documents in their own laptops. Plainly some degree of knowledge of arbitrator preferences is important. However simple or elaborate the presentation, if it does not appeal to the arbitrators in question then the advocate has failed themselves and their client.

---

42 Institutio Oratoria, Book VIII 2 at 24.

43 Doak Bishop, James Crawford and Michael Reisman, Foreign Investment Disputes – Cases, Materials and Commentary (Kluwer Law International The Hague 2005) at 1392.

44 Many advocates and arbitrators far prefer working with these more condensed and by far more portable bundles. Two of these folders – four times the amount of information - have the same weight and consume the same space as a single A4 folder.

V. Conclusion

Advocacy is the means by which an advocate discharges his duty to promote and protect his client's interests. On the one hand, counsel follows his client's instructions but on the other, he is free to conduct advocacy as he deems proper. As a general rule, codes of conduct of solicitors and barristers lay down general rules which determine the exercise of personal judgment upon the substance and purpose of the case a counsel is handling.[45] In other words, counsel has to provide competent representation which involves legal knowledge, skills, thoroughness and preparation reasonably necessary depending on the complexity of the case.[46] This establishes a duty to consider and establish, in cases involving large quantities of documents, appropriate means of organising, analysing and presenting that material.

No case requires a decision between either a rudimentary or highly sophisticated document management and presentation system. Sensible counsel will give close and serious consideration at the outset of each case to the likely numbers and types of documents that will be involved, and how they may wish to organise and present the documents, so that they can begin working with their opponents and the arbitrators at an early stage to fashion a system that best suits the case in question. In the vast majority of cases this will involve some sort of hybrid system that seeks to take the benefits, without the costs and other drawbacks, of the two extreme approaches.

Whilst in some cases funding alone will limit the parties' options, there are other variables to consider. One is the clients' and arbitrators' levels of sophistication and openness to technology. Some clients and arbitrators still view electronic processes with some scepticism; some, even, with disdain. The reasons are not always technophobia. Some people prefer working with paper; documents

---

45 Avrom Sherr, Legal Practice Handbook – Advocacy (Blackstone Press Limited London 1993) at 15.

46 John Cooley and Steven Lubet, Arbitration Advocacy (Notre Dame Ind. National Institute for Trial Advocacy 2003) at 41.

they can hold, scribble upon, remove and store in a special file containing what they consider to be core documents. For some, the need to use highlighters and post-it notes far outweighs the drawbacks of dealing with many bulky files. Particularly in the case of older arbitrators, the transformation from the review and analysis of paper documents to pixels on a screen is too visually and mentally demanding. The degree of client sophistication can also play a role. It is often a lost cause requesting clients to commit to the substantial investment in technology when they are unlikely to enjoy its benefits for themselves. And for arbitrators who do not know their email address from their elbow, the investment is also likely to be wasted.

Chapter 12

ADVOCACY BEFORE INTERNATIONAL TRIBUNALS IN STATE-TO-STATE CASES

James Crawford*

I. Introduction

Advocacy is the art of persuasion on behalf of a person or cause.[1] Forensic advocacy is that art or skill performed in the context of legal proceedings. In this chapter I deal exclusively with advocacy in international litigation, that is to say, in proceedings before an international court or arbitral tribunal which is distinct from any specific national legal system. Of course this covers a considerable range of possibilities – from the International Court of Justice to *ad hoc* tribunals; from inter-state arbitral tribunals to mixed tribunals of various kinds dealing with cases between individuals and states – even, on a certain view, to International Chamber of Commerce arbitration which is disconnected from any particular place where the parties worked and the dispute arose and is thus in some sense internationalized.[2] Given this wide range of possibilities, the level of distinctness or autonomy from national court systems will vary from

---

* James Crawford is a Whewell Professor of International Law, University of Cambridge. He was a member of the International Law Commission (1992-2001) and Special Rapporteur on State Responsibility. Professor Crawford is a member of the Australian and English bars and has an extensive practice before international courts and tribunals and as an arbitrator. The author wishes to thank Mr. Simon Olleson of Trinity College, Cambridge for his assistance with this chapter.

[1] Cf. SOED, vol. 1, "'advocacy'… the function of an advocate"; "'advocate'… A person who pleads, intercedes or speaks for another…"

[2] For a general review of the present situation see R Sands, R Mackenzie & Y Shany (eds), *Manual on International Courts and Tribunals* (Butterworths, London, 1999).

complete autonomy to relative subordination. Nonetheless, one aspect of each of these tribunals – in terms of advocacy, a key aspect – is that the people who appear to argue are not usually qualified or educated within any single legal system or tradition, nor are they subject to any common set of professional standards. The same is true for those who sit on these tribunals to decide. Lacking a single set of professional standards and rules and a more or less common legal grounding, these people must nonetheless interact, function and eventually reach agreement on what is to be said and decided, and must do so at an acceptable level. It is worth reflecting on some of the issues raised by this situation.

Before doing so, certain clarifications are called for, and some limitations upon the scope of the following discussion. First, in discussing "advocacy" in international litigation, it is impossible to limit oneself to oral argument in the way that common law works on advocacy tend to do.[3] When international litigation first began to take its modern form in the late nineteenth century, the question was whether the emphasis would be on oral or written argument and presentation of evidence. The first standing code of arbitral rules, associated with the creation of the Permanent Court of Arbitration in 1899, called for both a written and an oral phase, termed "preliminary examination" and "discussion".[4] The language may have been anachronistic but the combination of full written and oral phases set a pattern that has been largely followed since. International pleadings characteristically consist of two or three substantial rounds of written pleadings, with documentary appendices attached to each, followed by an oral phase which consists – to use the words of the 1907

---

[3] See, e.g., R DuCann, *The Art of the Advocate* (Penguin, 1964 (repr. 1993)); D Pannick, *Advocates* (Oxford, 1992).

[4] Convention [No. I] Regarding the Pacific Settlement of International Disputes, the Hague, 29 July 1899, 187 *C.T.S.* 410, 32 Stat. 1779, Art. 39. In the 1907 Hague Convention for the Pacific Settlement of Disputes, 18 October 1907, 205 C.T.S. 233, 36 Stat. 2199), the terms used were "pleadings" and "oral discussions" (see Art. 63). For the two Hague Conferences and their attempt to institutionalize international arbitration see DD Caron, "War and International Adjudication: Reflections on the 1899 Peace Conference" (2000) 94 *AJIL* 4.

Hague Convention – "in the oral development before the Tribunal of the arguments of the parties". Since new evidence (not otherwise in the public domain) is generally inadmissible after the close of written pleadings, the notion of "development" generally takes the form of recapitulation, emphasis and argument in the alternative. Indeed one might describe oral argument, at least before the International Court of Justice, as the continuation of written argument by other means.[5] Other tribunals may be somewhat more interactive, but internationally the free interchange of argument, question and analysis between bench and bar, based on a grasp of the dossier rather than a prepared text, is rather unusual.

Thus rather than talking about international advocacy in the sense of some national legal traditions, it is necessary to consider more generally the preparation and presentation of cases, that process being essentially a team effort and including the contribution of government lawyers and officials, external counsel (increasingly including members of law firms) and experts in other disciplines as required.[6]

Secondly, in order to make what follows manageable in scope, I propose to focus primarily on state-to-state litigation before judicial bodies (standing courts or *ad hoc* tribunals), and not to deal with the broader range of mixed cases between private parties and states.[7] It is true that in many respects mixed proceedings, at least before public

---

5 Cf. Clausewitz, *On War* (1832-4) Bk. 8, ch. 6.

6 On the preparation and presentation of cases at the international level see the symposium on "Problems in the Presentation of a Case" in C Peck and R Lee (eds.), *Increasing the Effectiveness of the International Court of Justice* (Kluwer, The Hague, 1997) 126-164; DW Bowett, "The Conduct of International Litigation" in DW Bowett & others, *The International Court of Justice: Process, Practice and Procedure* (British Institute of International and Comparative Law, 1997) 1-20; D Bethlehem, "Submissions on Points of Fact and Law: Written and Oral Pleadings Before the International Court of Justice" in F Weiss (ed.), *Improving WTO Dispute Settlement Procedures: Issues & Lessons from the Practice of Other International Courts & Tribunals* (Cameron May, London, 2000).

7 Still less is it possible to deal with the renewal after 50 years of international criminal trial advocacy. This appears to be based much more on oral evidence and argument, but its practice before the *ad hoc* tribunals would require a separate study.

international tribunals such as the Iran-United States Claims Tribunal or ICSID tribunals, are conducted on broadly the same lines as interstate litigation, and certainly the mixture of written and oral argument is similar. On the other hand, in mixed cases the initiative to litigate invariably – either in law or in practice – lies with the private party, and this makes a difference. Where possible some of the differences will be pointed out, but the focus here will be on interstate litigation.

II. The Pre-Litigation Phase

By contrast with advocacy at the national level, which is an aspect of standard professional training and has generated a quantity of literature, almost nothing has been written on international advocacy, and still less on what we may call the pre-litigation phase, i.e. the period after a dispute has crystallized and before any steps have been taken to bring it to some form of third party settlement. In truth it is this period (varying in duration from a few days to some years) which is so often crucial.

In the first place, there is always an issue of characterization: is the situation recognized by decision-makers as a "dispute" having a "legal" character? By this I do not mean, can an international court presented with the dispute decide it? It is not necessary to enter the well-trampled-on controversy as to whether there can be a *non liquet* in a contentious case at the international level. Whatever theory may say, that is a practically irrelevant issue: no government ever declined to refer a dispute to an international court or tribunal for fear of a *non liquet* – just as no international court or tribunal has so far declined to decide a contentious case referred to it for decision.[8]

---

[8] Classic treatments of this issue are H Lauterpacht, "Some Observations on the Prohibition of 'Non Liquet' and the Completeness of the Law", *Symbolae Verzijl* (Martinus Nijhoff, The Hague, 1958), 196 (reprinted in E Lauterpacht (ed.), Hersch Lauterpacht, *International Law: Collected Papers* (4 vols., Cambridge University Press, Cambridge, 1975), vol. 2, 213); H Lauterpacht, *The Function of Law in the International Community* (Clarendon Press, Oxford, 1933), 51-134; J Stone, "*Non Liquet* and the Function of Law in the International Community", *B.Y.I.L.*, vol. 35 (1959), 124;

The point is rather this: is the disagreement perceived by either or both parties as involving rights and obligations? Or at least is it perceived as one that could appropriately be referred to an international court or tribunal – either because of the answer that (it is hoped) will be given or because it will tend to remove the issue from the political agenda? The perception of a dispute as legal in this sense may inhere in discussions of it from the start – for example, if what is at stake is some form of boundary delimitation, land or maritime, and it is already clear that the interests of the parties diverge to such an extent that they cannot agree.[9] Or it may develop over time as the dispute develops, as one or both parties take action or as positions become more defined and entrenched. Indeed decision makers are probably more likely to seek legal advice because they are already predisposed to regard the issue as a "legal" one than they are to see it as legal because they have been so advised. And

G.G. Fitzmaurice, "The problem of non-liquet: Prolegomena to a restatement", *Mélanges offerts a Charles Rousseau; La Communauté Internationale* (Pedone, Paris, 1974), 89. So far there is no convincing example of a formal *non liquet* in contentious proceedings; in advisory proceedings a question can be asked in such general or hypothetical terms that it cannot be answered as such, and it may not be useful (or even possible) for the Court to reformulate it. In this sense, there may be advisory questions on legal issues which cannot or should not be answered – but nothing in the *Nuclear Weapons* advisory opinion (*Legality of the Threat or Use of Nuclear Weapons, I.C.J. Reports 1996*, p. 226) suggests that the Court could not have said, in any actual or imaginable case, that a specific use of nuclear weapons could not be judged – and the same considerations would apply, *a fortiori*, to other fields. See D Bodansky "Non liquet and the Incompleteness of International Law", in L Boisson de Chazournes and P Sands (eds.) *International Law, the International Court of Justice and Nuclear Weapons* (Cambridge University Press, Cambridge 1999), 153.

[9] It is true that with respect to maritime boundaries beyond the territorial sea, the primary rule appears to be that the parties should resolve their dispute by agreement so as to achieve an equitable result: UNCLOS, Arts. 74, 83. But the International Court has not made this into a significant prerequisite for judicial settlement (cf. *Land and Maritime Boundary Between Cameroon and Nigeria, Preliminary Objections, I.C.J. Reports 1998*, p. 275, 319-322) – and in general, the established international law test for a "dispute" is such that nothing a state wished to refer to the Court would be likely to fall short: *East Timor (Portugal v. Australia), I.C.J. Reports 1995*, p. 90, 99-100.

qualified advice may only be sought at a relatively late stage in the dispute,[10] when third person notes have already been written, positions on the substance not merely taken but articulated, and draft compromissory clauses drawn up and discussed. In short, the pre-litigation phase may be well and truly developed by the time those who will be responsible for the actual conduct of the litigation become involved.

But let us assume that governmental decision-makers anticipate or promptly perceive that the issue may lead to litigation at the international level, and seek advice at an early stage as to the possibilities, the form and venue of any litigation and its potential value relative to the dispute. What factors are to be taken into account?

A. Choice of Tribunal

It is not the function of those advising governments on an international dispute automatically to advise litigation, or to rush out in search of the nearest registrar. On the other hand, it is necessary at an early stage to explore the options. Are the States concerned parties to the Optional Clause and if so on what terms? Is there some regional dispute settlement agreement to which they are parties[11] (an option which has sometimes been neglected)? If the case in some sense concerns the law of the sea, are they parties to the 1982 Convention,[12] and what choices have they made pursuant to Article 282? If it is a fisheries dispute, are they parties to regional fisheries agreements, and how do these relate to the 1982 Convention and/or

---

[10] I am not of course suggesting that only external legal advice is qualified in this sense. But many governments lack a specialized legal office with experience of handling international litigation, and even where such an office exists, inter-departmental rivalries or other factors may contribute to excluding it or diminishing its influence.

[11] See, e.g., American Treaty on Pacific Settlement, Bogotá, 30 April 1948, 30 *U.N.T.S.* 55; European Convention for the Peaceful Settlement of Disputes, Strasbourg, 29 April 1957, 320 *U.N.T.S.* 24.

[12] United Nations Convention on the Law of the Sea, Montego Bay, 10 December 1982, 1833 *U.N.T.S.* 3.

the Fish Stocks Convention?[13] Are there potentially applicable bilateral treaties with jurisdictional clauses? Have these been registered with the United Nations? So far as bilateral treaties are concerned, the *United Nations Treaties Series* is woefully incomplete, a fact which the vastly improved accessibility of the register only serves to highlight.[14] If there is no existing title of jurisdiction, can one be created (e.g. by the deposit of a declaration under the Optional Clause) and if so, in what terms should this be done? Or have the parties agreed in principle to refer the dispute to third party settlement, so that it becomes a question of settling the terms of a special agreement or *compromis*? And if so, is that agreement in principle already binding on the parties, so that either party can rely on it if there is no concluded agreement on the precise terms of the reference?[15]

In these and other respects, there is a distinction between standing courts or permanent courts on the one hand and *ad hoc* tribunals on the other. If one is dealing with a standing court, there is already a body in existence with its own arrangements, its own rules, its own constitution and its own personnel, and the question becomes that of the appropriate presentation to the court or tribunal of a particular case. In relation to litigation before an *ad hoc* tribunal, the tribunal itself has to be created, resources have to be provided, a

---

[13] Agreement for the Implementation of the Provisions of the United Nations Convention on the Law of the Sea of 10th December 1982 relating to the Conservation and Management of Straddling Fish Stocks and Highly Migratory Fish Stocks, New York, 4 August 1995, UN Reg. No. 37924; A/CONF.164/37; 34 *I.L.M.* 1542.

[14] The prohibition of relying on unregistered treaties before organs of the United Nations (UN Charter, Art. 102) has not been enforced by the International Court – but it is as well to be safe. The Treaty of 1955 between Libya and France, crucial to the decision in the *Libya/Chad* case, was registered by France after the boundary dispute had arisen and just a few months before it was due to expire. See *Territorial Dispute (Libyan Arab Jamahiriya/Chad), I.C.J. Reports 1994*, p. 6.

[15] Cf. *Maritime Delimitation and Territorial Questions between Qatar and Bahrain, Jurisdiction and Admissibility, I.C.J. Reports 1994*, p. 112; *Maritime Delimitation and Territorial Questions between Qatar and Bahrain, Jurisdiction and Admissibility, I.C.J. Reports 1995*, p. 6.

secretariat has to be co-opted or established and the whole enterprise to be set up, as it were on a clean slate. In some cases there may be something intermediate between a standing tribunal and a purely *ad hoc* one, for example a standing secretariat with machinery for appointment of the tribunal, as with the Permanent Court of Arbitration or the ICSID Secretariat: this simplifies matters, reducing the range of questions about composition to the appointment of party-appointed arbitrators and a list of possibilities for the president of the Tribunal.

As to standing courts, these present relatively little difficulty in terms of the choice of forum, because it will usually be the case that there is only a single standing court to which a case may be brought. However, these days that is not always true. For example, one may be confronted with a choice between the International Court of Justice and the International Tribunal for the Law of the Sea. Australia and New Zealand arguably had such a choice in the *Case concerning Southern Blue-fin Tuna*, since the three states concerned (Japan as the potential respondent, Australia and New Zealand as the co-applicants) had all accepted the jurisdiction of the International Court of Justice under the Optional Clause. However, they shared the common reservation relating to other forms of dispute settlement, and the view was taken that this reservation might well apply so as to exclude the jurisdiction of the International Court. A further factor was the sense that the International Tribunal on the Law of the Sea might be more likely in the circumstances to give favourable consideration to an application for provisional measures, which was a core consideration in relation to the dispute.[16]

Although the choice between two standing tribunals rarely arises, it is by no means unusual to have a choice between a standing and an *ad hoc* tribunal, or between two *ad hoc* tribunals – particularly now that

---

[16] For the Award of the Annex VII Arbitral Tribunal, see *Southern Bluefin Tuna (Australia and New Zealand v. Japan), Award on Jurisdiction and Admissibility*, 4 August 2000, 119 *I.L.R.* 508; 39 *I.L.M.* 1359. Extracts of the Provisional Measures Order issued by ITLOS on 27 August 1999 are set out at 119 *I.L.R.* 525-529; the Order is reproduced in full in 38 *I.L.M.* 1624.

many investment disputes (and indeed many human rights disputes) may be brought both by the individual or company concerned in their own right or by the state of nationality in diplomatic protection proceedings, for example pursuant to the Optional Clause.[17] Indeed it may be possible for a claimant to proceed, at the same time or serially, before a human rights courts arguing on the basis of some denial of justice, for example under Article 6 of the European Convention of Human Rights, and before an arbitral tribunal under a bilateral investment treaty. For example, the claim by the Prince of Liechtenstein was brought before the European Court of Human Rights against Germany in respect of German litigation involving seized assets of the Prince; subsequently it was presented as part of an inter-state proceeding between the State of Liechtenstein and Germany in the International Court based on different grounds and with a different basis of jurisdiction.[18] In another case, the very same dispute concerning the Czech television station TV Nova was presented at the same time to two different UNCITRAL tribunals, in one case by a Dutch company, in the other by the ultimate United States investor, both against the Czech Republic. The irreconcilable awards of the two tribunals were issued within weeks of each other.[19]

A standard feature of bilateral investment treaties is that there is no requirement for exhaustion of local remedies. Many provide for a form of derivative or shareholder action which would presumably

---

[17] Under Article 27 of the ICSID Convention (Convention on the Settlement of Investment Disputes, Washington, 18 March 1965, 575 *U.N.T.S.* 159), measures by way of diplomatic protection are excluded where a matter has been submitted, or agreed to be submitted, to arbitration under ICSID. There is a question whether a similar limitation should not be implied into bilateral investment protection agreements – as it were by analogy with the exhaustion of local remedies rule.

[18] *Prince Hans-Adam II of Liechtenstein v. Germany* (App. No. 42527/98), E.C.H.R. (Grand Chamber), judgment of 12 July 2001. The claim presented to the International Court includes issues relating to property of persons other than the Prince, as well as claims by Liechtenstein as a state which were not presented to the European Court.

[19] *CME Czech Republic B.V. (The Netherlands) v. Czech Republic, Partial Award*, 13 September 2001 (Stockholm); *Lauder v. Czech Republic, Final Award*, 3 September 2001 (London), both available at http://www.cnts.cz.

not be allowed by the International Court.[20] Thus the flexibility in modern BITs conduces to a choice of forums, if not actual multiplicity of litigation. In the long run it may be that practices will emerge as to the most appropriate tribunal to select in these circumstances. For example, even if restrictive rules of shareholder standing such as those laid down in *Barcelona Traction* are avoided by the treaty, nonetheless there are sound prudential considerations for not allowing derivative actions by shareholders where the company itself has standing and is capable of presenting the claim – and *a fortiori* where it is actually doing so.[21]

B. Selection of an ad hoc Judge

A major question that is confronted with the respect to standing courts is the selection of an *ad hoc* judge. This matter has become more difficult because of the Practice Direction issued by the International Court of Justice in 2002, pursuant to which no person who has within three years acted as advocate or agent before the Court may be nominated as an *ad hoc* judge.[22] The result is that the normal pool from which *ad hoc* judges have been drawn has been drastically reduced: people are in effect given the choice of continuing to work as advocates in cases before the Court, or of adopting the perhaps rather solitary and chancy, not to say unremunerated, career of an *ad hoc* judge. Nonetheless there are individuals who, whether because they have previously served as judges on the Court[23] or for other reasons, are willing to fulfil that role. Thus it seems likely that a body of what may be called "professional *ad hoc* judges" will be created. It will be a very small group.

---

[20] Cf. *Barcelona Traction, Light and Power Company Limited, Second Phase, I.C.J. Reports 1970*, p. 3.

[21] This does not seem to have been considered relevant by the Tribunal in *Lauder v. Czech Republic.* The Tribunal noted that the Respondent had refused an offer to consolidate the two cases: para. 173.

[22] Practice Direction VII, 7 February 2002.

[23] Cf Practice Direction VIII, 7 February 2002, under which no-one who has served as judge or in registry in last three years to appear as agent, counsel or advocate.

There is always a tendency for a state, in particular a state unused to international litigation, to wish to have as an *ad hoc* judge someone (usually of its nationality) who can be guaranteed to take its side in the dispute, as if the *ad hoc* judge was a sort of "advocate" from within, someone who was sent by the appointing state in order to present its argument yet another time before the tribunal. No doubt there may have been *ad hoc* judges who clearly performed that role, but in general it is a mistake to choose the unknown partisan as an *ad hoc* judge – the person whose first task it is to write a judgment supporting his[24] own side, leaving it to fate to determine whether it will be a concurrence or a dissent. It is of course one function of an *ad hoc* judge to ensure that the case of the state concerned (one might indeed say its real case, reflecting its bottom-line concerns) is fully presented before the tribunal. In the practice of the International Court the *ad hoc* judges speak first in the oral deliberations, and at that stage they have the role of ensuring that the case is fully understood.

But beyond that the role of the judge *ad hoc* is not simply to take the position of the nominating state. It is, in the first place, to comply with the terms of the oath and to decide in accordance with conscience; and secondly, to seek to ensure that the court produces a result which the appointing state could accept. The primary function of international courts is to settle disputes, and in the context where no international court possess its own means of enforcement, this tends to mean that some level of compromise will usually be built in, often in a concealed or covert way, to the decision. Some cases – e.g., those concerning sovereignty over an island – can only be decided one way or another: the litigation has the appearance of a zero-sum game.[25] Moreover some cases are clear, and can only realistically be

---

[24] The two women so far appointed as *ad hoc* judges have shown conspicuous independence of mind: *Application for Revision and Interpretation of the Judgment of 24 February 1982 in the Case concerning the* Continental Shelf (Tunisia/Libyan Arab Jamahiriya) *(Tunisia v. Libyan Arab Jamahiriya), I.C.J. Reports 1985*, p. 192 (Judge *ad hoc* Bastid); *Arrest Warrant of 11 April 2000 (Democratic Republic of the Congo v. Belgium), I.C.J. Reports 2002*, p. 3 (Judge *ad hoc* van den Wyngaert).

[25] E.g., *Kasikili/Sedudu Island (Botswana/Namibia), I.C.J. Reports 1999*, p. 1045; *Sovereignty over Pulau Ligitan and Pulau Sipadan (Indonesia/Malaysia),* judgment of 23

decided in one way: the reference of the case to an international court may have been an advance recognition of this, a diplomatic means of effectively withdrawing a political claim. But even so, there can still be some reflection of the positions of the losing party in the choice and balance of the arguments chosen by the tribunal.

In other cases, especially those involving multiple issues, there is scope for a balanced judgment as between the parties. This has always been a feature of international arbitration, but it is not absent from decisions even of the International Court of Justice. We have seen possible examples of that in recent practice, for example in the *Gabčíkovo-Nagymaros Project* case between Hungary and Slovakia,[26] the decision between Cameroon and Nigeria on the *Land and Maritime Boundary*,[27] and the decision on *Navigational and Related Rights* between Costa Rica and Nicaragua.[28] Without in any sense acting as a delegate, an *ad hoc* judge can perform a constructive role even for a nominating state that fails to achieve an overall win.

At the other end of the spectrum is the *ad hoc* arbitrator as advocate. For example in the *Buraimi* arbitration between Saudi Arabia and the United Kingdom in 1954,[29] the Saudi arbitrator, the Deputy Minister of Foreign Affairs, seems to have regarded himself as the leader of the Saudi Arabian legal team. The matter reached a crisis when he passed a note to the principal counsel for Saudi Arabia suggesting what question to ask next. There were also suggestions of some degree of illicit persuasion behind the scenes; the result was that the United Kingdom's arbitrator withdrew from the proceedings. Subsequently the President of the Arbitral Tribunal, Judge De Visscher, also withdrew and the whole arbitration was frustrated. No-one suggests these days that matters

---

October 2001 (it was never suggested in argument that the two islands were separable in terms of the sovereignty claims of the parties).

[26] *Gabčíkovo-Nagymaros Project (Hungary/Slovakia), I.C.J. Reports 1997*, p 7.

[27] *Land and Maritime Boundary between Cameroon and Nigeria*, judgment of 10 October 2002.

[28] *Dispute regarding Navigational and Related Rights*, judgment of 13 July 2009.

[29] For an account see SM Schwebel, *International Arbitration: Three Salient Problems* (Grotius, Cambridge, 1987), 235-245.

be taken to this extent. But there have been lesser incidents which underline the counterproductive character of any attempt by the nominating state to persuade or urge their own arbitrator to take a position. In most cases, by contrast, the institution seems to have worked well enough to fulfil its limited aims.[30]

C. Joinder of Parties

In litigation before domestic courts it is not unusual to have to consider which among a number of potential respondents to sue, and provided jurisdiction can be obtained against one of them, it will normally be possible to join the others as necessary or proper parties. By contrast in international proceedings, jurisdiction is dependent upon consent and has to be established separately vis-à-vis each potential respondent State. In such cases difficult tactical choices may have to be made, and the matter is exacerbated by what seems an increasing tendency of states to act collectively, for example in imposing sanctions or taking countermeasures.

When the Republic of Nauru was considering whether to commence proceedings concerning the rehabilitation of the phosphate lands in Nauru – a claim was held against Australia, New Zealand and the United Kingdom as the partners in the phosphate industry in Nauru and as simultaneously constituting the administering authority of the Trust Territory of Nauru – the question was whether to commence the proceedings against all three or against only one. All three states were parties to the Optional Clause, but there were important reservations in the United Kingdom and New Zealand Optional Clause declarations whose effects on jurisdiction was difficult to determine in the circumstances. The

---

[30] Generally on the role of the *ad hoc* judge see the Separate Opinion of Judge *ad hoc* Lauterpacht in *Application of the Convention on the Prevention and Punishment of the Crime of Genocide, Provisional Measures, Order of 13 September 1993, I.C.J. Reports 1993,* p. 325, at p. 408-409 (paras. 4-6); Judge *ad hoc* Franck in his Dissenting Opinion in *Sovereignty over Pulau Ligitan and Pulau Sipadan (Indonesia/Malaysia)*, judgment of 17 December 2002, paras. 9-12. See also C Peck & R Lee (eds), *Increasing the Effectiveness of the International Court of Justice* (Kluwer, The Hague, 1997), 370-397.

decision was therefore made to proceed against Australia alone, a decision assisted by the fact that Australia had been the active party in the administration of Nauru, New Zealand and the United Kingdom in effect allowing the administration of the territory to be carried out on their joint behalf by Australia.

In the circumstances the choice turned out to be the correct one: the International Court held that the case was properly constituted against Australia alone, and that the claim was admissible brought against Australia alone. It left open the question whether the any eventual recovery against Australia would be limited in some way, by reference for example to its share of the profits arising from phosphate mining, or whether the normal principle would be applied that a state is responsible for the direct or proximate consequences of conduct attributable to it in breach of its international obligations.[31] In the event the case was settled when Australia itself paid the full amount that was claimed:[32] it subsequently recovered a proportion of that amount from the other two states. But if the case had been brought initially against the three states, it is not unlikely that jurisdictional objections made by New Zealand and/or the United Kingdom might have succeeded.[33] In that event the very act of bringing the case against all three states might have been thought to constitute a tacit admission: a second case started against Australia alone could have faced the psychological hurdle of Nauru having

---

[31] *Certain Phosphate Lands in Nauru (Nauru v. Australia), Preliminary Objections, I.C.J. Reports 1992*, p. 240, 258-259 (para. 48); p. 262 (para. 56). Cf the introductory Commentary to Part I, Chapter IV of the ILC's Articles on Responsibility of States for Internationally Wrongful Acts, *Report of the International Law Commission on the Work of Its Fifty-third Session*, UN G.A.O.R., 56th Sess., Supp. No. 10 (UN Doc. A/56/10 (2001)), 150-155, reproduced in J Crawford, *The International Law Commission's Articles on State Responsibility: Introduction, Text and Commentaries* (Cambridge University Press, Cambridge, 2002), 145-148.

[32] For the order removing the case from the list, see *I.C.J. Reports 1993*, p. 322.

[33] In his dissenting opinion, Judge Ago expressed the view that the NZ and UK reservations would not have been applicable – but the Court remained silent on the point and there is no certainty that Judge Ago's view would have prevailed: *Certain Phosphate Lands in Nauru (Nauru v. Australia), Preliminary Objections, I.C.J. Reports 1992,* p. 240, 326-328, particularly 327 (para.5).

apparently conceded, by its earlier conduct, that such a case would be improperly constituted. Consideration of these sorts of factors is clearly important at an early stage.

D. Constitution of ad hoc tribunals

I turn to the difficult problem of the constitution of *ad hoc* tribunals. In some cases, the tribunal has to be in effect created *de novo,* even if it notionally exists under the treaty – as for example an Annex VII Tribunal under the Law of the Sea Convention. Of course in modern practice there will always be a residual appointment clause, so that an appointing authority (whether the President of the International Court or the Secretary-General of the Permanent Court of Arbitration for example) will be able to make the appointment in the event that the parties do not agree. But the parties will want to retain a degree of control over the appointment of the tribunal and they will therefore strive to do it by themselves. If one party is not co-operating at this stage of the proceedings, the appointing authority will usually be able to appoint the whole tribunal; indeed it is desirable in that situation that the whole tribunal be named by the appointing authority so that inequality between the parties is avoided. Thus the appointment of party-appointed arbitrators is excluded if the one party is not co-operating.

Even assuming cooperation in principle, the actual process of selection of the members of an arbitral tribunal can be a harrowing one, because each party will be seeking to appoint persons who they believe will sustain their broad position. Yet it is improper (and potential nominees of any stature will refuse) to engage in anything that might remotely appear to be a negotiation as to the conditions of appointment.[34] So one approaches the person concerned and asks for a copy of their cv; one reads individual items which might give some insight into the way they think about the particular subject; there may

---

[34] Even later discussions as to the financial terms of appointment (if not already fixed, as under ICSID) can be difficult, and are best carried out on the record with both parties present.

be some general discussion about a possible appointment – but anything more specific is or should be excluded. Thus even the unilateral appointment of members of the tribunal (e.g. the first two appointees of the five person tribunal for which Annex VII of the Law of the Sea Convention provides) is to some extent an act of faith. One can only hope that appointees will perform their role in a way which is sufficiently satisfactory.

In terms of the method of appointing the remaining members of the tribunal (those whose appointment depends on agreement), it is common for the parties to exchange lists of persons who they would be prepared to see appointed. Persons common to both lists might then be appointed automatically, or at least there would be a presumption in favour of their appointment. These lists will often contain people whom the other party could not conceivably consent to, but there is no point in producing a list which contains exclusively persons who would be wholly unacceptable to the other party. The choice of individuals is a difficult and time consuming process, but it is one whose importance cannot be neglected.

E. Scope of the Dispute Referred to Arbitration

Of equal importance at the early stages is the question of the terms of reference, that is to say the provisions of the *compromis*, the definition of the dispute. As noted already, there can be problems when the parties to the dispute have themselves formulated the dispute as a legal dispute in precise terms. If States are contemplating commencing litigation it is desirable that they instruct counsel properly in advance as to the substance and form of the dispute, and give them time to think about the way in which the dispute should be formulated for the purposes of the *compromis* or special agreement.

The tribunal can itself assist in this respect, and a standing court will often try to do so. The International Court of Justice has become relatively adept in interpreting terms of reference in such a way as not to slant the case one way or the other – for example in the *Gabčíkovo-*

Nagymaros Project case.[35] In the *Qatar-Bahrain* case,[36] the parties could not agree on the way in which the dispute was to be formulated and the Court eventually, by a somewhat tortuous process, in effect took into account the different views of the parties, while managing *a priori* to uphold its jurisdiction over the merits irrespective of any precise formulation of the dispute. Perhaps the Court did for the parties what they should have done for themselves, but if the means chosen which did not find favour with all members of the Court, at least the outcome was broadly acceptable. In the context of advisory opinions, a further example of adroit refomulation of the question asked occurred in *Legality of the Use or Threat of Nuclear Weapons*. There the Court was asked whether the use or threat of nuclear weapons was permitted by international law in any circumstance. The Court avoided any implication that the use of nuclear weapons required specific authorization – a position that would have predetermined the answer, since the absence of any international consensus on the issue has so far excluded both specific authorization and specific prohibition.[37]

III. The Preparation and Presentation of the Case

I turn from the pre-litigation phase to the actual presentation of the case. Here I want to deal with four different subjects (among others that could have been chosen).

A. The Written Pleadings

In modern international litigation the phase of written advocacy is increasingly important, and much can be done at this stage to affect the outcome, one way or the other. Indeed there is often pressure to abbreviate the oral phase, in particular from judges whose own training is within the civil law tradition of summary hearings with a

---

35 *I.C.J. Reports 1997* p. 7.

36 See *Maritime Delimitation and Territorial Questions between Qatar and Bahrain, Jurisdiction and Admissibility*, *I.C.J. Reports 1994*, p. 112.

37 *Legality of the Threat or Use of Nuclear Weapons*, *I.C.J. Reports 1996*, p. 226, 238-239.

minimum of oral evidence. There is also the simple fact that long hearings take enormous amounts of resources both of the court concerned and of the parties, so that work on the written pleadings is frequently the dominant factor in the case.

On the other hand the oral proceedings retain their importance, in particular because they form the focal point of the presentation, the point to which the parties are working. It is psychologically difficult – and may be excluded in terms of instructions from the government concerned – to make anything that could be even remotely described as a concession at the stage of the written proceedings. The parties want to keep all issues open, and indeed it is not uncommon during the phase of the written proceedings that the issues proliferate, with new issues and new documents being introduced in the Counter-Memorial or even the Reply. The importance of the oral phase may be to refocus the attention of the parties on what is really important and to allow those presenting the case to make at least implicit (sometimes even explicit) shifts on particular issues. More generally the oral proceedings should provide a synthesis of each party's case when actually confronted by that of its opponent, thus allowing the Court to get to the points that are really at stake. It is for reasons such as these – and not only because of the tenacity of an oral tradition – that written proceedings must not be allowed to take over entirely.

The normal order of proceedings in the written phase depends on whether the case is bought by special agreement or unilateral application. If the case is bought by unilateral application the claimant will present its first written pleading (normally referred to as a Memorial); the respondent will produce a second responsive pleading (normally called a Counter-Memorial, and these will be followed by at least one further round of shorter written pleadings (normally a Reply and a Rejoinder). If the case is bought by special agreement there is technically no claimant and no respondent and the parties will normally present their first pleadings simultaneously. This presents a difficulty, since a party which is presenting its case simultaneously with the other side will almost inevitably reserve those parts of the case which depend upon what the other side may say –

for example, any pleading by way of the rebuttal of a potential defence or excuse.

Thus in practice, special agreement cases will tend to produce three rounds of simultaneous written pleadings. Each party will present what might be described as its affirmative case in the first round, in the second written round what may be described as their defensive or second-order case; then in a final round each will rebut the second order case of the other party. The International Court has now called on the parties by a practice direction to ensure that in special agreement cases the pleadings are not simultaneous. Thus one party will have the burden or the benefit of going first in the hope that the whole of the written phase can be completed with two pleadings by each party: the Practice Direction makes it clear that the party going first does not thereby assume any special burden of proof.[38] Whether this will save much time remains to be seen, but it should reduce the volume of the pleadings and will probably bring the whole case out more effectively than the combined process of guess-work and delay which is sometimes involved in the presentation of three rounds of simultaneous pleadings.

The purpose of the written pleadings is to present in substance the whole of a party's case together with all the relevant documents, maps and witness statements.[39] But it is not the function of a written pleading to present purely argumentative or rhetorical material. Unfortunately it is not uncommon for written pleadings to be presented in an overwritten – indeed at times hysterical – style. No doubt there can be legitimate differences in forensic taste, but in my opinion the written pleadings are better and more effective if they are relatively understated. They need to express the party's case, and to do so clearly, convincingly and without equivocation. But they do not

---

[38] Practice Direction I, 7 February 2002.

[39] As emphasized by the International Court in Practice Direction II, 7 February 2002: "pleadings are intended not only to reply to the submissions and arguments of the other party, but also, and above all, to present clearly the submissions and arguments of the party which is filing the proceedings."

need to pour abuse on the other side or to use language which is overblown or unsustainable. A feature of the written pleadings is that they can be and often are read and reread by the tribunal. In the context of such rereading and of the repeated study of key arguments, passages which are moderate in tone and which are clearly expressed tend to be more effective.

As noted, it is not unusual for parties to reserve to a later stage, whether to a second written pleading or even to the oral round, particularly sensitive issues, issues which will obviously have to be confronted at some stage and may well be decisive. Again it is a question of judgement whether tackle these at an early stage. My own feeling once again is that a party is not disadvantaged by a clear and forthright presentation of its case. On the other hand it is not necessary and is often undesirable in a Memorial to anticipate in advance points which are essentially defensive points, points to be made by way of rebuttal. What has to be presented in the Memorial is the party's own case in a sufficiently complete way, and accompanied by all relevant documentation.

Whatever approach is taken, the written pleadings should not be excessively argumentative, nor should they be academic or pedantic in their presentation. It is not the function of advocates (including those also known as professors) to give lectures to tribunals; it is not the function of written pleadings to substitute for text books. Cases can usually be presented clearly and eloquently without elaborate disquisition on legal issues. Where a legal issue really divides the parties it can be explored in more detail and often with more effect before the tribunal in the oral phase than by an elaborate presentation of legal argument in the written pleadings. So the function of the written pleadings (especially in the first round) is succinctly to set out the legal position, and to focus on the presentation of the dispute itself, both in terms of its historical origins, the essential facts, the diplomatic correspondence, attempts at its resolution, followed by the basis of the claim in factual and legal terms.

B. Issues of Evidence and Expert Opinion

I turn to issues of evidence themselves. In international tribunals the practice in terms of evidence varies greatly. In many ICC or similar arbitrations, there is a substantial presentation of oral testimony from witnesses of fact, in much the same way as would occur in a common law adversarial trial. But there are still differences between the two. In the first place although the arbitration laws of most states now allow the compelling of witnesses in aid of arbitration, it is still relatively uncommon for witnesses to be subpoenaed. It is frequently the case that each side will present as it were its "own" witnesses, without any attempt to bring in third party or neutral witnesses of fact. Thus modern international litigation seems to be very firmly set in the adversarial mode. Even two parties from civil law backgrounds, represented by European lawyers, will usually present their cases in a thoroughly adversarial way. But one must never underestimate the capacity of lawyers to adapt to new situations: United States lawyers characteristically argue with passion and vigour in favour of the costs-follow-the-event rule in international arbitration (at least if they have won or expect to win), while at the same time they abhor that rule in their own national practice!

As to the form of presentation of evidence, it is quite common for witnesses of fact in international arbitration to present their evidence exclusively through written means. Thus there may be substantial numbers of depositions or written witness statements presented on behalf of both parties, yet in the end neither party will call on the other side for cross-examination. It is not uncommon for a tribunal to be asked to assess conflicting witness statements without ever seeing or hearing the witnesses.

In particular in inter-state litigation the presentation of oral evidence is extremely unusual, and this is true whether the witness gives factual or expert evidence. Whether this is because of the acute pressures placed on presentation timetables by courts or for other reasons is unclear. It is certainly difficult to predict how much of a specific allocation of time a cross-examination will take, and the era of six-week International Court hearings is over. Instead testimony will be adduced through written witness statements supported by documents, and will constitute an aspect of the written case of the parties. As such they must be as complete, clear and concise as possible.

Turning to expert testimony, international disputes quite often involve issues on which non-legal expertise is required. This is true whether the disputes relate to hydro-electric dams, to scientific issues associated with deep sea fishing or to issues about freedom of trade or navigation under bilateral treaties It is also quite common for expert witnesses to be produced on legal issues, especially on national law but also conceivably on international law. My own view is that it is usually unhelpful for expert testimony to be produced on the very questions of international law which an international tribunal has to decide. For example, in the *Vivendi* annulment proceedings, both parties presented witness statements setting out particular positions in respect of the role of annulment and the relationship between the bilateral investment treaty, the ICSID Convention and the individual contract. This was the core issue, and the expert statements were careful arguments of the case. But they were not really different from written briefs, and it might have been more useful for the two distinguished persons concerned to have argued the case rather than making what amounted to *ex parte* statements in the form of expert testimony. In the event the Tribunal decided that it did not wish to hear evidence from either expert witnesses, preferring that the matter be argued by counsel.[40] In the context of oral argument before a small tribunal (as distinct from the International Court of Justice or the International Tribunal for the Law of the Sea), questions can be asked and the real issues of concern to the Tribunal exposed and developed, something which it is difficult to do in a written expert opinion.

The position may be different so far as concerns expert evidence on local law and practice. But again there is no objection to counsel

---

[40] See *Compañía de Aguas del Aconquija S.A. & Vivendi Universal v. Argentine Republic* (ICSID Case No. ARB/97/3), Decision of 3 July 2002, 41 ILM 1135, 1137 (paras. 6-7).

on each side simply presenting the legal materials, if necessary in translation, and making arguments as to their meaning which an intelligent tribunal can grasp. For example in *Tradax v. Albania* there was an important question of interpretation of the Albanian Law on Land; in particular, the question was whether the law providing for the privatization of land was immediately self-executing or was really a programmatic law which had to be given effect progressively. Since the claimant's case depended upon the assertion that the Law on Land carried out an immediate expropriation, this was an issue on which expert evidence of Albanian law could have been tendered. But in the end the matter came down to the interpretation of a law which, if properly translated, was a matter the tribunal could consider for itself in the precise context of the international law rule which made the issue of interpretation relevant.[41] It is doubtful whether the categorically opposed assertions of two Albanian lawyers on the point would have added much.

Expert witnesses on questions of scientific or other expertise are a quite different matter. Here the expert may have an extremely important role, although whether this material is presented by way of expert testimony or scientific advocacy will depend upon the approach of the parties and on the tradition of the court. In the *Case concerning the Gabčíkovo-Nagymaros Project* both parties independently decided to present their expert material in the form of scientific advocacy by the scientists who had prepared the relevant sections of the pleadings. One reason for that decision was that it was unpredictable how much time would need to be taken in cross-examination or how productive that would be: in the end, each party had greater control over the material if presented by way of advocacy rather than evidence. In the event, although the Court was very reticent about reaching conclusions on the purely scientific issues, the scientific material was presented skillfully on both sides, and there is no doubt that the Court's overall appreciation of the situation was informed by the scientific material.

---

[41] See *Tradex Hellas SA v Albania* (1999) 5 ICSID Reports 43.

By contrast, in the *Case concerning Southern Bluefin Tuna*, both parties presented written scientific evidence as to the existing and projected state of the tuna stocks, the crucial scientific issue which was in dispute between the parties. In the provisional measures phase, Australia and New Zealand also called their principal independent scientific witness to give oral evidence. Indeed he was subject to questioning on the *voir dire*, possibly for the first time in the history of international litigation, and then (having, unsurprisingly, been qualified as an expert) to a further brief cross-examination.[42] On the other hand counsel for the Respondent declined to call its own principal scientific witness. The outcome tends to show that where evidence has been called and subjected to cross-examination, it is incumbent upon the other side to produce its own expert for cross-examination.

Whether as scientific advocate or expert witness, a good expert – not too closely associated with the case of the party in question, and certainly not someone who has been intimately involved in the drawing up of the case, but who can speak authoritatively about the subject – can be invaluable. The search for such an expert is one of the most important roles of counsel in the pre-litigation phase of any case in which scientific or technical issues will be prominent.

C. Documents and Discovery

I turn to deal briefly with some questions relating to documents and discovery, although these could be the subject of detailed discussion in their own right.

One of the essential requirements of a good written pleading is that it presents the core documentation in an orderly fashion so that the tribunal has this before it in an accessible way. There is sometimes a tendency to present large numbers of documents in the order in which they are referred to in the pleading; in such a case, consecutive reading of the documents becomes difficult and may be

---

[42] See ITLOS/PV.99/20-21, 18 August 1999, available on http://www.itlos.org/start2_en.html.

very confusing. It is better to present – for example in the context of a diplomatic dispute between two states – the whole of the diplomatic correspondence in chronological order, even if it is not referred to in that order in the written pleading: this is a particular function of the initial Memorial which should be the basic statement of a party's case. Likewise it is better to present, at least so far as is necessary, the complete documentary dossier of correspondence relating to the dispute, even if particular items of it may not be referred to in the pleadings, and provided only that the volume of material is not such as to overwhelm the tribunal. In such cases simple chronological order is the obvious one to adopt; it has the virtue of allowing the documents to speak for themselves in the order in which they were created or received. Similarly, the separate presentation of all relevant treaties and other normative instruments to which reference will have to be made is useful, whether in chronological or some other evident order, and in a separate volume. Overall, the function of advocacy is not mere unilateral persuasion: it is the presentation of the case in a useful and workable manner.

In pure inter-state litigation, discovery is very unusual and the relatively few attempts that have been made by one state to get access to documents of the other have generally been ineffective. Moreover the International Court is simply told that it can draw an adverse inference from the failure to produce,[43] an inference which is rarely drawn (at least explicitly). Overall, discovery at the inter-state level performs a minor role.

Discovery at the level of mixed arbitrations in commercial and investment disputes is another question: increasingly, substantial discovery is being sought and (to some extent) given. On the other hand international tribunals are allergic, and with good reason, to the "fishing expedition" style of discovery, and the International Bar Association has produced guidelines on discovery, produced by a working group with membership drawn from a number of different

---

[43] Statute of the International Court of Justice, Art. 49.

legal traditions and legal systems.[44] These guidelines perform a useful role in confining and defining the discovery process at the international level. The emphasis in the guidelines is on the discovery of identifiable documents or relatively coherent defined classes of documents which are relevant to issues actually at stake in the litigation. The essential problem, here again, is that the normal disciplines which might prevail at national level (in terms ultimately of disciplinary sanctions for failing to make due discovery) only apply in an attenuated form, if at all, in international litigation. To some extent it becomes a matter of the professional conscience of the legal advisors rather than of any external sanction: this is another reason why the IBA rules and the rather moderate approach they take to discovery is useful.

D. The Oral Phase

For the reasons given above, oral argument remains in my view important in international litigation, perhaps more so in arbitration before smaller panels than before the International Court, but important before the International Court as well. A good advocate will focus on the key issues, if necessary at the expense of other questions posed by the written pleadings. It is at this stage that some level of gentle mockery, of criticism, even occasionally of denunciation of the other side's argument, can be effective, provided it is suitably phrased. In such a way the underlying weaknesses of the other side can be highlighted and exposed.

It may be assumed in well-conducted international litigation that the tribunal by the time that the oral hearings commence will be reasonably familiar with the written pleadings. However it cannot be assumed – whether of the International Court or an *ad hoc* tribunal – that all the judges are familiar with every document in the record. The practices of different judges and arbitrators vary; some take great

---

[44] See IBA Rules on the Taking of Evidence in International Commercial Arbitration (1999) in A Redfern & M Hunter, *Law and Practice of International Commercial Arbitration* (3rd edn, London, Sweet & Maxwell, 1999) 631-7.

care to read the whole dossier in advance, others prefer to be guided by the parties themselves in the course of the oral proceedings, and then to read the dossier thoroughly, informed by what the real issues now appear to be. Thus it is important at a relatively early stage of each side's oral presentation to draw the tribunal's attention to key facts and documents, and if necessary to do so in some detail. But this should not descend to the lengthy reading out from documents or decisions which used to be the practice in some English-speaking courts. But if it is necessary to read a crucial passage to the court, there should be no compunction about doing so, nor in pointing out why the passage matters, and which particular aspects of it are important. In that sense a presentation of variable focus, one which gives the tribunal both a sense of the overall shape of the argument and of important details, can be effective.

IV. Conclusion

International litigation presents its own challenges. The members of the tribunal will rarely be drawn from a single national legal system; rather they will come from diverse national legal traditions and may be attracted (or repelled) by different aspects of a presentation. The aim of the international advocate must be to gather the relevant material in a comprehensible, succinct way, for the understanding of judges who do not necessarily share either the presuppositions or the advocate's intimate knowledge of the dossier. To take perhaps a trivial example, anecdotes or maxims that may be effective and understood in one literary, linguistic or legal tradition may leave those in other traditions completely cold, indeed uncomprehending: the effective advocate will seek to appeal to some intelligent common denominator of the judges, without assuming knowledge which is culturally specific. At the same time it is possible and is often very effective to seek to encapsulate a particular case by reference to some element which is generally accessible for all of the judges – especially if it can be taken from the common dossier before the court. Advocacy which can present clear and concise images of what is at stake, especially where these are related to the history of the dispute, is much more likely to be effective than an unrelated or forced anecdote or allusion.

Evidently it is the function of the advocate to comply with the instructions of the government or other party, and to present the case in as forceful and vigorous a way as possible. At the same time it is not the function of the advocate simply to say things for money; nor unquestioningly to present the client's case in the way the client would have it, without regard to any of the actual difficulties. Rather it is the function of the advocate to seek to persuade the tribunal in such a way as to preserve the essentials of the client's case. This is a delicate matter, requiring trust between the client (through the Agent) and the advocate. In the search for a proper outcome, the advocate is not merely a mouthpiece but rather an active intermediary.

Part V.

ORAL ADVOCACY

Chapter 13

PRE-HEARING ADVOCACY IN INTERNATIONAL ARBITRATION

Lucy F. Reed and Alexander A. Yanos*

I. Introduction

What are the hallmarks of exceptional advocacy during the critical pre-hearing stage in an international commercial arbitration? This chapter describes advocacy practices aimed at winning the trust of the tribunal, building an optimal case, and protecting the client's interests – from the filing of the request for arbitration right through to the pre-hearing conference. To give away the ending: at each and every pre-hearing phase, the arbitral tribunal should perceive the advocate as confident (but not over-confident), thoroughly versed in the relevant facts and applicable law, master of a consistent case strategy, attuned to the client and its interests, reasonable, trustworthy and helpful.

The Pre-hearing Process: Broadly speaking, this chapter discusses ways in which an advocate can attempt to further his or her client's interests in seven main procedural phases of the pre-hearing process: (*i*) initiation of the arbitration; (*ii*) selection of the arbitral tribunal; (*iii*) preliminary sessions; (*iv*) interim measures; (*v*) document exchange; (*vi*) written pleadings; and (*vii*) pre-hearing conferences. Each phase represents an important opportunity to further the client's interests and counter the opposing counsel's efforts to do the same for his or her client.

---

* Partners, Freshfields Bruckhaus Deringer US LLP. The authors thank Paul Quigley, an associate with the firm, for his invaluable assistance in researching and preparing this chapter.

The Client's Interests: The U.S. football coach Vince Lombardi famously said "Winning isn't everything, it's the only thing." Many advocates follow the same approach to arbitration. However, the client's needs usually are more multifaceted. In many cases, the client will want counsel to balance the need to win the case against the client's desire to, among other things: (*i*) control costs; (*ii*) obtain a timely result; (*iii*) position the dispute for a favorable settlement; and (*iv*) protect business interests at risk of collateral damage by the arbitration. At the same time, the concept of winning – particularly in the international context – is more complex than often assumed. For example, certainly a win on the merits is good, but only as good as a positive award in the damages phase. A win against the wrong party (such as a single-purpose vehicle subsidiary instead of a multinational parent) can mean an award that is unenforceable.

A final introductory note on three overarching themes in this chapter: *First*, pre-hearing advocacy is largely determinative of the final outcome. A winning strategy requires an early understanding of the relevant facts and law and the client's overall goals, which means an investment in frontloading. The best approach is to reverse-engineer the steps that will lead to the desired final award: in other words, the effective advocate asks himself or herself very early what is the easiest and most robust way for the tribunal to decide in the client's favor on each of the outcome-determinative issues? *Second*, a balanced and reasonable approach to written and oral advocacy will almost always be the most successful. Tribunals may have to tolerate drama, but they do not appreciate it. Overstatement cannot be taken back. *Third*, the effective advocate always keeps an eye on settlement opportunities throughout the pre-hearing arbitration process. He or she also keeps an ear attuned to subtle (or not so subtle) messages from the tribunal about settlement. Just as von Clausewitz once explained that war is diplomacy by other means, so too must the advocate remember that arbitration is negotiation by other means.

II. Phase One: Commencing The Arbitration

Most arbitration proceedings are commenced with an exchange of initial submissions, typically a notice of claim and an answer. In the common law tradition, these are brief statements establishing the grounds for and defenses to a claim and the jurisdiction of the arbitral procedure. The claimant's initial submission would be the Notice of Arbitration in UNCITRAL proceedings or the Request for Arbitration in ICSID, ICC or LCIA proceedings.The respondent's would be the Answer in ICC proceedings, the Response in LCIA proceedings, or the Response to the Notice of Arbitration in the proposed revision to the UNCITRAL Rules. (At present the UNCITRAL and ICSID Rules do not provide for an opening submission by the respondent.) Some of these submissions contain more substance and detail than others, but in many cases it is not until the later substantive pleadings that each side sets forth in full detail its factual and legal position.

A. Early Mastery of the Case is Essential

When initiating arbitration or making the initial answer to a new arbitration proceeding, advocates should remember that "[t]he process of persuasion begins with the first document."[1] Thus, it would be a mistake to assume that the brevity of the document to be filed means that little work is necessary in its preparation. Critical decisions are involved in preparing the initial submission, all of which will have far-reaching consequences on the arbitral process. These decisions include: (*i*) which entity or entities should be named as the claimant(s); (*ii*) which entity or entities should be named as the respondent(s) (should non-signatories to the arbitration agreement be added?); (*iii*) what types of claims should be asserted (e.g., contract, tort, treaty?); (*iv*) should counter-claims be asserted; (*v*) should interim measures be requested; and (*vi*) in which forum should the arbitration

---

[1] Nicolas C. Ulmer, *Winning the Opening Stages of an ICC Arbitration*, 8 J. INT'L ARB. 33, 35 (1991).

be initiated (contractual forum, and/or treaty forum?). Importantly, arbitrators are often nominated with the initial filings; relevant advocacy considerations are discussed separately below.

In order to make the correct decisions on these critical issues, advocates will need to develop an early mastery of the key facts, documents and likely witness testimony. An early mastery of the case will also ensure that the initial submissions will be integral parts of the narrative to be presented to the arbitrators. Such a narrative is most effective when it is easy to understand, compelling, legally relevant and, of course, 100% factually accurate.

There are several reasons for attending carefully to the initial filings. *First*, if the story remains clear and constant, it will be more convincing and resonate more solidly with arbitrators over time. Conversely, a shifting narrative can appear opportunistic. *Second*, the initial pleadings may be the only documents in the hands of the arbitrators for months, and so will give them their initial – and lasting – impressions: "The arbitrators are fresh and eager to understand the case at the earliest stages of the case."[2] *Third*, the quality and strength of the initial submissions may influence the settlement assessment of the opposing party.[3] *Fourth*, if interim measures are contemplated or later prove necessary, the facts as pleaded in the initial submissions will be important to the arbitrators as they deliberate issues such as irreparable harm and likelihood of success on the merits. *Fifth*, document disclosure disputes, if they arise, will often be resolved with reference to the facts and claims as pleaded in the first submissions.

---

[2] Doak Bishop, *Advocacy from the Arbitrators' Perspective*, *in* THE ART OF ADVOCACY IN INTERNATIONAL ARBITRATION 441, 445 (Doak Bishop ed., 1st ed. 2004).

[3] Under the UNCITRAL Rules, initial pleadings may take on greater significance in the future. The most recent proposed amendments to the UNCITRAL Rules include adding an opportunity for the respondent to file a detailed response to the initial Notice of Arbitration. This may lead to more detailed Notices of Arbitration from claimant's counsel who wish to communicate their story to the arbitrators as early as possible in the proceeding, and are concerned about the respondent's story standing alone.

A final further reason to consider carefully the substance and tone of a first submission – a reason independent of the tribunal's likely views – is that it may serve as the summary document passed to the decision-makers on the other side. As such, it can also play a critical role in either progressing the dispute to settlement or inflaming the dispute and setting back settlement negotiations.

For claimants planning to commence a complex action or actions, an excellent first step is to compile a thorough written "audit" of the claims, including a description of the facts, an analysis of the applicable law, and an assessment of the likely outcome of each claim. Such an audit allows clients and counsel to make clear-eyed strategic calculations regarding which claims to press, when and where to press them, and even what types of settlements would be acceptable. Ideally, this audit will also include a calculation of the likely damages associated with each claim, prepared with neutral input by experts. Beyond its critical strategic value, such an audit is amortized with its use in drafting the initial request for arbitration, the memorial and other pleadings that require a description of the facts.

B. Consider Including Key Documents with Initial Submissions

One strategic question at the commencement phase always is whether to submit key documents with the initial submissions. In most (but not all) cases, key documents should be submitted, assuming procedural rules so permit. Structuring the case around the key documents from the beginning maximizes consistency in later filings. Key documents constitute persuasive evidence, and will give the arbitrators an earlier understanding of a party's case. "Holding key evidence or arguments in reserve is not generally consistent with the arbitrator's desires to understand the case at the earliest possible time and is not generally good strategy."[4] Educating the tribunal on

[4] Doak Bishop, *supra* note 2 at 445.

the issues of the case from the beginning may facilitate the arbitrators establishing a more efficient, tailored procedure:

> Counsel should appreciate that there are significant advantages to be gained in terms of case management from developing the issues in the case more fully from the outset. And the tribunal must commit to reading and becoming familiar with the written materials it is sent from the start of the proceedings. If this work is done, then the tribunal can work with the parties to develop bespoke procedures that are suitable for the case, thereby taking advantage of the flexibility that arbitration offers.[5]

Frontloading the work of identifying and collecting key documents can have ancillary benefits. Advocates can begin building files of the key documents which, even if not used with the initial submission, will support later filings. Based on early witness interviews and the early review of documentary evidence, advocates can begin compiling witness notebooks that will be useful for the later drafting of witness statements and witness examination.

If circumstances dictate – as they often do – that counsel must scramble to master the facts of a dispute before submitting the initial request or answer, counsel should consider noting this in the submission, thereby laying down a marker in case facts emerge to contradict or refine the position taken in their initial pleadings.

C. Style Issues

It goes without saying that, in drafting initial pleadings, advocates should not adopt local domestic procedural conventions regarding style, structure and formatting. This does not further the client's case before international tribunals.

---

[5] Christopher Newmark, *Controlling Time and Costs in International* Arbitration, *in* THE LEADING ARBITRATORS' GUIDE TO INTERNATIONAL ARBITRATION 81, 83 (Lawrence W. Newman and Richard D. Hill eds., 2008).

III. Phase Two: Constituting The Tribunal

Whether the tribunal will consist of one or three arbitrators, the process of constituting the tribunal is an opportunity for the advocate not only to affect the outcome of the arbitration but also the manner in which the proceedings are conducted.[6] Some arbitrators take charge early and run a fast-moving process leading to a prompt award. Other arbitrators remain removed from the process until the final hearing on the merits, allowing the parties to push their agendas, for example, for broad document disclosure and extensive motion practice, with little control. Thus, knowing the tendencies of the arbitrators and the relationship of those tendencies to the client's interests is critical.

A. The Party-Appointed Arbitrator

One mistake new arbitration advocates may make is to appoint an arbitrator in the hope that he or she will advocate (openly or otherwise) for the position of the appointing party client, without considering the effect that arbitrator's conduct will have on the chair of the tribunal. The danger of this strategy is that a non-neutral party-appointed arbitrator will negate whatever influence he or she might have had on the chair. Receiving a favorable dissent from one's own party-appointed arbitrator in an unsuccessful arbitration will be cold comfort to the client at the end of the process. It is wiser to appoint a truly independent party-appointed arbitrator who will have an influential voice on the tribunal.

Moreover, the appointment of an arbitrator who is (or appears to be) biased may result in challenges to the appointment or even impediments to enforcement of the eventual award. As such, any party-appointed arbitrator should be, and should comport himself or

---

[6] See Doak Bishop and Lucy F. Reed, Practical Guidelines for Interviewing, Selecting and Challenging Party-Appointed Arbitrators in International Commercial Arbitration, 14 ARB. INT'L 395, 395 (1998) (noting that "[i]t is a truism of arbitration that the process is only as good as the quality of the arbitrators conducting it.").

herself to be, impartial and independent. These two separate but interrelated requirements are defined in the International Bar Association's Ethics for International Arbitrators as follows:[7]

> Partiality arises when an arbitrator favours one of the parties, or when he is prejudiced in relation to the subject matter of the dispute. Dependence arises from relationships between an arbitrator and one of the parties, or with someone closely connected with one of the parties.

Within these parameters, the effective advocate will, of course, recommend appointment of a party arbitrator familiar with the client's legal system and expected to favor particular arguments or positions. The best advice to a client in this regard is this: "We do not and cannot promise you the vote of Mr. X or Ms. X. We *can* say that he or she will vote in your favor *if* you have the better case and we present it as such."

The practice of interviewing potential arbitrators in advance of appointment is now standard. Although any discussion of the merits of the dispute is off limits, short interviews may present an opportunity to test an arbitrator's schedule, his or her attitudes toward document disclosure and other procedural matters, and his or her opinions on potential candidates for chair of the tribunal. Another benefit from an interview, often underestimated, is the reassurance a client feels in seeing and hearing a potential arbitrator in person.

B. Selection of the Chair

The most important member of the tribunal obviously is the chair. Advocates should do all they can to retain a role in selecting the chair.

Too often, parties insist on rejecting out-of-hand any chair candidate proposed by the other side. Counsel should resist this

---

[7] International Bar Association, *Ethics for International Arbitrators*, 26 I.L.M. 583, 584-9 (1987).

because sometimes an opponent – for unknown and unknowable reasons – will propose a chair who is highly acceptable. The effective advocate listens with an open mind to each option proposed by the other side, always conducting careful due diligence.

The likely position of a proposed chair on the merits is the most important factor to consider, but it is not the only factor. It is also important to consider the tendencies of the candidate with respect to provisional measures, document disclosure, and management of the process. If the client's interests favor a prompt resolution of the dispute and careful attention to costs, a chair who is known to be overscheduled, slow to issue awards, or likely to let document disclosure and other motions drag on, could be a disastrous choice. Conversely, if broad document disclosure is necessary to the success of the claims, a chair with a restrictive view of disclosure could lead to a loss.

In considering potential candidates to serve as chair, the effective advocate uses all information available, including a review of published awards and other work, frank and confidential discussions with professional colleagues and, if possible, attendance at conferences at which the candidates speak.

It should always be a last resort – although, of necessity the norm in investor-state and other political arbitrations – to default to the appointing authority to select the chair. The input from the advocates is minimal or non-existent, and the appointing authority may or may not be an astute matchmaker. If this course has to be followed, it may be a good strategy to seek agreement with the other side that names discussed by parties or counsel will not be eliminated from the universe available to the appointing authority.

IV. Phase Three: Preliminary Sessions

After an arbitral tribunal has been appointed, a preliminary session normally follows. Whether through an agreement between the parties or the applicable rules, the preliminary session likely will result in an initial procedural order governing most of the proceedings. In modern practice, the tribunal (or the chair alone) will conduct the session by teleconference, following a winnowing of the outstanding procedural issues by counsel. The UNCITRAL Notes on Organizing Arbitral Proceedings (the "UNCITRAL Notes") contains a helpful "list of matters for possible consideration in organizing arbitral proceedings," with which experienced advocates are intimately familiar. These are the headings in that checklist:

1. Set of arbitration rules (parties may not have not agreed on a set of arbitration rules, or may have agreed on changes);
2. Language of proceedings (procedure for translations if needed);
3. Place of arbitration (location for hearing, other meetings);
4. Administrative services that may be needed for the arbitral tribunal to carry out its functions (establishment; payment for);
5. Deposits in respect of costs (amount, management, supplementary deposits);
6. Confidentiality of information relating to the arbitration; possible agreement thereon;
7. Routing of written communications among the parties and the arbitrators;
8. Telefax and other electronic means of sending documents;
9. Arrangements for the exchange of written submissions (scheduling, consecutive exchange?);
10. Practical details concerning written submission and evidence (e.g. method of submission, timing, number of copies, numbering, references);
11. Defining points at issue; order of deciding issues; defining relief or remedy sought (compiling a list of issues; is the relief sought adequately defined?);

12. Possible settlement negotiations and their effect on scheduling proceedings;
13. Documentary evidence (including submission of documents, enforced production of documents, standard means of dealing with large volumes of evidence);
14. Physical evidence other than documents;
15. Witnesses (degree of advance notice, requirement of witness statements, pre-hearing interviews or depositions);
16. Experts and expert witnesses (though these questions may be dealt with later in the proceedings, if the need for expert witnesses emerges);
17. Hearings (necessity, potential dates, time estimates – the majority of these issues will be dealt with later in the proceeding, and the granular details of the hearing will be dealt in a separate conference before it begins);
18. Multi-party arbitration; and
19. Possible requirements concerning filing or delivering the award.[8]

Not every issue on the UNCITRAL Notes checklist will apply in every arbitration. Nor is the checklist exclusive. Albert Jan van den Berg recommends adding two issues: the overall time schedule, and the possibility of bifurcating the proceedings.[9]

One of the fundamental characteristics (and attractions) of international arbitration is the parties' ability to tailor procedure. Hence, the parties should seek to reach agreement on points of

---

[8] U.N. COMM'N ON INT'L TRADE LAW, UNCITRAL Notes on Organizing Arbitral Proceedings, List of Matters for Possible Consideration in Organizing Arbitral Proceedings, U.N. Doc. A/CN.9/423 (Apr. 10, 1996), available at http://www.uncitral.org/pdf/english/texts/arbitration/arb-notes/arb-notes-e.pdf.

[9] Albert Jan van den Berg, *Organizing an International Arbitration*, *in* THE LEADING ARBITRATORS' GUIDE TO INTERNATIONAL ARBITRATION, *supra* note 6 at 149, 157.

procedure before turning to the tribunal. To the extent agreement cannot be reached, counsel typically advocate their positions on the outstanding issues in writing in advance of the preliminary session. This, in turn, should expedite and reduce the cost of arbitration.

When arguing for particular procedural points, the effective advocate avoids presenting the tribunal with a one-sided picture. The best submissions describe the context of the procedural dispute, acknowledge the other party's views, and plot a way from "here to there" for the tribunal, ideally in the form of a proposed order and schedule. An organized and balanced proposal is more likely to influence a tribunal than a partisan missive, and may even be adopted wholesale.

As early as the preliminary session, the parties may wish to resolve certain parameters for the final hearing. Some procedural issues – such as whether witnesses who submit witness statements must be produced for cross examination – will affect advocacy strategy from the very beginning.

If the tribunal schedules the preliminary session without circulating an agenda or checklist, the effective advocate will tactfully propose a list of issues in advance of the session. The UNCITRAL checklist is a natural and neutral proposition. Advocates should also consider offering draft procedural orders, although many arbitrators have their own preferred templates.

In this context, more is not always better. A clear procedural order is critical for efficient arbitrations, but should not be so detailed and exhaustive that it limits necessary flexibility and causes the very type of procedural disputes it aims to avoid.

V. Phase Four: Interim Measures

Interim, or provisional, measures are most frequently sought by claimants in arbitration proceedings to preserve assets necessary to satisfy a future award. Interim measures may also be sought on other grounds, such as to protect the contractual status quo from anticipated breach or to protect evidence from destruction. Parties may seek provisional measures from a court, often in the earlier stages of an arbitration, or directly from the tribunal, or from both. Although the advocacy techniques and skills required in interim measure proceedings are generally the same as those required in other written and oral submissions, some particular considerations do apply.

Most important, the very question of whether to pursue a request for interim measures is a weighty one. This question implicates varied and sometimes conflicting client interests, including the needs to: (*i*) control costs – interim measures can be expensive; (*ii*) obtain a timely result – interim measures can sometimes effectively conclude a dispute; (*iii*) position the dispute for a favorable settlement – interim measures can have substantial influence on settlement talks; and (*iv*) protect business interests at risk of collateral damage by the arbitration – for this, interim measures may be essential.

From an advocacy perspective, a request for provisional measures is an opportunity to demonstrate to the tribunal that serious interests are at stake and time is of the essence. In addition, a hearing on interim measures provides the advocate with an early opportunity to get in front of the tribunal and tell the client's story. If the story is compelling and the request for interim measures is successful, the client's position will be greatly strengthened.

A. Caution in Seeking Preliminary Measures

There are, however, several reasons why advocates should take a cautious and long view when considering whether to make a request for interim measures, especially if the case for the measures does not appear open and shut. *First*, interim measures are very hard to win, and an early loss obviously is not an auspicious way to begin an arbitral proceeding. *Second*, a request for provisional measures might lead to some consideration of the ultimate merits of the dispute by the tribunal before all of the evidence is in, and a loss might undercut the party's case. *Third*, a request for interim measures that is perceived to be spurious will lower the standing of the advocate as well as his or her client in the eyes of the arbitrators.

B. Structuring a Request for Interim Measures

An application for interim measures should be structured to be understood quickly by the tribunal, and provide the analytical skeleton for a favorable decision or order. Advocates must review and meet the essential elements for provisional measures under the relevant procedural rules. In proceedings under the ICSID Arbitration Rules, for example, an application for provisional measures must "specify the rights to be preserved, the measures the recommendation of which is requested, and the circumstances that necessitate such measures."[10] To facilitate speedy resolution of a request for interim measures, which by definition is time sensitive, the request should include a proposed decision or order.

C. Emergency Arbitrators

Several arbitration institutions – including the ICDR, the LCIA and the ICC – now provide for an "emergency arbitrator" procedure, whereby a temporary arbitrator (sometimes referred to as a referee) is appointed to adjudicate requests for urgent interim measures before the arbitral tribunal has been constituted. An emergency arbitrator has the limited role of adjudicating such an emergency application. The procedure can be remarkably speedy, with requests resolved in days or weeks.[11] Typically, any measures ordered by the emergency arbitrator can be lifted or modified by the arbitral tribunal once it is constituted.

---

[10] INT'L CTR. FOR SETTLEMENT OF INV. DISPUTES, *Rules of Procedure for Arbitration Proceedings*, Rule 39(1), ICSID/15/Rev. 1 (Jan. 1, 2003), available at http://icsid.worldbank.org/ICSID/StaticFiles/basicdoc_en-archive/ICSID_English.pdf.

[11] Paul Quigley & Guillaume Lemenez, The ICDR's Emergency Arbitrator Procedure in Action: A Look at the Empirical Data, 63(3) DISP. RESOL. J. 60 (2008).

VI. Phase Five: Document Disclosure

The effective advocate never assumes that any national standards of document disclosure (or broader discovery) or rules of evidence will apply. Tribunals typically include arbitrators from civil law and common law backgrounds. Even if counsel for both parties and the arbitrators are from the same domestic legal background, it would be a mistake to assume that the tribunal will apply domestic rules. U.S. attorneys, for example, cannot count on U.S.-style discovery even if they are before an all-U.S. tribunal.

The scope of document disclosure in an arbitration can have far-reaching consequences for the outcome of the dispute. Some claims by their nature, such as fraud claims, may require broad disclosure to be substantiated. If the tribunal refuses to permit such disclosure to proceed, the claims may be a dead letter. In other cases, document disclosure may not be necessary, but the process affords one or the other party the opportunity to delay the proceedings and wear down the other side.

The document disclosure stage is an important opportunity for the advocate to protect his or her client's varied interests. Although some arbitration rules address the scope of disclosure, it is almost always a highly contentious process. There is a premium on establishing parameters in the tribunal's procedural orders and the counsel conferences that precede preliminary sessions.

It is a reality that the degree of compliance with document disclosure orders – which often rely on parties acting against their interests – varies. Advocates must anticipate this possibly uneven playing field when considering the level of disclosure to seek. If the other side is unlikely to produce documents as ordered, there is little point in agreeing to broad disclosure; no advocate likes to have to explain to a client why it has produced documents and the other side has not.

A. Strategic Points

Advocates should be ready with their strategy for the document disclosure phase in advance of negotiations with opposing counsel and the preliminary sessions. The UNCITRAL Notes are not particularly helpful, as they flag only general issues of document disclosure and documentary evidence, as follows:

- Time-limits for submission of documentary evidence intended to be submitted by the parties; consequences of late submission;
- Whether the arbitral tribunal intends to require a party to produce documentary evidence;
- Should assertions about the origin and receipt of documents and about the correctness of photocopies be assumed as accurate;
- Are the parties willing to submit jointly a single set of documentary evidence;
- Should voluminous and complicated documentary evidence be presented through summaries, tabulations, charts, extracts or samples.[12]

In this day and age, advocates must also address issues concerning: (i) electronic discovery – yes or no? if yes, how much, and how?; (ii) privilege – what rules apply?; and (iii) document production from third parties.

In document disclosure, as in other contexts, the effective advocate is fully aware of his or her client's interests before speaking to the tribunal or launching into disputes. It is not uncommon, for example, for a client to value confidentiality of its own business information more than access to the other side's documents. One way to address such issues is with a detailed confidentiality agreement. Such agreements typically limit access to the documents produced (for example, only to persons actually involved in the arbitration) and provide for the destruction or return of documents after the conclusion of the arbitration. In some cases, where greater

---

[12] UNCITRAL Notes, *supra* note 8 at § 13.

sensitivity exists due to, for example, competition concerns, advocates may need to include provisions requiring that sensitive documents be disclosed only to counsel.

B. The IBA Rules

Parties and arbitrators in international cases often turn to the International Bar Association's Rules on the Taking of Evidence in International Commercial Arbitration (the "IBA Rules") to govern, or at least guide, document discovery. The IBA Rules provide that a request for production of documents should contain:

> (a) (i) a description of a requested document sufficient to identify it, or (ii) a description in sufficient detail ... of a narrow and specific requested category of documents that are reasonably believed to exist;
>
> (b) a description of how the documents requested are relevant and material to the outcome of the case; and
>
> (c) a statement that the documents requested are not in the possession, custody or control of the requesting party....[13]

Advocates need to know that the IBA Rules, providing as they do for production of categories of documents (albeit "narrow and specific" categories), may lead to a greater level of document disclosure than is typically expected by civil law practitioners. Of course, they may also lead to far less document disclosure than common lawyers desire. The effective advocate will adjust.

C. Use of a Redfern Schedule

In making a request for production of documents, advocates should disregard domestic formats – such as the "belt and

---

[13] INT'L BAR ASS'N, IBA Rules on the Taking of Evidence in International Commercial Arbitration, Rule 3 (1999) available at http://www.int-bar.org/images/downloads/IBA%20rules%20on%20the%20taking%20of%20Evidence.pdf.

suspenders" detail of document requests used in U.S. litigation – and employ specific requests. A particularly useful tool is the "Redfern Schedule," named after eminent arbitrator Alan Redfern. This is a table initially prepared by the requesting party with numbered entries: describing (*i*) each document or category of documents sought and (*ii*) the asserted relevance or materiality of the documents requested; stating (*iii*) that the requesting party does not possess and cannot reasonably obtain the documents sought; and leaving blank columns for (*iv*) the other side's identification of documents produced or detailed objections to the request; and (*v*) the tribunal's ruling on the request and objections. Few arbitrators enjoy ruling on extensive document disclosure disputes, and so most appreciate advocates who at least streamline the process with Redfern Schedules.

D. Electronic Document Disclosure

The transition from paper-based evidence (and, indeed, paper-based arbitral submissions) to electronic evidence such as emails can complicate document disclosure in international arbitration. Disclosure can be onerous: locating even "narrow and specific" categories of documents can require extensive and expensive searches by the responding party. The format of disclosure can be disputed: should files be produced in their original native form? with metadata? as images? If non-searchable image files are produced, should searchable files also be produced?

Advocates should confront these issues carefully and helpfully. For example, counsel should be prepared to be specific about how a given request for electronic data might (or might not) be onerous, rather than making *ad hominem* assertions. Counsel should adopt a reasoned position on the best format for electronic data and be prepared to solve the problem of electronic data disputes for the (often less IT-experienced) tribunal by presenting a user-friendly roadmap.

E. Privilege and Immunity from Disclosure

In an international arbitration involving parties and counsel from multiple jurisdictions, it is rarely clear which rules of attorney-client privilege, privacy or other privileges or immunities from disclosure apply to the proceedings. The laws of different jurisdictions may make differing demands on the advocates. Although it will not always be necessary to address this question, which usually arises in the context of disclosure disputes, advocates should recognize that the question will not be subject to easy resolution if it does arise. The normal rule applies: be prepared.

VII. Phase Six: The Main Substantive Pleadings

A. Dispositive Motions

Certain arbitral rules or procedural orders provide parties with an opportunity to make dispositive motions. These are motions arguing that the proceedings, or a particular claim or defense within the proceedings, should be resolved in favor of one party or another in advance of the final evidentiary hearing. If granted, such a motion can end the proceedings in favor of one party or narrow the scope of issues for the final hearing.

Dispositive motions remain rare in international arbitration, and success on such motions is rarer still. It is a major step for a tribunal to grant a dispositive motion, rather than take the safer path of leaving all issues to the final hearing.

To win a dispositive motion, the advocate must present sufficient evidence and law to resolve one or more jurisdiction or merits claims in his or her client's favor. The burden of establishing these facts and law is almost always on the moving party. The opposing party typically attempts to undercut the sufficiency of those facts and law.

For the advocate making a dispositive motion, clarity is critical. The facts and law should be presented as straightforward and undisputed, and as leading inexorably to the granting of the motion. Logical organization of key documents is critical to a clear narrative.

As with all written submissions, the motion should be structured to lead easily to an award (or partial award) in that party's favor by the tribunal.

For an oral hearing on a dispositive motion, the same advocacy tools apply as for the final hearing. Among other things, key evidence should be presented in a manner supporting the overall story. Depending on length, several oral advocates should speak, to hold and refresh the arbitrators' attention. Advocates should avoid using presentation slides that merely list the steps of their argument, as these can distract the arbitrators from the oral presentation and the key documents. In comparison, slides of graphics, charts and summary points, if well-prepared and used sparingly, do improve an oral argument and are useful to the arbitrators in deliberations.

B. Memorials

The memorials and counter-memorials are the key written submissions through which the claimants and respondents present the facts and legal arguments to support their claims, defenses and counter-claims. Although these submissions may go by different names under different rules (such as a Statement of Claim and Statement of Defense in the UNCITRAL Rules), and vary in number after the first exchange (reply, rejoinder and sur-reply), they remain the heart of pre-hearing advocacy in international arbitration proceedings.

The memorial and counter-memorial, as the first exhaustive submissions for each side, should set forth a case that needs little or no further development. A key advocacy tool is to structure these submissions by reverse-engineering from the desired award: what are the truly essential facts? applicable law? best cause of action? easiest damages calculation?

Where the advocate needs to present complex facts and multiple theories of law in a clear and simple manner in a memorial, an early and thorough planning session is critical. Gather the legal team, the existing submissions and the key documents, and pose the question: "How do we help the tribunal to help us win?" Ideas can be recorded on a flip chart or smart board, and the outline built, section by section. While all routes to a favorable outcome on each claim should be argued, the memorial ideally emphasizes the most direct ones. At this planning stage, an essential advocacy tool may be a one-page diagram of the straightest path to a win.

When deciding the emphasis and tone to adopt in drafting a memorial, the effective advocate always keeps the composition of the tribunal in mind. Regarding emphasis, and generally speaking, common law arbitrators may feel more comfortable with published awards, while civil law arbitrators may find policy arguments and the writings of prominent academics to be more persuasive.[14] Regarding tone, and still generally speaking, common law arbitrators may appreciate a more argumentative style, compared to the more dispassionate voice familiar to civil lawyers. When faced with a mixed panel, the editor of this book has advised:

> A non-argumentative format is likely to be acceptable to all arbitrators, while an inflammatory style may be considered offensive by some arbitrators. Thus, the academic style may be a suitable compromise style for mixed panels.[15]

A less argumentative style is generally expected and favored in international arbitration, but there are notable exceptions. The effective advocate knows his or her tribunal and drafts accordingly.

VIII. Phase Seven: The Pre-Hearing Conference

The goal of the pre-hearing conference is to set firm procedure for the final hearing. In most cases, the chair circulates an agenda or asks counsel jointly to draft one. Similarly, the chair may draft the resulting procedural order or ask counsel to do so.

Advocates must be fully prepared for the pre-hearing conference. They should comport themselves confidently and project mastery of

---

[14] Doak Bishop, *Advocacy in International Arbitration: United States*, *in* THE ART OF ADVOCACY IN INTERNATIONAL ARBITRATION, *supra* note 2 at 309, 340.

[15] *Id.*

the issues and procedural rules. The effective advocate will not be afraid to take charge (tactfully) of introducing issues if the tribunal seems inattentive or lacks initiative.

A. Balancing Certainty and Flexibility

In establishing hearing procedure through the pre-hearing conference, the tribunal and advocates should resolve the myriad of predictable issues, but also avoid trying to set rules for every eventuality. As one of the authors has co-written:

> Adopting very detailed guidelines will not help and should not be the goal. Quite to the contrary, excessively detailed procedural rules may cause difficulties of their own, namely inevitable squabbles with respect to the applicability and proper construction of such rules, and an unintended form of US motions practice.[16]

Finding the right level of detail for hearing procedure is not easy, and sometimes even apparently clear guidelines may be ambiguous. For example, even a "chess clock" approach to dividing time between the parties can lead to confusion; time and again, inexperienced arbitration counsel can be surprised to find that time spent cross-examining a witness counts against his or her own time.[17] Another common divergence in expectations concerns who has the last word at the hearing: the claimant or the respondent?

At the very least, the pre-hearing conference should raise and resolve questions regarding:

(i) Evidentiary Documents. All to be exchanged pre-hearing? Will the parties agree in advance on a set of undisputed documents?

---

[16] Laurent Lévy & Lucy Reed, *Managing Fact Evidence in International Arbitration*, in ICCA CONGRESS SERIES NO. 13: INTERNATIONAL ARBITRATION, BACK TO BASICS? 633, 641 (Albert Jan van den Berg ed., 2007).

[17] *Id.*

(ii) Timing. Length of day? Chess clock? Guillotine? Same amount of time for each party, even if one party is presenting more witnesses?

(iii) Location & Layout. Where? Who sits where? Access?

(iv) Use of Demonstratives. What types of demonstratives will be permitted? Must these be exchanged before they are presented?

(v) Oral testimony. Who and how? (See below.)

B. Witness Testimony

Given the importance of cross-examination in international arbitration hearings, experienced advocates know to use the pre-hearing conference to obtain ground rules for witness testimony. Finding that general pre-hearing guidelines are not always enough, one of the authors – with Laurent Lévy – has propounded "Notes on Organizing Fact Testimony in Advance of Evidentiary Hearing in International Commercial Arbitration" (the "Notes")[18] The purpose of the Notes is to identify issues on which advocates may have different expectations, and thereby minimize disruption and delay in hearings. The Notes are a starting point, allowing arbitrators to add and delete issues depending on the background and experience of the tribunal, parties and counsel involved, the number and identity of the witnesses, and the magnitude of the evidentiary record. The Notes, framed as questions to be considered by the tribunal, are as follows:

A. IBA Rules

Do you agree with basic principles in Art. 8 of the IBA Rules (arbitrator control, normal order of witnesses and questions, affirmation, scope of arbitrator questions)? If so, scope of conference can be abbreviated. (Note: This focuses counsel new to international arbitration on the IBA Rules.)

---

[18] *Id.* at 642.

B. *Why? Underlying Purposes for Fact Witnesses*

1. What is your perception as to the main purpose of fact testimony? To test the credibility of witness statements? Or to maximize fact-finding? Or both?
2. Would you welcome the arbitrator indicating in advance what fact testimony it most wants to hear? If so, by witness or by issue? If not, why not?

C. *Who? Details as to the Witnesses*

1. Subject to the time allowed (see below), what witnesses do you intend to present?
2. Are there witness statements filed for all? Critical amendments to be made?
3. Order of priority? Comfortable that they are not duplicative?
4. Are there witnesses from the other side you require?
5. Do you have witnesses you wish to call even if the other side indicates it does not want to cross-examine them?
6. Does any witness require a formal order or subpoena?
7. Do you anticipate bringing witnesses for possible rebuttal? If so, why do you anticipate a need for rebuttal?

D. *When? Scheduling and Order Issues*

1. In what order do you intend to present the witnesses? All of claimant's witnesses followed by all of respondent's? Or claimant-respondent by issue? Or a combination?
2. Are all your witnesses available?
3. Any special scheduling requests?
4. Do you have an estimate, however rough, of how much time each witness should take?

E. *How and What? Method and Scope of Testimony*

1. Do you agree that the arbitrator, specifically the chairman, shall be the umpire for all questioning?

2. Any special requirements/expectations for affirmations/ oaths? Any Islamic witnesses?

3. Witness preparation: What are your expectations/ intentions in relation to preparing your witnesses to testify? How much time do you intend to spend in cross-examination exploring the scope of preparation? How much preparation is likely to lead you to lodge an objection?

4. Sequestration of witnesses? Both before and after testimony? Special rules for party representatives?

5. Progression: Do you anticipate each witness going through direct, cross, redirect? Recross?

6. Progression: Do you anticipate limiting opening direct to thirty minutes, to affirm the witness statement and "relax" the witness?

7. Timing: Do you prefer the arbitrator to use the "chess clock" or "guillotine" timing system?

8. Timing: Does time spent on cross come out of the time "account" of the sponsoring side or the crossing side? How about time spent on arbitrator questions (asking and answering)?

9. Style: Do you anticipate using leading questions on direct as well as cross?

10. Style: On cross, do you intend to use a relatively aggressive US approach or a more conversational approach (subject to the chairman's control)?

11. Scope: Do you intend to limit direct and cross-questions to subjects covered in the witness statement? To object

if the other side goes beyond those subjects? What are your expectations as to the scope of the arbitrators' questions?

12. Privilege: What are your expectations as to privilege/confidentiality for witness testimony?
13. Objections: Do you anticipate making objections on relevance? Hearsay? Privilege/confidentiality? Repetitiveness? Delaying tactics?
14. Objections: How would you envision making objections? How do you envision the arbitrator should respond and rule on objections?
15. Use of documents: When you question a witness about a document, do you intend to refer him/her to an agreed hearing bundle or will you use loose copies (with copies for all)? Do you anticipate spending substantial witness time on documents, to focus the arbitrator on the record?
16. Visual aids: Do you intend to use new charts/maps/etc. with witnesses? If so, have copies available, as no surprises will be allowed.
17. Are you open to witness conferencing? If so, for which issues or witnesses?

Although, as noted, the format is a list of questions to be posed by the arbitrators in the pre-hearing phase, the effective advocate will be aware of these – and other questions – in preparing for and navigating this important pre-hearing phase. The goal is to set the stage for the final hearing, allowing the effective written advocate to make best use of his or her oral advocacy skills.

Chapter 14

OPENING STATEMENTS

Toby Landau and Doak Bishop

I. Introduction: The Significance and Function of the Opening Statement

"In my beginning is my end."
T. S. Eliot, *Four Quartets. East Coker*

The practice of international arbitration has evolved somewhat organically, and in its current form now embodies key elements of several different legal traditions. In particular, civil law approaches to written advocacy (e.g. the use of lengthy and all-inclusive written memorials) are often combined with Anglo-American approaches to oral advocacy (e.g. substantial hearings which include detailed oral submissions). Oral opening statements have become the norm, yet there is no fixed understanding as to their precise function. Some regard opening statements as relatively unimportant: a formal exercise in introducing a case that would already have been articulated in written briefs, and which the Tribunal would already have read and fully understood. Some regard them as an important opportunity to advance the debate between the parties beyond the written memorials; to distill the issues in the case; and to present a structure to the Tribunal in which witness and expert testimony might be placed. Others regard opening statements as more important than written briefs and oral testimony, allowing each party to educate and persuade the Tribunal, on the working assumption that written memorials may not have been read fully, or understood fully, and that witnesses and experts may not be believed.

In practice, the use to be made of the opening statement in any given case tends to reflect the particular background and experience of the counsel and arbitral tribunal concerned. For example, in US and English court proceedings, the customary role of the opening statement is to tell the judge / jury what the trial lawyer expects to prove during the course of the trial, and many US and English practitioners automatically assume that the same will apply in an international arbitration. But this assumption is without any foundation. For example, in US / English court proceedings, the parties may not have produced or deployed any evidence at the time of the opening statement, whereas in an international arbitration, the parties would typically already have submitted lengthy memorials, supporting documents, witness statements, and expert reports to the tribunal, and would have already "made" their basic cases in advance of the hearing, so the opening statement would serve no useful purpose if it is merely an introduction to the case.

Ultimately, in international arbitration there are no set rules on this issue, and so there should be no set preconceptions. But in deciding how to deploy an opening statement, the potential value of this component of the process in the overall presentation of one's case should not be underestimated. This is so for a number of related reasons.

Oral v Written Advocacy: The opening statement is often the first opportunity for the advocate orally and directly to address the tribunal, face-to-face; to make a direct impression; and to gauge the tribunal's reaction. As such, it can be an extremely valuable chance to clarify the facts and the law by correcting any misunderstandings created by the written pleadings; to answer questions from the arbitrators; to understand and dispel particular concerns; and, overall, to persuade the tribunal. To this, one may add that the opening statement allows the advocate to emphasize the "equities" of the case. The equities of the case refer to the key facts that implicate our human sense of right and wrong, of fairness and unfairness, and of suffering and injury. The "equities" go to the very heart of our sense of justice. By properly organizing and highlighting the key evidence and arguments, the advocate can communicate what is most important about the facts. This is more than just an intellectual exercise in reasoning; it can also convey a *feeling* that the client's case is *right* — that the equities of the case strongly support the client's position. When supported by the advocate's body language and voice tone, a message of conviction and credibility can be conveyed, and life can be breathed into otherwise sterile (and often dense) written submissions.

Clearly, the value of this opportunity increases in proportion to the volume of written material that may also be filed. Tribunals, like anyone else, have a finite capacity to absorb and distill lengthy and detailed written submissions and evidence, and whilst written advocacy obviously has its place, it can often be the face-to-face oral presentation that provides the essential path through the mass of written material. Once a theory and structure of the case has been conveyed, this may well guide the way in which the tribunal then addresses all other materials. Further, an oral presentation frequently allows a "connection" to be made between counsel and arbitrator that simply has no equivalent in terms of unsupervised reading.

Timing: Second, the opening statement has a special significance in terms of its timing in the overall arbitral process. Conceptions about cases are often formed early on, and once a particular theory has taken shape in the minds of the tribunal, it may well last, or at the very least "anchor" the tribunal in a particular perspective. And once a party has "anchored" a tribunal in a particular view, the burden passes to the other side to persuade it otherwise.

In this regard, one must consider the way in which people tend to receive and compute information. At this early stage of an arbitration, the tribunal is usually trying to understand the facts and organize them in their own minds into a narrative story that reconciles and makes sense of the evidence. Studies (described in other Chapters of this work) have demonstrated that people naturally think in terms of a narrative story, because this allows them an efficient mechanism to arrange, connect, store and remember facts – and because of the difficulty for most people to organize, remember or make sense of random information, or even a long list of connected facts. The opening statement provides the first in-person opportunity to supply the narrative story, and to structure how the arbitrators think about the case. This can be vital. Once the arbitrators have developed a strong first impression, and a mental structure of the evidence, it becomes more difficult later to change their minds (given the significant mental effort of discarding an entire structure of the evidence and constructing a new one). It is noteworthy that psychologists who study US juries have found that jurors start forming impressions of cases right after opening statements are concluded, and in 80% of the cases those impressions never change. Similarly, as observed by Waites and Lawrence in their study of the psychology of oral advocacy in international arbitration ("*The Psychological Dynamics in International Arbitration Advocacy*", Chapter 4 of this work):

> "A typical arbitrator concludes the initial stage of the decision making process with a single dominant story in mind. In fact, researchers have determined that a sizable percentage of arbitrators and other legal decision makers have established a clear leaning in the case by the end of the opening statement (prior to any exposure to witnesses or evidence). ...".[1]

And so the opening statement may in fact have a disproportionately important place in the overall task of persuasion.

Documentary v Witness Evidence: Third, the opening statement may well be the best and most direct means to take the tribunal through contemporaneous documentary evidence, which in turn may well be of far more probative value than the statements of witnesses. We have all become accustomed to highly polished witness statements drafted by lawyers on behalf of witnesses, often long after the events in question. The huge investment by lawyers in the process of witness testimony has, sadly, converted most witnesses of fact into advocates, and most witness statements into submissions. The notion of actual,

---

[1] Much of the advice discussed in this chapter is premised on some understanding of the psychology of persuasion. The reader is referred generally to the chapters addressing this topic by Dr. Richard Waites, James Lawrence, Sophie Nappert, and Prof. Dieter Flader. In those chapters the reader will find a basic primer addressing some of the psychological principles underlying the art of persuasion. This chapter applies those principles to the practice of advocacy.

untainted "recall" by witnesses of fact has long been lost. Witness testimony now depends upon a complex process of "production" by the party calling the witness, and "unraveling" by the opposing party, through cross-examination. The two procedures are closely aligned, and as witness preparation becomes more sophisticated, so the process of cross-examination must be correspondingly more rigorous. The result, in many cases, is increased costs; a relatively cumbersome process of limited evidential value, an increasing skepticism on the part of arbitrators, and a greater reliance upon contemporaneous documentary evidence. As one well-known practitioner put it in an opening statement in a recent international arbitration in which one of the authors was involved:

> "... What we're going to do is look at the documentary record and look at it in detail, look at it document by document, and there's a reason for that. ... Contemporaneous documents give us a real view of what happened at the time. Documents cannot be coordinated and prepared the way that we know witnesses can be. Documents can't change their stories the way we know witnesses can. Instead, documents take us back to the question that people really understood at the time. They take us back to what the parties' intentions were, their subjective intentions were at the time. It's easy for people today to remember things the way they'd like them to have been. Documents don't let them do that."

If in any given case special reliance is to be placed upon contemporaneous documentary evidence, the opening statement can be the prime opportunity for this. Indeed, it can be much more effective than the common process of taking witnesses through documents in cross-examination. Many advocates wish to show their tribunal the contemporaneous record, but do so by putting documents to witnesses. But this invariably ends up in a fruitless exercise by which the witness is asked to "confirm" what one can readily glean in any event from the document itself. The simpler approach is to take the tribunal directly to the documents, and to explain the relevance of each. This is effectively done in the course of an opening statement – and indeed this may be the only chance to do so. In many cases, there is no closing argument or the closing is effectively consigned to post-hearing written briefs or memorials, which may be served many weeks later, without the benefit of oral exposition, and at a time when hearts and minds may no longer be as open to persuasion.

In the end, the precise deployment of an opening statement is a question of strategy in each instance. Certain considerations, however, apply throughout, in terms of preparation, style and delivery, and it is these issues to which this chapter is devoted.

II. Preparation and Materials

Contrary to the impression seasoned advocates may seek to convey, a good opening statement is not the product of extemporaneous brilliance, but rather of meticulous and careful planning, preparation and organization. In the words of Thomas Edison, "Genius is one percent inspiration, and ninety-nine percent perspiration." The more thought, planning and (figurative) sweat, the better the opening statement is likely to be.

Written Notes: Most advocates prepare some form of written notes to assist them in presenting the opening statement, and thereby to ensure a structured and well-ordered presentation. This product can take the form of an outline (from the very simple, to the very detailed), notes, or even a script. The more incomplete the outline, the greater the danger of drifting "off-piste" mid-submission, or missing key points. The more detailed the outline, the greater the danger of reading aloud, and thereby losing all the benefits of oral advocacy (and most likely the tribunal's attention). A happy medium must be struck, which allows the advocate some flexibility, and in particular the ability to look away from his[2] notes, to secure eye-contact with the arbitrators, and to "connect" with his audience. One tip in this regard is to prepare one's notes with an extra-large

---

[2] The terms "he," "him" and "his" are used in this chapter for economy of style, and in the gender neutral sense, meaning any advocate of either gender.

font size and over-generous line spacing. The larger the font, the more the advocate will be able to keep a distance between himself and his script, and to look up, and then down, and find his place on the page. A 12pt font and single line spacing will deter the best of advocates from leaving his script.

Written Outlines: In addition to one's own written notes, another useful approach is to hand out to the tribunal at the beginning of the oral presentation a skeletal outline of the argument (or in the case of PowerPoint presentation, a print-out of slides). This serves several important purposes. Firstly, it can be the organizational vehicle for the oral presentation. It allows the tribunal to see the overall structure of the submission; where every point that is being made fits in terms of the scheme of the case; and where the advocate is in the argument, at any particular time. The ability to place each point in context in this way, and to follow the precise structure of the presentation, is essential for any audience's purposes. Second, the outline can be a useful means to provide citations to the tribunal, whether to documentary evidence, statements, or authorities, as well as quotations, excerpts, and diagrams, maps or schematics. Third, depending upon its length and detail, the outline can obviate the need for the tribunal to take extensive written notes. Fourth, a piece of paper in front of a tribunal allows it to look elsewhere than just at the advocate during the presentation itself, which may well improve the tribunal's concentration, and ease its overall task of listening.

Some advocates need only the barest of outlines of one or two pages, while others prefer a very detailed outline that can run in some cases to 20 pages or more. What is best for a particular advocate will depend upon his experience, skill and level of comfort. An advocate should use the vehicle that allows the presentation to be the most effective and persuasive – which invariably means the vehicle that allows the advocate to be the most comfortable while making the presentation. One word of warning, however: There is a tendency to over-burden written outlines, skeleton arguments, or PowerPoint slides, for fear of omitting important points. Once an outline starts to replicate a written submission, however, its utility has been lost, and one might as well simply refer to a full written brief. In so far as possible, the outline should be restricted to key points only, thereby leaving the detail for oral elaboration and exposition. The fuller the outline itself, the less need there is for any oral elaboration. Also, the fuller the outline, the greater the burden that may be placed upon the tribunal. In this regard, one might bear in mind a very recent admonition of counsel by the English Court of Appeal (albeit in the context of English litigation, in particular a challenge to jurisdiction in an arbitration matter):

> "71. It would not be right to end this judgment without expressing strong disapproval of the volume of papers with which the court was presented by Midgulf. There were 15 lever arch files. These included 5 volumes of authorities (totalling well over 100 authorities) and 3 files of documents (to which almost no reference was made) in addition to the core bundle. Midgulf's first 'skeleton argument' ran to 132 pages. Longmore LJ, as the supervising Lord Justice, ordered Midgulf to produce a proper summary of its argument. It produced a 15 page summary in which it complained that it was unable to develop its argument in proper detail and referred the court instead to the detailed argument contained in its previous document. The respondent's skeleton ran to 23 pages, about which I make no complaint in the circumstances. Midgulf served a supplementary skeleton argument running to 30 pages, in which it repeated many of its previous arguments and complained that GCT had failed to address in its skeleton argument a number of the arguments advanced by Midgulf in its original skeleton argument. In that respect Mr Nolan had shown good judgment because the matters either did not arise on the appeal or were of peripheral relevance.
>
> 72. I am afraid that the case is a grotesque example of a tendency to burden the court with documents of grossly disproportionate quantity and length. It is a practice which must stop. Far from assisting the court, it makes the work of the court infinitely harder. Hours had to be spent reading through Midgulf's voluminous skeleton arguments, and they were largely wasted hours. It will no doubt also have added greatly and unnecessarily to the costs of the appeal.

73. The central issue in this case was a very short one. As I said at the outset of the judgment, it turned on the effect of a small number of communications between the parties. All that the court needed in relation to that issue was to have the documents and a summary of each party's argument, which could have been provided in far less than 10 pages. The ordinary principles of contract law in this area are so well known there was no need for reference to authorities, let alone well over 100 authorities.

74. In Tombstone Limited v Raja [2008] EWCA Civ 1444; [2009] 1 WLR 1143 Mummery LJ said:

> "125. Practitioners who ignore practice directions on skeleton arguments (see CPR 52PD paras 5.10 "Each point should be stated as concisely as the nature of the case allows") and do so without the imposition of any formal penalty are well advised to note the risk of the court's negative reaction to unnecessarily long written submissions. The skeleton argument procedure was introduced to assist the court, as well as the parties, by improving preparations for, and the efficiency of, adversarial oral hearings, which remain central to this court's public role.
>
> 126. We remind practitioners that skeleton arguments should not be prepared as verbatim scripts to be read out in public or as footnoted theses to be read in private. Good skeleton arguments are tools with practical uses: an agenda for the hearing, a summary of the main points, propositions and arguments to be developed orally, a useful way of noting citations and references, a convenient place for making cross references, a time-saving means of avoiding unnecessary dictation to the court and laborious and pointless note-taking by the court.
>
> 127. Skeleton arguments are aids to oral advocacy. They are not written briefs which are used in some jurisdictions as substitutes for oral advocacy. An unintended and unfortunate side effect of the growth in written advocacy (written opening and closing submissions and "speaking notes", as well as skeleton arguments) has been that too many practitioners, at

> increased cost to their clients and diminishing assistance to the court, burden their opponents and the court with written briefs. They are anything but brief. The result is that there is no real saving of legal costs, or of precious hearing, reading and writing time. As has happened in this case, the opponent's skeleton argument becomes longer and the judgment reflecting the lengthy written submissions tends to be longer than is really necessary to explain to the parties why they have won or lost an appeal.
>
> 128. The skeletal nature of written advocacy is in danger of being overlooked. In some cases we are weighed down by the skeleton arguments and when we dare to complain about the time they take up, we are sometimes told that we can read them "in our own time" after the hearing. In our judgment, this is not what appellate advocacy is about, or ought to be about, in this court."

> 75. The problem has not lessened, and the present is a particularly egregious example. When [Counsel] was asked to explain why the court had been burdened with so many documents and such long skeleton arguments, he explained that it was his intention to provide it with all the written materials which might bear on any point which might arise during the appeal and to provide a full statement of his argument in order that his oral argument could be brief. That may accord with the practice in other jurisdictions, where it is customary for appellate courts to limit the time allowed for oral argument to a short period, but it is emphatically not the proper practice in this jurisdiction."[3]

The lessons for international arbitration, it is suggested, are clear.

Other Materials: In addition to a written outline or skeleton, opening statements are often effective when made by reference to documentary exhibits. This may entail cross-references to a main hearing bundle, and asking the tribunal to take up volumes at the

---

[3] Per Toulson LJ in *Midgulf v GCT* [2010] EWCA Civ 66 (10 February 2010).

actual hearing, as each cross-reference is made. This has the benefit of familiarizing the tribunal with the documentary record (as well as encouraging some physical movement by each arbitrator, thereby reducing chances of sleep, assisting blood circulation, etc). On the other hand, if there are many references to be made, this can be a slow, cumbersome and disruptive process, as each member of the tribunal tries to locate the correct volume, tab, page and paragraph. One way around this is to produce a specific bundle of documents for the opening presentation, comprising highlighted excerpts or select pages only, tabbed, and in the order in which the advocate intends to address them in the presentation. This can save much time, and allow for a more streamlined presentation. The downside to this is that it entails giving the tribunal more than one version of the relevant documents (the other being in the main hearing bundle). This can be intensely irritating to tribunal members who have marked up or intend to mark up their copies. The answer is to liaise with the tribunal in advance, and ascertain their particular desires and idiosyncrasies in this regard.

Dry-Runs: One way to increase an advocate's fluency and comfort, and to test the utility of a planned opening statement, is to practice its delivery. This can be done alone; before other lawyers working on the case; in front of the client; or all of the above as the presentation evolves. Among other benefits, practice can help the advocate tailor and prioritize the presentation to ensure that it can be made within the allotted time, while covering all of the key points. Indeed, it is time allocation that is often the most significant issue, and time is easily misjudged. Advocates who have inadequately prepared will often be cut-off midstream by a tribunal, when allotted time has expired, or face a high speed (and often unproductive) "gallop" through sections of their notes in order to cover important points within the allowed time.

Perspective: As the advocate prepares the presentation, it is essential to think of it at all times from the listener's perspective. The statement may have its own therapeutic or cathartic effects for the client, and may be intended to have intimidating effects for the opponent, but none of these points matter: all that matters is that the tribunal is actually persuaded. And so the only criteria must always be: what does the tribunal actually need to hear, how, and in what order? The advocate must put himself in the position of arbitrator, and determine what facts, evidence and arguments would grab and hold his attention, and how the intended "story" is best conveyed. In many situations, the most important element will be structure. Unstructured presentations are guaranteed to be of little persuasive effect, especially for a tribunal that may have relatively little understanding (as yet) about the case. Equally, much sound and fury about the opponent's bad faith may be nothing but an unhelpful distraction for a tribunal that needs to find an answer to the case, and to draft an award. To this end, and by way of example, the presentation might begin with a list of the issues to be decided by the tribunal, followed by an overview of the presentation's own structure and organization; a statement clearly and simply defining what the case is about; and then an explication of the legal principles to be applied. Such a background sets up the discussion of the facts by letting the tribunal know at the outset what is important to look for in the evidence. The better you anticipate the audience's specific needs and concerns, the more persuasive the presentation will be. And for most tribunals, their immediate need will be a map of the issues, a clear, precise and concise summary of each parties' case on each issue, and a solution to the case.

Anticipating Weak Points: A very important part of preparation is to anticipate the weak points of one's own case and the opposing side's likely responses. With this in mind, the advocate should then search for ways — both factually and legally — to bolster his case. This may require legal research into other claims, defenses, or exceptions to legal doctrines. It may require identification of other fields of law, codes or provisions to argue as alternatives. The advocate may identify areas of further factual investigation that are needed, such as additional document review and witness interviews. When done properly and aggressively, further factual and legal research can sometimes turn a weak point into a strong one, or at least neutralize likely opposing arguments. As with any other suggestion, however, there are dangers in excess. A common error in oral advocacy is to spend too long focused upon the case of one's opponent, rather than that of one's own. Whilst it is essential to be forearmed, the opening statement is the opportunity to present a coherent and compelling position to the tribunal, and it is infrequent that one's own position can be relayed effectively and persuasively by simply hammering and discrediting that of the opponent.

Responsiveness: A further essential aspect of oral argument is the ability, and willingness, to answer the questions of the tribunal. In international arbitrations, arbitrators may well ask questions of the advocates at any time. Some tribunals will wait until the conclusion of the prepared presentation, while others will interrupt the presentation as and when a query arises. Accordingly, a critical part of the preparation for any oral presentation is to prepare for this eventuality. This has several aspects. Firstly, and ideally, the structure and mode of presentation should be sufficiently flexible in order to allow the advocate to be interrupted, and to depart from his script, or change his order of issues if need be, in order to address a question. Deferring all questions until the end of a set piece presentation can be irritating to the arbitrator who has raised the issue. It can also appear evasive. Secondly, a list of the most likely and toughest questions concerning the case can usefully form part of the advocate's preparation, together with model answers. This preparation is crucial, and may itself shape the overall presentation. The authors have often modified their basic presentations after anticipating the hardest questions and preparing answers.

Language: Finally, in international arbitration, there is the added complication of language. In some cases, more than one language may be used, with simultaneous or consecutive translation. In other cases, one language may be used which is foreign to many participants in the arbitration. Each scenario raises crucial issues for the advocate, of which due account must be taken in preparing the opening statement. Consideration must be given as to how terms and phrases might be translated; what nuances may be lost or misunderstood in the process; and the pace of delivery that may be required. By way of general guidance in such cases, the advocate should use concrete words that translate into the other language as precisely as possible. Slang or culturally specific expressions should be avoided.[4] Sentences should be short. Where there are translators, they should be extended every reasonable assistance. This may include meeting with them in advance or providing them with a list of any technical terms to be used. In some cases, the translators may be given in advance a copy of the advocate's script, outline, PowerPoint, or skeletal outline to help them provide the most accurate translation. At times, the advocate may even provide his own advance translation. All of this assistance is the product of careful preparation, with due regard to the peculiarities and special needs of the international arbitral process.

III. Structure and Content

The Golden Rule – Simplicity: A fundamental principle of advocacy is to simplify the case and the presentation. The most persuasive presentation is often the most elegant and simplest one. If a position is difficult to follow, or lacks clarity, it is much less likely to stick in the arbitrators' minds. Only the subject matter that needs to be discussed should be addressed, and however complex the facts or the law, the story that is told must be easily and readily comprehensible. As the advocate prepares the case, and inevitably gets enveloped (and worse still, enthralled) by the minutiae, this fundamental principle must always be borne in mind.The authors have, at times, substantially changed a prepared presentation the night before a hearing, in order to simplify it. The process of simplifying usually brings clarity by clearing away unnecessary underbrush, and forcing the advocate to select and distill the points that, in the end, really matter.

Structure: The opening statement can be organized in any one of at least three ways: (1) by the topics to be discussed; (2) by the points to be made or propositions to be established during the presentation;

---

[4] In this regard, no assumptions should be made as to the familiarity of others with technical expressions that are in common usage in one's own legal system. One of the authors will take care in future before using the term "full and frank disclosure" where there is simultaneous translation, after its use in one instance led to the query: "Who is Frank?".

or (3) by themes. In addition, the factual discussion can often be organized into a narrative story. These methods of organization are not exclusive of one another, but may substantially overlap.

A topical organization might order the presentation based on the basic elements of the case: (1) introduction, (2) factual background, (3) the relevant law, (4) liability, and (5) damages. At times, the legal and factual topics may be reversed. Of course, there are many possible variants of this, and the advocate may need to emphasize one of the topics in much more detail than the others.

A presentation organized around the points sought to be made by the advocate may begin with a list of the propositions to be established in the presentation: "Mr. Chairman, I will cover [or establish] five points in my presentation, and they are, first, ... second ..." After initially listing them all, each point is taken up in turn and discussed in detail before moving to the next.

A thematic presentation may be facially similar, but the themes that provide the organizing structure may not necessarily be the same as the points or conclusions sought to be established. One definition of the term "theme" is "an idea, ideal or orienting principle that is dominant or persistent in a popular or tribal culture and often effective in controlling and activating belief and conduct in a specific direction."[5] In this sense, themes state the "principles for which the case stands,"[6] sometimes transcending the facts of the case, evoking powerful images, and establishing a greater significance for the case.[7] In effect, they link the parties' case to the values of the arbitrators. Of course, themes can also be more modest, characterizing "particular pieces of evidence."[8]

The facts of the case are more than just a collection of discrete or disconnected pieces of evidence. Properly conceived, the facts form a mosaic pattern that fits together neatly into a narrative story. In

---

5 Websters Third New International Dictionary (1966).

6 Richard C. Waites, *Courtroom Psychology and Trial Advocacy* (ALM Publishing, 2003), p. 328.

7 *Id.* at 329.

8 *Id.* at 328.

fact, to make sense the evidence must form a narrative story because, as already observed, as a matter of psychology that is how people think. In analyzing the evidence, the tribunal members will naturally construct their own story of the case. That story might be somewhat different for each of the arbitrators. In presenting the facts, therefore, the advocate should generally develop the evidence into a storyline. The story gives the arbitrators a way of organizing and remembering the facts. A story is also much more interesting and psychologically powerful than a mere discussion of discrete facts. Of course, the story must be built upon the evidence and be consistent with it. By providing a story into which to fit the facts, the advocate is structuring how the tribunal should think about the case, and this structure is greater psychologically than the sum of its parts.

Whichever organizing principle is used, the advocate should organize it methodically and systematically so that the presentation can be easily followed by the listener, resulting in good comprehension. The presentation should follow a logical and disciplined pattern, not skipping around whimsically in free-form fashion. For example, an opening statement might begin with an exposition of the applicable legal standards, followed by a discussion showing logically how the legal standards are satisfied by the evidence. The issue under discussion at a given moment should generally be exhausted before moving to the next issue. Through this issue-by-issue discussion, the case should be slowly built, block by block, as a symphony building to a crescendo.

Concrete Submissions: In terms of substance, the authors' experiences suggest that what persuades are concrete facts and logical arguments, not broad generalizations, sound-bites, paraphrasing, platitudes or conclusory statements. The authors have often seen arbitrators with their pens on the table when the advocates were speaking more abstractly about the case, only to pick up their pens and make detailed notes when a concrete fact or a new principle is addressed. When tested from the perspective of the tribunal, a submission is of use if it advances ones' understanding of an issue, and could be included in an Award. This immediately disqualifies broad, unspecific, and unsupported propositions. It also disqualifies gratuitous abuse, which many advocates spend at least part of their time heaping upon their opponents.

Thus, the advocate should build his presentation around facts, evidence and legal sources that are demonstrated precisely, accurately and concretely. The term "concrete" in this context means tangible, specific and particular, not abstract. In many cases, the presentation should quote — and often show — the basic source material and key evidence. This can be accomplished either by using a PowerPoint with slides that quote the key documents or (as suggested earlier) by handing out to the arbitrators a notebook containing the key documents, separately tabbed, and referring the tribunal to specific excerpts in the documents as they arise during the presentation. Of course, and again as noted above, rather than using a separate notebook for the opening, counsel may refer the tribunal to particular documents in binders that contain the full set of documents for the hearing.

The points to be made in the opening by the advocate should be sharply focused. An advocate should not be content with a presentation that generally discusses the facts and the law but should hone it carefully in order to show clearly the meaning of the law and precisely how the facts satisfy the elements of a legal claim or defense. Sharpening an argument also requires anticipating the opposing side's arguments and crafting one's points to take them into account and meet them. A tightly-reasoned argument is much more persuasive than one that is general in nature.

Admissions / "Common Ground": The advocate should also consider emphasizing any "admissions" of the opposing party – as long as they are in reality admissions or (to use the term frequently used by English lawyers) "common ground". "Admissions" means statements of a party that admit or recognize the existence of a significant fact or principle. Identifying and articulating aspects of the dispute that are in truth not in dispute is of significant assistance to tribunals, and may also provide important building blocks for one's case. On the other hand, care must be taken, since the incorrect assertion of "common ground" or the existence of admissions is entirely counterproductive, inflammatory for the opposing party, and singularly unhelpful for the tribunal.

Logical Flow: A compelling opening statement is also one that has a logical flow to it — the presentation flows smoothly from point to point, like a story, with each point giving rise to the next, and the next point building on the ones preceding it. This involves the advance preparation of smooth transitions when moving from the conclusion of one point to the commencement of the next one. Even an argument involving contract or statutory interpretation can be presented with a logical flow to it. Achieving this flow takes meticulous preparation, and often practice. But a submission that flows well is generally far more compelling than one with disruptive stops and starts, whether in terms of presentation or internal logic.

Points to Avoid: While in most cases there is much to be addressed in the opening statement, there are certain points that, as a general rule, should be avoided.

First, at this stage – before the witnesses have been cross-examined – the advocate should generally avoid relying upon evidence that could change once tested. For example, a point that relies solely on the statement of a witness and that is not corroborated by other evidence may be an unsafe foundation for the case. The advocate may not want to emphasize such evidence until the danger of cross-examination has passed. Similarly, there is obvious danger in opening one's case "too high", or overstating points that have yet to be proven, and may not ultimately be shown to the threshold one is expecting. Further, the advocate should generally avoid discussing the credibility of the witnesses and experts until they have concluded their oral testimony. Misjudging a witness' credibility may well infect the credibility of the advocate himself.

Finally, the opening statement is the time for the advocate to discuss his client's affirmative case. While the opposing counsel will necessarily be responding to many of the arguments, at this stage the advocate will generally not want to appear too defensive, so at times he may not wish to answer certain arguments put against him. Ultimately, which of the opposing side's arguments are to be addressed in the opening statement is a matter of fine judgment.

IV. Oral Presentation Style

There is then the all-important question of style.

Tone, Pace, Posture, Demeanor: Ultimately, the only consideration is to adopt the approach that is most likely to persuade in the instant case. There are any number of tones, paces, postures and demeanors from which to choose. Some advocates are aggressive; some are understated; some are indignant; others appear quietly wounded. In making this selection, it is obviously of enormous value to determine in advance (if possible) the expectations and foibles of the arbitrators with respect to oral advocacy; the style of oral advocacy, if any, to which they may be accustomed in their own legal system; and whether there are styles of argument that will strike a discordant tone, or even offend.

Further, even if the advocate can ascertain this information, a presentation must be crafted that will appeal to all of the arbitrators, who may be from different legal systems, with different expectations as to advocacy. Clearly, a single style of advocacy may not be appropriate when tribunal members are from different legal systems. This problem can perhaps best be addressed by a style of advocacy that reduces the subject to a universal common denominator: a presentation that is simple, clear and methodical.

As a guiding principle, the advocate should adopt a posture and attitude that is dignified, disciplined and sincere. But consistent with this attitude, the presentation should also demonstrate a reasonable measure of energy and enthusiasm in order to capture and maintain the attention of the tribunal. Arbitrators, like any other person, have limits to their attention span. In a long presentation, the arbitrators' attention may wax and wane. The arbitrators can "tune out" at times for many different reasons (e.g. because they have the parties' written submissions, and feel that nothing is being added; because they have a transcript of the oral presentations, which they can read later; because they have had a heavy lunch; etc). The advocate must be aware of these dynamics and must address them. A long, dry, and unenergetic presentation will likely ensure that the arbitrators "tune out" at some point. The same is true for a presentation that slowly meanders around with no clear structure or point. It is the responsibility of the speaker to capture and hold the tribunal's collective attention.

Body Language: An often overlooked but extraordinarily significant part of advocacy concerns the facial expressions and body language of the advocate. Since most people "read" facial expressions and body language to some extent (consciously or sub-consciously), albeit at times erroneously, it is important that the advocate's body language not "betray" the words used by indicating a lack of belief in what he is saying. Good communicators match their "phrasing" (*i.e.*, posture and gesture) to their message. American presidents generally thought to be excellent communicators like Ronald Reagan and Bill Clinton are considered to have had great phrasing, while George W. Bush did not. Advocates whose body language does not seem to match their statements may well be perceived by arbitrators as having a lack of conviction or credibility. A good advocate will be alert to this problem and guard against it.

Capturing Attention: There are certain techniques often employed to capture a tribunal's attention. The most fundamental technique is eye contact. At least in western cultures, eye contact is considered an important aspect of credibility and integral to persuasion. Eye contact attracts the attention of the listener and engages him. In western cultures, to "look one in the eye" is considered a demonstration of honesty and sincerity. This may not be true, however, in all cultures. In some eastern cultures, it is considered a sign of rudeness, aggression or confrontation. Thus, the advocate should know and understand the audience.

Second, attention is secured and sustained by structuring the presentation in a methodical and logical manner that is easily understood and followed by the arbitrators. The structure should convey to the tribunal that the advocate has carefully prepared the presentation, that it will address matters that will assist the arbitrators in properly deciding the case, and that the advocate will not waste time on tangential points. Promising an overly long list of points is certain to reduce the tribunal's morale, and focus them on their respective watches.

A third technique has already been mentioned — a reasonable amount of energy and enthusiasm in the advocate's voice, and a tempo to the presentation that moves it along at a brisk but reasonable pace. Such pace should not be too fast for the arbitrators to take notes, the translators to translate the speaker's words, or the transcriber to transcribe, but it should be fast enough to hold the arbitrators' attention so that their minds do not wander. This is important because listeners can usually digest information at a faster rate than people can speak, so maintaining a reasonably brisk pace keeps the presentation fresh. In this regard, the advocate should also consider the rhythm and cadence of the presentation. It should not always be the same, but should vary. It should rise and fall, quicken and slow. This again helps maintain the attention and interest of the tribunal.

A fourth technique is sometimes referred to as "verbal headlines." A verbal headline is a statement by the speaker of what topic will be discussed next or signaling the significance of the next point. "Mr. Chairman, I would now like to turn to my next point, which is of particular importance," or simply, "Mr. Chairman, this next point is very important." Such an introduction is likely to attract the tribunal's attention and have them reaching for their pens (if only for fear of subsequent criticism for missing an important element in the case).

A final, and quite easy, technique is simply for the speaker to pause for a few seconds. If the advocate pauses, after a brief interval the listeners will inevitably look up to determine the reason for the pause (special importance of the point just made; mislaid notes; departure of advocate; etc). This is a natural reaction. The power of the pause has long been acknowledged. It was notably a technique used by Abraham Lincoln, when he was a trial lawyer in Illinois, to gain the attention of the jury. It should be part of every advocate's repertoire. The advocate should also pause when he observes that the tribunal members are falling behind in taking notes or are having difficulty in finding a referenced document. This matches the pace of the presentation to the attention of the arbitrators.

Emotion: Except in very rare circumstances, the presentation should not be overtly emotional. But by the way the facts are fitted together, the presentation ordered, the words carefully chosen, and the story told, the advocate can sometimes create a subtle emotional undercurrent — a mood— that can assist in persuading. In this way, it is the words, the order, and the facts that create the emotion, not the advocate's voice or demeanor. The choice of words may be graphic and concrete when the facts permit, but should not be overstated with hysterical adjectives or hyperbole. Often, plain words with no accompanying adjectives will be more compelling. At least for English, the power of the language is in the verbs, which reveal the action, not in the adjectives or adverbs. Adjectives and adverbs provide character and color to the presentation, but the power of a statement emanates from the verbs. Active (not passive) verbs should be used whenever possible. As Mark Twain once said, "The difference between the right word and the almost right word is the difference between lightning and the lightning bug."

Metaphors, Similes & Analogies: The use of (measured) metaphors, similes and analogies can be helpful in explaining and clarifying concepts or for drawing colorful comparisons or contrasts. Metaphors and similes are generally fleeting, but can provide colorful and striking detail that can enliven any oral exercise. An analogy, by contrast, if carefully drawn, can reveal similarities to simple and easily understood examples that can be powerfully persuasive. A skillful advocate should make judicious but effective use of these tools.

Understatement: Following the points above, a word of caution is appropriate. A good presentation in international arbitration should be understated, and certainly not overstated. This advice stems from the nature of the audience. Arbitrators, like many judges - and unlike many jurors – tend to be professional, highly experienced, seasoned and critical thinkers. They subject the advocate's words and the evidence to a critical process, probing and testing their credibility and accuracy. An advocate who consistently overstates his case may cause a distraction, and may also lose credibility, with the result that his subsequent arguments are subjected to even greater skepticism. On the other hand, an understated approach involves less risk and leaves it to the arbitrators to a certain extent to draw their own conclusions from the evidence. The strongest convictions are not those received passively from another person strongly stating a conclusion, but those actively drawn by the decision-maker himself from his own review and analysis of the evidence. It is said that you can lead a horse to water but you can't make it drink. In most cases, leading an international arbitrator to the water is enough.

Similarly, the advocate should be sparing of his words and should stop when he has finished making his points. No words should be redundant. In this context, contrary to many advocates' instincts (particularly those on an hourly rate), less is certainly more. A point will either be good or bad. It will certainly not improve by repetition. A concise style that chooses words carefully, that says what is necessary and that concludes in advance of the appointed time is bound to be appreciated by the tribunal and, more importantly, to be more compelling and persuasive. Most arbitrators will not tell advocates they have used too many words in their presentations, but one suspects they often think so. A concise style that says only that which is strictly necessary — and then stops — is a virtue.

Credibility of the Advocate: The credibility of the advocate is integral to the art of persuasion. If you want a tribunal to believe in your case, they must believe in you. Credibility should never be assumed – it must be cultivated, and then maintained.

The credibility of an advocate is based on two factors: first, his honesty with the tribunal, and second, his mastery of the relevant facts and law. As to the first, honesty is primarily telegraphed by openness. If an advocate misstates or overstates any position, or appears evasive on any issue, severe damage will be done to his overall standing. At all times, he must be entirely frank[9] in his interaction with the tribunal. All questions put to him by the tribunal should be answered directly. Weak points and bad facts should be conceded once they are recognized as such. Case law that is inconsistent with the client's position but that is necessary for a full understanding of the law should often be cited and addressed, rather

---

9 But see Footnote 4, *supra.*

than buried. Such case law may be footnoted, and distinguished or explained. Aside from the issue of whether ethical rules require that inconsistent case law be cited, simply ignoring such decisions is bound to reflect badly upon the advocate himself. It is seldom that a client's position will be entirely correct, unassailable and free from any doubt in every single respect, whether in fact or law. Asserting this position will simply sow doubts in the tribunal's minds.

As to the second key element – mastery of relevant facts and law – the advocate must be as well prepared as possible. By demonstrating mastery of each relevant area, the advocate proves that he can be trusted to be technically accurate, which implies that his interpretation of the facts and law is more likely to be correct and dependable.

Paying Attention: At the hearing, the advocate should always pay close attention to the tribunal. Good advocates keep their heads up and out of their notes as much as possible during the presentations, carefully observing what is going on around them in the hearing room. Important intelligence can be obtained by keenly observing both the opposing side's reactions to the arguments and those of the tribunal members. Note their facial and bodily reactions to the arguments and testimony. Flag the points in the argument and testimony when the tribunal seemed to take notes furiously, when they seemed uninterested, and when they asked the transcriber to provide them with a particular portion of the transcript. Listen to the tribunal's questions carefully and analyze their concerns in detail. Most importantly, adjust the presentations to the reactions and concerns of the tribunal to the fullest extent possible.

Answering Questions: One of the most important advantages for both arbitrators and advocates of an oral hearing is the tribunal's opportunity to ask questions. Questions have a number of diverse functions, aside from simply soliciting more information. They may indirectly signal the tribunal's concerns about the case. They may reveal the tribunal's perspectives, and areas of particular interest. And they may reveal misunderstandings that might otherwise go undetected. This is a (sometimes alarming) window into the minds of the tribunal members, and so provides a critical moment for persuasion. Such an opportunity should be welcomed and openly encouraged by the advocate. Never show impatience or frustration with the arbitrators' questions. Accept the questions with a positive and constructive attitude. At times, the advocate should affirm a question by noting its importance. The authors have, at times, spent the better part of an hour during a presentation fielding and answering question after question from the tribunal. It is an invigorating and sometimes exhausting experience, but it can be a key moment for the case.

Because the tribunal's questions can be so important to the case, the advocate should carefully prepare for them in advance of the hearing. As previously noted, anticipate the hardest questions the tribunal could ask about your evidence and arguments and outline answers to each question. These answers must be accessible at a glance, so the advocate might prepare them in bullet point form, with the most important and direct point of the answer as the first bullet point, with the other bullet points arranged in descending order of importance. The advocate should also know the presentation well enough to be able to move in and out of it in order to answer questions as they arise with minimal disruption to the flow of the argument. Often a question will provide a segue to the advocate's next point. Generally, questions should be answered when they are asked because it is at that time that the tribunal is most focused and interested in the answer. Occasionally, the advocate might ask to delay the answer to a later point in the presentation if he has a lengthy and comprehensive discussion of it prepared for a later stage.

Most importantly, the advocate should address the arbitrators' questions seriously, honestly, forthrightly, and as fully as possible. If the advocate does not know the answer to the question, he should say so directly and honestly, rather than trying to make something up, but promise to research it and provide the answer at a later point in the hearing. Similarly, if the advocate learns he has made a mistake in answering a question, he should tell the tribunal at the earliest opportunity and correct it. It is the authors' experience that acknowledging an earlier mistake and correcting it generally builds credibility rather than detracting from it.

V. The Use of Technology: To PowerPoint or Not To PowerPoint?

The use of technology as an advocacy tool in international arbitration is now widespread, but there are marked differences of view as to its utility within the art of persuasion. Whilst an advocate may very usefully refer to documents, authorities and other materials in electronic rather than paper form, the key question in current practice is whether or not to make submissions by reference to projected slides and a PowerPoint or similar presentation.

The supporters of PowerPoint consider submissions as no different from any other form of presentation. Projected slides are seen as an extremely useful method of distilling key points, just as one would do in a written skeleton outline. Rather than just stare at the advocate, the tribunal is presented with a visually stimulating and streamlined display, often in colour, with animated elements, such as "pop-up" windows, and often highly poisonous (i.e. effective) schematic representations of the parties' respective positions.

The PowerPoint skeptics, on the other hand, point to a number of drawbacks to this medium. Unlike the use of a written skeleton outline, the use of a screen at the other end of a hearing room necessarily interferes with the direct connection the advocate would ordinarily seek to develop with each arbitrator he is trying to persuade. Rather than speaking directly to the tribunal, the advocate will often be faced with three people looking in a different direction. Eye contact is more difficult to maintain, as each member of the tribunal focuses in the distance on the screen. The problem is often compounded just after lunch, when the lights are dimmed, and eyelids become heavy. PowerPoint slides are frequently either over-burdened with information (and so difficult to read), or too brief to be meaningful (e.g with selective quotations from documents, given the lack of space on a slide). Even if a document is quoted on a slide, its impact may not be as immediate as putting a hard copy of the actual document in question directly under each arbitrator's nose. Further still, a PowerPoint presentation often solidifies the advocate's submissions into a set order, which cannot easily be changed. If an important question is raised by the tribunal early on, anticipating slides that will only appear subsequently, many PowerPoint advocates have no choice but to defer the matter and simply continue as planned. Written outlines do not impose the same straightjacket. Lastly, as experience shows, however advanced our IT systems have become, power supplies often fail; projectors often don't work on the day; laptops often refuse to co-operate with their users; and users often forget how to co-operate with their laptops. This can be an added and unnecessary source of stress for the advocate.

Whatever position one takes on this debate, there are a number of tips on the use of projected slides for opening statements.

Firstly, prepare and circulate a paper printout of all slides, in order to insure against a technology glitch; to allow the members of the tribunal to make notes on each slide; and to allow the tribunal to follow the slides without having to focus on a distant screen.

Second, do not try to cram too much information into each slide. A few key bullet points in a large font is usually optimal.

Third, consider the use of PowerPoint for the projection of key excerpts of documents to which frequent reference may be made (such as a statutory provision or contractual clause).

Fourth, try to arrange the hearing room in such a way that the screen is not too far away from the Tribunal and in a line of vision that – if at all possible – includes the advocate.

Fifth, test, re-test and then test again all equipment - and all users.

VI. Conclusion

Overall, if there is one point above all others that should be borne in mind with respect to opening statements, it is that there exists no single, correct form for such a presentation. Procedural flexibility remains at the heart of international arbitration, and the essential advantages of the process are directly undermined by the use of set formulas or national court precedents. The specific needs of each case, and each tribunal, must be assessed, free from all preconceptions, and the opening statement created and shaped accordingly.

Chapter 15

DIRECT AND RE-DIRECT EXAMINATION OF THE WITNESSES

Nigel Blackaby*

In a tome dedicated to the "art" of advocacy, no-one can doubt that the true advocacy skill lies in the art of cross examination. There is the work of the artist in all its colour and subtlety. Direct and redirect examination limit the work of this artist cross-examiner much as the frame of the painting. There is less art here but the overall impression of the work can be complemented or detracted by the way it is presented. So it is my task to speak of picture framing.

I. Direct Examination

Direct examination (also known as "examination-in-chief") is the process whereby a party questions the witness it has called to give evidence. In court practice it was traditionally the phase where the witness tells his or her story, guided gently by the lawyer. In modern arbitral practice, however, direct examination is positively frowned upon and sometimes even excluded. The usual practice of presentation of written statements[1] signed by the witness (usually a first statement and possibly a rebuttal statement) is deemed to replace the presentation of a witness's oral recollection of the events allegedly

---

* Nigel Blackaby is partner and head of Freshfields Bruckhaus Deringer's Americas arbitration practice, based in Washington D.C.

[1] See e.g. Article 4 of the IBA Rules on the Taking of Evidence In International Commercial Arbitration where the witness statement shall contain, inter alia, "a full and detailed description of the facts, and the source of the witness's information as to those facts, sufficient to serve as that witness's evidence in the matter in dispute."

relevant to the resolution of the dispute.[2] This practice has several advantages. First and foremost, there is no risk of "trial by ambush" since the evidence of the witness is known long in advance of the hearing thereby allowing the opposing party time to prepare properly for cross-examination. Second, much time will be saved when the witness's evidence is "pre-recorded" in a written statement rather than orally presented. In an international context where most participants will be away from home in a neutral city, this can result in important costs savings.

As a consequence of this practice, once a witness (let us call her Ms Smith) has been sworn in (usually by affirmation) by the tribunal, her direct examination is often limited to a ritualistic request by the party presenting her evidence to confirm that the written statements in front of her are indeed her statements and that it is her signature which is appended to them.[3] After a respectful twenty seconds of shuffling papers, Ms Smith invariably replies that they are indeed her statements and that the elegant flourish at the end of the documents is her signature. The advocate then asks her to confirm whether she wishes to change or add anything to her statements, to which she will normally reply in the negative. Sometimes to add authenticity to the exercise, she will correct an irrelevant date or add a missing comma. Ms Smith is then told by the advocate conducting the direct examination that an esteemed colleague sitting opposite will ask her a few questions. Then the real drama can begin. The preamble is complete.

I could end my contribution here by saying that such direct examination is a fine way to give junior associates their first true

---

2 See e.g. Article 8(3) of the IBA Rules on the Taking of Evidence in International Commercial Arbitration which provides "…The Parties may agree or the Arbitral Tribunal may order that the Witness Statement or Expert Report shall serve as that witness's direct testimony."

3 See e.g. Article 8(3) of the IBA Rules on the Taking of Evidence in International Commercial Arbitration which provides: "Any witness providing testimony shall first affirm, in a manner determined appropriate by the Arbitral Tribunal, that he or she is telling the truth. If the witness has submitted a Witness Statement or an Expert Report, the witness shall confirm it. …"

advocacy experience (a rather doubtful proposition if conducted in the manner set out above). Or I could suggest a few ways in which the initial framing exercise might be usefully engaged in a more effective manner.

I will first address the purpose and technique of direct examination in international arbitration (Part A) before considering the different ways in which that purpose can be served (Part B), how to protect the right to an effective direct examination within the procedural framework of the arbitration (Part C) and the scope of preparation of a witness for direct examination (Part D).

A. The Purpose and Technique of Direct Examination

Let us remind ourselves why direct examination is important: this is the first time that the tribunal and the party opposing the party adducing Ms Smith will have seen or heard her. Similarly, Ms Smith will not have met the tribunal nor the lawyers who are about to try and destroy her story and/or credibility. Nor in most cases will she have ever been confronted with the possibly unpleasant situation that suddenly faces her.

If she has been properly prepared by counsel, the nature of witness cross-examination and the roles of the respective actors will have been explained to her. But explanations are not the same as direct experience. A tourist who has been shown a postcard of the Eiffel Tower might be able to recognise it but will have no real sense of what it is like to stand beneath it or look around it. All this to say that in the first ten minutes of a witness's presence in the stand, the tribunal and opposing counsel will be "sizing up" the witness and the witness will be "sizing up" the tribunal and counsel. Opinions formed in those ten minutes will be critical to the credibility of the witness for the remainder of the examination.

This benefit may be less important to the expert witness who may have provided testimony on many occasions. Here, the benefit is the possibility of ensuring that the tribunal has followed the key messages contained in the expert report and provide the opportunity to the tribunal to ask questions in a mini "master class". For these reasons, it is beneficial to the arbitral process to allow limited direct examination. In this way, the witness is not immediately in a defensive posture and the tribunal can obtain an initial impression of the witness's character and demeanour before the crucible of cross-examination begins. Of course, in order to ensure that this opportunity exists it must be provided for in the relevant procedural order and so the issue has to be addressed clearly with opposing counsel when seeking to agree the terms of a procedural order or (if such agreement is not possible) at that critical first procedural meeting with the tribunal.

So how can direct examination be successfully used as a means of ensuring the acclimatization of the witness to her surroundings? First of all, what are the formal rules applicable to direct examination in international arbitration? The answer is "none". There are no strict exclusionary rules as would apply in domestic courts. However, whilst it is true that the tribunal will consider all evidence placed before it, it has the power to give evidence the weight that it considers appropriate.

So what direct examination will be given the most weight? The answer is only to ask "open questions." These are questions of the nature "who", "what", "why", "when", "how" or "where". Questions which suggest the answer and admit of a "yes" or a "no" answer (known as closed questions) are not expressly excluded but are of little assistance to the tribunal, although they can be used effectively in direct examination to establish certain preliminary or non contentious issues in order to "paint the scene" for the witness. The tribunal knows that the party will have had access to the witnesses presented and that questions of a closed nature effectively deliver the words to the mouth of the witness. The probative value of an open question is therefore far greater since the witness has to reflect on the question and respond in her own words. For example the closed question: "It is true Ms Smith isn't it that you did not attend the Board Meeting on June 10, 2006?" is of much less probative value than the two questions: "Were you able to attend all the company board meetings in summer 2006?" followed by "Do you recall the date of the board meetings you were unable to attend?"

An open question should not be confused with a broad question such as "what happened next". An effective open question in direct must be very specific and give to the witness a clear indication of the topic and scope of what is being asked.

Like any other piece of oral advocacy, preparation is key to conducting an effective direct examination. One should give careful consideration to the questions to be asked to elicit the key points and information from the witness. However, examiners should avoid relying too much on their notes and simply reading out questions that they have fully written out beforehand. There are several reasons for this.

First, as noted above, one of the aims of direct examination is to get the witness acclimatised to being "on the stand" and comfortable in answering questions. This is best achieved by asking questions in as relaxed and natural a manner possible rather than reading from a pre-written script. Second, when reading from questions in the order they have been written down, examiners can sometimes forget to look at and (more importantly) listen to their witness and the tribunal. The examiner must be prepared to react to the witness's answers and ask adequate follow up questions or change the order of the questions accordingly. It is surprising how often direct examiners do not listen to the answers of the witness they have presented. It is also wise to look at the tribunal's reactions to the witness's answers. If the tribunal seems perplexed by an answer, a follow up question may be in order. If the tribunal seems disinterested in a point, it would be best to move on. All this can be difficult to achieve when one is wed to a pre-written script. More importantly, appearing to be disinterested in the witness's answers may lead to the witness to disengage, or worse, the tribunal to lose interest.

In my experience, making a list of the key themes to be addressed and points to be elicited in bullet point form (with perhaps only a few questions on more complex issues written out in full) works best. This list of themes can then be used to signal to the witness and to the tribunal when changing topics. For instance, "Turning now to the meeting that took place on 16 January, could you tell us what was discussed? Ideally, the examination should flow naturally, like a conversation. Certain habits of examiners can, however, interrupt this flow, and create an annoyance such as repeatedly thanking the witness after each of her answers, or shuffling through papers.

B. The Content of Direct Examination

On the assumption that in most international arbitrations a written and signed witness statement will have been submitted, there is no extensive "story telling" direct as might be found in court. An effective direct examination in an international arbitration will therefore usually be limited to one or more of the following elements after the statement(s) have been confirmed: (1) a correction of the statement to address weaknesses; (2) the presentation of relevant experience; (3) a response to new matters in the other party's last written pleading or earlier oral evidence; (4) the updating of any new facts; and (5) in the case of complex expert evidence, the possibility of a brief "master class".

(1) Correction of the Statement and Address Weaknesses

The possibility to correct a statement can provide the opportunity for a witness to iron out minor inaccuracies or contradictions that inevitably appear as a case progresses, particularly where the facts may date back several years. More importantly, it provides a vital window to correct any errors that have appeared as a result of later documentary or witness evidence from the opposing party. An effective correction can defuse an otherwise harmful cross-examination question which would have exposed a contradiction. This is particularly important for witnesses presented by the Claimant since there will have been no procedural opportunity for them to respond to the last written witness statements presented by the Respondent. *A fortiori* if there has only been one round of pleadings and the witnesses presented by the Claimant have never had the opportunity of responding to the documents or witness statements presented by the Respondent. If there are documents or declarations in those witness statements which contradict witness testimony provided by Claimant's witnesses, direct examination is the only opportunity to defuse the risk of contradiction on cross-examination.

Imagine that in our hypothetical case, Ms Smith had given evidence for the Claimant in her rebuttal statement submitted by Claimant with the Reply Memorial that she did not attend the June 10, 2006 Board meeting. In the Rejoinder Memorial, Respondent attaches the minutes of that meeting which show that Ms Smith was in fact in attendance at that meeting. No doubt Respondent's counsel is looking forward to the moment when this contradiction will be exposed in cross-examination in order to damage Ms Smith's credibility. However, Ms Smith has the opportunity to correct that statement in her direct examination:

> "**Q.** Is there anything, Ms Smith, you would like to correct in your statement?
>
> **A.** Yes. At paragraph 22, I mention that I did not attend the board meeting on June 10, 2006. However, having seen the minutes of that meeting I see that I did attend although it appears that I left early. Since this was over three years ago, I based my evidence on my agenda and this meeting was not mentioned there. But the Minutes are quite clear and it appears that I was present for the first part of the meeting."

Whilst Respondent's counsel can no doubt still seek to prove that Ms Smith's evidence based on diary entries is not very reliable, she will no longer come across as someone who is lying to the tribunal.

(2) Brief Background

It is always useful to remind the tribunal who the witness is. Hopefully, the tribunal will have read the statement prior to the oral examination but a brief description of the relevant role of the witness by the witness herself in respect of the matters in dispute is helpful for credibility and context. You want the tribunal to believe that this is a clear and credible witness. To do that, it is important to highlight the positive aspects of her background – for example, a long service with the same company demonstrates consistency and loyalty; hands on experience with the industry will establish a basis for technical responses. With regard to the expert witness, this provides an opportunity to highlight the key experience relevant to the content of his report.

(3) Response to New Evidence in Last Written Pleading

Once the witness has been introduced, corrected any errors in the statement and briefly described their relevance to the dispute, the next step will depend on whether you are acting for Claimant or Respondent. If you are acting for the Claimant, the last submission to have been received will likely have been the Respondent's Rejoinder and accompanying rebuttal statements. There may be matters addressed in those statements or in documents attached to that Rejoinder for the first time to which Claimant's witnesses have not had the opportunity to respond. A typical open question to respond to new evidence might be as follows:

"**Q.** At paragraph 66 of his rebuttal statement, Mr Jones indicated for the first time that he remembers you insisting you would agree to pay US$ 5 million for control of Widgets Inc. at the January 16 meeting. Do you have any comments on this statement?

A. Yes. I was very surprised to see that statement. As is clear from the minutes of the meeting, I made it clear that the company would not increase its US$4 million offer for Widgets. I never offered US$5 million."

(4) Updating Evidence

The next possible area of direct examination is to update the factual situation since the last written submission. This may be necessary in the light of an evolving situation. For example, the contract at the heart of the dispute may have been terminated since the date of the last pleading. It would be important to draw that fact to the Tribunal's attention. Updating may be particularly important for expert witnesses. The quantum of loss may depend on the evolution of financial projections that seemed solid when the last pleading was prepared. However, these may need to be readjusted in light of supervening circumstances such as an economic crisis or the collapse (or climb) of the price of a relevant commodity such as oil or a specific metal. It is also the perfect opportunity to update a damages calculation which may have last been calculated at the Reply stage several months earlier.

(5) Expert Master Class

In cases where there is complex and conflicting expert evidence, often on valuation issues, a party should consider taking its experts step by step through their methodology and calculations. This cannot be done in a few minutes and will require a very flexible procedural order, usually based on the chess-clock concept (see below). However, in areas where the tribunal is not on familiar ground, it may be a very wise investment of time. If the expertise is in an area outside the law then the tribunal is in no better position to understand the issues than a reasonably intelligent lay-person. Whilst a well-written expert report is a good start, it is usually insufficient, just as reading a textbook on macroeconomics is unlikely to be fully intelligible to a reader who is unable to attend a class and ask questions of the professor. An expert "master class" recognizes that the tribunal needs an opportunity to clarify doubts on areas outside of its area of expertise.

We could call this the "masterclass" technique. An expert is asked to explain succinctly the manner in which the key conclusions have been reached, taking the tribunal step by step over the exercise undertaken. This is often assisted by presentation of visual aids (which usually must not contain any new information and have been exchanged with the other party prior to the examination). This gives the tribunal the opportunity to ask questions about the original process during an explanation of that process. Their questions will highlight to the party presenting the expert where additional clarifications might be needed in oral presentation.

There has been an increasing (and worrying) tendency of arbitral tribunals to instruct their own independent experts after the close of the final hearing to provide assistance on the question of quantum. This often gives rise to a long and complex exchange of views since the independent expert was not present at the final hearing. This practice appears to arise from the difficulties encountered by tribunals in working through the economic consequences of certain legal decisions. The "masterclass" technique minimizes this risk by providing the tribunal with the full opportunity to ask questions and understand the underlying methodologies in a much more effective way than simply reading the expert reports.

C. Protecting the Right to an Effective Direct Examination

As can be seen, depending on a series of unpredictable circumstances that will evolve during the life of the case, there may be quite a lot to cover in a brief direct examination. It is therefore critical to ensure at the beginning of a case that the right to ask those questions is protected. All of the above techniques can be rendered useless by a strict procedural order along the classic lines: "The signed statements of the witnesses shall constitute their examination-in-chief in the final hearing."

So how can parties be assured of a reasonable opportunity to engage in relevant direct examination? What if the tribunal is opposed to the idea at the procedural hearing? There are a number of solutions to this quandary. First, prior to the first procedural meeting with the tribunal, an agreement on direct examination should be sought with the other party. Most of the benefits of a more flexible direct examination can cut both ways and, if explained carefully to the counterparty, can result in agreement. If such agreement is reached, the Tribunal is unlikely to interfere. A possible agreement or order could read as follows: "The signed statements of the witnesses of fact and expert reports shall stand as the evidence-in-chief of that witness without prejudice to the right of each party to ask any questions in relation to: (a) the correction of any errors in the statement; (a) any new matters first mentioned in the last statements submitted by the opposing party to which the witness has not had an opportunity to respond; and (c) any supervening facts or circumstances of relevance to the case since the date of the last statement proffered by that witness."

Even with such an order, tribunals may seek to impose time limits on direct examination; ten to fifteen minutes is quite common. Whilst this would be more than sufficient in most cases, it will not be sufficient to conduct a "masterclass" with an expert which might need up to an hour. One way around the absolute nature of a fixed time limit for all witnesses is the "chess-clock" system whereby each party is allotted an equal fixed amount of time at the final hearing to engage in: (a) direct examination of its own witnesses; (b) cross-examination of the opposite party's witnesses; and (c) oral submission. Each party has complete flexibility to divide the time between any of these tasks. This will then allow each party to take into account the evolution of the case after the date of the procedural hearing in the assignment of its "quota". This is particularly useful for direct examination where more traditional procedural solutions will provide a fixed time limit. Tribunals often favour this technique since the parties are usually in a better position to know how to prioritise their time in order to prove their case. It also enables the tribunal to ensure that the hearings end on time.

D. Preparing Witnesses for Direct Examination

In the same way as the lawyer will have worked with the witness in the preparation of the witness statement to ensure that it only contains relevant material, it is permissible for the lawyer to assist the witness in preparing for direct examination.[4] This does not mean

---

[4] The IBA Rules on the Taking of Evidence in International Commercial Arbitration explicitly permit contact between a party, its counsel and a witness. See e.g. Article 4(3): "It shall not be improper for a Party, its officers, employees, legal advisors or other representatives to interview its witnesses or potential witnesses."

putting words in the witness's mouth. The key is to familiarise the witness with what can be an intimidating process so that she may comfortably and confidently testify truthfully based on her knowledge and recollection of the facts. In this regard, the witness should be guided as to what will happen when she takes the stand and what the "stand" (normally a chair at a table) and her surroundings will look like. The witness can also be guided as to the likely scope of the questions on direct as well as common sense issues such as (a) the need to understand the question (or else ask for it to be repeated); (b) the need to answer clearly and succinctly; (c) the need to maintain eye contact with the tribunal etc. However, there is such a thing as over-preparation. Answers that sound rehearsed will lose credibility.

A successful direct examination will have: (a) permitted the witness to acclimatize to her surroundings; (b) defused the impact of any difficult new documents or relevant evidence presented in the last written pleadings; and (c) brought the Tribunal up to date on any new facts relevant to the dispute.

II. Re-direct Examination

Once direct examination is complete, counsel presenting a witness has to observe in relative silence the cross-examination of opposing counsel. The witness is on her own whilst the lawyer on the other side of the table seeks to undermine her credibility and the value of her testimony. In the absence of firm rules of questioning, there are very few objections that can sensibly be made by counsel

---

However, contact with a witness may constitute a violation of lawyers' ethical rules of conduct in some jurisdictions which is why, for instance, Article 20.6 of the LCIA Rules provides that "Subject to the mandatory provisions of any applicable law, it shall not be improper for any party or its legal representatives to interview any witness or potential witness for the purpose of presenting his testimony in written form or producing him as an oral witness". See N. Blackaby, C. Partasides, *et als*, *Redfern & Hunter on International Commercial Arbitration*, 5th ed. (OUP, 2009) at paras 6.139-6.140, and E. Gaillard and John Savage, eds., *Fouchard Gaillard Goldman on International Commercial Arbitration* (Kluwer, 1999) at para 1285.

presenting the witness. There will inevitably be moments when the witness responds in a manner which appears harmful to the case. After what may seem an eternity, counsel may use the time-worn phrase "no further questions", at which point the tribunal will turn to counsel presenting the witness and ask whether there is to be any "re-direct".

Redirect examination (sometimes known as "re-examination") is the process whereby the party presenting the witness has an opportunity to clarify any harmful testimony given during cross-examination. This is the chance for counsel to try and "pick up the pieces" of any poorly answered cross-examination question. This is where the holes may be plugged (or enlarged!).

So what is "best practice" for re-direct in an international arbitration scenario? First, always contextualize the question by referring back to the question and answer. Second, don't ask leading questions. Third, remember that re-direct is an emergency solution – it should not be used lightly. Fourth, if it is used, try and ensure that you minimise the risk with documentary evidence to which your witness can be referred. Fifth, if you really have to ask a question where you cannot rely on a document, contextualize the question as much as possible.

A. *Identify the Cross Question and Avoid Leading*

Re-direct is limited to questions that arise directly out of the cross-examination questions.[5] It is not an opportunity to ask questions in direct that were forgotten at an earlier stage nor to engage in a general discussion with the witness on matters that have been drawn into focus by the cross-examination. The best way of not falling foul of this rule is to impose the discipline of identifying the cross-examination question and the response given. For example, let us imagine that Ms Smith, as Chief Executive of X Plc, the Claimant,

---

[5] See e.g. Article 8(2) of the IBA Rules on the Taking of Evidence in International Commercial Arbitration provides in relevant part that : "The Party who initially presented the witness shall subsequently have the opportunity to ask additional questions on the matters raised in the other Parties' questioning. "

was under an obligation to consult with the joint venture partner, Y Inc., the Respondent, before making any offer for Widgets Inc. In the cross-examination of Ms Smith, counsel for Respondent had asked a number of questions about the January 16 meeting of X Plc and then asked as a last question: "Did you later inform Y Inc. of your intention to make the offer?" Ms Smith responded "No, I did not." This was obviously a harmful answer to Claimant who needs to redress the situation. The redirect would commence as follows: "Counsel asked you a question about whether you informed Y Inc about the offer and you responded 'no'".

Even more so than in direct, it is critical NOT to ask leading questions for the re-direct to have credibility. As counsel for claimant, you think Ms Smith misunderstood the question and thought it related to whether such information was given in the JV partners' meeting held that same day with Y Inc. The least effective way to correct that statement would be to ask a leading question such as: "You were asked about whether you informed Y Inc about the offer and you said no, yet you did tell them a few days later didn't you?"

B. Re-direct is an Emergency Solution: Do Not Use Lightly

Re-direct is a blunt instrument that can easily cause more damage than it seeks to avoid. Since leading questions are off the menu and the witness will not be on the comfortable ground of their witness statement, the risks are great.

The first assumption that a tribunal will make when a re-direct question is posed is that the witness has answered a cross-examination question in a way that worries counsel presenting the witness. So the first question that counsel should ask is whether the answer given is sufficiently dangerous that it is worthwhile highlighting to the tribunal. Rarely does a witness answer as perfectly as counsel would like. But that is not good reason to engage in extensive re-direct. Indeed, extensive redirect is often the hallmark of an inexperienced counsel with a shopping list of slightly imperfect answers that might be polished on further questioning. The harsh reality is that witnesses often do not perform well on re-direct. So ask the question – does the answer really matter to the case? If it is peripheral, leave it. If it is material, but can be explained away in context, leave it and give the context in the closing statement. Only if the response really matters and cannot be easily explained should re-direct be attempted. Remember that if re-direct fails to achieve the clarification sought the error will have been highlighted to the tribunal and opposing counsel.

There is a quiet elegance and assurance to counsel who confirm they do not wish to pose any re-direct questions. The implicit message is "opposing counsel have failed to raise any material doubts as to the evidence or credibility of this witness". Such a message should not be given up lightly.

C. How to Minimize Risks of Re-direct through the Use of Documents

Having concluded that the error was a material one and that there is no easy way of explaining it away, look to see how the question might be posed by refreshing the memory of the witness by reference to a document on the record. It is rare that a witness will have an encyclopaedic recollection of the relevant contemporaneous documents. A quick (and erroneous) answer can often be corrected simply by referring the witness to a document on the record of which they should have knowledge which clearly contradicts the erroneous response. This is particularly the case where the witness may have been shown an incomplete extract from a letter or other document.

In the example above, counsel knows that there is a letter on the file authored by Ms Smith a few days later in which she writes to Y Inc to inform them of the possible offer for Widgets, Inc. The safest way to redirect would have been to ask: "Counsel asked you a question about whether you informed Y Inc about the offer and you responded "no". Can I ask you to turn to Exhibit C-15 [the letter showing that the offer was communicated to Y Inc.]? Was this letter written by you? [Answer: "yes"]. Please take your time to read it. [pause]. Do you wish to reconsider your answer to counsel's question?" Of course, having read the letter it will be clear that such communication did take place and there is a good chance the witness will correct the earlier statement but she will do so in her own words.

D. How to Minimize Risks of Re-direct through Context

But what happens if there is no document yet the answer was material to the case? How do you maximize the chances of the witness correcting the answer rather than digging the grave deeper? The best way is by maximizing the context before asking the question. Let us imagine in our hypothetical example that there was no letter communicating the proposed offer to Y Inc, but that the communication was orally made in the following meeting with the JV partner one month later. The re-direct could work as follows:

"**Q.** How often do you have high level JV meetings?
A. Once a month.

Q. You referred in your evidence to a meeting on January 16. When was the next JV meeting?
A. A month later – around February 15.

Q. What was discussed at that meeting?
A. The development of the business and the offer for Widgets, Inc.

Q. But counsel asked you whether you communicated the offer to Y Inc and you said "no". How do you explain your answer?
A. I thought he was referring to the January 16 meeting but that meeting was just a sales meeting. Of course we communicated the offer on the first occasion we had which was at the February 15 meeting."

Of course, the dialogue could have worked differently (and negatively if she had not recalled the February 15 meeting). However, by placing the meeting in context, the witness is given as many elements as possible to answer correctly and rescue the position.

One simpler use of re-direct with no documents is to enable the witness to complete an answer that was "cut short" by the cross-examiner. Sometimes the cross-examiner who cuts a witness off can be policed by a well-timed objection ("Mr President, please can the witness be allowed to finish her answer."). However, that is not possible if the cross-examiner has managed to get the witness to respond "yes" or "no" to a series of closed questions. In that circumstance, redirect may provide the opportunity to repeat the question and answer and to ask the witness to provide further context.

III. Conclusion

The "framing exercise" of direct and re-direct examination should not be underestimated. The first exercise enables the witness and evidence to be put into proper context. The second seeks to ensure that the often destabilizing techniques of cross-examination do not prevent the possibility of contextualizing and clarifying answers with the hope that nine times out of ten, counsel will respond with confidence when asked if there is any redirect: "No further questions."

In both exercises, the key is to keep the questions open. As Rudyard Kipling noted in the "Elephant's Child":

> "I keep six honest serving –men
> (They taught me all I knew);
> Their names are What and Why and When
> And How and Where and Who."

Chapter 16

CROSS-EXAMINATION AND RE-CROSS IN INTERNATIONAL ARBITRATION

Edward G. Kehoe

Cicero generally is perceived to have possessed one of the most versatile minds of ancient Rome. He was a philosopher, statesman, political theorist, and, most importantly for current purposes, a successful attorney and advocate. In one letter to his lifelong friend Titus Atticus, Cicero explains the art of cross-examination as he knew it. His letter began: "The gods know, dear Titus, that nothing an advocate does is simple, but of all the things an advocate must do, by far the most difficult, the most complex, and the most subtle is cross-examination." In the final paragraph of his letter, Cicero tells his friend: "The talent to cross-examine is a rare commodity. No more than three lawyers in all of Rome have it, and sometimes I wonder whether I myself am one of them."[1]

Much has been written since Cicero's day about the complexities, nuances, styles and art of effective cross-examinations. Some believe that cross-examination is so difficult and dangerous that a lawyer should forgo the opportunity absent compelling reason.[2] This practitioner disagrees. Cross-examination is not easy, but it need not be dangerous either. The keys to cross-examination in international

---

[1] Cicero was born in 106 BC. His original letter to Titus Pomponius Atticus is undated and remains intact. It was translated into English and edited by Irving Younger (1932-1988), and published in its entirety in Practicing Law Institute's *Winning Strategies and Techniques for Civil Litigators*, edited by James E. Lyons (1992).

[2] In his book "*The Devil's Advocate, How to be Seriously Good in Court*," (Sweet & Maxwell, 2d ed. 2009), for example, Ian Morley of England says of cross-examination: "The general rule here is **DON'T DO IT**...Every question in cross-examination is an **INVITATION TO DISASTER**. It is an opportunity for the witness to hammer you and your case." (emphasis in original).

arbitration lie in (i) understanding its purpose, (ii) preparing thoroughly, (iii) selecting the right witnesses to cross-examine, and (iv) executing well. When done effectively with the right witnesses, cross-examination should not expose your client to harmful testimony, and it can help to turn the case in your direction.

For purposes of this chapter, I will assume that the main dispute between the parties centers on a claim for breach of contract. If the rights and obligations of the parties are clear from the four corners of the contract, the arbitrators in most jurisdictions to my knowledge will not resort to extrinsic (*i.e.* parol) evidence to vary the terms of the agreement. When a contract is unambiguous, all testimony (direct and cross) will be largely irrelevant, because the contract will speak for itself. But if the contract is ambiguous concerning the disputed issue, then the rule in the United States (and most other jurisdictions to my knowledge) is that the arbitrator should consider extrinsic evidence such as written communications between the parties and earlier drafts of the contract to determine the true, objective intent of the parties to the agreement.[3] This makes the communications between the parties critical, as well as testimony concerning these communications.

Normally, the arbitrator is not concerned with the inner thoughts of the person who signed the contract. The uncommunicated, subjective intent of a party to an agreement generally is not relevant. Subjective intent can become relevant, however, if that intent is communicated to the opposite party before the contract is signed. That is the law, for example, in New York. If the recipient of this communication replies in some fashion, then clearly these communications will be important in resolving the ambiguity one way or the other. Accordingly, and once again, communications between the parties may be the deciding factor in assisting the arbitrators to rule in your client's favor concerning an ambiguous contract.

Some advocates in the field of international arbitration believe that a written communication, such as a letter, memorandum or email

[3] Michael Hwang addresses this issue in greater detail in chapter 17 of this book entitled *"Ten Questions Not to Ask in Cross-examination* in *Contractual Disputes."*

speaks for itself, and these advocates generally will not cross-examine a witness in order to have the opposing witness re-state words that he/she has committed to writing previously. If that is the mindset of the advocate—if questions that derive from the words previously written by the witness are eliminated from the cross-examination plate of options, then I would tend to agree with Mr. Morley that cross-examination could be an invitation to disaster. But a witness should not be immune to his written words during cross-examination. Indeed, prior written statements by the witness concerning a substantive issue in dispute should form the very core of the cross-examination.

A written statement by the witness on an important topic provides a "block" (as I like to call it) that essentially requires the witness to agree with the advocate ultimately. Without a block, little can be done to stop a witness from running past the examiner and defeating the purpose of the cross-examination. And cross-examining a witness with his own written words often breathes life and meaning into a writing that otherwise may not readily be apparent or convincing from a document. This is particularly so when the examiner uses a series of written communications to tell the story (usually chronologically) that cannot be gleaned from a single document. Finally, cross-examining a witness with his written words affords the witness the opportunity to disagree with the proposition that is put to him, and to say that his written words are being taken out of context or misunderstood. Obviously, this is not something that the advocate hopes for, but the ability of a witness to disagree with the examiner's interpretation of the witness' written words gives more credibility to the document than if the examiner chose to forgo cross-examination concerning the document altogether.

As detailed below, this does not mean that an advocate should present the witness with a document that the witness has authored, and ask whether the written statements are accurate. That is an extraordinarily ineffective means of cross-examination. Rather, the examiner should make the statement that helps to support his client's case (or undermine the case of the opponent), and ask the witness whether he agrees with the statement. This may require a series of questions, culminating in the one that supports the advocate's case or undermines the opponent's case. If the witness agrees with the statement, then the advocate has just accomplished the purpose of cross-examination. There is no need to confront the witness with the document once the witness agrees with the statement that is put to him. If the witness disagrees with the statement, or does not recall whether the statement is accurate, then the advocate will confront the witness with the document, and the point is made that way. In either instance, the important point that supports your case or undermines your opponent's case is made through the opposing witness—which is the purpose of cross-examination—as addressed immediately below.

I. Understanding the Purpose of Cross-Examination

The ultimate goal of the advocate in an international arbitration proceeding is to assist the tribunal in reaching the result that the advocate's client has put forward as its claim or defense, within all bounds of ethics. The purpose of cross-examination in this context is to obtain testimony from the opposing witness that either reinforces important substantive points that support the client's theory of the case or undermines important features of the opponent's case (or both). In other words, the questions that an advocate asks in cross-examination should fit within the advocate's theory of the case. Later, the advocate will weave these helpful statements into his closing argument and/or post hearing submissions to help demonstrate to the arbitrators why his client should prevail. The questions that an advocate prepares for cross-examination should be designed with this fundamental purpose in mind.

In popular culture, cross-examination is theater. Surely all of us have witnessed blistering cross-examinations by talented actors in movies and on television that essentially ends the case in favor of one side. It normally does not work that way. It is unlikely that any single statement by a witness on cross-examination will be the deciding factor in a case. And sometimes isolated nuggets of helpful testimony obtained during cross-examination will not appear particularly relevant to the witness or even the arbitrators at the time the statements are made. But the advocate who understands the purpose of cross-examination will forego attempts at theatrics and instant gratification, in favor of winning his case. He will move through his cross-examination methodically, asking short and mostly leading questions, gathering bits and pieces of helpful testimony one witness at a time. This takes discipline, and careful preparation.

After securing the helpful testimony that is sought from the witness on a particular topic, the advocate naturally is tempted to shine a bright light on the testimony in order to seize the moment and ensure that the arbitrators understand that a significant point has just been scored. Resist that temptation. The purpose of cross-examination has been accomplished—you have secured the testimony that you sought. Move on. You can (and will) explain the importance of the testimony to the arbitrators in closing arguments—not during the examination itself through additional questioning that can turn into argument and undermine all that you have accomplished.

Advocates also should resist the temptation to use cross-examination as a vehicle by which to pick away at the credibility of a witness on an irrelevant topic. If the credibility of a witness is implicated in important substantive topics in the case, then certainly that will be exposed during cross-examination. But little is served by showing that the witness is wrong on an irrelevant point. Again, questions on cross-examination should fit within the theory of the case.

II. Prepare, Prepare, Prepare

Much is written of the do's and don'ts of actually conducting a cross-examination during a hearing. But the real success of effective cross-examination almost always derives not from the sharp wit or quick thinking of the advocate during the cross-examination, but rather from thorough and uncompromising preparation. One hour of cross-examination should be preceded by many, many hours of thoughtful and careful preparation. Like an Olympic miler who logs thousands of miles over a four year period to compete in a race that lasts for less than four minutes, the substantial preparatory work prior to the cross-examination is the key ingredient of success. No matter how talented an advocate may be (or thinks he may be), the witness is likely to prevail if the advocate has not thoroughly prepared for the competition.

An advocate prepares for a cross-examination through a deliberate process that finds its roots in a cross-examination outline. A strong and detailed outline, backed by documents, will provide the advocate with a home-base to which he may always return to keep the examination on track.

A. Six Steps in Preparing to Cross-Examine a Witness

Step one. Create a written list of important topics in the case, and assign a number to each topic. This list of topics will form the basis of your cross-examination outline. A case can have any number of important topics, depending on its size and complexity, but it is likely that the advocate will cover a maximum of four or five major topics with any single witness on cross-examination. For example, if one of the main issues in the case relates to the course of conduct of the parties, then your outline will read: "Topic No. 1—Course of Conduct."

Step two. Study the written witness statement or expert report of the witness to be cross-examined, to determine each instance in which the witness provides testimony that falls into one of the categories on your list of important topics in the case. Take your pencil and circle each sentence or paragraph that touches upon one of the important topics, and write the topic number in the margin of the document. For example, each time the witness refers in his witness statement to course of conduct, circle that statement and write "Topic No. 1" or just "# 1" in the margin. By studying each witness statement in this fashion with a focused eye on the cross-examination topics listed in the outline, the advocate will determine the extent to which the witness provides testimony that is relevant to an important issue in the case.

Step three. Do the same for every document in the record of the case that is authored or received by the witness to be cross-examined, as well as documents that the witness cannot realistically refute, such as public filings by his company with a regulatory body. Documents received by a witness (either as the main recipient or as a "cc" on a letter or an email) usually are not as helpful as documents that the witness authored, but they can be helpful and should not be overlooked.

Step four. Study all of the statements that fall into each important "topic" on your outline and understand how they all fit together. After performing this step in the process, the advocate will be in position to determine whether to cross-examine the witness.

Step five: If you have decided to cross-examine the witness, develop and write into your outline (i) a crisp line of cross-examination questions, (ii) the answer for each question, and (iii) a citation to the document from which the answer is derived. Increase the font size on your computer so that the words in your questions appear larger than normal. You will be glancing down at your outline when asking the questions later—not reading from it—so a large font is important.

It is unlikely that any single question and answer will make the point on their own. The advocate most likely will need to piece statements together to make the ultimate point. Most questions should be backed by a prior written statement of the witness, so if the witness disagrees with any of the questions put to him, the advocate will keep the witness on course by directing him to the document he authored—which the witness cannot realistically refute. The advocate should possess written support for even the most simple and non-controversial of questions, because that is how the advocate keeps control over the examination and shows the witness (and the tribunal) that the advocate is the master of the facts and in command of the examination.

Track the witness's words essentially *verbatim* when writing the questions in your outline, and ask the question essentially using the witness's own words. When writing the questions in the outline, italicize or underscore the words in your question that you wish to emphasize.

Most witnesses begin a cross-examination by disagreeing with the questions put to them or, even more frequently, by providing a long-winded answer to a simple question in an effort to provide helpful testimony for their side. Allow the witness some leeway at the outset. The tribunal will not appreciate a witness who is unresponsive. Moreover, witnesses do not initially realize that their own words are being put back to them. Most witnesses catch on quickly, however, and after being confronted with their own written words two, three or four times, they tend to fall into a rhythm of agreeing with the questions put to them. This is because witnesses generally come to appreciate and understand that the lawyer has a document to support the question, and the efforts by the witness at advocacy or evasiveness are back-firing. *This too, creates important opportunities.* A good advocate may use the rhythm of cross-examination to ask some critical questions for which he does *not* have a block, and still secure the answers for which he hopes. This occurs only after the witness has become fully convinced that the advocate does not ask questions without having a document to support the point. This is an effective technique that must be used ethically and with care. As with all questions, these 'rhythm questions' should be a logical and accurate extension of the witness' prior testimony, and they can result in important testimony that close holes in a case.

Step six: Put each document that supports each question in a binder with tabs, highlight the language upon which each question is based, and write the document's hearing exhibit number, tab number and page in your outline next to the question and draft answer.[4] A sample outline appears in the section below. It is critical during a cross-examination that the advocate moves effortlessly from document to document, and that he can easily focus the witness on the words of the document when necessary. The effect of a cross-examination is largely defeated when an advocate fumbles around in search of a document.

---

[4] If the parties have exchanged core bundles such that the exhibits are pre-marked and tabbed, the binders will be unnecessary.

The preparation process seems tedious—and it is—but by *preparing* a clear and easy-to-follow outline, and organizing documents so that they can be accessed in seconds, the advocate glides smoothly and effectively through the cross-examination. As the Olympic miler appears to be almost jogging around the track while breaking the four minute mile, an effective advocate will make the cross-examination appear to be almost effortless. Moreover, an advocate's credibility is of paramount importance in all aspects of a case, including cross-examination. Without credibility, an advocate and his case essentially are doomed. The arbitrators must come to trust the advocate in all that he says, and this will occur when the advocate is truthful and accurate in his written and spoken word. The six-step process outlined above helps to keep the advocate's credibility intact in the cross-examination phase of the case, by ensuring a complete command of the issues and documents that relate to the theory of the case.

B. Sample Cross-examination Outline

A sample cross-examination outline is set forth below on two important topics in the case, based on the following hypothetical fact pattern.

In January, 2006, Seller Co. entered a three year, multi million dollar contract with Buyer Co. to supply high-grade steel that Buyer Co. uses in manufacturing aircraft. The contract contains a fixed price, and provides that Buyer Co. must pay for the steel by wire transfer within ten days of receiving it. The contract (unfortunately) does not elaborate on this point or provide for any consequences, such as interest or penalties, in the event of late payment. The Buyer frequently missed this ten day deadline—normally paying three, four or five weeks late. Mr. Smith, a senior manager of Seller Co. wrote two letters to his counterpart at Buyer Co., noting the late payment and asking for more prompt payment in the future. The letters were dated September 13, 2006 and February 10, 2007. As one might expect to see in correspondence from a supplier to one of its substantial new customers, the letters also contained language that Buyer Co. may use to its advantage.

In March, 2007, the market price of steel rose dramatically, and Seller Co. terminated the contract on a number of grounds that it claimed constituted material breaches by Buyer Co., including its repeated late payments. Buyer Co. commenced an arbitration claiming that its late payments were immaterial, and that Seller's termination thus was a material breach of a binding contract. Buyer Co. seeks damages primarily for the difference between its contract price and the higher market price.

Topic No. 1 (Buyer Co. was an Important and Valued Customer Despite Delay)

Q. Mr. Smith, you are a senior manager with Seller Co, is that right?
A. Yes. ("I am a senior executive with Seller Co."): Tab 1, Witness Statement, p. 1.

Q. As part of your job at Seller Co., Mr. Smith, you oversee the performance of all long term steel contracts, is that right?
A. Correct. ("As part of my job at Seller Co., I oversee the performance of all long-term steel contracts."): Tab 1, Witness Statement, p. 2.

Q. And this includes monitoring *the timing of payments* that each purchasing company makes under its long term contract with your company, isn't that correct?
A. Yes. ("I monitor the timing of payments that each purchasing company makes under its long term contract with my company."): Tab 1, Witness Statement, p. 3.

Q. Seller Co. and Buyer Co. signed the contract at issue in this arbitration in January, 2006, do you recall that?
A. Yes. ("My company signed the contract with Buyer Co. in January 2006"): Tab 1, Witness Statement, p. 3.

Q. Buyer Co. received 23 separate shipments of steel between January 2006 and September 2006. Correct?
A. Yes, that is correct (shipping records summary, attached to Mr. Smith's witness statement): Tab 2, p. 4.

Q. And Buyer Co. made all of its payments between 20 and 40 days after it received each shipment, right?
A. Correct. (Payment records summary attached to Mr. Smith's witness statement): Tab 3, p. 1.

Q. Despite this fact, Seller Co. was *pleased* that Buyer Co. was a customer as of September 2006, isn't that right?
A. Yes. That is right. ("We at Seller Co. are pleased that Buyer Co. is our customer"): Tab 4, Letter from Mr. Smith dated September 13, 2006.

Q. By February 12, 2007, Buyer Co. had made 36 separate purchases of steel under the contract, but had paid within the ten day period only twice, isn't that right?
A. I do not recall that level of detail.

Q. Please look at the February 12, 2007 letter from you to Buyer Co., found in tab 5 of the binder in front of you. Pause. Do you see where you wrote "Buyer Co. has made 36 separate purchases of steel under the contract, but you have paid within the ten day period only twice."
A. Yes, I see that. (February 12, 2007 letter): Tab 5.

Q. Was that an accurate statement when you wrote it?
A. Yes it was.

Q. Thank you. And despite this fact, your company did not declare Buyer Co. to be in breach of the contract as of February 12, 2007, is that right?
A. Yes. That is correct. But I did request that Buyer Co. make timely payments within the 10 day period going forward.

Q. Yes you did, but isn't it true, sir, that despite Buyer Co.'s payment history through February 12, 2007, your company continued to consider Buyer Co. to be an *important and valued customer* as of that date?
A. Yes we did. ("Despite your late payments, we continue to consider Buyer Co. to be an important and valued customer"): Tab 5, Letter from Mr. Smith dated February 12, 2007.

Q. And the monetary impact of Buyer Co.'s late payments was *insignificant* as of February 2007, isn't that correct?

A. Yes, that is correct. ("Although the monetary impact of Buyer Co.'s late payments is insignificant, we request that you pay more promptly in the future"): Tab 5, letter from Mr. Smith dated February 12, 2007.

<u>**Topic No. 2 (Seller Co. Terminated Due to Rising Steel Prices)**</u>

Q. Do you recall the fixed price established by the Contract for Buyer's purchases of the high quality steel?

A. Yes. It was $800 per ton. (Contract, p. 7): Tab 6.

Q. And $800 was the spot market price for a ton of this quality steel on the day that the Contract was signed, isn't that right?

A. Yes. (Contract, p. 7): Tab 6.

Q. The spot market price remained around $800 per ton through February 2007, isn't that right?

A. Yes. That is correct. (Spot market report pp. 3-7): Tab 7.

Q. What happened to the spot market price for this type of steel on March 1, 2007?

A. It increased.

Q. To what?

A. $1,200 per ton. (Spot market report, p. 10): Tab 7.

Q. Do you know why the spot market price for steel increased to $1,200?

A. Supply of this particular steel became limited due to a change in import regulations. (Monthly steel industry report): Tab 8; ("I have been in the steel industry for 20 years and I am an editor of the trade publication Monthly Steel Report"): Tab 1, Witness Statement, p. 2.

Q. When did Seller Co. terminate the Contract?

A. March 5, 2007. (Seller Co.'s termination letter dated March 5, 2007): Tab 9.

Q. About three weeks after your letter of February 12, 2007 describing Buyer Co. as an important and valued customer?

A. Yes, that is right.

Q. After terminating the Contract, did Seller Co. begin selling steel on spot market?

A. Yes. ("Seller Co. began selling its limited supply of high grade steel on the spot market in March 2007"): Tab 10, Seller Co.'s public filing with regulators.

Q. And Seller Co. currently sells the steel on the spot market, isn't that right?

A. Yes. (Spot market report, p. 11): Tab 11.

Q. I have no further questions, Mr. Smith. Thank you.

This outline presents virtually no risk to the examiner. If the witness had given different answers, the examiner had a specific document at hand to support the question and contradict the answer. This outline also helps to illuminate the underling theory of the claimant's case—that late payments were not a material breach of the Contract, and that a better opportunity rather than legal justification motivated the respondent to terminate the Contract. Also, while a party's "motivation" for breaching a contract is largely irrelevant in most jurisdictions from a purely legal perspective, an advocate who ignores motivation does so at his peril. The arbitrators want to know how all of the pieces of the puzzle fit together, and in this hypothetical, for example, the seller's apparent motivation for terminating the Contract helped to support the buyer's claim that its late payments did not constitute a material breach.

III. Selecting the Right Witnesses for Cross-Examination

While the fear of cross-examination causes some advocates to squander the opportunity to advance their case through cross-examination, an opposite camp of advocates feels obliged to cross-examine every witness who has submitted direct testimony in the proceeding. As with most issues in life, the right answer does not lie in either extreme. It may be best in some circumstances to forgo cross-examination of a witness.

The advocate should consider three things when evaluating whether to cross-examine a particular witness. First, has the witness stated anything meaningful in his/her direct testimony that touches upon an important substantive issue in the case? Second, has the witness authored any correspondence or other documents that may help your case? Finally, does the direct testimony from this witness cover the same subject matter as the direct testimony of another witness for the same party?

As to the first two questions: if the witness has not provided testimony that is relevant to one of the main issues in the case, then the advocate usually should forgo the opportunity to cross-examine. A cross-examination under these circumstances could make the witness more relevant than he or she otherwise would be. However, if this same witness has authored documents that either help the advocate's case or undermines his opponent's case, then cross-examination is in order to illuminate the helpful point.

When the direct testimony of one witness covers the same general subject matter as the testimony of another witness for the same party, there is great opportunity. Study each witness's direct testimony carefully. Look for areas where they may conflict. It is unlikely that you will find any meaningful conflict. But look deeper. The answer may lie in how forcefully one witness makes a point compared to another, or what one witness says that the other witness *does not.* Some witnesses are more inclined to stretch their alleged understanding of contract terms than others. So, when two witnesses signed the same contract, for example, and one witness provides lengthy testimony on an important point and the other witness barely touches upon the issue, you should focus on this latter witness. If the lawyers representing these witnesses could have legitimately, honestly and ethically gotten both witnesses to provide similar testimony on the same important topics, they would have done so. The fact that the latter witness did not support your opponent's substantive point on an important topic creates a tremendous opportunity. Simply put, focus on what the witness did *not* say in his witness statement. It is possible that the witness was weak on this point from your adversary's perspective, and a decision was made to keep that witness away from the topic. So that is exactly where you should consider going on cross-examination.

For example, in concession contracts to which a government entity is a party, two or more governmental officials sometimes sign the same contract on behalf of the government. The government may submit written direct testimony from three governmental ministers attesting to the same substantive issues concerning the contract at issue—essentially to support one another. If one of those witnesses, however, does not touch upon a topic that the others do, exploit it. Call that witness and discover whether he will undermine your opponent's case on that point about which he did not provide direct testimony. It is fair game to explore this in cross-examination because the witness provided testimony concerning the contract, so he opened the door for cross-examination questions as to the contract, whether or not he touched upon every disputed issue related to the contract. There is risk here—because the witness may simply re-affirm what the others have said already. But this may be a risk worth taking, even if you do not have a document to block the witness from running past you. In this practitioner's experience, if done correctly, these witnesses sometimes will undermine your opponent's case during cross-examination.

In this example of the concession contract, let's assume that an oil company and a sovereign State reached an agreement on the method of allocating the oil that each party would receive if oil were discovered in the country. Assume further that oil is discovered, and the parties enter into a new contract. A dispute arises concerning the terms of the agreement as it relates to allocation of discovered oil. The new contract is ambiguous as to the allocation formula. Both parties look to the earlier contract in arguing their case as to the meaning of the new contract. The oil company claims that the new contract simply clarifies the rights that already existed. The government claims that the new contract is a major modification of the earlier arrangement, and that the oil company relinquished substantial rights that it originally possessed. Assume that the three ministers who signed the second contract submitted witness statements on various topics in dispute. Assume that two of the ministers testified in their written witness statement that the second contract was intended to be a material modification of the earlier agreement between the parties, and the third minister did not mention this topic at all. The third minister focused only on the single issue of the term of the contract (which also was in dispute). In this circumstance, the advocate representing the oil company should call the third minister and cross-examine the minister on this critical issue of whether the second contract was indeed intended to materially modify the first. There is little to lose here, because the other two ministers already have advocated the government's case on this point. And the advocate may turn the case in his direction on a fundamental point by taking the risk.

The cross-examination in this hypothetical will be short. The advocate will develop the foundation; establish the importance of the first contract to the fullest extent possible with the witness; and then ask the witness if he intended to materially modify that first contract when signing the second one. This is advanced cross-examination technique. Normally an advocate would not consider wading into unchartered territory without a block or an established 'rhythm' on a topic that was previously supported with documents. nd usually, *but not always*, an advocate will only ask leading questions on cross-examination (more on that below). But this is the art of cross-examination. It is not a science. Judgment, experience, and a certain amount of risk is inherent in all that we do.

IV. Execute Well

In chapter 22 of this book, James Carter and Doak Bishop list and describe ten basic rules that appear to permeate the effective use of cross-examinations in international arbitration. Some of these rules find their foundation in preparation, and others in executing well. I agree with these ten basic rules, and I shall adopt them here, quoting each one below and elaborating on them.

First, "cross-examination should be conducted in a civil and respectful manner." This includes being patient and cordial with a witness who seeks to command the stage with long, self-serving responses that do not answer the question put to him. An advocate normally hurts his case, his credibility and even possibly his reputation when he is sarcastic or rude to a witness on cross-examination, or when he cuts the witness off mid-answer—even when the witness otherwise might deserve such treatment. This does *not* mean that the advocate should allow the witness to take control of the examination with unresponsive answers. Rather, the advocate should politely insist on an answer to the question. For example, after a long and rambling answer that advances the witness's case, the advocate might say: "Thank you for that Mr. Smith, but I did not ask you about your understanding of paragraph 5 of the contract, I simply asked you whether you had read the entire contract. Can you answer that question, please?" An advocate may need to ask the same question three or even four times before receiving a responsive answer. The tribunal will not appreciate a witness who constantly attempts to side-step questions. But even when the advocate perceives that the tribunal is losing its patience with an evasive witness, the advocate should not follow suit. The advocate should allow the witness to dig his own grave by alienating the tribunal—and the advocate should remain composed, professional, polite and patient. Indeed, the witness's reluctance to answer the question helps to validate the point.

In addition to conducting the examination in a respectful manner, the advocate should be mindful that his pace and tone will play an important role. This generally comes with experience. The advocate should strive for a relatively rapid tempo on cross-examination, but also should ensure that the tribunal is keeping pace with the issue and the questions, particularly when reviewing a document. Notice that I wrote "Pause" in the sample cross-examination outline above, when directing the witness to the document. This is a reminder that the witness and the tribunal need a few moments to find a document in their binder or bundle. This will come naturally with experience, but it does not hurt to write it in the cross-examination outline.

It is not a good idea to look often at the tribunal while questioning a witness on cross-examination. The advocate should be focused like a laser on the witness, the answers and the important issues at hand. Also, it may appear to be bad form if an advocate seems to be seeking approval from the tribunal during a cross-examination. Nevertheless, it is a good habit to look at the tribunal after you have directed a witness to particular language in a document, to ensure that the arbitrators have found the document and the relevant language, and that they are following along. The tribunal is likely to interpret this exactly as it is intended—to be helpful. It also gives the advocate an opportunity to read any body language that the tribunal may be displaying, and react accordingly.

The advocate's tone should be confident, but not strident. Also, be mindful of speaking loudly enough to be heard clearly and easily by the witness and the tribunal. A weak voice that is difficult to hear will frustrate a tribunal and may convey weakness in the advocate and his position. Similarly, voice inflection is particularly useful in cross-examination. Although the competitive exchange between examiner and witness normally should keep the attention of the arbitrators, a monotone voice with little inflection can cause even an artful cross-examination to lose some of its effect. It simply is difficult for the human ear to listen carefully and at length to a monotone voice. Voice inflection also enables the examiner to place particular emphasis on important words in the question, as shown in the sample outline above.

Second, "cross-examinations should generally be brief and to the point." Some of the most effective cross-examinations are those that last less than 15 minutes. The examination will be based on the advocate's written outline, and the outline is based almost exclusively on documents. It should move along efficiently. If the witness agrees with the question put to him, the advocate moves to the next question. If the witness evades the question, the advocate will continue to ask the question until the witness answers it. This obviously will increase the length of time needed to complete the examination, but that is unavoidable. If the witness disagrees with the question put to him, the advocate normally will confront the witness with the document supporting the advocate's point, the witness then agrees, and the advocate moves on to the next question.

Third, "counsel should know the purpose for examining the witness and have a well thought-out plan, complete with a contingency plan and an exit strategy, before commencing." The advocate accomplishes this in the preparation process that I describe above. Clearly, the advocate must have a fully developed plan for examining the witness on important topics where the witness can either help the advocate's case or undermine the opponent's case (or both). The advocate executes on this plan by following his written outline during the cross-examination and securing the answers that advance this goal.

Fourth, "the advocate should rarely plan on making his or her case by cross-examination." Although an effective cross-examination can help to turn a case in your direction, the advocate should not count on it. As stated at the outset of this chapter, cross-examination is based largely on the documents in the case that are written (or to a lesser degree, received) by the witness being cross-examined. The advocate is likely to use those same documents in presenting his direct case, and in closing argument. So cross-examination is unlikely to reveal additional facts that cause a case to be won. But cross-examination breathes life into those helpful documents, enables the examiner to present his case through the opposing witness, which is quite effective, and also creates opportunities for a witness to discredit himself by denying the obvious, being evasive or otherwise attempting to contradict the written words. Cumulatively, these aspects of cross-examination can contribute to a successful outcome, but they are unlikely to be dispositive on their own.

Fifth, "the force of a good cross-examination is found in the substance of the questions asked." This is why the advocate should identify the topics that are important in the case and prepare the cross-examination outline around these important topics. Little is gained in cross-examining a witness on ancillary issues.

Sixth, "the advocate must exercise some level of control over the witness." This is usually (but not always) accomplished through short, leading questions that can be answered with a "yes" or "no" response. Of course, a witness normally will be permitted to explain his answer, and that is fine. An advocate does not lose control of the witness merely because the witness wishes to explain his answer. If the explanation is particularly long winded, the advocate may wish to reaffirm the helpful answer. For example, "thank you for that explanation as to your busy schedule, Mr. Smith, but the answer to my question was 'no' — you did not read the entire contract before signing it, isn't that right?" But the advocate should allow the witness to finish his answer, and the advocate should not expressly demand a yes or no answer. Indeed, an advocate who attempts to exercise too much control over a witness is likely to alienate the tribunal in the process. As one noted American trial lawyer once observed, "Too much witness control is like your neighbor who uses a choke leash to walk his dog. You may not start out liking the dog, but before long you sympathize with him for the way he's being treated."[5]

As stated above, the advocate should not allow a witness to evade a question. If the witness filibusters repeatedly, and each side is allotted a limited amount of time during the hearing, the advocate may calmly say to the witness: "I appreciate that you wish to make these points that you believe help your case, Mr. Smith, but I did not ask you about that. And the time that we spend on this cross-examination is counted against the time allowed to my client during the oral hearing. So could you please listen to the question that I am asking you, and answer that question?" A statement such as this can only be made after the witness has clearly established himself to be evasive and unresponsive. A critically important feature of this, of course, is that the advocate has asked a pointed, clear and specific question which the witness has not answered. If the question is long or unclear, then the advocate has failed in his mission and has provided the witness with an opportunity to advocate and filibuster.

It is best for an advocate to handle an evasive witness himself, rather than to seek assistance from the tribunal. Assuming the advocate's questions are pointed and clear, the tribunal will intervene and direct a witness to be more responsive when the tribunal sees fit to do so, especially if the advocate continues to be polite,

---

[5] James W. McElhaney, McElaney's Trial Notebook. Fourth Ed. American Bar Association 2005.

professional and patient with the evasive witness. In asking the tribunal for assistance with an evasive witness, an advocate unnecessarily states that he has lost control of the witness. And the tribunal will appreciate an advocate who does not ask the tribunal to take sides in this situation.

An advocate also should take the blame if the witness claims to be confused by a question or rambles on without answering the question. This is easily accomplished. After the witness talks at length about his busy schedule, the advocate may say: "I am sorry Mr. Smith, I meant to ask you whether you read the entire contract. Can you answer that question please?"

Notwithstanding conventional lore of cross-examination technique, an advocate does *not* risk losing control over a witness by asking non-leading questions. When performed correctly, a non-leading question can be a powerful tool in cross-examination, with no risk. First, when an advocate possesses a document that makes the point which the advocate wants the witness to admit on the witness stand, it often is more effective to have the witness say the words out loud than to simply agree with the advocate. For example, in the sample outline above, the advocate asked "[d]o you know *why* the steel price on the spot market increased to $1,200 per ton?" There was no real risk in this question, because the witness had already explained the reason in a written communication, and the tribunal often wishes to hear more from a witness than "yes" and "no". So while it is important to keep control over the witness, it also is important that the advocate not conduct the examination in a manner that completely chokes or stifles the witness. Asking non-leading questions where there is little or no risk of harmful answers is appropriate and helpful. Second, witnesses often do not understand or appreciate all of the various issues that comprise an entire dispute, and as a result, witnesses sometimes make statements on cross-examination that unwittingly help the examiner's case. When a witness does this during cross-examination, the advocate should seriously consider asking the witness "why" he believes such a fact to be accurate. This is because the opposing advocate is likely to attempt to unwind or blunt the harmful testimony during re-direct examination. Having the witness elaborate on his helpful answer during the cross-examination by asking open-ended, follow-up questions makes it more difficult for the opposing advocate to reverse the damage to his case during re-direct examination.

Seventh, "be prepared for the unexpected answer." This can occur when the advocate departs from the documents and asks the witness an important question for which the advocate does not have a "block". Such questions should be asked sparingly, but sometimes the risk is worth taking. When the advocate takes this risk, he should be ready to immediately ask a short series of questions on a related topic with which the witness must agree. This is designed to make an unhelpful answer seem less relevant, and to get the cross-examination back on track with the examiner winning the battle. Also, the advocate cannot let it appear that the answer was damaging. This may be difficult, but it is important. An advocate who appears visibly stung by an answer makes the answer even more damaging than it already is. Moving quickly to the next question helps the advocate to avoid unintended visible reactions to the hurtful answer.

Eighth, "the advocate should begin and end the cross-examination with the two strongest points that he or she is confident can be successfully made." In other words, start strong and finish strong. First impressions are important, and the first series of questions will set the tone of the cross-examination. Also, because the tribunal normally will be most alert and focused at the outset of the cross-examination, the most important points should be made promptly—saving one important point for the end. Ending strong is important. The impact of an otherwise effective cross-examination will be diminished by a weak conclusion. Similarly, an otherwise uneventful cross-examination can become memorable for the tribunal if a direct hit is scored just before the examination concludes.

Ninth, "avoid arguing with the witness or asking questions that are primarily argumentative in nature." This is axiomatic. If an advocate argues with a witness on a point during cross-examination, the point is lost. Cross-examination is the time for establishing and confirming important facts that are central to the theme of the case—not for arguing points in dispute. In the sample outline above, the advocate ended with the question: "[d]oes Seller Co. currently sell the steel on the spot market?" knowing full-well that the answer is "yes". The purpose of that final question was to plant in the minds of the arbitrators that Seller Co. terminated the contract so that it could make more money by selling the steel on the spot market. The advocate will argue this point in his closing argument. The advocate should not argue this ultimate point with the witness on cross-examination, and doing so almost certainly will undermine the point that the advocate attempted to make. For example, the advocate in the sample above did not proceed to ask: "Isn't it true, sir, that your company terminated the contract *not* because Buyer Co. paid its bills late, *but rather* because your company concluded that it could make more money by breaching the contract and selling the steel in the spot market?" This is argument. An advocate may dream of winning a case with such questions, but that is where such questions should remain—in one's dreams.

Tenth, "listen to the answers of the witness." This is important for at least three reasons. First, it is important to receive an answer to the specific question asked. Witnesses often seek to evade tough questions. If an examiner does not listen carefully to the answer, he may fail to realize that the witness has artfully evaded the question by rephrasing it and thus answering a different question, or by talking around it. That is bad enough on its own, but to make matters worse, the arbitrators will probably realize that the question was not answered, and this will cause them to question the skill of the advocate. Over the course of a hearing, a bond of trust should develop between the advocate and the tribunal. The tribunal should come to view the advocate as a master of the facts and a respected guide to the truth. If the guide gets lost, the bond of trust is diminished. Second, the witness may expose a weakness that can be exploited by follow-up questions. If the advocate has prepared well for the cross-examination, it will be unnecessary to look ahead to the next question as the witness is answering the pending question. Finally, the witness's answer may touch upon a different topic in the advocate's outline. When that occurs, the alert and attentive advocate will move to that section of his cross-examination witness. This type of nimbleness impresses a tribunal, and it occurs when an advocate is prepared and listens well.

IV. Re-Cross-Examination

To the extent the international arbitration tribunal allows re-cross-examination, the advocate must decide quickly whether it will be helpful. It usually is not, except for purposes of re-asserting critical points and seizing the opportunity to end the examination on your terms and not on the terms of your opponent.

In re-direct examination, the opposing counsel will have attempted to rehabilitate the witness in important areas, but if the cross-examination was effective, the witness will not effectively unwind his prior testimony. And if the advocate wades in to re-cross-examination to "follow-up" on some of the points advanced on re-direct, it is likely to become an unfocused argument with the witness, which is a disastrous end to a cross-examination. Nevertheless, it is unfortunate to allow the opposing side to have the last word on an important topic, particularly if the re-direct examination seems to have confused or clouded the good points that you made on cross-examination. So an entirely appropriate, and safe, re-cross examination is one that goes right back to the cross-examination outline and re-affirms the ultimate and critical points with which the witness must agree. This is consistent with the eighth rule of cross-examination above—start strong and end strong.

So, for example, if Mr. Smith provided a long explanation during re-direct examination as to his utter disappointment and outrage with Buyer Co.'s practice of paying its bills well beyond the ten-day period allowed by the Contract, a re-cross-examination might go something like this:

Q. Mr. Smith, during your testimony a few moments ago when Ms. Wills was asking you questions, you stated that you were offended and outraged by Buyer Co.'s late payments, do you remember that testimony?

A. Yes I do.

Q. But it is correct, isn't it Mr. Smith, that despite its late payments, you and your company continued to consider Buyer Co. to be an *important and valued customer* just three weeks before you terminated the Contract?

A. Yes. That is right. ("Despite your late payments, we continue to consider you to be an important and valued customer."): Tab 5, letter from Mr. Smith dated February 12, 2007.

Q. Thank you sir, I have no further questions.

This re-cross was based on both documents and on the prior testimony of the witness, so the witness had no choice but to reaffirm the ultimate point that the cross-examination had established. This must be done quickly. The advocate must get straight to the point on re-cross. The arbitrators will have absolutely no patience for anything that comes remotely close to a repeat of the cross-examination. But a short, crisp and focused re-cross that hits a critical point or two that the witness sullied on re-direct can be effective, and it ends the entire examination on the right note.

V. Conclusion

In his famous letter to his friend, Cicero said of cross-examination: "To do it better than competently, to do it superbly, requires a convergence in one cross-examiner of three qualities. The first quality is experience. The second quality is talent. And the third quality is technical mastery. . . .The chief, the central principle of advocacy in all its parts and in every aspect, is preparation."

As international arbitration practitioners, we may discuss and debate the utility of cross-examination, and the manner by which an advocate molds the cross-examination to make it most effective. There is, of course, no right answer for all circumstances. The art form is refined and polished over time, with experience that is derived from conducting cross-examinations, determining what works well (and what does not), and sharing ideas.

Chapter 17

TEN QUESTIONS NOT TO ASK IN CROSS-EXAMINATION IN INTERNATIONAL ARBITRATION

Michael Hwang*

I. Introduction

This chapter identifies ten questions that an international arbitration practitioner should take pains to avoid in cases concerning contractual interpretation and breach. The recommended abstinence applies mainly to cross-examination where the governing law is common law, but the majority of the questions from which Counsel should abstain in common law should in most cases be likewise avoided during cross-examination where the arbitration is governed by civil law. The lesson to bear in mind is that, in his preparation for cross-examination, Counsel must have a firm grasp of his case theory, before trying to establish the facts that are the foundation stones of that theory. He must first understand the rules of contractual interpretation and contractual breach (these being the two most common issues in practice), and focus his mind on the significance of questioning witnesses in contract cases and whether certain questions should be asked. Even where questions are permissible, they may not be (1) relevant to the legal issues at hand, or (2) helpful to the Tribunal in deciding the key issues.

---

* Barrister and Arbitrator, Singapore. I am grateful to my associates, Charis Tan and Su Zihua, for their assistance in the preparation of this chapter.

II. The Ten Questions to Avoid

1. Questions about the unarticulated intention of witnesses, e.g. *what did you mean when you wrote this letter/these minutes?*

2. Questions about the motives of witnesses relating to actions or omissions, e.g. *why did you insert this clause in the agreement? Why did you do/not do something?*

3. Questions about a witness' interpretation of letters or contractual documents unless it impacted on his subsequent actions, e.g. *what does this clause of the contract mean to you? What do you think the writer of this letter meant by paragraph X?*

4. Questions to demonstrate what is or is not in a document, e.g. *where in this document does it say [whatever]? Do you agree that this clause does not say anything about [something]? Look at this document – does it contain any reference to [x]?*

5. Questions for dramatic effect which do not add to the knowledge of the Tribunal, e.g. *I put it to you that you are not telling the truth* (unless Counsel has built up a foundation for this suggestion by previous questioning). *Could you please read out the third paragraph of your letter?*

6. Questions designed to make the witness concede facts in favour of the opposing party which are apparent from the record and are not denied, e.g. *do you agree that you never replied to my client's letter?*

7. Questions solely aimed at attacking credibility or creating prejudice, i.e. having no direct relevance to the issues, but designed to question the witness' credibility or character by asking him questions on other matters outside the events covered by the existing arbitration.

8. Questions that seek to argue a legal issue with a lay witness, e.g. *do you agree that Clause X means…? Do you agree that my client acted lawfully in terminating your employment?*

9. Questions which take a witness through facts and documents with a view to making the witness agree with the other party's interpretation of a document or characterization of events (rather than the actual facts themselves), e.g. *do you agree that my client behaved reasonably under the circumstances?*

10. Questions which end – "*answer yes or no*" when the question is not a "yes or no" question.

III. Why Avoid the Ten Questions?

A. *The principles of contractual interpretation render such questions pointless (Questions 1, 2 and 3)*

(1) The approach to contractual interpretation is objective (Question 1)

Under English law, interpretation of a contract is the ascertainment of the meaning which the document would convey to a reasonable person having all the background knowledge which would reasonably have been available to the parties in the situation in which they were at the time of the contract.[1] In short, the English approach to interpretation is an objective one and is so without controversy.[2] The objective approach is also applied in Australia,[3]

1 *Investors Compensation Scheme Ltd v West Bromwich Building Society* [1998] 1 WLR 896 ("**Investors Compensation**") at 912, reaffirmed by the House of Lords in Chartbrook Ltd v Persimmon Homes Ltd [2009] 1 AC 1131 ("**Chartbrook**")

2 Sir Kim Lewison, *The Interpretation of Contracts* (Sweet & Maxwell: London, 2007) ("**Lewison**") at [2.03].

3 In Australia, courts have adhered to an explicitly objective approach to the construction of contracts, particularly of written contracts signed by the parties. Both in determining what terms have been incorporated in a contract, and in interpreting those terms, the task of construction is not to ascertain the subjective

New Zealand,[4] Singapore,[5] the United States,[6] and Canada.[7] Thus, common law embraces an objective approach to interpretation.

In the common law context, the aim of interpretation is not to probe the real intentions of the parties but to ascertain the *contextual meaning* of the relevant contractual language. The question to be asked is what a reasonable person, given the factual matrix in which the contract was made, would have understood the parties to have meant by the use of specific language. The answer to this question is to be gathered from the text under consideration and its relevant

---

intention of the parties, but rather to determine what a reasonable person in their situation would have intended or assumed. See N C Seddon and M P Ellinghaus, *Cheshire and Fifoot's Law of Contract*, 9th Australian Ed. (LexisNexis Butterworths: Australia, 2008) ("**Cheshire Australia**") at 394 and 429. Accordingly, it is unequivocal that the court cannot receive evidence from one party as to its uncommunicated intention, understanding or expectation of the contract. Such extrinsic evidence of subjective intention is in principle not admissible. *Cheshire Australia,* at 411 to 412.

4 *Lewison,* at 26.

5 *Zurich Insurance (Singapore) Pte Ltd v B-Gold Interior Design & Construction Pte Ltd* [2008] SGCA 27 ("**Zurich Insurance**")

6 Contractual interpretation in the United States similarly takes such an objective approach. The object in construing a contract is to ascertain the meaning and intent of the parties as expressed in the language used in the contract. Primary importance is placed upon the words of the contract, and therefore, the actual intent of the parties is ineffective unless it is expressed in some way in the writing. Thus, the court should not inquire into the actual mental processes of the parties in entering into the particular contract; rather the law presumes that the parties understood the import of their contract and that they had the intention which its terms manifest. Richard A. Lord, *A Treatise on the Law of Contracts*, vol. 11, 4th ed. (West Group: United States, 1999) ("**US Contract Law**") at 271 to 277. It is clear, therefore, that it is not the real intent but the intent expressed or apparent in the writing which is sought; it is the objective, not the subjective, intent that controls. *US Contract Law*, at 281 to 283.

7 In Canada, it is similarly accepted that an objective approach is necessary to make sense of the words used in a contract. When asked to give meaning to the words the parties have used, courts have to start from the position that the interpretation of those words has to be established objectively, i.e. as they would be understood by the reasonable person as familiar as necessary with the business and the likely shared understandings of the parties. John Swan, *Canadian Contract Law*, 1st ed. (LexisNexis: Canada, 2006) ("**Canadian Contract Law**") at 492.

contextual scene.[8] However, where the contract is complete on its face, the language of the contract constitutes *prima facie* proof of the parties' intentions[9] and it is only in limited circumstances that the courts can seek to interpret the document using information from beyond the four corners of the contract.

Where the courts indicate that they will give effect to the intention of the parties when interpreting a contract, the intention referred to is the articulated rather than the actual intention of the parties. In other words, what is important is not one party's subjective intention, or even what he might have conveyed, or attempted to convey to a third party (i.e. a non-contracting party) about his understanding of what he was doing.[10] What is important is what was *expressed*, and what a reasonable person would have understood from what was expressed.

Consequently, the subjective intentions of the parties have no role to play in contractual interpretation. This is why questions aimed at demonstrating the parties' subjective intentions at the time of the contract (i.e. Question 1-type questions), are unhelpful and irrelevant to the legal issue at hand. It makes no difference to the outcome of the case, even if it can be established what the witness meant when he penned a letter or typed a document. It makes no difference *why* the witness inserted a particular clause into the agreement, or phrased the clause the way he did at the time of the agreement, since both these questions go to the question of what was in the parties' own minds and their uncommunicated intentions.

There is one exception where the subjective intention of the parties of the parties can override the clear meaning of the written words, which is when one party applies for rectification[11] of the

---

8 *Per* Lord Steyn in *Sirius International Insurance Co v FAI General Insurance Ltd* [2004] 1 WLR 3251.

9 *Zurich Insurance* at [40].

10 *Pacific Carriers Ltd v BNP Paribas* (2004) 218 CLR 451.

11 In *Chartbrook*, the House of Lords also clarified the scope of application and test for allowing rectification. According to the House, rectificiation is not confined to cases where there was a concluded antecedent contract with which the final contract did not conform but is also available when there was no binding

contract so that the written words will reflect the actual intention of the parties but, unless such an application is made, the remarks made above will apply.

While a civil law court or tribunal is theoretically required to interpret a contract by way of discerning the parties' common intention[12] or real intention,[13] which suggests that a subjective approach need be taken in the interpretation of a contract, courts and tribunals adopt an objective approach[14] to interpretation in practice.

---

antecedent agreement but the parties had a common continuing intention in respect of a particular matter in the instrument in respect of which rectification is sought. In both cases the question is what an objective observer would have thought the intentions of the parties to be. In order to get rectification it has to be shown that the parties were in complete agreement on the terms of their contract but by an error wrote them down wrongly. If, by looking at what the parties said or wrote to each other in coming to their agreement and then comparing it with the contract they signed, it can be predicated with certainty what their contract was, and that it is by common mistake wrongly expressed in the document, the document can be rectified, but nothing less will suffice. Rectification is rarely sought as a remedy, but such a claim would justify a more liberal approach to cross-examination of the actual intentions of the parties as manifested by what they said or wrote.

[12] This is the French position under Art 1156 of the Code Civil (French Civil Code) which says that the primary role of interpretation is to discover the *commune intention des parties* (common intention of parties). See Konrad Zweigert and Hein Kötz, *Introdution to Comparative Law,* 3rd ed. (Clarendon Press: Oxford) ("**Comparative Law**") at 402.

[13] The German position under Section 133 of the Bürgerliches Gesetzbuch (German Civil Code) is that the aim of construction is to 'discern the real intention' and the crucial thing is the actual historical will of the parties. See *Comparative Law* at 403.

[14] The French courts incline towards the subjective approach to interpretation. Nonetheless, where no common intention can be found, the judge is supposed to ascertain the 'hypothetical' intention of the parties or to adopt the interpretation which in all circumstances, objective and subjective, must be regarded as the one the parties would reasonably have intended. Further, since a judge will very rarely able to discern any actual intention common to the parties, he generally has no option but to focus on 'objective' considerations and ask how the term in question should and would normally have been understood in that particular context by a reasonable man and remains free to come to his conclusion on the basis of objective considerations and call it the *commune intention des parties contractantes* when he comes to write his judgment. See *Comparative Law* at 402. While Section 133 of

In short, they interpret a contractual term by reference to what a reasonable person would have understood it to mean in that particular context. Consequently, questioning exercises seeking to expose the unarticulated intention of witnesses are limited in value and Question 1-type questions should also be eschewed even where civil law governs the contract.

(2) The court only looks at a limited factual matrix (Question 2)

Questions on motives should be avoided. The common law position (taken in England,[15] Singapore,[16] Australia,[17] Canada[18] and the United States of America[19]) is that the background factual matrix

---

the German Civil Code explains that the aim of construction is to 'discern the real intention', thus suggesting a subjective approach must be taken, other parts of the same Code presuppose that an objective approach to interpretation be taken and there is a certain tension between the objective and subjective tests. German case law has suggested that contracts will generally be interpreted objectively although this is subject to certain important qualifications, for instance, where the true intention of both parties coincides but deviates from the objective meaning of their declaration, the literal meaning need not prevail. The classic example is the famous *Haakjöringsköd* case, in which parties intended to buy and sell whale meat, but described it as shark meat. The court took the view that the contract was for the sale of whale meat and that the delivery of shark meat was a breach of contract. See Basil Markesinis, Hannes Unberath and Angus Johnston, *The German Law of Contract*, 2nd ed. (Hart Publishing: Cornwall, 2006) at 133-135

[15] See for instance, *Investors Compensation*

[16] See for instance, *Zurich Insurance*

[17] See for instance, *Codelfa Constructions Pty Ltd v State Rail Authority of NSW* (1982) 149 CLR 337

[18] Similarly, in Canada, it is accepted that words cannot be understood apart from their context. Contractual language cannot be understood without some knowledge of their context and the purpose of the contract. Words, taken individually, have an inherent vagueness that will often require courts to determine their meaning by looking at their context and the expectations that the parties may have had. *Canadian Contract Law*, at 493.

[19] In the United States, extrinsic evidence at the time the contract is made, is also admissible. The circumstances surrounding the execution of a contract may always be shown and are always relevant to a determination of what the parties

surrounding the execution of the contract may be taken into account to aid the court in the interpretation of the written words of a document. This is because words used in a contract cannot be divorced from the circumstances prevailing at the time the contract was made, and a court seeking to ascertain the meaning of a contract must look to the factual matrix surrounding its execution.

The significant point to note is that, under the common law position, background evidence that is admissible is limited to *facts, circumstances in reality,* and *factual matrices.* The emphasis is upon *what happened,* and *what a party did or did not do*, there is no question of *why* a party did what he did. A party's motivations for doing what he did or did not do do not impact upon the interpretation of the contract (or whether he has been in breach) and should be disallowed as irrelevant (although questions of admissibility are not decided in arbitration on the basis of rules of evidence but on the Tribunal's perception of what is relevant or helpful to its decision). Cross-examination questions that concern the surrounding facts, circumstances and factual matrices, go to the background and context of the transaction, and are therefore relevant. In contrast, questions which seek to cast light on a party's private intentions and motivations, are not.

There are two exceptions to this principle:

A. the contract itself makes motive a relevant element (e.g. a clause that allows a right to terminate a contract if one party has reasonable cause to believe in a certain state of facts).

---

intended by the words they chose. In construing a contract, a court seeks to ascertain the meaning of the contract at the time and place of its execution. Thus, the circumstances surrounding the execution of the contract will always bear upon the contract's meaning. *US Contract Law,* at 435 to 436. The term "surrounding circumstances" refers to the commercial or other setting in which the contract was negotiated and other objectively determinable factors that give a context to the transaction between the parties. It would include, for example, whether one or both parties was new to the trade, whether either or both had Counsel, the nature and length of their relationship, as well as their relative age, experience, education and sophistication. *US Contract Law,* at 439.

B. the issue is assessment of damages, the principle of mitigation is important, and questions may legitimately be asked about the innocent party's attempts to mitigate his damage which will often involve questions about the reasons for the innocent party's acts or omissions in mitigation.

Consequently, these exceptions apart, Counsel in a common law international arbitration would be ill-advised to subject the Tribunal to questions about *why* Mr X did or did not do something, or questions which explore each individual party's motivations for how they negotiated, or even internal emails within each individual party (where the party is a company) which discussed the clauses of the contract, such questions being inadmissible where the applicable law of the contract is common law.

Questions on motives, however, may potentially find applicability in arbitrations governed by civil law, which places fewer restrictions on the admissibility of evidence. For instance, French law does not place *a priori* limitations on the admissibility of materials deemed relevant for that purpose: all materials likely to help shed light on the parties' actual intention in principle are admissible, including materials pertaining to such contextual factors as pre-contractual, collateral, or subsequent statements or actions by the parties, even such materials as may pertain to one party's intention undisclosed to the other.[20] However, even civil law tribunals do not in practice find questions on unarticulated motives or intentions relevant to questions of contractual intention.

---

[20] Catherine Valcke, "Contractual Interpretation at Common Law and Civil Law—An Exercise in Comparative Legal Rhetoric", 2008, in *Exploring Contract Law* (University of Toronto, Faculty of Law) ("**Catherine Valcke**") at 23 to 24.

(3) Questions of construction are a matter for the Tribunal or dictionaries. Further, pre-contractual negotiations and post-contract conduct may generally not be taken into account for contractual interpretation. (Question 3)

Aside from avoiding questions on unarticulated intention and motives, Counsel should also abstain from asking questions about the witness' interpretation of letters or contractual documents (unless the interpretation impacted on that witness' subsequent actions). This is for two reasons.

First, questions of construction, whether of domestic or foreign documents, are matters of law and not of fact and belong exclusively to the court and the opinions of experts thereon are irrelevant.[21] In short, the interpretation of contractual or commercial documents is a matter for the Tribunal to decide, and it makes no sense for Counsel cross-examine a witness on his interpretation of a particular document unless his understanding of the document (right or wrong) is helpful in explaining why he took a particular course of action (provided the reasons for his action are themselves relevant in deciding the critical issues in the case).

Second, where the Tribunal is unable to interpret certain terms in a written instrument, its first course of action would be to construe the terms by reference to dictionaries and other material[22] and a witness' interpretation will seldom be relevant. Accordingly, Question 3-type questions should be avoided.

Of course, some Counsel believe that it is good advocacy to develop a case (which is capable of argument on the documents alone) through the mouths of witnesses, particularly by forcing witnesses on the other side to agree with the interpretation canvassed by cross-examining Counsel. While it is debatable whether this

---

[21] Michael Howard & others, *Phipson on Evidence,* 16th ed. (Sweet & Maxwell: London, 2005) at 1032. See also *LHS Holdings Ltd v Laporte PLC* [2001] EWCA Civ 278 reported at [2001] 2 All ER (Comm) 563.

[22] *Investors Compensation* at 913

achieves a greater forensic effect than a well-reasoned brief, I suggest that, in commercial arbitration, cross-examination should generally be confined to matters of fact rather than matters of argument.

Questions about a witness' interpretation of letters or contractual documents can relate to the witness' knowledge of contractually related matters before as well as after the making of the contract. Another reason for discouraging 'why' questions about a witness' interpretation of letters or contractual documents is that the common law generally excludes from evidence, the pre-contractual negotiations and post-contract conduct of parties[23] (this general

---

[23] The English position is that evidence of pre-contractual negotiations is generally inadmissible in support of the construction of a contract because, in the course of negotiations, parties' positions are constantly changing, and their agreement is only recorded in their final agreement. Lord Wilberforce in *Prenn v Simmonds* [1971] 1 WLR 1381. This position was re-affirmed in *Chartbrook*, where the House of Lords was invited to reconsider the rule in *Prenn v Simmonds* but declined on the basis that to allow such evidence would create uncertainty of outcome in disputes over interpretation and add to the cost of advice, litigation or arbitration given that statements in the course of pre-contractual negotiations were subjective and could, if oral, be disputed, and it was not often easy to distinguish between statements which reflected the aspirations of a party and those which embodied a provisional consensus which might help in the interpretation of the contract eventually concluded, Under English law, the exclusion of pre-contractual negotiations is not absolute and evidence of pre-contractual negotiations is admissible to establish (a) that a fact was known to both parties; (b) where the parties have agreed on the meaning of a word or phrase in negotiations; (c) to decide (in a consumer contract) whether a term has been individually negotiated; and (d) to determine which party put forward a particular term. *Lewison* at [3.08]. Pre-contractual negotiations could also be used to support a claim for rectification or estoppel. *Chartbrook*. In respect of the subsequent conduct of parties, the general rule is that English courts do not look at subsequent conduct to interpret a written agreement. However, where the agreement is partly written and partly oral, subsequent conduct may be examined for the purpose of determining what were the full terms of the contract. Additionally, the subsequent conduct of the parties may be examined where an estoppel by convention is alleged; where it is alleged that the agreement was a sham; and probably for the purposes of determining the boundaries of an ambiguous grant of land. *Lewison* at [3.15].

In Singapore, there is no absolute or rigid prohibition against previous negotiations or subsequent conduct, although, in the normal case, such evidence is likely to be inadmissible for non-compliance with the three conditions that (a) the material must be relevant; (b) the material must have been reasonably available to all contracting parties; and (c) the material must relate to a clear and obvious context. *Zurich Insurance* at para.s [125], [127] to [129], and [132(d)]. In *Goh Guan Chong v Aspentech, Inc* [2009] SGHC 73 at [58], Ang J opined that in addition to previous negotiations and subsequent conduct, drafts of contracts which satisfy the three conditions could also be admissible. This was because there was no reason, in principle, to differentiate drafts from contractual negotiations. Ang J also commented that documentary evidence of negotiations as they appeared in drafts would tend to be more reliable than oral evidence though where the parties' respective positions changed with each draft, drafts would provide only scant assistance and ultimately, the weight (if any) to be given to drafts as extrinsic evidence would have to differ from case to case depending on the factual matrix.

In Australia, where parties have recorded the terms of their contract in a document, the parol evidence rule applies to exclude evidence of pre-contractual terms that "subtract from, add to, vary or contradict the language of a written instrument". In respect of whether the subsequent conduct of the parties is admissible, the Australian courts have not been unanimous. The objection to such evidence is that post-contractual conduct may be deliberately tailored so as to give veracity to a meaning not intended at the time of formation of the contract. Many courts have professed adherence to the rule that subsequent conduct is inadmissible, but at the same time, the dogmatic application of this view has been openly criticised by others. *Cheshire Australia,* at 416.

In the United States, the admissibility of pre-contractual negotiations between the parties is also one of difficulty. On one hand, pre-contractual negotiations are not admissible to prove that the actual intent of the parties is at variance with the words of the written instrument when those words are given their appropriate local meaning. On the other hand, pre-contractual negotiations are admissible to prove that the parties were dealing in regard to a particular matter or to secure a particular object, or under circumstances where the local usage would give a particular meaning to the language. Negotiations are also admissible to, where the local meaning is ambiguous, to show that the parties attached one appropriate meaning to their words, rather than another equally appropriate meaning. *US Contract Law,* at 836. The United States is quite likely the most liberal where admission of evidence of the parties' subsequent conduct is concerned. The American courts take the position that, given that the purpose of judicial interpretation is to ascertain the parties' intentions, the parties' own practical interpretation of the contract, i.e. how the parties actually acted, thereby giving meaning to their contract in the course of performing it, can be an important aid to the court. *US Contract Law,* at 491 to 492. The American courts therefore give great weight to the parties' practical interpretation, unless it is contrary to the plain meaning of the contract, or clearly one sided. The conduct of the parties therefore provides nearly conclusive

exclusion is of course subject to exceptions). Hence, the answers to questions asking what the witness interpreted certain pre-contractual letters which deal with the price of goods to be sold or questions

---

evidence of the parties' contractual intentions, this is particularly true when the contract is ambiguous. *US Contract Law,* at 507.

The Canadian position in respect of pre-contractual negotiations is not absolute. Evidence of what took place during the negotiations may or may not be considered by the court that is asked to interpret an agreement. If the agreement is held to be the sole and final expression of the parties' agreement, evidence of what occurred during the negotiations will be irrelevant. On the other hand, what happened during the negotiations may provide useful and important evidence of the meaning to be given to the words and expressions used by the parties and of their expectations. Evidence, for example, of what one party knew (or should have known) of what the other expected may be sufficient to deny the first party the right to enforce the contract on any terms but those accepted or proposed by the other party. *Canadian Contract Law,* at 525. However, a balance has to be found between an examination of every scrap of evidence that a party may offer to prove that the agreement does not mean what it appears to mean, and a refusal to consider anything outside the four corners of the agreement. The Canadian courts find the necessary balance by considering a number of factors: (a) is the transaction or the relation created by the agreement and the language of the agreement standard or common? (b) Is the language (or at least on a first impression) clear and are the consequences of applying the plain words reasonable? (c) Is the position of the party who is claiming that the agreement is not the final expression unreasonable and implausible? (d) To the extent that the agreement is a standard agreement governing many similar cases, is there an argument that similarly situated parties should be treated in the same way? (e) Does the relation between the parties, their relative sophistication, knowledge, access to legal advice and bargaining power, indicate that one party does not need protection from the other? To the extent that these five questions can be answered in the affirmative, the party who seeks to adduce evidence of prior negotiations or other external factors will bear a heavy burden to persuade the court that these external factors are relevant. *Canadian Contract Law,* at 526. In Canada, there is no prohibition against the use of subsequent conduct to aid in interpretation of the contract. The rule with respect to subsequent conduct is that if, after considering the agreement itself, including the particular words used in their immediate context and in the context of the agreement as a whole, there remain two reasonable alternative interpretations, then certain additional evidence (such as subsequent conduct) may be both admitted and taken to have legal relevance if that additional evidence will help to determine which of the two reasonable alternative interpretations is the correct one. *Canadian National Railways v Canadian Pacific Ltd* [1979] 1 WWR 358 at 372.

seeking to show that the witness behaved in a manner inconsistent with the words of a contract after the dates of the contract (to show that the contract does not mean what it says) may (depending on the governing law) be irrelevant (unless some argument based on estoppel is being mounted) and it would make little sense to waste the Tribunal's time on such questions. Consequently, unless a careful scrutiny of the laws of contractual interpretation has been conducted, Counsel may wish to reconsider questions seeking to uncover a witness' interpretation of pre- or post-contractual documents or even post-contractual behaviour as a tool of contractual interpretation.

As mentioned above, civil law (theoretically) places a different emphasis on the relevance of evidence of contractual intention. Consequently, while Counsel in a common law case should abstain from doing so, Counsel in a civil law case theoretically starts with the right to ask questions about the witness' interpretation of letters or contractual documents. However, because civilian lawyers in practice adhere to the objective technique of contractual interpretation, questions about the parties' actual intentions do not generally interest civilian trained arbitrators, who tend to interpret contracts based on the actual words used and their normal meaning. Unless, therefore, there is a reason to believe that both parties to a contract understood particular words in a contract differently from their plain and ordinary meaning (as in the *Haakjöringsköd* case), cross-examination of the actual intentions of the parties in agreeing to the words used in a contract are unlikely to be of great interest, even to a civilian arbitrator.

B. As a matter of practice, "forensic" questions (questions 4, 5, 6 and 7) are not helpful and merely waste time unnecessarily

"Forensic" questions are questions which do not enlighten the Tribunal but are solely designed to introduce what are largely uncontroversial matters and are therefore asked either as "throat-clearing" exercises for the cross-examiner, or because Counsel wants to use the witness to demonstrate his own folly or lack of credibility, to prejudice the Tribunal or simply for dramatic effect. These types of questions will seldom be welcome by arbitral tribunals, and should be avoided by Counsel whether at an arbitration governed by common or civil law.

The first thing that arbitration neophytes have to learn is that arbitrators (even common law arbitrators) both in Europe and Asia do not like fixing long evidential hearings to the same length as a court trial. This is particularly true if the arbitration is institutional rather than *ad hoc*, as institutional rules like SIAC (2007 version), ICC, BANI (Indonesian Arbitration Institute) and KCAB (Korea's national arbitration institution) fix fees by reference to the value of the claim rather than by the time spent. Accordingly, a Tribunal held under the auspices of these rules will often be disinclined to fix long hearings because the arbitrators are not going to be paid anything more for the longer hours that they will spend. The institutions value efficiency in disposing of a case, so arbitrators are under an incentive to complete a hearing as soon as they decently can consonant with the principle of giving each party a (reasonably) full opportunity to present its case.

Even if parties have a large number of witnesses, the Tribunal is more likely than not to adopt some form of case management system to bring both time and costs under control. The Tribunal may therefore exhort parties to get together to agree the maximum time each witness will have, subject to the final discretion of the Tribunal to extend time. The Tribunal may even adopt the "chess clock" method and confine parties to a total amount of time and then making all parties stick to it no matter what excuses may be made.

Under such circumstances, Counsel in such fixed time arbitrations will need to be frugal with use of time, and will have to be very selective about the line of cross-examination he wants to adopt. In short, he needs to get to the point very quickly and there is no room in arbitration for forensic questions.

International arbitration does not allow a time budget for questions which are purely designed to rattle a witness without advancing the knowledge of the Tribunal about the matters in issue.

With regard to questions which demonstrate what is or not in a document, Counsel should note that most tribunals respond better to a reasoned and structured argument from Counsel on undisputed facts rather than hearing them emerge in piecemeal fashion on cross-examination. Consequently, such questions serve little practical purpose and should not be asked. Instead, Counsel should concentrate on developing his points about what emerges from the documents in his Opening or Closing Submissions so that facts and documents can be blended into a proper theory of the case.

With regard to questions for dramatic effect or questions which do not add to what is in the record or knowledge of the Tribunal (as well as questions designed to make the witness concede facts in favour of the opposing party which are apparent from the record and not denied), Counsel should note that such questions are only exercises in forensic skill which do not assist the Tribunal in its decision but serve to spend (if not to waste) valuable hearing time. Further, if the witness is not co-operative in answering, a disproportionate amount of time will have been lost by such techniques which in turn will destroy the value of this weapon in Counsel's armoury, and simply frustrate the Tribunal if one party runs out of time. While some Counsel will be skilful enough to achieve their desired effect (depending on their forensic skill and the defensive ability of the witness), such questioning, is, in arbitration terms, a luxury which will generally not be tolerated and should therefore be eschewed.

Although the common law rule in litigation is that cross-examination need not be confined to evidence-in-chief of the witness but may extend to any relevant issue in the case, courts generally allow cross-examination questions which are justified as testing the credibility of the witness, even if they do not relate to any relevant issue to be decided. However, given that, in the great majority of commercial arbitrations, the credibility of a witness is not usually the key factor in determining whether or not the Tribunal accepts that witness' evidence, most arbitral tribunals are unlikely to be so generous, and would be unwilling to give a roving commission to Counsel to ask a series of questions about an unrelated matter simply to demonstrate that the witness is generally untruthful or unreliable. Questions attacking credibility should thus be avoided unless necessary to prove a critical element in the case.

Questions aimed at prejudice are closely related to questions aimed at attacking credibility and are questions which, while related to the factual narrative or background of the case, nevertheless do not bear on the legal issues of liability or quantum, but are asked solely to establish that a witness (being a party representative) has acted in a questionable manner viewed from a moral perspective, but not directly bearing on the issue of liability. Many lawyers forget that the law of contract is based on strict liability. For better or worse, the law of contract is not concerned with who is the "good guy" and who is the "bad guy", but rather who has acted in breach of the terms of the contract. Admittedly, however, the position is somewhat different in civil law where the concept of good faith is an important feature in the law of contract, but even then, good faith is not an excuse for roving attacks on a witness' character and it is only relevant under clearly defined principles where the conduct of the contracting party can be said to have breached the legal standard of good faith. In the result, aside from abstaining from questions attacking credibility save when absolutely necessary, questions which aim to prejudice should also be avoided.

C. Legal issues are matters for submission (Question 8)

Nothing pains a Tribunal more than to hear a Counsel trying to debate a point of law with a lay witness. "*Is it not clear that Clause X means…?*". Any Tribunal should (and usually will) stop Counsel with the pained admonition "*is that not a matter for Counsel's submission?*".

D. Questions which take a witness through facts and documents with a view to making the witness agree with the other party's interpretation of a document or characterization of events (rather than the actual facts themselves) are generally not worth the time (Question 9)

The questions are a variant of the Question 4 to 7 type. They are forensic to a degree but involve a high degree of argument with the witness as Counsel seeks to take an undisputed fact or document and put a spin on it which he endeavours to persuade the witness to accept. As the saying goes, "*nice work if you can do it*", but realistically, in the limited time available for cross-examination in international arbitration, such an exercise is likely to end in frustration as the Tribunal is not going to be generous in allowing Counsel extra time to persuade a witness to agree with Counsel's version of interpreting or characterizing facts or documents.

E. "YES" or "NO" questions may be unfair (Question 10)

A favourite technique of some cross-examining Counsel is to tell a witness to "please answer YES or NO". While this technique is justifiable to some extent in ensuring clarity in the position taken by witnesses, there are times when such an approach is unfair, when the question is not really capable of a "YES" or "NO" answer (the classic example taught in law school being "*and when did you stop beating your wife?*").

This warning can further be extended to include questions based on a false or unproven premise. An alert opposing party (or Tribunal) will usually spot the impropriety of such questions and make an objection. Some of such questions, however, inevitably fall through the cracks and can lead a witness to be confused and give an answer which will give cross-examining Counsel temporary satisfaction but which will eventually have to be explained or modified when the misunderstanding of the witness is revealed.

Like the server in tennis, cross-examining Counsel has an advantage in his interaction with a witness of being able to frame a question in the way he likes, but if he abuses that privilege and frames a question in an unfair way, he will lose the sympathy of the watching Tribunal without corresponding strategic gain. These warnings apply equally whether the arbitration is conducted under common or civil law.

IV. Conclusion

The importance of cross-examination in international arbitration is often over-rated. It is not a pre-requisite of natural justice[24] and can be eschewed completely or substantially if the case is primarily about interpretation of documents, or if there are no substantial disputes of fact. Common lawyers are familiar with the litigation procedure known as originating summons, where the court rules on a case without hearing oral evidence, simply on the basis of affidavit evidence alone, so it is possible to conduct an arbitration on the basis of documentary evidence alone, with no or minimal oral evidence in support.

Arbitrators have more often than not been disappointed by how little they have learnt from hearing the witnesses, as opposed to reading their witness statements and reviewing the relevant documents. Indeed, what arbitrators find lacking in international arbitration is the time spent on oral advocacy, where Counsel explain their written submissions before the Tribunal, which can then exercise a Socratic dialogue with Counsel in clarifying and testing those submissions. If more time is spent on oral submissions, that would add more value to the Tribunal's appreciation of the facts and issues and arguments than long hours with the witnesses. But if we are to have oral witness evidence in an international arbitration, then Counsel should bear the following precepts in mind: He should ascertain what the rules of contractual interpretation and liability are under the applicable law, and plan his cross-examination based on what is necessary to establish or deny contractual liability (as the case may be) under that law. And considering the time constraints in

---

[24] *The University of Ceylon v Fernando* [1960] 1 WLR 223

international arbitration, Counsel should limit cross-examination to areas which are most necessary. As a rule of thumb, he should test his proposed questions by asking himself: "*what use can I make of the answers to these questions in my Post Hearing Brief?*". If he cannot answer his own question, then he should probably omit that question. The mantra for cross-examination should be "*less is more*".

Chapter 18

ATTACKING THE CREDIBILITY OF WITNESSES AND EXPERTS

Guido Santiago Tawil*

I. Introduction

The practice of international arbitration comprises elements of both the common law and the civil law legal traditions. However, one of the aspects where approaches still differ significantly is the way in which oral examination of factual witnesses and experts is conducted. In general terms, the goal of witnesses and experts examination is to confirm or rebut each parties' allegations. In doing so, establishing or attacking their credibility and qualifications could play a significant role. The strategy for conducting such examinations in arbitral proceedings, the style, tone and pacing or the way in which the witness or expert is approached by the examiner evidence both the relevance of tactical and practical considerations and the increasing sophistication that can be observed to this respect.

This chapter will discuss different strategic aspects that are normally involved when questioning the credibility or qualifications of witnesses or experts in international arbitration.

---

* Chair Professor, University of Buenos Aires; Senior Partner, M. & M. Bomchil; Co-chair IBA's Arbitration Committee (2009-2010); Council Member, ICCA; Court Member, LCIA; Member, ICC's Latin American Arbitration Group. The author wishes to thank Federico Campolieti for his assistance in the preparation of this chapter.

II. First Step: Submission of Written Witness Statements and Expert Reports

The most developed practice in international arbitration is to submit written witness statements and expert reports, together with the main pleadings.[1]

A. Written Witness Statements

A witness' credibility will first be tested by the way that his or her written statement is presented before the tribunal. Although it is a common practice for counsel to collaborate with the witness in drafting or reviewing the written statement[2] it is crucial to understand what should be the scope and limits of such participation. Including

---

[1] The wide acceptance of this practice in international arbitration is best evidenced by the number of institutional rules which recognize it. *See*, for instance, Article 4(4) of the Rules on the Taking of Evidence in International Commercial Arbitration, adopted in 1999 and reviewed in 2010 by the International Bar Association ("IBA Rules"); article 20(3) of the London Court of International Arbitration's Rules on Arbitration adopted in 1998 ("LCIA Rules"); and article 36 of the International Centre for Settlement of Investment Disputes Arbitration Rules ("ICSID Rules"). *See also* V.V. VEEDER, *Introduction*, Dossier of the ICC Institute of World Business Law: Arbitration and Oral Evidence, 2005. *See also* MICHAEL BUHLER & CARROLL DORGAN, *Witness Testimony pursuant to the 1999 IBA Rules of Evidence in International Commercial Arbitration: Novel or tested standards?*, 17(1) Journal of International Arbitration 3, Kluwer, 2000, at 12: "The submission of witness testimony in written form is well suited to international arbitration. The use of written witness statements can enhance the efficiency and shorten the overall duration of the proceedings, thereby potentially reducing costs…".

[2] This practice has not been exempt from criticisim. As explained in paragraph 61 of the 1996 UNCITRAL Notes on Organizing Arbitral Proceedings ("the UNCITRAL Notes"), "some practitioners favour the procedure according to which the party presenting witness evidence submits a signed witness's statement containing testimony itself. It should be noted, however, that such practice, which implies interviewing the witness by the party presenting the testimony, is not known in all parts of the world and, moreover, that some practitioners disapprove of it on the ground that such contacts between the party and the witness may compromise the credibility of the testimony and are therefore improper…"..

facts or constructions not learned or developed by the witness itself could not only pose ethical or legal issues for counsel but hinder the credibility of the entire testimony from the very beginning.

Written testimonies should be short, to the point, expressed in a polished but plain language and, as mentioned before, avoid including legal argumentation or other information that would be reasonably beyond the witness personal knowledge. Ignoring this basic rule could not only affect the witness credibility before the eyes of the arbitral tribunal but also open the door to further damage in cross-examination. To the extent possible, hearsay should be avoided.

Particular care should be taken when two or more witnesses address the same topic or, what is worse, say the same things. A skillful cross-examiner can easily gain some benefit from that situation at the hearing by exploiting either contradictions or excessive similarities among the testimonies.

B. Expert Reports

Use of party-appointed experts is a common and widely spread practice in international arbitration. While experts are usually required to provide a written report summarizing their opinions, conclusions, and bases of rationale, prior to the hearing,[3] there is an increasing demand to request the parties to identify any party appointed experts that they intend to use and the subject matter of such testimonies at earlier stages of the proceedings.[4]

---

[3] This is recognized in several institutional rules on arbitration. See, for instance, Article 5(1) of the IBA Rules, Article 20(3) of the International Chamber of Commerce's Rules of Arbitration, adopted in 1998 ("ICC Rules"), Article 20(2) of the LCIA Rules, and Article 36 of the ICSID Rules. Paragraph 73 of the UNCITRAL Notes highlights that "if a party presents an expert opinion, the arbitral tribunal might consider requiring, for example, that the opinion be in writing, that the expert should be available to answer questions at hearings, and that, if a party will present an expert witness at a hearing, advance notice must be given or that the written opinion must be presented in advance, as in the case of other witnesses".

[4] The new text of Article 5 (1) of the IBA Rules,states that " A Party may rely on a Party-Appointed Expert as a means of evidence on specific issues. Within the

Although counsel generally plays a less active role in the drafting or preparation of expert reports, there are still certain pitfalls which could eventually undermine the expert's credibility. Particular care should be given by experts when submitting their opinions and by counsel when drafting the letters of instruction. An expert report could be easily undermined if it becomes clear from the instructions received or the statement itself that he or she have only been provided with limited documentation or a partial and inaccurate construction of the facts.

Inexperienced counsel may be tempted to push the limits of what the expert is prepared to say or encourage such expert to defend untenable positions in his or her report. To the extent that the expert is prepared to support such positions, it can be easily and effectively hurt by a skilled cross-examiner or rebutted by an opposing expert.

While most expert reports generally include a disclosure of the scope and terms of the instruction received, a statement of the facts on which the expert is basing his or her opinion and conclusions and a list of the documents reviewed, newer rules are reinforcing the need of a broader disclosure in such aspects as relationships and authorship of the reports.[5] At the same time that they evidence the

---

time ordered by the Arbitral Tribunal, *(i)* each Party shall identify any Party-Appointed Expert on whose testimony it intends to rely and the subject-matter of such testimony; and *(ii)* the Party-Appointed Expert shall submit an Expert Report".

[5] The new text of Article 5 (2) of the IBA Rules states that "The Expert Report shall contain:

(a) the full name and address of the Party-Appointed Expert, a statement regarding his or her present and past relationship (if any) with any of the Parties, their legal advisors and the Arbitral Tribunal, and a description of his or her background, qualifications, training and experience;
(b) a description of the instructions pursuant to which he or she is providing his or her opinions and conclusions;
(c) a statement of his or her independence from the Parties, their legal advisors and the Arbitral Tribunal;
(d) a statement of the facts on which he or she is basing his or her expert opinions and conclusions;
(e) his or her expert opinions and conclusions, including a description

continuing efforts for broader transparency in international arbitration, such requirements open new fronts that should be duly covered by both parties counsel when planning the expert examination.

III. Second Step: The preparation for Cross-Examination

Prepping[6] of witnesses and experts prior to their oral testimony at the hearing is a practice generally accepted in international arbitration.[7] Witness prepping may consist in reviewing pertinent documents with a witness, discussing the applicable law, explaining the general format of the proceedings, encouraging the witness to tell

---

of the methods, evidence and information used in arriving at the conclusions. Documents on which the Party-Appointed Expert relies that have not already been submitted shall be provided;

(f) if the Expert Report has been translated, a statement as to the language in which it was originally prepared, and the language in which the Party-Appointed Expert anticipates giving testimony at the Evidentiary Hearing;

(g) an affirmation of his or her genuine belief in the opinions expressed in the Expert Report;

(h) the signature of the Party-Appointed Expert and its date and place; and

(i) if the Expert Report has been signed by more than one person, an attribution of the entirety or specific parts of the Expert Report to each author.[...]".

[6] In the context of this chapter, "witness prepping" is considered different from "witness coaching." While the former involves familiarizing a witness with the facts of a case or with the formalities of courtroom procedures, the latter often raises ethical concerns because it may involve an examiner improperly influencing the testimony of a witness.

[7] Article 4(3) of the IBA Rules, and Article 20(6) of the LCIA Rules expressly providing for witness preparation and interviewing. *See* ROBERT S. RIFKIND, *Practices of the Horseshed: The Preparation of Witnesses by Counsel in America*, Dossier of the ICC Institute of World Business Law: Arbitration and Oral Evidence, 2005, at 55. *See also* FOUCHARD, GAILLARD, GOLMAN, *On International Commercial Arbitration*, Kluwer, p. 702, at 1287; *See also* PETER R. GRIFFIN, *Recent Trends in the Conduct of International Arbitration: Discovery Procedures and Witness Hearings*, 17:2 Journal of International Arbitration, 19, 2000.

the truth, and conducting a mock direct or cross-examination. Mock examination of witnesses and experts is in many cases a crucial part of hearing preparation. Checking how a particular witness or expert will react when faced with tough questioning or sensitive issues being raised in public is always a learning experience both for witnesses and counsel.[8]

The witness reaction to sensitive questions such as those related to personal motivations, ethical or monetary issues, or any other topic which could test the witness's credibility could evidence aspects of his or her personality that should be known to counsel in advance. If the witness does not cope well under pressure during mock examination, counsel should decide whether further prepping would solve this problem or whether that witness should be called by the proffering party to the hearing. Even in cases when witnesses are called by the opposing party for cross-examination, witness absence is not entirely unusual, even if that means that such testimony will be struck out.[9]

In any case, it should always be clear that reactions to real examination usually differ to those observe in mock examination and that rehearsing in excess a witness examination could produce as bad results as the lack of preparation.

---

[8] Mocks have become so common that, in some larges cases, companies have even gone through the whole mock litigation of a case (therefore hiring mock counsel for both sides and a mock tribunal) just in order to test the strength and weakness of a particular case before submitting it to arbitration.

[9] The general practice to this respect is reflected in new Article 4 (7) of the IBA Rules ("If a witness whose appearance has been requested pursuant to Article 8.1 fails without a valid reason to appear for testimony at an Evidentiary Hearing, the Arbitral Tribunal shall disregard any Witness Statement related to that Evidentiary Hearing by that witness unless, in exceptional circumstances, the Arbitral Tribunal decides otherwise").

IV. How to Attack the Credibility of Witnesses and Experts Through Cross-Examination

A. Questioning an Adverse Witness's Credibility

Preserving witness credibility is usually a crucial element to win a case. Therefore, knowing how to effectively question witness credibility, forcing a tribunal to doubt how much weight, if any, it should give to a testimony is a powerful tool in counsel's arsenal. However, the first and most important decision that counsel should take is whether cross-examination is necessary or convenient in the particular case.[10] Cross-examinations may be risky. A witness may reveal or highlight facts or evidence that the attorney was not anticipating. In trying to weaken its opponent's case through the witness' testimony, the attorney may in fact be doing the opposite.

Further, if counsel realizes that bringing an opposing witness to the stand can potentially hurt more than help his case, it could decide not to call that witness to the hearing or, if called by the proffering party, seek –if any- a very limited cross-examination. In many cases it helps more a party's case that strong witnesses from the opposing party pass unnoticed during the hearing.

Thus, when preparing for a cross-examination, a practitioner should keep in mind that in some circumstances, no cross-examination at all or a very limited one might in fact be the most effective strategy. A cross-examination conducted for the mere sake of procedural formality or that reveals immaterial, irrelevant or directed only to confirm already established facts will provide no assistance in order to decide the case and bears the risk of unnecessarily upsetting the arbitral tribunal.

If the practitioner decides that it is worthwhile to call the witness for cross-examination, he must have in mind whether he intends to use the witness to promote his case, undermine the one of his

---

[10] GREGORY A. HEARING & BRIAN C. USSERY, *Guidelines for an effective cross-examination: The science behind the art*, available at: http://www.bna.com/bnabooks/annual

opponent, or a combination of both. He should ask himself, 'How can I best use this witness to benefit my case?', 'Can this witness corroborate any facts to support my case or to advance my theories?' Then, he should consider how he may best question the witness.

One of the most effective ways of conducting a cross-examination is to prepare in advance not a number of independent and unrelated questions but different alternative lines of subsequent questions closely related between them. During preparation, the cross-examiner should foresee potential answers and be prepared to switch to a different line of subsequent questions depending on the answers effectively provided by the witness during oral testimony. In doing so, experienced examiners normally conduct witnesses through simple and apparently innocent questions that encourage them to admit facts that cannot be later denied when, as a result of the subsequent questions, the witness finally discovers where is the examiner leading to.

To achieve such result, examiners will normally tend to privilege close-ended questions, requiring either "yes" or "no" answers from a witness, instead of open-ended questions,[11] which could afford the witness both the opportunity to escape from the planned examination road as well as further develop or amend errors in which he or she could have incurred.

A strategy that is also often useful when commencing interrogation is to use that witness to corroborate relevant facts of the examining party's case. It is normally easier to obtain favorable information from a witness at the outset of the cross-examination as the witness will be naturally less hostile at this point towards counsel and more open in his responses.

In order to prepare an effective strategy, a skillful cross-examiner must not only know in detail what the witness has said in his written and oral testimonies, but also who the witness is; his profile, his personal interests, his experience in testifying, etc. Learning as much as possible about his life and experiences, reading his publications or

---

[11] R. DOAK BISHOP & ADAM P. SCHIFFER, *Effective Advocacy in International Arbitration*, The Metropolitan Corporate Counsel, 2005, at 25.

researching in his web sites constitute essential stages of the preparation needed prior to the examination. The more the examiner knows about the witness, the best are the chances to perform a good cross-examination.

Some of the most frequent tactics followed in order to challenge a witness's credibility through cross-examination are to: (i) highlight inconsistencies, errors or areas of confusion in the witness' testimony; (ii) establish the witness's bias or prejudice, either in favor of the proffering party or against the examining party; or (ii) establish the witness's pecuniary interest in the dispute.[12] The first one is clearly the most effective one for discrediting a witness. Indeed, while evidence of bias or financial interest could generally be a useful way of discrediting a witness, it will be limited in their application to the particular facts of a case. The examiner should not question a witness about his alleged bias if nothing in the facts or evidence support such a claim. In contrast, focusing on inconsistencies or areas of confusion in the witness' testimony will always be an effective means of deemphasizing the reliability of the witness in the eyes of the arbitral tribunal.

An experienced examiner will try to identify and construct contradictions between the witness' written statement, other evidence produced, and his testimony during the oral phase of the proceedings in order to undermine his credibility. He should concentrate on those areas where there appear to be discrepancies in the facts.[13] Although each of these inconsistencies may not appear to have, on their own, the power to crush an opponent's case, when taken in their entirety, they can raise questions concerning the accuracy of the witness's memory or the credibility of his testimony.

---

12 MARK A. CYMROT, *Cross-Examination in International Arbitration*, 62 Dispute Resolution Journal, 52, 2007, at 55.

13 For example, if a witness claims that he clearly remembers seeing a document a certain number of years before but cannot remember the context in which he saw it (where, with whom, etc.); if a witness says that he remembers writing a specific letter but is unable to recall on his motivations to do so, etc.

In certain circumstances, witnesses could destroy their own credibility through evasive answers or a visible lack of collaboration.[14] If a witness does not respond directly to precise questions put forward by the examiner, sometimes it could be enough for the examiner to evidence such evasive attitude through some simple and obvious questions directed to make sure that the arbitral tribunal notices it with no need to pursue further questioning. In some cases, examiners appear more concerned in thinking about the next question or line of questions to pose to the witness while he is testifying rather than in hearing what the witness effectively says. A good examiner should be extremely alert and prepared to do both things at the same time. Witness may make, especially during long cross-examinations, surprising statements[15] that can be very effectively used by a diligent counsel.

No matter how the examiner intends to question the witness's credibility, one thing is certain: the examiner who has a strong command of the facts and issues of a case will have greater chances of success on a cross-examination than the one who mainly relies on his dramatic skills to intimidate a witness or impress the tribunal. Indeed, although examiners should always maintain their composure during a cross-examination before an arbitral tribunal, this should be particularly remembered when appearing before tribunals consisting of arbitrators from different legal backgrounds as some of their members may react differently to some verbal or physical tactics used by the examiner during his questioning.[16]

---

[14] GREGORY A. HEARING & BRIAN C. USSERY, *Guidelines for an effective cross-examination: The science behind the art*, available at: http://www.bna.com/bnabooks/annual

[15] R. DOAK BISHOP & ADAM P. SCHIFFER, *Effective advocacy in International Arbitration*, The Metropolitan Corporate Counsel, 2005, at 25

[16] While some tribunals might allow an examiner to assume a more dramatic stance or aggressive tone with an evasive or non-responsive witness, other tribunals might caution counsel against doing so. Moreover, while some arbitrators might permit an examiner to control a witness through short, direct questions requiring short, direct answers, others might interject on the grounds that the examiner is not allowing the witness to speak or explain his positions.

B. Attacking an Expert Witness's Credibility and Qualifications

Francis Wellman stated in 1903 that: "it is unwise for the cross-examiner to attempt to cope with the specialist in his own field of inquiry."[17] Although experience shows some remarkable exceptions and results, that still seems to be the wiser approach to expert witness cross-examination. If an expert has some sort of advantage, it is naturally in his field of knowledge.[18] Attempting to prevail on a discussion with a skilled expert witness in matters covered by his expertise will usually end in reinforcing his authority and credibility. Technical discussions should in general be left to party appointed experts and, in most cases, it should be through their testimony that a party should prevail in those issues.

Thus, in preparing for cross-examination of an expert witness, counsel should consider the following options:

First, the examiner must identify from the outset potential weaknesses to be highlighted during the interrogatory. One obvious place to begin with is checking whether the expert is legitimately qualified in his claimed field of expertise. Although it is unlikely that this tactic will often be applicable since most experts will be accepted as qualified before the tribunal, counsel should always keep in mind the steps that experts must take to become certified in their respective field. For instance, if the expert has no practical experience but merely academic knowledge of the field of practice that he is testifying in, the examiner should consider bringing this information out on cross-examination.

---

[17] DAVID B. BAUM, *Taking on the Opposing Expert: An Approach to Cross-Examination*, 780 Practical Law Institute, New York, 2008, at 905, citing FRANCIS WELLMAN, The Art of Cross-Examination, 1903, at 82.

[18] Attacking party-appointed experts' credibility based in their written opinions will generally become a harder task than doing so with factual witnesses. Counsel is usually not familiar with expert's technicalities, opinions, conclusions, and bases of rationale. Therefore, it is not generally advisable to enter into a discussion with the expert about the core of his opinion, unless counsel is certain that there is no risk or very limited risk to do that at all.

Second, if facts or evidence do not suggest that the expert is unqualified in his field, the practitioner should consider examining whether the expert's qualifications actually apply to the specific dispute at issue.[19] One way to achieve this is to show that the expert's qualifications do not relate to the opinion that he is offering before the arbitral tribunal. Suppose the expert is a civil engineer. While civil engineers may be able to offer general opinions concerning the design, construction or maintenance of building structures, they may not necessarily have expertise in designing offshore structures, like oil platforms. In such a scenario, the examiner shall draft a set of questions directed to show that the expert's qualifications do not advance the opponent's case.

A third effective means to challenge an expert witness testimony is to question the bases or rationale for his opinion. An examiner may do this by showing that the expert relied on factors that others in his field would not typically have relied on in formulating an opinion. A slight variation on this tactic consists in establishing that the expert does not have personal or accurate knowledge of the facts on which he is relying or have been misled in the facts placed before him and, therefore, his conclusions are based on unreliable evidence.

For instance, if all the information on which the expert bases his opinion was provided by the opponent's party and no independent examination was carried out, it could be effective to pose to him questions like 'Do you consider that facts are important in this case?' 'Were the facts of the case exclusively provided by the opposing party?' 'On what basis do you believe the facts you have relied upon to be true?' 'If the facts were different than those which you had been provided, would that affect your opinion?'.

Fourth, a skilled examiner should research how many times has an expert testified in favor of the opponent's position. If so, the examiner may be able to successfully establish a clear bias underlying the expert's proffered opinion, ultimately eroding his independence.

---

[19] *See* RICHARD H. KREINDLER, *Benefitting from Oral Testimony of Expert Witnesses: Traditional and Emerging Techniques*, Transnational Dispute Management (TDM), Volume 4, Issue 3, 2007.

Fifth, as it happens with factual witness, researching the expert's profile, career, experience, publications or web pages is a crucial aspect of hearing preparation. Interesting information could appear through such research in order to contradict his statements in the case. For example, the expert may have published a paper where he expressed his views on a similar topic to the one addressed in his testimony, supporting the same or similar general principle or rule yet now constructs an exception or alternative never discussed in his publication. Bringing up such inconsistencies before the arbitral tribunal could certainly help in challenging the expert's credibility.

Additional strategies that an examiner should consider when confronting an expert witness include some of those previously discussed for factual witnesses. Highlighting inconsistencies, gaps or facts omitted in an expert's report is usually a very effective tactic.[20] Hammering on them or in other elements that could pose doubts in the expert's analysis, research, or memory could affect the credibility of the expert's testimony, regardless of his qualifications.

V. Final Remarks

The experienced counsel knows that while cases will generally not be won in an examination they can certainly be lost there. Devoting enough time and resources in order to attain due preparation for a hearing is always a basic recommendation in this regard. In weighing of evidence in international arbitrations, no credit will usually be given to testimonies coming from witnesses or experts who appear as unreliable to the arbitral tribunal, irrespective of how reasonable or logical their opinions could seem. Although awareness of the topics and tactics described hereinbefore should benefit examiners when cross-examining a factual witness or expert, some strategies will show more effective than others depending on the case, witness or expert confronted to.

---

[20] DAVID B. BAUM, *Taking on the Opposing Expert: An Approach to Cross-Examination*, 780 Practical Law Institute, New York, 2008, at 907.

No single tactic has proved to be effective in every case. Strategies for cross-examination should be considered on a case by case basis.[21] A diligent counsel should rely on more than one approach in order to question the credibility of witnesses and experts, and be prepared to change his strategy even in the middle of the cross if the situation requires him to do so.[22] One of the worst mistakes that counsel can make is pursuing the same line of questioning before a witness or expert that instead of being discredited by it keeps building the opposing case. In those situations, pride should be forgotten and the examination should quickly change its course or even end in order to avoid further damage.

---

[21] The following war story is a good example of how an expert can be easily disqualified. During the hearing on the merits, an expert –whose report had been submitted with the reply memorial– was first questioned about his independence, which he strongly reaffirmed. Then, he was asked if his testimony was prepared by himself or was made together with the other party's counsel. He totally denied that suggestion, and affirmed that he had prepared his report alone without even reading the parties pleadings. Immediately after that answer, the examiner asked him why there were more than thirty paragraphs in his report that were copied verbatim from the previous claim memorial of the party that had appointed him. The examiner evidenced this incredible "coincidence" through a power-point presentation and immediately ended the examination without entering into technical discussions. The credibility of the expert was completely destroyed. The counter-party did not perform any re-direct examination and that expert report was not even mentioned in the final award.

[22] If the examiner notes from the witness' responses that the line of questioning may prove more problematic than beneficial, he should gracefully retreat towards another line of questioning. *See* R. DOAK BISHOP & ADAM P. SCHIFFER, *Effective advocacy in International Arbitration*, The Metropolitan Corporate Counsel, 2005, at 25

Chapter 19

CLOSING ARGUMENTS

Audley Sheppard

I. Introduction

What advocate does not imagine himself or herself presenting a closing speech as articulate and as persuasive as that of Portia in the Merchant of Venice. Or that of Atticus Finch in To Kill a Mocking Bird:

> "To begin with, this case should never have come to trial. The state has not produced one iota of medical evidence that the crime Tom Robinson is charged with ever took place... It has relied instead upon the testimony of two witnesses, whose evidence has not only been called into serious question on cross-examination, but has been flatly contradicted by the defendant. Now, there is circumstantial evidence to indicate that Mayella Ewel was beaten - savagely, by someone who led exclusively with his left. And Tom Robinson now sits before you having taken the oath with the only good hand he possesses... his RIGHT."

Unfortunately, the practice of international arbitration is generally much more prosaic and there is limited opportunity for such drama. Nevertheless, oral and written closing arguments are a common feature of international arbitration, although some arbitrators and counsel consider that they are unnecessary or at least overrated. Some arbitrators and counsel would replace closing arguments with a question and answer exercise (oral or written). Some arbitrators (but probably few counsel) would happily close proceedings with the last answer from the last witness or expert at the hearing. This short chapter considers the advantages and disadvantages of these various approaches and the styles of advocacy that may be adopted for each.

II. Questions and Answers

It is increasingly common for experienced tribunals to put questions to the parties at the end of the hearing and for counsel to answer them orally and/or in writing. This approach has advantages for both tribunal and parties, because it enables the tribunal to get specific answers to the questions that concern them and enables counsel to seek to explain clearly their position on some of the matters that the tribunal considers important and/or unclear. I generally invite the tribunal at the very start of the hearing to consider putting questions to the parties at the end of the hearing and to schedule that into the timetable, so that the tribunal can be thinking of questions they might want to ask as the trial proceeds. I prefer for the tribunal to provide its questions on the penultimate day so that it provides at least one evening (or the whole night!) to prepare considered answers.

If there is to be written closing argument, the tribunal may dispense with oral answers and suggest written answers to its specific questions, or it may invite the parties to answer orally but allow longer written answers as well. As counsel, one tries to infer from the questions in which direction the tribunal is heading: for or against your case. This can be an encouraging or dispiriting exercise. However, an experienced tribunal should ask the questions neutrally. And should, in my opinion, ask a series of questions, some of which might appear to indicate a leaning towards the claimant's arguments and some of which might appear to indicate a leaning towards the respondent's arguments.

III. Whether to Have Closing Arguments

One popular guide to advocacy in England goes as far as to state: "The closing speech is the reason the advocate exists. It is their weapon, their art, the moment for persuasion. Some say the advocate' greatest weapon is cross-examination. Not so. A good speech can recover bad cross-examination. But a bad speech can lose an otherwise winnable case, even after a good cross-examination, especially if your opponent makes a good closing speech." (The Devils' Advocate, A short polemic on how to be seriously good in court, by Iain Morley).

Even if arbitration counsel do not believe that closing speeches are the reason they exist, most counsel want to have the opportunity to remind the tribunal of the more salient and persuasive elements of their case and in particular to explain that their case has only become stronger as a result of listening to the fact and expert witnesses at the trial. On the other hand, many arbitrators consider that they already understand each side's case and do not want it repeated yet again and that they have remained alert during the trial and are satisfied with the view that they have formed on where each side's case has been strengthened and weakened as a result of examination and cross-examination. Most arbitrators will not deprive counsel of presenting a closing argument, if they insist, but seek to limit the time for an oral closing or put a page limit on written closings.

IV. Oral or Written Closings

Experienced advocates, especially in England, tend to prefer oral closings. They prefer to summarise the evidence and arguments whilst it is fresh in their and the tribunal's minds. Oral closings also allow the advocate to stop thinking about that case and move on to the next.

In addition, oral closings may be preferred because the arbitrators intend to start their deliberations immediately after the close of the hearing and are likely to form a view on most of the issues, which it may be difficult to shift if only a written closing is served some weeks later. For this reason, counsel are willing to compromise the advantages of having more time to prepare the closing argument in favour of making an oral argument while the tribunal is still impressionable.

Some counsel and arbitrators prefer written closings, because by allowing the parties more time it is more likely to ensure that the tribunal receives the arguments clearly presented and complete. That may also give comfort to the tribunal that they have been presented with the arguments that are most important to the parties and so long as they address all those issues in their award, they cannot be criticised for not dealing with an important point and risk having the award challenged by the losing party on that ground.

Written closings should be presented reasonably soon after the end of the hearing. Depending on the complexity of the case, two or three weeks is common. Arbitrators should not necessarily reject a request for a longer period, especially if it comes from both parties, because it might be a window for the parties to settle the case, after having ad their "day in court".

Most advocates want to have the last word and do not like leaving an argument unanswered. Counsel often ask for a second round of written closings, but a second round rarely clarifies matters for the tribunal and is to be resisted.

V. Purpose and Content of Closing Argument

It is often said that the closing argument should be the first thing that an advocate writes, before the Request for Arbitration and any other submission. This may be unrealistic or at least rarely applied in practice, but it reflects a worthy objective: consistency and coherence. You should have already explained your case theory, in your written submissions and/or written or oral opening. The closing argument is the opportunity to add reference to the oral evidence that supports your case. The related purpose is to deal with any evidence that might appear to undermine your case theory. It is best not to ignore the inconvenient, but to deal with it head on. Some counsel like to describe the general veracity or persuasiveness of each fact and expert witness. This can appear very partial. It is better to focus on the content of the evidence itself and whether it is plausible or consistent with the contemporaneous documents.Interposing counsel's personal opinion may serve to irritate the tribunal and distract from the argument.

The closing argument is also likely to include a section applying the law to the facts.

The purpose of closing argument, whether oral or written, is of course to persuade the tribunal to decide in your favour and therefore should reach a crescendo that leaves no doubt in the tribunal's mind that you have the better argument. It can be a useful approach in many cases to present a closing argument as if you were writing the award. This comes more easily once you have sat as an arbitrator. But the objective is for the tribunal to cut and paste your written closing into their draft award (sometimes literally, so always provide an electronic soft copy). This may mean that the closing argument has to be presented in a more reasonable and conciliatory style, and this is more likely to find favour with the tribunal in any event. It may also be necessary to discard some arguments. It may be difficult to persuade the client to drop arguments that the client believes in, or has spent a lot of money in pursuing, but reducing the closing argument to one's best arguments is likely to more persuasive. If the tribunal has not asked for it (and they should), it is useful to reiterate the relief that is being sought. Some relief may have become redundant or inappropriate, so it helps the tribunal for it to know what each party is still asking for.

VI. New Evidence or Authorities

A thorny issue for counsel is whether new evidence or authorities can be presented in post-hearing written closing arguments. Some tribunals make a ruling that no new evidence may be introduced. However, if the new evidence is compelling, counsel has no option but to try to introduce it. This is best done before the closing argument is served, so that if it is accepted then both parties can address it. Likewise, tribunals are likely to take a very dim view of the introduction of new authorities, unless it the decision has only been issued or made public after the last hearing and it is clearly relevant. Again, it would be prudent to inform the tribunal and other side before serving the closing argument so the other side can also address it.

If new evidence or authorities come to light after closing argument and before the award, the tribunal have a hostile reaction to its introduction, but if it is clearly relevant, then counsel has a duty to his or her client to inform the tribunal and indeed a duty to the tribunal itself to inform it of any new decision that could materially affect the result.

VII. Conclusion

I hope that, like a good closing argument, this guidance note is relevant, focussed, informative and persuasive. But if ever in doubt, apply The Bellman's Rule of Three and repeat your argument three times, which will make it true and undoubtedly persuade any tribunal!

"Just the place for a Snark! I have said it twice:
That alone should encourage the crew.
Just the place for a Snark! I have said it thrice:
What I tell you three times is true."

The Hunting of the Snark (An Agony in 8 Fits), Lewis Carroll

Part VI.

REGIONAL DIFFERENCES IN INTERNATIONAL ARBITRATION

Chapter 20

THE BRITISH PERSPECTIVE AND PRACTICE OF ADVOCACY

Peter Leaver and Henry Forbes Smith

I. Introduction

This chapter outlines best practices in the advocacy and resolution in England of international commercial disputes. It compares English litigation and arbitration, and highlights features which may make England distinctive from other jurisdictions.

The art of advocacy is the art of persuading another person to decide or act in accordance with one's wishes. In international commercial dispute resolution in England, the art of advocacy is influenced by two central features.

The first feature is the object of persuasion. Whether in litigation or arbitration, this will usually be a court or tribunal comprising one or more middle-aged lawyers who will know little or nothing of the facts, may know little or nothing of the law relevant to the issues they have to decide, and may have no assistance other than the advocates appearing before them. The court or tribunal is likely to be motivated, above all, to decide the case in a manner: (1) which accords with legal principle and due process; (2) which it personally believes is just, fair and reasonable; and (3) which it hopes will be respected by the parties, appellate courts, and enforcing courts.

The second feature is the inherent complexity of the exercise. The parties will disagree about what happened, why it happened, and what is the right outcome. The facts may be extensive, and expert assistance may be required. The law is simple in essence, but complicated in detail. While all of this is true of wholly domestic disputes, disputes involving parties or facts from more than one country present special difficulties. Facts which arise abroad may be more difficult to understand and to prove than facts which arise in a purely domestic context. International cases tend to be larger than purely domestic cases. Law tends to become more difficult when different countries are involved. Problems of choice of law arise. Foreign or international law may be more difficult to identify and apply than local law. Enforcement may be required abroad.

Although always dependent upon the circumstances, effective advocacy in England lies generally in providing the court or tribunal with a clear, simple, and reliable path to a solution which is right (and is sought by one's client). Everything should be made as simple as can be. The court or tribunal should be told what happened, what it must decide, what the relevant legal principles are, and how they apply. A path through the complexity should be provided. The path should be consistent with the contemporaneous documents: oral evidence is less likely to be believed if it is inconsistent with the documentary record. Problems should be addressed; inconsistencies should be explained; irrelevant matters should be ignored. What is said should instil in the court or tribunal the confidence to decide that the proposed solution is, indeed, the right solution.

Effective advocacy is not limited to the final hearing, but is required from the outset of the dispute. The parties' legal teams must understand the facts and evidence, and must decide their strategy and case which they must advance and adjust as events unfold. Every contact with, or document prepared for, the court or tribunal is important, from the first statements of case, through procedural hearings, disclosure, evidence, submissions and trial. Every statement made or document put forward involves advocacy: it should all, in its own way, be calculated to instil confidence in the solution that is proposed.

Although litigation or arbitration may be accompanied by negotiation with the other side, it is not itself negotiation. One does not negotiate with a court or tribunal: one tries to persuade it. This requires honesty and candour. This does not preclude novel legal arguments or fall-back positions, but it does mean that, in general, it is unlikely to be advantageous to take factual or legal positions which are clearly wrong. The adverse consequences of taking bad points may go well beyond the loss of the point itself. It gives the other party something to attack; wastes the time of the court or tribunal; distracts from one's other positions; and most problematic of all, reduces the credibility of the person taking the bad point, be that the party, its advocate or its factual or expert witness. The saying goes, "when in a hole, stop digging"; better still, do not get in the hole at all. Once taken, positions can be difficult or impossible to retract. Clients accustomed to commercial negotiation sometimes require time to understand this.

Effective advocacy, and effective dispute resolution, is the same whether the international commercial dispute is being resolved in the English High Court or in international arbitration. It is therefore unsurprising that recent years have brought convergence in best practices in the resolution of international commercial disputes in litigation and arbitration in England.

By a series of reforms over the past thirty years, the English High Court has abandoned what was once a primarily oral procedure. The High Court now pursues a mixed written and oral procedure which seeks to be responsive to the size and nature of the case (and, within limits, the wishes of the parties); which involves written evidence and submissions; and in which the function of oral hearings, culminating in the final trial, is to enable the court to hear oral argument and to test the written evidence by cross-examination.

International commercial arbitration now follows much the same approach. A written procedure is supplemented (even in continental Europe) by an oral hearing in which written evidence and submissions are tested by cross-examination and oral argument.

Increasingly, therefore, the choice between litigation and arbitration in England is finely balanced. This convergence is something to be welcomed, whether one calls it the 'judicialisation of arbitration' or the 'arbitralisation of litigation'. Litigators and arbitrators have much to learn from each other, as they strive to provide the commercial community with first class dispute resolution. For their part, those responsible for forum selection agreements should ensure that such agreements record, as precisely as possible, the kind of dispute resolution that the commercial parties they represent want.

II. English lawyers, courts and arbitrators

A. English lawyers

For historical reasons, English lawyers are divided into barristers and solicitors. Until recently only barristers could appear as advocates in the English High Court. However, clients could not instruct barristers directly. Only solicitors could instruct barristers. Barristers could not practise in partnership, and therefore formed 'chambers' with other barristers with whom they shared costs but not profits. Solicitors formed law firms with other solicitors with whom they shared profits.

The result was a split profession. Large commercial litigation in England has traditionally been conducted by a unified team combining barristers and solicitors. Although regulatory-driven, this arrangement was largely non-prejudicial to clients. All members of the team contributed, and the teams became well used to working together efficiently and effectively.

The difference in arbitration was that there were never any restrictions upon who could appear as counsel. (However, clients still could not instruct barristers directly.) Accordingly, many solicitors and foreign lawyers have long conducted arbitrations in England to great effect without using barristers. Others have long used barristers for arbitrations, or have alternated on a case by case basis. Many English commercial barristers and solicitors, therefore, have extensive experience in arbitration.

We are now in a period of regulatory change. Since 1990, solicitors have been able to qualify to appear as advocates in English litigation. Foreign or in-house lawyers may now instruct barristers directly, whether for litigation or arbitration. Accordingly, those responsible for the conduct of dispute resolution in England now have wide choice. They can use just solicitors, or just barristers, or both, or neither.

B. English judges

Commercial litigation worth more than £50,000 is generally heard in the High Court, which is based in London at the Royal Courts of Justice on the Strand. It is heard by a single High Court judge without a jury.[1]

There are about 100 High Court judges. They are assigned to specialised divisions, one of which is the Commercial Court. The Commercial Court comprises about 20 judges, who resolve cases without wigs, gowns, or excessive formality. The great majority of cases in the Commercial Court are international commercial disputes: only a small proportion involves domestic commercial disputes. The Commercial Court judges, therefore, have very extensive experience in the resolution of international commercial disputes. They are well versed in dealing with jurisdiction, choice of law, foreign facts, foreign witnesses, foreign languages, and foreign law.

High Court judges are generally appointed at about the age of 40 to 55. The appointment is professional rather than political, and is generally made from the ranks of successful barristers. Most Commercial Court judges are successful former commercial barristers. A few High Court Judges are successful former academics or solicitors.[2]

International commercial litigation in England is, therefore, usually resolved by an experienced and successful lawyer who has

---

1 This has been a gradual development in tandem with the gradual abandonment of the jury trial. Until 1846, all civil cases in England were heard by a jury. Between 1846 and 1980, jury trials steadily declined. Since 1981, the rule has been that a party may apply for a jury trial where the claim concerns fraud, libel, slander, malicious prosecution or false imprisonment, save where the trial requires a prolonged examination of documents or accounts or any scientific or local investigation which cannot conveniently be made with a jury (section 69 of the Supreme Court Act 1981). The effective result is that many large commercial disputes cannot be resolved by a jury even if fraud is alleged.

2 Lord Collins, a member of the Supreme Court (the highest English court), was formerly a successful commercial solicitor, and was (and remains) the author of Dicey, Morris & Collins on the Conflict of Laws, the leading English book on the subject.

spent 20 years or more practising as a commercial barrister, and thus has very extensive experience in resolving international commercial disputes. Most High Court judges are English, but some very successful English judges have come from other commonwealth countries.[3]

C. The composition of an English arbitral tribunal

The parties have first choice how the tribunal is to be constituted, who it is to comprise, and how it is to reach its decision. In so far as the parties do not agree, the *lex arbitri* will supply default rules. A typical result is that each party may select one arbitrator, and that the party-nominated arbitrators, or a third party, may select a third arbitrator who will preside or chair, will not share the nationality of any party,[4] and will have the deciding vote if the party-appointed arbitrators disagree.[5]

Parties often select as arbitrator a professional, neutral lawyer who is experienced in the resolution of international commercial disputes, and whose general approach they feel may suit them. They hope that such an arbitrator will not only decide in their favour, but will be persuasive to the other arbitrators on the tribunal. Selecting a partisan arbitrator may secure one vote, but cede influence within the tribunal. A party may find that an arbitrator from the *lex arbitri* has more influence on the tribunal than an arbitrator from the party's home region, if different. In any case, it is obviously sensible to select an arbitrator fluent in the language of the *lex arbitri*. The parties should also take account of the fact that the governing law, or the language of witnesses or documents, may be foreign to the *lex arbitri*, and should try to anticipate how the other party may choose.[6]

---

[3] Lord Steyn and Lord Hoffmann, former members of the House of Lords (now the Supreme Court), are from South Africa.

[4] LCIA Rules Article 6.

[5] English Arbitration Act section 20(4); LCIA Rules Article 26.3; ICC Rules Article 25.1.

[6] For example, if the governing law is foreign to the *lex arbitri*, an arbitrator trained in that law may have significant influence within the tribunal. Each party

It is also common for the chairman to be a professional, neutral lawyer who is experienced in the resolution of international commercial disputes. The chairman's view will often be dispositive if the party-appointed arbitrators do not agree; moreover, the chairman will usually take the lead in running the case and drafting the award. Generally, therefore, the view of the chairman is crucial to the outcome of the dispute.

Given these factors, the composition of an English arbitral tribunal will often resemble closely the composition of the High Court in deciding an international commercial dispute, save that (1) the arbitrators may often come from different countries, while the judge will usually be English, and (2) there will often be three arbitrators rather than one judge, although the view of the chairman will often be dispositive.

The parties should investigate their arbitrators, both before making their selection, and once the tribunal as a whole is known. Arbitrators who are or have been judges or advocates, or who have published or spoken, may have a publicly available record showing their approach. This should influence how the parties approach the case. A number of (but by no means all) former Commercial Court judges become successful arbitrators.

D. Communication

Once the tribunal is selected, it becomes the object of persuasion, and its identity should influence the parties' every step. A style of presentation which English and European lawyers often find persuasive is a measured and neutral tone which explains a party's case in a clear, concise, accurate, reasoned and authoritative way. This style can sometimes appear underdone or unpersuasive to some lawyers, particularly American lawyers. Conversely, an argumentative or overdone presentation can seem distractive and less persuasive to

---

must consider whether this is desirable, and how its opponent may choose. One may wish to avoid the situation in which one's opponent has appointed the only arbitrator trained in the governing law.

many English and European lawyers. In England, the key point is that one must explain one's case in a reasoned way. This requires more than tending simply to state one's position or conclusions, a habit of some European courts which many English lawyers find unpersuasive. It is always necessary to consider one's audience: the members of the tribunal, and in particular the chairman.

A good style of presentation is required not only for legal submissions (written and oral), but also for fact and expert evidence (written and oral). Everything that is said by or on behalf of a party to the tribunal should meet the central requirement of advocacy: it should be persuasive to the tribunal. A party whose evidence or submissions are confusing, too short (providing insufficient explanation or ignoring relevant issues), too long (repetitive or containing too much irrelevant detail), or argumentative and overdone, is not giving its case the best possible exposition.

Additional care is required when communicating with arbitrators, counsel, witnesses or experts whose native language is not English. If the *lex arbitri* is English, the arbitrators and counsel will usually speak some English. However, dispute resolution places special demands on language, and it should never be assumed that those whose native language is not English will feel wholly comfortable with this. Moreover, important witnesses and experts may speak no or little English (or any other language common to the tribunal and counsel), so that communication to or by them may need to be translated. Translated communication must be clear if it is to succeed.

The advocates and the tribunal should therefore ensure that their written and spoken communication will be understood by all involved: the tribunal, advocates, witnesses and experts. This means speaking in a clear voice and not too fast. It also means speaking and writing using clear and simple language which is not colloquial and which the audience has the best chance of understanding. The overriding goal is that language should be clear, simple and concise, and neither overstated nor understated. Rhetorical flourishes are to be avoided, not only because elaborate language tends to be unpersuasive, but also because such flourishes tend to be difficult for non-native speakers of English to follow. For the same reason, language should not be understated, but should clearly state one's position. Excessive subtlety can be missed altogether.

III. Jurisdiction and arbitration agreements

The parties' first opportunity to control the resolution of their dispute is the inclusion of a forum selection clause in their contract. This is an opportunity to set the resolution of any dispute on the desired path.

Under English law, commercial parties have great freedom to agree upon the kind of dispute resolution they want. They can choose litigation (by making a 'jurisdiction agreement'), arbitration (by making an 'arbitration agreement'), or some other kind of dispute resolution. They can choose in what court or tribunal, and under what rules, any dispute should be resolved. They can make their choice exclusive (so as to preclude alternatives) or non-exclusive (so as to permit them). They can agree what law or rules the court or tribunal should apply, or that the court or tribunal should apply no law or rules at all, but decide the case as it thinks fair (*e.g. ex aequo et bono*) or in its absolute discretion. They can agree that their judge or arbitrator should not be impartial, or that one of them should have no legal or procedural rights. They can agree whether there should be disclosure or depositions. They can agree whether their dispute should be decided on paper or following an oral hearing. They can agree whether the decision should be final or subject to appeal. They can agree who will pay the costs of the dispute. They can agree whether any judgment or award may (or may not) be enforced, either generally, or in particular countries or against particular assets.

In general, English law will seek to give effect to the agreement that commercial parties have made. There are limits to this freedom. Some rules of procedure are mandatory, and may not be departed from by private agreement. Other rules may not be mandatory, but one may find that they form part of a definition of a 'court' or 'tribunal', so that their removal may rob a judgment or award of enforceability. However, many rules of judicial or arbitral procedure can be modified by private agreement, often without risk to enforceability. Even where they cannot, a well-formulated agreement may nonetheless entitle one party to recover from the other party loss caused by the resolution of the dispute in a manner which was not agreed.

The scope for party autonomy makes it too simplistic to describe the choice between litigation and arbitration as a choice between two competing sets of procedure. It also means that it is not entirely fair to blame the dispute resolution community for the 'judicialisation of arbitration' or for the 'arbitralisation of litigation'. Nor is it entirely fair for Americans to complain about a lack of deposition rights, or for Europeans to complain about document disclosure. If commercial parties are not satisfied, the solution is straight-forward: they should rewrite their forum selection agreements. Commercial parties are their own best judges of the dispute resolution they require. Many have sophisticated internal or external counsel quite capable of selecting what is wanted. If commercial parties do not agree, this may of course be because they cannot agree: but still less should the arbitrators or judges then be blamed.

A. Finality

The parties may agree a precise balance between the finality of an award or judgment, and rights of appeal. Jurisdiction or arbitration agreements may seek to secure finality by ousting the right of appeal,[7] or by providing a contractual right of enforcement anywhere or against any assets. Conversely, jurisdiction or arbitration agreements may seek to restrict finality. This may be done by agreeing a contractual right of appeal to another tribunal or to a court, or by agreeing to support (or not oppose) permission to appeal. It may also be done by contractually limiting enforcement, either generally, or in particular countries or against particular assets.

The parties may seek to enhance the right of appeal in more subtle ways. For example, English litigation and arbitration is often

---

[7] *Shell Egypt West Manzala GmbH v. Dana Gas Egypt Limited* [2009] EWHC 2097.

conducted under foreign law. In some legal systems, foreign law is applied as a question of fact of a special kind, and is, therefore, subject to more limited rights of appeal than the application of the *lex fori*, in part because of the practical difficulty of recalling expert witnesses on appeal. This is the position in England, where the effect of section 82(1)(a) of the Arbitration Act 1996 is that the (already highly limited) right under section 69 to appeal an award on a question of law is restricted to a question of English law. This can, however, be departed from by agreement. The result is that an agreement to arbitrate in England a dispute which is governed by foreign law should expressly permit an appeal on a question of foreign law if that is a desired possibility. A further possibility, in litigation as well as arbitration, is to agree that foreign law is to be decided on the basis of submissions of counsel. This may bring foreign lawyers into the legal team, reduce the expense and risk of expert evidence, and further enhance the prospect of appeal on foreign law.

B. Confidentiality

Confidentiality is more difficult to secure. It is widely supposed that commercial parties may agree to conduct arbitration in private, but may not agree to conduct litigation in private. This is traditionally said to result from *Scott v. Scott* [1913] AC 417, 436, where Viscount Haldane LC said:

> "... where all that is at stake is the individual rights of the parties, which they are free to waive, a judge can exclude the public if he demits his capacity as a judge and sits as an arbitrator. The right to invoke the assistance of a Court of Appeal may be thereby affected, but the parties are at liberty to do what they please with their private rights. In proceedings, however, which, like those in the Matrimonial Court, affect status, the public has a general interest which the parties cannot exclude, and I am unable to see how their consent can justify the taking of an exceptional course."

Viscount Haldane did not clearly address the question of whether commercial parties could agree that their private rights should be resolved in private by a judge as judge. The problem is not the right of the parties to a public hearing, from which commercial parties can contract out by agreeing to arbitrate in private,[8] and therefore can also contract out by agreeing to litigate in private. The problem is rather the public interest in maintaining confidence in the courts.[9] Although it remains unclear to what precise extent this public interest is inconsistent with protecting the confidentiality of what goes on in litigation, and requires public access to confidential documents and statements produced in commercial litigation, it remains easier to protect the confidentiality of what goes on in arbitration than in litigation. This has been a significant reason for the growth of arbitration in England.

It must be emphasised, however, that full confidentiality can be difficult or impossible to secure even in arbitration. Regulatory or other disclosure obligations may require the disclosure of information relating to the arbitration, or the publication of all or part of an award. For example, a confidential arbitration award may have to be disclosed in related litigation (lest injustice there be done), and may thereby become public knowledge. Moreover, the content of an arbitration award may become public knowledge if the award is appealed to a court or enforcement is contested.

Commercial parties who want what goes on in the resolution of their dispute to be confidential should agree this in their forum selection agreement. They should also select arbitration rather than litigation. Ousting the right to appeal to or resist enforcement in a court may also help secure confidentiality. (If the parties want the right to appeal or resist enforcement, they could agree to do so one or more arbitral tribunals.) However, the parties should understand that these measures may not ensure complete confidentiality.

---

8 *Suovaniemi v. Finland*, 23 February 1999; *City of Moscow v. Bankers Trust Co* [2005] QB 205, 226B.

9 *Werner v. Austria* 26 EHRR 310, 330, [62]; *City of Moscow v. Bankers Trust Co* [2005] QB 205, 225G.

Judges and arbitrators should write any judgment or award that may become public in a manner which intrudes upon confidentiality to the minimum extent necessary. Where the parties have agreed that their dispute is to be resolved in a confidential manner, judges should consider whether and how they can give effect to this agreement. At the same time, it must be acknowledged that it is in the best English legal tradition for a persuasive judgment or award to explain the relevant facts and law openly and clearly.

C. Other differences between litigation and arbitration

Confidentiality aside, the scope for party autonomy, and the commercial expertise of English judges and arbitrators, makes the choice between litigation and arbitration in England finely balanced. However, there remain important practical differences.

Some points favour litigation. The High Court is a free public institution: commercial parties pay relatively nominal court costs. In arbitration, however, the parties must pay the costs of the arbitrators and of the accommodation used for hearings. Further, the High Court is a standing tribunal in which hearings can be readily scheduled, while an arbitral tribunal takes time to create, and can be difficult to bring together, at all or for any length of time. Moreover, the High Court has greater powers than an arbitrator to compel the production of evidence, consolidate related litigation, and restrain parallel litigation. These powers can greatly assist in the effective resolution of many types of dispute, particularly those involving multiple parties or serious allegations of fraud. These powers can sometimes be made available in support of arbitration, but are more naturally available in support of litigation.

Other points favour arbitration. In particular, the High Court has less ability to accommodate the wishes of the parties than an arbitral tribunal. Confidentiality is a traditional example, but there are others. For example, an arbitral tribunal can more readily sit in a foreign country or conduct litigation in a language other than English than a court can. (However, the High Court regularly hears translated evidence, and videoconferencing is available). Further, although High

Court judgments are widely enforceable throughout Europe, and indeed outside Europe, particularly where the parties agreed an English jurisdiction agreement, nonetheless an arbitral award may more readily be enforced outside Europe under the New York Convention, which has not been matched by any parallel global convention for court judgments (and indeed may never be).

It is by reference to factors such as these that commercial parties should choose between English litigation and arbitration. Whichever they select, they should seek to agree the procedural rules that they want as precisely as they consider appropriate.

IV. Case management

Justice delayed is justice denied. Yet a 'kangaroo court' (that is, one which denies due process in the name of expediency) is no better for being a 'kangaroo arbitral tribunal'. Moreover, no two cases are the same: each requires its own balance between speed and care. All this makes effective case management critical. It is the responsibility of the tribunal as a whole to ensure that the case is resolved as speedily as is consistent with due process in light of its specific features.

The parties play a leading role in case management, and their agreement is one of the surest signs of due process. Once the dispute has arisen, the parties should consider how they wish the case to be conducted, and when the tribunal is constituted, it should convene a procedural meeting or hearing to decide this: in the High Court, this is called a 'Case Management Conference'. Procedural meetings or case management conferences can be reconvened as necessary. A not insignificant task is to decide when the substantive hearing will be held. Finding a time that suits the court or tribunal and the parties can be difficult; the temptation to agree too short a time period should be resisted.

The tribunal should ensure that the parties are aware of the available flexibility. The parties may not appreciate that the tribunal may be willing to sit, not in London, but on the other side of the world, if that is more convenient (as it often may be, e.g. for parties based in the Pacific). The parties may not appreciate the financial or legal significance of appeal, confidentiality, disclosure, or deposition rights. They may not appreciate that they can reduce the arbitrators' costs by permitting the chairman to engage a cheaper, younger, lawyer to help administer the case and to research issues which will be dealt with in the award. Now is the time for them to consider in detail how they want their dispute decided, in light of its size and complexity, and the position they find themselves in. Do the parties want a cheap, quick procedure? Or something moderate yet reasonably rigorous? Or the full treatment? The parties are free to supplement, or to agree to revise, the content of their jurisdiction or arbitration agreement.

If the parties can agree, their agreement can be recorded in a procedural order which will govern the arbitration or litigation. A procedure which is agreed by commercial parties should largely be safe from procedural irregularity. If the parties cannot agree, the tribunal or court will have to decide. It will record its decision in the procedural order. The suggestions that follow are premised upon the parties not agreeing to the contrary.

Much will depend upon the size, nature and complexity of the case. If the arbitration is for a small amount, and does not involve allegations of fraud, a cheap and quick procedure may be appropriate. Often, however, international commercial disputes are for very substantial amounts indeed, or involve very serious allegations of fraud. One can understand that commercial parties may not wish to entrust the power to decide important questions to a 'rough and ready' procedure. A finding of fraud by an arbitrator may have the same damaging effect as a finding of fraud by a judge.

A. Arbitration documents

The purpose of documents which are produced in the course of the arbitration, such as statements of case, witness statements and expert reports, is to set out a party's case, to provide the other party with notice of the issues to be decided, and to permit an effective and efficient hearing in which the court or tribunal can decide the issues.

If these documents do not do their job, the hearing is likely to be fragmented, unwieldy and unsatisfactory, causing delay and wasted cost. Moreover, the due process requirement that each party should know the case against it may potentially be infringed.

However, the timing of and relationship between these documents varies from country to country. Arbitration is able to draw on best practices.

In Switzerland, the parties will sequentially exchange a full brief (a 'memorial') which will set out in one place their factual and legal case, and will attach the documents on which they rely. There may then be rounds of reply. The judge will use these briefs to decide which witnesses to question, and how. The questioning of witnesses is reserved exclusively for the judge. The parties' lawyers are permitted neither to question witnesses nor to assist in the preparation of written witness statements: to do so is considered to influence the witness.

In England, statements of case ('pleadings') originated before the introduction of written witness statements, and were for many years the only formal notice of a party's case prior to trial. They are expected to state the central propositions of fact and law on which each party relies. In complex cases, they are often extensive documents, and in English litigation each party must confirm that its statements of case are true. Following statements of case, the parties exchange written witness statements and expert reports, which to some extent duplicate the content of lengthy statements of case. The practice in the Commercial Court is typically to exchange fact witness statements simultaneously, and expert reports sequentially with the claimant's expert going first.

In English litigation, it is the job of the parties' lawyers to investigate the facts and to orchestrate their presentation. They may question the witnesses of the party they represent, and in large cases will usually write these witnesses' statements, subject to the close review and agreement of the witness, and subject to the professional obligation to ensure that the statement reflects the evidence of the witness and not anything else. This is sometimes misunderstood by continental European lawyers, who fear that it may distort or suppress evidence. However, it produces a clear benefit, particularly in large cases. It helps the parties to understand their case, focuses the evidence of the witness, and tends to produce a clearer statement of evidence, which better addresses the relevant issues and can more effectively be understood by the judge or arbitrators and cross-examined in the hearing, than a witness statement produced by the witness alone. It is, however, expensive, and it presupposes high ethical and professional standards in the practice of law.

In the United States, initial statements of case are sometimes brief, just identifying claims and defences. However, they may need to be expanded to resist a motion to dismiss the claim or defence. English and European lawyers find it concerning that a party can commence litigation or arbitration without providing any detailed explanation of its case. They worry that this permits 'fishing trips', that is, the launching of a claim in the hope that something will turn up in disclosure or depositions.

Arbitration is able to draw on the best of these practices. One approach which is used increasingly is, in effect, the Swiss approach described above, modified to accommodate disclosure, cross-examination, and lawyer involvement in the preparation and presentation of written evidence. Under this approach, the claimant will serve a statement of case attaching its fact and expert evidence; the claimant will then give disclosure; some time later the respondent will serve a statement of defence attaching its fact and expert evidence; the respondent will then give disclosure; there will then be time for replies. This approach may help to bring forward the identification of each party's case, and to reduce duplication between statements of case and written evidence. However, care is required to ensure that factual and expert evidence is identified with sufficient clarity to permit effective cross-examination. The evidence should therefore be attached to the statement of case, and not scattered (still worse, unattributed) therein.

The English approach is also often used, in which sequential statements of case are later followed by written evidence. This serves to focus the issues increasingly as the case goes on. It is good practice for the later written evidence to be provided sequentially, so that the claimant's witnesses go first, and the respondent's witnesses do not waste time addressing issues which are not raised. Sequential exchange focuses the dispute and reduces the risk of issues not been addressed by the time of the hearing.

B. Depositions

Parties to American litigation may take advantage of extensive pre-trial fact finding procedures. In particular, they may conduct 'depositions', which are a form of pre-trial cross-examination in which the parties may question witnesses (from the other side, or third parties) in the presence of the other party's lawyers but without the presence of the judge. This produces an extensive evidentiary record in advance of trial.

Depositions are unknown in modern England (save in the limited guise of written interrogatories) and continental Europe. They are popular with many Americans, and sometimes bring forward the identification of the truth and enhance the predictability of trial. However, depositions are expensive, and can be an unjustified intrusion on witnesses. Moreover, unless special arrangements are made, the deposition will be conducted in the absence of the tribunal, and may be less valuable, and less concentrated, than cross-examination in the hearing itself. In general, depositions tend to be more useful in cases which involve fraud or turn on oral evidence, and tend to be less useful in commercial disputes which turn largely on documents.

Depositions are not widely used in international arbitrations, especially outside the U.S. There are limits on the ability of arbitrators and courts outside the United States to order depositions. Where the parties have agreed deposition rights in their jurisdiction or arbitration agreement or procedural order, the court or tribunal can enforce this by refusing to permit a party to put forward a witness whom it has failed to produce for deposition. Where deposition rights have not been agreed, however, the most common approach in English and European litigation and arbitration is not to expect or order depositions. This remains a significant difference in comparison to litigation in the United States. Parties who want deposition rights in English or European litigation or arbitration should agree those rights in their forum selection agreement.

C. Disclosure

In continental European litigation, the parties are generally required to disclose only those documents on which they rely. They are generally under no obligation to disclose documents within their possession or control which are unhelpful to their case. The judge may order production of such documents, but this is not common (unsurprisingly, since it may not be known what they are).

This has long been of concern to English and American lawyers, who worry that a party may conceal relevant documents and have the court or tribunal decide the case on a false basis. Accordingly, in England and the United States, the parties have long been required to search for and disclose to the other party all relevant documents within their possession or control, whether helpful or unhelpful. However, this approach has become extremely expensive over the years, as cases have grown in size and electronic documents have proliferated. Vast quantities of relevant documents are now routinely disclosed. All such documents must be individually reviewed first by the disclosing party's lawyers (e.g. for privilege) and then by the receiving party's lawyers. Much of the expense of large commercial litigation in England and the United States involves disclosure.

In England, the harshness of the exercise is reduced by the fact that the required search can be limited by proportionality, materiality and relevance. In a large case, the parties are expected to seek to reach agreement on the extent of the necessary inquiry. The court will monitor the process through frequent procedural meetings (case management conferences). Much, as always, depends upon the nature of the issues: a fraud case may require extensive disclosure; a simple breach of contract case very little. Proportionality and relevance are also relevant to United States disclosure, but in practice English judges appear to have kept the extent of disclosure under somewhat tighter control than their American colleagues. This may particularly be so in relation to electronic documents.

International arbitration often follows an approach by which parties may request production of categories of documents where this is proportionate to the case. This is quite close to the English approach, and can also be expensive. The IBA Rules on the Taking of Evidence in International Commercial Arbitration can be useful as guidelines in relation to discovery. However, in the experience of one of the authors, the IBA Rules should not become the procedural rules for discovery as the tribunal's discretion can be fettered by their use as such, and their adoption as rules can lead to unnecessary procedural disputes.

Where a party is told that no documents exist and does not believe this, it may be reasonable to ask the other party what searches it has undertaken before giving this confirmation. If the answer reveals that the search was inadequate, it may be reasonable to request a further search, and it may be possible to persuade the tribunal to order this. But if it appears that an adequate search has been conducted, then that is usually the end of the inquiry, and the matter is one for submission in the hearing and the drawing of inferences by the tribunal. As always, European or other commercial parties who are unhappy with the cost or intrusion of disclosure should exclude it in their forum selection agreement.

D. Interlocutory applications

Unless the parties agree a fast-track process, large international commercial disputes generally take some time to resolve, whether in arbitration or litigation. Between one and one and a half years is a common life-span. Given this, it is understandable that a party may wish to seek an early ending to the case, perhaps on the basis that the court or tribunal should not decide the case on jurisdictional or other grounds, or on the basis that the claim or defence is hopeless and should be disposed of without factual inquiry. Or a party may seek to advance the case more quickly than would otherwise occur, by early determination of some preliminary issue.

Such applications may require a lengthy early hearing. Experience tells that it may be better to resolve the case just once in a final hearing, rather than embarking on what may prove to be a series of expensive satellite or preliminary skirmishes (potentially involving appeals), at points in time in which the parties' cases may remain undeveloped, only to culminate in a final hearing in any event.[10] It is therefore unsurprising that courts and tribunals tend to be reluctant to grapple in detail with the issues at an early stage. Moreover, a tribunal that may have struggled to find time in its diary for the final hearing may be reluctant to schedule a sizeable early hearing, particularly if this would defer the date of the final hearing should that still be required.

Yet justice is not always served by letting the case run on. It is wrong to allow a plainly unmeritorious case to continue until trial, with all the expense and disruption of business and personal life that this involves. A jurisdiction challenge may turn on undisputed facts, or discrete facts which can readily be determined at an early stage. Or a party's case may simply be hopeless, and quite insufficient to justify subjecting the other party to the stress, inconvenience and cost of trial and preparation. In practice, however, a compelling case may be required to persuade the tribunal to arrange a substantial interlocutory hearing, and to persuade a court or tribunal to grant dispositive early relief.

Any application for early determination should ideally be made at the first available opportunity. It may be sensible for the parties to discuss any proposed application with the court in a procedural hearing (or case management conference). This may help to indicate whether an application for early determination should be brought at all.

---

[10] Early resolution of a jurisdiction challenge or other skirmish may sometimes exercise a useful influence on the outcome of the case, allowing the parties to size up the strength of their position at an early stage. However, it is dangerous to assume that this will occur, or that it will occur for the right reasons and in the right way.

From time to time, the court or tribunal may also be asked to resolve ancillary matters on which the parties cannot agree, from disputes over disclosure, to requests for further information about a party's case, to applications for security for costs, to a wide range of other matters. Periodic meetings can be scheduled to resolve such matters.

V. The Hearing and preparation

The hearing of a large international commercial dispute can occupy a long time. Unless the parties agree a fast-track format, many large commercial arbitrations involve a final hearing lasting several weeks, just like large commercial litigation, although the vast majority of arbitrations last for less than a week.

The main purposes of the hearing are to permit oral argument on the issues that must be decided, and to enable the written evidence to be tested by cross-examination.

Sufficient time should be reserved for the hearing, including overspill time. The last thing anyone wants is for the hearing to be adjourned until all involved can next meet – which may be months or years away. Generally, it does not help to seek to compress too much into too little in the hearing, or to have the court or tribunal sit for long hours to make up for a lack of sufficient time. This tends to be an inefficient method of proceeding, and may lead to a judgment or award that is challengeable on grounds of due process. Hearings work much better if they are concentrated for five or six hours a day, with all involved having time to prepare for the following day. The typical practice of the Commercial Court in a long trial is to sit four days a week.

It is often helpful to schedule a short pre-trial review. This should be well before the hearing. Its purpose is to review the conduct of the hearing, including the order and timing of evidence. It should be possible to indicate when individual witnesses are likely to give evidence, enabling practical arrangements and reducing intrusion upon them. It may also be important to discuss how and when any necessary oral argument will occur, i.e. on legal issues or the meaning of documents. Any outstanding practical arrangements, such as translation, trial bundles, or the use of live transcripts during the hearing, should also be decided. If such matters can be largely agreed by the parties, it may be possible to hold the pre-trial review by telephone or to dispense with it.

It is generally helpful for the parties to provide the court or tribunal with written opening submissions in advance of the hearing and written closing submissions after it. These documents should explain the parties' cases and provide a guide to the key issues of law and fact which must be decided. These are key advocacy documents, and should be clear, concise, reliable and persuasive. The written opening submissions should be provided sufficiently in advance of the hearting to enable the court or tribunal to read them properly. If they are lengthy, it may be sensible to divide them, for example into 30-page chunks which can be digested in one sitting. Schedules can be an effective way of providing detail without cluttering the thrust of what is being said.

Oral opening submissions are generally brief in arbitration: one usually has an hour or so. Here there remains a distinction between the practice in arbitration and that in English litigation, in which oral openings can occupy several days (or even longer) as a supplement to the written opening submissions. Particularly in cases where the documents are important, this can ensure the judge is well-equipped to hear the witnesses.

After opening submissions comes evidence. The usual order of evidence is to begin with the claimant's fact witnesses, followed by the respondent's fact witnesses, and then to conclude with expert evidence, tackled in the same way and discipline by discipline. However, it may sometimes be sensible to depart from this. In a complex case, for example, it may be better to begin with experts, to set the scene for the fact evidence. These matters should be decided by the time of the pre-trial review.

The use of written witness statements has made examination-in-chief (i.e., the questioning by a party of its own witnesses) largely redundant, in both litigation and arbitration. Some arbitrators, particularly from continental Europe, can be distrustful of lawyer-assisted witness statements, and can therefore seek to hear the witness' evidence in his or her own words through examination-in-chief. It is suggested that this concern is misplaced. The persuasive value of a witness statement depends on its consistency with the documents, its explanatory power and the ability of the witness to withstand cross-examination. There is no reason to disbelieve a clear and coherent witness statement which is consistent with the documents and other evidence and survives cross-examination. Any desire for examination-in-chief should be raised in the pre-trial review.

This brings us to cross-examination, which serves the second of the two main points of the hearing: to enable the evidence to be tested. Cross-examination remains an essential tool in establishing the truth. It may not always achieve this, but it should always be undertaken. It should be emphasised that due process does not require that a party be given unlimited time to make oral submissions or to conduct cross-examination. On the contrary, due process requires only that a fair opportunity to present one's case. A party should not be permitted to cross-examine forever or to ask irrelevant questions: unless it has been agreed, there is no right to filibuster a court or tribunal. However, a party should be given a proper opportunity to conduct cross-examination. As always, much depends upon the nature of the case and on any agreement between the parties. In a large case, however, proper cross-examination for a significant witness (expert or fact) may require days (or even weeks) rather than minutes or hours. Modern arbitration is therefore moving away from the old continental model. The time that is likely to be required for cross-examination should be discussed in advance or in the pre-trial review. The parties sometimes agree time-limits to ensure the arbitration runs to schedule; but the tribunal must ultimately take responsibility for the proper conduct of the case.

It is sometimes suggested that expert evidence should be heard by an 'expert conference', in which all the expert witnesses give their evidence together in the hearing. This sometimes occurs in litigation in Australia, where it is known as a 'hot tub'. In similar vein, it is sometimes suggested that it may be helpful for the experts to meet following their reports, but in advance of the hearing, to see whether they can agree a joint experts' report. This often occurs in English litigation.

An arbitration tribunal can adopt such processes if they are agreed by the parties, but, it is thought, should be reluctant to impose them. These processes tend to favour experts who are fluent in the language of the tribunal and accustomed to giving evidence (i.e., 'professional' expert witnesses) over experts who may not speak the language of the tribunal and may be unfamiliar with litigation. A live 'hot tub' or 'witness conference' also places a burden on the advocates and the court or tribunal to ensure it is effective and efficient. In the absence of the parties' agreement, it is therefore thought that the experts should be presented and cross-examined one at a time and in the usual way, so that the court or tribunal, and the opposing advocate, can give each expert the full benefit of their attention. For similar reasons, it is thought that a tribunal generally should not require the experts to meet before the hearing unless the parties agree to this.

VI. Award

The parties can agree that the tribunal should deliver either a reasoned or unreasoned award; but if they do not agree, reasons should be given (in practice, most parties want and are willing to pay for reasons, which are an inherent part of justice).

The purpose of any judgment or award is to do justice and to be seen to do justice. The judgment or award should command the respect of the parties and of any appellant or enforcing court or tribunal. To this end, it should meet the basic requirement of advocacy: to persuade. However, this requires neither endless detail nor unnecessary discussion of confidential material. What is required is a clear explanation of whether the court or tribunal has jurisdiction and how; what due process was observed; what it has found to have happened and why; and what it has decided and why. The judgment or award should address each party's case, making it clear why points have been rejected. It should deal with alternative arguments, in case the primary ground for decision should be found wanting on appeal. All this should be done concisely. Many arbitrators err by producing excessively long awards which risk not being understood. Arbitrators should aim to produce persuasive awards of reasonable length. At all cost, however, an arbitrator should not produce an excessively short award which tends to command rather than to persuade, and which tends to state propositions or conclusions rather than to provide reasoning. That is appropriate only if the parties have agreed to an unreasoned award.

VII. Conclusion

Advocacy plays a major role in all aspects of litigation and arbitration. In England advocacy is both written and oral, but wherever it is deployed, the hallmark of good advocacy is the clear, concise and persuasive presentation of a party's case.

Chapter 21

THE CONTINENTAL EUROPEAN PERSPECTIVE AND PRACTICE OF ADVOCACY

Teresa Giovannini*

I. Introduction

Referring to a "Continental European Perspective and Practice of Advocacy" in international arbitration might seem somewhat odd and old fashioned in light of the number of tools which currently exist providing for a harmonized approach to arbitration practice (e.g. UNCITRAL Model Law, IBA Rules on the Taking of Evidence in International Commercial Arbitration or the IBA Guidelines on Conflicts of Interest in International Arbitration, ICDR Guidelines for Arbitrators concerning Exchange of Information). Nonetheless, cultural differences remain embedded within these harmonized rules, stemming from those practices generally accepted and recognized in certain parts of the world as compared with others; and notably from the legal background, culture, values and languages of arbitrators and counsel.

The purpose of this chapter, dedicated to the peculiarities of Continental European Advocacy, is not simply to recall that these differences exist, but rather to provide counsel with tools to understand the background and expectations of those clients, opposing counsel, and arbitrators based or trained in continental Europe. This will enable counsel to maximize the flexibility that characterizes international arbitration, and prompt "*to make the process*

* Partner, Lalive, Geneva www.lalive.ch.

work'[1] with *"some baseline concept of "how do things work" for these diverse participants".* In addition, this study will assist counsel to exercise their discretion to organize arbitral procedures, by picking and choosing those tools that appear better suited to each given case. This approach is feasible under most national laws and arbitration rules, which leave wide powers to the parties to tailor their arbitral procedure.

II. Adversarial versus Inquisitorial Legal Systems

Despite the above-mentioned trend towards harmonization of many arbitral rules and procedures, the European continental litigation culture remains deeply entrenched in an inquisitorial logic. In the context of litigation, this way of conceiving the procedure gives the court, and not the parties, the primary role in steering the procedure. As stated by J. Lew: *"In the inquisitorial system, the court "takes the initiative in directing the ascertainment of the facts and the law"*, the role of the parties being limited in this respect to *"merely assist the tribunal in this task".*[2] As emphasized by a learned international legal writer: *"[i]t is an essential feature of civil law proceedings that the courts assume the obligation to investigate the case themselves and to find the "truth"".*[3]

This fundamental nature of the inquisitorial system triggers the application of several basic principles that constitute recurrent themes in the approach taken throughout the proceedings in general, in particular with respect to the manner in which the arbitration is

---

[1] Madges S. Thorsen, *The Whole Enchilada: Cultural Differences in International Arbitration,* MSBA ADR Section, 8 May 2007, p.3, http://www.mnbar.org/sections/adr/WholeEnchilada.pdf.

[2] Julian D.M. Lew, *Inquisitorial v. Adversarial Proceedings,* ASA Special Series N° 26, *Best Practices in International Arbitration,* July 2006, pp.167 ff, 169, with reference to Lew, J D M/Mistelis, L A/Kröll, S.M., *Comparative International Commercial Arbitration,* The Hague, London, New York, 2003, p.533, # 21-34; and to Redfern, A/Hunter, M/Blackaby, N/Partasides, C, *Law and Practice of International Commercial Arbitration,* 4th ed. , London, 2004, p.320, # 6 – 10.

[3] Hans van Houtte, *Counsel-Witness Relations and Professional Misconduct in Civil Law Systems,* Arbitration International, Kluwer, 2003, Volume 19, Issue 4, pp.457 ff, 457.

initiated and to the issue of evidence. Cultural legal background has also an impact on certain aspects of the decision making process and the attitude of the arbitral tribunal towards settlement discussions. In addition, the continental legal culture leads to some peculiarities with respect to the ethics of advocacy, both towards the client and towards the opposing side and the arbitral tribunal.

The judge's power to ascertain the truth is reflected for example in the French New Code of Civil Procedure (French NCPC), which reads: *"[t]he Judge has the power to order ex officio any legally admissible measure of investigation"*.[4] In practice, this power is enforced by the authority vested in the judge to e.g. order a fact-finding procedure, to set time limits, to identify the facts which have to be proven by the parties[5] or to order one party to produce evidence in its possession.as provided for example explicitly in Article 871 of the Belgian Judicial Code. This power of the judge is accompanied by the parties' duty to cooperate with the court in its task to ascertain the facts.[6] If this duty is violated, the judge is empowered to impose sanctions. This is the case for example in Belgium[7] or in France[8] where the court can issue a subpoena order (*astreintes*) when a party refuses to produce documents. Interestingly this inquisitorial approach is somehow reflected in the International Court of Arbitration's Rules of Arbitration (ICC Arbitration Rules). These provide that the Arbitral Tribunal may decide *"of its own motion"* to hear the parties together in person, as well as witnesses or experts appointed by the parties or

---

[4] French NCPC, Article 10.

[5] J. A. Jolowicz, *Adversarial and Inquisitorial Models of Civil Procedure,* The International and Comparative Law Quarterly, Volume 52, Number 2, April 2003, pp.281 ff, 290 and 291.

[6] French NCPC, Article 11.

[7] Alan Redfern, Claude Reymond, Andreas Reiner, Bernard Hanotiau, Lord Eveleigh, Ian W. Menzies, Allan Philipp, *The Standards and Burden of Proof in International Arbitration,* Arbitration International, Kluwer, 1994, Volume 10, Issue 3, pp.317 ff, 344.

[8] French NCPC, Article 134.

"any other person" and it may also appoint experts and may *"summon any party to provide additional evidence"*.[9]

Once the fact-finding process is completed, the judge is responsible for determining and applying the correct rules of law (the principle of *Jura Novit Curia*). This principle is expressly contained in the French NCPC: *"[t]he judge decides the case in accordance with the rules of law that are applicable to it"*; and in particular *"[h]e must give or restore the exact characterization to the facts or acts in dispute without limiting himself to the designation proposed by the parties"*.[10] The principle of *Jura Novit Curia* has also been recognized in the UNIDROIT Principles of Transnational Civil Procedure of 2004 (The 2004 UNIDROIT Principles),[11] which confirm the judge's authority in the fact-finding process and his responsibility for ascertaining the law: *"the court is responsible for considering all relevant facts and evidence and for determining the correct legal basis for its decisions..."*.[12]

The corollary of the inquisitorial approach to facts and law consists in the strict application of the principle of Contradictory Debate, *"whose effect is to ensure that the judge takes nothing into account for the purposes of his decision that has not been open to contradictory debate by the parties"*. This principle does not require legal recognition for instance in English law *"for the simple reason that the information on which the decision will be based is presented – in the classic adversary process- orally by the parties in open court...*[and] *is therefore subjected automatically to contradictory debate"*.[13]

Another principle that characterizes continental European legal systems is the Burden and Standard of Proof. In fact, as a result of their legal training and practice, continental lawyers understand that they bear the entire burden of proving their case.[14] The rule is expressed in various continental civil or procedural codes. For

---

[9] ICC Arbitration Rules, Article 20(2).

[10] French NCPC, Article 12.

[11] Adopted by the American Law Institute (ALI) in May 2004 and by the International Institute for the Unification of Private Law (UNIDROIT) in April 2004.

[12] 2004 Unidroit Principles, Article 22.1.

[13] JA Jolowitcz, *op.cit.*, pp.282 and 283.

[14] Madge S. Thorsen, *op. cit.*, p.6.

instance, in France Article 9 NCPC provides: *"[I]t is incumbent upon each party to prove the facts necessary for the success of its claim in conformity with the law"*. It is specified further that *"in no case can a judicial investigation be ordered with a view to compensating the party's deficiency in the evidentiary process"*.[15] The Swiss Civil Code (cc.ch)[16] likewise provides that *"[e]ach Party must prove ...the facts alleged by it to support his claim"*. Article 2697 of the Italian Civil Code (cc.it.) contains a similar rule, stating that: *"[w]hoever seeks to claim a right in court must prove the facts that constitute its base"*.

The rule set out above governing the Burden of Proof has one particularly important consequence, namely that a Party should not – as a matter of principle – be compelled to produce evidence detrimental to its case.[17] This may be at odds with other legal cultures. Indeed, as stated by Richard Kreindler: *"from a US point of view this might suggest an unacceptable, even naive honour system, in which clearly neither party would voluntarily produce documents not favourable to its cause"*.[18]

As to the Standard of Proof, it is common knowledge that while the approach to standard of proof in Anglo-Saxon legal systems is the balance of probabilities, *"[c]ontinental laws seem to establish a much higher standard"*.[19] Thus, for example, Austrian law uses the term "full conviction" (*"volle Überzeugung"*), and Swiss case law refers to the notion of "conviction".[20]

---

[15] French NCPC, Article 146.2.

[16] Cc.ch, Article 8.

[17] Urs Martin Laeuchli, *Civil and Common Law: Contrast and Synthesis in International Arbitration,* Dispute Resolution Journal, August-October 2007, p.2, with reference to Bernardo M. Cremades, *Managing Discovery in International Arbitration,* 57 (4), Dispute Resolution Journal, November 2002-January 2003.

[18] Richard H. Kreindler, *Arbitrating with Different Legal Traditions: Civil Law,* The International Journal of Arbitration, Mediation and Dispute Management, Volume 75, Number 2, May 2009, pp.199 ff, 202; ***contra:*** 2004 Unidroit Principles, Article 16.2, providing that: *"It is not a basis of objection to...disclosure that the evidence may be adverse to the party or person making the disclosure"*.

[19] Alan Redfern, Claude Reymond, Andreas Reiner, Bernard Hanotiau, Lord Eveleigh, Ian W. Menzies, Allan Philipp, *op. cit.,* p.334.

[20] See for instance ATF 118 II 235.

The principles outlined above are the cornerstones of the entire procedural approach adopted in continental advocacy. They therefore facilitate a greater understanding of the characteristics of the continental legal process in general as compared with the common law legal culture.

III. The Procedural Approach

From the continental European perspective, two elements must generally be considered with respect to legal procedure in general. The first is that since the burden of proof lies with the party making its claim, this party must provide the evidence on which it relies to prove its case. Accordingly, a party cannot seek to rely on evidence [held or] presented by the other party to build up its case. As stated by a learned practitioner, *"[t]he concept of filing first, and filling out the details only after obtaining documents in the adversary's possession, strikes most Continental practitioners as reckless and unfair"*.[21]

The second element in the civil tradition is that written evidence is generally held to prevail over oral evidence. In other words, *"in most civil law systems, the case is presented on documents before a hearing occurs, if a hearing occurs at all, and documents are viewed as the single most credible type of evidence"*.[22] Thus in Spain, a tradition of written pleadings has prevailed since the 19th century.[23] A similar practice has been adopted in Germany, where *"in a typical international commercial arbitration with German elements between two enterprises, witnesses will not be the sole or even the primary focus"*.[24] This approach is also affirmed in international arbitrations located in Switzerland, where *"the parties' written submissions usually play a very important, if not determinative, role in the decision-making*

[21] Siegfried H. Elsing, John Townsend, *Bridging the Common Law-Civil Law Divide in Arbitration,* Arbitration International, Kluwer, 2002, Volume 18, Issue 1, pp.59 ff, 59.

[22] Madges S. Thorsen, *op. cit.,* p.4.

[23] Doak Bishop, *The Art of Advocacy in International Arbitration,* New York and Bern, 2004, Inigo Quintana and Alberto Fortun, *Advocacy in International Commercial Arbitration: Spain,* p.151.

[24] Richard M. Kreindler, *op. cit.,* p.202.

processes of the arbitral tribunal".[25] In sum, it can be affirmed along experienced international arbitrators' view that *"European continental arbitrators rely on written pleadings and documentation".*[26]

A. The Statement of Case

As a consequence of the two features mentioned above, continental European lawyers are generally expected to initiate the arbitration proceedings with a full statement of their case, including the evidence supporting it. Thus, in Germany, Section 1046 of the Code of Civil Procedure (*Zivilprozessordnung, ZPO*) relating to arbitration taking place in Germany requires that, in the statement of claim, the claimant *"shall state his claim and the facts supporting the claim"*, and the respondent *"shall state his defense in respect of these particulars"* and that *"[t]he Parties can submit with their statements all documents they consider to be relevant or other evidence they will submit"*. As emphasized by Richard Kreindler, *"the case is meant to be properly and fully framed, and to be ripe for decision, at the beginning of the dispute, as opposed to making the case up or discovering the case as one goes along, benefiting from a discovery process which, in the German context, may never come or in any event not in the same manner and same scope as the US user might have expected".*[27] Likewise in Sweden the parties are expected to indicate at the outset the evidence, both documentary and oral, they wish to rely on,[28] an approach that clearly implies that the initial statement of case is detailed. According to Spanish principles of advocacy, the plaintiff pleads the case in full in its first written statement: *"the practice is to present fully detailed pleadings of fact and law at the opening stage of the proceedings".*[29]

---

[25] Gabrielle Kaufmann-Kohler & Blaise Stucki, *International Arbitration in Switzerland, A Handbook for Practitioners*, Kluwer, 2004, David P. Roney, Anna K. Müller, *The Arbitral Procedure*, p.65.

[26] Oliver Bolthausen and Peter H. Acker, *Obtaining Discovery in International Arbitral Proceedings: The European v American Mentality*, CIArb Arbitration Journal, Volume 74, Number 3, August 2008, pp.225 ff, 225.

[27] Richard M. Kreindler, *op. cit.*, p.202.

[28] Doak Bishop, *op. cit.*, Kaj Hobér, *Advocacy in International Commercial Arbitration: Sweden*, p.181.

[29] Doak Bishop, *op. cit.* , Inigo Quintana and Alberto Fortun, *op. cit.*, p.160.

B. Evidence

Evidence in international arbitration takes on particular features from the continental European perspective specifically with respect to legal privilege (*infra,* # III.3.1), relevance, identity, preparation and interrogation of witnesses (*infra,* # III.3.2), discovery (*infra,* # III.3.3.) and experts (*infra,* # III.3.4.).

(1) Legal Privilege

Continental European multilateral legal instruments generally recognize a person's right to refuse to give evidence in so far as he or she has a privilege or a duty to refuse. Thus, Article 11 of the Hague Convention on the Taking of Evidence Abroad in Civil and Commercial Matters of 18 March 1970[30] (the 1970 Hague Convention) provides that *"[i]n the execution of a Letter of Request* [to obtain evidence] *the person concerned... may refuse to give evidence in so far as he has a privilege or duty to refuse to give the evidence...a) under the law of the State of Execution; or b) under the law of the State of origin..."*.

The 2004 UNIDROIT Principles also contemplate the protection of privilege, providing that: *"[e]ffect should be given to privileges... concerning disclosure of evidence or other information"*.[31]

Finally, the European Code of Conduct for European Lawyers[32] (The CCBE Code of Conduct) applicable where the seat of the arbitration proceedings is located in Europe contains a strict professional obligation of confidentiality. This obligation is identified as being *"a primary and fundamental right and duty of the lawyer"* that *"serves the interest of the administration of justice as well as the interest of the client"*.[33]

---

30 The 1970 Hague Convention is not directly applicable to arbitration proceedings.

31 2004 Unidroit Principles, Article 18.1.

32 The CCBE Code of Conduct was originally adopted at the Council of Bars and Law Societies in Europe (CCBE) Plenary Session on 28 October 1988. It was subsequently amended in 1998, 2002 and 2006.

33 CCBE Code of Conduct, Article 2.3.1.

The above definition sets out the primary distinction between common law and civil law litigation systems. Under the former, attorney-client privilege is a foundational principle implemented by well-defined exclusionary rules of evidence. It is the client's right to waive the privilege and introduce attorney-client communications as evidence.[34] Under the civil law tradition, professional secrecy is a matter of public policy enforced by criminal sanctions; it cannot be waived by the attorney even if the client has waived any privilege.[35] Thus, in France, pursuant to Article 226-13 of the Criminal Code, disclosure of a communication deemed privileged may be sanctioned by up to one year of imprisonment and a 15'000 Euro fine. In Switzerland, Article 321 of the Criminal Code provides for imprisonment of a maximum of three years or a fine.

This principle is limited to outside counsel in Switzerland, France, Sweden and Italy.[36] In Belgium, Denmark, the Netherlands, Germany and Spain, in-house counsel have also traditionally been able to rely on legal privilege to refuse to disclose communications between themselves and the company for whom they work,[37] provided that these communications relate to provision of legal opinion and advice.

The situation has been clarified by the well-known *Akzo Nobel Chemicals Ltd and Akros Chemicals* decision of 17 September 2007.[38] In this case, the European Court of First Instance held that internal corporate communications seeking the legal advice of in-house counsel are not covered by legal professional privilege. The fact that in-house counsel is a member of a national bar association does not

---

[34] Marc J. Goldstein, *Crossing The Common Law-Civil Law Divide in International Arbitration: A Primer for the Perplexed Practitioner*, 2006, www.hodgsonruss,com/ files/1_2_1/MJG_Common_Law_Civil _Law_ Divide. pdf , pp.10 and 11.

[35] Pierre Heitzmann, *Confidentiality and Privileges in Cross-Border Legal Practice: The Need for a Global Standard ?* ASA Bulletin, 2008, Volume 26, Issue 2, pp.205 ff, 206.

[36] Klaus Peter Berger, *Evidentiary Privileges : Best Practice Standards versus/and Arbitral Discretion,* Arbitration International, Kluwer, 2006, Volume 22, Issue 4, pp.501 ff, 504 and references.

[37] Pierre Heitzmann, *op. cit.,* p.209.

[38] Joined cases T-125/03 and T-253-03, *Akzo Nobel Chemicals Ltd and Akros Chemicals Ltd vs Commission of the European Communities*, 17 September 2007.

have any effect on this principle. The European Court stated that documents must have been exchanged with an outside counsel in the context of the defense of the company in order to attract legal privilege. The Court specified however that documents prepared within the company for the purposes of gathering information to assist outside counsel in understanding the facts on which he or she is required to give legal advice remain confidential, provided that they had been created with a view to obtaining a legal advice.

As regards the contents of the privileged information, two questions are of particular importance when considering the characteristics of the continental European legal context. The first question concerns the privilege of mediation or settlement discussions. It is worth noting here Directive 2008/52/EC of the European Parliament and of the Council of 21 May 2008 on certain aspects of mediation in civil and commercial matters that is applicable to cross-border disputes (the Directive 2008/52/EC). This applies when *"one at least of the parties is domiciled or habitually resident in a Member State other than that of any other party on the date…(a) the parties agree to use mediation after the dispute has arisen; (b) mediation is ordered by a court; (c) an obligation to use mediation arises under national law"* or when *"the court…invite* [s] *the parties to attend an information session on the use of mediation…"*.[39] Article 7 of this Directive provides for a clear confidentiality obligation as follows:

> "1. *Given that mediation is intended to take place in a manner which respects confidentiality, Member States shall ensure that, unless the parties agree otherwise, neither mediators nor those involved in the administration of the mediation process shall be compelled to give evidence in civil and commercial judicial proceedings or arbitration regarding information arising out or in connection with a mediation process, except:*
>
> *(a) where this is necessary for overriding considerations of public policy of the Member State concerned, in particular when required to ensure the protection of the best interests of children or to prevent harm to the physical or psychological integrity of a person; or*

[39] Directive 2008/52/EC, Articles 2 and 5.

> (b) *where disclosure of the content of the agreement resulting from mediation is necessary in order to implement or enforce that agreement"*,

it being further specified that:

> "2. *Nothing in paragraph 1 shall preclude Member States from enacting stricter measures to protect the confidentiality of mediation"*.

The CCBE Code of Conduct likewise contains a provision aimed at protecting the parties' intentions to keep particular settlement discussions confidential as follows:

> *"If a lawyer intends to send communications to a lawyer in another Member State, which the sender wishes to remain confidential or without prejudice he or she should clearly express this intention prior to communicating the documents"*.[40]

On a national level, the situations vary. In France, any correspondence exchanged between French attorneys is considered confidential by nature and cannot even be disclosed to their own clients with the exception of the information contained in such correspondence that can and should be disclosed to the client[41] In Italy, labeling a communication as "confidential" is presumed to mean that the receiving attorney cannot disclose the document to the adjudicating tribunal and can require that confidentiality be maintained even with respect to the receiving attorney's client.[42] The same situation prevails in Portugal.[43] Conversely, in Belgium and in

---

[40] CCBE Code of Conduct, Article 5.3.

[41] Pierre Heitzmann, *op. cit.*, p.211.

[42] Gary B. Born, *Legal Representation and Professional Conduct in International Arbitration – c. Professional Conduct of Legal Representatives in International Commercial Arbitration,* in Gary B. Born, International Commercial Arbitration, Kluwer, 2009, pp.2304 ff, 2314 and FN 112; Catherine A. Rogers, *Fit and Function in Legal Ethics: Developing a Code of Conduct for International Arbitration,* Michigan Journal of International Law, Winter 2002, pp.341 ff, 373.

[43] Catherine A. Rogers, *Fit and Function in Legal Ethics: Developing a Code of Conduct for International Arbitration,* Michigan Journal of International Law, Winter 2002, pp.341 ff, 373.

The Netherlands, there is no specific settlement privilege. However, cases have been reported in Belgium providing that statements made during mediation proceedings cannot be used in litigation, consistent with the applicable rules governing mediation proceedings.[44]

The second question relates to the issue of self-incriminating information. Under French and German procedural laws for instance, no litigant is required to provide "weapons for his opponent's case".[45] In Switzerland, under the new Federal Code of Civil Procedure of 19 December 2008 (the 2008 Federal Code of Procedure),[46] the parties and any other person can refuse to cooperate in the evidentiary process when such cooperation might trigger civil or a criminal liability[47]. Conversely, the 2004 UNIDROIT Principles provide that *"[i]t is not a basis for objection to…disclosure that the evidence may be adverse to the party or person making the disclosure".*[48]

The rule contained in the ICDR Guidelines for Arbitrators Concerning Exchanges of Information provides that when confronted with privilege or professional ethics and other legal impediments, *"[w]hen the parties, their counsel or their documents would be subject under applicable law to different rules, the tribunal should to the extent possible apply the same rule to both sides, giving preference to the rule that provides the highest level of protection".* This suggests that the issue of privilege must be carefully examined, taking into account the specificities of the seat of the arbitration and the relevant applicable national laws and bar rules.

---

44 Pierre Heitzmann, *op. cit.*, FN 20.

45 Matthieu de Boisséson, *Evidentiary Privileges in International Arbitration,* ICCA Congress Series 2006 Montreal 13, Kluwer, 2007, pp.705 ff, 709 ; Fabian von Schlabrendorff & Audley Sheppard, *Conflict of Legal Privileges in International Arbitration: An Attempt to Find a Holistic Solution,* in Liber Amicorum in honour of Robert Briner, ICC Publishing, 2005, pp.743 ff, 754

46 The 2008 Federal Code of Procedure, entering into force on 1 January 2011.

47 2008 Federal Code of Procedure, Article 163 and 166.

48 2004 Unidroit Principles, Article 16.2.

(2) Witnesses, relevance, identity, preparation, interrogation

As mentioned above, continental European arbitrators tend to place **little added value** on oral testimony, which they view with skepticism.[49] While in the common law tradition the hearing constitutes the climax of the entire proceedings, in the civil law culture the hearing completes the written evidence but is not a tool for the taking of evidence in its own right.[50] As noted by a renowned practitioner, "*in the civil law there is a deep distrust of the testimony of fact witnesses*";[51] and this all the more the case when these fact witnesses are affiliated with or employed by a party.

As to the identity of potential witnesses, unlike under the American system, the European approach is to distinguish between witnesses and party representatives. Lawrence W. Newman gives the example of the Iran-U.S. Claims Tribunal, where a party representative cannot be sworn in or sit in the witness chair, but may make an informal presentation.[52] Witnesses, contrary to party representatives, are generally excluded from the hearing room and must swear or affirm to tell the truth.[53] This approach is adopted for example in Germany, where party representatives are not permitted to testify.[54]

As to the preparation of witnesses, in some continental European countries such as Austria, Germany, the Netherlands and Sweden, counsel may approach and interview a prospective witness, a practice strictly forbidden in other countries such as Belgium, France, Italy

---

[49] Lawrence W. Newman, *International Arbitration Hearings: Showdown or Dénouement ?* Tulane Journal of International and Comparative Law, Spring 1997, pp.393 ff, 395.

[50] Yves Derains, *La Pratique de l'administration de la preuve dans l'arbitrage commercial international,* Revue de l'Arbitrage, Volume 2004 Issue 4, pp.781 ff, 787.

[51] Pierre A. Karrer, *The Civil Law and Common Law Divide : An International Arbitrator tells it like he sees it,* Dispute Resolution, Journal of the American Arbitration Association, 2008, pp.72 ff, 76.

[52] Lawrence W. Newman, *op. cit.,* p.398.

[53] Lawrence W. Newman, *op. cit.,* p.398.

[54] Yves Derains, *op. cit.,* p.795.

and Switzerland by ethical bar rules and/or criminal laws.[55] While not applicable as such to international arbitration, attention must be paid to these traditions and customs that might result in an uneven playing field if not taken into consideration at the outset of the proceedings.

Particular attention has been given to **witnesses of the opposing side** by the CCBE Code of Conduct. This provides that:

> *"A lawyer shall not communicate about a particular case or matter directly with any person whom he or she knows to be represented or advised in the case or matter by another lawyer, without the consent of that other lawyer (and shall keep the other lawyer informed of any such communication)".*[56]

Regarding the examination of witnesses, the striking feature of continental European legal culture resides in both the fact that the procedure is generally based upon documents rather than oral testimony on the one hand, and in the role of the judge who, as set out above, is the actual manager of the procedure, on the other.

Thus, in civil law countries the judge is expected to have read all pleadings and submissions (including written witness statements) before the hearing. In addition, he or she will take the lead in interrogating [examining] witnesses, the role of the lawyers being generally limited to suggesting to the judge questions that should be asked[57]. This practice is mirrored in the field of international arbitration, where continental European arbitrators will often actively participate by confronting and questioning witnesses and, as appropriate, select which witnesses they want to hear while excluding others, despite the parties' requests.[58]

(3) Discovery

Under most continental European legal systems, the practice of **pre-trial discovery** (consisting of requests for disclosure, interrogatories, requests for production, requests for admission and

---

[55] Hans van Houtte, *op. cit.,* p.457; Gary B. Born, *op. cit.,* pp.2308 and 2309.

[56] CCBE Code of Conduct, Article 5.5.

[57] Siegfried H. Elsing, John M. Townsend, *op. cit.,* p.3.

[58] Lawrence W. Newman, *op. cit.,* p.395.

depositions) is unknown. Generally, it may be said that only in instances where a prospective witness may become unavailable due to overriding circumstances may a court order a so-called "preliminary examination".[59] As regards discovery, from the continental European perspective, it has been said that discovery does not exist. This is not entirely true, inasmuch as discovery is allowed, but in a far more limited way than in common law countries. Claude Reymond, a well known civil commentator, notes that civil law courts are generally reluctant to assist with the extraction of evidence as a consequence of the principle, discussed above, of *Onus Probandi Incumbat Allegandi*[60].

As stated by Pierre Karrer in response to the argument that the IBA Rules of Evidence present a good compromise: *"Yes…but it is still not entirely predictable to what extent discovery, or production of documents…will be granted in any particular case"*.[61] The legal background of the participants concerned will therefore be of paramount importance in determining the scope and nature of discovery [or "document production" as it is better known in international arbitration]. German courts, for example, while empowered to order a party to disclose documents in its possession[62] will rarely use this tool in practice.[63] Marc Goldstein gives the example of a civil law chairman denying all involuntary document production except that which a Tribunal-appointed expert might require.[64]

A practical consequence of this general reluctance of continental European lawyers to require compulsory production of documents[65]

---

[59] Hans Smit, *Roles of the Arbitral Tribunal in Civil Law and Common Law Systems with Respect to Presentation of Evidence,* ICCA Congress Series 1994 Vienna 7, Kluwer, 1996, pp.159 ff, 161.

[60] Claude Reymond, *Civil Law and Common Law Procedures: Which is the More Inquisitorial? A Civil Lawyer's Response,* (1989) 5 Arbitration International pp.357 ff, 360.

[61] Pierre Karrer, *op. cit.,* p.76.

[62] ZPO, Article 142.

[63] Rolf Trittmann and Boris Kasolowsky, *Taking Evidence in Arbitration Proceedings Between Common Law and Civil Law Traditions – the Development of a European Hybrid Standard for Arbitration Proceedings,* UNSW Law Journal, Volume 31 (1), pp.330 ff. 336

[64] Marc J. Goldstein, *op. cit.,*p.5.

[65] Olivier Bolthausen and Peter H. Acker, *op. cit.,* p.226.

is that discovery may be allowed only after the parties have submitted all documents on which they respectively rely.[66] This is consistent with the principle that the parties are expected to establish their case on the basis of the facts and evidence that they know or dispose of, and not on the basis of the (possible) evidence in the possession or control of the opposing side or of third parties. Both parties can accordingly anticipate that they will most probably obtain a specifically described document in the possession of the other side if this document is relevant to the facts alleged (which implies that the burden of allegation remains with the party seeking discovery) or if the requesting party is entitled to demand the production of the document under the relevant provisions of law.[67]

(4) Experts

The continental European practice is for the tribunal to appoint its own expert at the request of the parties or of its own motion, according to terms of reference established by the tribunal itself. The tribunal expert will conduct his or her own inquiry into the relevant matters at issue. This inquiry may be fairly elaborate and will often include hearing from the parties or from experts nominated by the parties. The tribunal's expert then reports to the tribunal. While the parties may be given an opportunity to challenge the findings of the tribunal's expert, the tribunal expert's report to the tribunal often becomes the finding of the tribunal on the subject entrusted to the expert.[68]

It must be emphasized that under the continental European practice, an expert appointed by a judge or arbitrator is not subject to cross-examination: he is not a witness. Nor can experts appointed by arbitrators be impeached by party-appointed experts.[69]

---

[66] Richard H. Kreindler, *op. cit.,* p.202.

[67] Siegfried H. Elsing, John M. Townsend, *op. cit.,* p.60.

[68] Siegfried H. Elsing, John Townsend, *op. cit.,* p.64; Yves Derains, *op. cit.,* p.799.

[69] Olivier Bolthausen and Peter H. Acker, *op. cit.,* p.226.

C. The Decision Making Process

It is not uncommon in continental European legal systems for the arbitral tribunal to provide the parties with a pre-evaluation of the case before the tribunal issues the final decision. This interim evaluation must be specifically authorized by the parties. This approach is rooted in the German legal tradition with the view of facilitating a settlement in court.[70] The parties may then submit their comments on this interim evaluation of the case,[71] generally in their post-hearing briefs.

The cultural underpinning of this approach may be identified also in Article 15.2 of the World Trade Organization Dispute Settlement Understanding on Rules and Procedures governing the Settlement of Disputes (WTO/DSU) as follows: *"Following the expiration of the set period of time for receipt of comments from the parties to the dispute, the panel shall issue an interim report to the parties, including both the descriptive sections and the panel's findings and conclusions".*[72]

D. Settlement Discussions within the arbitral process

It is an inherent part of the civil law tradition that the judge is also entrusted with the task of preventing disputes, by helping the parties to reach an amicable settlement.[73] Article 21 of the French NCPC provides that: *"To conciliate the parties is part and parcel of the judge's task".* Likewise, Article 197 of 2008 Federal Code of Procedure stipulates that: *"the proceedings on the merits are preceded by an attempt at reconciliation before a conciliation authority".* A similar provision is contained in the Italian Code of Civil Procedure.[74] Arbitral tribunals located in continental Europe or rooted in civil law traditions might therefore – much to the surprise of common law lawyers – suggest

---

[70] German ZPO, Article 278.1

[71] WTO/DSU, Article 15.2.

[72] Doak Bishop, *op. cit.,* Duane W. Layton, Jorge O. Miranda, *Advocacy before the World Trade Organization Dispute Settlement Panels in Trade Remedy Cases,* pp.75 ff, 124.

[73] Pierre A. Karrer, *op. cit.* p.80.

[74] Italian Code of Civil Procedure, Article 183.

that they might assist the parties to resolve the dispute amicably. This behaviour will not be considered as constituting bias or pre-judgment under national laws on arbitration in civil law countries.

IV. Advocacy Ethics

A final reference shall be made to some peculiarities in the ethical rules of continental European lawyers governing relations with the client, the opposing side and towards the arbitral tribunal.

A. Relations with the Client

In addition to the rules governing confidentiality, mentioned above, a particular aspect of the relationship between continental European lawyers and their own client is the express and generalized prohibition of contingent fees arrangements. Article 3.3. of the CCBE Code of Conduct provides: *"A lawyer shall not be entitled to make a* pactum de quota litis*".* It is specified that: *"By* "pactum de quota litis" *is meant an agreement between a lawyer and the client entered into prior to final conclusion of a matter to which the client is a party, by virtue of which the client undertakes to pay the lawyer a share of the result regardless of whether this is represented by a sum of money or by any other benefit achieved by the client upon the conclusion of the matter".* The prohibition is reaffirmed in Switzerland, Germany, Austria, France, Belgium, Denmark, Finland, Norway, Portugal and Spain (but not in Italy).[75]

However, the so-called *pactum de palmario,* according to which – in addition to an hourly rate – a premium is agreed upon in case of success, is generally[76] admissible and indeed often used in important commercial cases. Under the general procedural duty to act in good faith (see *infra,* Relations with the Tribunal), lawyers have a duty to disclose to the arbitral tribunal accurate and complete cost statements and any conditions on counsel's entitled to fees.[77]

---

[75] Daniel Wehrli, *Contingency Fees/Pactum De Palmario "Civil Law Approach",* ASA Bulletin, Kluwer, 2008, Volume 26, Issue 2, pp.241 ff, 243 ff

[76] With the exception of Germany.

[77] Daniel Wehrli, *op. cit.,* p.254.

B. Relations with the Opposing Counsel and with the Tribunal

Article 11 of the 2004 UNIDROIT Principles sets out a general principle of good faith as follows: "The parties and their lawyers must conduct themselves in good faith in dealing with the court and other parties". It is specified that "[t] he parties share with the court the responsibility of fair, efficient, and reasonably speedy resolution of the proceeding. The parties must refrain from procedural abuse, such as interference with witnesses or destruction of evidence".

This duty of good faith is transposed from the duty of good faith in civil law. As mentioned by V.V. Veeder,[78] quoting Bernard Hanotiau, it is: "... a basic principle of international commercial arbitration that the parties have the duty to co-operate in good faith in the performance of their agreement as well as in the arbitral proceedings", the source of that obligation, according to Antonias Dimolitsa, residing in "the international principle of the inviolability of the arbitration agreement" that "is actually just a special application of the principle of pacta sunt servanda which, together with the parallel application of good faith, is strictly applied to arbitration agreements".

V. Conclusion

Awareness of the cultural legal differences of the participants involved in international disputes as outlined in this chapter will ensure that lawyers and arbitrators can better adapt dispute resolution procedures as they deem fit, maximizing the flexibility provided in national laws and rules on international arbitration. Cultural legal differences are immensely valuable when they are not seen as a divide, but as a means to enrich everyone's own vision of the mechanisms for international dispute settlement that are being employed or can be employed. On a practical level, lawyers will *"make the process work"* having some baseline concept of *"how things work"*.

---

[78] V.V. Veeder, the 2001 Goff Lecture, *The lawyer's Duty to Arbitrate in Good Faith*, Arbitration International, Kluwer, 2002, Volume 18, Issue 4, pp.431 ff, 438 and 439.

Chapter 22

THE UNITED STATES PERSPECTIVE AND PRACTICE OF ADVOCACY

Doak Bishop and James H. Carter

I. Introduction

For better and for worse, U.S.-trained lawyers' practice of and perspective on advocacy in international arbitration proceedings is influenced heavily by U.S. litigation experience. This advocacy training emphasizes delving deeply into the facts of a dispute and using a variety of discovery and motion procedures to shape an adversary proceeding prior to the trial or merits hearing. But this training and experience teaches advocates to leave no stone unturned in the search for the facts and cultivates what some see as an "overstated" style, in which counsel argue their case as strongly and confidently as possible, leaving little or nothing to be inferred. This contrasts sharply with the "understated" British style, in which it is often left to the judge to draw the conclusions.

Although the written brief plays an important role in American judicial advocacy, oral advocacy is at the heart of the American style of advocacy. The reason may be found in the emphasis in U.S. legal education and experience on advocacy intended for a jury system. The jury system was introduced into the United States by Great Britain when the original States of the United States were colonies. Following independence in 1776, the United States maintained and even expanded the jury system. When the jury system was in its infancy in England, many jurors (even aristocrats in the early days) could not read or write, so all evidence was introduced to the jury orally.[1] All documents, for example, were read to the jury. This

[1] Lord Wilberforce, *Written Briefs and Oral Advocacy*, 5 Arb. Int'l 348 (1989).

tradition of a largely oral trial has continued in the United States to the present day, and rules of evidence and procedure are shaped to protect lay jurors from improper exposure to categories of information that are considered unreliable or unduly prejudicial.

But in fact, very few commercial cases are tried to juries, or even tried at all. The great majority are either settled or resolved on the basis of written motion papers that usually are prepared after extensive fact discovery. Indeed, one of the prime motivators for this motion practice is a desire to resolve cases without jury trials if possible. Such trials, if used widely today in commercial disputes, would be impossibly expensive and time consuming. In addition, lawyers for defendants often fear that jury trials may result in unpredictable outcomes or even "runaway" verdicts in very large amounts.

The cases that are not tried are either settled or dismissed. Although a motion to dismiss a case may be made near its beginning, typically on the basis of legal grounds, the most common motions are those for summary judgment. Such a motion may attack all or only a portion of a case, and a decision to grant even a motion for partial summary judgment could simplify issues and lead to settlement. A summary judgment motion is based on a showing that there is no genuine issue as to any material fact in the case. There may be factual issues, but the moving party seeks to show, from the discovery that has been taken in the case, that they are not "genuine" or do not involve a "material" issue. When a motion for summary judgment is filed, it is the burden of the moving party to show as a matter of law either that the opposing party cannot meet its burden of proving an element of its cause of action or defense or that the moving party can meet its burden of establishing a claim or defense as a matter of law. This is a difficult burden, because all presumptions are against the moving party. All fact issues are presumed to be resolved in favor of the non-moving party unless established conclusively.

As a consequence, the search and development of important factual information during discovery is of paramount importance. Wholly aside from how the evidence will be used at trial, the documents brought to light from an opposing party's files become the bargaining chips in the motion practice maneuvering that either leads the parties to settle or resolves cases by court rulings. This is one reason why U.S. lawyers are accustomed to casting their nets widely to "fish" for any and all potentially useful material. The presumptions built into the U.S. legal system broadly encourage this type of discovery, perhaps in part because it does lead to a large number of settlements.

It follows inevitably from this search for facts in an opponent's files that there are likely to be disputes about the scope of that effort, leading to disputed motions seeking to compel or resist aspects of the disclosure. American lawyers are accustomed to spending significant portions of the discovery period litigating these issues.

Finally, most U.S. litigation lawyers also spend a considerable part of their time in oral depositions of witnesses, conducted in lawyers' conference rooms. The lawyer conducting a deposition is entitled to examine any adverse witness, such as an employee of an opposing party, on the basis of cross-examination questions that may be leading, accusatory and generally designed to put the witness in as bad a light as possible. The examiner's goal often is to create "sound bites" composed of short snippets of testimony in the form of admissions that can be inserted in summary judgment papers in an effort to show the presence or absence of factual issues. These depositions almost always occur outside of judicial supervision and, particularly if they are not videotaped, sometimes can lead to unrestrained verbal behavior by counsel. They also can involve formalistic disputation over questions of evidence or legal privilege. Lawyers who spend much of their time engaging in these exercises may acquire advocacy habits that carry over when they become advocates in international arbitration proceedings.

Not all U.S. lawyers who act as either advocates or arbitrators in international arbitration are trial lawyers, and thus they are not all influenced by U.S. litigation practices to the same degree. Probably most U.S. lawyers who act as counsel in international arbitrations are trained and experienced as trial lawyers in U.S. courts, although a few U.S. advocates are international business lawyers or professors. U.S. trial lawyers who are novices in international arbitration may approach document discovery with a fishing net and have at times advocated their cases too aggressively, treating the arbitral panel like a U.S. jury or seeking to "score points" on formal issues as though in a deposition rather than before decision makers. Of course, U.S. trial lawyers who are experienced in international arbitration generally recognize the differences in the styles of advocacy required before a U.S. jury or used in a deposition and what is effective before an international arbitral panel.

II. Advocacy in the United States

A. Litigation in U. S. Courts

(1) Juries

In the United States, parties have a right to a trial by jury in most cases, including civil disputes. Juries may consist of six or 12 persons (depending on local court rules) who are called randomly from the community. The qualifications to be a juror are not high: jurors are required to speak English, they must be able to read and write, and they cannot have been convicted of a felony. They also cannot be related to the parties and generally know nothing about the facts of the case. The jurors do not have expertise in the subject matter of the case or the law and (except for other experiences as a juror) have no experience in deciding cases.

Cases in the United States are tried not only to the jury, but also to a judge. The judge acts as the gatekeeper for the evidence, deciding if the offered evidence meets the "admissibility" standards of the rules of evidence, which are designed to prevent the jury from being influenced by unreliable evidence. The judge also decides the applicable law and instructs the jury as to the legal standards. The jury then decides whether the party that bears the burden of proof on a given issue has met its burden of proving facts that meet the legal standards. Thus, the jury is the decision-maker on the facts as applied to the legal standards. The judge must ultimately decide whether to enter judgment based on the jury's verdict or to set the verdict aside.

If the case is not one in which the parties are entitled to a jury, or if the jury right is waived, the trial is to the "bench," meaning the judge alone. In bench trials, judges often are more relaxed about strict enforcement of evidentiary rules designed to protect lay jurors; but generally, the procedural rules and advocacy styles are the same as in jury trials.

In a jury trial, time is precious because the jurors are called away from their jobs to hear and decide the case. They are generally paid very little for their jury service, often just enough to pay for parking near the courthouse, and they do not want to spend any more time than necessary. As a result, jurors are not generally given the documents admitted into evidence to read until they retire to deliberate at the conclusion of the evidence. Photographs may be passed to the jurors during the taking of the evidence, but generally nothing else is given to them. Jurors also, generally, are prohibited from taking notes or asking questions while the evidence is being taken. A court reporter transcribes the testimony verbatim, and if the jurors have a dispute among themselves during deliberations about what a given witness said, they may ask the judge to have the disputed testimony read to them. Because the jury is often in a hurry to decide the case at the conclusion of the evidence, it is generally believed by trial lawyers that the jurors do not usually read the documents introduced into evidence – certainly not carefully. This has led to the practice among trial lawyers of "talking" all important evidence into the record, including reading key provisions of contracts and letters, "blowing them up" into a large oversized form that can be seen and read by all the jurors simultaneously or scanning them into a computer and showing them on a large television monitor.

(2) Pleadings

Pleadings in most courts in the United States consist of what is referred to as notice pleadings. This means that the parties are not required to plead their case in detail or to plead the evidence upon which they rely to prove their case or establish a defense. They are only required to plead sufficiently to put the other side on notice of their claims or defenses. The facts are then developed by the discovery process. A complaint or petition filed by the plaintiff to initiate the case may be a brief document consisting of a few paragraphs outlining the general nature of the case and the ultimate facts, followed by a listing of the legal causes of action or legal claims being asserted.

The defendant then files an answer. In many jurisdictions, the answer must admit or deny each fact and claim asserted by the plaintiff in a rigid, numbered paragraph format, while in others a general denial may be asserted in a single sentence, denying all claims and facts. If the defendant wishes to plead an affirmative defense, it must do so in its answer by asserting the legal defenses upon which it relies. A defendant may also file a counterclaim, a cross-claim against a co-defendant, or a third-party complaint against a person who may be liable for all or part of the plaintiff's claim. Generally, a plaintiff must file an answer to the counterclaim. Amended and supplemental pleadings may also be filed by the parties, although many jurisdictions require court approval to do so.

(3) Discovery

Discovery as practiced in the United States is often misunderstood abroad. Because the legal paradigm on which the system is based is a trial conducted in a single setting of consecutive days or weeks before jurors who are taken away from their normal jobs for that time, pre-trial discovery has evolved as a means of developing the evidence and preparing the case so it can be presented to the jury quickly and relatively concisely. Pre-trial discovery does not take place before a case is filed in court, but over a period of months or even years after the pleadings are filed and before the trial commences, although in rare instances a future litigant can take a deposition with a court's permission prior to the commencement of litigation in order to perpetuate testimony relevant to a future lawsuit.

Pre-trial discovery includes an array of procedural devices and may consist of requests for disclosure, interrogatories, requests for production of documents, requests for Admissions, and depositions. Once the pleadings are filed, typically counsel for each party sends to the other party a request for disclosure of certain basic facts and documents, a set of interrogatories (written questions propounded to the opposing side, which must be answered under oath), and a request for production of documents (which typically seeks the opposing side's internal documents and correspondence by broad category). This written discovery quite often results in motions to compel answers to interrogatories or the production of documents, which may involve judicial hearings to determine whether the party to whom the discovery requests were addressed has fully responded.

A request for production of documents may ask the opposing party to produce documents described only by broad general categories. U.S. judges usually permit broad and wide-ranging document discovery unless good cause is shown to quash certain categories of the document request. Good cause may include legal privileges such as attorney-client and work product or the lack of relevance of the documents to the issues in the case. As a practical matter, U.S. courts typically put the burden on the party responding to the request to show why the documents should not be produced. This is probably due to the large docket of cases over which the judges preside and the press of time. It is considered a fail safe procedure to order the documents produced, even at considerable cost, and then sort out the consequences later. The fact that documents are produced does not mean they are admissible before the jury.

Interrogatories consist of a set of questions, usually limited to 30 questions or fewer, which one party may submit to the other. The party receiving the interrogatories must answer each question within a period of time, typically 30 days, under oath. Answers usually include extensive objections as well as some information.

Requests for admissions ask the receiving party to admit or deny a specific fact that is stated in the request. If a fact is denied but later proved to be true, the requesting party may move to recover its costs for having to prove the fact. Facts that are admitted by a party cannot later be denied or controverted without permission of the court for good cause shown. Requests for admission are conceived as a method for narrowing the scope of the trial by making it unnecessary to adduce proof of uncontroverted facts, but they often are used principally to secure absence of evidentiary objections to admissibility of documents.

In the U.S., a deposition typically consists of a proceeding in which counsel for one party orally questions either the other party or a non-party witness before a court reporter or stenographer, who transcribes counsel's questions and the witness' answers verbatim and types them up into a transcript. In larger cases, depositions often also are videotaped. Depositions are taken informally, usually in a conference room at one of the lawyers' offices. The witness, the court reporter (also sometimes a videographer) and the lawyers representing both parties are present. The parties themselves may also attend. Before answering the questions, the witness is administered an oath to tell the truth. Each side's counsel may direct oral questions to the witness, with the side initiating the deposition completing its questions before the other side begins. The witness must answer orally unless a question falls within a legal privilege (*e.g.* the attorney-client privilege or a qualified immunity for a lawyer's confidential work product). In recent years, many courts in the U.S. have begun imposing time limits on the taking of depositions, often in the range of four-to-eight hours per deposition.

Depositions may serve various purposes. Typically they are taken both to learn about facts and also to attempt to pin the witness down to a particular version of those facts that it will be difficult to alter at trial. Depositions allow oral testimony to be preserved and read – or if videotaped, played – to the jury, particularly if the witness is unavailable for the trial. Depositions may be used to impeach a witness who testifies at trial inconsistently with the testimony given during the deposition. Perhaps most importantly, depositions allow counsel to take the measure of most adverse witnesses in advance of the trial so the cross-examination of the witness at trial can be narrowed, honing in on certain areas while avoiding others.

(4) Rules of Evidence

The rules of evidence provide guidance to the trial judge as to what evidence is admissible before the jury. In the U.S., the terms "admissible" and "inadmissible" are used to describe the trial judge's ruling as to whether certain evidence may be introduced or admitted before the jury. If the evidence is admissible, the jury is entitled to see or to hear the evidence. If it is inadmissible, then the jury does not get to see or hear the evidence. If evidence is ruled inadmissible, a record may he made of the nature of the evidence for purposes of appealing the ruling at the conclusion of the trial.

In the U.S., evidence that the jury is allowed to see or hear is "introduced" into the record or "admitted" into evidence. A careful record is kept of admitted or introduced evidence so the record will be clear as to what the jury may consider in reaching its verdict. In a non-jury trial, this is the evidence that the judge will include in the record. He or she will disregard the evidence ruled inadmissible, at least in theory. Appeals may be based on whether the evidence in the record was sufficient or insufficient to justify the jury's verdict or court judgment.

The rules of evidence in the U.S. typically consist of technical rules concerning the relevance of certain types of evidence such as character and habit, settlement discussions, and liability insurance (among others); legal privileges not to provide certain evidence; cross examination of witnesses; opinion evidence such as that of expert witnesses; authentication of documents; and "hearsay." "Hearsay" is usually defined as a statement made by a person other than while testifying under oath in the case and offered into evidence to prove the truth of the matter asserted in the statement. Hearsay is a major topic consisting of a general rule that hearsay evidence is inadmissible, followed by numerous exceptions that admit hearsay testimony under certain conditions. Thus, if a witness to an automobile accident is called to testify at trial as to what one of the drivers said at the scene about the cause of the accident, that statement is hearsay. If the statement is against the interest of the person making it – the driver admitted the accident was his fault –

then it falls within an exception to the hearsay rule and is admissible. Hearsay exceptions are based on the likely credibility of the statements.

(5) Witness Preparation

Because testimony is presented to the jurors so quickly, with no opportunity for them to stop the witness and ask questions, and also because of the importance of impressions in a jury trial, witness preparation is a well-honed art in U.S. jury trials. U.S. trial lawyers consider it virtually malpractice not to carefully prepare their witnesses to testify. Such preparation may be as simple as interviewing the witnesses and telling them what questions to expect. On the other hand, it may consist of rehearsing the witness several times, going through the questions to be asked on direct examination and letting the witness practice answering with time spent refining the answers. It may also include a mock cross-examination so the witness can practice answering the key questions likely to be asked by the opposing side and to acclimate the witness to the potential hostility of the cross-examiner's tone of voice and the pointed nature of the questions. Finally, at the extreme, the preparation may consist of placing the witness in a mock courtroom with a mock jury, possibly with a video camera to tape the performance, and allowing lawyers for the side sponsoring the witness to examine and cross-examine the witness. The mock jurors are then debriefed giving their impressions of the witness and the testimony.

Of course, the trial lawyer in preparing a witness is not supposed to change the facts or the substance of the witness' testimony. The purpose of preparation is to help the witness to be more accurate, less susceptible to techniques that may be used in cross-examination that may give a misleading impression, and enable the witness to articulate the key points more directly, more concisely and more persuasively.

(6) Conclusion

Certain key elements of this system can be identified in the conduct and arguments of U.S. counsel based on their training and experience. For example, U.S. counsel sometimes argue that they should be allowed to discover the facts fully before any step viewed as an evidentiary hearing commences, assuming a single sitting at which all evidence must be adduced. U.S. counsel will often seek documents described by broad categories. They may also seek to "introduce" or "admit" documents "into evidence," which is a concept foreign to civil law. Occasionally, an American advocate may voice technical objections to the "admissibility" of evidence, based for example on the hearsay rule.

Non-U.S. counsel may consider these techniques of advocacy to be over-blown, spending too much time, effort and money on what should be a simple search for truth. But as long as a jury may render a verdict in the U.S. for millions or even billions of dollars, and do so based on impressions, the art of advocacy in the U.S. will continue to focus on these skills.

B. Domestic Arbitration in the United States

Domestic arbitrations in the United States tend to involve a flexible, hybrid procedure. American arbitrators will virtually always allow any procedures agreed by the parties when such agreement can be obtained. In rare cases, U.S. trial lawyers may agree to use the Federal Rules of Civil Procedure, the Federal Rules of Evidence, or the procedural or evidentiary rules of a given state. These rules import into the arbitration process broad document discovery, depositions and technical objections.

Even without regard to technical rules, however, domestic arbitrations in commercial cases are generally characterized by some amount of discovery prior to the evidentiary hearing (usually broad document requests and sometimes a few depositions), increasingly with specified time limits. In some cases, however, no depositions may be allowed. Since there is no jury, the hearing is usually conducted without reference to any technical rules of evidence and often with a minimum of technical objections to the admissibility of evidence. U.S. arbitrators, however, may be careful to make a record of what documents have been "admitted into evidence."

U.S. arbitrators are very reluctant to appoint independent experts, usually preferring simply to allow the parties to present their own experts. Because of the emphasis in U.S. courts on oral testimony, American arbitrators often expect all key evidence to be at least mentioned during the testimony at the oral hearing, and some allow full oral direct examination of the witnesses.

However, in recent years written witness statements have begun to be used as direct testimony. Broad cross-examination of witnesses is generally allowed, with the proviso that it be civil in tone and not argumentative. Some arbitrators will limit the cross examination to the scope of the witness' direct examination. In cases involving direct oral testimony, U.S. counsel often request two weeks or more for an evidentiary hearing. More and more often, however, U.S. arbitrators are setting shorter time limits for the evidentiary hearing, or at least imploring the parties to move the case along.

C. Lessons in Persuasion from U.S. Jury Psychology Studies

Several companies have been created in the United States in the past 25 years specializing in jury psychology for trial lawyers. These companies are mostly composed of professionals with masters and doctorate degrees in psychology. They use scientific and quasi-scientific techniques to study mock jurors and help parties and lawyers prepare for trial. Jury psychology companies offer several services to lawyers. First, they conduct focus groups with people selected to resemble the likely jury demographically. These focus groups involve lawyers (live or on videotape) role-playing both sides giving their final arguments. The focus group members then answer a written questionnaire designed to determine their individual feelings about the case, followed by a group deliberation to decide the case. The latter involves group dynamics and often points out the importance of strong personalities – opinion leaders – on the jury.

The purpose of the focus group is to determine how certain themes and arguments will be received by a jury so the lawyers can discard those that are not persuasive and refine the others.

Second, these companies conduct mock trials before a mock jury demographically similar to the expected circumstances of the real jury. Witnesses or counsel present the evidence that the real witnesses are expected to give. Sometimes, some of the real witnesses will testify, while at other times actors will be used to portray the role of a real witness and present his or her testimony. The purpose of the mock trial is to gauge how the real jury is likely to decide the case. Often, several mock juries (in one case in which one of the authors was involved, four mock juries) will be present at the mock trial but will deliberate separately to determine how demographically different juries may react to the case.

Third, jury psychology companies often include graphic artists, computer programmers and other professionals to help design charts, blow-ups of documents and computer simulations to enhance the visual effect of the case, and thus its ability to persuade.

Finally, jury psychologists may design telephone surveys to determine objective means of detecting potential jurors with certain attitudes that are relevant to the case. For example, such a survey might show that two-thirds of the people in a given geographic area who read the magazine, *Psychology Today*, have strong negative views about companies that pollute the environment. This may be important in an environmental case. These same psychologists may assist at trial in the selection of the jury, occasionally using jury questionnaires or the jurors' oral answers to the lawyers' questions during the jury selection process to rank the jurors in terms of their suitability for the case. The rankings are made, of course, from the perspective of their client's case.

From the thousands of jury studies conducted in recent years, there has developed a literature on jury psychology and what techniques may be persuasive. The most important determinant of how a juror decides a case is the juror's own values, attitudes and beliefs. Although the creation of a favorable "mood" by a lawyer during witness examination and argument may influence and move a juror to a certain extent, counsel is unlikely in a trial to change the values of the jurors. Instead, those values must be taken as the starting point of advocacy, and counsel's case should be designed to show how it implicates the juror's values, compelling a favorable result. "Know your audience" is good advice for any public speaker and critical for trial lawyers in large cases. This helps explain the growth of jury psychology studies.

From a technical perspective, the juror's values may be raised by developing themes for a party's case – no more than three or four – that serve to link the party's case to a particular value or values. Those themes may be stated in a single sentence or phrase, like "a man's word is his bond," or a theme that the respondent has been "unjustly accused." Themes are typically used in the opening statement of a case to establish what the case is about and what is at stake.

One revelation that has resulted from psychological studies of juries is that most jurors come to preliminary conclusions in a case immediately after opening statements are concluded. What is surprising is that in 80% of all trials, those preliminary conclusions never change throughout the trial. This shows that not only are first impressions important, they are disproportionately important. Once a juror has reached a preliminary conclusion, the playing field becomes tilted, and the disadvantaged party must make a stronger evidentiary showing to overcome this first impression.

Another psychological principle that is important is the theory of primacy and recency. This theory hypothesizes, and studies have confirmed, that people tend to remember best the first and last things they hear. This theory has implications for how counsel order their evidence – the order of witnesses and the order of the points they plan to make with each witness. Thus, for example, many lawyers plan each cross-examination to start and end with the two strongest points.

Eye contact is another key to persuasion. When arguing to the jury, it is critical that counsel make and maintain eye contact. This does not mean that counsel may never look away to consult notes, but continually reading from a text is usually fatal to persuasion. Eye contact demonstrates interest and sincerity in the integrity of one's positions. It also bonds the advocate with the jurors.

Since jurors are not usually allowed to take notes, ask questions or read the documents during the evidentiary phase of the case, they are passive observers in the courtroom. They are often overwhelmed by the amount of information that flows past them from the witnesses. For these reasons, jury psychologists opine that what jurors remember and base their decisions upon is only 10% the substance of the case, while 90% is based upon their impressions. In this system, the trial lawyer's role is to manage the impressions of the jury – the impressions of the facts and of the parties. The credibility of the parties, witnesses and the lawyers is important. At the conclusion of the case, the jurors may not be able to remember the details of a given witness' testimony, but they will remember that a particular witness was straightforward or evasive, honest or not credible, and these impressions will influence their decisions.

Credibility is also critical to persuasion. Jurors come to court looking for an anchor, someone on whom they can rely consistently. In a jury trial, that figure is usually the judge because of his or her neutrality and authority. But an advocate can also assume this role by demonstrating consistent honesty with the jury. This can be done, for example, by readily conceding weak points and indisputable facts. Credibility creates a receptive attitude, opening a juror's mind to what the advocate has to say, not suspending judgment on it, but at least dispensing with an initial skepticism toward a lawyer's argument.

Psychologists who specialize in jury studies have also opined that people's retention of information may go from 15% of what they hear to 85% of what they hear *and* see, because most people's dominant sense for learning is sight, not hearing. Visual aids, graphics and demonstrative evidence, such as charts, graphs, maps, diagrams, blow-ups of documents and computer animations, are used as much as possible (often at considerable expense) to focus the jury's attention and tell the party's story visually, as well as orally.

The foregoing discussion mentions only a few of the many principles of oral persuasion discovered in jury studies. Not all have significant implications for persuasion before an arbitral panel, but some do.

D. Mindset of the U.S.-Trained Lawyer

The U.S.-trained lawyer, then, comes to an international commercial arbitration proceeding with a set of mental habits based on his or her own education and experience. It commonly will include some degree of suspicion about evidence that is not taken in oral form and an expectation that virtually all witnesses will have been subjected to a round of depositions before they actually testify, a habit of robust oral presentation and a liking for visual aids, timelines and other graphic tools to assist in persuasion. As a consequence, a U.S. lawyer may require persuading that written witness statements can provide meaningful discovery in advance of the evidentiary hearing, will be read by the arbitrators and can be an effective means of presentation of direct evidence. The U.S. lawyer is likely to want to negotiate at least some degree of direct oral testimony in addition to a written statement rather than submit the witness at the outset to what the lawyer assumes will be aggressive cross-examination.

Similarly, the U.S. lawyer may be reluctant to abandon the possibility of at least some depositions prior to hearing. There may be good reason to permit depositions to preserve testimony of witnesses who otherwise could not be available at the hearing, but the U.S. lawyer will feel uncomfortable, and to some degree disadvantaged, if he or she has not actually seen the key witnesses in the other camp under the fire of a deposition examination prior to the hearing. The U.S. lawyer is likely to think in terms of visual aids, often including blow-ups of important contractual language. This runs the risk of failing to recognize that in some legal cultures arbitrators consider it relatively insulting to be confronted with enlarged contractual language that they consider sufficiently presented in the documents themselves.

Finally, the mental tool kit of the U.S. lawyer will include the concept of motions, which play such a prominent role in his or her litigation experience. This is likely to lead to challenges to document discovery in arbitration and to consideration of the possibility of a "motion" for interim measures or for separate consideration of potentially dispositive issues on the merits in arbitration.

III. Suggestions for the U.S. Lawyer Regarding Advocacy in International Arbitration

The U.S.-trained lawyer confronting his or her first international commercial arbitration usually feels to some degree uncomfortable because of the difference between its structure and typical U.S. litigation. He or she may be disconcerted by the relative absence of detailed procedural rules and time limits for a series of steps leading to "trial" and the lack of detailed rules of evidence about what is "admissible." But in fact, the skills learned in U.S. litigation can be adapted without great difficulty to the needs of advocacy in international arbitration.

A. Know Your Audience-The Values of the Arbitrators

A basic concept of persuasion is that the advocate should understand the motivation of the decision-maker and design the case to appeal to his or her values, attitudes and opinions. The paramount motivation of most arbitrators in deciding a case is probably to reach a decision of which they can be proud – one that upholds the values of the international commercial community by fairly and justly deciding the case according to the relevant law and commercial standards. If the award were published, the arbitrator would like to be able to point to it with pride to demonstrate the arbitrator's competence and wisdom. Without doubt, there is also a commercial motive – we would all like to receive payment for our time and expertise.

It is little discussed in international arbitration, but certainly understood at some level, that a tripartite panel of arbitrators from different cultures and legal systems may have values that differ to a greater or lesser degree. Without intending any stereotyping, it seems indisputable that a variety of values may be found among arbitrators from different legal systems, such as a United States international lawyer, a British barrister, a French professor of public international law, a practicing lawyer in South America, a professor of private international law from Africa, an Islamic lawyer trained in Shari'a law, and a Chinese law professor. Arbitrators from professions other than the law – engineers, accountants, and insurance or shipping executives – may bring still other values to the case. Even within each of these descriptions, differing values may certainly be found.

The generic term "values" is divided by some psychologists into three categories: (1) values, which are basic, deep-seated beliefs such as religious beliefs; (2) attitudes, which are lasting convictions that are more flexible than deeply-felt values; and (3) opinions, which may be considered as current or temporary impressions. Although religious beliefs are generally not involved in commercial disputes, they may be injected in some circumstances, such as when necessary to evidence the establishment of customary international law or in seeking interest on a debt in disputes with parties from Islamic countries.

In light of these differences, how should the advocate prepare his or her case? The first step is to realize that even among such a diverse group, there are common values. To a significant extent, the values of each country are embodied in its laws. Arbitrators who are lawyers have an understanding of – and allegiance to – the laws of their own countries. Consequently, the starting point for determining a lawyer-arbitrator's values must be the legal system in which the arbitrator is trained. Even for arbitrators who are not lawyers, the legal system of their country is quite important.

One common denominator of various legal systems is found in the private international law or conflicts-of-laws rules that may direct an arbitrator to a different country's laws. One authority has written that international arbitrators should be "internationally minded."[2] By this, he meant that international arbitrators should be open minded to other legal regimes than their own and should not be chauvinistic about their own system. Experienced international arbitrators generally have expertise in applying conflicts-of-laws rules and determining – and applying – the laws of foreign legal systems. Thus, another value that will undoubtedly vary among arbitrators, perhaps

[2] Pierre Lalive, *On the Neutrality of the Arbitrator and of the Place of Arbitration*, in Swiss Essays on International Arbitration 23, 24 (1984).

depending on their experience, is their willingness and ability to apply laws different from their own legal system.

Public international law, to the extent relevant in a given case, is also likely to represent a value of many international arbitrators. Treaties, customary international law and general principles of law[3] constitute a value of supreme importance in some international cases. Another value may be found in the customs, usages and standards of various industries and professions. Certain arbitral rules even direct that the arbitrators "shall take account" of trade usages.[4] Standard practice and the ethics of certain professions such as accounting, engineering and construction, for example, create values against which particular conduct is judged. These standards, to the extent they are articulated and understood, are probably generally honored and applied by international arbitrators.

There are other values likely to be common to experienced international arbitrators. The first is an unstated assumption that the international system of commerce and private enterprise are of substantial value to the world, and their proper functioning should be maintained by arbitrators when disputes arise. Most cases and laws assume the significance of the system of international commerce, but some – such as expropriation cases in which extreme positions have been taken – may challenge the very nature of the system. Future challenges may come from non-governmental organizations ("NGOs") that protest environmental and international trade policies and decisions of the World Bank, the World Trade Organization and even the International Centre for the Settlement of Investment Disputes ("ICSID"). A view that arbitrators should decide cases in a manner that allows international commerce to flow and businesses to prosper (at least reasonably and according to law) is likely an unstated, but important, value of most international arbitrators.

It is virtually universally recognized that contractual commitments should be honored. This value is embodied in the phrase, *pacta sunt servanda.* Of course, there are excusing factors recognized by various

---

[3] Statute of the International Court of Justice, Art. 38.

[4] ICC Rules of Arbitration, Rule 17(2); UNCITRAL Arbitration Rules, Art. 33 (3).

legal systems for failing to comply with agreements, but in general the sanctity of contracts is a time-honored value. Other values may be found in multilateral and bilateral treaties, *the lex mercatoria*[5] and general principles of law.[6]

Still further clues to an arbitrator's values may sometimes be found in religious beliefs, political beliefs, national loyalty, the economic system to which the arbitrator is accustomed, published arbitral awards,[7] published articles, speeches, papers and opinions expressed as an expert witness. To the extent possible, careful counsel should review whatever sources are available to determine the arbitrator's values, attitudes and opinions. The advent of computerized research makes this task far easier to complete than previously. This is not unlike some types of jury research.

B. Strategy and Case Preparation

(1) Strategic and Tactical Decisions

The most important – and most effective – work of the advocate in an international arbitration comes not in brilliant oratory, but in the strategic and tactical decisions made. It is the judgment of the advocate in advising the client on these decisions that may add significant value to the case. The strategic and tactical decisions of a case may include such things as what investigation to undertake, which claims or defenses to assert, which person to appoint as arbitrator, which country's (or non-national) law to assert for application to the case, which documents to use and which to

---

5 *See, e.g.,* UNIDROIT Principles of International Contract Law; Lord Justice Mustill, *The New Lex Mercatoria: The First Twenty-Five Years,* in Libor Amicorum for the Rt. Hon. Lord Wilberforce 149 (1987).

6 *See, e.g.,* Note, *General Principles of Law in International Commercial Arbitration,* 101 Harv. L. Rev. 1816 (1988).

7 *See, e.g.,* the Yearbook of Commercial Arbitration, published by the International Congress of Commercial Arbitration (ICCA) and Kluwer's. Kluwer's markets a CD containing the Yearbook. One may run an electronic search of the CD by arbitrators' names to determine the published awards of potential arbitrators.

emphasize, which witnesses to use to prove the case, which witnesses to call at the hearing to testify orally, and the order of calling witnesses and introducing documents. Should an application be made for interim measures? Are there issues that can be isolated for separate, early treatment, in the nature of a "motion?" These are among the crucial strategic decisions of the case.

Every case has both a factual and a legal component to it. There must be a legal route to accomplish the client's goal, but the engines of the case are the equities of the client's position – the "wrongs" that were or were not committed. The advocate should identify and find the means to emphasize those equities to the arbitrators. The law is generally broad and vague and can be interpreted – or in rare occasions even changed – to accommodate the equities. The stronger the equities, the more compelling the need for the law to accommodate them. One of the equities is the consequence of the wrongs, which may range beyond recoverable damages. This should not be neglected.

Some commentators in the United States have distinguished between structural equities and those that are more malleable. Structural equities are those that are unchangeable – the undisputed facts and background information. The more malleable equities are those that rely on disputed oral testimony and characterizations of the facts. In U.S. litigation, the structural equities are sometimes neglected as trial lawyers expend much of their time and effort tussling mightily to obtain admissions from the opposing party in depositions and cross-examination. But the structural equities provide the foundation for the case and should be fully developed by the advocate. Sometimes the arbitrators will decide the case based only on those equities, especially if they cannot find a principled way to decide between disputed testimony.

One example of a successful strategy comes from a well-known international arbitration counsel who noted a case in which he was approached by a client desirous of filing an international arbitration against a breaching party. But the breach occurred several years earlier. The law of the country with the closest connection to the transaction would have barred the claim as untimely. Research revealed that the laws of one country with at least some connection to the contract contained a six-year prescription or limitations period for the claim to be asserted, and the contract revealed no choice of the governing law by the parties. At the inception of the case, counsel for the claimant was able to negotiate an agreement with the respondent to apply the law of the country with the six-year prescription period, thus solving a major problem in the case.

One of the authors handled a ticklish tactical issue in a case brought by the U.S. subsidiary of an Asian state-owned company against U.S. and Peruvian companies under the Arbitration Rules of the Inter-American Commercial Arbitration Commission and the International Bar Association's Supplementary Rules of Evidence for International Commercial Arbitration. The claimant's key witness, an Asian-American, seemed unlikely to be a good oral witness at the evidentiary hearing on the merits, and yet he was a key witness, and his appearance was necessary. His testimony focused on the contract and several meetings with the respondent's key witness. The problem was solved by the ordering of the witnesses. Since the claimant was privileged to introduce its case first, claimant called as its first witness an expert on the type of international contract at issue for the purpose of walking the arbitral panel through the contract provisions. The contract provisions provided the strength of claimant's case. Once the Panel fully understood the contract, claimant then called to the witness chair the key witness of the opposing party, whom he suspected would be a poor witness and whose anticipated testimony would be inconsistent with several documents that witness had authored. With the opposing witness' credibility severely damaged on cross-examination, claimant then called its key witness, who made a better-than-expected showing, drawing strength from the problems of the opposing witness. Claimant concluded its liability case by calling its independent consultant, who was very credible and who had been present at many of the important meetings. He verified much of the testimony of the claimant's key witness. In sum, claimant framed its most important witness with an expert on the contract (a subject of the key witness' testimony), the opposing side's key (and weak) witness, and an independent consultant who could verify many of the facts. The tactical ordering of the witnesses was successful, allowing the party to make a strong first impression and soften the impact of its own problematic witness.

The arbitral equivalent of motion practice also presents strategic and tactical issues. Virtually all arbitration laws and rules now offer the possibility of requesting interim relief, and an application for some form of conservatory or injunctive order from the arbitrators at an early stage of the case can be a powerful way to bring the equities of the matter to the decision makers' attention when they are forming their critical first impressions. It may prompt a brief oral hearing much earlier in the process than otherwise would have been possible. However, the equities of the application should be compelling, or it may backfire. The standards for granting such applications are not well settled, which is a complicating factor.

Similarly, laws and rules now recognize and in some cases even encourage early attention to the possibility that specified issues – in particular, issues that could be dispositive of the entire matter – might be segregated for early arbitral decision. This is sensible and naturally attractive to the U.S. litigator trained in summary judgment motion practice; but such an application or "motion" (a term the international arbitration rules do not use) has its difficulties. The arbitration system is not well adapted to a process of organizing individual issues for decision on a separate basis, and arbitrators' experience often inclines them against this unless the parties all agree on it. Will document discovery and preparation of witness statements be confined in an initial round to this issue alone? What standard of proof would suffice to dismiss a case or a portion of a case, if the party resisting the application claims that the issue cannot be considered in isolation or that still more discovery is necessary before it can be addressed? Would segregating issues by "motion" merely extend the arbitral process if the party seeking early resolution failed in its proof?

(2) Themes

Another lesson from U.S. jury studies is that the advocate should develop one or more cohesive themes that will reverberate throughout the argument. The theme should be capable of being summarized in a single sentence or possibly even a phrase. The theme should serve as a link between the values of the decision-makers and the evidence to be presented. In fact, each theme should appeal to a particular value. The themes provide the arbitrators with an organizing principle around which to fit the details of the evidence.

The rule of thumb in U.S. jury trials is that the advocate should limit the themes to no more than three or four. More than that may unduly complicate the case and be difficult to remember. While themes are important, the details of the case should not be sacrificed to the themes. Arbitrators are detail-oriented professionals who will read the documents and memorials, usually before the oral hearing, and at the hearing they may take notes and examine the witnesses themselves. They are more likely to be persuaded by the concrete facts than by generalized statements. Nevertheless, themes may be significant as an organizing principle and as a link to values and should not be neglected.

(3) First Impressions

Still another lesson that is translatable from jury studies in the U.S. to international arbitration is that decision-makers begin reaching conclusions about a case at an early stage. In fact, jury studies have shown that jurors reach preliminary conclusions about a case after hearing opening statements by both sides, and 80% of the time those conclusions never change. This is partly because of the psychological principle of *primary* – first impressions – and the lesson of these studies is that first impressions not only count, they count disproportionately. Once the decision-maker has developed an impression of the case, it can be changed, but it is difficult. The party that made the weaker first impression is working uphill, like Sisyphus rolling the stone up the mountain.

In the authors' experience, the same principle is true in arbitration, although probably to a lesser extent.[8] Arbitrators may come to the evidentiary hearing with only tentatively formed impressions from their reading of the witness statements and materials, strive to keep an open mind through the entire evidentiary process and certainly listen to all of the evidence presented; but they develop impressions and even reach tentative conclusions with each witness presented. Many arbitrators will discuss the most recent witnesses and evidence at lunch breaks. From day to day, their conclusions may be refined and sometimes even changed significantly, but often what is heard at an earlier point is of disproportionately greater persuasive value.

This does not mean that the respondent is disadvantaged or that the last witness in the respondent's case is of no value. But if the final witness presents surprise testimony that is contrary to impressions already developed by the arbitrators, it is more difficult for the arbitrators to take the organization of the case they have developed in their minds – supporting evidence organized around certain conclusions – and completely revamp it. At that late stage, it is easier for arbitrators to discount the evidence, perhaps even believing that if it were critical, surely the advocate would have referred to it earlier. They may consider it an after-thought by the party and give it lesser weight.

The lesson from this psychological principle is that counsel should seek to structure the arbitrators' thinking at an early stage of the case – in the pleadings, the pre-hearing memorials and in the opening statements. Each succeeding pleading and memorial should include additional detail and evidence, providing a cascading effect.[9] Important claims, defenses, arguments and evidence should be introduced to the arbitrators early. If witnesses with important

---

[8] *See* Nicolas C. Ulmer, *Winning the Opening Stages of an ICC Arbitration*, 8 J. Int'l Arb. 33, 34, 36 (1991).

[9] *Id.* at 33, 36-37.

evidence will not be heard until late in the hearing, the arbitrators should be warned that this is the case. If the arbitrators know that an important witness will testify late, they will strive to keep an open mind and not allow any tentative conclusions to become too rigid. Therefore, advocates should provide the arbitrators at the outset of the hearing with an agenda for their case, including an idea of the significance of each witness.

In order to counter the effects of the psychological principle of primacy and provide due process, arbitrators should ensure they are mentally fresh for receipt of the respondent's evidence and not compress the respondent's time because of scheduling problems or weariness. It should be a fundamental tenet of due process that the arbitrators give the same careful attentiveness and alertness to the respondent's case as they do to the claimant's, and to the last witness the same as to the first.

(4) Proving the Case

U.S. trial lawyers learn to make their case through the witnesses, using them to talk every point into the record. There is no need for this in arbitration. Unlike juries in the United States, arbitrators generally read the important documents, in advance of the hearing whenever possible. Thus, questions designed to establish omissions from the documents such as, "Is there anything in the contract that addresses this point," are unnecessary and a waste of time. Counsel can save time by simply pointing the Panel to important omissions from the documents, which often can be discussed in detail in opening statements.

(5) Documentary Evidence

In countries with a strong oral tradition, such as the United States and the United Kingdom, oral testimony can be very important in a case. But even in these countries, the contemporaneous documents of the parties are often the strongest evidence. In civil law countries, which generally do not have a strong emphasis on oral evidence, the historical documents created by the parties are likely to be of overwhelming importance. With arbitrators from either system, the advocate should focus on the documents as the most persuasive weapon in his or her arsenal.[10]

But careful consideration should be given to the possibility of disputing, or not, the propriety of the scope of documentary production that is made by the other side. It is natural for a U.S.-trained lawyer to expect that there will be such skirmishing, and international arbitrators have somewhat grudgingly accommodated that process, typically through use of "Redfern Schedules" in which counsel detail their reasons for seeking or objecting to, respectively, the production of each requested document or category of documents. However, arbitrators tend to have a limited patience for a large number of challenges in this form and may react badly to conduct that can be characterized as a "fishing expedition." It may not be the best strategy to fight over every document production disagreement.

The advocate should review the documents carefully before the hearing – several times if necessary and beginning at the earliest time possible. Counsel should master the crucial documents, know their chronology, how they fit together and what the critical passages are. In this way, the advocate can select the best documents to use and can immediately point to particular documents and language to refute the opposing side's points raised at the oral hearing.

Marshaling the documents for their most effective use is another facet of advocacy. Counsel must decide first how many documents to introduce into the record. Second, if the documents are voluminous, the advocate may desire to create a set of "key" or "core" documents so the arbitrators will have both a full set of the documents and a smaller, more manageable set of key documents. Counsel may also wish to highlight the important passages in the key documents so the arbitrators can quickly find what counsel believes are the crucial points. Some arbitrators may not desire any

---

[10] Charles N. Brower, *Evidence Before International Tribunals: The Need for Some Standard Rules*, 28 Int'l Law 47, 52 (1994).

highlighting – or may perhaps even be offended by it – because they may view it as influencing their judgment of the passages or as drawing attention away from the remainder of the document. Thus, highlighting is an issue that should sometimes be raised at the preliminary hearing.

Counsel must decide how to organize the documents. The possibilities may be listed as follows: (1) introduce the documents one at a time, each separate from the others; (2) organize the documents loose within a file folder; (3) put the documents in a three-ring notebook or notebooks with a tab to separate the documents and make them easy to locate; or (4) bind the documents in a soft-cover binding such as spiral binding that will lay flat, also tabbing them. A binding that will lay flat is easier to use at the hearing at which several documents may be referred to simultaneously, sometimes requiring that one binding of documents be stacked on top of another. Three-ring notebooks are awkward for this purpose, although they allow documents to be added or taken out, while a set of bound documents does not have this advantage.

Once the means of organizing the documents is decided, the Advocate must decide the substantive organization. Should documents be organized chronologically, or by issue, or both? Another possibility is to arrange the documents in the order in which counsel intends to use them at the evidentiary hearing. For example, counsel can hand the arbitrators a separate notebook for each witness, including all the documents to be used with that witness, in the order in which they are to be used. The problem with this method is that documents are often used more than once, and documents arranged in order of use may be difficult to find after their initial introduction. The arbitrators may see different copies of the same document many times, but do not have the opportunity to work with a single document with their highlighting and notes. The authors prefer to organize a discrete set of documents chronologically, but when the documents are voluminous, they might be organized by issue. Within each bound set of documents concerning a discrete issue, the documents should generally be organized chronologically.

Within each binder or notebook, each separate document should be tabbed by number or letter, and an index should be provided in the beginning of each binder. In this way, each of a voluminous set of documents can be located quickly and easily at the hearing.

The final organizational issue is whether all documents should be included in a single unified set or whether each side should introduce its own set. Generally, arbitrators prefer a single set of documents for use. If counsel for the parties cannot agree on a single set, then the advocate should consider creating a set that would include at least most of the important documents that will be used at the hearing by both parties. It is likely that the arbitrators will most often use and refer to the single set that is most comprehensive and easiest to use, and by developing such a set, counsel may ensure that the arbitrators will use his or her set most of the time at the hearing. There are advantages to having your set used. First, counsel knows and can locate and use his or her set of documents more easily. Second, counsel can highlight his or her set of documents in advance, provided the arbitrators do not object to this procedure, resulting in the panel using a set of documents highlighted to emphasize one party's case.

Another variation is for the parties to create a unified set of documents which they agree are at least relevant to the issues, allowing both sides to highlight them, and then allowing each side to supplement this set with its own set of documents.

(6) Expert Witnesses

When presenting complex technical evidence, the good advocate should not throw the arbitrator into the deep end of the pool without swimming lessons. In complex cases, the advocate should define – and even provide a written legend to the arbitrators defining – the technical terms used by the experts. Photographs, diagrams and demonstrative evidence should be used to illustrate technical terms and processes so the Panel can visualize them. Once the arbitrators visualize the concepts, verbal descriptions can be understood and can refine them. But the advocate should provide sufficient background in the experts' reports, pre-hearing memorials, opening statements and the early moments of the experts' oral testimony, gradually building the arbitrators' knowledge and understanding before honing in on the disputed points. An alternative approach is to proceed immediately to the disputed points, pausing then to provide background on each technical point sufficient to fully understand it before moving to the next.

Expert witnesses should be selected carefully for their expertise in the particular issues of the case. But if they are expected to give oral testimony, they should also be selected for their ability to articulate clearly their opinions, and even more importantly the reasons for their opinions. It is the reasoning of the expert that sells his or her opinions. The experts should also be quick enough on their feet that they will not be confused during cross-examination.

(7) Mock Arbitrations

In significant arbitrations in the U.S. and internationally, counsel have begun to use techniques similar to mock trials for jury cases in which mock arbitrators – with similar backgrounds to the real arbitrators – are hired, and mock presentations are made to them. The mock arbitrators then either talk directly to counsel about their views of the case, assessing the strengths and weaknesses, or conduct mock deliberations, which may be videotaped or conducted in a room with a one-way mirror so counsel can view the deliberations.

Counsel also can determine the likely views of the real arbitrators on witness testimony. Even if the witnesses are not presented, a mock arbitration can be held in which counsel talks the mock arbitrators through the evidence and then obtains their impressions of the parties' cases and arguments.

C. Written Advocacy - Memorials

Because most arbitrators are likely to be visual learners – people whose predominant learning sense is reading – and also because of the lack of a strong tradition of oral advocacy in many civil law countries, the most important opportunity for persuasion often lies in the written argument – the memorials and briefs – rather than in oral advocacy. Thus, counsel should fully argue the case in the memorials and not leave important points solely for oral advocacy. The memorials provide the best and fullest opportunity to argue the case and persuade the arbitrators.

One issue that arises is what to emphasize in argument. Memorials of lawyers from civil law countries tend to focus more on the law, while U.S. counsel's briefs tend to emphasize the facts. These tendencies reflect what is considered most problematic – and most important – to decision-makers from their respective legal systems. To a significant extent, it reflects the difference in how the law is established in civil and common law countries. In the U.S., the doctrine of *stare decisis* makes case law binding, at least when the facts are substantially similar, and therefore U.S. lawyers concentrate on arguing the few cases that are factually most similar. Their efforts tend to be bent toward showing that their case is factually analogous – and not distinguishable – from previous precedent. In the civil law, the law is often established by debating the applicable legal theory by reference to the treatises of reputable legal scholars, often tracing the theory from the Roman law through the Napoleonic Code and on to the civil or commercial code of the relevant country. Much space is taken with the policy reasons for applying one code provision instead of another. The writings of leading scholars are often deemed more persuasive than case law, except in the few instances in some civil law countries when case law may be considered as binding precedent.

It follows that counsel should know the decision-maker. If the arbitrators are all from the U.S., counsel may wish to focus briefs more on the facts and the published case law and develop them more fully. If all arbitrators are from civil law countries, the lawyer should emphasize the theory of the law and develop the legal argument in depth. If the arbitrators are mixed – from both legal systems – the advocate should develop both the law and the facts in detail, discussing in depth the legal theory and citing case law, and not neglect either.

Another question for the advocate is the style to use in the memorials. U.S. lawyers tend to use a very argumentative style in which counsel's points are made in a highly adversarial and confrontational manner, focusing on one side of the argument, and often "overstating" their points, leaving nothing to be inferred by the decision-maker. In some civil law countries, on the other hand, advocates craft their memorials in a more academic, non-argumentative style. Once again, the advocate needs to know the audience. If the arbitrators come from a tradition in which the academic style of memorial is common, then counsel should write in a non-argumentative style. If the arbitrators are U.S. lawyers, however, then an argumentative style may be more appropriate. And if the arbitral panel is mixed, then counsel should consider a compromise, or perhaps use a non-argumentative style. A non-argumentative format is likely to be acceptable to all arbitrators, while an inflammatory style may be considered offensive by some arbitrators. Thus, the academic style may be a suitable compromise style for mixed panels.

D. Oral Advocacy

(1) Credibility

The credibility of the parties – and of counsel representing them – may be of great significance to the arbitrators in deciding the case.[11] Particularly in a complex case involving technical issues and close questions, the arbitrators may be more trusting of the arguments made by a party or counsel who has established credibility with the Tribunal. Counsel may create credibility by showing competence, and even mastery, of the subject matter of the dispute, honesty in dealing with the facts and law (including the citation of facts or law that are not helpful to the party's case but that are necessary for a full understanding, and conceding a weak point when necessary),[12] sincerity, and a fair approach to issues of procedure and evidence.

---

[11] *See* Nicolas C. Ulmer, *Winning the Opening Stages of an ICC Arbitration,* 8 J. Int'l Arb. 33 n.3, 34-36, 42 (1991).

[12] *Id.* at 43.

Similarly, a party may establish credibility by displaying honesty and competence and by being forthcoming and straightforward, not evasive, in answering the questions of the Tribunal.

The importance of credibility cannot be overstated. If one party establishes greater credibility than the other, it is natural for the arbitrators to trust that party. Trust, in turn, can be very important when the arbitrators confront close or technically difficult issues. In one case in which one of the authors acted as counsel, both sides' counsel were asked a question by the Tribunal. The author answered strongly, disagreeing with opposing counsel. After proceedings were adjourned for the day, technical experts opined that the author's statement was not entirely correct. The issue was an important one to the outcome of the case, and it was tempting to let a strong statement stand. But candor is a key value necessary for the proper functioning of the international arbitral system, and credibility of counsel is crucial to persuasion. The next day, the author asked for leave at the outset to make a statement and, recalling the questions to the Tribunal, stated that his previous answer was incorrect and opposing counsel's statement was correct. In this way, credibility was maintained, and the Tribunal was not misled. The author's case ultimately prevailed.

(2) Organization and Precision in Presentations

In all oral presentations, counsel should be thoroughly prepared, well organized and demonstrate a mastery of the facts and documents. To accomplish this, counsel must meticulously review the key documents and witness statements more than once, creating a chronology of major events and noting important passages. Counsel must also understand the relationships of the critical facts and documents to one another and to the applicable law. A good command of the facts demonstrates expertise and builds credibility with the arbitrators.

When counsel has completely mastered the facts, he or she should prepare the presentation carefully, always keeping in mind the goal of persuasion. Arguments should be logically organized and clearly stated.[13] Obfuscation and lack of clarity can be fatal to the efforts of persuasion. Counsel should also be as precise as possible at all times in dealing with the facts and arguments, avoiding the rhetoric of generalizations.[14] Concrete facts are far more persuasive than general observations and conclusory statements.

The facts and law should be stated as strongly as they reasonably allow, but avoiding overstatement and exaggeration. Key verbs, adverbs and adjectives should also be selected with care to create word pictures and mood. Precise word selection should not be overlooked. As Mark Twain once said, "The difference between the right word and the almost right word is the difference between lightning and the lightning bug."

(3) Opening Statements

Counsel should view the opening statement as one of the prime moments in the case for persuasion. The arbitrators are mentally fresh and interested. The Tribunal is eager to understand the case. This is the opportunity to make a strong first impression and structure the way the Tribunal views the case. Moreover, in many arbitrations, final oral argument is not allowed, instead permitting post-hearing memorials to serve this purpose. Thus, opening statement may provide the only opportunity to orally argue the case.

The advocate should accomplish three goals in the opening: (1) provide a road map of the case so the Tribunal will understand the issues and what evidence and witnesses will be forthcoming; (2) provide important background information necessary to understand the case such as the definition of technical terms, explanations of technical standards, tests and procedures, diagrams to visualize the technical matters, and an explanation of the key terms of the contract; and (3) persuade the arbitrators that the party

---

[13] Jack J. Coe, Jr., *International Commercial Arbitration: American Principles and Practice in a Global Context* §9.12.1 at 249 (Transnational Publishers, Inc., 1997).

[14] *See generally* Stanton Belland, *The Iran-United States Claims Tribunal; Reflections on Trying a Claim,* 1 J. Int'l Arb. 237, 247-48 (1984).

has a meritorious case by telling a compelling story that puts the evidence into an overall structure, quoting some of the best evidence and demonstrating the compelling nature of your logic and arguments.

Making a strong first impression can influence the way the Tribunal views the case. If the Tribunal believes at the inception that you have a strong case, it may influence how they view the witnesses – their credibility, the plausibility of their story and the strength of their testimony. A strong first impression can skew the Tribunal's impression of the entire case. A weak first impression can do the same – to your disadvantage.

The advocate should consider beginning with a list of the issues the Tribunal must decide. With that understanding, the Tribunal can then listen to the facts, recognizing what is important and why. Counsel should next tell the story of what happened. The story should be told from the client's point of view, usually chronologically, although there may be good reason to skip around at times. From time to time, counsel may pause to explain technical terms or draw the Tribunal's attention to the language of the contract. Visual aids can be used to assist the Tribunal in understanding technical issues.

Try to avoid short time limits for opening if you have a story that benefits from a fuller telling. The story should be supported whenever possible by actually showing the precise language of key documents and testimony. The more specific and concrete the evidence, the more persuasive it will be. If the structure of the contract is important to an understanding of how its key provisions were intended to operate, walking the arbitrators through the document can be useful at the outset. Experienced arbitrators are accustomed to "lawyer talk" in which issues are "clear," evidence is "compelling" and the opposing witnesses are not credible. Arbitrators are likely to disregard, or at least discount, such U.S.-style "lawyer talk" – unless it is supported by concrete evidence. To be persuasive, avoid the lawyer talk – show, don't tell.

(4) Direct Examination of Witnesses

In most international cases, all direct testimony of witnesses takes the form of written witness statements rather than oral direct examination of the witness. Oral testimony of the witness may be limited to cross-examination and rehabilitation or rebuttal examination by the sponsoring party's counsel. This saves time at the oral hearing, but it sometimes leads to tactical problems for the sponsoring party. If the Panel hears only the cross-examination and rebuttal, but not an oral direct examination, some counsel are concerned that psychologically the Tribunal may give the oral cross-examination greater weight than the written testimony. Counsel therefore often ask that, while all direct testimony has been reduced to writing, the witness nevertheless should be allowed to "warm to the seat" by responding to a limited direct mini-examination by the sponsoring party's counsel to highlight the key points.

When full oral direct examination is allowed, counsel should consider certain rules, partly to save time at the evidentiary hearing and partly to increase the persuasive effect of the evidence. First, counsel should consider introducing the witness' written resume or curriculum vitae in order to save time, but orally highlighting a few key events in the witness' background either by counsel's or the witness' narrative or by question and answer. The witness can be asked to verify his or her resume. Second, the witness should be asked to verify the accuracy of any written statement or expert report. At the very outset, and in a matter of seconds, counsel has technically made a relatively full record with the witness and can move to the most persuasive points. Of course, if the written statement or report needs to be supplemented or changed, doing so at the outset may be best in order, for example, to establish credibility. Orally verifying a resume, witness statement or expert report at the outset of a witness' testimony is likely to ease any concerns the arbitrators may have about the accuracy of and their ability to rely on the written evidence and allow them to concentrate on the oral testimony.

Counsel should have the direct examination well organized and prepared in advance, with any documents to be used with the witness within arm's reach and in the order to be used. The Tribunal and opposing counsel should be informed at the beginning of the witness' testimony of the documents to be used so they can pull their copies and be prepared, unless counsel intends to hand copies of the documents to each as the need arises.

The direct examination should be crisp and concise, emphasizing the key points. The examination should move as quickly as possible consistent with the Tribunal understanding the points. Counsel should watch the Tribunal during the examination to a reasonable extent, and if an arbitrator appears perplexed, counsel should stop and have the witness elaborate upon a point. If the Tribunal takes notes, counsel should not move too quickly for the arbitrators to keep up the pace. When documents are used with a witness, the advocate should pause until all Tribunal members have found the passage in the document upon which the testimony will focus. The advocate should always remember the audience – if the play moves so slowly that the audience gets bored or so quickly that they cannot keep up, then counsel and the witness are merely talking to themselves.

If the examination is lengthy, even the most alert arbitrator will have times when his or her attention will wane. Counsel should ensure that the key questions and answers are not lost in the background noise of a long day. Pausing for a few moments before a crucial question changes the rhythm of the questioning and will likely result in the arbitrators turning their attention to counsel to determine the reason for the halt. This will re-establish attention. Abraham Lincoln, in his prime as a trial lawyer in Illinois, was renowned for this technique. Using verbal headlines to tell the Tribunal something important is about to happen is another way of regaining attention. "Mr. Smith, the next question goes to the key issue in this case and is very important. Please think about it carefully before you answer." The Tribunal will likely tune in and pay careful attention to the next question.

Partly because of the principles of primacy and recency – people remember best the first and last things they hear – the advocate should carefully design the examination to begin and end on two of the most important points to be made with the witness. Beginning and ending strongly are important for persuasion. A good examination should not just trail off into matters of little or no import. One of the strongest points should be saved for the conclusion of the examination.

In the evidence itself, both written and oral, whenever possible, the witness should tell his or her story in narrative form. Much of the story should be chronological, told from the single point of view of the witness and should state the little details that lead to an inference that the facts are plausible and credible. The motives of the witness in key events should not be overlooked because, even if not critical – or even relevant – to the issue to be decided, decision-makers' curiosity usually leads them to want to know why a person acted as he or she did in order to fill out the story. Also, in that stated motive an arbitrator may find credibility and plausibility to support the remainder of the testimony.

(5) Cross-Examination of Witnesses

A noted professor of trial procedure and evidence in the United States developed what he called the "Ten Commandments of Cross Examination."[15] Those "commandments," which are well known to U.S. trial lawyers, are:

1. Be brief, short, and succinct (limit on juries capacity to acquire information). Never make more than three points on cross-examination.
2. Use short questions and plain words.
3. On cross-examination never ask anything but leading questions. Put words in the witness' mouth.
4. Be prepared. Never ask a question to which you do not know the answer. This is not the time to find out what the case is about.

---

[15] Irving Younger, *The Art of Cross Examination*, A.B.A. Litig. Sec. Monograph No. 1 (1976).

5. Listen to the answer.
6. Don't quarrel with the witness.
7. Avoid repetition – never permit the witness to repeat what he said on direct examination (if jury hears it twice they probably will believe it).
8. Never permit the witness to explain anything.
9. Avoid the "one question too many."
10. Save the ultimate point for summation (pull it together and explain it on summation).

Implicit in Commandments 3 and 8 is that an advocate never asks a hostile witness a "why" question, that is, a question beginning with the word "why," unless the cross-examiner knows the answer. Otherwise, the witness is allowed an open-ended question to explain his or her position. This is the anathema of artful cross-examination in the United States, where counsel attempts to control the jury's "impression" of the witness and the testimony on cross-examination by limiting the witness' ability to state and explain his or her position.

Cross-examination of witnesses is an important aspect of advocacy in the U.S. and British legal cultures, but many countries employ little or no cross-examination in their judicial systems. Thus, the practice of cross-examination varies widely from country to country. Certainly, the Ten Commandments of cross-examination in U.S. courts are not entirely applicable in international arbitration. In particular, the wisdom of saving ultimate points for summation is doubtful. Nevertheless, certain rules for cross-examination may be derived from the practice of international arbitrations.

First, cross-examination should be conducted in a civil and respectful manner.[16] This is so partly because it is the proper way to conduct oneself. But it is also correct because a disrespectful or discourteous manner is offensive not only to the witness, but also to

[16] Paul Friedland, *A Standard Procedure for Presenting Evidence in International Arbitration*, 11 (4) Measley's Int'l Arb. R. 25, 28-29 (April 1996).

the arbitrators. The slashing, sometimes sarcastic, style sometimes used by U.S. trial lawyers in depositions and before juries has little place in an international arbitration. The only exception might be a situation in which a witness is caught in a series of material lies, and the lies are obvious to all observers. Even then, however, lack of courtesy may undermine the helpful contrast between the respectful interlocutor and the dishonest witness. In most situations, of course, the arbitrators want to believe that witnesses are honest, and they will have little tolerance for counsel abusing a witness in a strained attempt to create an impression to the contrary. Of course, there is no place in international arbitration for attempts to intimidate a witness, and if an interpreter is necessary for a witness, the examiner's tone of voice will likely be lost in any event.

Second, cross-examination should generally be brief and to the point. The days of a trial lawyer like Earl Rogers cross-examining a witness for four days just to ask eight key questions at the end when the witness was tired are long gone in American courts and never existed in international arbitration.[17] Counsel should focus on three or four points to make in cross-examination, seldom more. Although some set-up questions may be necessary to make a point, counsel should get to the point as soon as possible. Cross-examination is not the time for a fishing expedition to learn what the case is about. A cross-examination that rambles or fails to make points is not likely to be well received by the arbitrators. The authors, when serving as arbitrators, have often heard other members of the Tribunal say at breaks after a long and futile cross-examination that they thought the purpose of cross examination was to make points, not just fill time.

Third, counsel should know the purpose for examining the witness and have a well thought-out plan, complete with a contingency plan and an exit strategy, before commencing. If there is no purpose to be gained by cross-examination, don't ask any questions. Remember, things can always get worse; cross-examination can harm the examiner's case. The advocate should have a purpose for every question posed to the witness. There are generally three

[17] Adela Rogers St. Johns, *Final Verdict* 325-29 (Signet 1972).

purposes for cross-examining a witness: (1) to bring out favorable facts neglected by the opposition; (2) to impeach the credibility of the witness, often with a prior inconsistent statement, if it truly is inconsistent; or (3) to establish background facts or authenticate documents, when necessary.

Fourth, the advocate should rarely plan on making his or her case by cross-examination. In U.S. practice, the predominant custom is to concentrate on obtaining admissions from opposing parties by forceful cross-examination. These admissions become a central point of the case, either in motions or at trial. By contrast, a party's case is usually carried in an international arbitration by its own witnesses and documents. This is due in part to the lack of pre-trial discovery, such as depositions, in international arbitration. Because of the lack of depositions, there is a reduced opportunity to discredit witnesses. For these reasons, the advocate should keep cross-examination in perspective and rarely plan on it being the key to the case.

Fifth, the force of a good cross-examination is found in the substance of the questions asked. They should be carefully thought out and meticulously phrased to be very pointed, like a sharpened scalpel, not a blunt instrument. The questions should go to the very point to be made. They should be simple and clear in order to avoid any claims of misunderstanding. A carefully calculated question can instantly raise the arbitrators' eyebrows in anticipation of exposing inconsistencies or unconsidered difficulties with the witness' positions.

Sixth, the advocate must exercise some level of control over the witness. It is within the Tribunal's discretion, of course, as to how much or how little to allow a witness to say in response to a question from counsel; but the Tribunal should not allow cross-examination to be frustrated by speech-making, filibustering and evasion by the witness. The advocate is justified in insisting that the witness answer a legitimate question, and that he do so directly and responsively and not repeat his position endlessly to carefully circumscribed questions that do not inquire about his position. This does not necessarily require a "yes" or "no" answer to every question because if the answer would be incomplete or misleading as the question is posed, then the Tribunal should allow the witness to explain the answer.

Seventh, be prepared for the unexpected answer. Without a deposition of the witness in advance as practiced in United States litigation, counsel must cross-examine without knowing how the witness will answer many questions posed. Thus, cross-examination should often be conducted in the British style, as the authors understand it, with the first question of a line of examination being general and tentative, allowing counsel to retreat gracefully if nothing can be obtained. The authors usually save a failsafe question that must almost certainly be answered in a manner that is helpful to the examiner's case in the event an unexpected and unhelpful answer is given to a question. The examiner then has the next question ready to ask the witness immediately and without hesitation to get the examination back on the right track and is not lost at sea. Moreover, the impression that the examiner is winning the battle with the witness is not lost or unduly disrupted.

Eighth, the advocate should begin and end the cross-examination with the two strongest points that he or she is confident can be successfully made. Since arbitrators generally take notes, this principle is less important in an arbitral proceeding than in a U.S. jury trial, but it still has force. The arbitrators are freshest and listen most carefully at the outset of an examination and are likely to be most receptive at that time. Moreover, the first questions set the tone of the cross-examination. The Tribunal should see immediately that the questioner is going to get to the point quickly and make points with the witness. Similarly, a pointed ending marks the examination as much more persuasive than a cross-examination that limps to a close.

Ninth, avoid arguing with the witness or asking questions that are primarily argumentative in nature. Proper cross-examination is factual in nature. Ask questions designed to bring out the facts. Save argument for the proper time.

Finally, listen to the answers of the witness. Good follow-up questions can be asked if the questioner listens to the witness instead of thinking ahead to the next question while the witness is answering. Listening carefully means noting any evasions, subtle distinctions or nuances in the answer that deserve further scrutiny.

(6) Demonstrative and Graphic Evidence

In the United States, it is commonplace to use demonstrative and graphic evidence in trials to juries. It is also quite common for graphic evidence to be used in arbitration proceedings in the United States. Demonstrative and graphic evidence may include charts, graphs, maps, diagrams, schematics, time lines, physical evidence, documents that are enlarged so everyone in the hearing room can focus on a single document, documents available on a computer so they can be shown on a video screen, use of an "Elmo" (which contains an overhead camera to show documents on a video screen in real time), an overhead projector, computer animations or simulations and models.

The study of demonstrative and graphic evidence is so advanced in the U.S. that psychologists who specialize as jury consultants purportedly have identified locations and colors as key aspects. For example, most people in the U.S. – where people read from top left to the bottom right – will direct their attention first to the top left of a chart. Therefore, the first message should be located in the top left-hand side of the chart. Psychologists have also identified colors they claim are associated with certain feelings. Particular colors are used for specific messages. But counsel should remember that these lessons may be – and probably are – culture-bound and not universal.

The general rules for effective visual aids created for a jury trial in the U.S. include the following: (1) they must contain a single, clear message; (2) they should contain no distractions or ambiguities; and (3) they should be appealing, including bold colors, use of contrasts and distinctive shapes or objects. The latter rule is of far less importance in an international arbitration.

Use of demonstrative and graphic evidence in international arbitration is not common, although it is growing as more U.S. counsel use it in international proceedings.[18] Some Continental and British arbitrators have indicated a disdain for such evidence. One of the authors, participating in an arbitration before English barrister

---

[18] *See generally* Stanton Belland, *The Iran-United States Claims Tribunal: Some Reflections on Trying a Claim*, 1 J. Int'l Arb. 237, 249 (1984).

arbitrators, saw American counsel for the opposing party instructed to take down a visual aid blowing up language from the contract, which the arbitrators found insulting. In this atmosphere, counsel should be careful and conservative about the introduction of such evidence. If in doubt, ask the arbitrators at the preliminary hearing about their attitudes towards its use.

(7) Language Interpretation

When a simultaneous translation of counsel's argument by an interpreter is required because all parties do not speak the same language, counsel must be conscious that his or her direct words will not be heard by all persons in the hearing room – including one or two of the arbitrators. To be persuasive in a simultaneous interpretation is far more difficult than when speaking to the arbitrators directly.

If possible, counsel should prepare the interpreter in advance. Review the material and even the presentation, at least in concept, with the interpreter. Review the specific words of the presentation when possible, especially any technical terms. If it is possible for counsel to select the interpreter, this should be done carefully to ensure competence in the technical translations.

Counsel should avoid rapid speech and should carefully select words to ensure they will translate properly.[19] In particular, counsel should avoid idioms, slang and metaphors that may be well known in one culture, but are unknown or maybe misunderstood in another. This is equally true for written advocacy. Precise and clear word selection will generally serve the advocate better than colorful regional speech.

(8) Closing Argument

Closing argument is an important part of U.S. litigation, for it usually provides the last message that counsel will be able to convey

---

[19] Jack J. Coe, Jr., *International Commercial Arbitration: American Principles and Practice in a Global Context* § 9.12.1 at 249 (Transnational Publishers, Inc., 1972).

to a jury before the judge instructs them for their deliberations. In a bench trial or arbitration, there may be post-hearing memorials or briefs. In such cases, closing argument will not be the final word. In arbitration, sometimes the question of whether to have oral argument, post-hearing memorials, or both, is left until late in the evidentiary hearing. If the arbitrators decide to hear oral argument, it may be on short notice, perhaps even at the end of a number of days of hearing. In such circumstances, there may be temptation for counsel to forego a hastily prepared oral argument and rely entirely on the post-hearing memorials.

This temptation normally should be resisted. Every opportunity to speak directly to the arbitrators about the issues should be welcomed. Closing argument can help to address specific issues that the arbitrators may have on their minds while the evidence is fresh. Also, arbitrators may deliberate and come to at least some provisional decisions about the case promptly following the close of the hearing, when they are together at the hearing site. It is dangerous to let this happen without taking advantage of the opportunity for closing argument.

IV. Conclusion

There are significant differences in the styles of advocacy necessary to succeed before a U.S. jury and before an international arbitral panel. Nevertheless, there are lessons to be learned from advocacy in the U.S. jury system that can be applied to the art of persuasion in international arbitration. Some of those lessons derive from the studies of jury decision-making by psychologists. The thoughtful advocate should be aware of those lessons and the techniques necessary to make use of them. Careful and prudent employment of those techniques in the service of the merits can substantially aid in the presentation of the case and will go a long way in helping the advocate succeed in the task of persuasion.

Chapter 23

THE ASIAN PERSPECTIVE AND PRACTICE OF ADVOCACY

Christopher Lau

I. Introduction

In no other region in the world is there as great a diversity in race, language, culture, religion and legal systems as in Asia. India alone lists twenty-one distinct languages with twenty-one distinct cultures and nine religions. Western colonialism in Asia, as elsewhere, left a legacy of western law, which over time has merged with Asian legal traditions and continues to influence many Asian legal systems with varying degrees of intensity and visibility.[1] Whereas arbitration as a tool for resolving disputes in Singapore and Hong Kong is widely used, in other Asian jurisdictions such as Vietnam, the use of arbitration is relatively new. Most Asian states have ratified the two major international arbitral Conventions,[2] some states have adopted or adapted in their arbitration legislation the UNCITRAL Model Law

---

1 H. Patrick Glenn, "Legal Traditions of the World: Sustainable Diversity in Law", at p. 329

2 To date, the New York Convention on Recognition and Enforcement of Foreign Arbitral Awards (1958) has been ratified in: Afghanistan, Australia, Bangladesh, Brunei Darussalam, Cambodia, India, Indonesia, Iran, Kazakhstan, Kuwait, Kyrgyzstan, Laos, Malaysia, Marshall Islands, Mongolia, Nepal, New Zealand, Pakistan, Philippines, People's Republic of China (PRC), Singapore, South Korea, Sri Lanka, Thailand, Uzbekistan and Vietnam. The Washington Convention 1965 has been ratified by the following countries: Afghanistan, Australia, Bangladesh, Brunei Darussalam, Cambodia, Fiji, India, Indonesia, Japan, Kazakhstan, Kuwait, Kyrgyzstan, Laos, Malaysia, Micronesia, Nepal, New Zealand, Pakistan, Papua New Guinea, Philippines, PRC, Samoa, Singapore, Solomon Islands, South Korea, Sri Lanka, Thailand, Timor-Leste, Tonga, Turkmenistan and Uzbekistan.

on International Commercial Arbitration but others have not[3]. Major political changes in China, not only opened its market to foreign investors but also brought along arbitration as a preferred dispute resolution mechanism. However, "in the light of the striking mosaic of physical, economic, linguistic, cultural and political differences it is hardly surprising that there are substantial variations in legal systems and approaches to dispute resolution across the continent".[4] This chapter which discusses advocacy in Asia is written in the context of such Asian diversity.

II. The Art of Advocacy

Advocacy as Socrates points out "[...] is not [to] teach juries and other bodies about right and wrong – [the orator] merely persuades them".[5] International arbitration absent the procedural rules and legal guidelines that one finds in litigation, enables counsel comparative and greater freedom in the use of the tools of persuasion.

Put simplistically, the art of advocacy before a tribunal is nothing more than putting a party's case across as clearly and as convincingly as the factual matrix or the evidence and the law permit in order to persuade the tribunal of the merits of a party's case. The art of persuasion in advocacy when stripped of its frills, it is suggested, comes down to three essential principles. First, counsel cannot force the tribunal to accept his submissions, as it is indisputable that coercion or force often has the opposite effect. Secondly, counsel must ensure that the case he advances is either credible or plausible in that it must contain a modicum of logic and it must be supported by law and the facts. Thirdly, the argument is more likely to be accepted if it is presented positively and is not contrary to the tribunal's basic beliefs.

---

3 States that have passed national arbitration legislation on the basis of the UNCITRAL Model Law are: Australia, Bangladesh, Cambodia, India, Hong Kong Special Administrative Region, Macao Special Administrative Region, Japan, New Zealand, Philippines, Singapore, Sri Lanka and Thailand.

4 Michael Pryles/Michael J. Moser, "Introduction" to the Asian Leading Arbitrators' Guide to International Arbitration, p. 2

5 See James Boyd White, *The Ethics of Argument: Plato's Gorgias and the Modern Lawyer*, 50 U. Chi. L. Rev. 849 (1983).

These three principles are equally applicable to arbitrations conducted in Asia. But it is important when applying these principles to realize that different cultural influences may be at play when a party to or a witness in the proceedings is Asian. Given that communicating successfully with someone from one's own background can be difficult enough in the best of times, communicating without any regard to the different cultural influences at play can only lessen the probabilities of success.

III. Mind the Gap!

Whilst it is stating the obvious, a gap does exist between cultures in Asia and elsewhere and even within Asia. In East Asia, the basic aspects of Taoism and Confucianism still define how East Asians behave and communicate.[6] These aspects can be conveyed in three Chinese words: *li*, *mianzi*, *guanxi*[7]. The same concepts, although in a different cultural context, also describe behaviour patterns of other Asian cultures such as Indian and South Asian in general.

Reasonable English equivalents for *li* are "propriety" or "virtue", conveying a sense of the individual's proper behaviour and obligations in society. The requirements of *li* are largely influenced by Confucius' model of society which explicitly defines relationships (business, family, social, etc.) in a hierarchical manner. The stress on deferring to those higher-up in the hierarchy largely accounts for the instinctive unwillingness of East Asians to confront authority. The same used to be true of all South Asians, Hindu, Muslim, Buddhist or Sikh though to a lesser degree today because of Western influences on the middle classes but the instinctive unwillingness remains for most rural people. Due to the effect of *li* on business life, individual workers in East Asia tend to adopt the goals and behaviour of their

---

[6] One must keep in mind that these are tendencies, not ironclad rules. Individual East Asians also vary, of course, and, cultural norms are always changing.

[7] The paragraphs that follow under this heading, when not otherwise indicated, is based on the article "*Through the Wall: A cross-cultural guide to doing business in China*" by David M Lenard, published in Asia Times (June 2006).

leaders to a much greater extent than is normally the case elsewhere. This applies in South Asia as well. In East Asia and for most rural people in South Asia, other manifestations of *li* include a certain formality in social relations such as speaking softly, in the need to avoid a confrontational approach that brings conflicts into the open, and not losing one's temper or making physical gestures such as pounding one's fist on the table. The typical result of such behaviour is that it both alienates the other person and results in a loss of face.

The word *mianzi* is known in the West as the concept of "saving face", the essence of which is that East Asians expect, at all times and in all ways, to be treated according to their position in the hierarchies they personally occupy. This was also true of all South Asia until at least 1947 and of Pakistan, which is less democratic than India, even today. In politics and hierarchical organisations in India as in for example, the Indian defence forces and to a certain extent in the Indian civil services, this persists even today. Asians are extremely sensitive to any behaviour they perceive as implicitly diminishing their position. On loss of face, East-Asians may become cold, distant and unhelpful. Another aspect of this concept is to avoid having to say "no" to a direct request because doing so is perceived as helping the other person to save face and to preserve harmony. The unwillingness to say "no" is likely to create communication problems, especially with cultures at the other end of the bluntness-tact scale. If a stranger, for example, asks for road directions in India or in Pakistan, he is more likely to receive imprecise road directions than to hear the person asked admit that he does not know the way. To communicate effectively, it is necessary to become attuned to some of the most common verbal and non-verbal substitutes for "no", such as a pledge to "seriously consider", a change of the subject or negative body language. Certain gestures on the other hand, may mean quite the opposite. In India, for example, a shaking of the head in response to a comment or even a question does not mean "no". Instead, it means "yes" or "I agree". Cultural sensitivity is needed for effective communication. Patience, firmness as well as cultural sensitivity will in most cases work better than open confrontation.

Guanxi can be defined as "a special personal relationship in which long-term mutual benefit is more important than short-term individual gain".[8] A related issue is *collectivism* which describes a tendency to define an individual rather by his membership to a group (e.g. family, clan, town, school class, company, section, official bureau) than by his achievements. There is a reciprocal obligation in that the group is expected to support the individual for which the group, in return, expects unquestioned loyalty. *Collectivism* is still the rule in the more backward parts of India, where people are still identified by their religion, caste, town, region or mother tongue but less by school or college class membership which following British tradition is a very upper middle class concept. Being employed by a company in South Asia, except in a few industrial towns, is not a South Asian identity creator and an employee in the civil services usually does not identify himself with the bureau with which he works. The exception is service in the Indian defence forces.

The practical implications of Taoism are numerous such as an aversion to absolute statements or value judgments manifested by the difficulty of "pinning down" an East Asian to a specific position.

IV. Bridging the Gap

Successful advocacy as with successful communication begins with knowing and being aware of these cultural differences and to the make up and sensitivities of the tribunal. Building "rapport" may otherwise be difficult.[9] Rapport in this context means bonding, in other words, the ability to make others feel that one understands them. It is fostered through sharing common ground or commonality. This does not mean that building rapport is only achievable between those of the same background. It is also achievable by creating the

---

8 Jonathan M. Zamet/Murray E. Bovarnick, "*Employee Relations for Multinational Companies in China*" in The Columbia Journal of World Business, Vol. 21, No. 1 (Spring), reprint (1986)

9 The reader is referred to Martin Hunter's article "*Reflections on advocacy and the art of persuasion*", The Litigator [1995], at p. 275 et. seq., where an extensive analysis of what comprises "rapport" is given.

perception of common ground or commonality, so long as the effort to create this perception is sincere. In Asia as in any culture, insincerity can lead to a loss of credibility.

To this cultural gap must be added the significant differences in the legal systems of Asian countries. Indonesia, Japan, South Korea, Taiwan and Thailand have adopted or inherited a civil law system whereas Bangladesh, Brunei, India, Malaysia, Pakistan, Singapore and Hong Kong SAR have a common law system. The Philippines and Sri Lanka have a combination of both civil and common law. The People's Republic of China, North Korea, Vietnam, Laos and Cambodia have "socialist legal systems" and Myanmar a mixture of socialist legal systems and common law. In addition, the underlying legal system, whether civil or common law, has been influenced by religious law such as Islamic law in Brunei, Indonesia, Pakistan and Malaysia. [10]

Accordingly in the context of arbitral proceedings, to bridge the cultural gap and differences in legal culture, it is necessary to address and neutralize perceptions of ignorance of any sensitivities that the tribunal, parties and witnesses might have of counsel coming from a different cultural and legal background. This can be achieved by displaying sensitivity and demonstrating awareness and in doing so, establishing common ground or commonality.

V. Pre-arbitration

In jurisdictions strongly influenced by Confucian ideals, parties generally prefer disputes resolved by negotiation or mediation/ conciliation than by the decision of a third party. In the "conciliation culture" of East Asia in particular, "[l]itigation was condemned as a moral wrongdoing to society and to the other party. A good judge was not supposed to give a judgement but to try to bring about a good conciliation.[11] [...] Under such ideology, it is not a socially

---

[10] See Veronica L. Taylor/Michael Pryles, "*The Cultures of Dispute Resolution in Asia*" in Dispute Resolution in Asia, 3rd ed. at p. 8

[11] Yasuhei Taniguchi, "*Is there a Growing International Arbitration Culture? An Observation from Asia*", in International Dispute Resolution: Towards an

correct thing to litigate in order to win one's supposed right without first conferring with the other party to find a reasonable solution."[12] Such was also the prevalent attitude in pre-British India and to this day, it appears that Indians will try first to conciliate before litigating. In this sense, Asians in general perceive arbitration to be no different from litigation.

In institutional arbitrations in Japan, Korea, People's Republic of China and Taiwan, combining conciliation or mediation with arbitration in the same proceedings is common.[13] In Hong Kong SAR and in Singapore,[14] the relevant arbitration legislation allows the arbitrator, with the express consent of the parties, to also act as the mediator in the same dispute. Indeed, in some arbitrations in Asia, Asian members of the tribunal have been known, in the course of the arbitration, to suggest to parties settlement of the dispute although it does not follow that a tribunal member in so suggesting, is evading the task of having to decide the dispute. In Kashmir for example, settlement of the dispute is often suggested to parties.

Counsel should be alive to this cultural disposition. It is consistent with Asian culture. In the same vein, counsel should not be concerned that were he to suggest mediation or conciliation that this would be viewed as a lack of conviction in his own case.

VI. First Impressions Count

The display of sensitivity and awareness should be made evident from the beginning: in correspondence, pleadings, memorials, witness statements, affidavits of evidence-in-chief, applications and submissions to the tribunal. First impressions do count. These often

---

International Arbitration Culture, Albert Van Den Berg, Gen. (ed.), ICCA Congress Series No. 8, at p. 31

[12] Taniguchi, supra note 7 at 36

[13] As was noted by Michael Pryles and Michael J. Moser in the "*Introduction*" to the Asian Leading Arbitrators' Guide to International Arbitration, at p. 13; see also Art. 8 of the International Commercial Mediation Rules of the Japan Commercial Arbitration Association and Art. 40 of the CIETAC Rules which permits arbitrators to switch roles and act as conciliators/mediators.

[14] See Sec. 17 of the Singapore International Arbitration Act (CAP 143A)

have a bearing on the view the tribunal subsequently takes of the merits of a party's case. Clarity, brevity, probity and integrity in all communications, methodical and effective organisation of documentation, proper marshalling of the evidence, responsiveness and reasonableness are qualities which can only endear parties to any tribunal.

VII. Pleadings

Party autonomy in arbitration provides parties with considerable flexibility to fashion their respective cases. There being no fixed precept in international arbitration as to how each party is to present its written case, this often depends on whether the particular arbitration is institutional or *ad hoc*. In institutional arbitration conducted for example under the rules of the Singapore International Arbitration Centre ("the SIAC Rules"), these rules provide for the party wishing to commence arbitration to submit a Notice of Arbitration and for the opposing party to file an Answer to the Notice of Arbitration[15] and if not already included in the Notice, for the claimant to subsequently send to the respondent a Statement of Case to which the respondent is to then file a Statement of Defence.[16] Under the Rules of the Hong Kong International Arbitration Centre ("the HKIAC Rules"), the claimant and the respondent are required first to submit a Notice of Arbitration and an Answer to the Notice of Arbitration respectively[17] followed by a Statement of Claim from the claimant, unless this was already contained in the Notice for Arbitration or if the claimant elects to treat its Notice of Arbitration as the Statement of Claim[18] and a Statement of Defence[19] by the respondent.

The Arbitration Rules of the China International Economic and Trade Arbitration Commission ("the CIETAC Rules") require the

---

15 See Rules 3 and 4 of the SIAC Rules

16 See Rule 16.3 of the SIAC Rules

17 See Articles 4 and 5 of the HKIAC Rules

18 See Article 17 of the HKIAC Rules

19 See Article 18 of the HKIAC Rules

party initiating recourse to arbitration to submit a Request for Arbitration and the respondent to submit a Statement of Defence.[20] The Korean Commercial Arbitration Board Rules ("the KCAB Arbitration Rules") similarly provide for submission of a Statement of Claim and Defence[21] as do the rules of the London Court of International Arbitration. The Rules of Arbitration of the ICC International Court of Arbitration ("the ICC Rules") refer to a Request for Arbitration and an Answer to the Request.[22] In *ad hoc* arbitrations conducted pursuant to the provisions of the UNCITRAL Arbitration Rules, the rules provide for the submission of a Statement of Case and a Statement of Defence.[23] However such documents are described, whether it is pleadings, memorials or requests, the function of these documents is to set out the principal elements of each party's case, leaving to parties to decide how detailed these should be, with references as appropriate, to documents and law. This requires counsel to ensure that the claim or defence is set out concisely, clearly arranged and in a manner easily understood by the tribunal.

VIII. Burden and Standard of Proof

It is for counsel to persuade the tribunal of the merits of his case and in order to do this, he has first to determine what the burden of proof is as well as its standard. In Asia's common law jurisdictions, the burden is generally considered a procedural issue whereas in Asian civil law jurisdictions, it is usually regarded an issue of substantive law; the standard of proof may not only be a matter of substantive law, but it can also reflect subjective standards ("inner conviction") of the arbitrators[24] Generally, it appears to be "[t]he practice of [...] international arbitral tribunals [...] to require each

---

[20] See Article 10 and 12 of the CIETAC Rules

[21] See Articles 11 and 12 of the KCAB Arbitration Rules

[22] See Articles 4 and 5 of the ICC Rules

[23] See Article 18 and 19 of the UNCITRAL Arbitration Rules

[24] See Julian D M Lew/ Loukas A Mistelis/ Stefan M Kröll, Comparative International Commercial Arbitration, at p. 560 et seq.

party to prove the facts upon which it relies in support of its case. [...] The only exceptions relate to propositions that are so obvious, or notorious, that proof is not required. The degree of proof that must be achieved in practice before an international arbitral tribunal is not capable of precise definition, but it may be safely assumed that it is close to the "balance of probability"."[25]

Whilst there appears to be a global standard of proof in international arbitration, counsel however, ought to be cautious and not assume that "propositions" which are "so obvious" that no proof would be required in his home jurisdiction would be the same when arbitrating in Asia.

IX. Evidence

Arbitrators – unlike common law judges in state court proceedings – do not act as a "kind of referee"[26] administering the rules of admissibility with regard to evidence while leaving the decision as to the evidence to be adduced almost wholly to the parties. In international arbitrations whether in Asia or elsewhere, there is no pre-existing detailed set of procedural rules governing the proceedings as there is in state courts. The tribunal and parties are free to adopt the most appropriate and efficient procedure, including the reception of evidence, for a particular dispute since the tribunal has a broad discretion as to the evidence it wishes to receive and to rely on. Even in international arbitrations conducted in an Asian jurisdiction with common law traditions,[27] a common law practitioner needs to be acutely aware that the process of obtaining evidence and

---

[25] Alan Redfern/Martin Hunter, Law and Practice of International Commercial Arbitration, 4th ed., at p. 297. However, in cases of fraud, bribery, corruption or extortion, a higher standard of proof may be required; see Robert Pietrowski, "*Evidence in International Arbitration*", LCIA Arbitration International, [2006], at p. 380

[26] Alan Redfern/Martin Hunter, Law and Practice of International Commercial Arbitration, 4th ed., at p. 295

[27] See e.g. Tan Chuan Thye/John Cheong, "*Disclosure of Documents in Singapore International Arbitrations: Time for a Reassessment*", Asian International Arbitration Journal, [2005], p. 49 et seq.

discovery that would have been appropriate in proceedings before his national state courts would be quite inappropriate in arbitration proceedings. This is notwithstanding the fact that an Asian arbitrator sitting in arbitrations conducted in English is likely to have had exposure to the common law even if originally his training was in a civil law jurisdiction.

In an international arbitration, the evidence to be presented to the tribunal comprises essentially of the following:

(A) Documentary evidence
(B) Witness evidence
(C) Expert evidence

A. Documentary Evidence

It is expected that counsel will voluntarily disclose all documents which he considers necessary to establish his case as is reflected in institutional arbitration rules and practice in ad hoc arbitrations.

Compelled disclosure of documents by way of applications for discovery has long provoked controversy in international arbitration because there appears to be a consensus today that "zealous advocacy in arbitration must be tempered by an appreciation of the need for speed and efficiency and wide-reaching discovery based on possible relevance can be incompatible with these goals."[28] This consensus is equally applicable in Asia. Recent initiatives undertaken by arbitral institutions to provide guidelines on discovery recommend that "[a]rbitrators should weigh the costs and burdens of production against the likely value of requested documents – and should either deny requests imposing "substantial" costs and burdens or

---

[28] James H. Carter/John L. Hardiman/Joseph E. Neuhaus, "*Discovery in Arbitration: Recent Developments*", in The Arbitration Review of the Americas [2009] referring to the draft of the "CPR Guidelines on Pre-Hearing Disclosure of Documents and Presentation of Witnesses in Commercial Arbitration" ("the draft CPR Guidelines") of the International Institute for Conflict Prevention & Resolution (CPR) at 1

condition production upon the requesting party bearing the costs of such production".[29]

Accordingly, subject to any pre-existing agreement between the parties on discovery, counsel should confer with the tribunal at the earliest convenient time to determine the scope of discovery permitted, in what form and address the issue of preservation of electronic documents which may become relevant once arbitration proceedings have been commenced and that might otherwise be routinely destroyed. The IBA Rules on the Taking of Evidence in International Arbitration ("the IBA Rules"), the provisions of which aim also to balance common and civil law approaches in respect of discovery, are increasingly agreed to by parties and the tribunal in arbitrations conducted in Asia. This said, in international arbitrations seated in India, Indian parties have not generally been receptive to the application of the IBA Rules preferring instead to continue the practice with which they are more familiar and to apply their national law on the taking of evidence even though the *lex arbitri* of India provides for the inapplicability of the Indian Evidence Act to the arbitral proceedings.[30] Nevertheless, wide-ranging discovery in international arbitrations also in India is not the norm. In any event, counsel making applications for discovery should be alive to the sensitivities of the tribunal and parties, particularly if they are from different legal cultures and with differing discovery traditions.

Discovery of electronic documents (also known as "e-discovery") in the context of international arbitration has become a focal point of attention[31] largely because "the biggest single factor driving up costs

---

[29] Draft CPR Guidelines at 6

[30] See Hindustan Prefab Ltd. v Dosajh & Co., 2004 (2) Arb LR 91 (del); Ganges Waterproof Works (P) Ltd. v Union of India (1999) 4 SCC 33 and see generally "Law relating to Arbitration and Conciliation", PC Markanda, 7th ed., at pp. 496 and 497

[31] The International Centre for Dispute Resolution (ICDR) in May 2008 issued "Guidelines for Arbitrators Concerning Exchanges of Information" and the International Institute for Conflict Prevention & Resolution (CPR) is drafting "Guidelines on Pre-Hearing Disclosure of Documents and Presentation of Witnesses in Commercial Arbitration". In June 2008, the ICC formed a working

of discovery in U.S.: litigation today, at least in large cases, is e-mail".[32] The "consensus" reached permitting only limited disclosure of documents in arbitration proceedings applies equally to e-disclosure.[33] In this regard, the Chartered Institute of Arbitrators' Protocol for E-Disclosure in Arbitration may serve as a useful guideline when making discovery applications.

B. Witness Evidence

The practice in international arbitrations which are generally not "documents only" arbitrations, is for tribunals to permit oral evidence to be adduced by way of cross-examination and re-examination (redirect examination) with the respective witnesses' evidence in chief (direct evidence) admitted in proceedings in the form of an affidavit sworn or affirmed by the witness or by way of a signed witness statement. The same is true of Asia.

It is good practice to state in the witness statement or affidavit that if the statement has been prepared by lawyers acting for the party for whom the witness is giving evidence, that it has been so prepared on the basis of information provided by the witness, which he has since read and confirmed as to its veracity and accuracy.[34] This is to

---

group to examine e-disclosure issues and the IBA has launched a review of its 1999 Rules on the Taking of Evidence. In October 2008, the Chartered Institute of Arbitrators released a Protocol for E-Disclosure in Arbitration.

[32] James H. Carter/John L. Hardiman/Joseph E. Neuhaus, "*Discovery in Arbitration: Recent Developments*", in The Arbitration Review of the Americas [2009]

[33] Draft CPR Guidelines divide requests for production of electronic documents into three categories:

(1) For production from 'active or archived files of key witnesses or in shared drives used in connection with the matter at issue,' the requests should generally be 'reasonably specific.' (2) Production from 'a wide range of users or custodians' should be permitted only with a 'showing of extraordinary need.' (3) Requests for 'back-up tapes, deleted files and metadata' should only be granted 'if the requesting party can demonstrate a reasonable likelihood that files were deliberately destroyed or altered by a party in anticipation of litigation or arbitration and outside of that party's usual and customary document-retention policies."

[34] e.g.: "This witness statement has been prepared by counsel for Claimant, [counsel], based on my correspondence and telephone calls with them. An initial

address any perception that the statement is not that of the witness and therefore not in reality his evidence.

Whether the statement states the minimum or gives a full and detailed account of events depends on the witness although it must be borne in mind that a bare statement could result in a longer hearing time and a consequential increase in costs, quite apart from any possible negative inferences that an opposing party could try and raise on the reliability and credibility of the evidence proffered. Article 4 of the IBA Rules[35] provides a useful guide as to the form such a statement should take. In any event, the evidence in the statement should be presented precisely and concisely. It must also avoid making submissions in respect of the party's case or argue the party's case since that is not its function.

Cross-examination of witnesses is now commonly accepted in international arbitrations in Asia as it is elsewhere. When cross-examining an Asian witness, counsel should consider the witness' culture because this will facilitate his communication with the witness and render examination of the witness more effective. The cultural background of the witness is likely to have an influence on how he testifies and how he reacts to questions. Indian witnesses for example in answer to a question, as a matter of course, will often respond with a "yes" before actually answering the question when it then becomes obvious that the answer to the question is in fact "no". So the observations made earlier regarding Asian cultural make up should be borne in mind particularly during cross-examination.

The cultural background of the party and the witness may also be key to placing the events the witness testifies on in their proper context, explaining his actions, conduct and communications at the material time. In East Asia, laws, contracts and formal dispute resolution tend to be treated as less important than the relationship

draft was prepared by [counsel], upon which I commented in a series of correspondence with [counsel]. I have read this witness statement in its entirety and the statements expressed herein are my own. I have not been influenced by [counsel] or anyone else in making this witness statement."

35 This is suggested also in cases where the parties did not agree on the application of the IBA Rules.

between the parties. Consequently, East Asian parties do not perceive a contract as the conclusion of a deal but rather as the beginning of a commercial relationship. Matters such as personal goodwill and the need to look at changed circumstances are regarded as more important than the words of a contract. That is why East Asians expect the subordination of law and contracts to evolving circumstances and, as in South Asia as well, relational values.[36] In other Asian states however, such as Singapore, Hong Kong and India, parties are more likely to litigate commercial disputes and laws and contracts have much the same significance as in the West.[37] In general, individuals as well as companies in Asia that have not been exposed to Western business standards are likely to keep to the approach inherent in their own culture. Counsel needs to keep this cultural disposition in mind particularly when cross-examining a witness in a case in which a subsequent oral amendment to a contract is in issue. Absent clear evidence, counsel should also be slow to challenge the credibility of a witness.

When cross-examining a witness, the old adage in proceedings in the common law courts "Watch his Lordship's pen!" applies equally to international arbitrations. It can be of little value if counsel cross-examines at a pace and in a manner which the tribunal is unable to follow. Overly aggressive cross-examination of any witness and particularly an Asian witness may be counterproductive both in respect of the evidence the witness will then give as well as the impression such aggression might create in the tribunal.

Increasingly, in Asian arbitrations seated in Singapore and in Hong Kong, parties and the tribunal especially in complex matters agree on a hearing time table based on equality which is often referred to as "chess clock" procedure. Such a time table effectively requires counsel to focus his cross-examination on the most

---

[36] Philip J. McConnaughay, "*Rethinking the Role of Law and Contracts in East-West Commercial Relationships*" in International Commercial Arbitration in Asia, 2nd ed., at p. 494

[37] Michael Pryles/Michael J. Moser in the "*Introduction*" to the Asian Leading Arbitrators' Guide to International Arbitration, p. 3 et seq.

essential matters in issue. This emphasizes even more the need for skilful advocacy.

When cross-examining a witness and even more so when an interpreter is required, counsel should be careful to keep the questions simple and precise in order to reduce the risk of the object of the question being lost in translation, particularly when the subject matter of the dispute involves technical terms. Sarcasm should be avoided at any cost since this could easily give rise in translation to misunderstandings. Counsel should also refrain from making humorous remarks during proceedings in a language not easily understood by the witness or a member of the tribunal since this may well cause offence.

C. Expert Evidence

Expert evidence may be adduced by experts appointed by the tribunal or by a party. It is important to remember that the fundamental principle of expert evidence is to provide the tribunal with information which is outside the experience and knowledge of the tribunal and thus, if direct evidence is available and it is admissible, expert evidence is unnecessary. Equally important is the principle that the expert's opinion must be based on facts either on the record or within the expert's own knowledge. If not, the credibility of the expert could be in issue. Article 5 of the IBA Rules provides a useful guide as to what the statement of an expert should contain.

Whether appointed by the tribunal or by a party, the expert is expected to be independent and it is good practice in the expert's witness statement that the expert states in an introductory paragraph that he understands his evidence must be independent and that the purpose of this objective and independent evidence is in order to assist the tribunal.

Tribunals, in an attempt to narrow the areas of dispute between experts, often now direct the experts to meet before issuing their reports and attempt to agree on a list of issues and to prepare a list setting out what has been agreed and where not agreed, stating what these are and why.

In Asia as elsewhere, tribunals are often encouraging parties to have the evidence of expert witnesses given in a simultaneous and joint hearing by way of a discussion amongst themselves and with the tribunal. This is also referred to as "witness conferencing". One of the advantages of this procedure is that it reduces the confrontational dimensions of cross-examination and counsel should tailor his cross-examination style accordingly since such procedure often results in the evidence taking the form of an academic discussion.

X. Conclusion

Counsel, when opening or closing a case, should keep his submissions simple and precise. In complex cases, a skeleton of counsel's opening or closing submissions and a crib sheet of the undisputed facts made available to the tribunal in advance of the hearing, will ease the task of counsel in telling the party's story. The submissions should address the critical issues with reference to the law and to the facts where necessary. In addition to having full mastery of the facts and law, counsel must also be honest and frank as doing so can only but help maintain credibility with the tribunal. Arbitration unlike litigation provides parties largely with the forum and the flexibility they need to resolve their disputes. This flexibility is well suited to Asia, with its kaleidoscope of cultures and legal traditions. To advocate successfully, counsel should take full advantage of this.

Part VII.

ADVOCACY FROM THE PERSPECTIVE OF THE ARBITRATOR

Chapter 24

ADVOCACY FROM THE PERSPECTIVE OF THE CIVIL LAW ARBITRATOR

Bernardo M. Cremades* and Ignacio Madalena**

I. Introduction

The purpose of this chapter is to analyze various issues related to advocacy in arbitration from the perspective and experience of a Spanish arbitrator. This chapter does not endeavor to cover every element of arbitration. It provides an insight to the functioning of arbitration in practice, discussing the main functions of arbitration practitioners and the advocacy skills required at each stage of the proceedings.

Within the broad mandatory limits of the seat, parties and arbitrators enjoy a high degree of freedom and discretion in designing the proceeding. This makes arbitration a less predictable dispute resolution mechanism, in comparison with ordinary law courts and requires a thorough specialization from counsel and arbitrator. Most arbitration rules include a written and an oral phase with a hearing. In the preparation of the different written submissions, counsel is free to adapt the structure of the pleadings and modes of presenting the factual and legal issues to the nature of the case. The oral phase is also flexible in comparison to an ordinary courtroom. The arbitration hearing is free from the technicalities of litigation. However, this informality still requires specific advocacy skills from counsel –to

---

* Senior Partner, B. Cremades y Asociados, Madrid. President of the Spanish Court of Arbitration. E-mail: *bcremades-mad@bcremades.com*

** Associate, B. Cremades y Asociados, Madrid. Georgetown University Law Center (LL.M.), Universiteit Katholieke Leuven (LL.M.). E-mail: *i.madalena@bcremades.com*

persuade the arbitral tribunal in the presentation of the case– and also special skills from the arbitrator –to conduct the proceedings efficiently and to render a well-reasoned award.

II. Designing the Arbitration Proceedings

Arbitration is a private remedial device found on party autonomy, as expressed in the arbitration agreement, which is the jurisdictional cornerstone of arbitration. The possibilities that the parties have of tailoring the rules of the proceedings distinguishes arbitration from the formalities of domestic judicial processes.[1] In regular court proceedings, little discretion is left to the parties or the judge, as there will be specific rules governing almost every aspect of the adjudication process. There is no prototype arbitration. Each case will be different, even when the same rules apply. As long as the parties and the arbitrator adhere to the mandatory rules of the seat, the particulars of the proceedings are left to the parties' agreement or the arbitrator's discretion.[2]

In the past decades there has been tendency of harmonizing arbitration proceedings. This is in part due to globalization, the

---

[1] The principle that the parties are free to determine and design the arbitration proceedings is recognized by: (1) the most important international arbitration conventions [Arts. II and V(1)(d) of the NY Convention; Art. IV(1)(b) (iii) of the European Convention]; (2) the arbitration laws of the major trading nations [namely those implementing Art. 19(1) of the Uncitral Model Law]; and (3) the rules of the leading arbitration institutions, including the ICC (Art. 11), the LCIA (Art. 14.1) and ICSID (Rule 20.2). See GARY B. BORN, *International Commercial Arbitration* (2009) vol. II at 1748 – 1758.

[2] Unless the parties' agreement or the applicable arbitration rules otherwise provide, the arbitrator has the discretion to determine the arbitration procedure. Such discretion is recognized by: (1) the most important international arbitration conventions [Arts. IV(4)(d), V(1)(b) and (d) of the NY Convention]; (2) the arbitration laws of the major trading nations [namely those implementing Art. 19(2) of the Uncitral Model Law]; and (3) the rules of the leading arbitration institutions, including the ICC (Art. 15.1), the LCIA (Art. 14.1) and ICSID (Rule 20). Also, Art. 15 (1) of the Uncitral Arbitration Rules allows the arbitral tribunal to conduct the arbitration "in such a manner as it considers appropriate" provided that the principles of equality and due process are respected. See BORN, supra note 1 at 1758 – 1765.

modernization of national arbitration laws and the contribution of different international soft law instruments, such as the "IBA Rules on the Taking of Evidence in International Commercial Arbitration," the "IBA Guidelines on Conflicts of Interest in International Arbitration," or the "Uncitral Notes on Organizing Arbitral Proceedings."[3] The practice of arbitration further reveals that arbitrators often adopt quite uniform standards, which ultimately reconcile the different legal traditions leaving behind local considerations, in such matters as interim measures, document production or admission of certain witness or expert evidence.[4]

The standardization of arbitration proceedings has been accompanied by the use of electronic tools, including the use of emails for communications and notifications, the electronic submission of documentary and expert evidence via CD or USB drives, and video-conference examination of witnesses over the Internet. Furthermore, the International Chamber of Commerce (ICC) has taken the initiative of creating an *online* platform called *NetCase* which enables, if agreed by both parties, the presentation of all submissions and exhibits by Internet, eliminating the use of paper. The main advantage of this system is in terms of costs saving and round-the-clock access to the entire file from any computer.

All arbitrations require the active participation of the arbitrator from the outset. He or she will conduct a preliminary review of the case and identify the facts and essential legal issues involved. This will serve as a basis for the arbitrator's proposal to the parties of an outline of the proceedings tailored to the needs of the case. In the context of the ICC, the arbitral structure is established in the "Terms of Reference" and the first procedural order.[5]

---

3 Karl-Heinz Böckstiegel, "Past, Present and Future of Arbitration," *Arbitration International,* vol. 25, issue 3 (2009) at 298. See also Gabrielle Kaufmann-Kohler, "The Globalization of Arbitral Procedure," *Vanderbilt Journal of Transnational Law,* vol. 36, issue 4 (2003) at 1313.

4 Id.

5 Article 18 of the ICC Rules requires the arbitral tribunal that "...as soon as it has received the file from the Secretariat..." to draw up in a separate document the "Terms of Reference". This document shall identify the parties and their

However, given that at the beginning of the arbitration the parties will only have submitted a brief description of their claims and defenses, the arbitrator may not have enough information to draw and accurate list of issues. Furthermore, parties might have filed detailed submissions, but the description of the issues could still be confusing. In these cases, the arbitrator may avoid making a closed list of issues, without limiting his discretion to consider other issues at a later stage in the proceedings.[6] This will ultimately affect the length of the submissions, the number exhibits, expert reports and witness statements, with the resulting increase in time and costs of the arbitration.

Saving time and costs in arbitration requires the active participation of the parties and the arbitrator from the outset of the proceedings. Parties are advised to make sure that the arbitrator has enough information about the subject-matter of the dispute from the very beginning of the arbitration. This will allow the arbitrator "...to understand the key issues at an early stage and adopt procedures to address them in its procedural orders..."[7] and to draw, prior consultation with the parties -usually via conference call- an effective plan for the proceedings.[8]

Efficiency and timesaving during the proceedings are overarching principles governing the entire process. Freedom to design the arbitration proceedings is limited by the mandatory rules

---

representatives, establish the seat or place of arbitration and applicable law, the language to be used during the proceedings, the manner in which pleadings and exhibits are to be submitted, or the manner in which communications and notices are to be validated, as well as any other rule that the nature of the particular arbitration may require.

6 Michael E. Schneider, "The Terms of Reference," The New 1998 ICC Rules of Arbitration Special Supplement – The ICC International Court of Arbitration Bulletin (November 1997) at 26.

7 ICC Commission on Arbitration, "Techniques for Controlling Time and Costs in Arbitration: Report from the ICC Commission on Arbitration," ICC Publication no. 843 (2007) para. 46 in relation to paras. 17, 22-23 and 32. Available at http://www.iccwbo.org/uploadedFiles/TimeCost_E.pdf

8 CHRISTOPHER NEWMARK, *The Leading Arbitrators' Guide to International Arbitration -2nd Edition* (2008) at 83 - 84.

to ensure that due process and equal treatment of the parties is at all times respected.[9]

Equal treatment applies before and during the arbitration proceedings. First and foremost, all agreements the parties make regarding the appointment of arbitrators must respect this principle. At the same time, all parties should be treated and regarded equally during the arbitration –namely, in relation to the presentation of evidence, the opportunity to submit claims, and the establishment of deadlines according the needs of the case.

Due process requires that each party has a "reasonable opportunity to present its case," in terms of Article 15(2) of the ICC Rules. Other institutions include a similar wording in their rules. All pleadings and written submissions should be filed within the agreed deadlines and both parties should have the opportunity to present –at the agreed procedural stage– all evidence in support of their claims and defenses. Both parties should also have access to all the information and documents presented by the other party. However, due process does not necessarily require an oral phase, unless the specific nature of the case so requires or the examination of witnesses or experts is necessary.

III. Effective and Persuasive Pleadings

The objective of every lawyer and the essence of advocacy is "the persuasive communication of a party's case to the arbitral tribunal"[10] Effective and persuasive pleadings: (i) adopt a logical and persuasive reasoning; (ii) are well structured and have the appropriate length in accordance with the objectives of the presentation; (iii) use clear,

---

[9] The Constitutions of most nations recognize the right of every person to effective legal protection in exercising his/her rights and interests, thus prohibiting a lack of proper defence. On the international sphere, the 1948 Universal Declaration of Human Rights (Article 10) and the 1966 International Covenant on Civil and Political Rights (Article 14) expressly recognise the universal nature of this right. Equality and due process apply to all areas of Law, including arbitration.

[10] David J.A. Cairns, "Advocacy and the Functions of Lawyers in International Arbitration", *publication forthcoming* (2010).

precise and neutral language; and (iv) provide a thorough but concise presentation of the facts and the applicable law.[11] These principles apply to all forms of submissions (oral or written) between counsel and the arbitrator.

A. Logical and Persuasive Reasoning

The first requirement is that counsel should resort to a logical and persuasive reasoning when presenting their case. Logic is achieved by correctly linking propositions, the explanation of the facts, the Law and the relationship between facts and law. This is definitely the model followed by counsel in their pleadings and the arbitrator in the award.

The legal art does not end at applied logic, which will not always lead to a single answer, but rather, it will provide different solutions, which may at times be contradictory. Therefore, a fair application of the law will sometimes require the adoption of alternative decisions; other those resulting from pure applied logic. This is achieved through "legal reasoning" and "legal argument," techniques that provide the arguments supporting the relief sought or a fair solution in the award.

The first factor to be considered in legal writing is the audience. Defining the audience helps organizing and presenting information and communicating more effectively. In arbitration, the tribunal is the audience that must be persuaded. It is the arbitrator who must be convinced of the reasons that support a certain claim and not one's client or the other party's counsel.

Different scholars have addressed a number of legal reasoning theories, some of which have identified factors to be considered

---

[11] Id. David Cairns explains that there are six skills of the advocate in case presentation, which overlap and interact and include: (i) 'legal expertise' or profound knowledge of arbitration law and its international legal framework; (ii) 'legal reasoning' or the facility of logical thought; (iii) 'question and answering techniques' of witnesses and experts; (iv) 'expression' or the form that an advocate structures his speech or written pleadings and expresses or conveys the arbitral tribunal; (v) ethical behaviour; and (vi) 'tact' which fine tunes an oral or written presentation.

when structuring effective legal arguments.[12] The facility of logical thought in legal reasoning requires identifying: (i) the thesis that is to be proven; (ii) the supporting reasons or evidence; (iii) the argument that frames the facts within the general rule; and (iv) the legal grounds in support of the argument. But effective and persuasive legal reasoning does not end here. It requires further support based on the application of universally accepted principles such as good faith, legitimate expectations or equal treatment, among others.

B. Structure and Length

The second feature of persuasive writing is the structure chose to organize the presentation of the factual and legal arguments. "Structure is the backbone of expression" and will guide the arbitrator throughout the presentation.[13] This will require the use of certain connectors between sentences and ideas, letting the arbitrator know where counsel is going and allowing him to follow a logical route. This is done through various techniques clarifying the organization of thoughts. The choice of one structure or another distinguishes an ordinary from an outstanding submission.

Further, counsel should always bear in mind that the object of the arbitration is not to engage in an academic debate over theoretical questions that have little relevance on the relief sought. This should always be kept in mind when structuring the presentation of the case, to avoid unnecessary and irrelevant discussions.

In the common law civil procedure, pleadings have traditionally been brief and more schematic than in continental jurisdictions where these are much more extensive, providing a detailed description of the factual background of the case –by constantly referring and cross-referencing to the documents and expert reports that accompany the pleadings– and explaining all the legal supporting

---

[12] See CHAÏM PERELMAN, La Lógica Jurídica y la Nueva Retórica (1979); ROBERT ALEXY, Teoría de los Derechos Fundamentales (1993); MANUEL ATIENZA, Las Razones del Derecho: Teorías de la Argumentación Jurídica (2003).

[13] Cairns, supra note 10.

arguments in greater detail. In arbitration, pleadings resemble the civil law tradition as far as length and detail in the description of the facts, the evidence and the applicable legal reasoning.[14]

In arbitration, the internal structure of a pleading does not need to adhere to the traditional model of "facts" and "legal grounds" – typical of the structure followed by civil law practitioners– as sometimes the particular needs of the case will require an alternative internal structure. For instance, in the case of certain arbitrations with long and complex factual allegations and copious correspondence – such as construction and engineering disputes– it is possible to draft a core pleading, legal in nature, that would be accompanied by several addenda explaining in detail all the supporting technical facts and exhibits. This would prevent any loss of power of the fundamental legal arguments while trying to include in the same document, a long, complex and sometimes technical explanation of the facts.

The structure chosen should allow an accurate explanation of the facts of the case, as it is impossible to apply a law in the abstract. In general, structure should be well adapted to the objectives of the case, but should be logical itself and easy to follow. This is done applying different techniques, including:

(a) parallel structure, which means using the same grammatical structure –e.g., parallel adjectives– for ideas that are logically parallel;

(b) clear and logical organization of thoughts addressed within paragraphs and sentences, headings and sub-headings;

(c) the use of logical links between paragraphs and sentences, putting sentences in logical order, choosing the most effective structure for phrases and sentences, introducing accurate transitions and making numbered and bulled point lists; or

---

14 See Pierre A. Karrer, "The Civil Law and Common Law Divide: An International Arbitrator Tells it Like He Sees It," *Dispute Resolution Journal* (February-April 2008) vol. 63 at 72, 75, stating that "…the days of common law notice pleading are gone in international commercial arbitration. Full narration is required."

(d) ensuring that each paragraph is not overloaded with different ideas. Usually each paragraph should not contain more than one idea; and[15]

(e) always allowing for a non-defensive and positive structure.

The use of the appropriate language is dealt with in the following section.

C. Language Choice

The specific audience directly influences the choice of language in legal writing. In international arbitration, the individual counsel is addressing is the arbitrator, which in many occasions might not share the same mother tongue. Even where the arbitrator appears to be fluent in the language of the arbitration, special care should be taken in choosing the most neutral and international expressions.[16]

First, pleadings should be brief and clear, avoiding the accumulation of unnecessary details without deviating from the line of argument.[17] It is true that certain arbitrations might require a more detailed explanation of the facts –often due to the technical aspects of the case– but in these cases it is best to include a preliminary summary of the facts. In all cases, explanation of the facts will never be clear unless counsel follows a chronological description, and the clarity can further be enhanced by including a brief summary of the facts at the end of each heading or sub-heading.

It should be bear in mind that concrete words create clearer images in the arbitrator's mind than abstract ones. Concrete words should be chosen for the description of facts which favor the relief sought, while abstract ones may serve to de-emphasize certain

---

[15] MARY BARNARD RAY, JILL J. RAMSFIELD, *Legal Writing: Getting It Right and Getting It Written* (1993) at 162, 194-196, 203 and 205.

[16] Cairns, supra note 10.

[17] See FRANÇOIS MARTINEAU, *Argumentación Judicial del Abogado* (2008) at 24 – 28.

questions. Also, creating and repeating certain key words along the pleading might also strengthen persuasiveness.[18]

D. Presentation of the Facts and the Law

When setting out the facts, counsel must be specific and list the facts in chronological order. Unless the arbitrator is thoroughly familiar with the issues in dispute, neither the exhibits, nor the legal arguments will capture his attention. Sometimes, it is very useful for the arbitrator if the pleading includes a preliminary section summarizing the dispute, followed by a brief list of the main headings or summary of contents.

International arbitration requires expertise in different legal areas. In addition to the different national laws, international conventions and soft law instruments that apply, counsel should be aware of all the underlying legal materials that apply to the subject matter of the dispute, which in one single arbitration may range from the civil, administrative and constitutional laws of a country to legal instruments which are typical of public international law, such as treaties. Being a lawyer specialized in international arbitration means being a "generalist" and requires high versatility and enormous adaptation to different jurisdictions.

IV. Documentary Evidence

Documentary evidence is undoubtedly the most important type of evidence. Oral statements and examination of witnesses and experts have a secondary role. Notwithstanding the relevance of witness and expert evidence, documents outweigh testimony.[19] The presentation of documents during the arbitration raises different issues as to when, how and by whom these documents should be filed.

---

[18] RAY, supra note 15 at 218-219.

[19] Karrer, supra note 14 at 76, stating that "...documents provide the best skeleton of the animal we are trying to reconstruct and the recollection of various people may help us put flesh around those bones...".

Regarding the first question –i.e. the appropriate procedural stage to submit documentary evidence– arbitrators tend to require, unless the parties have otherwise agreed, that all pleadings be accompanied by the documents that are cited in the pleading, including correspondence, witness statements and expert reports. Usually, further submissions of documents are allowed if the documents are filed with the purpose of responding or rebutting the evidence previously submitted by the other party. This limits the submission of unnecessary, redundant or irrelevant evidence.

In practice, under exceptional circumstances, arbitrators admit documents that a party was unable to submit at the agreed procedural stage, when the documents in question might have a direct and relevant impact on the outcome of the case. When acting under such discretionary powers, arbitrators often allow the other party to present counter-evidence to ensure that both parties are treated equally.

Arbitrators tend to rely on counsel's management and presentation skills to determine how to present documents during the arbitration. The preparation and presentation of documents requires from counsel a proper allocation of resources, coordination of a legal team and eventually the appropriate use of technology –i.e. an electronic database– to facilitate identification, search and classification of scanned documents and correspondence.

Both parties should ensure that there is no duplication of exhibits during the arbitration. This can be confusing for both parties and the arbitrator. Therefore, arbitrators often require parties to prepare and coordinate the presentation of joint list of exhibits to avoid that parties and arbitrators end up with unnecessary duplicates. In other occasions, arbitrators instruct the parties to number exhibits consecutively and to assign a letter –"C" for the claimant's and "R" for the respondent's documents– before the exhibit number.

It should always be bear in mind that overproduction of documents weakens credibility. Parties often file numerous volumes –and sometimes boxes– of unnecessary documents, resulting in additional but unnecessary work, with the obvious impact on time and costs.

Parties are generally allowed to submit photocopied documents, which are considered authentic and complete, unless the other party challenges its authenticity, in which case the original must be provided. In any case, after hearing both parties, arbitrators usually have the discretionary authority to decide on the probative value of any document. Parties are also allowed and advised to present the documents on a CD-ROM or on any other electronic support, helping the arbitrator to access, find or re-print any documents at any time.

Finally, reference shall be made to the question of document production, very common in international arbitration, which raises important strategic decisions for counsel and procedural issues for the arbitrator in relation to procedural efficiency. Most international arbitrations often raise discovery issues, reflecting the legal cultural clash that arbitration seeks to reconcile.[20] While lawyers are influenced by their legal tradition, arbitrators should ensure adapt to the nationalities involved in the proceedings as to how much document production will be allowed. Most arbitration rules leave "ample degree of flexibility," as it is the case for the ICC Rules.[21]

Finally, arbitrators find in different soft law instruments –such as in IBA Rules on the Taking of Evidence– a persuasive source to decide the extension of the requested production of documents. Generally, every request for document production shall be filed within the agreed calendar and should also meet certain standards as to form, specificity and relevance.[22]

---

[20] Bernardo Cremades "Managing Discovery in International Arbitration," *Dispute Resolution Journal* (November 2002 – January 2003) at 73 – 77.

[21] Bernard Hanotiau, "Document Production in International Arbitration: A Tentative Definition of 'Best Practices'" – *2006 Special Supplement of the ICC International Court of Arbitration Bulletin* at 114. Under the ICC Rules "…the Arbitral Tribunal shall proceed as short a time as possible to establish the facts of the case by all appropriate means…" (Article 20.1) leaving arbitrators with the discretion to proceed accordingly with the limits of equality and due process (Article 15.2). In addition, the tribunal has the discretionary power to request any "additional evidence," from the parties "at any time during the proceedings" (Art. 20.5).

[22] Yves Derains, "Towards Greater Efficiency in Document Production before Arbitral Tribunals—A Continental Viewpoint," *2006 Special Supplement of the ICC International Court of Arbitration Bulletin*, p. 114. The ICC Rules of Arbitration contain

V. The Hearing

A. The need and place of a hearing

Due process does not require that a hearing always be held. Indeed, many arbitration rules allow parties to agree on "documents only" arbitrations –i.e., based only on the parties' written submissions and the exhibits attached thereto.[23] However, national laws and arbitration rules general provide that a hearing should be held if one party so requires.[24] Therefore, oral presentation and interrogation of witnesses and experts continues to be regarded as a one of the main roles of an advocate.

International arbitration reconciles the common law practice of "oral" trial with the historical written tradition of continental

---

no provision dealing specifically with the production of documentary evidence, but Article 20, which refers to the means by which the arbitral tribunal establishes the facts of the case, allows the tribunal to request additional evidence from the parties, at any point in the proceedings. In general, any request for production of documents should identify the documents sought with a high degree of specificity and sufficient detail. Or else, if only a category of documents can be identified, that category must be narrowed down to a limited period of time, to documents of a given kind, of specific authors and in relation to a specific question. Furthermore, in ruling on the request for production of documents, the arbitrators may consider the prima facie relevance of the documents, having regard to the factual allegations made by the parties.

[23] For example, in the context of Uncitral, Article 24 (1) of the Model Law provides: *'Subject to any contrary agreement by the parties, the arbitral tribunal shall decide whether to hold oral hearings for the presentation of evidence or for oral argument, or whether the proceedings shall be conducted on the basis of documents and other materials. However, unless the parties have agreed that no hearings shall be held, the arbitral tribunal shall hold such hearings at an appropriate stage of the proceedings, if so requested by a party.'* Also, Article 15 (2) of the Uncitral Arbitration Rules states: *'If either party so requests at any stage of the proceedings, the arbitral tribunal shall hold hearings for the presentation of evidence by witnesses, including expert witnesses, or for oral argument. In the absence of such a request, the arbitral tribunal shall decide whether to hold such hearings or whether the proceedings shall be conducted on the basis of documents and other materials.'*

[24] See Article 20.6 ICC Rules; Article 19.1 LCIA Rules; Article 15.2 Unictral Arbitration Rules; Article 25.4 of the Swiss Rules of International Arbitration; Rule 29 of the ICSID Arbitration Rules, among others.

jurisdictions.[25] In arbitration, the general practice is an initial written phase consisting of pleadings, witness statements and expert reports, followed by a compulsory oral phase (unless the parties jointly agree otherwise) subject to time limitations.

Generally, the hearing will be held at the seat of the arbitration, but the provisions of the leading institutions allow hearings to be held at any other location agreed by the parties or deemed appropriate by the tribunal based on considerations of costs, safety and logistics. Even in cases in which one of the parties demands that the hearing should held at the place of arbitration, arbitrators retain certain margin of discretion to decide otherwise.[26] Sometimes, in order to save time and costs, it may be possible to hold a hearing via conference call or videoconference, which is accepted if suitable for the case and the arbitrator allows it.[27]

B. The nature of the hearing

The nature, structure and duration of the hearing are usually left to the discretion of the arbitrators, subject to previous consultation with the parties, and will depend on several factors, including: (i) the parties' agreement (within mandatory limits of the seat) and the provisions of the applicable arbitration rules; and (ii) the limits imposed by the principles of equality and due process.

One of the main goals of the hearing, together with the examination of witnesses and experts, is to offer the tribunal a direct, face-to-face presentation of the case, including the opportunity to make brief synthesized closing arguments. In general, the modes of presenting the case at the hearing are informal and flexible, but a persuasive presentation of the case requires strong oral communication skills emphasizing or stressing the crucial factual or legal issues. The same remarks addressed for the preparation of

---

[25] Cairns, supra note 10.

[26] For example, Article 14(2) of the ICC Rules allows the arbitral tribunal, after consultation with the parties, to "*...conduct hearings and meetings at any location it considers appropriate unless otherwise agreed by the parties...*".

[27] ICC Commission on Arbitration, supra note 7, para. 74.

pleadings –in relation to structure, choice of langue and legal reasoning– apply to the oral presentation of the case.

The still cultural difference between common and civil law advocates is sometimes perceived during the hearing. In general terms, common law attorneys are noticeably concerned with the transcript and the recording of the hearing, with the resulting risk of losing eye contact with the arbitrators. Continental lawyers often lack the oral advocacy techniques developed in common law jurisdictions and they seem more concerned on the content than in the form of their message.

One of the most sensitive issues for the arbitration tribunal is to determine the amount of time that each party will have to intervene, as well as the whole duration of the hearing. Common law attorneys are not so used to the narrow times limits during the hearing to present the case and to examine witnesses, and may expect to have as much time as necessary to accomplish all the necessary tasks.[28] On the contrary, lawyers from civil law jurisdictions are often accustomed to strict time limitations. In international arbitration, time limits exist for the duration and length of hearing, but arbitrators tend to be flexible regarding the allocation of time to cross-examine a witness or an expert. Generally, due process and equal treatment do not require giving each party the same exact amount of time to intervene and to conduct the examination of a witness.[29]

Flexibility in time allocation is coupled with the discretion of the arbitrators to interrupt and pose questions at any time during the hearing.[30] The value that these questions have to show the issues that

---

[28] See H.M. Holtzman, "Streamlining Arbitral Proceedings: Some Techniques of the Iran-US Claims Tribunal," *Arbitration International,* vol. 11, issue 1 (1995) at 39, 46 – 47.

[29] Bernard Hanotiau, "The Conduct of the Hearings", in LAWRENCE W. NEWMAN, RICHARD D. HILL (EDS.) *The Leading Guide to International Arbitration* (2004) at 269, 383.

[30] Article 21(3) of the ICC Rules provides that the "…Arbitral Tribunal shall be in full charge of the hearings…." See also Article 8(1) of the IBA Rules on the Taking of Evidence recognizing the arbitrators have "…at all times…complete control over the evidentiary hearing…."

can be addressed on the final written submissions (conclusions) outweighs the impact of these questions on the time frames of the hearing. The best closing submissions are those that give an answer to questions raised by the tribunal during the hearing.

Unless there is an explicit authorization from the Arbitration Tribunal, hearings are private. Most arbitration rules provide that it shall be discretionary with the arbitrator to determine the possibility of the attendance of any other persons other than those participating in the arbitration. In fact, the rules of most arbitration institutions make a specific reference to the privacy of hearings.[31] Moreover, under the discretionary authority that arbitrators have in organizing the hearing, witness and experts are generally not allowed to stay at the hearing room before or after they have been examined.[32]

C. The presentation and examination of evidence

Perhaps one of the most remarkable differences between arbitration and court proceedings relates to the rules as to the admissibility of evidence. Most arbitration rules confer the arbitrator full and exclusive authority to decide the relevance and admissibility of evidence.

In common law jurisdictions, there is a strong belief in the value of witness testimony, perhaps due to the severity of the penalty for perjury and to the fact that proceedings were historically entirely oral and documents were introduced through witnesses.[33] In continental jurisdictions, where the written form has traditionally prevailed, oral presentation of the case has nevertheless become an important

---

[31] For example, Article 21(3) of the ICC Rules provides: "...save with the approval of the Arbitral Tribunal and the parties, persons not involved in the proceedings shall not be admitted..." at the hearing.

[32] Such discretionary power is implicit under Article 21(3) of the ICC Rules [See YVES DERAINS, ERIC A. SCHWARTZ, *A Guide to the ICC Rules of Arbitration* (2005, 2nd Ed.) at 289-291]; Article 20(4) of the ICDR Rules and Article 25(4) of the Unictral Rules, among others.

[33] For the differences between the Common Law and the Continental approach to witness testimonies, see Karrer, supra note 14 at 76.

element of civil procedure, but there is still greater reliance on documents as the more probative form of evidence.

In international arbitration, one of the main purposes of the hearing is to allow the examination of a party's own witnesses (through "direct examination") or the witnesses of the other party (through "cross-examination"). Generally, examination requires rigorous training that mainly comes with practice. Cross-examination includes challenging the credibility of the witness, which requires from counsel specific questioning techniques. Most of these have been developed in the context of common law jurisdictions, including "...the use of leading and non-leading questions, the appropriate use of open and closed questions, keeping questions brief, incremental questioning, repetition and emphasis, techniques for linking questions, and the importance of structure and chronology…."[34]

During the examination of expert and witnesses, the atmosphere is very different from a courtroom. In practice, arbitrators and counsels maintain a friendly spirit, far from the technicalities of regular court litigation. Furthermore, the tendency is to encourage parties to use written statements as direct evidence, rather than oral testimony, and if there is to be cross-examination, arbitrators will usually limit the time available for such examination.[35]

VI. Advocacy and the Arbitrator's Adjudicatory Function

A. The Role of the Arbitrator

Arbitration is a form of adjudication. The arbitrator is not a mediator or a conciliator and it does not fall within his role to try to secure a compromise settlement. The arbitrator's main function - primarily jurisdictional- is to render a final and binding award based

---

[34] Cairns, supra note 10. See also, Bernardo M. Cremades, Bernardo M. Cremades & David J.A. Cairns, "Cross-Examination and International Arbitration," in *Between East and West: Essays in Honour of Ulf Franke* (Kaj Hobér, Annette Magnusson & Marie Öhrström eds., 2010).

[35] See ICC Commission on Arbitration, supra note 7 at paras. 81 and 84.

upon the evidence and the arguments presented. The arbitrator is neither a representative of the party who has appointed him (in the case of a tribunal) nor a negotiator, as the service the arbitrator provides "resolves a conflict" "...exercising a jurisdictional authority" and thus enabling the parties to "...achieve the same objectives as they would before national courts...."[36] The award has the force of *res judicata* and can only be set aside in exceptional circumstances.

Arbitrators act under the restraints imposed by the applicable arbitration law, mainly in relation to their independence and impartiality. For this reason, national laws grant arbitrators a series of rights that enable them to carry out their functions, but it also assigns them duties and responsibilities so as to protect the rights and interests of the parties.[37] Thus, arbitrators might be liable for a breach of those duties, but otherwise they are only subject to their own conscience.

Arbitration, like court adjudication, implies an authoritative determination by the tribunal imposing a solution upon the parties to

---

[36] Decisions of the Spanish Constitutional Court no. 15/1989, Ninth Point of Law; 62/1991, Fifth Point of Law; 288/1993, Third Point of Law; 174/1995; 1996/75; 1996/146; 1996/176; and 1997/196, defining arbitration as "...a jurisdictional equivalent, whereby the parties can obtain the same objectives as in the civil jurisdiction, i.e. obtain a decision settling the dispute with the force of res judicata." See Bernardo M. Cremades, "Constitutional Aspects of Arbitration in Spain" in KLAUS PETER BERGER, GEORG BORGES, HARALD HERRMANN (EDS.) *Zivil- Und Wirtschaftsrecht Im Europaischen Und Globalen Kontext / Private And Commercial Law In A European And Global Context - Festschrift für Norbert Horn* (2006) p. 909.

[37] The most important arbitration laws, institutional rules and codes of ethics recognize that arbitrators are under the following duties: (i) to be impartial and independent of the parties and remain so during the entire proceedings; (ii) to conduct the proceedings in such a way that they lead to a valid and enforceable award; (iii) to complete their mandate and not to resign without good cause; (iv) to conduct the arbitration fairly and without undue delay; and (v) to keep the arbitration confidential. The breach of these obligations –mainly when negligence is involved– may raise the arbitrator's liability and the resulting obligation to pay damages. Further controls are further established by the market and arbitration institutions against those arbitrators which do not comply with the abovementioned duties.

a dispute. The award is the consequence of the authority of the tribunal conferred by the parties in the arbitration agreement. When the award is rendered, the losing party is supposed to comply with it. If it refuses to do so, court intervention will be necessary to ensure recognition and enforcement. This will obviously imply that the judge will verify whether the award was duly made.

In addition to its binding effects, arbitral awards shape international law and may have political or economic implications. Such an impact requires careful decision-making and specialized techniques in drafting and reasoning the award. This is achieved through similar skills as an advocate, through legal expertise, logical reasoning and choice of language,[38] but also through tact and diplomacy, with the view of enabling a fair and just resolution of the dispute.

B. The Impact of Good Advocacy

Arbitral awards follow the typical structure of a decision by a binding adjudicative body. Every award shall clearly identify the parties and outline the procedural background, referring to the most important procedural steps of the arbitration and naming all the participants, including witnesses and experts that appeared during the arbitration. The award should also cite the pleadings and refer to the exhibits presented, indicating the relevant dates of submission and notification. There are of course certain formalities than need to be complied with,[39] but the preparation of a well-reasoned award is greatly assisted by good advocacy skills of the lawyers representing the parties.

---

[38] Cairns, supra note 10.

[39] The law of the seat, the applicable institutional rules or any agreement of the parties, may provide the formal requirements that must be fulfilled by the arbitral award. Article 31 of the Model Law establishes the following usual requirements: the arbitral award: (a) "shall be issued in writing" (31.1); (b) "shall be signed by the arbitrator or arbitrators" (31.1); (c) "shall state the reasons upon which it is based, unless the parties have agreed that no reasons are to be given or the award is an award on agreed terms..." (31.2); and (d) "shall state its date and the place of arbitration..." (31.3).

Detail description in the award of all proven facts is required to allow a proper application of the law. There is no need to go through, in the same detail as the parties did in their pleadings, every single event, piece of correspondence or document related to the facts of the case. The award may only refer to those facts that the arbitrator considers to be proven, but this task requires a detailed analysis of all evidence presented. This is easier when counsel has presented the evidence within an adequate structure, chronologically describing with clear a neutral language only the facts.

Systematic presentation of the documents, avoiding duplicates and overproduction allows a better understanding of the facts. When drafting the award, arbitrators use the pleadings and any indexes of exhibits as a guide to their analysis and this should also be bear in mind when preparing the pleadings.

The award should include a concise description of the positions of the parties in relation to the different claims and defenses. An accurate summary in each heading of the pleadings helps arbitrators to identify the essence of each party's position. Structure is the essence of advocacy. Arbitrators will retain a clear and organized structure of the pleadings' factual and legal arguments and, if appropriate, will reproduce it in the award.

The transcript of the hearing plays an important function. The tribunal's review of the oral testimony is more effective when the parties' closing submissions provide a summary explanation of the facts, bearing in mind that most questions regarding unclear facts are addressed by arbitrators during the hearing.

Arbitrators should reach their decision in the award by applying a previously established rule or standard. This task requires knowledge and expertise in the legal science, just as any advocate in presenting and defending a case. It also requires the arbitrator to search for logical formulas of applying the relevant laws to the facts of the case, in order to reach a correct decision. Even if the tribunal is familiar with legal issues in dispute and the applicable law, parties are encouraged to instruct arbitrators on the relevant legal principles and provide the tribunal with all the appropriate legal materials.

The tribunal will often follow its own legal reasoning, influenced by the most reasonable and logical propositions addressed in the parties' pleadings. The more logical is the counsel's thought in the written submissions the more clear and concise is likely to be the tribunal's reasoning. Where both parties provide a logical line of reasoning that allows the arbitrator to weigh the alternative positions in the most effective way.

In practice, an international arbitration may raise questions where there appear to be no previously established rules, or where the rules are still in a phase of development. The arbitrator will first seek to apply a previously established national or international rule that applies to the merits; but if no formal source of law settles the problem the arbitrator may resort to internationally accepted – sometimes non-binding– principles which may provide a reasonable and fair justification of the award.

An illustrative example is found in the filling-in function of Lex Mercatoria and the different soft law instruments that conform what has been called the *Ius Mercatorum.*[40] Parties are therefore to refer, as complement to the applicable, to any universal principle which might a persuasive impact on the tribunal to demonstrate the relief sought is not only the most logical, but also provides the most equitable, reasonable and fair resolution of the case.

Finally, the award must contain an operative decision or ruling declaring rights or requiring action. In view of the fact that arbitration is a form of adjudication, the award needs to be clear and precise, declaring or granting specific rights and obligations, and eventually ordering specific action from a party.[41] This is largely ensured when the parties' pleadings provide a clear, concise and complete description of the relief sought.

---

[40] José Carlos Fernández Rozas, *Ius Mercatorum: Autorregulación y Unificación del Derecho de los Negocios Transnacionales* (2004) at 187 – 200.

[41] Bernardo M. Cremades, "The Arbitral Award," in NEWMAN, HILL (EDS.) supra note 29 at 397 – 414, 402.

VII. Conclusion

The role of an arbitrator is to resolve disputes that the parties have agreed to submit to arbitration, rendering a final and binding award. The role of the arbitrator also includes conducting the proceedings in an efficient and effective manner, in accordance with the parties agreement, the provisions of the arbitration rules or discretionally, within the limits of the applicable mandatory laws.

Arbitration is a private remedial device different from court litigation that requires specific skills, both from counsel and the arbitrator. Within broad limits, parties and arbitrators may design the proceedings in accordance with the nature of the case. Such freedom and flexibility is perhaps the appealing aspect of arbitration. Coupled with its neutrality, arbitration is the most suitable mechanism to resolve disputes, including those of an international nature.

Within the limitations imposed by the principles of equality and due process, the parties and the arbitrator (within his discretionary authorities) can freely set up the proceedings and adapt them to the needs of the case. Today, international arbitration practice is relatively uniform as a result of a gradually increasing tendency to globalize and standardize proceedings. The traditional distinction between the Anglo-Saxon and Roman Law advocate has become obsolete, at least as far as arbitration is concerned, which requires truly global and transnational training. In a global market, the international arbitration practitioner has become a generalist with expertise in different areas of the law from a diverse array of jurisdictions.

Advocacy in international arbitration is far from the rigid standards of domestic procedural laws, and arbitration lawyers enjoy greater flexibility in the presentation of the case than domestic litigators, who find themselves tied to strict ritualistic formalities, namely in continental jurisdictions. Notwithstanding the flexibility of arbitration, it still requires careful decision-making by counsel when designing a procedural strategy, research expertise, written and communications skills, and the ability to manage the simultaneous application of binding rules and soft law instruments.

The arbitrator, as an independent adjudicator chosen by the parties, will always offer the possibility of analyzing and processing each of the parties' claims and contentions, in the most effective and speedy way, without unnecessary formalities.

An international arbitrator plays a crucial role in the development of the law governing cross-border transactions, including international investment law. It is generally accepted that an award rendered in an international arbitration is not a legally binding precedent. In practice, arbitral tribunals very carefully analyze and rely upon the reasoning employed by other arbitral tribunals. Therefore, a well-reasoned award provides and contributes to the formation and shaping of transnational law.

Chapter 25

ADVOCACY FROM THE ARBITRATOR'S PERSPECTIVE

L. Yves Fortier* and Stephen L. Drymer**

I. Introduction

Plutarch wrote that "the good have no need of an advocate." Would that that were always the case. As many good yet poorly represented parties have learnt, in arbitral proceedings it is not enough to be right, let alone good; it is essential that the rightness of one's case be apparent to the person or people invested with the authority to determine the dispute. Therein lays the advocate's challenge. Ask any arbitrator what he or she really wants from an advocate. The answer, if truthful, is likely to be along the lines of "simply, everything". Arbitrators want it all. And why not? If our role is to determine the outcome of a dispute, the role of the advocate is to persuade us to determine the matter one way or another and ideally to show us not only why but exactly how to do so.

It is often said that the best advocates do the arbitrators' work for them. At the very least, they simplify the arbitrators' job enormously. As Doak Bishop wrote in the first edition of this book: "The advocate should think through the case from the standpoint of the arbitrator – putting himself in the arbitrator's position – defining the issues to be decided and considering what is necessary to prove those issues." In doing so, the best advocate lays the groundwork for a decision or award that, from the standpoint of the arbitrator, effectively writes itself.

---

* Chairman Emeritus, Senior partner, Ogilvy Renault, Montréal, Canada

** Partner, Ogilvy Renault, Montréal, Canada

This comes as no surprise to the seasoned lawyer. Oliver Wendell Holmes famously declared that "Judges are apt to be naïf, simple-minded men, and they need something of Mephistopheles. We too need education in the obvious." Many parties and counsel may well recognise any number of arbitrators in this description. And many arbitrators may well recognise themselves, if they are frank. For as compared to the parties themselves and their representatives, at the outset of an arbitration the arbitrator – if not quite simple-minded, one hopes – is certainly relatively unsophisticated. Compared to the parties and their advocates, the arbitrator possesses at best an unrefined knowledge of the issues in dispute and the multiple ways in which those issues may be construed and ultimately determined. As did Faust, the arbitrator requires a guide.

Arbitrators look to counsel to guide them through the thicket of facts and law, allegations and opinions, claims and counterclaims, hard science and red herrings, evidence and puffery, rhetoric and bombast that make up the typical adversarial proceeding. We expect the advocate to lead us unerringly toward conclusions that, with the benefit of the advocate's assistance, come to seem obvious. The best counsel is part humble servant, part all-knowing teacher and very much part psychologist. This, in addition to being deeply versed in all facets of the case at hand and keenly attuned to our every grimace, smile, understanding nod or uncertainty stated or otherwise. In short, we want the advocate to be and to do simply everything.

As if that were not enough to ask, the experienced advocate also understands full well that for every arbitrator "everything" mean something different. When one speaks of arbitrators, especially international arbitrators, there exists no monolithic "we" or homogeneous "they". In contradistinction to judges, who in any given jurisdiction hail from roughly similar cultural, educational and legal backgrounds and tend to operate exclusively within the confines of a particular juridical regime and code of procedural conduct, international arbitrators are as diverse in their experience and expectations as can be imagined; and they function within a system that but for a few fundamental principles – party autonomy, equality of treatment, due process – in theory is almost infinitely variable and in practice varies tremendously from case to case.

As was noted in the foreword to the first edition of this book, however great the challenge of becoming an effective persuader at the bar of a national court, it is greater still in the international arbitral field. In our field the race is not to the procedurally profound, but to the nimble adapter who is ready to try every case in an entirely new way depending on rules of play and the identity and predilections of the decision-makers of the day. The successful international advocate understands this variability, and thrives on it. He or she embraces the challenge of contending with laws and rules, customs and manners that are not his or her own, and is able to appear equally comfortable before any arbitrator in any hearing room in any region of the world.

If there is one immutable rule in a field that is well defined by its very limited number of immutable rules – a field in which the notion of a one-size-fits-all arbitration belies the fundamental nature and promise of this potent and widely-used dispute resolution mechanism – it is that the successful advocate must tailor his approach to the varying nature and exigencies of the tribunals before which he appears, and to the varying means of communicating with, guiding and ultimately persuading the arbitrators by whom his client's case is to be determined. Above all else, the advocate in international arbitration must be incredibly, yet credibly, flexible. If there could be said to be a single key to success, a so-called golden rule of advocacy in international arbitration, it must be this: *Adapt as required, and do unto arbitrators as they would have you do.*

It is because of the cosmopolitan and almost infinitely variable nature of international arbitration, and thus of what constitutes effective advocacy in that forum, that there cannot be said to be a single best way to advocate a case successfully in an international arbitration. In a field in which even the most experienced counsel are unlikely to find themselves pleading the same issues under the same law in accordance with the same rules before the same three arbitrators twice in the course of their careers, there can be few hard and fast rules. Certain issues recur. Institutional rules are well known. The applicable law is in many cases well settled. Certain tools available to the advocate are invariably the same. Yet still the changing identity of the decision-makers before whom a case is presented requires the effective advocate to select and wield those tools differently than he might do in other instances.

Thus the answer to the question *What do arbitrators really want?* is not simply "*everything*". The complete answer is that the advocate must strive to be *everything to all people.* This is not to suggest that there is nothing more concrete to say about how best to present a case to an international tribunal – a simple perusal of the fascinating and highly instructive essays contained in this volume illustrates that this is not so. Yet the fact remains that the great challenge facing the advocate in international arbitration is to adapt his skills and style so as to communicate with and persuade an ever-changing array of decision-makers far more diverse than he or she could ever encounter during a lifetime of domestic trial or appellate practice.

In the remarks below we do not propose a set of detailed must-*do*s or *don't*s. Rather, what we hope to convey is a sense of the multiple ways in which the unique challenge facing the advocate in international arbitration is manifested. What we hope to offer are certain ideas – not so much rules as rules of thumb – that the successful advocate in international arbitration constantly bears in mind as he embraces this challenge.

II. The Role of Counsel

Lawyers are sometimes compared to actors. And so they should be. Both are called upon to deliver performances that vary according to the nature of the plays and productions in which they are engaged from time to time. Both cloak themselves in the garb of the character of the moment. And for both, the consummate professional is capable of playing a role without seeming to do so. It may well be that all the world is a stage. For professional actors, however, the stage ends at the footlights; the play itself is a series of meticulously rehearsed cues; and the drama commences with the rise of the curtain and closes with the dispersal of the crowd each night. No such thing for the advocate. The advocate not only plays his role in person; he also appears before his audience in writing, on the telephone and by videoconference, delivering lines from a script that he constantly revises, perhaps discards entirely, and then consults again as the need arises. His performance begins upon first contact with an arbitrator or tribunal and ends upon the conclusion of the case, sometimes several years later. His stage could be said to be defined less in spatial than in temporal terms.

As this book illustrates, the role of counsel – summed up in the concept of "advocacy" – informs the advocate's behaviour from the moment of his first entrance on the arbitral stage (the parties' initial administrative conference call with a tribunal, or in prior correspondence with an arbitral institution that is eventually transmitted to the tribunal) until his final exit (the submission of post-hearing briefs, or submissions on costs, or comments on a request for correction of an award). It cannot be too strongly emphasised that advocacy encompasses far more than oral pleading. Advocacy is manifested in counsel's every interaction with the arbitrators appointed to determine the case at hand. Here too, the finest international counsel understand and thrive on this challenge.

Too many advocates lose sight of this important point. They act as though exchanges that take place out of the physical presence of the tribunal or far removed in time from the hearing are less meaningful or have less impact on the arbitrators' perceptions of the dispute than the moments – generally fleeting – spent in the hearing room. In many respects that may be the case. However, international arbitrations typically play out over long periods of time and across far-flung regions of the globe and diverse cultural lines. Many important matters are dealt with either well before or after the hearing or hearings. The advocate who neglects to keep his eye on the ball and to consider how his conduct is likely to be perceived from "the standpoint of the arbitrator" at every turn, in every letter or request or document produced, in every telephone meeting or video conference, does so at his client's risk.

Arbitrators come to hearings with an open mind, of course. Few, however, come to hearings without having formed some sort of provisional view of the case based on the parties' written submissions, documents and witness statements filed and the many exchanges with counsel that will already have taken place. Nor is this very human predilection limited to an arbitrator's *prima facie* view of the dispute. Perhaps even more so, arbitrators are apt to form initial impressions of counsel themselves – Are they polite? knowledgeable? effective? Can they be relied on to describe facts and issues fairly? Is he a more trustworthy "guide" for the tribunal than his adversary? – on the basis of counsel's tone and approach often long before the arbitrators and counsel may actually meet each other for the first time.

This process, largely subliminal, continues throughout the proceedings and is nourished by every message or impression conveyed by counsel and received, formed or revised by the arbitrator. At in-person hearings in particular it encompasses not only the words spoken by the parties' advocates but, equally important, their non-verbal communication – their "body language", often as powerful as it is subtle, expressed in the smallest of gestures, smiles or scowls. The finest advocates understand that communication occurs on many levels and they are careful to use every means of interacting with the tribunal – whether in person or otherwise, in speech or print, tone or comportment – with the aim of conveying the key message: I am an honest broker who can be trusted to assist the tribunal to reach a just and fair resolution of the dispute.

III. Know the Case

Just as in many industries the paramount rule for professionals who interact with the public in an advisory capacity is the so-called "KYC" rule – Know Your Client – so too advocates are well advised to KYC: Know Your Case. Knowing one's case means, most fundamentally, knowing the facts and the law of the case at hand. Advocates must master all aspects of the dispute; not only their own briefs but those of their adversaries. Yes, arbitrators do enjoy the occasional "*gotcha!*" moment, when we are able to correct counsel or otherwise demonstrate that we have in fact read and considered the materials submitted by the parties, which we perhaps interpret differently than does counsel. But the truth is that we prefer that the parties' advocates not appear taken aback by anything that we might have to say or any question that we might ask. If we are to trust our advocate-guides, as we truly wish to do, then we will ideally be reassured that they have traversed the relevant ground before us and know the terrain better than do we. At the end of the day, nothing is worse from the standpoint of decision-maker in an adversarial process than to come away from a hearing feeling – and most likely sharing this view with his co-arbitrators – that he has not been helped by counsel's presentation of their respective cases.

This rule presumably applies in all legal systems, before all national courts or other adjudicative bodies. However, it is perhaps nowhere more important than in the international arbitral arena due to the unique challenges involved. Before national courts, much of what there is to know about one's case – everything having to do with procedure, for example – is common knowledge (or at least presumed to be). The expectations of all concerned with respect to the use of mechanisms such as pre-trial discovery or cross-examination are shared, as are the nature and degree of deference expected to be exhibited toward the presiding judge. Even the significance of certain facts, the importance of certain words spoken or gestures made by one party to another, may be commonly understood by all concerned. Not so in international arbitration.

The advocate's toolbox is not necessarily the same when he appears before an international tribunal as when he is before a domestic court. Out goes one's well-worn copy of the Code of Civil Procedure or the Federal Rules of Evidence. Out goes the habit of addressing juries or cross-examining fact and expert witnesses; or for many civil lawyers, the habit of deferring overmuch to judges to control the administration of evidence and examine the facts of the case. Out goes a lifetime of experience with motions practice and procedural manoeuvring; or a reluctance to have parties examined under oath. Out go many assumptions that, upon reflection, one realises are premised on cultural factors that are specific to oneself and one's client alone. In their place may be two slim volumes – the UNCITRAL or LCIA or ICC Rules, perhaps; and the IBA Rules on the Taking of Evidence in International Commercial Arbitration.

Those, plus the willingness and ability to check one's national baggage at the door and to do things differently than are done at home. Hot-tubbing anyone?

The advocate before an international tribunal must be prepared and able to put aside his preconceptions regarding the proper conduct of adversarial proceedings. What is appropriate and perhaps even necessary in a courtroom in one's home jurisdiction is not necessarily welcome or effective in an arbitration. This is so in our view even in domestic arbitrations – but that is another matter. It is certainly true in international arbitration, and not only in cases where the parties' counsel and the arbitrators hail from different countries.

Knowing your case also includes knowing the rules, whether institutional or *ad hoc*, according to which the parties have agreed the arbitration is to be conducted. These on their own usually indicate fairly clearly that what is allowed and expected of counsel is very different than how he or she might be expected to act in a courtroom. One example that is occasionally used to illustrate this basic point concerns the burden of proof. To the question *Which party bears the burden of proof?* most lawyers' reflex is to answer that the plaintiff/claimant bears the burden. However, Article 24(1) of the UNCITRAL Arbitration Rules states clearly that "each party shall have the burden of proving the facts relied on to support his claim or defence"; and indeed this principle is frequently applied by tribunals constituted under other arbitration rules. The distinctiveness of international arbitral procedure is reflected as well in the responsibilities and powers typically accorded international arbitrators, certain of which are widely codified in institutional or other rules – the responsibility to establish the facts of the case as it considers appropriate, for example, or the power to call for the production of additional evidence *proprio motu* – and certain of which – such as the duty to ensure that proceedings are conducted not only fairly but efficiently and expeditiously, on occasion more expeditiously than even the parties might wish – are generally understood to rank among the arbitrator's core duties.

The point is that the rules of international arbitral institutions and tribunals do not mirror the procedural rules of any particular jurisdiction. On the contrary, international arbitration rules are typically an amalgam, fairly skeletal, of procedures derived by compromise from diverse national traditions that are fleshed out on a case by case basis according to the diversity of experience and expectations of the parties and the members of the tribunal. Further, to the extent that the practice of international tribunals becomes increasingly harmonised, reflecting a coalescence of diverse national experiences, the more experienced arbitrators are more likely to consider themselves the guardians of that practice and of its distinctiveness. International tribunals, far more than domestic arbitral tribunals, will not hesitate to remind parties that by choosing arbitration they have deliberately chosen a dispute resolution method that, for all its similarities with litigation, is nonetheless a very different beast. It is not unusual in the course of a hearing for counsel to be reminded by the arbitrators, when necessary, that they are not in a courtroom in Sydney/Paris/New York/London. Not that international arbitrators are not firm believers in the fundamentally consensual nature of arbitration. They are; and it is precisely on this basis that experienced international arbitrators do not hesitate to wield the authority conferred on them expressly or implicitly by the applicable rules to conduct proceedings in the manner that they consider most appropriate in the circumstances of the case, and most in keeping with the basic precepts of international arbitration.

IV. The Outcome

One of the most valuable lessons generally learned early in the career of an advocate is that he or she cannot and will not win every case. By the same token, few cases are on their own necessarily fated to be won or lost. All counsel have lost cases that they felt certain to win (their clients usually even more so), just as they have won cases that initially they may have believed were hopeless. From this we appreciate that fate, if it could be said to exist in the context of adversarial legal proceedings, can be fickle indeed. We also learn that although the outcome of any given case ultimately rests with the tribunal, counsel play a significant role in shaping that result. Cases may be won despite poor advocacy, or lost despite the best. Good advocacy, however, in all cases can only increase the chance of success.

Effective advocacy is about understanding and working with the material – the facts and law – at hand, seizing the attention of the decision-makers, interesting them in the story that one wishes to tell, communicating with each of them and subtly leading the way toward the desired outcome, or at least the best possible outcome in the circumstances. Again, this much is true of advocacy in general. However, the ability of the advocate to influence the outcome of a case is arguably greater in international arbitration than in domestic litigation. The diversity of experience and expectations of arbitrators and the variable nature of the arbitral process as compared with litigation before the courts of a particular jurisdiction, mean that what might seem evident from the standpoint of a judge may be far less so to an international arbitrator. Similarly, the members of an international tribunal may not initially anticipate (with the same degree of certainty as might a judge) that certain techniques or arguments will be employed by counsel and that certain elements of the case will only become apparent as a result. And in any event, on a three-person international tribunal what appears black-and-white to one arbitrator may well seem quite gray to another.

V. The Tribunal

Counsel who also serve as arbitrators in international cases understand that the perspective of the arbitrator differs greatly depending on whether "the arbitrator" is sitting alone or as a member of a tribunal, and on whether he or she is chairman of a tribunal or party-appointed. These counsel also understand that a dynamic is invariably established among the members of a tribunal that encompasses both their interpersonal and professional relations.

Invariably, individual tribunal members involve themselves to varying degrees in certain areas of the tribunal's work. The chairman, for example, typically assumes the lion's share of responsibility for resolving procedural disputes and for drafting the final award. An arbitrator familiar with the applicable law will naturally be deferred to by his colleagues with respect to legal issues. Another arbitrator may demonstrate at the hearing a knowledge of or fascination with a particular technical facet of the case, a sure sign that he will ask the chairman (if he is not actually requested) to draft the part of the award that describes the technology or industrial process in question.

The advocate who is attuned to the dynamic between arbitrators will adjust his approach accordingly. Yet he will never cease attempting to engage and persuade all members of a tribunal, which may in fact mean directing the greater part of his attention to the arbitrator who appears least convinced of a particular point. Majority decisions are not unusual. However, it is no secret that most awards in international commercial arbitrations are rendered unanimously and that tribunals tend to seek unanimous outcomes. Getting there requires that each arbitrator feel comfortable with both the process and the result.

It may seem trite to observe but it is nonetheless true that the surest way for an advocate to guide a tribunal toward a desired result is to engage each of its members. Certainly, any arbitrator who acts regularly as chairman will disclose, without violating the "*secret du délibéré*", how important it is for the smooth and efficient conduct of the tribunal's work that his colleagues on the tribunal to feel that they are treated with due respect by all counsel. Indeed, this is often as important as "winning" each arbitrator outright to one's view of the merits of the case. The experienced advocate does not expect to win all cases. Neither does he expect always to persuade all members of a tribunal that his position is more sound than his adversary's. Effective advocates understand that arbitrators are as apt to be persuaded to decide a case a certain way by their colleagues on the tribunal, in the course of the tribunal's deliberations, as they are by counsel during the proceedings. And they appreciate that even a reluctant arbitrator is more open to reconsidering his views if he feels that he has not been written off by the party in question, but that his concerns were acknowledged and squarely addressed in counsel's written and oral submissions.

Experienced arbitration counsel are also prudent to ensure that they do not appear to focus overmuch on "their", i.e. their party-appointed, arbitrator. This is not only because all members of a tribunal are subject to duties of impartiality and independence, which requires that they act in effect as members of a collegiate body. It is, rather, because that is the way most tribunals work in practice. Further, experienced counsel understand that they are better off in the long run if their party-appointed arbitrators defend the integrity of the arbitral process and earn the respect of their tribunal colleagues than if those arbitrators act as advocates – a sure way to derail deliberations and even imperil the appointing party's case.

VI. The Indirect Effect of Advocacy

This leads to the observation that advocacy has both direct and indirect effects. It has direct effect on an arbitrator reading a brief or watching the examination of a witness or listening to an advocate's closing argument. It has an indirect effect, as when an arbitrator, persuaded by the position presented by the advocate, then attempts to convince the other members of a tribunal of the wisdom of that position.

Advocacy, good or bad, also has a more prolonged, occasionally delayed, effect than many counsel may realise. The import of certain elements of a witness's testimony or an advocate's submissions may not be immediately apparent to an arbitrator. The eureka moment may arrive only later, in the privacy of the arbitrator's study or during the tribunal's deliberations. Advocacy is often described as a process of planting seeds, the fruits of which are later harvested and eventually transformed into a favourable judgement or award. The best lawyers understand that advocacy is also a bit like tossing stones into a pool, the ripples from which continue to be felt long after the stone itself has sunk from view.

VII. Conclusion

The advocate in international arbitration faces an awesome challenge if he or she is going to represent his or her client's interests efficiently and convincingly. As in so many facets of like, the task becomes easier with experience. Experience is an indispensable teacher. But if the arbitrator expects the advocate to do "everything", as we have sought to demonstrate, the arbitrator himself must never forget, that in the classroom of any specific arbitration, he also has a responsibility to contribute to the education of every lawyer who aspires to become the complete advocate. In other words, and we end on that note, the arbitrator must never forget that, once upon a time, he was an advocate or that, in the near future, he may be on the other side of the bar!

Chapter 26

ADVOCACY REGARDING DAMAGES IN INTERNATIONAL ARBITRATION

Craig S. Miles*

> "The *only* goal of trial is to get money for your client."
> — *David Ball on Damages* xxi (NITA 2005)

I. Introduction

David A. Ball, Ph.D, ends the preface of the second edition of his treatise with the above maxim. While his book is geared toward U.S. plaintiffs' lawyers in personal injury and wrongful death cases, the maxim is undoubtedly true in international arbitrations as well. Barring the relatively rare instance where a claimant seeks non-pecuniary remedies, the claimant's primary goal is to obtain the highest monetary award possible. Conversely of course, the respondent's goal, if unable to prevail on liability, is to minimize the damages award. Yet damages often get short shrift in the preparation of an international arbitration. Parties often spend months developing complicated factual details and arcane legal theories, only to wait until relatively late in the game to develop their damages story. This is a mistake. Damages should be foremost in the minds of advocates at every stage of an international arbitration. Whenever possible, prior to even filing a claim, claimant's counsel should be well advanced in the preparation of his damages evidence, through the early identification of appropriate documents and witnesses to the quick retention of a damages expert or experts. This in turn will inform the approach at each subsequent step in the process, from the selection of arbitrators to closing statement.

---

* Partner, International Arbitration Group, King & Spalding, Houston.

This chapter will present damages from the standpoint of the claimant's advocate. This is logical. Claimants of course have the burden of proof on all issues. Respondents, on the other hand, in effect have two chances to defeat a damages claim – on liability and on the merits of the amount claimed. It is for claimants to develop powerful, compelling evidence on damages. Respondents, by contrast, rarely will offer a true alternative damages valuation. In most instances, respondents are happy to focus first on defeating liability and then, only in the alternative, to merely poke holes in the claimant's damages evidence without risking setting a "floor" for damages by offering their own figure. There are exceptions to this of course – when liability is clear or even stipulated, a respondent will want to present a compelling alternative damages model. But in most cases the onus is on the claimant, so that perspective will be the focus of this chapter. Where appropriate, however, I will make occasional comments from the respondent's perspective.

I will begin with a discussion of certain general principles of persuasion that influence decision-makers when awarding damages. I will then discuss relevant damages considerations at each of the main stages of an arbitration. I wish to emphasize here that this chapter supplements the other chapters of this book dealing with those stages. In the main, I fully endorse the techniques discussed in the preceding chapters regarding opening and closing statements, cross-examination, *etc.* This chapter's purpose is to emphasize the complementary yet critical role that damages advocacy should play in the overall presentation of a case.

II. Basic Principles of Persuasion Regarding Damages

David Ball identifies the basic principles that guide decision-makers when awarding damages.[1] While his focus is on lay jurors, many of these principles apply to arbitrators as well. Although arbitrators are generally more sophisticated than lay jurors, and while the commercial disputes that are the typical focus of international

---

1 *David Ball on Damages* 1-12 (NITA 2005).

arbitrations are less likely to be susceptible to the emotional triggers that influence decision-making in, say, personal injury and wrongful death cases, arbitrators do not cease to be human beings influenced by emotions. The main psychological and emotional elements that arbitrators will consider in awarding damages include the following: (i) degree of harm and loss; (ii) proportion of time spent on harm, losses and money; (iii) the respondent's conduct; and (iv) the claimant's conduct. I will address these in turn.

A. Degree of Harm and Loss

Ball notes that the degree of harm and loss is rarely the most important decision-making factor, but it carries significant weight.[2] Yet claimants' advocates often fail to explain in clear terms the full degree of harm that the respondent's conduct has caused. A routine breach of contract through a counterparty's failure to timely pay may seem relatively mundane and straightforward. Yet that failure could have significant knock-on effects. The lack of income could cause the claimant to fall in arrears with its own creditors, damaging relations – sometimes permanently. Likewise, existing or potential lenders may view the business less favorably due to the resulting liquidity issues. Expansion plans could be derailed. The business could even fail. Moreover, if the business is a small business, the individual owner or owners may suffer significant stress and anguish.

As Ball explains, "harm and losses" means all the bad things that happened because of the respondent's conduct.[3] In order for arbitrators to sympathize with a claimant, they need to know the full range of harm that it suffered. Even if not all of the harmful ancillary effects are recoverable as damages in and of themselves, making their presence known to the arbitrators makes it more likely that the arbitrators will award the full measure of direct damages that the claimant seeks. Thus, the good advocate will spend time developing a story that exploits all of the proximately-caused negative consequences of the respondent's conduct.

---

2 *Id* at 2.

3 *Id.*

B. Proportion of Time Spent on Harm and Loss

As Ball observes, a sprinkling of testimony about damages followed by a brief summation in closing will not make the arbitrators think that the claimant's focus is on receiving a large damages award.[4] And the arbitrators will award accordingly. Ball thus argues that a third to half of time should be spent on damages.[5] While that may not be realistic in many arbitral hearings, appropriate time should be allocated to damages. Any fact witnesses with relevant information about damages should have that information prominently included in their witness statements. The memorial itself should include a significant section on damages, and damages should be mentioned early and often. I have seen many 200-plus page memorials where the damages section is merely a 10-page summary at the very end of the memorial, after 190 pages of detailed factual recitation and legal arguments. This is generally a mistake, although it is somewhat understandable – the temptation may be to defer the detailed discussion to the accompanying report of the damages experts. But there is a fine line to be walked here. The expectation is of course that the arbitrators will give full and careful consideration to the damages reports. Yet those reports cannot exist in a vacuum. They must be carefully tied to the claimant's overall story in a compelling way. It is critical to mention the damages story prominently and clearly in the first few pages of the memorial. The separate damages section of the memorial should summarize the key valuation elements and figures in a clear and persuasive way. Of course it should not repeat in great detail what is already in the damages reports; but nor should it merely summarize the figures and say "For more detail, see the accompanying damages reports."

Likewise, a significant portion of the opening and closing statements should be devoted to damages. As with memorials, I have occasionally seen two-hour opening statements where only the last

---

[4] *Id.* at 3.

[5] *Id.* at 4. Ball quotes Don Keenan as saying: "Liability is defense turf. Damages is your [*i.e.*, the claimant's lawyer's] turf." *Id.* at 5.

couple of minutes are devoted to summarizing the damages figures. I disagree with this approach. The key issues on damages should be addressed in the opening, and the respondent's best arguments should be tackled and persuasively rebutted. Little is gained by deferring these issues to the expert testimony and/or closing. The closing statement itself should re-emphasize the best case on damages and supplement it by highlighting the most helpful damages testimony that was elicited during the hearing.

In sum, proportionate time must be devoted to damages, no matter how much attention the liability case needs. As Ball says, "Time is money."[6]

C. The Respondent's Conduct

Decision-makers tend to look at two factors to gauge respondent conduct: the respondent's state of mind at the time of breach, and then its subsequent conduct.[7] If a respondent breaches a contract inadvertently or out of an unavoidable necessity, arbitrators are unlikely to think badly of it. Indeed, arbitrators will expect a respondent to have behaved the way others in the same position would have acted (a sort of "commercial reasonableness" test). Thus, the claimant advocate's goal should be to show how the respondent's conduct violated reasonable commercial behavior (and the more outrageous the violation, the better).[8] For example, a respondent who breaches a contract knowingly and for commercially unreasonable reasons (*e.g.*, the contract has become marginally uneconomical due to unanticipated price fluctuations), with no consideration for its impact on the claimant, is likely to anger the arbitrators, which in turn will make the arbitrators more likely to award the claimant the full measure of damages sought.

Similarly, the way the respondent behaves subsequent to the breach can have a material impact. Did the respondent ignore the

---

[6] *Id.*

[7] *Id.* at 5-6.

[8] *Id.*

claimant's phone calls or written requests for a negotiated solution? Did it deny any responsibility for the breach? One case of ours involved a government's expropriation of private property. On several occasions, the expropriation was enjoined by the domestic courts of the host State. The government's response in every instance was simply to ignore the rulings and issue new decrees of expropriation. In their award, the arbitrators described this as "the most egregious element of the whole affair." Surely this conduct played a role in the arbitrators' assessment of damages, however indirectly.

The respondent's conduct in this respect can also extend to its handling of the arbitration itself. Has it "lost" or failed to produce critical documents? Has it raised frivolous defenses or jurisdictional objections? Has it failed to offer witness statements from key figures in order to avoid subjecting them to potentially damaging cross-examination? While such conduct may give rise to an award of costs (which can be quite significant in their own right as a separate element of damages), it can undoubtedly influence the core measure of damages. In the same case I just described above, the host State repeatedly asserted untimely jurisdictional objections or re-raised the same jurisdictional objections as ostensible merits issues. The arbitrators were not pleased, and criticized the respondent's actions as "greatly increasing the costs of these proceedings." The claimant's advocate would be foolish not to emphasize both types of conduct. Arbitrators will not generally award speculative or unproved losses, but they are human beings — "bad" respondents anger arbitrators, and angry arbitrators are much more likely to make respondents pay. Thus, the claimant's advocate should be as thorough as possible in searching for and highlighting such evidence, so long as it is reasonably relevant to the issues in the case.

D. The Claimant's Conduct

If "bad" respondents anger arbitrators, the converse is also true — unsympathetic claimants are not good candidates for damages at all, let alone significant awards. Thus, the skillful respondent's attorney will look for ways to present the claimant in as negative a light as possible.

This could include commercial overreaching by the claimant, prior unethical conduct, or conduct that misled or sought to take advantage of the respondent. In investment arbitrations, for example, one of the most common emerging defense tactics is to scour the record for evidence that the claimant obtained its investment improperly, such as through bribery or by misrepresenting its financial wherewithal or commercial expertise to acquire the investment. When this happens, the claimant's advocate's task is to emphasize the claimant's good works – being a responsible corporation in most instances, for example, or having behaved commercially reasonably toward the respondent in other circumstances.

Personal demeanor has a role to play as well. If the claimant is an individual, or for witnesses who will acts as the "face" of a corporate claimant, ill-perceived characteristics such as haughtiness or defensiveness must be avoided. Counsel should keep this in mind in selecting such witnesses. To the extent that "bad" witnesses are unavoidable, such characteristics can be softened with careful preparation or through work with external consultants. Bear in mind, however, that not all legal traditions look favorably on extensive witness preparation (or sometimes any preparation at all). Counsel should know their arbitrators and their expectations, and avoid having witnesses whose testimony appears too polished or rehearsed. At the end of the day, a lawyer cannot convince the arbitrators that the client is deserving of a large damages award by merely saying or providing some documentary evidence that the client is good and deserving; the client must demonstrate its worthiness through words and actions that allow the arbitrators to make their own judgments and to feel comfortable awarding large sums of money.

With these basic principles of persuasion in mind, we turn now to the key stages of an international arbitration and the role that damages advocacy should play in each. For purposes of this discussion, I will assume that the case involves a contract or treaty breach that substantially impairs the profitability of a significant on-going business – the result being that the claimant will be obliged to demonstrate losses rigorously through sophisticated expert testimony and accompanying valuation models.

III. Getting Started: Managing Client Expectations to Your Benefit

A key element of being a good advocate on damages is managing client expectations at the outset. While client management in general is critical in any case, it is particularly important when it comes to damages. Even the most sophisticated of claimants will often have an inflated sense of entitlement to damages in a particular case. This is not surprising. The claimant will normally feel victimized by the actions of the respondent, and that sense of injustice, combined with the claimant's often egocentric view of its own situation (*e.g.*, business prospects), can lead to heightened, and occasionally unrealistic, expectations. I once had a prospective client open an introductory meeting by declaring that its case would be the biggest damages case in the history of the arbitral institution administering the claim. While there may be instances where such expectations are well grounded, clients nonetheless need to understand that awarding damages in international arbitration not a science. They need to know that arbitrators will generally be skeptical of large damages claims and will demand rigorous proof; that new or untested businesses are unlikely to generate large lost-profits-based awards; and that arbitrators are, in the main – and for better or worse – conservative when it comes to awarding damages.

This need not be a negative, however. Having this discussion with the client early on can help assist in the process of obtaining the best damages evidence available, and as early as possible. Business plans, forecasts, financial models, analysts reports, financial statements, tax returns, regulatory filings, government files, e-mails, key current and former employees, *etc.*, are all sources that need to be unearthed, secured, and analyzed in as much detail as possible. Engaging the client early on in this process and investing it in this key element to the success of its damages case is critical. It is time and money well spent and will normally pay off in the end. It is also information that the damages expert will inevitably need – so the sooner, the better.

IV. Retention of the Damages Expert

The retention of a qualified, persuasive, independent damages expert in the type of case under consideration is critical. Its importance cannot be underestimated. Clients sometimes feel that their own business plans and cash-flow models should be sufficient to serve as competent evidence of how the business would have performed in the absence of the breach. They are wrong. While such evidence can be relevant and useful, arbitrators will simply not award significant damages in a complex commercial case based on such evidence. An independent valuation expert is invariably needed.

Moreover, the valuation expert should be retained as early as possible – ideally well before the claimant even files its request for arbitration. As mentioned above, the valuation expert can assist the client in focusing on gathering the appropriate documentary evidence to support the damages claim. In many (if not most) instances the valuation expert will be better positioned than counsel to identify the full scope of documentary evidence needed. In addition, early retention and commencement of the valuation expert's work can help identify evidentiary gaps that may need to be filled with particular witness statements or additional experts. For example, evaluating damages concerning the client's recent entry into a new line of business may require additional independent expertise on the market for that line of business and the client's ability to have obtained a particular market share in the absence of the breach.

Further, early commencement of the valuation expert's work can aid in the decision of when to file the request for arbitration. Depending on the particular arbitral institution in which the claim is filed, the process may move relatively quickly. In some instances, the claimant can expect to file its principal claim memorial (with accompanying damages evidence) in as little as two to three months after filing the request for arbitration (sometimes even less). If the valuation expert commences work before filing and determines that the complexities of the case will require, say, six months to provide a thorough and detailed valuation report, the claimant can take this into account in determining the appropriate date to file. By contrast, if the claimant files first and searches for a damages expert later, the claimant may find itself with insufficient time to prepare the type of valuation report needed to support the damages sought. The lesson is simple: sooner is almost invariably better.

V. Selecting Arbitrators

An arbitrator's view on damages issues should certainly be a relevant consideration in analyzing candidates for party-appointed arbitrator and chairman. By no means should this take precedence over the key attributes that a prospective arbitrator should have – integrity, intelligence, personality and stature, attention to detail, and expertise. But a general predisposition on key issues, including damages, can be important, and even critical in certain cases. For example, in a case involving a nationalization of a 30-year oilfield concession, where the claimant is seeking lost profits for the life of the project while the respondent advocates for awarding only the book value of the assets and reserves, the candidate's views on such issues can be dispositive. Where available, past writings and awards should be carefully scrutinized to determine patterns regarding damages. Needless to say, this applies both to the claimant and the respondent.

VI. To Bifurcate or Not to Bifurcate?

Some practitioners advocate bifurcation of liability from damages. This may depend on which side of the case one is on. As Larry Newman and David Zaslowsky explain:

> This is an approach that frequently appeals more to respondents than to claimants. Claimants may oppose bifurcation because they sense that they will have a more persuasive case if they can show not only the wrongful conduct of the respondent but the harm that that conduct has caused. Conversely, the respondent may well favor bifurcation because he or she hopes to defeat the claimant's case on the merits and never have to address the issue of damages. Possible bifurcation of the proceedings should, in appropriate

cases, be one of the topics to be discussed among the parties and the arbitrators early in the proceedings.[9]

As a general rule, I do not favor bifurcation. From the claimant's perspective, a compelling liability case is indeed more often than not better presented with the accompanying quantification of harm. Likewise, a respondent that is confident on liability need not fear the absence of bifurcation, and can even use it to strengthen the perception of its view on liability (notwithstanding the attendant cost of dealing with damages before having the chance to prevail on liability). Of course, in some instances bifurcation may make sense even from the claimant's perspective. For example, if there is a thorny jurisdictional issue, the claimant may be better off avoiding the cost of a damages expert (which is usually the single most expensive element of an international arbitration, aside perhaps from the arbitrators' fees) until the jurisdictional issue is resolved. In other instances, more mundane considerations may come into play. Some clients may need time to raise the funds necessary to pay a damages expert, and so could be aided by the attendant delay resulting from bifurcation. Similarly, given the increasing prevalence of third-party funding in international arbitration, an interim liability award can be a compelling tool for attracting such financing. Regardless, I certainly agree with Newman and Zaslowsky that bifurcation is a matter that should be addressed early in the proceedings.

VII. Memorials and Witness Statements

I have already briefly mentioned above the role of memorials in the damages story. To repeat, it is a mistake to relegate damages to a short summary section at the very end of the memorial. Damages should be front and center. They should play a prominent role in the introductory description of the case. Moreover, the factual section of the memorial should describe the full range of harm that the claimant

[9] Lawrence W. Newman and David Zaslowsky, *Grappling with Damages in International Arbitration*, 242(63) NYLJ.COM (Sept. 29, 2009).

suffered due to the defendant's breach, even if not all of that harm is directly claimed as monetary damages. The legal analysis should cogently and persuasively support each of the elements of damages that the claimant seeks to be awarded.

A special word is in order about causation. Claimants often jump from the legal analysis of breach directly to the quantification of damages, without establishing a causal link between the breach and the damages sought.[10] Not only is this logically flawed, it can be legally fatal. Every legal system of which I am aware requires a claimant to establish proximate cause between breach and damages. More often than not the link is straightforward or even self-evident. But sometimes it is not. Examples include where external factors (*e.g.*, macroeconomic factors, changing market conditions, rise of competition, *etc.*) may be concurrently devaluing a business independent of the respondent's breach. Or the tribunal may find that the respondent committed only one or two breaches rather than the multiple breaches that the claimant alleges. In investment treaty arbitrations, for example, respondents often argue that a finding of breach of only one standard of protection in the treaty (*e.g.*, fair and equitable treatment) should not entitle the claimant to the "full" measure of damages that the claimant might otherwise receive if, say, the tribunal were to find that the respondent's acts were tantamount to an expropriation.

In such circumstances, the claimant may need to establish the specific damages that were caused by the specific breaches found. In complex cases, it may even be necessary for the claimant to provide a detailed chart listing each alleged breach and the specific damages resulting from each such breach. In this way, in the event the tribunal rejects one or more breaches, it need not throw out the whole damages award with the bath water on the grounds that the claimant has not sufficiently identified how the breaches found proximately caused a specific measure of damages.

---

[10] For that matter, some arbitral awards are guilty of making the same conclusory leap.

VIII. The Damages Report

A. General Considerations

In the type of case under consideration (*i.e.*, substantial impairment if the profitability of a significant on-going business), the valuation report will almost surely be the single most important determiner of whether the claimant will receive the full measure of damages sought. The report should be thorough, detailed and well written. Each element of the valuation model should be rigorously supported and independently researched and confirmed (preferably with objective, third-party evidence). While the independent expert is not an advocate for the claimant, it is an advocate for its own conclusions. Although valuation issues are often quite technical, the expert's writing must be cogent, persuasive, and accessible. Jargon should be avoided.

Further, unless the parties have agreed or the tribunal has ordered otherwise, all of the supporting materials should normally be provided along with the report. This includes back-up spreadsheets supporting the principal calculations, the underlying data supporting the spreadsheets (*e.g.*, invoices, contracts, market research, *etc.*), and relevant academic literature. Respondent's counsel will often scour the damages report to identify every single conclusion or citation that lacks supporting evidence, then argue either that the data is unsupported, or that its own expert is unable to fully respond due to the lack of data, *etc.* – which can then in turn be used to justify an extension in preparing its rebuttal memorial and expert report. Including all the supporting data upfront avoids such problems. Given the frequent breadth of such data, it is normally advisable to include it on a CD.

B. Valuation Methodologies

As to the substance of the report, valuation experts should normally consider all available approaches, discard those that are not appropriate for the case at hand, and select a core approach that can then be "sanity checked" against the other viable approaches. In general terms, valuation methodologies come in three basic approaches: income, asset and market. Income approaches determine fair market value by multiplying the benefit stream generated by the business times a discount or capitalization rate. Discounted cash flow (DCF) is among the most common of the income-based approaches. "In essence, to use the DCF is to view a company's fair market value as being equal to the discounted present value of its expected net cash flows (*i.e.*, gross cash flows minus expenses), which can be considered to some extent as the discounted value of its future profits."[11] The discount rate is thus a key variable in determining a DCF valuation.

Asset-based approaches are based on the theory that the value of a business is equal to the sum of its parts. Under accounting principles, most assets are reported on the books of the company at their acquisition value, net of depreciation where applicable. In contrast to income-based approaches, which require the valuation expert to make (somewhat) subjective judgments about such elements as the discount rate, book value is relatively objective. But the value of a going concern's intangible assets, such as goodwill, is not well captured in book value, which generally leads book value to understate the fair market value of a business. For this reason, claimants are generally loath to use book value alone.

The market approach to business valuation is based on the idea that in an arms-length situation, the market will drive the price of a business to a certain equilibrium. In other words, a buyer would not pay more for the business, and a seller would not accept less, than the market price of a comparable business enterprise. A valuation expert can thus look at transactions for comparable businesses to identify how the sales price compared to a set variable, such as book value or earnings. By determining the price-to-book-value or price-to-earnings multiple of the comparable transaction, the valuation expert can apply the multiple to the subject business to arrive at its indicative

---

[11] R. Doak Bishop & Craig S. Miles, *Lost Profits and the Discounted Cash Flow Method of Calculation*, 1(1) WORLD ARB. & MED. REV. 33, 35 (2007).

value. It is thus similar to the "comparable sales" method that is commonly used in real estate appraisal. The difficulty in this approach lies in identifying the companies that are sufficiently comparable to the subject company for this purpose.

C. The Use of Multiple Approaches

At the end of the day, the expert should generally settle on a preferred "base" approach and a single valuation. As some commentators have observed, when a single expert presents "various calculations of damages based on varying assumptions," this "may generate confusion and uncertainty."[12] Some experts attempt to work around this by arriving at a single valuation by using multiple approaches, but assigning a relative weighting to the different approaches. For example, the expert may calculate both a DCF value and a book value and then, to account for both the uncertainties of DCF and the inadequacies of book value, assign a weighting of, say, 70% to DCF and 30% to book value to arrive at an overall damages figure. This allows the expert to present a single valuation while still showing two or more different methodologies to value the company. The arbitrators could then theoretically choose from among the different valuations, or reach their own valuation by assigning a different weighting percentage to the respective methodologies. The expert could also present a single valuation but provide sensitivity tables that demonstrate the affect on the valuation of small changes to the most sensitive variables. For example, the expert's "base" case in a DCF valuation will necessarily assume a certain discount rate, which will invariably be subjected to intense scrutiny by the respondent's expert. In response, or in anticipation, the expert could demonstrate the impact on its "base" case of varying the discount rate up or down by, say, two percentage points. This enhances the expert's credibility while at the same time demonstrating resolve as to the propriety of the expert's "base" case.

---

[12] Lawrence W. Newman and David Zaslowsky, *Grappling with Damages in International Arbitration*, 242(63) NYLJ.COM (Sept. 29, 2009).

There may be situations, however, where the advocate may want to put forth different methodologies by different experts. One example where this approach could be useful is when one or more approaches is each problematic individually, but when presented together can support one another and give the arbitrators comfort in awarding damages under one or the other approach. Another is when the subject matter of the approaches is sufficiently different that a single expert cannot plausibly be found with the requisite expertise to support both methodologies.

An example where both situations existed in the same case was a case of ours that involved a hotel and casino project that was expropriated about halfway through the construction phase. Consequently, the project never operated. Due to various domestic court cases, the arbitral hearing did not take place until 12 years after the expropriation. Because the project never operated, it would normally be challenging to obtain an award of damages based on a DCF valuation. Nonetheless, due to the passage of time and the presence of similar resort projects in the region that had developed in the interim, we felt that a DCF could be justified by utilizing revenue data from the nearby projects as a proxy for how the client's project would have fared in the absence of the expropriation. But we were not comfortable advocating a DCF as the sole valuation methodology, so we also included a comparables valuation that attempted to determine a fair market value for the expropriated property by looking sales transactions and offerings involving comparable properties in the same region, even though there were relatively few such contemporaneous transactions (which would normally make a comparables valuation problematic). This required local real estate market expertise that was quite different from the expertise needed for a traditional DCF valuation.

As it turned out, the DCF and comparables valuations ended up being very close to one another. In the end, the arbitrators rejected the DCF but accepted almost in full the comparables valuation (applying only a somewhat higher margin of error than that advocated by our real estate expert). We felt that the extensive evidence presented with the DCF likely comforted the arbitrators in their acceptance of the comparables valuation. Of course, it may well be that the arbitrators would have reached the same result even if we had only presented the comparables valuation, but this is probably a good example where presenting multiple approaches was the best, or at least the safest, course of action.

It is also generally a good idea to provide the arbitrators with a full electronic copy of the damages model, in a format that allows them to modify the key assumptions as necessary. In the event the arbitrators choose to adopt your model as the baseline, you are already halfway home – you have won the larger war, subject only to prevailing on some key remaining skirmishes (which, to be sure, may have significant impact).

To sum up, a competent, persuasive, independent damages report is the *sine qua non* to an award of substantial damages in a complex commercial case. One respected tribunal in an investment arbitration, in adopting the claimant's damages valuation almost in full, pointed out that the claimant's experts' reports "are, in the Tribunal's view, an example as to how damages calculations should be presented in international arbitration; they reflect a high degree of professionalism, clarity, integrity and independence by financial expert witnesses."[13] This is the standard to which advocates should strive when presenting damages in such cases.

IX. The Hearing on the Merits

I have already mentioned that sufficient time should be devoted to damages in the claimant's opening statement. The key issues on damages should be covered, and the respondent's best arguments should be tackled and persuasively rebutted. Little is gained by deferring these issues to the expert testimony and/or the closing argument. Arbitrators rarely interrupt opening statements, so the floor is yours to make your most persuasive case on damages in the hearing's opening moments. Covering damages in only summary

---

[13] *ADC Affiliate Ltd. v. Hungary* (ICSID Case No. ARB/03/16), Award of Oct. 6, 2006, ¶ 516.

fashion may leave the arbitrators with the impression that the claimant's case is weak on liability, which is certainly not the impression that any claimant wants to leave. Demonstrate confidence on liability by devoting a significant amount of the opening statement to damages.

With respect to direct examination of damages experts, the "norm" in international arbitration is for directs to be very limited or for no directs to occur at all. The theory is that the respective experts' damages reports speak for themselves, and that the hearing is only for cross-examination. From the claimant's perspective, agreeing to this approach is a mistake, at least in the usual scenario where the respondent submits a rejoinder memorial and accompanying expert rejoinder reports. This means in effect that the respondents' damages expert has had the "last word" (in writing) on the key issues, and has had time to fully and carefully rebut in writing the last written report of the claimant's damages expert. In that scenario, the absence of meaningful direct examination of the claimant's expert deprives the claimant of the last real opportunity for its expert to rebut – even in summary form – what is usually an extensive written rejoinder report by the respondent's expert. Thus, in my view, the claimant should always seek a sufficient amount of time (at least one hour in a complex case) for direct examination of its damages expert. This time can be used to rebut the respondent's expert's rejoinder report, and to re-emphasize the main themes of the claimant's damages case.

When it comes to cross-examining damages experts, it is generally necessary if only to avoid the appearance of acquiescence, although more often than not little headway is made. In a complex, high-dollar commercial case, the parties will normally retain experienced, well-qualified, confident quantum experts. The issues are usually sufficiently complex, and the experts' positions sufficiently hardened, that advocates will generally find themselves fighting on the expert's turf. If an expert has left low-hanging fruit to be picked, by all means it should be exploited. Otherwise, the cross should re-emphasize the party's themes and strengths through leading questions; then the advocate should move. Rarely is a damages case won on cross-examination of the quantum experts. This is precisely why the written damages reports are so critical.

The testimony of the damages experts should ordinarily be received at or around the same time so that the arbitrators can more readily compare their positions. As an alternative or supplement to cross-examination, the arbitrators may wish to hear the experts together in a procedure known as "witness conferencing," by which the arbitrators and counsel question the expert witnesses in one another's presence – either before or after they have testified separately – so as to narrow down the areas of differences. In my view, such witness conferencing can be useful but should not replace traditional cross-examination.

As with opening, substantial time should be dedicated to damages in the closing statement. This is the opportunity to hammer home the themes on damages that you have shaped throughout the case. The psychological factors that most influence arbitrators to award damages – degree of claimant's harm and loss and respondent's conduct – should be re-emphasized. Favorable damages testimony that may have emerged during the hearing should be highlighted. Conclude with a simple request: "We are not here seeking sympathy. We are here to collect a debt." "The award should be the difference between what could have been and what is."[14]

X. Tribunal Damages Expert

In some cases, the tribunal may determine that it needs to retain its own independent damages expert. Taking this step may be appealing to the tribunal in the face of radically different valuations from the parties' experts, as sometimes occurs. More often than not, the arbitrators will take this step at the end of the hearing. From the advocate's perspective, this raises important issues. For one, the parties will not normally have the opportunity to cross-examine the tribunal's expert. Thus the form of the expert's assistance to the tribunal should be carefully controlled. Ideally from the claimant's

---

[14] *David Ball on Damages* 246-47 (NITA 2005).

perspective, terms of reference should be drawn up that explicitly delineate the scope of the independent expert's assignment, which should normally be limited to commenting on the parties' respective valuations, rather than offering up wholly novel ones of its own. The independent expert should also provide a draft report that gives the parties and their experts sufficient time to provide comments before the independent expert issues its final report. Similarly, the parties should be provided a full and fair opportunity to comment on and critique the final report before the tribunal issues its award.

XI. Conclusion

The claimant's main goal in most arbitrations is to receive as much money as the circumstances of the case fairly allow. The job of the claimant's advocate is to make the client's goal a reality. The joint interests of client and advocate are best served by focusing on damages issues from the very outset of the case, and shaping each stage of the arbitration accordingly. "Time is money."